A DEEPENING ROAR

A DEEPENING ROAR

Scotch College, Melbourne, 1851–2001

James Mitchell

*for Courtenay Shrimpton
on his visit to Scotch
29 February 2008
Jim Mitchell*

ALLEN&UNWIN

First published 2001

Allen & Unwin
83 Alexander Street
Crows Nest NSW 2065
Australia
Phone: (61 2) 8425 0100
Fax: (61 2) 9906 2218
Email: info@allenandunwin.com
Web: www.allenandunwin.com

National Library of Australia
Cataloguing-in-Publication entry:

Mitchell, Jim, 1946– .
A deepening roar: Scotch College, Melbourne, 1851–2001.

Bibliography.
Includes index.
ISBN 1 86508 576 6.

1. Scotch College (Melbourne, Vic.)—History. 2. Private schools—Victoria—Melbourne—History. I. Title.

371.02099451

Designed and set by Steven Dunbar
Printed and bound by Ligare Pty Ltd, Sydney

10 9 8 7 6 5 4 3 2 1

In history he is urged to summarise more, and to connect History with Geography, ... He must master the leading events, group others round these, fix them all with a date or two (taught in class by mnemonics) and thus get a grip on the whole.

JAS JAMIESON (HEADMASTER OF THE PREPARATORY SCHOOL 1905–22), REPORT ON ALEX BUCHANAN, TERM II, 1915.

In writing the Annual Report of a Public-School, where the work done, and the results sought to be obtained, are, year by year, necessarily the same in kind although differing perhaps in degree, it would require no small amount of originality and ingenuity to produce something new. If I state that during the past year our numbers have increased, that the conduct of the pupils has been good, that the amount of work done has been satisfactory, that there has been a keen contest for Prizes, that the efficiency and usefulness of the Institution have, I modestly venture to assert, been fully maintained, I have, perhaps, said all that the public care to know. I could not, however, dignify such a statement as the above with the name of a Report; and I believe that to many of our Friends a more detailed account will be acceptable.

ALEXANDER MORRISON (PRINCIPAL 1857–1903), PRINCIPAL'S REPORT, 1862.

God or fate has crowned our school with honour and length of days.

THE REV. ALEC FRASER (CHAPLAIN 1945–67), DIVINE SERVICE IN THE MEMORIAL HALL, 19 OCTOBER 1947.

CONTENTS

List of boxes

List of maps, plans and aerial views

ABBREVIATIONS AND GLOSSARY

acre: approximately half a hectare.

ADB: *Australian Dictionary of Biography*.

AISV: Association of Independent Schools of Victoria.

APS: Associated Public Schools.

Arthur Rob: Arthur Robinson House.

ASCM: Australian Student Christian Movement.

Assembly: (i) the regular meeting of the whole school, combining religion and announcements. At Eastern Hill held in Number 1, and at Hawthorn in the Memorial Hall, daily and later thrice weekly. At the start of the day until 1999 when it moved to 10.30 am. (ii) General Assembly of the church.

A/V: audio-visual.

CAT: Common Assessment Task, a form of assessment during the 1990s VCE.

CRA: Common Room Association.

CSIRO: Commonwealth Scientific and Industrial Research Organisation.

E&F: Executive and Finance Committee of Council.

Elder: in the Presbyterian Church, a lay member of the parish council (Kirk Session).

Form I: Year 7.

Form II: Year 8.

Form III: Year 9.

Form IV: Year 10.

Form V: Year 11.

Form VI: Year 12.

GHC: General House Committee.

Grades 1–6: Years 1–6.

Group Master: Head of Year.

HOD: Heads of Department meeting.

HSC: Higher School Certificate (Year 12).

kirk: Church (Scots).

Kirk Session: The council of the local Presbyterian parish.

Matric : Matriculation, Year 12.

MCEGGS: Melbourne Church of England Girls' Grammar School.

MLA: Member of the Legislative Assembly of Victoria.

MLC: Methodist Ladies' College.

MMBW: Melbourne and Metropolitan Board of Works.

Moderator: Usually the head of the state Presbyterian Church. In the Presbyterian Church, moderator means chairman and thus applies to the chairmen at each level. The local minister is moderator of the Kirk Session.

NCIS: National Council of Independent Schools.

NFRC : National Fund-Raising Counsel.

OSCA: Old Scotch Collegians' Association.

PE: Physical Education.

PLC: Presbyterian Ladies' College.

pound: One pound of money (£1) became $2 on the introduction of decimal currency. One pound of weight (1 lb) is a little under half a kilogram.

Pre(s): Prefect(s).

Prep(room): Preparatory work for the next day's schooling, done by boarders in the Preproom.

Presbytery: A regional body of the Presbyterian Church. Scotch lies within the Presbytery of Melbourne North.

Pro(s): Probationer(s). The school officers next below Prefects.

PROV: Public Records Office of Victoria.

Q: Indicates a questionnaire response.

SEC: State Electricity Commission (the government-owned provider of electricity).

Senior Subject Master: Head of Subject.

Session: Parish council.

VCAB: Victorian Curriculum Advisory Board.

VCE: Victorian Certificate of Education.

VFL: Victorian Football League, forerunner of the AFL.

VIII: A rowing crew (of 8 members).

VISE: Victorian Institute of Secondary Education.

XI: A cricket or hockey team (of 11 members).

XV: A rugby team (of 15 members).

XVIII: An Australian Rules football team (of 18 members).

ACKNOWLEDGEMENTS

I am indebted to Stuart Macintyre, Ernest Scott Professor of History at the University of Melbourne, for his confidence in selecting me for this task and for his generous help thereafter. I am indebted to the School Council for commissioning me, and to Council's History Committee— Professor Weston Bate, Dr Gordon Donaldson, Professor Stuart Macintyre, Pam Marshall, Dr Janet McCalman, Leigh McGregor, Dr Barrie Orme, Professor David Penington, Professor Sam Ricketson, Ian Savage, Geoff Speed, Dr Alistair Thomson—and especially its Chairman, Dr Robin Stewardson, whose patient support has been unstinting.

At the school, I am especially grateful to Dick Briggs (Archivist) and David Paul (erstwhile Senior History Master).

I have a profound debt to the people who read my drafts. The whole draft was read by the committee, and by Dick Briggs, Dr Ian Britain, Dr Peter Fullerton, William Henderson, Edward Hunter, Sonia Hunter, Alec Lyne, Dr Janet Mackenzie, Campbell McComas, Paul Mishura, David Paul and Michael Robinson.

Draft chapters or parts of chapters were read by Ron Anderson, Matt Bahen, David Baillieu, Sir James Balderstone, Brian Bayston, Ivo Beattie, Dr Graeme Blanch, Ron Bond, Dr Syd Boydell, David Boykett, the Rev. Graham Bradbeer, David Brand, Nick Browne, Ken Clayton, Sir Zelman Cowen, Peter Crook, the Rev. Archie Crow, Keith Darling, Garry Disher, Alex Dix, Ken Evans, John Ferguson, Doug Galbraith, Dr Desmond Gibbs, Ken Gifford, Sir Archibald Glenn, Tony Glover, Robert A. I. Grant, Dr Lucy Healey, Margaret Healey, Tim Healey, Dr Katie Holmes, Tim Hurst, Bruce Lithgow, George Mackenzie, Ian Mackenzie, Donald Macmillan, Mary Macmillan, Ken Mappin, Bill Marshall, David Mason, Guy Mason, the Rev. Dr Davis McCaughey, Mr Justice Ray Northrop, Graham Nowacki, the Rev. Norman Pritchard, Neil Roberts, Philip Roff, David L. Scott, Prof. Richard Selby Smith, Dick Shirrefs, Frank Stuckey, Prof. Ron Taft, Dr Joanna Tapper, Elaine Tarran, Neville Taylor, Alan Watkinson, the Rev. David Webster and Don Wirth.

Julia Hare and Jane Mosley rendered great service administratively.

It was invaluable to use the interviews conducted by Hilary Webster or Geoff Tolson with Dr Archie Anderson, Brian Bayston, Harold Blenkiron, Henry Bowden, Rice Clayton, the Rev. Alec Fraser, Bruce Lithgow, Philip Roff and Prof. Richard Selby Smith. I drew also on an interview with Harry Baker conducted by John Bannister. I thank, also, George Wood, author of Scotch's Diamond Jubilee history, and Harvey Nicholson and David Alexander who edited the centenary history.

The school's librarians, especially Dr Desmond Gibbs, were unfailingly welcoming and supportive, as was Christine Palmer, Archivist of the Presbyterian Church of Victoria.

I am indebted to Sam Anderson for allowing me to quote from the papers of Dr Archie Anderson; Ruth Campbell for permission to quote from Ross Campbell's *Urge to laugh*; Tim Healey and the Healey family for permission to use Colin Healey's writings; Kirk Alexander for permission to quote Kirkland Robertson; Donald Skene Larkin for permission to use the diary of William Skene; Catherine Sullivan for permission to quote from the diary of Alexander Campbell; and Chris Wallace-Crabbe for permission to print three poems.

My thanks go to Robert Abbey, Aaron Abell, Andrew Abercrombie, Chris Adam, Bruce L. Adams, Ken Adams, Brett Aisen, Doug Aitchison, David Alder, Keith Alder, Alan Ames, George I. Anderson, Peter J. Anderson, Stuart J. Anderson, Jason Andrew, Jonathan A. Andrew, Bruce Andrews, Max Annand, Chris Appel, Lesley Armstrong, David Ashton, Peter M. Ashton, Sheila Atkins;

Brett Bahen, Dan Bahen, Yvonne Bahen, Brian Bainbridge, Dee Baird, Geoffrey R. Baker, Greg Baker, Andrew Bales, Daniel Barrie, Warwick Barry, Victor Barton-Smith, Doug Batten, Bill Baxter, Don Beaurepaire, Matthew Bell, James Bennett, Jack Berryman, Ken Bethell, Charles Birch, Sam Black, John Blaine, Robert Blair, Mim Blomquist, Geoff Bolger, Ian Borrie, Geoff Bowden, Tom Bowen, Suzette Boyd, Glen Boyes, John Boykett, Rohan Braddy, David Bradshaw, Lindsay Brand, Charles Bridges-Webb, Brian Bromberger, Geoff Brooke, Bruce Brown, David Brown, Helen Brown, Howard Brown, John C. Brown, Stan Brown, Wesley Bruce, the Rev. John Buchanan, Anthea Bundock, Jon Burke, Ian K. Burnett, Tim Burns, the Rev. Jerram Burrows;

Tom Cade, Geoff Cadogan-Cowper, Ron Caffin, Ian Cairns, Bill Callister, Bruce Cameron (1928),

Donald J. G. Cameron, Roger Cameron, Frank Campbell (1928), M. Ross Campbell, Rob Carmichael, Graham Carrick, Tania Castles, Michael Cathcart, Alf Chandler, Brian Charlton, John Chenhalls, Wei Ch'ng, Colin Christie, Andrew Clark, Avril Clark, David Clark, Jean Clark, David Cliff, Donald Clues, David Clunies-Ross, Kim Coillet, Ihan Coker, Peter Colclough, John Collins (1927), Julian Collins, Mark Collins, Bill Comerford, Chris Commons, Tony Conabere, Geoffrey P. Cook, Nick Corker, Russell Coutie, Russell Coutts, Neil Cracknell, John Craigie, John G. Cromie, Max Cromie, (Robert) Bruce Crow, Murray Crow, John Cumming, Fiona Curran;

Richard Dalitz, Kate Darian-Smith, Don Davenport, Ronald Davey, Jim Davidson, Dick Davies, Bruce Dawson, Gary Day, Gareth de Korte, Donna Delporto, Keith Dempster, Jim Denham, Jill Diedrich, Stephen Digby, Will Digby, Ric Dillon, Lesley Dixon, Ken Don, Geoff Donaldson. Lachie Donaldson, Tim Downey, Mark Dreyfus, Julian Duband, Campbell Duncan, Hugh Duncan, Alistair Dunn, Jan Dunn, David Dyson;

David Earle, Matthew Earle, Andy Edwards, Michael Edwards (1970), Ed Ellis, Michael Evans, Hamish Ewing, Lee Ewing, Rowan Ewing;

Lachie Fairbairn, Frank Falconer, Howard Farrow, Michael Favaloro, Douglas Fearon, Michael Feller, Rob Fincher, Fred Findlay, Ken Fisher, Bill Fisher, Gordon Fisher, Tom Fisher, Helen FitzGerald, Gary Fitzpatrick, Allan Fleming, Bill Fleming, Ken Foletta, Graeme Fraser, Ken Fraser, Lachie Fraser-Smith, Richard Freadman, Anthony Freemantle, Max Frew, Bill Fullagar;

Rod Gabriel, Dud Gay, Keith Gaze, Ian Gelling, Greg Gillespie, John Girvan, Ian Glaspole, Bill Gleadell, Gordon Goldberg, John Goldsmith, David Gordon, Peter Gration, John S. Green (1947), Max Griffith, David Grounds;

Di Hall, Hartley 'Jock' Hall, Leslie Hall, Alan Hamley, Peter Hammond, Ian Hansen, David Hardie, Don Hare, Jim Hare (1967), James Harkness, Peter Harkness, Mairi Harman, Ian Harper, Ian Harris, Ian Harrison, Don Hart, Alan Hartman, Brett Harvey, Chris Hayes, David Head, Richard Heath, Sir Lenox Hewitt, John Hewson, Jon Hickman, Jonathan Hiller, Alec Hilliard, David Hilliard, Patricia Holdaway, Baxter Holly, Ted Holmes, Grevis Howe, Peter Howe, Roger Hughes, Francis Hui, S. E. K. Hulme, Angas Hurst, Neville Hurst, Ross Hyams,

Kathy Hyde, Geoff Hynam;

Geoff Ingham, Rhys Isaac;

Ross Jackson, Robert Jacobson, Ken James, David Jamieson, Rodney Jane, Dana Jankovic, Max Jelbart, Stephen Jelbart, David Jewkes, Martin Jilovsky, Barrie Johns, Chris Johnson, Colin Johnston, David Johnston, Mark Johnston, Adrian O. Jones, Gail Jones, John P. Jones, Peter Joyce;

Geoff Keep, Jim Kelso, Leonard Kemp, Geoffrey Kerr, Jeff Kiddle, George Klein, Sir Harold Knight, Steve Kong, John Koraus, Steven Kunstler, Andy Kuo;

Scott Lacey, Alexander Laing, Tom Lane, John Lavett, Jim Lawson, Peter Lawson, Fay Leong, Neville Leybourne-Ward, Peter Lindsay, Gordon Logan, Margaret Long, Geoffrey Love, James Luke, Tim Luke, Col Luth, Bruce Lyman;

Jed Macdonald, Andrew Grant Mackay, Angus Mackenzie, George Mackenzie, Chris Mackey, Kathryn MacKinnon, Alan MacQuarrie, Finlay Macrae, Douglas Mactier, Josh Maddock, Alan Malcolm, Geoff Maple, Ian Marks, Robert Marks, Pieter Marseille, Ashley Marshall, Ian Martin, John S. Martin, Gordon Matthews, Peter Mayman, Geoff Mayor, Bill McAlaney, Jim McAllester, Bill McAuley, Don McClean, Eric McCowan, Alan McDonald, Bill McDonald, Robert McDonald, John McFadyen, John McFarlane, Hugh McKay (1946), Malcolm A. McKenzie, Rob McLaren, Sir Ian McLennan, John McMeekin, Russell McNaughton, Andrew McNicol, Hilary McPhee, Gus McQueen, Hunter McWhinney, the Rev. Ken Melville, Patricia Melville, Bill Meyer, Alexander Millar, Hugh Millar, Arthur Mitchell, Cal Mitchell, Eileen Mitchell, Ross Mollison, Graham Monk, Rob Moodie, Derek Moore, Bob Moran, Keith Morgan, Jim Morrison, Sir Laurence Muir, Ian Murray, Sophie Musci;

John Nairn, Robert Negri, Faye Newman, Jamie Neyland, Lynley Nimmo, Bruce Nixon, Phil Norman, Bill Norris;

Simon O'Byrne, Jim Olifent, Bob O'Neill, Lloyd Owen, Hal Oxley;

Pam Pappas, Robert Papuga, Craig Parsons, Ian Parton, Willis Parton, Colin Paterson, Frank W. Paton, Max Paton, Michael Paton, Nick Pavlovski, Edwin Peatt, Helen Pepyat, Bruce Pettigrew, Peter Petty, John R. Philip, Bill G. Philip, Ian Phipps, Ian Picken (1937), Ralph Pickford, John Sandham Pilkington, Inocentes Porciuncula, the Rev. Gordon Powell, Barry Price, Richard Price, Bill Pugh, Philip Pullar, Mark Purvis, Catharine Pye;

Jim Ramsay, Andrew Ramsey, Noel Ramsey, Sir Benjamin Rank, Lindsay Rattray, Sir William Refshauge, Duncan Reid, Michael W. Reid, Rob Reid, Richard Reyment, Robert Reynolds, John Rickard, James Ridell, Peter Ritchie, Stephen Ritchie, Ian Roach, Leonie Robbins, Guy Robertson, David Meredith Robinson, David Murray Robinson, Ian Robinson, John Roddick, Ian Roper, David Rose, John Munro Ross, Andrew Rubins, Elaine Rudd, Paul Runting, Gilford Rush, Nicholas Ruskin, Robert Russell, Susan Russell;

Fraser Samuel, Rodney Saulwick, David Schloeffel, Andrew Schreuder, Rex Schurmann, Chris Scott, Malcolm Scott, Rod Scott, Graham Sellars-Jones, Steven Sewell, Ravi Sharma, David Sharpe, Bill Shattock, David Shave, Ken Shave, Sam Shields, Dylan Shirley, Alan Shugg, Bill Sides, Harrie Scott Simmons, Bob Simpson, James Simpson (1971), John Simpson, Carlos Sinay, Alan Skurrie, Maurice Smith, Rob Smith, George Smyth, Bill Snaddon, Bryan Speed, Gordon Spence, John C. H. Spence, Roy Spratt, Trevor Steer, Sir Ninian Stephen, Frank R. I. Stephens, Geoff Stevens, Chris Stewardson, Ron Stott, Charles Su, Stuart Sutherland, Ian Swain, Tim Swain, Bill Swaney (1937), Robert Swann, Don Symington, Bruce Symon, Roger Syn;

Peter Tainsh, Garth Tapp, Jan Tarver, Rod Tasker, Chris Taylor, David Maxwell Taylor, Hugh Taylor, Ian Teague, Trish Teesdale, Donald Telfer, Keith Thom, Ian Thomas, Keith Thomas, Geoff Thompson, David Thomson, Bill Tingate, George Titmus, Ashley Tucker, Greg Tucker, Rod Tucker;

Bob Vines, David Vines, Dick Vines;

Peter Waddell, Bob Wade, Peter Wade, Bill Walker, Peter Walker, Ken Walton, Jane Walton, Don Ward, John Ward, Sue Ward, Nick Waters, Campbell Watson, Don Watson, Keith Watson, Geoff Wemyss, Ken Wheat, Arch White, Hugh White, Edward Whitehead, Bruce Whittaker, Peter Wickens, Charles Widdis, Jules Wilkinson, Drew Williams, Hugh Wilson, Keith Wilson, Len Wilson, Peter R. Wilson, Will Winspear, Frank Wood, Simon Woods, Brian Woolacott, Rob Wootton;

The Rev. Prof. George Yule;

Desmond Zwar.

The vastness of such a list means that this book is my amalgam of perceptions of the school and does not reflect the views of any of the above in particular, and is certainly at odds with some of their views, just as they were often at odds with each other. Many comments and suggestions have not been included, due either to lack of space or the author's obtuseness.

In publishing photographs and cartoons, I am indebted to the courtesy of Rick Altman (p. 306), Big Shots Photography (p. 430), Commercial Photographers (p. 254), Chris Commons (p. X), Dickinson-Monteath Studios (p. 233), Lachlan Fairbairn (p. 516), John Fisher (p. 262), Mrs J. Granger for permission to publish the work of her husband George K. Granger (pp. 146 and 350), Mrs Christina Hallett (p. 1), Hebfotos (p. XIIIb), The Herald & Weekly Times Photographic Collection (pp. 81, 151 and 168), Edward Hunter (pp. 134, 459, Vb, VIb, VIIIb, IXb), John Ingham (p. II), Peter Jeppesen for permission to publish the work of his father Max Jeppesen (pp. 141, 195, 312 and 508), Stephen Kong (p. XVI), La Trobe Picture Collection at the State Library of Victoria (pp. 32 and 84), Peter Lew (p. 332), Muntz Studios (p. 242), Pilbeam Pic (p. 392), *Pix* (p. 502), Andrew Rahni (pp. 35, 153, 277, 280, 338, 343, 371, 439, 441, 463, 491 and 501), Philip Robertson (pp. 399 and 448), Gay Robson (pp. 465 and XIVa), Sabre Air Snaps (p. 205), Skyview Aviation (p. VII), Mark Strizic (pp. 286, 289, 303, 394, 419, and 484), Robert Sutherland (p. 20), Graham Whitford (pp. 187 and 314), and Whitney Bros. (p. 415). The illustration on p. 117 appears by permission of the Australian National Library Manuscript Collection. In the case of some old photographs, we have not been able to trace the copyright holder.

Steen Vestergaard helped greatly with the photography. Edward Hunter designed the timeline and graph (pp. 517 and XII).

Colin Golvan ably represented me in negotiating my contract with the school.

I am deeply indebted to Dr Deborah McIntyre's wisdom and encouragement, and to Edward Hunter's intelligence and taste as he helped carry this book to completion in its final months.

Dr Peter Fullerton has as ever been a constant support and guide. Without him, this book would not have been written.

Introduction

To be 150 years old is no mean achievement and Scotch College, Melbourne, has commissioned this history in celebration. For the school, that is reason enough for a history.

Other readers may dip into these pages out of a curiosity born of Scotch's foremost role in Australian society. In *Who's Who* Scotch's Old Boys appear more often than those of any other school in the country, and in the *Australian Dictionary of Biography* more than any other school except Sydney Grammar School.[1]

This achievement reflects partly on the school and partly on the church-school system in the State of Victoria, of which Scotch is the oldest surviving member (and the ninth oldest surviving secondary school in Australia).[2] In Victoria (created just 14 weeks before Scotch opened), the oldest secondary schools have had a particular status. For boys, there were six of them, founded between 1851 and 1878. They called themselves Public Schools, to claim the status of the great schools of England. Two were Church of England (Melbourne and Geelong Grammars) and by belonging to the same church as the Queen they catered to the social upper crust. One, Xavier, was Catholic, and its clientele was thus socially apart. Of the other three, the Presbyterian Geelong College was small and distant. The remaining two schools—Presbyterian Scotch College and Methodist Wesley College— were the middling schools, serving a wider social mixture and affording a conduit for the upwardly mobile. Of these two schools, Scotch had three advantages over Wesley: it was older; it grew larger earlier; and Presbyterianism was more socially respectable than Methodism, not least because in Scotland it was the established religion.

In New South Wales, by contrast, a quite different school system emerged. There, the men listed in *Who's Who*, for example, are most likely to have attended a selective high school, like Sydney Boys' or Fort Street Boys'.[3]

One could write a history of Scotch College with a broad focus. Such an approach might see Victoria's Public Schools not so much competing as co-operating, mutually confirming (by their rivalries) each others' status as components in a single system. Or one could write a history of the school as manifesting educational themes, placing it within the context of work by Gwyneth Dow, 'Bon' Austin, Richard Selleck, Marjorie Theobald and others.[4] Or one could write about Scotch's role in shaping the membership and ideology of Australia's privileged circles of wealth and power. Or one could conduct a sustained examination of Scotch boys' later professions and careers (engineers, surgeons, lawyers, and so on). Such an enquiry is now at last possible because parallel to writing this history, and greatly facilitating it, Paul Mishura has created a comprehensive and accurate register of all Old Scotch Collegians. This realises one of the school's long-held dreams, and builds on the work of Percy Serle (1887)* and Bruce Symon (1945).

This book touches on those wider topics, although it may not set the school in context as much as some readers would like. Rather, I aim to look at Scotch more from inside than outside. The lived experience of the school breathes life into its own history, and the perspective of its pupils and teachers helps our understanding of larger themes as illuminated by the example of one school.

For Scotch's Diamond Jubilee in 1911, the history committee jettisoned many items worthy of inclusion.[5] I have followed in their steps. As in 1911, many readers of the present work may be hurt or puzzled that they, or someone they admired, are not mentioned. Many correspondents may wonder at the omission of material they sent me. For this I can only apologise, and offer as an explanation the practicalities of compressing 150 years and 32 000 boys into a single book (with 1500 words per year and 7 words per boy). This has meant that I have left out much that is worthy and interesting. From the initial drafts, I have cut well over 100 000 words.

My own experience is perhaps typical: this history mentions neither the School Captains and Vice-Captains I admired, nor the prefect who in his chosen school activity most awed and inspired me. Neither do I write about the activities that most engaged me, nor my school-friends, although a few appear in the footnotes because they returned questionnaires.

The questionnaires went out with the December 1997 issue of *Great Scot*, the school community's quarterly magazine. They invited all members of the Scotch community to play a part in writing this history. The questionnaires asked open-ended questions designed to stimulate memory. I received over 300 replies. These responses are not quantitatively representative, but I have treated them as qualitatively representative because they voice a very wide range of opinion. With a majority of respondents, I had a dialogue from sending follow-up questions.

Respondents ranged from six knights of the realm, through seven Duxes and six Captains of the School, to men who left early to escape or who swore never to send their sons there. Russell Coutie (1932) said of Scotch that he could 'make no criticisms whatsoever',[6] and others rhapsodised about 'the best days of your life' (1952),[7] or 'a brilliant and easy going time' (1981).[8]

* A date in brackets indicates the year a man left the school. The appearance of such a date after a man's name thus designates him as a Scotch Old Boy.

In sharp contrast, boarder James Lawson (1952) 'cannot recall any enjoyable experiences'[9] and Bill Fisher (1951) thinks that 'while it was probably good for me, the happiest day of my life was when I left the school.'[10] Dick Davies (1941) 'hated the place'.[11] Alan Moorehead (1926) wrote decades later of 'the sense of loathing—yes, positively loathing—that still overcomes me whenever I think of that place.'[12]

There seems little chance of reconciling such a divergence. Indeed, I have not tried to do so, for each man has written the truth about Scotch as he experienced it. There are as many Scotch Colleges as there are boys and teachers. All have a story, and the story of each is true. There is no single correct history of Scotch.

Another problem for the historian is that often an individual's experience does not seem compressible into an institutional history. For example, the noted biologist Professor Charles Birch (1935) writes of the school that

> my direction of life professionally was set there. This was mainly due to that wonderful biology teacher Mrs a'Beckett [staff 1921–36]. She not only enthused me for biology but from her I learned more about life and little details of living such as not having hot buttered toast as the butter prevents the first enzymes that digest the bread from acting. So it helps you to get indigestion. Secondly was the Natural History Society and wonderful nature excursions to learn about plants and insects especially. I found the students very friendly but did not form any life-long friendships. I learned much from particular ones such as Zelman Cowen [1935] who was in the same class. At one of his birthday parties I heard for the first time Beethoven's Emperor Concerto and that began my interest in music.[13]

The questionnaire respondents would concede that 'memory is a selective and hence unreliable source of information' (1969).[14] 'These days I wonder how many of my recollections truly reflect historical fact and how much they owe to the fond embroidery of the intervening years' (1950).[15] Throughout, we are dealing not just with people's memories but also with how they remember those memories, with an overlay of judgements and myths. In an organisation, history is concerned not only with what actually happened, but also with how events were felt and understood by the actors and how they became legendary for individuals and for the school itself. Also, all the memories about each period are (obviously) all from men of the same age. The younger men are more frank about sex, the older men more frank about family penury. Moreover, half the school's history lies beyond the reach of living memory. The oldest Old Boy with whom I have had contact left school in 1917.

As well as drawing on personal recollection, this book uses records kept by the school and associated organisations. Their survival has depended on the accidents of history. 'Not a single school record can be found prior to 1857.'[16] In 1998 the staff moved to a new common room, and emptied their cupboards into a large rubbish bin. Rummaging through it, I found useful documents and also several cheques, long out of date, made out to the Glenn Centre Sports Club. Dare one say that when Scots are even throwing out money, then much else of value is being lost.

Publications about Scotch are rare. There are a few articles. Richard

Selby Smith (Principal 1953–64) and Colin Healey (Principal 1964–75) published articles soon after leaving office.[17] David Merrett (1962) wrote about Scotch in the Great War.[18] The richest published sources are autobiographical and biographical, discussed in Chapter 7.

I was commissioned to write this book by the school Council, and have worked closely with the History Committee mentioned in the acknowledgements. My contract with the school gave me unrestricted access to all documents, save only that in using confidential documents I should not reveal the identity of the people concerned. The contract, also, gave me full freedom to write as I chose, except that the committee would have the final say in any dispute between us over matters of taste or appropriateness. No such dispute occurred.

The commission from the school was to write a history of the full 150 years. (The school's previous histories, in 1911, 1921, 1926, and 1952, each also preferred to gather in the whole tale from start to finish.[19]) Among the difficulties this entailed for the present work is that the Principal of the last two decades, Dr Gordon Donaldson, remains in office. I have therefore preferred for these most recent years to attempt to consider broad developments rather than to make the same sort of assessments open to the historian of more distant periods.

The book's structure combines narrative and themes. This can be disconcerting. When themes or topics recur in the school's life—like the teaching of French or the ideals of sportsmanship—it seemed best to deal with them just once, rather than consider them eight times under each headmaster. This means that even chapters 3 and 4, apparently 19th-century chapters, range to the end of the 20th century. It means, conversely, that a principal like Healey appears in many chapters outside the one that bears his name.

Endnotes are used chiefly for quotations. Quotations without endnotes are from questionnaire responses that did not authorise citation by name. Much of what I say on recent years comes from conversations with staff, boys, and recent Old Boys. The school archives have been in storage this last year, leading to some bibliographical raggedness in the notes.

I have often standardised my sources' spelling and use of apostrophes. I have kept or introduced capitals at the start of quotations.

I speak often of Scotch as an agentic force—as *doing* or *deciding* or *wanting*—and I hope the reader will forgive this shorthand for Council or some other authority in the school. As I also make clear, a large school is a complex organisation often internally at odds with itself.

As author, I should declare an interest in my subject. I attended Scotch as a boy, benefited from it, and was happy there. I imagine that some of this rosy glow suffuses what I have written. But I have not been an active Old Boy and had not been there for over 30 years until invited to write this book. I imagine this gives me some distance from my subject and some hope of a historian's objectivity. Even so, one day when I was researching at the school it was raining and the library was very crowded; one of the librarians asked me where we went in my day when it was raining, and I found that I couldn't remember it ever raining.

This book is a homage to those I knew and loved at Scotch as a boy. My world then was filled by Skewes, of course, and by Drew and Car, Rick, Ref, Mac, Bill, Jessup, Rossiter, Ron, and Young. I have not seen most of them for decades, but I find, as I look back, how fresh my memories of them are. Three teachers also stand out: Ivan Collins (staff 1954–60) in the Junior School, Alec Lyne (Dux 1928, staff 1942–74, Senior Geography Master and Drama Master), and above all the Rev. David Webster (Senior History Master 1963–70) who shaped me as a historian. They taught me, in their different ways, how to see the world, and how to talk about what I saw. If this book pleases you, much of what is good in it comes from them.

And now at last I can feel what Alexander Morrison wrote in his diary on 18 December 1884: 'relief of work over and boys gone'.

North Fitzroy
St Andrew's Day 2000

1

LAWSON
1851–1856

Thirty years before Melbourne's first permanent European settlers, on 7 February 1803, the Surveyor-General of New South Wales rowed up the River Yarra through what is now Richmond and Heyington and came to a pleasant spot where a creek flowed in. Gardiner's Creek would be its name one day. 'Saw some natives', recorded one of the party, James Fleming. 'The land in general is a fine black soil, ten to eighteen inches deep. Timber—gums, Banksia, oak, and mimosa of all sorts, but not large except the gum. The river appears to rise to the height of eight or ten feet at times by the wreck on the trees.'[1] Here they stopped for a picnic. The next day they rowed back down the river and sailed out to sea and away. Perhaps it is true, that once you have looked at Scotch College there is nothing else in Melbourne worth seeing.

On the other side of the world, in Edinburgh, the Rev. Thomas Chalmers advocated education 'impregnated with religion'. One of his disciples, the

Robert Lawson, at his school outside Bacchus Marsh, several years before his death.

1

Rev. James Forbes, is celebrated as the founder of Scotch College. Many of his legacies still abide: a fissile Presbyterianism; a Christian rebuttal of 'mere secular instruction';[2] and a passionate belief that education can make a difference and is the only way to make good citizens, honest neighbours, dutiful children, and dutiful parents.

Aged twenty-five, Forbes came in 1838 to three-year-old Melbourne as its second Presbyterian minister. He founded a parish school, and campaigned vigorously for education. In 1846 he walked away from all he had created, when he left the Presbyterian Church to help form the Free Church of Australia Felix, as part of the Presbyterian Disruption that spread from Scotland. Forbes soon built up a new parish and school. He also advocated a secondary school, to furnish teachers for parish schools, and in 1850 the church authorised him to ask the Free Church of Scotland 'to send out an accomplished Teacher to take charge of an Academy for instruction in the higher branches of science and literature, and in which young men might pursue their preparatory studies with a view to the office of the Ministry'.[3] It was 'to be open and accessible to all without denominational peculiarities'.[4] Scotland responded warmly.[5] To pay the new teacher's salary, the Misses Mure put up £200 for the first two years,[6] and economised by dispensing with their footman. The views of the footman are not recorded.

The Free Church in Scotland chose Robert Lawson, a teacher aged about thirty, to be 'Rector of the Academy at Melbourne'.[7] They gave him maps, books, and up to £50 for an *Encyclopaedia Britannica*, school books and apparatus.

Forbes died by 'the afflicting hand of God' on 12 August 1851, the month before Lawson arrived.[8] As to the impact of his death on Scotch, we can only speculate. Arguably the school lost a father who might have supported it for another forty years, and defended its Principal within the church. Equally arguably, Forbes might have proved a difficulty for the school. With his passionate views on education he might have been unable to let the Principals find their own way. His life manifested the view that there is a time to plant and a time to pluck up what is planted, and he might have abandoned Scotch as he had his earlier schools. Or he might have opposed the Free Church's union with other Presbyterian churches in 1859, and kept Scotch marginalised in the hands of a rump church. As it was, his death let darkness cover Scotch's birth. The new teachers from Scotland were unlikely to dig out old colonial newspapers and never mentioned Forbes's earlier writings. Even his name died, and the school's first histories called him John instead of James.

Lawson's charter came not from Forbes but sailed with him from Edinburgh, as four succinct 'suggestions'.[9] Firstly, that he see himself as a Christian missionary, teaching classes with a Christian purpose, like the Free Church schoolmasters in India. Secondly, that he inspire young men to become Presbyterian clergymen. Thirdly, that he arrange lectures open to the public. And fourthly, that he report annually to Scotland. Explicit educational goals were soon developed in Melbourne, where they wanted a school rather than a missionary school.

Lawson arrived in Melbourne on 11 September 1851, advertised in the newspapers on 1 October, and opened school on 6 October 1851, now celebrated as Foundation Day.

Of that first day we have no record beyond knowing it was a fine spring day. He and his wife, Isabella, an Irishwoman, were the only teachers. She took the junior boys, and she spoke French and German fluently, so conversation in these languages was an inducement to boarders, who lived with the Lawsons at 198 Stephen Street, now Exhibition Street, Melbourne.

Who were the first Scotch Collegians? The Register is lost, but we can identify 40 boys in that first year. Among them were John Alexander Adamson (grandfather of Alec 'Tiger' Lyne) and Joseph Wright Cade (great-great-grandfather of Tom Cade, Captain 2000). In 1911 at the Diamond Jubilee old William Tait signed his menu: 1851 First Boarder. As in Presbyterian primary schools, enrolments reached beyond the church. Only one-third of the boys were Presbyterians, whilst another third were Church of England. They were not predominantly Scottish. Birthplace evidence is slight, but Australian-born were the largest group, followed by Scots (all Lowlanders) and English, and soon Irish.

In 1851 the Rev. William Miller (or Millar) became Convenor of the church's new Academy Committee. As Lawson is reckoned the school's first Principal—albeit in temporary accommodation with his wife as his first teacher—so we may count Miller as the first Chairman of the College Council.

Scotch's life has been shaped by a trinity of forces: church, Principal, and Committee (later Council). Each played a different role in the school's life. The church was founder, sustainer, and judge. The Rector or Principal was the school in action, teaching, leading, hiring and firing staff, and disciplining. The Committee or Council sat in between, focusing the energies of the church, supporting the Principal, and managing any dialogue between church and Principal. By the end of the first year these three forces were in place and at work.

The school opened in a small bluestone cottage, already a Free Church School, in Spring Street, between Lonsdale and Little Lonsdale Streets. It was destroyed by fire in 1943 but a pavement plaque marks the spot. The school moved to 61 Spring Street, on the corner of Spring and Little Collins Streets. This building was before and afterwards a hotel. The large bar-room held the main classes simultaneously. A gate led from the yard into Little Collins Street where the town roughs heckled the academicians. One night a burglar with a knife wounded a teacher, George Hanson, who slept in the downstairs dormitory to keep order.

The first site of Scotch College at Spring Street, Melbourne.

Within a year the church sought to obtain land and erect a permanent building.[10] The Committee was told to raise money to buy land, and—no harm in trying—it asked Lieutenant-Governor La Trobe for a grant of land.[11] The Free Church abhorred government control of religion, but welcomed grants for education. A century later, when Presbyterians opposed Scotch's receiving government grants, this went beyond the original, pragmatic Free Church stance.

The school got its grant of land. It was Scotch's good fortune to be born in the same year as the gold rush. Whether or not this made La Trobe or his successor feel wealthier, it did make them anxious about keeping order as adventurers flooded into the colony. Men of property supported the churches as a bulwark against disorder. Also, pastoralists and merchants wanted to avoid the need to send their families to schools overseas. Between 1851 and 1856, government aid to religion doubled, doubled, and doubled again.[12] A few years later, men of property were less fearful of revolution and, as inter-denominational rivalries swelled, the flood of government money to the churches dried up.

Two acres (one hectare) on Eastern Hill were granted to the church for a grammar school in 1853, to be held by trustees nominated by the church: Miller, the Rev. John Tait (the Moderator), the Rev. D. M. Sinclair, Archibald Bonar, merchant of Melbourne, and John Armstrong of Bush Station,

Geelong. Trustees were the church's usual means of holding property or entering into contracts. When college property was insured, for example, it was in the names of the Trustees, and it was the Trustees, not the Committee, whom the church instructed to proceed with the building.

To help pay for the construction, the Presbyterians received one-seventh of the government funds allocated to the five leading denominations to build schools. But wages were startlingly high, as labour left for the goldfields, and the Trustees borrowed on their personal security— presumably this meant Bonar and Armstrong, for the three clergymen may not have had many assets. Costs reached £10 000 (500 times annual fees).

In January 1854 the school opened on Eastern Hill, on the corner of Lansdowne Street and Grey Street (now Cathedral Place). It is now (2000) occupied by the Peter MacCallum Cancer Institute.

The new classrooms seemed large and bare, less homely but more scholastic. The boarders slept in a dormitory and the second master slept there too, to prevent rowdyism. The *Argus* in 1855 described the boys as healthy and cheerful, notwithstanding the strict discipline maintained.

The site was small and became ever more cramped by new building over the next fifty years. In the 1870s in a humpy in a corner of the playground an old couple sold sweets.[13] By the turn of the century,

Our playground was but a scrap of asphalt, inclined at an angle of about 15° with a 3 ft [1 m] drop at the lower end. It was bounded by a brick wall … and a row of solid outbuildings ranging from bike shed, past tool shop to gents only. Recess-time kick-for-kick on this terrain was not a pastime for weaklings and only the reckless dared to go up for a mark. The going up was all right but the coming down offered the dangerous alternative of a crashing descent over that 3 ft drop and a head-on collision with the unsympathetic wall.[14]

Although the site was small it was well-situated, being open and high. To the north, St Patrick's Cathedral was yet to be built. To the east, the boys played in the future Fitzroy Gardens, a wilderness with a gully that Henry Jennings (entered by 1859) could jump even at its widest. They played cricket (one boy died from a blow on the forehead) and other games in which Lawson often joined. Traffic on Lansdowne Street was slight, and the gardens were in effect extensions of the school. Alexander Morrison included them in his definition of College bounds. Boys ate lunch there. Over the decades the gardens grew in beauty with trees and statues, and Scotch's 'high-spirited youths' protected the trees from vandals.[15] Later, a nude figure of Psyche aroused lust in Ross Campbell (1928, Rhodes Scholar) as he ate his apple turnover.

The second advantage of Eastern Hill was that it was high ground at a time when the only drainage was natural. Morrison marketed it as naturally healthy, and attributed its freedom from epidemics to its elevated, open position surrounded by so many public reserves, although he did attribute it also 'to our spacious and lofty class-rooms, and to the great amount of personal attention I always give to ventilation, drainage, and cleanliness'.[16] Infectious diseases were harder to avoid. In 1884 measles raged for a week.

Here on this hectare the school settled for 70 years.

Enrolments rose rapidly to around 150 and then levelled off. The gold rush continued to suck people into Victoria, grown more populous than New South Wales.

Lawson had at least a dozen teachers. Andrew Burn (staff 1851–55) was principal assistant master in 1853–55 until he left to become Headmaster of the Free Church School at Geelong, the first of many headmasters groomed at Scotch. The most notable master was Dr John Macadam (staff 1855–64), who taught Natural Science, Chemistry, Botany, and Geology. From 1861 he also lectured at the university. A commanding figure with a powerful voice, he was clean-shaven, which was uncommon. His hair was worn long. Some say it was red and others say it was black.[17] It is a reminder that all our information comes through the prism of fallible human observation.

The Melbourne Academy was also called Mr Lawson's Academy, or the Grammar School, or names more reflective of its religious and ethnic roots—the Scots' College (that is, the college of the Scots) or the Scotch College (that is, the college that is Scottish). For a few years all these names occurred side by side until by the 1860s usage settled on 'the Scotch College'. One further change remained, that of becoming simply 'Scotch College'.

At the end of 1856 Lawson resigned. 'Nothing whatever is known to us of the circumstances', wrote the school's historian 55 years later, in 1911, when at least some oral explanation might have endured.[18] The resignation of a principal in the prime of life without any convincing explanation will always raise questions. Lawson did not resign because he was leaving Melbourne or leaving teaching, for he opened a school in Fitzroy, and later in rural Victoria.

Perhaps he tired of the church, or the church of him. Rumours and conjectures can be found to illustrate either of these possibilities. Perhaps he could not work with the Academy Committee's convenor, Miller, who was replaced after Lawson. They had arrived on the same ship, where perhaps they had disliked each other? Or perhaps the reverse is true, that Miller was closely associated with Lawson and left when Lawson left?

Perhaps, finally, we should believe a hearsay account of the opinion of Lawson's sister, Mrs James Muir, that his zealous labour was checked by a report from a Hamilton parent that 'lack of discipline gave the young students an excess of freedom calculated to undermine their moral make-up'. An investigation cleared Lawson's honour, but his 'fair and naturally sensitive mind' brooded upon this until he resigned to found a school of his own.[19]

In 1869 he committed suicide by stepping overboard on a voyage between England and Australia.

It is hard to say much about Lawson. He stayed only a few years, and by the time the school became interested in its own history—say at its Diamond Jubilee in 1911—few of his estimated 276 boys were left. We hear briefly that he could run fast, was a splendid teacher, a strict disciplinarian (his favourite tawse was a brass-bound carter's whip without a lash), had a mild sense of humour, and was generally liked by the boys. His nickname of 'Bobby' suggests affection, but was also the slang word for the newly invented policeman. The histories lapse into a kind of caricature, reciting that his hands were as soft as a lady's whilst Mrs Lawson's manner was masculine. Lawson is said to have been of medium height, well-proportioned, and of fair complexion. A photograph of him (see p. 1) is here published for the first time. Previously the school has used only one picture of him (below), which some Lawsonites said is not a good likeness.[20] In 1951, the centenary historian detected in it 'a lurking sense of humour' whilst Allan Dawes (1917) saw a 'wild eye [that] belied a stern Scots forthrightness.'[21]

Robert Lawson, first principal, 1851–56.

2

MORRISON
1857–1903

Many small schools collapse with the loss of their founder-teacher, but Scotch had an exoskeleton in the form of the Free Church which provided institutional continuity. Or almost so: not for the last time Scotch was a casualty of fights within the church. The Rev. William Miller was at loggerheads with his successor as convenor, the Rev. Dr Adam Cairns. Miller refused to attend Committee meetings or to hand over the correspondence and minute books, which are now lost. The Committee expressed 'regret and surprise'.[1]

In 1857 another Miller, John Stevens Miller, 'succeeding Mr Lawson in the Rectorship' of Scotch, offered 'a sedulous attention to … approved modes of tuition'. Mrs and Miss Miller cared for the boarders.[2] Enrolments fell. Many boys may have followed Lawson to his new school. Mrs Miller died. By August 1857 Scotch had only about 50 day boys and six boarders. Miller moved on, and in 1872 was ordained. We know little about him, and Scotch pays him no honour nor counts him as a Principal. Later histories call him Acting Rector. If Scotch had then had several short-term Principals, Miller might have been remembered, but instead Scotch now embarked upon the 46-year reign of Alexander Morrison.

It became customary to call Morrison a farmer's son—'the son of a simple Scotch farmer', says Colin Gilray (Principal 1934–53).[3] Perhaps this made later eminence more glorious, or perhaps it implied an inner strength or straightforwardness supposedly linked with working the land. In fact, Morrison's father was also the local road engineer, and his mother's family owned property. Yet as the sixth son he had to make his own way, and at university supported himself by bursaries and teaching. He was educated at his local parish school, at the Elgin Academy, and at the University of Aberdeen, so this young man knew little of the world but one part of Scotland. His elder brothers were already clergy or schoolmasters, and he became Rector of St John's Grammar School in Hamilton, near Glasgow. Unfortunately, many of the pupils went instead to the new private school set up by his predecessor. But soon he doubled the numbers, and developed the study of Science and Commerce.

His wife, Christina, was described by their daughter as 'sent to good schools', a good linguist, and with some knowledge of music. She 'wrote excellent, well-expressed letters in an elegant and by no means characterless handwriting', with a quill pen and violet ink.[4]

In an age when letters and people travelled only as fast as wind, hoof, and steam could carry them, the church replaced Lawson with commendable speed. Commissioners in Scotland offered the post to two elder Morrison brothers and then to young Sandy. He was already on his way when the Melbourne Synod learnt his name in May 1857.

He was 28 years old.

YOUR LOCKS WERE LIKE THE RAVEN

The Morrisons reached Melbourne in July 1857, with a baby in arms, a nurse, and Christina's elder sister. The school's version is, romantically, that he went at once to the school where the boys were hard at work and gave them a half-holiday.[5] The family memory is that they were not met, and spent the first night in a wharf-side hotel.[6] Nor had the school prepared for them: the house of the childless Lawsons was too small and lacked a garden for the growing family.

Morrison and the Committee began awkwardly. Morrison had been told he could spend £1000 on 'outfit passage money and necessary expenses'. (This seems a large amount; a century later the Selby Smiths' fares and furniture cost the same.) When he asked the school to meet these costs, the Committee had not heard of the arrangement and could obtain no details from the estranged William Miller who had authorised the expense. The Committee expressed concern for Morrison's 'awkward and painful position' but denied liability to pay his costs, and obliged him to write an unconditional acceptance of this decision. Morrison's response to financial obstacles—to all obstacles—was to meet them head on. He decided to pay off this unexpected debt as speedily as possible.[7] The only way to do so was to expand the school and increase its revenue. The school did not pay him a salary, but all its revenue went to him, out of which he met the running costs and paid up to 10% to the church. What remained, he kept, so he stood directly to gain from increasing enrolments and keeping costs low. It was even worth his while to contribute towards the cost of expansion.

In a year he quadrupled enrolments to 201 with an average enrolment of 150. By 1860 he enrolled 284 and averaged 225. Thereafter numbers levelled off. There were 340 in 1874. The drop-out rate was high. 'It will scarcely be credited that nearly one-half of the Pupils attending the Scotch College enter annually, remaining only a short period with us. In explanation of this fact, a variety of causes, arising partly out of the still unsettled state of the country, frequent changes of residence, &c., might be adduced.'[8] Morrison wisely made each term's fees payable in advance. This also helped his cashflow and slightly increased what he earned in interest. Even small sums compound well when extended over forty years. For each of the four terms he charged five guineas for day students, ten guineas for day boarders (who ate at the school), and 25 guineas for resident boarders (with a 10%

reduction for brothers). The Preparatory School fee was three guineas. Fees remained unchanged for the rest of the century.

Morrison's higher enrolments needed accommodation. Within two months of his arrival he asked for two new rooms. The Committee appointed a sub-committee to commission an architect, set a maximum cost, and appointed another sub-committee to raise a loan. These three decisions herald the stamp of the school's governance to this day: a determination to get good professional advice, a frugal resolve to control costs, and a never-ending endeavour to raise money. Soon, the Building Sub-Committee was also 'to see that the work is done in as substantial a manner as possible'.[9] This is how Scotch has always tried to build. Gilray, for example, decided against a principal's house when wartime restrictions meant it could be built only of timber.

In another two months Morrison had them add a room for the use of 'a juvenile class', and 1858 was scarcely begun before he obtained further enlargements, and in 1859 he asked for a new building. Opened in 1860, it meant 'that two classes are never taught in the same room at the same time'.[10] He also wanted water laid on and piped drainage. (Their absence reminds us that the Scotch of those days was not a smaller version of today's but, even with good natural drainage, was a different, smellier kind of place.)

The cost of additional rooms was met by the 10% of revenue Morrison paid the church and by borrowing from a bank although, unwilling to wait, Morrison erected a wooden classroom at his own expense, on terms agreed with the Committee. For the new building, the Committee chose a plan that allowed the work to occur in stages, thereby combining expansion with commonsense money management. Cairns sent a letter and a lithographed sketch to leading Presbyterian gentlemen, asking them to be guarantors for a loan. They wrote promissory notes, each guaranteeing to pay a certain amount in a year's time; these notes were renewed annually for

A raven-haired Alexander Morrison and daughter Eliza. The photographic technology of the day obliged sitters to remain motionless for some time and this prevented them from smiling.

diminishing amounts as the loan was paid off.[11]

The money went to Morrison himself, and the church guaranteed him against being personally responsible for repaying the loan. This was a simpler arrangement than having the money go to Morrison through the church. It was monitored by the audit process, but also reflects a confidence in Morrison's probity. The drive to expand the school served the interests of both Principal and church, and we can detect by 1859 a mutually satisfactory relationship. When the school had difficulty borrowing, it was Morrison who advanced the necessary £600. The Committee undertook to repay him capital plus interest. That Morrison had the money to hand shows how quickly he was turning a profit. He paid no board or lodging and there was no income tax.

Joseph Reed was the architect, now and later. (In 1883–90 he was in partnership with Anketell Henderson (1868) who became a leading Melbourne architect. A century later another architect, Bill Corker (1962), of Denton Corker Marshall, helped stamp a new face on Melbourne's public buildings and freeways.) Among Reed's works are the Exhibition Building and Ormond College, but he proved unable to give coherence to Scotch's repeated expansions, which had what Morrison called 'a want of uniformity'.[12]

Next, Morrison proposed 'an Infant and Preparatory School'. The Committee agreed and allowed him to advance them 'a sum sufficient for the necessary outlay', with repayment and interest deferred until after the present debts were paid off.[13] It was built by early 1862, when two of Sir Redmond Barry's sons were among the first to enter. In 1865 it fluctuated between 10 and 30 boys.

The external loans were quickly paid off, as the Committee refinanced them for diminishing amounts from a succession of banks. By the mid-1860s, Morrison's strategy of borrowing to build and then paying off the debt from the increased enrolments was seen to be a success, and the annual call for promissory notes from Friends of the College became over-subscribed. Promissory notes had proved a good way to manage loans: Scotch raised loans, lenders felt guaranteed, and the benefactors did not actually have to part with any money, which no doubt enhanced Morrison's financial reputation.

As a businessman, Morrison was good at marketing. He positioned his product as comparable with 'the best conducted Educational and Boarding Establishments in the mother country.'[14] From 1861 he occasionally called Scotch a Public School, and at Speech Day in 1864 he summarised a recent Royal Commission on English Public Schools and concluded that 'we may fairly venture to assert our superiority, inasmuch as the course of study … recommended is exactly what we have been pursuing for many years.'[15] Having dispensed with Eton and Harrow, Scotch's main competitors were the local one-man private schools, 'where much is professed but little done, except in a very superficial, unsubstantial way'.[16] Morrison sought to distinguish Scotch from these. He always called his school *the Institution*. He emphasised its organisational depth by representing himself as a Headmaster supervising departments, such as the 'Commercial Department', and in the school's *Annual Report* he published departmental reports. In doing so, though he gave up the role of all-knowing Principal, he showed the high quality of his staff. This he did also when he engaged a scholar to take charge of senior classes, and especially the classes preparing for the university 'as have hitherto devolved upon the Principal'.[17] Instead, Morrison devoted more time to the junior classes, where he could form 'an estimate of the ability and character of each pupil, a knowledge of which is of considerable importance in enabling me to guide him in his future course of study'.[18] In this, Morrison compared himself favourably to English headmasters. For the same reasons, in 1867 he appointed a Vice-Principal (1867–69), the Rev. John Moir of Aberdeen. ('When roused he'd hurl an ink-pot or the chalk, / Or anything at hand. / His marksmanship was bad, he seldom scored, / Though in his teaching he took better aim.'[19])

Morrison probably let departments devise their own courses, since there were subjects taught at Scotch in which he is not known to have had expertise. Nevertheless, he exercised 'a careful Superintendence over all the Departments of the Institution' and took 'an active part in the Teaching of every Class'.[20] In a cramped school he had 'almost daily opportunities of witnessing' how teachers conducted their classes.[21]

As a businessman, he moved quickly to sell new products as they came onto the market. In 1862 the Victorian Government set up a Civil Service Examination, and Scotch at once began to prepare students for it. Most senior boys sat for both this and matriculation.

He also developed Speech Day. In 1851 the church examiners presented prizes on the spot, but in 1857 Morrison published a prize list and from 1860 he delivered an *Annual Report*. Parents were uninvolved in the school and this was their chance to size up the Principal. They liked what they saw, this tall young man in his early thirties, with his upright stance and that genetic mixture of the Celts, black hair and blue eyes (and his were pale blue, not the deep blue painted in his portrait[22]).

His annual speeches were clear, concise, ordered, and informative, and each year he told parents something new or found new ways to tell them what had to be repeated. He was a good teacher, as the parents experienced for themselves. He blew the school's trumpet (only to be expected), and he did so not with high phrases but (as a careful Scot) with facts and figures— the number of hours per week on each subject, the number and percentage of students who passed the university-run examinations in final year, and with how many exhibitions, and whether Scotch boys were more likely to pass than other boys. He prepared a table of how subjects interlocked, and made calculations of average marks. From 1870 he recorded Scotch boys' achievements at university, on the grounds that boys' success there depended on the teaching imparted at school. Scotch's worth was measurable. He soon added lustre to Speech Day by inviting distinguished visitors like the Governor to preside and distribute the prizes.

Morrison also exercised a schoolmaster's prerogative in training parents to train their sons. Homework was part of boys' chores from as early as 1862, in preparing the next day's lessons. Morrison urged parents to see that boys did this work. All boys had a timetable showing what subjects they had next day. For the rest of the century he laboured the point that low marks meant that 'home lessons have either been neglected or imperfectly prepared', and he chided parents that 'Written excuses … for non-preparation of lessons are still given much too freely'.[23]

When boys qualified for university while still aged fifteen or sixteen, Morrison instead offered them a further year at school in a small class that

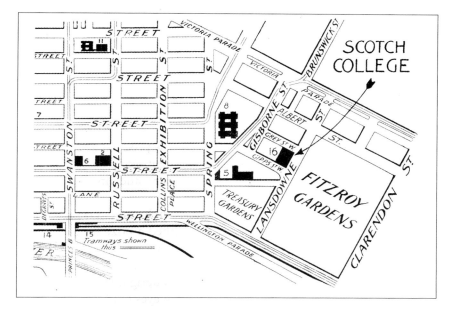

Map of East Melbourne.

read the first year's university work, run by a teacher chosen at Oxford like Albert Weigall (staff 1863–66). It prepared them well for entering university. It made them more likely to win exhibitions and so boosted Scotch's prestige.

Sport, too, began. In February 1858 Scotch played cricket against Geelong Grammar. Two brothers, George and John Tait, who played for Geelong Grammar in 1858, played for Scotch in 1859, their father having moved to Melbourne. The Tait Cup commemorates them, and Scotch was pleased to win it when it was first contested in 1998.

Among the boys' other games, one in retrospect became important when in August 1858 Scotch and Melbourne Grammar played a game resembling Australian Rules Football. In teams of forty a side, at Richmond Park under the auspices of a fine day and their respective magnates, the juvenile presbytery and episcopacy came out uncommonly strong. Both masters and boys appeared to reach the acme of enjoyment, and most jubilant were the cheers that rang out amongst the gum-trees and the she-oaks of the park when the Scotch College achieved a goal. This event occupied nearly three hours in its accomplishment. The compliment was shortly reciprocated by the opposition, who made a grand effort to do the deed. Evening's anxious shades cut short the amusement which, to judge from the evenly balanced scales of results and the apparently inexhaustible physique of the combatants, must otherwise have been interminable.

The game spread over several days. 'Twice or thrice the Scotsmen prematurely rang out the slogan of victory' but the outcome was likely to be resolved only 'if masters were barred'.[24] This new game had a promising future.[25] The result was a draw. The Cordner-Eggleston cup commemorates this match.

In rowing, the first Head of the River race occurred in 1868, after Charles Field wrote a challenge to Melbourne Grammar. Scotch won, and won the hundredth race in 1967 in a boat given to Scotch by Field's son Hugh.

In 1859 the school's ownership changed, passing from the Free Church to the Presbyterian Church of Victoria newly formed by the union of several Presbyterian churches. Some Free Church parishes joined the Presbyterian Church only later, in 1867, and a few parishes of Scotch's founder exist to this day (2000). The new church named new Trustees, all laymen. The absence of clergy suggests that experience had proved the need for men of property in this position.

In the mid-1860s the church loosened its control over its schools. By then there were several Presbyterian secondary schools, and the church asked them to state 'the amount of superintendence on the part of the Church which they would desire'.[26] The church for its part no longer wanted a committee for each school, and so in 1865 Scotch lost its governing committee and from 1868 reported to the church's Education Committee. In any case, supervision seemed less necessary. The church expressed a 'lively satisfaction' with Scotch's prosperity,[27] and year after year commended Morrison for his 'able and successful management of the Institution, and the eminent services rendered by him to the Church'.[28] Otherwise Scotch drew little attention.

THE EXPULSION FROM THE GARDEN

Morrison sweetened his next building scheme, in 1869, by linking it to the education of rural Presbyterian ministers' sons. Their fees would be reduced, and subsidised by bursaries whose donors could nominate the recipient, subject to approval by the Committee. Tacked on to this was a proposal to raise a new loan to build a principal's residence and new dormitories. A church enquiry confirmed that 'the accommodation for the Principal and his family is extremely defective'. The house was pokey, and the small storeroom prevented Morrison from cutting costs by buying wholesale. 'There is no study, nor any room which the Principal can regard as exclusively his own', for 'the office is utilised in the evenings for the practice of music'.[29]

The church adopted Morrison's proposal. But much grief was to come of it.

Previously in raising money, the Committee had borrowed (from banks or from Morrison) and paid the debt out of Morrison's percentage payments to the church, the loan being secured by promissory notes from wealthy Presbyterians. Instead, the Education Committee, perhaps because it disagreed with the methods of the former Scotch College Committee, perhaps because of the large amount needed, chose to guarantee the loan with a mortgage. What could Scotch mortgage? Not its land, as that was an inalienable grant from the Crown. Instead, the school would mortgage its revenue. (Church minutes also talk of mortgaging the buildings.)[30]

Delays ensued while the church named new Trustees: Sir James McCulloch, Robert Simson, John Matheson, (Sir) James MacBain, and James Wilson.[31] Meanwhile, the Committee accepted an offer from Morrison that he pay the church 12.5% of gross revenue instead of 10% as hitherto, until the building debt was paid, provided the Committee went straight ahead with extending the buildings.[32]

By May 1870 the formalities were overcome and financiers clamoured to lend money, but Scotch had already met another problem, which delayed the mortgage, split the church and damaged Morrison's good name.[33]

The issue was a dispute with the school's neighbour and parish church, Chalmers Church, which used part of Scotch's land as a manse garden. Scotch's legal ownership of this land had been recently reaffirmed by the Crown, and the Education Committee told Chalmers Church 'that the portion of the College site now in their occupation will be required for the new additions about to be built'.[34] The minister of Chalmers Church, he whose garden was at stake, was the same Rev. Dr Adam Cairns who had convened the Scotch College Committee from 1857 to 1865, but he now flung himself against Scotch's expansion with all the fervour with which he opposed trains running on Sundays. He insisted that he and Lawson had verbally agreed to swap this land with another block. Could Cairns have forgotten that he only obtained permission to build, on this land granted to Scotch for educational purposes, by representing his house as 'a Professor's House'?[35]

The dispute burst upwards through the Education Committee, the General Assembly and Parliament.

The Education Committee proved unable to defend Scotch. Cairns and

CRICKET

Cricket is older than Scotch, and the earliest prizes included one for cricket. In 150 years, Scotch has seen almost every possible cricket result. In 1962 it won every cricket match except one which it lost to Carey Grammar by one run. In 1975 Scotch lost the premiership by the last ball of the season. Scotch's greatest score was 646, against Wesley in 1898, captained by John Graham. Scotch's worst score was 5, against Geelong Grammar in 1900, despite which Scotch were still premiers that year, captained by Albert 'Prince' Treeby.

Among Scotch's bowlers, Leslie Freemantle (1917 Captain of Cricket) in a match against Wesley in 1917 took 16 wickets for 92 runs, an average of 5.75. Derek Leong (1969) in a match against Caulfield in 1969 took 15 wickets for 70, an average of 4.67. Tom Crow (1950 School Captain, Captain of Cricket 1948–50) over a season managed 31 wickets for 312 runs, an average of 10.06. (*Satura* called him 'a bowler with frequent spasms of excellent batting'.[36])

John Smith (1954), a fast bowler, took four wickets with four balls against Xavier in March 1952, a feat achieved only once before in Scotch's history. He actually took 5 wickets in 6 balls, but 'unfortunately a search of the records could not give any comparable feats, as such things are not usually recorded.'[37]

The greatest individual score was 293 by Ian Fleming (1928) against Xavier in 1928. Daniel McLeod (1891) hit 204 not out in 1891 against Geelong Grammar, and Robert Hodges hit 204 against Caulfield Grammar in 1983. George Meares (1924) scored a century in each innings, 131 and 122 not out, against Wesley in 1924.

Scotch's greatest cricketing sons have been batsmen, like Colin McDonald (1946) and Bob Cowper (1958 Captain of Cricket), later the only player to score a triple century in Australia, 307 against England in 1966. McDonald was never elected Captain of Cricket. Gilray allowed this to happen, respecting the boys' democracy. Instead, he added a unique footnote on the honour board, setting out McDonald's centuries. Cowper played in the First XI for four seasons, starting in Year 9 aged 14. His youthfulness sparked jokes about his playing in shorts. Tim Downing (1999 School Captain) spent five years in the First XI starting in Year 9.

The number of teams levelled off at around 30 in the 1970s.

Some boys found cricket 'so boring',[38] but others found it full of feelings. Being an opening batsman could be stressful. 'In year 7 and 8, I couldn't handle the pressure of opening the batting and was always so nervous about playing that I dreaded each training session and each match' (1996).[39] Facing fast bowlers could be frightening (1936).[40] But cricket's leisurely pace gave 'time to mix with other members of the team when your side is batting. … gave me the chance to get to know boys outside my own class' (1929).

During the 20th century Scotch developed superb facilities, playing on turf pitches when even suburban sides played on matting.

A drive flashes from the thick meat of my bat,
Leaving extra cover for dead. All around us,
Touched by a pastoral brush,
Midges hover and glint:
Chiaroscuro daubs the river-gums.
The serene hour brims with oceanic feeling,
Drowning these four green ovals deep as a
    dream
In which I move at ease, for Morrison's off-
    spinners
Aren't going to turn an inch this afternoon.

Goings and dwindlings: my stupid adolescence,
Bone-dry years of hollowness and blank,
Thirsting, fills out again with fields and games
Till my lifelong model
Of happiness or poise becomes
A well-timed leg glance taken off my toes.

Chris Wallace-Crabbe (1950)[41]

'Men who've made their name as demons with the ball' (The School Song). Scott Lacey (1982), shown here bowling, writes, 'The photographer Andrew Rahni was courageous enough to actually stand in the net to take it. In only a few deliveries he realised that accuracy was definitely my short suit. He wasn't badly injured'.

one of his parishioners, James Balfour, a businessman, were members of the Committee and publicly advocated the Chalmers Church case. There was no requirement that Committee members abstain from voting when there was a clash of interest. Probably the men who sided with the school also had other loyalties. The Rev. Irving Hetherington, minister of the Scots' Church, said Scotch should build where it thought best, but perhaps this was a skirmish in some wider war among Presbyterian clergymen?

Since Balfour threatened to appeal any decision he did not like to the General Assembly, the Committee sent the whole problem there. Scotch was handicapped by the lack of a Scotch College Committee to represent it within the church system. It fell to Morrison to argue the school's case at the Education Committee, and again at the Assembly where he had no right to speak and was denied a hearing.[42] This was a disastrous position for any principal to be in.

The Assembly, consisting of gentlemen with gardens, upheld the parish's claim on the school's land, and instructed it to give Scotch some land in

ROWING

Of all sports, rowing most captured the school's soul. 'A little bit out of proportion you know,' said one Chairman of Council.[43]

Rowing's attractions are several. Months of synchronised teamwork and training are tested in a burst of 'intense physical pain'. It combines 'strength, balance and dexterity'.[44] It requires a level of subordination of the individual to the team not found in most other sports, what one winning Captain of Boats calls the harmony of a very fast crew.[45] With rowing, 'teamwork was everything'.[46] 'To always show up, to rely on others and to know that others relied on you, I think are very important lessons that stand one in good stead throughout life.'[47] If one of the crew 'catches a crab' (loses control of his oar), this 'can be dangerous because an oar could break, or rowers on their sliding seats can collide,'[48] whilst the oar slews into the water beside the boat and acts as a brake.

> I saw the crews a-rowing in the College House
>   Regatta,
> The ones in front were Morrison and Monash
>   were the latter.
>   Yes, Monash were the latter …
>
> Lest Morrisonian heads should swell, I wouldn't
>   like to flatter,
> But their oars, as they drew well ahead, made
>   quiet a rhythmic patter,
> While the Monash oarsmen's blunders caused a
>   really frightful splatter
> Though the cox exhorted shrilly non-stop: 'Atter,
>   fellows, atter!'
> But suddenly the green boys stopped—we saw—
>   despite the chatter
> Of 'Monash hasn't got a chance'—that some-
>   thing was the matter.
>
> At this dramatic moment we'll conclude this
>   little patter
> For Morrison's most *crabby* on the subject of
>   Regatta.
>
> *Robin Stewardson* (1955)[49]

Rowers see Melbourne from down in the river cuttings.[50] Each section of the river had its own smell. On early morning rows past the brewery, 'the beer they were making smelled like cooking biscuits'.[51] Rowing itself smelt 'of grease that we used around the leather on the oars, the wood of the boat and the unspeakable things that we dredged up from the Yarra' (1975).

Scotch has won the Head of the River 32 times. Perhaps the most famous victory was in 1919, with Cecil McKay (School Captain 1918 and 1919, OSCA President 1951, Deputy Chairman of Council 1950–53) as Stroke. Scotch and Xavier each repeatedly spurted ahead then fell back. Just before the finish 'Xavier, by desperate efforts, pushed ahead … but with a final rush Scotch caught them, and the judge posted "Dead Heat" … The crowd was wild with excitement.' In the row off, Scotch led from the start but towards the end Xavier made up practically all lost water. It was 'neck and neck, but this time Scotch got their sprint in first, and although Xavier fought it out to the bitter end, they could not quite get up, and Scotch passed the post a canvas to the good.'[52] William Littlejohn (Principal 1904–33) had opposed the row-off, believing that the dead heat should have stood. There were concerns that a second row was not medically advisable.

Since 1950, 200 or more boys have rowed each year, peaking at 285 in 1975, and in 2000 the numbers are stable at about 220.

Coaching came from staff and Old Boys. Let Don Macmillan's (staff 1959–87) dedication stand for all. Cycling along the river bank 'pedalling like crazy, stop watch in hand, shouting to a crew', he did not see a water-ski ramp sitting on the bank before being put into the river. 'Up he went and over. He came down in an appalling crash. But he didn't hesitate. He jumped up and ran the last 20 yards to the judges' box to get the right timing. Only later did he come back to pick up his hideously wrecked bicycle.'[53]

The boats' names told Scotch's history (the *Thistle*, the *Glen*), and proclaimed its leaders (the *Arthur Robinson*), heroes (the *Cecil McKay*), benefactors (the *O. J. Addison*) and servants (the *Ron Roberts*—he who looked after the boats from the 1930s until 1971).

The concentration of rowing's effort into such a short space of time seems to have its counterpart for the spectators. Of all the school's sports, rowing most energises Scotch boys. In 1992, 700 of them were at the Barwon, half the Senior School. No other school activity engages so many spectators.

The famous 1919 Head of the River crew, stroked by Cecil McKay (deputy chairman of Council, 1950–53). After a dead heat, Scotch won the row-off, despite some medical doubts about the wisdom of allowing a second race.

Dark blue to right of them,
Light blue to left of them,
Wetness in front of them
Shouted and thundered;
Stormed at with pie and shell,
Boldly they threw and well,
Into that awful smell,
Ran the six hundred.

Steeped in the battle's hue
They were all black and blue;
Prefect and Pro
Reeled from the numbers shock
Shattered and winded.
Many an egg was popped,
Many a face was clocked,
While round the fight they flocked,
Dauntless six hundred.

David Clunies-Ross (1953)[54]

Council was as passionate. It has discussed rowing more than any other sport. It described a new boat in 1951 as 'a gift from Council',[55] which is extremely odd. No other purchase by Council was ever called that. In 1961 the Executive and Finance Committee, led by Douglas Bain (1917, Chairman of Council 1959–63), bought new boats and a boatshed with such a unique disregard for all Council's usual procedures of reports, quotes and capped expenses, that one Council member, Dr Robert Lawson (1925, Council 1959–74), protested. In response, Council increased the allocation.[56]

Boys, too, have deplored or approved the amount of money spent on rowing, for example in the letters column of *Satura*.[57] In 1971 Scotch spent $4100 on rowing (boats, oars, trailer and outboard motors) compared to $2700 on teaching aids and equipment, $2200 on musical instruments and $2100 on office machines.

Rowing's auxiliary, the Cardinal Club, was founded by 1981.

From 1948 to 2000, the Head of the River was all but once on the River Barwon at Geelong. 'The train trip there and back was good; especially the tunnel. I got mobbed, jobbed and robbed of my ticket, watch and junk in the 20 seconds we were in the tunnel. Luckily I got them back.'[58]

All along the Barwon,
    The crowd is on the watch,
Boys are a-shouting,
    Come on, Scotch!

Red caps, blue caps,
    The crowd is a-quiver,
Still the boats are out of sight,
    Far down the river.

Everyone for what he likes!
    We want to see
Our crew, the Scotch crew,
    Rowing free!

High in the stand above.
    The judge holds his watch,
We are down a-shouting
    Well done, Scotch![59]

'Rowing Machine', a cartoon in Satura *of 29 March 1963.*

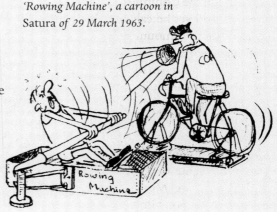

return. Three of the five Trustees, however, refused to alienate what was entrusted to them, and gave legal notice to eject Cairns. Cairns initiated an Act of Parliament to overrule the Trustees, but was defeated by the school's supporters.[60] So the church had to accept that Scotch had a right to its land, but it punished the school by ordering that boys could not play there.[61] Effectively, Cairns kept his garden.

Morrison paid for fighting for Scotch. The church set up a threatening enquiry. It found that the Principal held office under the church's 'control in all respects'.[62] To demonstrate this, the enquiry ruled that the Principal could engage teachers for no more than twelve months. For the church to claim control of staffing was new. It was also unhelpful, for it overturned Morrison's practice of three-year contracts. (The journey from Scotland was a long one for a one-year appointment.) Equally unprecedented, the church extended its financial control of the school by stipulating the fees for ministers' sons. Morrison was compelled to agree to all this in writing. The Rev. Peter Mercer, Secretary of the Education Committee (and previously and later of the Scotch College Committee), scoffed at the idea that Morrison's view carried any weight. That would be 'absurd'.[63]

Thus Morrison, Principal for fourteen successful years, was publicly put in his place. When the interests of his school were threatened he had no choice but to speak up, especially when there was no other spokesman. The church could have praised his dedication to his school, even while overruling him, but that would have entailed a different conception of duty—duty to follow one's conscience. The church saw both school and principal as its servants, whose only duty was obedience. Relations between Morrison and the Education Committee deteriorated to the extent that Morrison declined to attend.[64]

Instead, he counter-attacked but he did not choose his ground wisely. (Perhaps he did so as a fiery Scot, a side of him we do not see in his sage and immobile portraits (see pp. 10 and I). Having lent money to the school, he now presented a bill for interest. But he overreached himself in two ways. First, although the Committee had agreed to pay interest, no rate had been mentioned, and yet he calculated it at 10% *compound*, so that the interest due was twice the amount he had lent. Secondly, he had never mentioned the interest before, though he had regularly submitted accounts to the Assembly. The church in its turn hit back by deciding that it owed Morrison no interest at all, as he had never claimed it, and that the capital he was owed would not be repaid until the school had paid off the earlier debt owing to the banks.

Cairns—now out to destroy Morrison—successfully moved motions in which the Committee censured 'the tone of Mr Morrison's letters', and appointed an accountant, Thomas Dickson, to examine Morrison's accounts from the beginning. Morrison refused to produce his accounts, and when Dickson waited upon him for that purpose Morrison found it 'inconvenient to enter upon the matter at present'.[65] The Committee handed the problem to the Assembly. The school's accounts had long been audited, and annually laid before the Assembly. No evidence was advanced that Morrison had engaged in financial impropriety, and it may be that the enquiry's vindictiveness started to embarrass people. MacBain resigned from the investigation.

On all other matters, the church insisted on prevailing. In 1872 the Assembly by 56 votes to 10 combined menace with insult when it laid down the procedures to be followed if Morrison was charged with heresy, immorality, inefficiency or misconduct. It instructed Morrison to withdraw his claim for interest on the advances made by him. It reiterated the Assembly's power to veto staff. It ordered him to 'recognise the authority and jurisdiction of the Assembly in regard to the internal management of the institution'. It even required six months' notice if he intended to resign (though it may have hoped to drive him to do so). All this was set down as an agreement between Morrison and the Moderator, which Morrison was obliged to sign.[66]

Yet another enquiry began in 1872 as a part of a broader enquiry into educational policy, with particular attention to religious teaching. Its report snapped at Morrison's heels—it wanted more religious education, examined annually by church-appointed examiners—but it had 'no hesitation in declaring' that the school deserved the church's 'confidence and support', and that under Morrison it had attained a high degree of 'prosperity and efficiency'.[67]

So Morrison emerged from the crisis still Principal of Scotch. By the

THE CAMERA CLUB

The 1909 *Collegian* published photographs taken by boys. A Camera Club began early. Membership peaked at 80 boys in the early 1950s, when it had the 'biggest and best-equipped school darkroom in Victoria'[68]. Ilford (Aust.) Ltd supplied chemicals and papers, whilst Kodak sent visiting experts. In 1961 the club was 'virtually non-existent' and by 1975 had recovered to 25. Today photographic work is part of the curriculum.

Three boys, Andrew Rahni (1983), Philip Robertson (1983) and Peter Lew (1980), took several of the photographs used in this book. Two other photographers, outsiders, are also well represented among this history's illustrations, Max Jeppeson and Mark Strizic. Untrammelled by Scotch's myths and visual traditions, their photographs of the school and its people are fresh and delightful.

end of 1874 the Assembly was shamed into something approaching an apology, when it gave him 'Special thanks … for the liberal terms on which, from time to time, he has made advances of money towards the improvements of the buildings, and more particularly for his donation of £1450, which is simply to bear interest at 4 per cent. during the term of his principalship, and thereafter to be handed over free of all obligation to the Church'.[69] This was his most recent contribution, and both sides were scrupulously careful to record the terms in full.

Morrison had discovered the need for a seat in the Assembly. He seems to have sat as an elder from Chalmers Church in 1868, but not thereafter. He now secured himself a seat as an elder from Mornington, where he and his family worshipped when at Craigie Lea, his substantial country home.

The Education Committee emerged less creditably. It had magnified the difficulties it should have managed, and it was implicitly rebuked when the Scotch College Committee was recreated in 1872.

That revived Committee was overshadowed by another group of winners in the dispute, the school's Trustees, who now took up a prominent role in the school. They had been the school's most effective defenders within the Presbyterian community, and although nominally they were merely holders of property in trust, they were sucked into the vacuum left by the abolition of the Scotch College Committee and by the church's diminished confidence in Morrison. When in 1871 the boys 'utterly ruined' Cairns's garden (most likely in retribution for his attacking their Principal), the Education Committee turned to the Trustees for help,[70] that is, to intervene in the school and its discipline of the boys. The Trustees sat on the new Scotch College Committee and graced the school's advertisements whilst the Committee went unmentioned. In any case, in 1883 the Committee again disappeared. Morrison probably did not stir himself to preserve it, for its secretary was Mercer, who had publicly castigated him, and its convenors were successively the Rev. James Nish (1872–74) and the Rev. T. Mackenzie Fraser (1874–79), who in 1870 had moved and seconded the motion in the Assembly that Morrison be not heard. Fraser also had opposed all new building. Its final convenor, from 1879, was the Hon. John Cumming, whom we may regard as the first layman to be Chairman of the School Council.

The abolition of the Committee left the Trustees in unchallenged superiority. Indeed the 1883 *Annual Report* called them the 'Governing Body'. Eminent, wealthy and powerful Presbyterians, they presided at Scotch functions and stood as its guarantor, having won their spurs when a majority of them defended Scotch against the church. The Trustees were not a united group. They split in the Chalmers Church dispute, and in Parliament the conservative MacBain opposed the liberal McCulloch. Five in number, later Trustees included Francis Ormond and Duncan Love. At last in 1897 came the blind Member of Parliament and pastoralist Malcolm McKenzie (1868), 'an Old Collegian'.[71] For the first time, 47 years after its foundation, an Old

Boy held a key position. Soon afterwards, the church replaced the Trustees with the Presbyterian Trusts Corporation.

Council was recreated in 1890, with the Rev. John Mackie as Convenor until 1897.

In 1872–73, as the Chalmers Church dispute subsided, the Trustees took out a mortgage and erected new buildings. The new principal's house was roomy and comfortable, welcome for a large family whose eldest child was only in his teens. The new boarding accommodation was 'constructed on the most approved principles'. Instead of dormitories, there were bedrooms with two or three boys in each. 'By special arrangement a boy may have a room for himself. There is a large dining-hall, a spacious library and sitting-room, and music-rooms for the exclusive use of boarders.'[72] The church limited the number of boarders to fifty.

Now Morrison could afford to show the strain he had been under. Exhausted by overwork and worry, he asked for a year's leave and in 1875 went to Europe. On the way home he fell ill with 'Roman fever' and at Melbourne was so weak he had to be carried ashore.[73]

The Vice-Principal (1870–1904), Robert Morrison, managed the school in his brother's absence. When Frederick Armitage took overseas leave from the King's School at Parramatta it collapsed in 1865 and closed until 1869. That Scotch survived the absence of its Principal reveals that it had come of age as an institution, with a life separate from even its most significant personality.

YOUR LOCKS ARE LIKE THE SNOW

Morrison's year overseas stimulated him. In the colony he had tried to recreate the old country, and now aged 45 he caught up on twenty years of change back home. On returning to Melbourne, he introduced short written examinations in every subject fortnightly, which ensured a steady industriousness, and he introduced 'result cards' recording boys' marks and the class average. Boys who failed attended special classes on Saturdays. (This helpful response had deteriorated by the 1920s into a punishment, a Saturday detention.[74]) He subscribed to American educational literature, and enrolled the sons of the American consul. He increased Science teaching, and with H. M. Andrew of Wesley persuaded the University of Melbourne to include science subjects in the matriculation examination, and to found chairs in Engineering, Chemistry and Physics.

Morrison was more often in rivalry with Wesley, as each intended their boys to win the exhibitions. Scotch has long measured itself against the other Public Schools, especially the other five old schools, and especially against Melbourne Grammar and Xavier. Indeed, much as Scotch would like to define itself from a single self-referenced standpoint, it is as true for institutions as for people that what enables them to know themselves is the presence of the *other*.

BROTHERS

From the start, Scotch contained brothers. Three Ralston brothers were enrolled in 1851. Later, seven Chambers brothers spanned 22 years, and nine Benjamin brothers possibly spanned 35 years.

Were the older brothers welcoming? Younger brothers seemed to have little to recommend them. From below, the relationship was clear: 'Give cheek—take shit. That's what being a little brother was about' (1964).[75]

Older brothers had several quite different uses. At their best they were heroic figures, always bigger and faster because they were always ahead in the race to grow up, so they were always a challenge against whom younger brothers measured themselves. Or a source of exhortation. Geoffrey Baker (1938) became school welterweight boxing champion in 1938 after his older brother Bill threatened: 'win the boxing or cop a hiding from me'.[76] More practically, Edwin Peatt's (1932) elder brother Norman (1929) 'used to frequently find a girl for me to escort'.[77]

Equally, older brothers can show what to avoid. 'I remember arriving as an 11 year old and seeing my older brother getting a hard time because he was "different" and consciously determining to "fit in" as much as possible to gain acceptance' (1977).[78]

Several brothers shared the school's highest achievements. Westmore (1911) and Frank (1914) Stephens were both Captains of the School. Hugh (1897) and Percy (1909) Wilson, Angas (1940) and Neville (1950) Hurst, Christopher (1959) and Peter (1965) Selby Smith, Charles (1982) and John (1983) Su were all Duxes of the School.

It is harder for a younger brother to have his achievements seen in their own right.

When James Macneil (1950) became a prefect he merely followed his brothers Rowan (1946) and Peter (1947). Less exalted precedents can oppress. 'Chesty Bond [staff 1946–85] (excellent teacher) on my first day at school dubbed me as he had done to my brother before me, "Gertrude" which stuck all through school life. He should have been sacked!'(1956)

A boy with a smarter younger brother has a problem. 'Would recommend that he be separated from his younger brother if possible. He worries unduly' (Blue Card, Form IV, 1947).

It is common for brothers to go to the same school. Most families have an inertia in this regard, and for the school it is a straightforward way of securing new enrolments, all the more so with large 19th-century families. By 1861 Morrison offered a 10% fee concession, which was a sensible business decision; families were likely to want to send their boys to the one school, and a small concession would encourage them to do so. From 1960 the 10% concession was to apply only to the second and subsequent brothers.[79] Healey wanted to do away with it except in necessitous cases, but 'it never seemed quite the right moment!'[80]

Brothers followed each other away from Scotch, too. Four Grounds brothers attended Scotch—Arthur 'Boggy' Grounds (1916), Marshall 'Marshy' Grounds (1920), Haslett 'Hassy' Grounds (1919) and Roy Grounds (1920), later Sir Roy the architect. When Littlejohn expelled Haslett, an incorrigible rule-breaker, their father took Roy away as well and sent them to Melbourne Grammar, where Haslett, an outstanding sportsman, helped defeat Scotch in cricket and football.

Melbourne Grammar has always held first place in Scotch's demonology—'you couldn't help noticing that the Grammar boys came from the wealthiest homes, were C of E and Establishment'.[81] Whether in 1908 or 1978, the *Collegians* call it 'our old rival' and 'the old enemy'.[82] Onto it Scotch has projected teenage boys' worst fear, voiced in Parliament in 1997 when Old Scotch Premier Jeff Kennett (1965) abused Old Melburnian Leader of the Opposition John Brumby: 'If you can't get a girl get a Grammar boy'.[83] As for Grammar's becoming a coeducational school, Scotch snorted, it had long been that way.[84] Xavier College was most easily defined by emphasising its Irishness and Catholicism: Scotch boys by the turn of the century mocked these 'Micks' with calls of 'Look out boys, it's Friday'.[85] Cecil McKay, Stroke of the Crew in the famous 1919 race against Xavier, called out 'Now it's porridge against potatoes!'[86]

Christina Morrison died in 1883, when Morrison was only 53. He was 'grief-stricken and aged beyond belief'.[87] At her grave in Kew Cemetery he busied himself to get railings for his darling's grave. He planted violets, febrifuge and verbenas, and tended this 'precious plot—It looks beautiful after the rain'.[88]

In his first devastation Morrison thought of resigning, but instead stayed to reap the harvest he had sown, as in the second half of his reign his pupils became leading citizens, and spread the school's reputation and influence. They were academics, doctors, architects and lawyers. They were businessmen in brewing, newspapers, tobacco, mining, pastoralism and shipping, among them David Elder (entered 1862) whom the *Bulletin* dubbed the Napoleon of capitalists.[89]

In the realm of education, Old Boys were perhaps influenced by being Morrison's students. Robert Ramsay (entered 1852) was in 1870 Scotch's first Member of Parliament. He was Minister for Education in 1875–77 and oversaw the creation of much of Victoria's state education system. Sir Harry Lawson (1891), Minister for Education in 1915–17, also had a particular interest in education. George Tait (1859) and Andrew Harper (1858) were Principals of the Presbyterian Ladies' College in 1875–88, where they set a high academic tone.

William Shiels (entered 1862) became Premier of Victoria in 1892, having risen to fame in sponsoring divorce reform that widened the grounds for divorce over the objections of the churches.[90] Since then Scotch has provided four more Victorian premiers (Sir Harry Lawson, James McPherson, John Cain and Jeff Kennett) as well as premiers of NSW (Sir George Reid, 1858), South Australia (Vaibin Solomon, entered 1866), and Tasmania (Jim Bacon, 1967).

Sir Joseph Hood (Dux 1863) was in 1890 the first barrister born and educated in Melbourne to become a judge.[91] Edmund Armstrong (1880) became State Librarian in 1896, and David Martin (said to have attended Scotch) Secretary of the Departments of Agriculture and Public Works

1890–1908.[92] Frederick Clendinnen (1879) was the first Melbourne doctor to take an X-ray, and became one of the first medical radiologists in the world.[93] He suffered mutilating injuries because protection from radium was little understood.

In 1899–1900 the Australian contingent to the Boer War included (Sir) Julius Bruche (1890) and Colonel Tom Price (1860)—he who in 1890 gave the order against striking trade unionists to 'Fire low and lay them out'. The war's opponents included William Maloney (1872) and Arthur Griffith (1877). Maloney in 1889 began 51 years as a left-wing parliamentarian, supporting female suffrage and a republic.[94] Griffith, also a republican, became a Labor MP in 1894, and sat in the first NSW Labor Government in 1910.

Strengthened in stature by the reputation of his Old Boys, Morrison's later decades passed more serenely than the first decades. In 1890, further additions provided new bedrooms, studies, lavatories and baths, and three large classrooms, making twelve separate classrooms in all. But the general financial collapse of the 1890s and the drought of 1902–03 shook Scotch severely. The elderly Morrison coped only by battening down and soldiering on. Enrolments shrank to an average of 237. Though he saw in the new century, he always wore the black frock-coat of an earlier epoch. Warm-hearted and genial, a white-haired and powerful man of stern appearance, the Doctor—the 'Doc', as the boys called him,[95] still walked erect, and his handwriting remained fully legible.

He died on a Sunday afternoon, 31 May 1903, as he sat in his study in his usual easy-chair. His grand-daughter recounts that he said: 'The only sign of advancing age I feel is that sometimes I find myself a little short of breath'. Then his head fell forward.[96] His daughter wrote that 'without warning, without pain, with little more than a sigh—"God's finger touched him and he slept".'[97]

Alexander Morrison made Scotch

Alexander Morrison in old age. 'Your locks are like the snow'.

College. When he arrived, although he inherited handsome buildings, the nature of the school was in flux. When he left, the school's central myths and aspirations were in place, and it bore the characteristic stamp of educating boys' minds and character which we shall explore in the next two chapters. The fledgling school had grown into an adult, its body shaped and its predispositions settled. Later Principals could, like hormones, stimulate or slow it down, or could, like viruses, infect it with new ideas, but many an infection it threw off. Its Old Boys were already distinguished. Sir John MacFarland (Chairman of Council 1919–34) said 'The Scotch Collegians are his best Memorial'[98]

The Rev. Dr Alexander Marshall in 1902, Chairman of Council 1897–1919. He helped choose the new site at Hawthorn. 'I claim a Monday morning rest when I can get it'.

CADETS

CADET CORPS

The Cadet Unit began in 1884; it is older than the Australian Army. The unit trains boys to be soldiers, instructing them in weapons and military manoeuvres both formal and in the field. Alongside this simple goal the unit, like any long-lived organisation, like the school itself, has repeatedly changed its aspirations. It began as a drill body, shifted to learning warfare only just before World War I and only in earnest after World War II, when leadership also became an aim, and shifted again, as the Cold War ended, to become more focused on outdoor skills.

Military Drill began earlier, as physical exercise. In 1877, Sergeant-Major White-head became drill-master and expanded drill into the beginnings of a cadet unit. Major-General Sir Julius Bruche (1890), later Chief of the Australian General Staff, praised Whitehead handsomely as 'my military father … He was a most lovable character, and a very fine man'.[99] Additional impetus came in 1884 from Victoria's Minister for Defence, Colonel Sargood, and in 1910 from Commonwealth legislation requiring six hours a week compulsory military training by all boys aged over 14. The unit flourished, and in 1888 provided the Guard of Honour for the Governor, Sir Henry Loch, at the opening of Melbourne's International Centennial Exhibition. The officers were masters including a Major Major (staff 1904).

The main activity was drill, although its rationale changed. To Morrison, drill improved 'carriage and physique' and imparted 'habits of smartness and prompt obedience.'[100] To Gilray, it summoned each boy to do his best, 'one of the greatest lessons a citizen needs to learn'.[101] Drill still has its place, climaxing in the annual tattoo, and has always woven its spell: 'After some years in the Scouts,' David Shave (1952) 'feigned headaches to watch the cadets from the "secrecy" of the hill. Transferring to the cadets, I was marker in the winning Quarter Guard in 1952. I enjoyed the precision of drill and this continued after school.'[102]

Despite the later broadening of military training, the unit's earliest period produced its greatest soldiers, Lieutenant-General Sir John Monash (Dux 1881, OSCA President 1927), Major-General Sir James McCay (Dux 1880) and Brigadier-General Robert Smith (1898). Hence the warcry:

All the Scotchies then did cry
Hi, Hi, Hi, Generals Monash, Smith, McCay
We'll be with you wet or dry,
Ready to do or die (Hooch-aye).

Of the period between the wars, it is possible to say either that 'clean boots and shiny buttons was about all that was required … Certainly cadet training bore no relevance to the conflict that was about to ensue' (1940), or that 'the training in cadets was a great advantage' (1938),[103] and helped one get an early commission (1932).[104]

Beyond drill, boys actually fired weapons. Guns appeal to boys as fine pieces of machinery, as a means of projecting power,

The cadets in 1886 outside Dr Morrison's residence.

and as a means of testing and improving a skill. Military training legitimised these pleasures. Cadet camp allowed 'playing with big guns—6-pounder anti tank gun—they don't get that chance any more!' (1951).[105]

Camps occurred at least as early as 1904, when they consisted entirely of parades, inspections and drill. Such camps could be a boy's first time away from home.[106] Memories range from the location—Puckapunyal was 'the only place in the world where you could be up to your neck in mud, and get dust in your eyes!' (1967)—to 'the regimentation and the cold and basic living' (1979).[107] As well as military lessons, camps taught boys socially 'about living with and working with others' (1995).[108] As one company commander said about a four-day exercise near Mt Hickey in 1962, 'I don't care if we find out nothing at all about the enemy, if all

of you can learn to tolerate each other's weaknesses and live together we will have achieved a great deal'.[109]

Militarily, Lieutenant-Colonel Bond (Commanding Officer 1961–66) intended to train boys to act like troops in the field. In April 1963 in the Lerderderg Gorge, Bond 'was hit by a sizeable rock which fell from a considerable height down one of the cliffs by the river… He was seriously hurt … The boys who were with him showed much initiative and good sense, and managed to bring him up the cliff, and on to a track, very quickly and carefully.'[110] One boy produced a flask of medicinal whisky.

The first such bivouac was held in 1958, a two-day exercise with boys eating and sleeping in the field. The physical and social aspects were probably much the same on any cadet bivouac:

Eldorado State Forest, sleeping under a wet poncho with the wind and rain freely pouring in both ends of the tent.

Scotch College at Eastern Hill with the cadets on parade in Lansdowne Street. Morrison's residence is on the left. On the far right is the original 1854 building.

... And who can forget the ration vegemite tins exploding in the fires at night after they had warmed up a bit, and eating the sweetened condensed milk from the tube. And the highlight of cadet camps must be my witnessing a fart being lit—truly memorable! [1975][111]

The sacrifice of luxuries like mess hut and tents meant that greater discipline was required, and that the boys learnt a bit about 'roughing it'.[112] The emphasis on loss and hardship contrasted with scout bivouacs which stressed bush skills and comradeship.

Few Old Boys report learning bush skills through cadets, and David Ashton (1965) was put off 'going out into the bush at all, for about 20 years, until my son joined the Scouts and I went away with him on father/son hikes. I then found out that the bush wasn't as hostile as the cadets had made it seem, and later I even became president of the Old Scotch Bushwalking Club!'[113] Yet Howard Brown (1963) loved the bush: 'The smell of wattle bloom ... takes me immediately to cadet camp (September holidays) and manoeuvres out in the field. The wattle would be in bloom and we would often camouflage ourselves with sprigs of wattle.'[114]

Other training covered automatic weapons, tactics, and map reading. '"Piston, barrel, butt, body, bipod." I still recall the sequence for disassembly of a Bren gun' (1964).[115]

As the school's aims changed, the cadets followed. By the middle of the twentieth century cadets offered 'character building, discipline, team-work and leadership, ... while preparing themselves for responsible citizenship'.[116] Boys learnt to give and take orders, and to shoulder 'the burdens of responsibility and command—something every boy should try to experience'.[117] Boys found these leadership skills 'more value in later life than all the academic subjects' (1946).[118] 'You ... experience what it is like for people to be relying on you' (1995).[119] 'Left school ... aged 16 and was able to cope with new life as Jackeroo in Western Queensland before war service because of educational advantage and training from Cadets to handle people' (1939).

As the unit grew in size and complexity it gave its leaders 'a better appreciation of administration and of being personally organised and effective' (1952).[120] 'A chance to see real outcomes quickly. To mix the physical with management and planning' (1958).[121] Other boys felt that 'the power went to some of the boys' heads' (1975), and that it 'was a brutish and bullying environment' (1967) of 'mindless regimentation by ego-fed little Hitlers' (1962)—the 'regimented encouragement of institutional bullies' (1964).[122] Yet one critic later enjoyed the army immensely and has 'no idea' why he disliked the cadets (1949). Boys' likes and dislikes do not always make sense, even to themselves.

The military side of the unit has risen and fallen. In the early 1930s, when another war seemed unlikely, Gilray said that cadets was not militaristic.[123] In the late 1960s, as World War II receded and the Vietnam War raised doubts about war, the unit began to emphasise other goals and even to play down its military purpose. The 'aim of the Unit', said *Satura* in 1968, is 'not to turn out soldiers'.[124] Healey at the Church's Educational Policy Committee had to defend cadet training in church schools.[125] At least one former cadet, a crack shot, says that 'I now feel that it is morally wrong to teach children to shoot guns. The fact that the school still has cadets is a factor that makes me think I will not send my son to Scotch' (1965).

In the century's three final decades, the likelihood of war faded, government support waned and the war-seared teachers who had fought World War II retired. The military nature of the unit fell ever more into the background (just as the role of the Army itself changed from war-making to peace-keeping). Training swung more to the skills needed for the challenges of bush, water and mountain.[126] By the 1980s, the unit's goal was

by predominantly voluntary effort, better to equip young people for community life by fostering initiative, leadership, discipline and loyalty through training programmes which are also designed to stimulate an interest in the Services ... The main aim is character development—a preparation for life by supplying many opportunities to learn co-operation, responsibility, loyalty, working for the common good. ... Development of leadership is our secondary aim ... To bring honour to the Cadet himself, his family, his Unit and his school. Self-respect and pride in doing a good job under trying conditions.[127]

It was a far cry from a sar-major's drill and how to strip a Bren gun.

Periodic contractions of government support for cadet units have left the Scotch unit linked with the Army, but essentially operating independently, and free to compete for boys' interest by developing its own programme, which in 1998 included bushcraft, mountaineering, day and night navigation, abseiling and boating. When at the end of the century the government decided that school cadet units might revert to fully supported status, Scotch did so only after confirming it could preserve such programmes.[128]

In size the unit during the 1950s contained nearly 600 boys, and by 2000 was half that size.

3

A THOROUGH AND LIBERAL EDUCATION

The task of schools is to teach what is not taught elsewhere in society. This apparently simple statement shapes the history of Scotch College. Society keeps changing what needs to be taught, and it keeps changing what needs to be taught by schools. Society itself, moreover, is divided into groups with diverse and conflicting aspirations, which a school must meet or manage as best it can, or carve out a niche to serve particular interests. Disciplines come and go—such as Russian. Concepts of necessary lessons come and go—such as being a gentleman. Aspects of education move from families to schools (such as clothing or sex education), or are still possible in families but no longer at school (such as corporal punishment). A school will interact with these trends. It will follow when it must, and lead when it can.

At first, merely being a secondary school was important. Private secondary schools like Scotch came into existence to meet a need in the educational system. The government elementary schools taught only the 'elements' of knowledge, breaking it down into pieces that had little meaning or use outside the school. By contrast, in the private secondary schools, when literature or Euclid was studied, 'a meaningful and complete entity was offered to students—a play, a theorem, a book of Virgil. However badly taught, however obscured by a dreary pedagogue, an original intellectual creation was brought into the classroom—and there was always a chance that Virgil or Homer might work his magic'.[1]

THE EDUCATION OF YOUNG GENTLEMEN

Lawson's advertisement to open his school said he would teach what was 'essential to the education of any young gentleman'. Morrison, too, promised 'an education … for young gentlemen'. The school existed within a social context which required it, most of all, to educate gentlemen. This meant that the teachers themselves were 'none but Gentlemen',[2] and that what they taught was Classics, Geography and Modern Languages.

The Classics and the Good Book

The Free Church bought Lawson the books that formed Scotch's first library, and they show both the scope and limit of what he taught: Virgil, Horace,

Livy, Sallust and Xenophon. Such books distinguished the Academy from schools that taught the basic skills of literacy and numeracy. To have studied Latin or Greek was the mark of a well-educated man, not because he continued to read them, but because through them he met the thoughts of another civilisation.

So boys at Scotch met Icarus who invented wings but flew so close to the sun that it melted the glue on his feathers and he plunged to his death. Aim high but do not overreach yourself. Or, for Scotch boys: Aim high but plan well.

Horatius and two soldiers held a narrow bridge against a thousand attackers. A righteous stand on well-chosen ground will triumph.

Xenophon's *Anabasis* tells of Greek mercenaries whose Persian employer died. To get home, they sought the coast, where Greek merchant shipping plied. Their excited cries when at last they saw the sea—*Thalatta! thalatta!*— would have made sense to the boys of the seafaring British Empire, and might have moved them.

Regulus, they read, was taken prisoner by Rome's mortal enemy Carthage and obtained release by promising to persuade Rome to make peace. But back in Rome he urged Rome to redouble its war efforts. Then he returned to Carthage to face their punishment, for he had broken his word. So the boys of Scotch learnt about honour and morality, in stories based not on religion (for the Romans' pagan religion was ignored) but on a code of civic virtue.

Such stories were gripping enough for the moral to be digested unnoticed rather than force-fed. And lest too much wisdom should seem oppressive, there were even stories of boys getting the better of sage old men, as when a father and son sat drinking wine and the father warned the lad not to drink too much or the two candles in front of them on the table would start to blur into looking like four candles. 'But Dad,' the son replied, 'there's only one candle'.

Told in English such tales might go in one ear and out the other, but laborious translation was more likely to fix them in the memory.

Morrison's emphasis on Classics was no personal foible, for the university required them. Many boys with no natural ability for Latin had to toil at it to get to university. Law and Medicine required Latin long into the twentieth century and for another generation, until the 1970s, it remained a staple part of Scotch's education of brighter boys. Morrison had boys begin Latin early, but limited it to 'only one school hour daily until they have attained considerable proficiency in English and Arithmetic'.[3] Boys delighted in the random chance that makes a word in one language sound rude in another, and IIIc in 1939 attended carefully to M. D. Close's (staff 1939–40) exposition on the pronunciation of *causas*.[4]

Latin teaching was usually dogmatic. Words had to be learnt by heart— '*paro, paras, parat, paramus, paratis, parant. I prepare, you prepare, he, she, it prepares, we prepare, you prepare, they prepare!* What a foundation for life!' (1955).[5] Grammar is either right or wrong, and its rules had to be learnt, not debated.

> The ablative is used, they say
> With *sub* and *sine*, *ab* and *de*.
> Other words we ought to know
> Are *cum*, along with, *ex* and *pro*.[6]

Thus doggerel gave a pattern to the arbitrary. Latin was long taught by William 'Bumpy' Ingram* (staff 1892–1934) who was Vice-Principal from 1912. He was 'a dark, dreamy man who after hearing a boy speak his lines from Virgil in the usual halting fashion would repeat them in a delicious murmur and then go on without stopping for perhaps fifty or a hundred lines more, rapt in his own enjoyment of their euphonious cadence'.[7]

The application of Latin knowledge was translation. When Ingram translated Caesar's *Gallic War* to Bruce Pettigrew's (1934) class, he would dictate

> at a rate of knots and few were able to keep up with him. At first we tried
> two or three of us to take turns in writing the sentences and then filling in
> the blanks after class. Before long we discovered that printed translations
> could be purchased but there was a problem in that Bumpy did not agree
> with some of this translation and was able to spot at minor exam times those
> who had so cheated. The remedy was to take the printed work into class and
> make amendments where the Ingram translation differed.[8]

Later teachers were more creative. Paul Radford (staff 1935–45) 'tried to get away from strictly text book stuff. I think he had us acting in short plays in Latin for instance. Also we were given Latin names (not necessarily kindly ones—my friend … who could have used some orthodontistry, was Tuscus). I have a vague memory of making models of a Roman villa.'[9] Charlie 'Noso' Boyes (staff 1929–65), gruff but gentle, even used his (well-earned) nickname as a teaching springboard when he explained the Roman system of nomenclature using Ovid's full name, Publius Ovidius Naso.

Latin's later years were under Ron 'Chesty' Bond (staff 1946–85). He too was Vice-Principal (1968–85), so to teach Latin was clearly good preparation for the purple. His teaching was firm, didactic and intimidating as boys were summoned to stand in front of the class before the master's desk— 'Up before the Tribunal! What's the Latin for *seldom*? Quick now! Uh One. Uh Two. Uh two-and-a-bit. Uh Three! Clang! Gong! In the pound! Half an hour's detention tonight, my child' —and though this put some boys off Latin completely,[10] others were captivated by his hauteur and 'his commitment to, knowledge of and love of a difficult and apparently irrelevant subject'.[11]

One advantage of Latin was that at least you didn't have to speak it.[12] Even at its worst, the dull drummed-in Latin could later help an Old Boy in

* He was so brainy that the bumps of knowledge stuck out all over his skull. (McInnes, *Road to Gundagai*, p. 104.)

southern Europe and South America. It was also 'a great help in substantially enlarging one's English vocabulary' (1941).[13] At its best, 'I found its logical structure quite fascinating, all the declensions and conjugations following in orderly patterns, … The extreme economy of Latin intrigued me, too: typically, a 10-word English sentence might translate into 4 or 5 words of Latin, with no loss of meaning' (1970).[14]

In 1865 four of the eight Latin classes also learnt Greek, but were not as advanced as with Latin. Greek would always delight a few Scotch boys. 'Like English, and quite unlike Latin,' it seemed 'a vast field of wild flowers in its beauty of expression'. Thus Bill Fullagar (1945) who wanted to say of the Greeks: 'I *know* these people. They talk to me'.[15]

The other people who talked to the boys were the Old and New Testament writers. Although the formal purpose of its study was salvation, the Bible also introduced boys to the thinking of other times and places. Indeed, since the text of the Bible was fixed, it exposed boys to a much wider range of human behaviour than came through the Classics, whose rude or suggestive passages did not appear in schoolboy primers. The Bible told of lies, murder and genocide in its opening chapters, and went through adultery, swindles, seduction, masturbation, homosexuality, treason, infanticide, murderous abuse of power and bloody vengeance, as well as courage, victory, endurance, wisdom, self-sacrifice and the love poetry of the Song of Solomon. Boys would have read a great deal of this in an age that encouraged Bible reading.

The Classics and the Bible were the backbone of Scotch's intellectually disciplined, humanist, religious, liberal education.

English

The foundation on which Morrison built all learning, however, was a thorough education in English. Morrison regretted how schools in England emphasised the Classics to the neglect of English.[16] He did not want boys who could 'throw off Latin verses by the score, [but were] quite unable to produce a creditable letter in their mother tongue'.[17] In this, he reflected his university, Aberdeen, a centre of studying English literature at a time when it was regarded as secondary to the Classics. Morrison 'was the first in Australia to introduce the study of English literature into the curriculum' and was widely imitated.[18]

Spelling was the basic building block. As early as 1866 'throughout the whole school the spelling is generally very good … mainly due to the constant practice'.[19] A century later Miss Dorothy Goodenough (staff 1920–58) 'was very, very hard on spelling. It took hours of practice with my mother to master "difficult". I think it was then that my mother helped me with homonyms like "stair" and "stare". … a "stair" goes into the "air"!' (1955)[20] After spelling, boys learnt grammar, and by 1877 the subject was well enough understood for a joke to turn upon it: 'A pupil asked to compare the adjective "cold" replied—cold, cough, coffin'.[21]

Older boys had to apply these tools. They wrote essays, and each week paraphrased a portion of Milton or Shakespeare, Addison or Pope, which drew out 'latent powers of thought, which no other exercise could, perhaps, so effectually have urged into activity'.[22]

The English exam papers in 1860 reveal the course. Boys had to sketch the life of Shakespeare or Milton; to explain the plot of *Much Ado About Nothing* or the argument of *Paradise Lost* and to show some knowledge of either work, its characters and its language, and to give a prose version of a passage provided. They had to show some knowledge of word origins, distinguishing between words derived from Latin and Greek or between Celtic and 'Saxon', and to 'mark the changes the words have undergone in spelling and meaning'. Also, they were asked for 'examples of words purely Australian that are now deemed good English'.[23] A composition was then required on a topic that would engage them, like Garibaldi, Australian exploration, or sport. Such Australian themes dispel the idea of a cultural cringe.

Boys also read aloud. This was a custom of the time. Families read novels and the Bible in this way, and authors toured to read their works aloud. Before microphones, any boy who hoped to be a public figure had to develop

'If you don't be quiet, boys, I'll sit on you', 1982. Miss Pat Berry taught Junior School boys from 1957 to 1983.

voice production and the accompanying, often formalised, gestures to semaphore his meaning.

At government schools, reading meant reading aloud, with less attention paid to comprehension, for it is possible to read something aloud without having much idea what it means. At Scotch, Elocution made sure this did not happen. Junior classes learnt pronunciation, articulation, and accentuation. For senior boys it was also a mental subject, for they had to gain a thorough understanding of a passage so that in speaking it aloud they could bring out 'delicate niceties of taste ... by judicious modulation, intonation, and inflection'. In any passage read, a boy had to know every word's meaning, synonyms, and opposites, and had to provide full explanations of every incidental allusion, whether mythological, historical, geographical, or biographical.[24] Recitations and readings graced every Speech Day (hence the name).

An early Elocution teacher was T. P. Hill (staff 1862–75), using his own *Oratorical trainer*, the first example of Scotch's practice of employing teachers of the calibre to generate text-books in their discipline. Hill overcame Morrison's doubts that elocution could be taught in large classes,[25] and so long as he had Hill to teach it Morrison made elocution compulsory, but from the late 1870s it faded out. By the 1970s, the long cycles of educational practice had brought it again into vogue as Scotch boys recited Russian poetry for the Pushkin prize.

In 1870 Morrison appointed Frank Shew (1867, staff 1870–1922) to the staff, where he taught for 53 years and became the only mere teacher whose portrait hangs in the Memorial Hall. He was one of the first Old Boys to come back as a teacher. He played cricket and football for St Kilda. He had knowledge, taste and his love of literature

> (quite beyond the ordinary love of the scholar) would transfuse his reading— for part of his teaching consisted of reading to his class poems and passages from our English classics—and transfigure his whole being so that the boys nearly always came under the spell. But also he could instantaneously be put out of his happy mood and would tremble white and speechless with rage ... [his] thin brown ascetic face pale in fury with trembling lip.[26]

French and German

To speak French was another mark of a gentleman. To teach it, Lawson and Morrison employed a succession of Frenchmen. They emphasised conversation. At the 1862 Speech Day a dozen boys held a *'Conversation entre les jeunes gens de Paris, de Londres et de Melbourne'*.[27] Later, Henry Bowden (1907, staff 1913–56, Vice-Principal 1935–56) emphasised grammar and told his pupils they would pick up the speech quickly when they went to France.[28] Teachers were anglophones, and even a German, Dr Bernard Mendel (staff 1941–77). Peter Wilson (1947 Dux) compared 'the Oz-accented French of 'Bosh' Bowden* with the precise Germanic accent of 'Doc' Mendel'.[29] Laurie 'Percy' Provan (1934, staff 1950–81) 'spoke French with a distinctly Australian drawl'.[30] But they grounded boys solidly in the language, and inspired them about French culture. Bowden's affection for the French people and their culture led Doug Batten (1946) into a ' "love affair" with France, its history, literature and other arts, food and wine, and above all its people's *joie-de-vivre*'.[31] Alan Shugg (staff 1967–99) ensured that the 1994 Language Centre had a kitchen to demonstrate the dishes of the target language, and female staff have encouraged boys to do the cooking themselves.

As with Latin, there was much rote-learning, and mnemonics like Provan's 'Canadian National Railways and don't forget the Puff Puff', CNRPP being the key to *cage, nage, rage, page* and *plage*, the only French words ending in 'age' to be of the feminine gender. Frank 'Walter' Kirby (staff 1920–55) 'encouraged the learning of French by "or-al re-pet-ition" while Boyes railed against the learning of Latin "parrot-fashion" to the same form'.[32] Kirby was deaf, perhaps an understandable act of self-defence for a man teaching French to Australian boys, 'and we'd mouth words while he increased the volume of his hearing aid. We'd then speak a little louder.'[33] Kirby used to teach the *Marseillaise* by marching up and down the classroom playing it on his violin. 'He also used to be seen walking his cat on a lead, like a dog. A bit out of the ordinary, but I can still remember every word of the *Marseillaise*' (1956).

For boys who found it easy, French had a language's advantage, that it required no reasoning power,[34] but many boys found it hard or pointless.[35] Yet afterwards, an Old Boy who enlisted as an airman in World War II and trained in Canada found Bowden's lessons stood him in great stead with the French-Canadian girls. Another boy found it, relevant or not, 'a break from my science-based subjects'.[36]

Since around 1960, the idea has revived of learning to speak French. Dr Joseph Jordens (staff 1959–61) spent his whole first lesson talking only in French, and simply enough to be understood. *La chaise est sur la table. Où est la chaise? La chaise est sur la table.* 'Est sur' sounded like azure, so one had yet to break the sound down into words, but one left that first lesson already knowing what that sound meant. A sustained approach of this method— the early 1950s French textbook, *Mon Livre*, contained no English—risked students feeling lost.[37]

German was in the early days offered only as an extra subject, costing a few additional guineas, and so was not always taught at all levels. In Mendel's final-year German, only three boys failed in 30 years.

Hebrew

For gentlemen who were Jewish, Hebrew was an optional extra subject, costing a couple of guineas, but with a reduced rate for more than one boy

* Some say that Bowden's nickname of 'Bosh' was short for *boshter*, meaning *bonzer*. Others attribute it to his stories of fighting the Boche (the Germans) in the Great War.

per family. It was taught during the 1860s and 1870s. By the 1880s the Jewish community seems to have had its own classes.

In 1872, 27 Jewish boys learnt Hebrew, taught by the Polish-born Morris Myers (staff 1870–77). No Jewish theology was taught (though explanations were given on the Jewish feasts and other historical observances) and 'the work was limited to acquiring a knowledge of the Hebrew language'. Presumably this course met the expectations of the Jewish parents, but the 1872 church enquiry into Scotch found that most of the time went on 'the merely mechanical work of mastering the difficulties of pronunciation and reading; in translation and analysis the pupils were very deficient'.[38]

Penmanship

Lawson himself taught penmanship, a necessary skill in the era before typewriters and printers. As befits its antiquity as a discipline, the position of Writing Master became hereditary, later passing from Edmunds father to son. Father Edmunds (Walter, staff 1907–37) 'always signed his name alongside a sketch of a Quill pen'.[39] He tied left-handed boys' left hands behind their backs.[40] He smashed John Blaine's (1932) new Waterman pen, 'and told me I should use a Dawson Nib. My Waterman pen was a present from my father and probably cost a guinea'.[41]

Interest in handwriting occasionally revives. In the late 1950s, Mrs Rose Turnbull (staff 1943–59) encouraged italic hand-writing in the Junior School. Japanese and Chinese influences may yet reinvigorate Australian calligraphy.

Geography

Geography was another necessary study for a gentleman who belonged to a world-wide empire. Edinburgh gave Lawson maps and globes. The 1860 examinations expected boys to have a wide and up-to-date knowledge of geographical systems and processes. Darwin's *Origin of Species* was only just published, but boys were asked 'What are the four kinds of Coral Formation; give examples of each, with Mr Darwin's explanation of their formation'.[42] They were asked about stratified rocks and their characteristic fossils, about volcanoes in Iceland, river systems in South America, categories of lowland, and the difference between continental and Pelagic islands. Even if many

Robert 'Nutty' Wilson in 1954. He and Alan 'Stonk' Ross wrote a staple mathematics textbook and earned substantial royalties.

of the answers were parroted, they equipped the boys with a range of ways of reading landscape.

Practical boys liked Geography because 'it was there to see without any argument' (1938),[43] full of 'facts which were relevant to everyday life' (1952).[44] The imaginative found it awoke interest in the world at large, other peoples and other lands. The thoughtful gained a new way of looking at the world, seeing not just a landscape or a town, but complex systems at work. In the 20th century it grew practical and scientific, but in the 19th century it could be more conjectural, and perhaps never more so than in Morrison's later years under 'Spot' Chadwick, 'a tall hatchet-faced but good-looking athlete'.[45] He was 'undoubtedly the greatest teacher of geography the world has ever seen or is ever likely to see again, now that geography has been annihilated by aeroplanes. Chadwick, however, luckily belonged to the age of balloons'.[46] At Scotch, the atlases

> had to be by Alex Keith Johnston 'Geographer in Ordinary to Her Majesty for Scotland'; but as maps were Mr Chadwick's hobby he did not confine himself to the works of that renowned geographer but used maps of every provenance, even German and French. Not an inch of the wall of Mr Chadwick's classroom but was covered with maps, and these were changed according to the particular subject of the day's lesson. ... he would sit in his classroom in the midst of his maps like a spider in his web gloating over the wrecks and disasters that befell this and that expedition, navigator or explorer who had daringly but unthinkingly paved the way 'for the urbanized Europeans to pour like vermin into the solitary places of the earth destroying and devastating the beauty and the power of nature.' ... Chadwick was torn between that love of unknown lands and strange peoples, which has lured so many great travellers and been the subject of so many epics and poems, and a hatred—quite alien to the nineteenth century—of the consequences of these discoveries.
>
> He bewailed the population explosion and the spread of industrialisation, all manufacturing the same goods in astronomical quantities. The populations will grow larger and larger and more standardized in order to consume them. Nobody sees the fatal writing announcing our doom or notices how rapidly the earth is shrinking to the size of a tennis ball. Long before some of you are dead it will be impossible to read on any map the words 'Desert,' 'Unknown Country,' 'Impenetrable Forest,' 'Waterless Region'. In the place of these names of hope and inspiration you will only be able to read: 'First-class Hotel,' 'City Reservoir,' 'Electric Power Station,' 'Refuse Dump', ... and 'Large Asylum for the Insane.' Such was the discourse of 'Spot' Chadwick.[47]

Leisure

The leisure activities of a gentleman were also attended to. Lawson advertised for a drawing master within weeks of his arrival, and by the

FOOTBALL

Football is 'the noble art of kicking goals and preventing others from doing likewise'.[48] At Scotch it had its own song, now in disuse, *Scotch! Boot the Leather, O!*

Much of football is true in every age, so the conditions at the 1908 Scotch v. Xavier match sound familiar: 'It was wet, very wet; it was muddy, and slushy and slippery—to be brief, it was anything but dry. During the first half we had it all our way, and when the second bell rang, the scores were 2–9 to 0–2. Hartkopf, Morrison and McCracken were just magnificent, wallowing about in the mud as if to the manner born. Nevertheless they found it impossible to keep their feet, and were often deposited in an inch of slush greatly to the deterioration of their new colours. The most natural thing to do in the circumstances was to wade out and take serious measures with the culprit. But though Scotch and Irish blood do not seem to blend well in a mud-pie, we parted in perfect friendship and with no ill-feeling on either side.'[49]

In 1877 the football team, captained by Charles Baker, did not lose a match. As an innovation, a team photograph was hung in the dining hall. The next year, the same happened and since the cricket team was undefeated, it too earned a photograph.

Other great teams arose every generation or so. The 1942 First XVIII won every match, defeating Melbourne Grammar by the then highest score ever kicked against that school, 20.15 (135) to Grammar's 12.12 (84) and in its Associated Public Schools (APS) matches that year scored 684 points which was 3.5 times the 192 points kicked against it. It was coached by Charlie Boyes (staff 1929–65), and captained by Doug Heywood (1942) who went on to play 53 games for Melbourne and became a football legend. Four times champion—1942, '43, '45 and '47—Scotch won 19 matches and lost none in those golden years. In the four years from 1941–44 they won 17 games and lost only two.

In 1996, captain Charles Lunn, coach Timothy Gallop (staff 1991–97), Scotch beat Melbourne Grammar 142 to 56, and in 2001, captain Campbell Brown, coach Steven Holding (staff 1987–), beat Melbourne grammar 145 to 8.

The 1953 First XVIII—captain Alan Cobham, coach Frank 'Faf' Fleming (1925, staff 1930–63)—were undefeated champions. Physically fit and with a will to win, in the match against Melbourne Grammar from a seemingly hopeless position at half-time the team fought back courageously to win the match, taking the lead only five minutes before the end.[50] In 1954 Scotch again won every match (captain Peter Hawthorne, coach 'Ocker' Ferres, staff 1946–69). The 1955–57 teams, coached by Fleming (captains: Michael Winneke, 1955 School Captain, Ian Law and Tony Olsson) produced four of the players that won Hawthorn its first premiership in 1961: Law, Malcolm 'Basher' Hill (1956), John Winneke (1956) and Colin Youren (1957). In 1967 Scotch missed the premiership by a missed goal after the siren.

In 1958, a century after the first match, Scotch's premiership inspired so many boys to play that a Seventh XVIII was formed, (and Xavier perhaps had the same over-supply, for when they played the Scotch Seventh they were found to have 19 men on the field).[51] The 1974 team, led by Tim Ashton and coached by Mick Eggleston (1947, staff 1958–87), was the best Scotch team Ewen 'Ginner' Davidson (1927, staff 1932–73) had known, and 'the best school-boy football team' Healey had seen 'in all the three codes I have known in about fifty years'.[52]

By contrast, in 1884 Scotch lost every match. In 1924 they lost every match but the last and won that, against Wesley, by only one point 8.13 (61) to 8.12 (60). In 1955 also they lost every game but the last which was again against Wesley.

Alexander McCracken (1871) was first President of the Victorian Football League 1897–1915.

The number of Australian Rules football teams peaked at 25 in the 1960s, and fell back to 19 teams by 2000.

They first wore a tough sailcloth-like fabric (little insulation on a cold day but presumably harder to tackle) then went to wool, for warmth. Later, acrylics kept the warmth in and lengthened the garments' lifespan. Most recently, the First XVIII wore jumpers of a light synthetic fabric that is tough, wind-proof, washable and warming, with a slippery texture that helps players elude opponents.

The smell of football was of liniment,[53] Oil of Wintergreen (Methyl Salicylate), applied to the players legs.

Glen Maginness marks the ball in front of the green grandstand, 1979.

Rick Fewster, Dave Yunghanns, Scott Bennett, Brian Hodge (back to camera) in 1980.

1860s there were prizes for human figures in chalk, landscape, architectural and engineering and ornamental drawings, displayed at Speech Days.

Music also began in the 1850s. In 1865 Morrison attempted to make it a routine subject 'without extra fee', but this quickly reverted to an extra few guineas to learn an instrument. As early as 1861 one of the instrumental music teachers was Mrs Trickett, apparently the first female non-primary teacher. She was still teaching in 1883.

Dancing, too, was taught for a few extra guineas by a visiting teacher. Few boys took it, but it continued under Littlejohn as an optional subject.

At some point in the above pages of gentlemen's requirements, we have moved from talking about knowledge to talking about skills. Morrison's Scotch taught both. Over Scotch's 150 years, definitions of knowledge and skills have wandered. Latin was once central but is now a curiosity. Handwriting was a skill, as were elocution and dancing. In the 19th century these skills were necessary for a young man's advancement.

MODERN KNOWLEDGE, USEFUL SKILLS

As well as subjects to shape gentlemen, Morrison offered subjects because parents wanted them or because he thought they were useful. Here, too, we find a mixture of knowledge and skills.

Science

The centenary history said that Morrison disliked Science. Yet in 1862 Morrison said Natural Science's 'importance in Education can scarcely be over-estimated' because 'it cultivates, beyond all other studies, "the faculty of observation and the love of truth" '.[54] He retained Lawson's Macadam to teach 'his valuable and full course' to all classes.[55] Only at the top of the school was it not taught, because those boys had to focus on the nine subjects the university set for the matriculation examination: Greek, Latin, English, French or German, Arithmetic, Algebra, Euclid, History (England, Greece, Rome), and Physical Geography. After Morrison's death, half the money raised for a memorial went to supply Physics apparatus.

Macadam encouraged boys to record his lectures in well-written and well-drawn note-books,[56] and we can discern the course's details from his examinations. Younger boys studied 'Elementary Chemistry: Heat' and were asked about thermometers, freezing and boiling points of water, the effects of heat, conductors (good and bad), preceded by questions on oxygen, the composition and properties of water, and the sources, properties and uses of sulphur. Older boys studied 'Chemistry of the Non-Metallic Elements and their Compounds; Geology; Physiology; Botany'.[57] They were asked 'How can the Chemist recognise Hydrogen Gas from Oxygen Gas and both from Nitrogen?', and about thermometers, smelting furnaces, crystallography, the properties of potassium, the uses of mercury, and the 'laws of Chemical combination by weight'.[58] This was almost entirely rote-memory work; nevertheless the course covered a substantial amount of material. Practical Chemistry was for boys destined for agriculture and mining. It required 'apparatus, and re-agents'[59] and was throughout the 19th century an optional subject costing a few guineas extra. Scotch thus taught a soundly based science course with sensible practical applications for the pastoralist, industrialist and miner.

Among Macadam's many other interests, he was the organising Secretary of the Burke and Wills Expedition, and his enthusiasm may have contributed to an optimistic painting by the art master, H. L. van den Houten (staff 1862–75), whose *The Exploring Party Coming Upon an Encampment of Natives* was painted in 1861 before the expedition failed.

Macadam died in 1865 and his work was taken over by the Principal's brother Robert Morrison, who used his influence to increase the Science budget. In 1873 a new building contained separate Chemical and Physical Laboratories and the requisite apparatus. Serle says that Scotch was the first school in Australia to have a science laboratory.[60] From 1887 Physics and Chemistry were a regular part of the senior curriculum. Robert Morrison had won honours in Natural Science and Chemistry at Edinburgh University. He taught science at Scotch until the end of the century, by which time Macadam was forgotten and Robert and Science seemed to

Bunsen burners and beakers: Doc Scholes's Chemistry class, 1930s. Small window panes were easily repaired.

explain each other's presence. That at least was how Walter Turner (1901) saw it:

> the most obvious character among the masters was the Doctor's slightly built younger brother, … who was quite incapable of teaching anything and no doubt had therefore been allotted by his brother—in the righteous contempt of a classical scholar—the department of science. Even in those … days there were a few maniacs who wished their sons to have a scientific education. There were not many of them in Melbourne because Scotchmen predominated in Melbourne and the Scotch, we know, are a hardheaded race with a very exact sense of values. A good Scotchman is impervious to rationalism, whether by defect or superfluity of intellect I do not know. Perhaps it is because he is trained in argument from his cradle that reason seems to him to be merely a by-product of porridge and one must then give him the credit for concluding that it is hardly likely that a by-product of porridge should be the key to the universe.
>
> There were, however, sufficient rich or important Saxons in the city of Melbourne to make a Science class a desirable appendage to the curriculum; besides there was the much more important question for the Doctor, namely, what to do with his brother Robert who belonged to that very superior class of gifted and characterful men usually described officially as 'unemployable'.[61]

Mathematics

Alongside Science came Mathematics, which included Arithmetic, Algebra, Geometry and Trigonometry. Morrison gave Mathematics more time than did Eton, Harrow and Rugby. Boys learned Arithmetic first, then Algebra or Geometry, 'never less than five hours weekly and … with the University Class, about ten hours weekly'.[62]

Like Latin, Mathematics had a set of rules to be mastered and then built upon. Like any subject, it could be difficult—'never understood a thing about it' (1964)[63]—or 'boring (all those numbers). No passion, no emotion, no human condition or dynamics' (1978).[64] One boy 'didn't have a clue what it was about; always in total misery' (1959). Yet there was delight in its 'closed logical system, challenging to the intellect, which could be played as a game' (1950).[65] 'The symbolism fascinated me and still does' (1958).[66] Other boys talk about it in terms that are almost moral. 'It is one of the few things in life where there is a right and a wrong answer' (1973)[67]—'the questions did not let one go astray' (1945).[68] In Algebra and Physics, the answers 'were honest and predictable once the clue was revealed. (Good gospel sermon material here!) Once you know the Truth other things fall into place' (1944).[69] The moral side of Mathematics was most evident in Geometry, often called Euclid because it comprised his theorems: a collection of problems and solutions famous for two thousand years. The solutions lay partly in applying the correct theorems. Each proof always ended with the letters QED (*quod erat demonstrandum*, meaning *which was to be proved*), so that the circle of thought was complete and intellectually satisfying, and returned, like a minuet, to its beginning.

Algebra plagued many boys, for it 'made simple mathematics complicated with unknown factors!!! e.g. Let x = the number'.[70] As early as 1860 an examination paper asked: 'How many different arrangements can be made of the letters of the word "Boroondara?"'[71] Keith 'Tiny' or 'Shorty' Elliott (staff 1946–79; he was of course very tall) 'knew how to teach Algebra, and if you could get him telling a war story, would entertain you for hours' (1981).[72]

The 1860s Arithmetic and Algebra examinations for senior boys tested skills. The Algebra paper set complicated expressions that had to be simplified, requiring perseverance and the careful application of a range of rules in the right order. Perhaps this was not unlike learning Latin. The Arithmetic paper tested skills rather than creativity; at its most creative it asked boys to move from one system to another. Compared to today it matched Year 10. The Geometry paper was the most intellectually challenging as it required a creative application of proofs to the situations described. 'If two chords of a circle, AB and CD intersect each other in the point F, show that the rectangle AF FB is equal to the rectangle CF FD whether the point F be within the circle or without.'[73] We cannot tell if boys were already trained to answer these questions, or if the examination genuinely invited boys to apply their knowledge in unforeseen ways.

Boys studying Arithmetic at Scotch mastered the use of decimal and vulgar fractions, and ratios, and learnt arithmetical skills directly applicable to the merchant, the speculator and the employer, like compound interest, and various complicated propositions in the style of 'If 3 men can mow 8 acres in 2 days …'[74]

Commerce

As early as 1857 Scotch gave a prize for Book-keeping, and by 1878 for Commercial Arithmetic and Correspondence. This part of the curriculum shows most clearly that Morrison modelled Scotch on his own school, the Elgin Academy, and followed the tradition of the Scottish academies and of English Dissent as opposed to the English grammar schools' concentration on the Classics.[75] Morrison made his fortune running Scotch as a business. By the 1890s he sat on the board of the National Mutual Life Association. He saw 'Mercantile Life' as a natural destination for his pupils, and made it one of his four-pillared 'English, Mathematical, Classical, and Commercial Education'.[76] Vigorous young Melbourne saw no shame in commerce. The Rev. John Ewing urged the Presbyterian congregation of Toorak to advance civilisation and amass wealth.[77] Scots were prominent in Melbourne's commerce and finance.

Morrison refuted any idea that all Scotch taught was Classics. Except for the 20 boys in the University Class, 'only one hour per day is devoted to Latin, the same amount of time as is given to Arithmetic; while Writing, Book-keeping, Spelling, Grammar, Geography, and Composition—all practical subjects—occupy a prominent place in our programme, and engage a large proportion of our time and attention'.[78] The commercial room was 'spacious, airy, and well lighted' when compared to other subjects' quarters.[79] In 1866 the course covered book-keeping, 'Single and Double Entry, Usual routine of a merchant's office, Commercial nomenclature, money, banking, public companies (formation, principles, liabilities, duties of persons employed by), Merchant service (Ships, freights, … custom dues…), Bills, stocks, mercantile correspondence'.[80] Employers appreciated this. Morrison repeatedly pointed 'with much satisfaction to many of my former Pupils now engaged in some of our best mercantile houses'.[81] Indeed, he became part of the process and recommended eligible youths to fill vacancies. He noted that 'Some of the cleverest boys take to business'.[82]

Scotch's aim to train boys' character, as well as their minds, fitted them well for commerce. At the 1878 Speech Day, Sir James McCulloch, former Premier of Victoria, urged the boys always to be honest in commercial life so that 'your word is your bond. My hope is that it may be said of the merchants of Victoria, as was said of the merchants of Tyre, "Her merchants are princes, her traffickers the honourable of the earth".'[83]

TEACHING METHODS
Biblical models

Various models were available to 19th-century teachers. The Enlightenment influenced Scotch's insistence that its teaching was systematic.[84] The Bible's first example of teaching is that Adam and Eve were told a rule, failed to learn it, and were expelled. Pedagogically this has two aspects, the use of punishment and the use of explanation.

James Forbes would have made fear the central plank in education at Scotch. The fear of the Lord is the beginning of wisdom, so schools had a duty to 'teach you the fear of the Lord (Psalm xxxiv.11)'.[85] Fear as a teaching model has lingered long, and as late as the 1960s John Cumming (1967) sensed at Scotch 'the smell of fear in the corridors that the place ran on'.[86] Small boys can fear adults even without its being policy. Bill Gleadell (1966) was scared of George Logie-Smith (staff 1959–78):

> he would enter my piano lesson without warning and make 'constructive comments' to my teacher, Mrs Limb [staff 1937–73] and myself. He would appear overbearing and threatening, so much so that I became terrified when he entered the room. … I have spoken to George on several occasions over the past twenty years and wondered what I was so worried about.[87]

Robert Blair (1963) 'was petrified of Garth Tapp [1939, staff 1948–77, Secretary of OSCA 1978–88] to the extent that more than 10 years outside school I was shaking in his presence at a fund-raiser, even with my wife by my side.'[88] Another boy recalls 'absolute terror' (1950).

Punishment for failing to learn a lesson has several intensities and purposes. It can be done as an example. Adam and Eve received no chance to learn from their mistake. The learning opportunity was for others. It is not by chance that such strong, pre-emptive discipline occurs near the start of the Bible, and many masters have adopted the same strategy of beginning as fearsomely as possible. Men with military training had already used this technique in the armed forces. As late as the 1970s, Bond began the year with a thunderous entry to the classroom. A long ruler whacked down hard on a desk, and a manner that brooked no weakness, set the tone from the start. With a solid frame established, some mellowing would be possible, and learning could proceed. The military model of learning is said to be that 'when you fear the instructor more than the task, learning will take place'.[89] By century's end, however, Rob McLaren (1973, staff 1987–) writes that 'it is only when a student feels comfortable and safe in his immediate environment that any real learning can take place'.[90]

In the 1920s Edmunds taught writing to the Junior School with 'a bunch of keys with which he chastized children'.[91] In the 1930s Charles 'Chassa' Pawsey (1908, staff 1922–43)—fearsome in appearance and attitude, unsmiling, and overbearing—used a 'rubber hose to chastise for smallest infringement i.e. not knowing the answer to questions one did not understand'.[92] In the 1960s 'there was one master who would extract information from students by pinching tightly a small patch of their hair and slowly screwing it around until the correct answer was provided'.[93] Another master is described by Old Boys decades apart as 'sadistic' and one who 'enjoyed beating boys' (1951, 1972).[94]

A more flexible model of punishment allowed for the possibility that he who is punished might learn. Thus Pharaoh underwent increasingly severe punishments until he achieved the desired behaviour which had been explicitly stipulated from the outset—for learning is greatly helped when pupils are given clear targets. The educational model employed is that a mistake is best followed quickly by a rebuke or punishment. This was how Morrison taught Latin. He put 'the boys through conjugating verbs and declining nouns and those who failed too ignominiously received a few hard strokes with the taws on their open hands. There was no newfangled nonsense about old Dr Morrison.'[95] The taws was a Scottish leather strap, slit at the ends. Gordon 'Gunner' Owen* (staff 1946–74) ended a boy's spelling mistakes by threatening to cane him.

A lesser level of physical pain was not so much a punishment as a means of punching the truth in. When 'Bill' Adams (1911, staff 1920–28 and 1936–64 when he was called 'Cakey') taught Greek to Alec Lyne 'His methods were simple and partly physical. There was much repetition in unison of declensions and conjugations and as he walked round the class he would

* 'Gunner' Owen, nicknamed after the Owen Gun.

stop and punch your shoulder to the rhythm of the chant. Similar physical reinforcement impressed the correction of mistakes we had made.'[96] 'He said as he thumped your bicep with his huge hairy fist that there was a direct link between the bicep and the brain.'[97]

> One Master ... tried to fit the punishment to the crime. A boy caught eating a sweet during class was made to pass the remaining confectionery around to be shared by all. Those who talked in class were sent out to talk continuously and in an audible voice to the elm tree in the middle of the quadrangle. One who was making a whistling noise with the cap of his pen was instructed to use it to play the national anthem while the class stood to attention. If any laughed during the recital the miscreant would be detained for one hour after school.[98]

Much of the physical punishment seems to have been considered unexceptional. Lyne later became friends with Adams, and together they ran Scotch's branch of the Australian Student Christian Movement (ASCM). Another Old Boy recently extolled the virtues of Littlejohn, several times expressing his admiration of the man, and concluding with a final emphasis that, after all, 'I knew him quite well for he often caned me'.[99] 'They say corporal punishment scars a boy—which is a lot of cock! We treated it as a great joke—those bloody detentions really hurt!'[100] Morrison concurred: a public rebuke 'was more stinging than a flogging'.[101]

For boarders, caning was common. One in 1929 was caned 24 times in one term; once the cane broke. Otherwise, officially only the Principal could administer corporal punishment,[102] so conceptually caning seems to have been regarded as different from the routine physical intimidation that occurred in the classroom. It was an era that accepted a level of physical violence between teacher and pupil. A good deal of whacking and pummelling had no reason other than the doing of it. When the school later moved to Hawthorn, the buildings were not ready and two grades were in marquees. Littlejohn would walk outside the tents thwacking at any boy whose shape made a bump in the side of a tent, and he roared with laughter as he did so.

Unabashed by post-Freudian anxieties about physical contact, the old propensity to hit boys was part of a broader enthusiasm for touching which let many masters throw a comradely arm round boys' shoulders. In primary school boys learnt their ABC from Miss Hay (staff 1862–70) literally sitting on her knee.[103] As late as the 1940s, Gilray could hug a boy. David Grounds (1946), although aiming for Medicine, still wanted to study English Literature, evoking a spontaneous embrace from Gilray in the middle of the quadrangle.

As early as the 1870s, corporal punishment had its critics. The Government wanted to limit its use in the state system, but Scotch said this would weaken teachers' authority. As for alternative punishments, like detention after school hours, to deprive boys of outdoor exercise 'is far more injurious to health, and, consequently, more truly cruel than a few strokes of a strap or cane'. 'The fact is that the old Scottish tawse was the most humane means ever used in school government.'[104]

The second pedagogical aspect of the story of Adam and Eve is that God did not explain why they should not eat the apple. At the theological level, this relates to faith. Educationally, too, it has profound implications. Must a teacher explain everything always? Or are there times when it is best just to instruct? Must boys chiefly be taught how to reason, or are there basic facts and skills which boys must learn whether or not they make sense at the time (or ever), like the value of pi or the spelling of phlegm? As Philip Roff (Principal 1975–81) told the Junior School Mothers' Association, for a boy studying Mathematics 'there are certain things such as his tables … which it is more efficient for him to know rather than to have to work out each time he uses them'.[105]

To tell rather than to explain thus has its place. Turner described it in the hands of Robert Morrison.

Of all the masters, even including the Head, Robert Morrison spoke in the broadest Gaelic of his native heather … but that did not matter because Robert Morrison belonged to that class of inspired beings whose speech you do not understand with your intellect but with your appendix. No scientist has yet discovered the use of the appendix but this is what it is for. And if you have no appendix the utterance of such men remains for ever dark to you. …

It reveals the nature of the Vice-Principal's teaching that at the end of years … we had never learned even the names of the chemicals he used or what were the operations which he conducted with such deliberation and care that if they did not enlighten us they at least mystified and thrilled us. …

When we were all collected in the classroom at the proper hour Robert Morrison, a smaller and slighter man than his brother, wearing a rather shabby frock-coat, with none of his brother's this-worldliness, would glide behind the table and begin scribbling some figures in chalk on the blackboard … Sooner or later, after sentences more or less in-coherent had been visibly addressed to us, he would open a bottle, light a Bunsen burner, sprinkle some powder on a metal disk, hold it over the burner and perhaps a marvellous cobalt light would dance momentarily in the air. … After one such successful experiment there would be at least half a dozen

Robert Morrison, second Vice-Principal, 1870–1904. '…lifting the tails of his frock coat and calling out "Skedaddle noo!", he would be the first to fly from the room… .'

failures. It was these alone which moved Robert Morrison to any flow of speech and what we then heard was something like this:

'Wha' now, what divil's got into the thing. Weel, weel, I shouldna ha' thocht it. Let me see now, I'll gi' 'em a bit of a surprise. Now this is $B_2F_6KL_{20}$ and that is $PQR_{14}F_6LMNO_{16}$. If this sounds compleecated ... weel, if you remember H_2O is just water then you needna be surprised at $PQR_{14}F_6LMNO_{16}$. It's a rare form, a lovely rare form of $PQ_7RF_5L_{14}$ and MNO_9. Wha' the devil won't the Bunsen burner burn?'

At this an excited boy might rashly call out:

'It's not lit, sir,' upon which Robert Morrison would say:

'Hoold your gab you unlettered divil. Now what can be the matter with this God-forsaken gob of a Bunsen burner? Niver trust any one named Bunsen. Weel, weel, niver mind we'll try something else. Noo this is $KP_{10}RS_{16}$ and we shall see what happens when it meets $RS_{14}KP_6$. This is a sort of chemical incest, boys, but you wouldna understand that. Niver mind, nothing happens. Noo then you see yon wee powder, it is $X_{14}Y_7Z_{21}$. It doosna do a thing itself but it's a catalytic and in its presence $RS_{14}KP_6$ and $KP_{10}RS_{16}$ combine to produce an entirely new thingamagig $KR_{22}PS_{14}$ and P_{56}. Sich is a Berselius catalysis; it canna be explained but if ye wee ignorant bawbees were properly instructed in zoology ye would understand that it's what happens when an elephant and giraffe mate in the presence of another camel'—BANG!

At such a crucial moment in the Vice-Principal's chemical lecture one or other of the retorts which he had cooking was sure to explode to the immense satisfaction of the class. But nothing of this sort ever disconcerted Robert Morrison who seemed to be just as pleased when anything went wrong as when a demonstration was successful. Every now and then he would look at his watch to see how the hour and a half allotted to his class was going. Occasionally, when nothing would go right and he was in a particularly gloomy mood he would deliberately bring the lesson to a premature conclusion by emitting from some jar a vast quantity of sulphuretted hydrogen whereupon lifting the tails of his frock-coat and calling out 'Skedaddle noo!' he would be the first to fly from the room.[106]

Whether or not boys understand what they learn, and whether they learn their lessons to avoid penalties or to gain rewards, all these teaching models are authoritarian. 'As the heavens are higher than the earth, so are my thoughts higher than your thoughts. For as the rain and the snow come down from heaven, and return not thither but water the earth, making it bring forth and sprout, so shall my word be that goes forth from my mouth; it shall not return to me empty, but it shall accomplish that which I purpose' (Isaiah lv.8–11). Within this top-down model, the ways of learning and of reaching the truth are many. Most teachers at Scotch have known their Bible and had in their minds all these models of how to impart knowledge.

Sometimes knowledge comes through a clear didactic voice, as with Christ in the Sermon on the Mount. Sometimes it comes from the force of example, as in a laboratory demonstration: 'Go and do likewise' (Luke x.37). Sometimes it is a steady repetition that pushes the message home, as when, in Genesis chapter 1, the account of each of the seven days of creation ends the same way: 'And God saw that it was good'. Sometimes the pupil does not understand what has been said and teachers need the patience to repeat themselves, even in the face of a sustained lack of understanding. So God called repeatedly to Eli before the boy understood (1 Samuel iii.4–10). Herbert Bower's (staff 1940–75) 'satisfaction was obvious when a less-gifted student suddenly saw the logical solution to a problem'.[107] Sometimes it seems that only a struggle can bring knowledge, as Jacob wrestled with the angel: Jacob could not win but would not let go (Genesis xxxii.27). Sometimes a teacher can find an argument that is simple, like 'If God be for us who can be against us' (Romans viii.31), and sometimes the argument has to be complicated, a sustained sequence of reasoning like St Paul's Epistle to the Colossians. Sometimes those who have made a mistake are told about it all too bluntly, as when Nathan confronted King David with murder (2

Rex Saunders at work in 1979. Rolling up his sleeves, he engages the boys in a variety of modes. Such photographs are rare, for the school has virtually no pictorial record of staff engaged in their primary task of teaching.

Samuel xii), and sometimes they are allowed to discover the truth for themselves, as when Joseph postponed his self-revelation to his brothers (Genesis xlii).

Assessment and emulation

The test of education, said Morrison, is not what is taught but what is learnt.[108] So he measured boys' achievements in a variety of ways.

Under Lawson, examination was done externally, by the church, which considered doing so again during its attack on Morrison in 1872.[109] This proposal was not adopted, not least because Morrison's *Annual Reports* for a decade had catalogued how very well his boys were doing at the externally run matriculation and Civil Service examinations. Within the school, results were by 'daily class markings' and by 'searching written examinations'.[110] Examinations were meant to be educative, and boys who fell short were subjected 'to a second, and sometimes even to a third examination, so that we insist on having the work done'.[111]

The suggested preparation for examinations was timeless. The student should 'subject himself to rigorous self-tests; he should systematically work out past examination papers, carefully noting all points in which he fails, and afterwards endeavouring to overcome any difficulties he may have met with'. In the exam, he should remain calm, read the whole paper, and start with the questions that seem easiest.[112]

Morrison knew that boys measure themselves against each other. He split classes into Divisions of boys of like ability, 'stirring up to a great diligence many a boy who would never have exerted himself, if he had had to contend with … thirty competitors instead of with ten'.[113] In each subject Morrison named not just the prize-winner but the boys who came next, at first naming only the top three and later the top half. Comparing the average and a boy's mark 'affords the fairest means of estimating how a boy has done'.[114] He gave prizes for improvement, too, and to boys who came second or third in several subjects. One boy in fifteen won a prize. For Dux of the school, Morrison published the names and scores of the runners-up. 'With the generality of boys these methods are sufficient to secure hard earnest work, but as every teacher knows, to his sorrow, there [are boys] who are swayed by no such motives, and can only be reached by the fear of punishment … if all other means fail.'[115]

STAFFING

Morrison was neither threatened by other men's talent, nor did he think all teachers should be alike. He employed 'some rare personalities not all likely to fit comfortably into a very rigid conception of what a schoolmaster should be'.[116] Their very diversity was educational, such as, in 1861, the first Ph.D. on the staff, Carl Adler (staff 1864–65), from Leipzig. When Melbourne was only decades old and all staff had to come from overseas, the school was more multicultural than in its middle years, between 1880 and 1980, say, when most teachers were Anglo-Celts from Melbourne.

The first appointments happened by proxy, through 'a Committee of gentlemen … in the mother-country, who … selected for me Masters … who come out to me under an engagement of three years' service'.[117] The contract was renewable. To the end, in obtaining staff for higher classes, he used 'commissioners at home' to locate appropriate men, but made the appointments himself by correspondence.[118] The better he chose, the more quickly they left to more senior positions in other schools (Weigall left to be Headmaster of Sydney Grammar School) or in the state education system (Gilbert Brown (staff 1856–57) became Inspector-General).

A BROAD AND STREAMED EDUCATION

One aspect of Morrison's greatness is that he held the whole process of education in his mind. He saw everything Scotch did as inter-related. He knew why each subject was taught and the order in which subjects were taught, and he had the gift of making it sound simple to parents. Within the intellectual realm he sought breadth by providing 'a complete English, Mathematical, Classical, and Commercial Education'. In each branch he gave 'an *equal* education'.[119]

In the Senior Department there were two parallel courses, 'the one preparing for the Universities and the Learned Professions, the other for Mercantile Pursuits, and generally for those Professions in which a critical knowledge of the Learned Languages is not essential'.[120] By 1875 Morrison called these two streams *Classical* and *Modern*.[121] 'The difference in the courses [is] that Pupils pursuing the former devote to Greek and Latin the time which those following the latter spend on Modern Languages, while both prosecute together the study of Mathematics, English Language and Literature.'[122] By 1875, the Modern side learnt Natural Science as a regular part of this course.

With breadth Morrison sought length, and in 1862 began a Junior Department to improve standards in later classes where 'at present, the progress of the Pupils is seriously retarded by their having to devote so much time to Elementary … knowledge … which should have been acquired at an earlier age'.[123] An 1866 junior timetable allocated two-thirds of the week's 30 hours into four main areas: English, Writing, Arithmetic, and Latin. The 1872 enquiry found the education there was as thorough and complete as for senior boys. From 1879 it was placed under a master.

The climb from junior to the two-streamed senior level was set out in 1860 on a chart. It showed how each subject built on its predecessor and showed when a pupil should commence each branch. For example, after so many years at English a boy should commence Latin, 'and after being two years at Latin, Greek is taken up'.[124]

Morrison's 'two leading Principles' were that English was of primary importance, and that 'Great care is taken to have the Pupils well grounded in every Branch, so that whatever knowledge they acquire is *thorough*'.[125] A 'good general education, as wide as is consistent with thoroughness'.[126]

There were 'about ten different stages of advancement'.[127] In a town only 20 years old, and at the end of the earth, Morrison found an educational muddle, with boys 'at all stages of advancement, weak here and strong there'.[128] To cope with this he allocated boys to classes by a four-part classification—English, Mathematics, Classics, and Modern Languages. 'All the boys are classified according to their proficiency in each of these four divisions without any reference to their rank in the other three, and so it frequently happens that a boy is in a high class in one of these departments, while he may be in a low one in the others.'[129] (In 1878 John Monash (Dux 1881) was in classes in the Lower Fifth, Upper Fourth, and Lower Fourth.) Educationally this was excellent. It ensured that each boy could work at his best ability without being obliged to hurry or dawdle so as to fit in with a class determined primarily by physical age. Instead a boy went where his strengths took him, carried 'forward as fast as he can go in each branch, irrespective of his progress in the others'.[130]

Sir John Monash (Dux 1881) as a youth.

A disadvantage was that it entailed more teachers. It was administratively time-consuming, as every boy had to be individually classified, and reclassified during the year to reward ability and performance. As no class had a permanent membership, it was not easy for a class to develop a distinctive character, or for class rivalry to be engendered.

As well as breeding gentlemen and training them usefully, Morrison broadened their minds. He arranged lectures from people passing through Melbourne, and he widened his range of subjects by charging a few extra guineas to employ Visiting Teachers for subjects that involved additional cost (Practical Chemistry, Gymnasium) or for which there was a limited demand (Hebrew, Drawing, Instrumental Music, Dancing, and Elocution in its later days). He drove boys on by intensifying competition among them and by allocating each boy to the class in each subject that would challenge him.

4
EDUCATING THE WHOLE MAN

As well as trying to make boys smart, Scotch hoped to make them wise. Morrison rejected the utilitarian view that boys should 'learn nothing but what can afterwards be turned to a directly practical account; what will—commercially speaking—pay, without any reference to their mental and moral training'.[1] Instead, he wanted 'to educate the whole man; combining intellectual, moral, and religious training, with a sound healthy physical development'.[2] This multi-directional outlook shaped the school motto *Deo et Litteris*—For God and Learning. From 1914 it was *Deo Patriæ Litteris*—For God, Country and Learning. Unlike mottoes with a single strand of thought, Scotch summoned its boys to a diverse world.

As with academic knowledge and skills, moral education has changed in the passage of 150 years, as each generation tackles it afresh. Its continuous thread is that Scotch hopes to produce men who can tell right from wrong, and act accordingly; men whose inner life is one of self-discipline and whose outer life is one of service to others.

RELIGION AND MORALS

Morrison held that 'moral and religious training should be the paramount end of all education' and to it he 'always devoted much anxious attention'.[3]

His Religious Instruction course encompassed several issues at once. He found boys had little knowledge of the Bible and were 'generally very ignorant of religious matters'.[4] He therefore made Bible study part of the school's curriculum but 'of course, not compulsory',[5] so that 'pupils whose parents object are not required to attend',[6] although 'most' pupils did attend.[7] To make this optional subject attractive it was non-Denominational and 'strictly Scriptural',[8] with the Bible as, prosaically, 'the text book'.[9]

Morrison challenged older boys to think about the Bible and to apply modern scholarship. The 1860 New Testament examination tested not only knowledge of Bible events, but asked about the date and authorship of New Testament books, or about the argument in Galatians compared to the first eight chapters of Romans. Similarly the Old Testament exam asked about dating the Book of Job.

Boarders' Religious Instruction paralleled how Morrison raised his own family. His children had a Bible as soon as they could read, at age six. He held family prayers each day before breakfast, when each child had to recite a biblical verse. (They naturally chose short verses, one of his sons memorising 'Jesus wept'.) On Sundays toys were put away, though bricks were allowed 'on the understanding that only churches and their accompanying manses were built'.[10] Boarders had to learn verses and the Presbyterian *Shorter Catechism*, hear Scripture and attend church.

For the whole school, the day opened and closed with prayer. Classes had Bible lessons two hours a week (run by Morrison as much as possible) or had to learn verses. Only the classes studying for university entrance were excused. The church in 1872 favoured Religious Instruction every day for every class, but Morrison avoided this. He taught the boys morality not as an evangelist but as an educator, and his optional, creative, and scholarly approach to Religious Instruction drew on all his skills. He hoped boys were Christians, but he never gave this as one of his goals, and instead repeatedly stated a more humanist goal. 'With religious instruction, I have combined every effort to make my boys truthful, honourable, upright, and kind to each other.'[11] Even in this apparently secular statement, Morrison would have had in mind Philippians iv.8: 'true ... honorable ... just ... pure ... lovely ... gracious'.

B's Without Stings

B truthful, B honest, B upright, B fair,
 B kind to a class mate or friend;
B noble, B good, and B-have as you should,
 Then B sure you'll B right to the end.[12]

In teaching boys to be truthful, honourable, and upright, the school drew on the Christian and classical traditions. Once a boy was old enough to know the difference between good and evil, 'he is morally bound to strive after the one and to avoid the other. And all education, rightly considered, means nothing else.'[13] Littlejohn taught truthfulness by never calling a boy a liar (which would have implied that the boy habitually lied). Instead he would suggest that 'on this particular occasion what you had said was not the truth'.[14] Half a century later the *Collegian* described this approach as condemning an act but not the person.[15] Littlejohn expected boys 'to own up when we did something wrong, even though punishment might result'.[16] In 1932 'Doing the right thing was a fact and not a hackneyed saying'.[17] Old Boys of the 1960s felt they were taught 'Understanding right from wrong'[18] and the importance of honesty.[19]

As for Morrison's goal of being honourable, in 1965, during a building appeal, Scotch raised fees by 20%. To have postponed it until after the appeal, said Colin Healey (Principal 1964–75), 'would have been dishonourable'.[20] In the 1930s during Ingram's classroom tests, cheating was rife.

Boys opened their cribs under the desk while he walked solemnly up and down gazing ruminatively from time to time at the cricket field and announcing the score … But should he leave the room placing one of us in charge, the cribs would immediately vanish. It was all right to cheat when Bumpy was there but not when he was absent.[21]

Moral education at Scotch has always been three-pronged: to teach religion, to create a moral atmosphere, and to model behaviour. The staff were not so much an alternative to religious instruction as religious instruction in action. Good behaviour would be 'caught' rather than 'taught'.[22] In class, Morrison wanted masters 'to cultivate and maintain a high tone of moral feeling and upright honourable conduct', and out of class he expected them to 'mix with the Pupils as much as possible'.[23] Every subsequent Principal has followed this policy; all that has changed is that successive generations have wanted to model different things.

Morrison wanted to teach good habits, and he hired his own relatives or religious men, preferably students of divinity (especially for resident masters). His successors continued to appoint teachers who would give the boys more than an academic eduction. When asked what he owed to Scotch, Sir Archibald Glenn (1929) thinks first of 'the association with fine people, good masters with high moral standards'.[24] It is said of Frank Fleming (1925, staff 1930–63) that he did not teach History or English, he taught boys. Long after they forgot the gerunds and dates, they remembered his lessons of life. A boy who failed English Literature nevertheless names the teacher, Owen, as his best teacher because 'he taught me so much about life, people, personalities. He was also my house master in Arthur Rob—very strict but *always* fair and *always* consistent'(1967).

Littlejohn shared Morrison's doubts that Religious Instruction was the best way to teach morals. Instead, moral instruction should be given 'incidentally and unobtrusively', the teacher making a wise use of opportunities, 'speaking the word in season rather than in some lesson planned for the purpose'.[25] Later principals and chaplains concurred. The Rev. Archie Crow (1938, assistant chaplain 1965–67, chaplain 1968–85) in 1969 said 'that religion was the corporate responsibility of all the staff', who should develop class discussion from boys' questions.[26] Explicitly religious occasions like Assembly were only a beginning, and no discipline was immune from moral issues.

William 'Bumpy' Ingram, third Vice-Principal, 1912–34. During his tests, boys cheated only when he was present; otherwise it seemed unsporting.

Beyond personal influences, boys' character was shaped, said Morrison in 1887, by the discipline and surroundings of a Public School.[27] Public School life, said Littlejohn, was

> a spiritual thing … stimulated by wisely ordered discipline and by the demand for honest intellectual work; kept fresh and wholesome by organised school games, so long as they do not play too exclusive a part in fixing the standard of personal distinction among the pupils; …fostered by the … Old Boys; and intensified by the assembling of the whole school daily for acts of common worship.[28]

Gilray put it more simply: 'to convey certain standards of value through the very sharing in the common life of the school'.[29]

Morrison also made good use of the boys themselves. As a Christian, Morrison believed in original sin: that after Adam all men are sinners. Yet if Morrison pondered whether boys were intrinsically wicked it seems that he felt they were not. He spoke fondly of 'my boys' or 'my young friends',[30] and he seems to have thought most boys were disposed towards good behaviour if properly led in that direction.[31] Without overlooking their misdeeds, he concentrated on what was good. This enabled him to notice and make use of the ways boys behave. Their tribalism and their propensity for hero-worship were moulded to serve authority rather than revolt against it.

> In taking advantage of the *esprit de corps* so prevalent among boys, I have always tried to enlist their sympathy and co-operation, so as, by *their* means, to create and foster a sound and healthy public opinion, by which boys can do so much to teach each other, putting down whatever is low, mean, and cowardly … The conduct of the boys, with very few exceptions, has been exemplary, while many of them, who have been pre-eminently distinguished for honor, truthfulness and gentlemanly conduct, have exerted a most beneficial influence over the whole school.[32]

Here is one of Morrison's lasting achievements—a challenge to be good, based on a belief that they would rise to that challenge and throw up leaders who set an example worth following. Of course, not all Scotch boys proved to be good or to be good leaders.

CHARACTER

What teachers and older boys were meant to model was *character*. Morrison in 1869 declared that one of Scotch's 'great missions [was] to form and discipline character'.[33] By character he meant 'habits of exertion, self-denial, self-control, and desire for self-culture'.[34] Littlejohn concurred that the task of the school was 'the formation of character', and that 'the most potent factor is the personality of the teacher'.[35] What Littlejohn meant by 'character' is captured in his reference for Kenneth Bridge (1923), who 'had developed into a lad of much strength and grace of character, entirely straight and reliable'.[36] *Character* embraces both morals and something more. By the second half of the twentieth century it was used mainly in phrases like 'character development'[37] or 'character building' (cadets was 'character building'[38]) which was most likely to refer to no more than what one gained by overcoming adversity.

Self-control and hard work

A boy in his inner world should have habits of order, self-control, and self-reliance.[39] How does one teach such things? Probably in many ways, and a new way appeared in the 1870s: the obituary. When Scotch was young, so were the Old Boys. Old Boys died young, from illness, drowning or accidental shooting, but from the 1870s Old Boys were old enough to have had a career before they died, and so to warrant a panegyric. When William Rees (1861), the first medical graduate of the University of Melbourne, died in 1879, his obituary not only described his achievements but also held up for emulation his 'thoroughly-disciplined ability'.[40] Self-discipline has remained one of Scotch's touchstones. It became second nature for Jim Olifent (1938), whilst Ross Hyams (1980) felt Scotch 'Taught me excellent work habits—the discipline required for study and for organising time/work schedules'.[41]

In organising time, *Young Victoria* (the school magazine 1877–85) advocated 'punctuality', 'regularity' and 'a methodical and orderly disposition of time and resources', and deplored procrastination. 'What is done at its proper hour, and with calmness, can well be done with care and exactitude', for 'the clock is the sternest ruler of our daily lives; its warning hand cannot be disregarded with impunity'.[42] In the twentieth century the clock's face found a voice

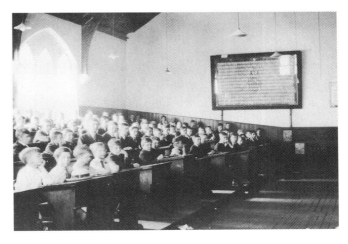

Morning prayers for the last time in No. 1 in East Melbourne. The morning glare regularly gave headaches to masters.

as Littlejohn and Healey shouted '*You boy!*' at miscreants late for class. Coordinating a thousand boys into dozens of classrooms was done by a document called, appropriately, the timetable. At a school full of activities, boys learnt time management ('an asset for life'),[43] but an unmotivated boy felt that 'Nobody really instilled the idea of time management to get through the academic work load'.[44]

Other forms of self-discipline alluded to darker forces: boys' battle with their own 'tempers, passions, and evil desires'.[45] Self-discipline also had an outward focus: obedience and 'Subordination to just authority',[46] a 'prompt and cheerful obedience which wins for us the favour of our superiors, and renders us fit to command in our turn'. A 1991 Old Boy believed cadets 'teaches the wrong examples of discipline … a military based discipline, rather than one derived from oneself'. James Simpson (1971), now Professor of Medieval and Renaissance English at Cambridge, wrestled with this from a different perspective, asking whether obedience to rules was the sign of a Christian community? The answer, he believed, was that discipline at Scotch was imposed just as often by fear, and that true Christian discipline should be self-imposed.[47] Scotch has always tried to teach both kinds of discipline.

'Binding together and confirming all the other habits … is the grand habit of industry', said *Young Victoria* in 1879.[48] In every later generation Scotch instilled a strong work ethic. This could mean respecting it in others: 'No schoolboy loves a swat, but we did learn to appreciate the results achieved by the lad who, through hard work, made full use of the brains he had and to value his success above that of the brilliant brain to whom success came easily'.[49] It could mean what Colin Scott (staff 1958-64) taught Hugh Taylor (1964) in Years 9 and 10, that 'it was alright to do well and work hard—in fact it was good'.[50] Old Boys of the 1990s talk about it as a trade-off: 'if you want to achieve you must work hard'.[51] 'Mr Cracknell [staff 1973– , Group Master 1995–] was right, there is no substitute for hard work. But it didn't get in the way of the social life, which continued. Everyone still went out every weekend' (1996).

Self-control also applied to property. Fleming as a boarding-house master trusted the boys, thus encouraging them to be worthy of his trust. Locks were permitted only on food lockers (he knew the temptation to take food was too much for a hungry boarder). The worst sin to him was deceitfulness. 'Youthful transgressions or exuberance were seen for what they were and were punished promptly and then forgotten.'[52]

Manners maketh the man

An outward sign of character is manners. Morrison in his practical way recommended 'Neatness of attire, gentleness of speech, and gracefulness of action [as] a passport to success'.[53] Littlejohn was more romantic. At the 1924 OSCA Annual Smoke Concert he said that:

> The public school, essentially English in origin, had become the most potent factor in the Empire. A mystery to the foreigner, an enigma even to the democratic American, the public school was the most severely criticised of all English institutions, and yet the most religiously copied. To what did it owe its mighty influence? Not to its numbers, nor to its literary achievements in school work, nor to its supremacy in sport, but to the ancient public school motto, 'Manners maketh man.'[54]

Some manners are perhaps ephemeral. Morrison disapproved of hands in pockets. Littlejohn berated a boarder 'at breakfast for what he called bad manners, said I held cup in 2 hands'.[55] That boys should 'keep quiet when

TIMEKEEPERS

Scotch's most romantic bell hangs outside the boarders' dining hall. Captain Frederick Tickell (1875) carried it off from Peking when he commanded the Victorian naval contingent that helped suppress the Boxer Rebellion in 1900.

Scotch at Hawthorn usually used a bell to regulate activities. In 1929 boarders were summoned to eat by the kitchen's steam whistle but were woken by a hand bell until at least the 1970s. At the day-school, the bell regulated the periods. Boys not in their place when the bell stopped received a detention (Rule 15). At first this bell was rung by a rope and if the rope broke, recess had to be ended with an auctioneer's bell. By the late 1940s, a new teacher at the start of his first day, listening to the rising noise of boys outside the common room, was startled by 'the shattering discords of some mechanical engine which must be the school bell. At first it seemed to rouse an even greater gust of catcalls, laughs, cries of pain, heavy blows, and treble blasphemies outside. Then the tide receded, as the angry swarm sullenly consented to kill each other in another place.'[56]

For decades the bell was rung by a bell-boy, a responsible lad who slipped out of class at the appropriate time. When he blundered ('I once rang the bell ½ hour or so too early') he incurred the wrath of teachers.

In 1964 the master clock moved from the Pavilion to outside the Bursar's Office and was used to make the school bell automatic (as it already was in the Junior School), with an IBM system.

The Music School in the 1960s had a siren, louder than any music, and boys advocated a siren for the quadrangle, as its sound would carry further. Instead, the school as it expanded installed more than one bell, and in the Lithgow Centre broadcast an electrically generated chime.

The constraints of time spread even to sport, and though cricket continued at its own unperturbed pace, and the first football match lasted as long as they wanted, more modern games had quarters of specific lengths. So boys became timekeepers, and had 'the minor thrill for a teenager of operating the siren at regular intervals',[57] a great boon in a world where boys are so often told to be quiet.

appropriate' (1979), 'remaining silent until spoken to' (1945),[58] is no longer emphasised. The social custom of standing when teachers entered a classroom surprised a 1991 new boy.

Old Boys throughout the twentieth century recall Scotch teaching them courtesy and good manners. Boys learnt how to thank or praise someone even when they had no wish to do so. Sometimes their choice of words shows what a struggle good manners are with basic human instincts: 'we must congratulate',[59] 'we must feel very grateful'.[60]

For most of Scotch's life, manners were part of being a gentleman. Indeed, many of the school's aims were explicitly framed in these terms. Morrison's Rules required 'gentlemanly conduct', and *Young Victoria* advised boys to 'wear the white flower of blameless life which is the surest indication of a gentleman'.[61] In the new century, Gordon Scholes (staff 1924–40) told the boys, 'You are here to learn to be *Christian* gentlemen'.[62] 'Christian gentleman' was how Rice '45' Clayton (Senior History Master 1925–63) praised Gilray, and how Bill Callister (1941) praised David Bradshaw (1924, staff 1930–53, Junior School Headmaster 1945–53).[63]

In the 1940s *gentleman* applied to everything from sex education—'To behave as a gentleman'[64]—through to the ultimate accolade of hero worship—'the School Captains of the day were such … gentlemen, that they exerted a terrific influence on most of us'.[65] Tapp in 1958 asked classes to define a gentleman as a way of identifying conduct to emulate. At the same time Miss Goodenough discerned an even more archaic virtue, asserting that 'chivalry is kept alive in the modern boys by their kindly remarks and acts'.[66]

At the Centenary in 1951, the oldest Old Boy present, Henry Brook (1878) recalled that Morrison gave three rules to every boy leaving school —love and honour God, honour the King, and remember always that you are a gentleman and a Scotch Collegian.[67]

PRIVILEGE AND RESPONSIBILITY

As well as producing men of character and courtesy, Scotch aimed to produce men of value to the community. The inner life had an outer manifestation.

Scotch is expensive and generally its poorer families are wealthier than the average Australian family. Scotch has never really found a way of saying this comfortably, but it is most at ease in doing so when linking privilege to duty. The Christian version of this, as Tapp put it, is that 'we hold our gifts in trust from God and have a responsibility to develop them. That development must embrace a concern for all people, and emphasize the attitude of service.'[68] A more secular version is Morrison's view that those with wealth and position should do their duty to their country.[69] Littlejohn 'expected all of us to understand that we were privileged to attend a private school of this standing and that we had a responsibility to society and our fellow man as a consequence'.[70] Gilray 'taught me that I was a privileged person, that I owed the world

The rulers of tomorrow. Nonchalantly confident Scotch boys at Eastern Hill.

something and not the reverse'.[71] Selby Smith told boys 'that their gifts and powers have been given to them as a trust and not an outright gift, and that they must use them at times for purposes beyond their own'.[72] Gordon Donaldson (Principal 1983–) says life 'can best be lived fully if it is lived in service to others'.[73]

This approach at least addressed the inequalities in our society, though it did not rectify them. 'I like the school, but I'm not sure how healthy it is to mix with a privileged minority for years and years. Perhaps the same things would have happened wherever I was' (1980).[74]

In the 1870s Old Boys entered Parliament, and Morrison began to talk about a new aim for Scotch, that of equipping boys for 'their duties as citizens', 'to leave their country better than they found it'.[75] Where men are entrusted with power, said McCulloch, a former premier, their education should 'qualify them to deal intelligently with political and social questions of the day'.[76] Fifty years later, in 1927, Littlejohn asked:

> What should parents desire their son to gain by sending him to a good school? Is it merely that he should acquire knowledge and pass examinations? That certainly is a desirable object, but it is not a high ideal. Is it rather that he should have all his powers of body and mind and spirit directed and developed? That is a higher ideal, nor does it exclude the lower one. But the present day objective of a liberal education is wider still. Briefly, it is to fit the boy to live his life as a citizen, to make him able and willing to shoulder responsibility, and to be of service to the community. … Service to the community is the greatest duty in life, and … They must be trained and inspired to face their duties as citizens.

Littlejohn envisaged this happening in a quite practical way. 'A big school teaches the value of co-operative effort for the good of the whole. … It affords a training in discriminating between … what is just and what unjust.'[77] Old Boys concur. They learnt the 'standards of behaviour as a good citizen' (1927),[78] 'how to live, and to conduct myself, in a community' (1929). Being at Scotch was an 'effective process of learning in citizenship' (1967).[79] Under Healey, proponents of Adventure Training said that living and working in a group would develop citizenship skills.[80] Earlier statements of the benefit of living together would not have used this phrase.

In the 1920s, *Christian* citizenship was postulated. The Rev. Frederick Hagenauer (1890) preached to Old Boys and parents that a man should carry Christian principles into his nation's life, and should enter that life to the fullest extent.[81] The 'development of Christian ideals of citizenship' became formally one of Scotch's goals when the school became incorporated in 1980.[82]

A more cynical concept of citizenship is seen in a master's comment on one boy's blue card: 'Very quiet, passive, inert. Doesn't have much academic ability, or apparently any will or drive to succeed. Likes the outdoor life. He will grow up into a sound enough citizen' (Form V, 1964).

Citizenship's most fervent manifestation, patriotism, was one of Scotch's aims for much of the 20th century. In 1934 the chaplain thanked God for the good things in the school's life, including patriotism.[83] Such language receded after World War II.

Morrison's Presbyterian values about character infused the school's discourse about itself and do so to this day: truthful, upright, kind, hard-working and duty-bound to service. Gordon Fisher, Captain in war-time 1941, around halfway between Morrison and ourselves, draws together much of the above when he reflects on Scotch:

> encouraging concern for others (less fortunate) ... tolerance towards other races, religions, and people who were different. ... to turn out young men who were self reliant, confident, able to accept responsibility, patriotic, prepared to sacrifice one's life for one's country and able to achieve leadership in whatever field of endeavour one chose, the assumption being that students were privileged and had access to an 'education' superior to that provided by the state. Personally I'm not sure that I was prepared or mature enough for adult life as it took some time to adjust to life in the lower ranks of the Army after 13 'privileged and sheltered' years at Scotch.[84]

Similarly, Healey proposed 'respect for hard work and delight in hard striving; a sense of dignity both of the individual and of society; a condemnation of snobbery and a sense of modesty. This is the kind of discipline which is self-imposed after it has been learnt.'[85]

Even so, there are Old Boys who could be described as ambitious, putting themselves before the public good, contemptuous of opinions other than their own, and determined to have their own way.

SPORT

Scotch is old enough to predate the modern adulation of sport, and may outlast it.

At the start there was no sport, just games like Prisoner's Base, which Lawson joined in. (Two sides occupy contiguous 'bases' or 'homes'. Any player running out from his base is chased by one of the other side and, if caught, is made a prisoner.) Morrison was not much interested in sport, for which he had the condescending tolerance of 'a man of superb physique who had never in his life taken any exercise for its own sake'.[86] He established the school's reputation on its academic results. When he praised boys who 'exerted themselves strenuously to maintain the honor of the College', he was referring to examinations.[87] His vision was that Scotch offered an 'intellectual, moral, and religious training', although 'we are careful also not to neglect the physical'.[88] As a businessman, however, he acknowledged customer interest in 'the athletic sports and exercises now so much in vogue',[89] and in the early 1860s he offered Cricket, Foot Ball, Boating, Swimming, a Gymnasium, and Military Drill. He limited the boat club to

those who could swim, and boys swimming at Sandridge or St Kilda baths had to be accompanied by a master. The gym had the 'newest and most approved apparatus and appliances' and was run by a 'scientific teacher',[90] but it was an optional extra for which fees were charged, so only a handful of boys in each age group participated.

In 1868 Morrison inaugurated a Scotch College Athletic Sports Day. Graced by the Governor, it may mark the advent of Scotch as a school that officially lionised sport. William Freeman (entered 1860) won the first Old Collegians' Cup. In those days all the Old Boys were young. As the oldest of them entered their thirties their interest in the school revived, and at 12 guineas their silver cup was worth two terms' fees.[91] Morrison made a fuss of the Cup and ranked it after Dux and Champion, presumably to elicit more Old Boy generosity. Because he saw that the Old Boys were as interested in the school's sporting achievements as in its academic laurels, from 1868, also, his *Annual Report* listed sporting leaders and achievements. From 1870 Morrison secured use of a cricket ground. The cricketers developed the skills that were hampered by playing on grounds pockmarked

LONG JUMP

The longest swearword Lewis Campbell (1907) ever heard was uttered at the long jump. It 'started as the contestant missed the take off board and finished at the far end of the sand pit, just one word. "Jonah" Whyte [1880, staff 1890–1927] turned his back and walked away, I suspect to hide his grin.'[92]

In 1919 (the year of the dead heat in rowing), the Combined Sports were equally undecided until the last minute. With one event to go, there was a three-cornered contest between Scotch (74.5 points), Wesley (78) and Melbourne Grammar (74).

The last event was the Open Long Jump, and each of the three schools was well

represented. Norm Tranter (1919) had to win the Long Jump to win the Sports for Scotch. Champion of Athletics in 1918 and 1919, Tranter had already won the 100 yards and the 220 yards. But his luck was out. After two 'no jumps', he recorded a fine 20 feet 9 inches, but Sargent of Grammar jumped 21 feet 11 inches in his last jump, so that Tranter had to break the record to win the Sports for Scotch. The challenge galvanised him to leap 32 centimetres further than he had ever jumped before, setting a record of 22 feet 1.5 inches (6.74 m) that stood for 37 years until broken in 1958 in the first Combined Sports at Olympic Park, on cinder tracks.

from other sports. Scotch built a handsome pavilion and spent large sums preparing the turf. Quoits and lawn tennis were also played. Scotch was taking sport seriously enough to let Old Boys put money into it. The crowning achievement came in 1891, repeated in 1892, when Scotch held the Public Schools Championship in Cricket, Football and Rowing, the first time any school held all three. The victory on the river was especially hard-won. Scotch, Wesley and Geelong Grammar were neck and neck the whole way. Scotch won by a metre, whilst Wesley beat Geelong for second place by even less.

But should boys play sport? And if so, how much? Morrison was dubious. Ultimately, he allowed games only because 'all schools have them, and it would, therefore, be impossible to dispense with them'.[93] He took care that boys 'should not train too much'[94] and he worried at injury to 'the weak and delicate'.[95] Nowadays Scotch would shrink from such labels. Nowadays Scotch still makes every effort to prevent injuries, but accepts that they will occur and values sport's benefits over this cost.

Another danger is no longer troublesome. Using cups as prizes was contentious within the church, and Morrison preferred medals, but donors favoured cups, and he acquiesced.

He worried that frequent matches distracted boys from study and 'give a disrelish for the more important literary work of the school', and he was surprised to discover that sport was 'not prejudicial to the pupils' studies, as in nine cases out of ten those who are successful in the sports also take prizes'.[96]

A more intractable problem was that success in sport received 'an undue amount of importance', 'too much éclat'.[97] Éclat (general applause or social distinction) was Morrison's word of opprobrium for sport throughout his last 20 years, for he saw sport's 'undue prestige'[98] as dangerous, and he disapproved of its power to inspire boys' souls. Perhaps he saw it as idolatrous if his boys spoke about sport as did twentieth-century boys, with phrases like 'enshrined in our hearts' (1909)[99] and with words like 'love' and 'obsession' (1931)[100]—or declared of sport 'It's my life!' (1976).[101] By 1913 the religious nature of sport was well enough established to be played with: 'There is only one God, and the captain of Football is his prophet'. 'I must play games with all my heart, with all my soul, and with all my strength.'[102] This last mocked the First Commandment, and was surely blasphemous.

In 1876 Morrison restricted the time given to sport and from 1880 he allowed only one cricket and football match with each other school. In 1889 he conceded *two* matches with each school, but when it interfered with many boys' studies he raised the matter with the other headmasters, an early sign of how Principals' freedom of action is constrained by having to work with their peers. At Wesley, Adamson heightened the importance of sporting success, and Scotch had to adjust to this.

Morrison is not known to have played any sport. Littlejohn fished and played tennis and golf. All subsequent Principals were raised after sport had established itself at schools. Gilray, Selby Smith and Donaldson played rugby, Healey was a cross-country runner, and Roff rowed. Also, Gilray was an athlete, and Selby Smith played hockey. Later Principals have also tried to diminish the adulation for sport. Gilray did so in conjunction with (Sir) James Darling of Geelong Grammar. One reason for ceasing to hold the Head of the River on the Yarra was to lessen public adulation. Selby Smith wrote that 'the boy who has been a leader in sporting activities has often been given too much of the limelight, and gained too much prestige among his fellows. Far too much attention, certainly, has been paid by the press, and by some of the "old boys" of these schools.' Echoing Morrison, he wrote that 'many boys developed high levels of skill, but this is of little importance; and while all should strive to do their very best, it must always be clearly understood that the production of skilled athletes is in no sense the true purpose of school sport'.[103]

Sport as a moral activity

During the nineteenth century, successive waves of ideals about physical activity rolled over Scotch. First, Muscular Christianity valued sport as a way of teaching young men wholesome activity and the moral usefulness of co-operation and self-sacrifice. At the turn of the century, the new Australian nationalism rather scorned sport as immature and encouraged young men instead to undertake more practical activities like military service.[104]

Morrison's doubts about sport were due not to an objection in principle—'I have always encouraged boys to take suitable outdoor exercise'—but to what he saw as sport's limited benefits. He did not approve of sport that was tiring. He saw sport in purely physical terms: 'a means of maintaining health, affording relaxation and supplying an outlet for pent-up physical energy'.[105] That is, he did not see sport as educational. In the closing decades of the nineteenth century, however, he made concessions to the view that sport could educate by shaping character. Morrison would have preferred to teach character by example, Christianity and the Classics, but his instincts as a teacher led him to make use of whatever engaged the boys. This meant sport.

Winning and losing

At root, sport's educational claims attached to what was most basic about sport: winning and losing. These were elevated from mere muscular or dexterous achievements by the addition of a view about how one should handle them, teaching what Morrison called 'two important lessons, to endure defeat without a grudge, and to bear success without undue elation'.[106] Such lessons run counter to human nature, and to learn them is to learn a social behaviour. At Scotch they became part of the way the school talks about itself, and briskly appear in the School Song: 'Glad if winners, but if beaten never sore'.

Scotch loves winning. As well as the 'joy and pride' of it, winning is what

carries boys to find in themselves skill and courage that they might not know they had. Boys are urged to have a 'will to win'.[107]

As for losing, 'We learned to ... receive the kicks with at least some show of equanimity; to meet disappointment, if not with a smile, at least with a grin'.[108] A good loser was like the First Crew in 1958, which 'has not tried to offer any explanation for their defeat, but has accepted it like true Scotch Collegians and true sportsmen'.[109] Hal Oxley (1933) learnt 'to lose happily, congratulating the winner'.[110]

'. . . because strong is good'. Don Davenport, Teacher-in-Charge of Athletics since 1988.

'Do your best'

Several different views played down winning. 'Play to win,' said Healey, 'but remember that the worst impediment to the enjoyment of school games is the belief that nothing matters so long as the game is won'.[111] So 'winning was not everything, it was more important to participate' (1937).[112] Even when 'our teams were not conspicuously successful', Selby Smith was pleased that 'we had still more boys taking an active part, and the level of sportsmanship was good'.[113]

Scotch's most sustained attempt to value participation over winning was in 'standards'. One of the burst of new activities under the early Gilray, standards were the idea of Mel Clayton (staff 1923) after a trip to England.[114]

Coach of First XVIII pep talk: 'We don't want good losers. What we want are gracious winners'. (*Satura*, 17 August 1965, p. 13.)

Boys ran, jumped or threw in competition not against each other but against a standard set within the reach of the average boy. A boy could have as many goes as he wanted. A boy with no hope of representing his House in the annual sports but who qualified in six standards won a point for his House in the competition for cock house. Within weeks the number taking part in athletics doubled. Boys liked or disliked standards according to their ability. Ian Martin (1947) 'couldn't run or get the standards', though 'in retrospect it was character building'.[115] Maurie Smith (1942) most disliked the mile event, for 'as House Captain it was a "Must" for me to qualify in the required number of events ... and I failed repeatedly to get the mile standard. Repeating the sprints is one thing but repeating the mile!!!!'[116]

At the start, standards forced the day-boys to stay after normal hours in those days of few extra-curricular activities. Boarders had no choice and 'many of the more reluctant participants, it is rumoured, were even carried down to Standards in leg-irons, with the whips cracking ominously in the background'.[117]

Standards spread from athletics to rowing in 1945–51 (to increase numbers), and to swimming (in 1968, replacing Swimming Certificates), and to music, where Bill Pugh (1951) played the same piece for five years to earn house points.[118]

Even though standards had boys competing against an average rather than against other boys, the context remained one of winning or losing. An earlier doubt about winning was that an easy win had little value. As Archie Anderson (1909, OSCA President 1950, Chairman of Council 1954–59) said: 'we learned, be it acknowledged with difficulty, that hard fought failure may be more honourable than easily achieved success'.[119] Another version of this was to congratulate a losing team on its fighting spirit.[120]

This set winning and losing aside, and praised trying. In 1913 the football team 'earned high praise even when they missed'.[121] Praise for trying spread outside sport, even to academic work. 'The best things about Scotch were the teachers who encouraged me to use whatever skills I had, to do as well as I could, regardless of the standard that was ultimately achieved. The values [like] "try hard" … have been an important "benchmark" since leaving school' (1966).[122] Howard Brown (1963) believed he was made a Probationer because 'I was not outstanding at anything but was prepared to have a go'.[123] Healey challenged his staff: 'Have you commended the also-rans who obviously tried hard?'[124] Littlejohn 'felt the function of schools was to develop every boy to the utmost of his capacity. And for that reason he did not smile on making too much fuss about exam successes, because the boy who had a 60% brain and developed to 60% had been just as well done by the school as the boy who had 120% brain and came out top.'[125] Roff believed 'that every child should do as well as he is capable'.[126] Donaldson wants 'each boy to achieve to the limits of his potential'.[127] Even an ordinary mark may be a triumph: Anne Colman (staff 1985–95, Head of History 1991–95) had her 'most thrilling result' with a boy who scored only 59. Alan Watkinson (Head of English 1985–) spoke of 'boys who really looked as though they would fail yet managed not just to scrape a pass, but who strode well into the 50s, helped by teachers who gave up much of their free time'.[128]

In the end, however, a House Captain who said that trying was enough,

Dr Archibald Anderson (1909), Chairman of Council, 1954–59. Preferring to act as an impartial chair, he felt obliged to exercise leadership as Council's attendance and expertise declined.

was ambivalent. 'We can justly claim to have *tried*, and that, after all, is the essence of the House competitions ... but near enough is not good enough'.[129] When an Old Boy of 1948 writes about 'doing one's best (or better)', he shows the clash between the two different aims of trying and winning.

At Scotch, *trying* slides into *trying to do one's best*, which slides into *trying to exceed one's best*. 'I tried to do everything as well as possible' (1923).[130] 'Gunner' Owen 'encouraged us to "reach for the limits"—stretched your thinking'.[131] Bond House in 1990 thought being equal cock house was not good enough.[132] Scotch, said Chris Johnson (1968), 'stretched me in ways I would not have chosen if I hadn't been "expected" to do these things—particularly sport. (Who would have expected—or allowed—a very short-sighted, very small boy to play Rugby? But no hint or comment that some other winter sport might have been a better idea.)'[133]

To try meant trying whether or not there was hope of winning; 'the game is not lost until it is over'.[134] Arthur 'Eggy' Rush (staff 1936–63), who coached the First XI 1942–54 and won three premierships, could 'inspire those under him to do their best regardless of the state of the game'.[135] In a race where the leaders had finished, Frank Falconer (1954) kept going to the finish, even though exhausted.[136] Once when 'Footy training on the main oval was nearly over, the top 16 and 17 year old boys at the peak of their fitness stood or sat panting on the ground ... Around the outside of this exhausted group, Mr Dean [staff 1946–49 and 1972–79] a spry 60 year old JOGGED throwing and catching the ball. Apparently he ran up to 10 km per day to keep fit' (1975). 'Scotch emphasized persistence.'[137] It did so academically, too. Bond taught 'stickability',[138] and Ian Harrison (staff 1967–84) was 'patient beyond belief'.[139]

Selby Smith thought that one of the two real justifications for the time and attention paid to games 'is that boys who are interested in games soon come to appreciate the value of training and of practice—to recognize that inconvenience and discomfort may often be necessary if one is to give of one's very best, and to accept them readily in order to improve their performance and in the hope of success'.[140]

Fair play

When the game's the thing, rather than winning, there is room for the idea of fair play. Littlejohn said that 'to play the game' fostered ethical qualities.[141] 'Playing the game—sounds priggish now.'[142] What it meant in practice, said the Rev. Rowan Macneil (1911, chaplain 1925–34) in one of his prayers, was 'clean sport and honourable dealing'.[143] Bob Horne the elder (curator 1895–1929) said sport should at all times be clean and keen.

Fair play meant respecting opponents—'Respect your opponents but fear none'[144]—and even befriending them. Fair play extended beyond the players to those who watched. Gilray said boys who booed were blackguards.[145] Healey abhorred booing and any abuse or contempt for the other side or the umpire.[146] Characteristically, he wrote a guide to sportsmanship and advised the audience to 'Be generous in applause of good play by either side'.[147] At much the same time, the APS (Associated Public Schools) also tried to lay down how spectators should behave. In tennis, for example, they should not applaud errors or double faults. The admixture of the fair-playing winner and gracious loser coalesced into the idea of the 'sportsman'. Littlejohn's reference in 1924 for William Dobbie (1923) said that he 'displayed a true sporting spirit',[148] a comment not about his prowess but about his character. Bob Wade (1949) recalls the School Captains of his day as 'good sports and gentlemen'.[149]

All these moral virtues about winning and losing, couched in sporting terms, can be simplified into the one concept of self-control, which has both a moral and a psychological meaning. Selby Smith believed that self-control was the other real justification for the time and attention paid to games. Games,

> especially those which involve bodily contact, lead those who take part in them into situations where it is the easiest thing in the world to lose one's temper, or to blame the umpire, rather than one's own shortcomings, for one's lack of success. In these ways, games of various kinds can be a real training ground for character and self-control, and this can be as true for those who are not at all skilful in them as it can be for the real experts.[150]

Team spirit

There is a tension at Scotch between the desire for heroes to idolise in gold letters upon the honour boards, and the desire to stress team, duty, playing one's part and the self-effacing, modest, Christian gentleman.

Another of sport's educational benefits, in the air by 1883, was in 'fostering a commendable *esprit de corps* amongst the boys'.[151] Through sport the school could touch on something profound. When in 1879 Sir James McCulloch urged boys to 'be forgetful of self, and nobly live for others',[152] we may imagine that many a boy was unmoved. In a sporting context, the idea packed more punch. 'We learned that self is a paltry thing compared with the common good, that the selfish player is in value far below that of his perhaps less gifted fellow who plays, not for himself, but for his side' (1909).[153] The *Collegian*, even on an obscure page in reference to an obscure team like the 1951 Under 15A Cricketers, records that 'This team … had a very successful season, being undefeated and topping the ladder for school teams. Their success was due, not to outstanding performances, but to every member playing his part.'[154] At the Junior School Mothers' Association, a retiring president, Barbara Tolson, thanked her committee: 'things only run smoothly if a captain has a good team'.[155] In 1990 Scotch's basketball newspaper, *Great Shot*, reminded boys that 'No one player is the whole team. "*We*" win or lose—never "*I*"'.[156]

ATHLETICS

Running, jumping and throwing may seem straightforward, so that their history ought to report merely a satisfying list of faster, further or higher. In trying to do this, we are obstructed by a steeple-chase of obstacles.

The cut-off date for age-groups has changed from the start of the year to the start of the term. Earlier records were therefore set by older boys. Metrification makes the 100 metres race 9 yards 1 foot longer than the old 100 yards race. A sprinter now travels further, but on a better track.

A long jumper in the 1960s took off from a metre square marked with lime. The distance was measured from the shoes' imprint nearest to the jumping pit. Today the runner must lift off from or behind a board which has its margin defined by a narrow strip of plasticine. Comparison with old records no longer occurs. Shotput started at a 15lb weight, adopted the men's standard of 16lb, then fell to 12lb in the open level and is now on the rise again. Hurdles went from 3 feet 6 inches to 3 feet 3 inches. But some achievements leap the metrification hurdle, like Tony Olsson's running a mile in 4 minute 15.5 seconds in 1956. Even adjusted to 1500 metres in 3 minutes 58.2 seconds, his time remains a record.

In jumping, boys once hurled their whole bodies as best they could, whilst today's high jumper lifts each limb separately (see High Jump).

Speed and consistency go to Joseph Ischia (School Captain 1991) who set a record for the 800 metres in every age group. Breadth belongs with Albert Hartkopf who at the 1909 Combined Sports won and set records in the 100, 220 and 440 yards, and Long Jump. He also won the Shot Put and was third in the High Jump. The oldest record still on the books belongs to Eddie Cohen (1930), whose under-15 100-yard run corresponds to 11.64 seconds for 100 metres. (Sir Edward Cohen became President of the Law Institute, Chairman of Carlton and United Breweries for 17 years, Electro Zinc for 24 years and Commercial Union Assurance for 20 years, and also Vice-Chairman of the Herald and Weekly Times Ltd.)

Tony Briggs, multiple record holder in athletic events, 1982.

Being part of a team could be enormously satisfying. It 'taught you to be part of a unit and to be pleased when your team mates achieved'. Ken Don (1944) found the 'competition was wonderful with a team around you. Friendships made on the field are ever-lasting.'[157] Aaron Abell's (1991) fondest memories of Scotch are of being in a crew; 'what ever you did, you always did it with your crew mates … it was a very special relationship between all nine of you, I guess you would spend so much time with the same guys you would inevitably become great mates'.[158] A predisposition towards team activity may be phylogenic, so that Scotch's hope to teach moral selflessness through team sports builds on a strong foundation.

The cost of belonging to a team is loss of personal choice. In 1951, as rowing expanded, Arthur Mitchell* (staff 1940–57) declared that 'Persons who do not turn up for their row spoil the row for others. They are therefore not worthy of any consideration.'[159]

* Arthur Mitchell was nicknamed Mitchell/2. That is, half a Mitchell.

Sacrifice of self for the greater good had other applications, too. Boys learnt that it was noble to die in war. One boy even felt he should not study, so that his lower mark would 'let another get a better place'. What children make of adult ideas can be unexpected.

The concept of the team is at odds with the concept of the individual. Some boys resolved this simply by defining themselves as 'not a team player', and others now regret 'not getting involved in non-team sports e.g. running, tennis, maybe golf'.[160] The school's way of resolving the apparent conflict between team and individual has been to emphasise that though the individual must be subordinate to the team, it is the individual who makes the team's victory possible.

Bill Comerford (not an Old Boy) was at the 1947 Combined Sports, and later recalled what was perhaps the 880 yards final.

> One of your boys, the smallest in the field, established a big early lead only to be slowly cut down in the straight. They started to pass him and he was almost out on his feet, but he struggled on to try and score at least a point for his school. It was one of the bravest and most emotional sporting efforts I have ever seen … Your boy collapsed on the finishing line with the hope of scoring at least the place but unfortunately he had not completely cleared the line. It was a memorable and moving event with everyone on their feet cheering him on.[161]

More often, Scotch boys did win a place. Indeed, in athletics 'our success has come, not from a huge number of first placings, but from a great number of seconds and thirds in all events. In other words, all-round strength, and not merely a few individual stars, has been the dominant feature of our wins.'[162] Thus *Satura* looking back from 1962. In 1978, the year of the Grand Slam, Scotch won in athletics with only three wins (Under-15 800 m Alan Fearn-Wannan, and Peter Hyett Under-16 800 m and 1500 m). Similarly, in swimming, at century's end, success was due to boys being 'competitive' rather than winning, although in the early 1990s Richard Kleine (staff 1986–) as swimming coach saw Scotch win a majority of events, with winners such as future Olympic medallists Matt Welsh (1994) and Dean Pullar (1990).

Overall, in rowing (from 1868 to 2000) Scotch has either won as many times as Geelong Grammar School or one less, depending on how one views the war-time 1943 result (when Geelong Grammar was unbeaten in Geelong, and Melbourne Grammar was unbeaten in Melbourne). In Football (1891–2000) Scotch and Melbourne Grammar have won an equal number of times. In Cricket (1891–2000) and Athletics (1905–2000) Melbourne Grammar has won most often and Scotch second most often. In these four sports, since the Associated Public Schools expanded to 11 schools in 1958,[163] Xavier College has won most often, with Scotch in second place. Donaldson's instruction since 1989 that any Scotch team should come among the top three in its competition, challenges boys to achieve and yet sits within Scotch's past performance. As Brent Anderson, Captain of Selby Smith House in 1989, proclaimed: 'We are not a team of champions, but a champion team'.[164]

Compulsory sport

Morrison limited sport to 'only the best',[165] but his successors made it a universal activity. Littlejohn in 1904 made it compulsory except on production of a medical certificate. By 1945, Gilray had a majority of the school playing sport. When Selby Smith handed over to Healey, 'about 90% of the school played sport regularly'.[166] Healey wanted every boy to undertake some sporting activity, and Roff conducted a census and enquired into the reasons why 300 boys were still not playing. At last, on Saturday, 1 April 1977, Roff found 'virtually the entire Senior School of 1260 was involved either in rowing, orchestra practice, or … cricket, basketball, volleyball, tennis, swimming, cross-country, golf, table tennis, hockey,

SCOTCH COLLEGE VERSUS MELBOURNE GRAMMAR SCHOOL, 1907

Given perfect weather, the playing area in splendid order, and two evenly matched teams, one naturally expects a great game, and the crowd who attended at the E.M.C.G. [East Melbourne Cricket Ground] to see our Grammar match were not disappointed. We had played a shocking game against Geelong, but it was recognised that our true form was still to be shown, and we hoped that a mighty effort would bring us out on top. The Grammar were fully represented, while Gair, who was crippled in the Geelong match, was absent from our team. He pluckily stood a trial in the morning, but as his leg seemed weak, no chances were thrown away, and Evans took his place forward.

Bowden, as usual, lost the toss, and

Grammar decided to kick with a slight wind behind them to the railway end. Grammar were first on the ball and attacked, but the Scotch defence was strong, and it was not till after seven minutes' play that they found the opening, a remarkably clever bit of ruck work giving Lewers a chance to snap a goal. Scotch then attacked, and Hartkopf from a free kick scored a fine goal, followed soon after by a magnificent angle by Ballenger from another free. Grammar then forced the play, and a beautiful mark by Martin right in front brought their second goal. Lewers then missed a very easy snap, and at quarter time they were leading by one point, 2–1 to 2–0. Scotch so far had played a great game against the wind, were always in front of their opponents, had a bit more dash and determination, and thus early many of our sanguine supporters were predicting a win. With the wind Scotch at once moved forward, and set up a sharp attack, but nothing but behinds came of it, and as Grammar broke through with a fine rush and scored a goal, they still led at half-time with 3–2 to 2–6. Our hopes were now not so high as before, as with our chances we should have had a substantial lead, but our forwards were crowding in, mainly owing to the backs and wings, who kept pressing in towards the goal and bunching the play.

At the bell Scotch forced the play, but Payne was marking brilliantly, and time after time drove the ball well away from danger. At the other end, Richards, Gray and J. O. Robertson had set up a stone-wall defence, and kept driving the ball on. Slowly we crept up, and when the lemon bell rang we had a small lead, 4–8 to 4–5.

The final quarter began in almost hysterical excitement, which increased as Grammar, playing with more vim than they had hitherto shown, charged forward and rattled up three behinds, followed almost immediately by a great dash by Fraser, which ended in a goal. The tension was now painful. Hundreds of excited Grammar supporters were shrieking, "You've got 'em, Grammar. Keep 'em going!" Hundreds of equally frantic Scotchmen were screaming, "Come on, Scotch. Now then, boys!" Hats were flying, umbrellas waving, and all Melbourne seemed let loose, when Bowden tore away across the centre and slammed the ball to Ferguson, who immediately smashed it through the posts. Scores again level. A couple of behinds followed, and we led by 2 points, when Hotchin, squirming through a couple of opponents, bagged another sixer, and Scotch, with 8 minutes to go, were 8 points ahead. Grammar, seeing their chances fast going, tore into it with redoubled vigour, and with a great dash surged forward. A fine long kick into the [Grammar] goal was taken by Knox, who had no difficulty in scoring a goal. Two minutes to go, two points to get. Could they do it? Again they rushed forward, but the Scotch back line beat them back. A towering kick was marked by Bowden, who drove it on to Ferguson, and as he whopped it through, the bell rang; leaving Scotch winners by 7 goals 10 behinds to 6 goals 8 behinds. A great finish to a great game. Indeed, the general verdict was "The best game for many years," its chief merits lying in the marking, kicking, dash and determination, but above all in the absolutely pure character of the game, not a single instance of unfair or unduly rough play calling for adverse comment from the onlookers.

H. H. Bowden[167]

badminton, debating, chess, shooting, squash or archery'.[168] Such universal sport (and counting music, debating and chess as sports) had three requirements: a range of sports wide enough in Australian society to engage all boys; Saturday sport to provide enough time outside class; and enough opponents to play against. In 1904 no Saturday sport was played, and to generate competition Littlejohn had cricket and football matches between classes. There were then no houses.

Making sport compulsory changed the nature of the school's internal discourse about sport. The boy who played no sport now contravened school policy, and so the school found it increasingly hard to find anything positive to say about him. Since sport was not just exercise but morally uplifting, the boy with no interest in it must be morally wanting. Gilray pontificated that 'the boy who does not play team games ... is not so likely to make as good a citizen as the one who does'.[169] Yet among Scotch's great non-sportsmen we need look no further than Sir John Monash, who as a boy 'did not box, shoot, camp, or play football' and, in the eyes of his friend, George Farlow (1881), 'took no part in games or appeared to be in any way athletic'.[170] As Monash's biographer Geoffrey Serle put it, 'Like all great men, and most great soldiers, John Monash was a mother's boy'.[171]

Doubts about keeping sport compulsory are aired from time to time. The issue is often the compulsion rather than about sport. 'I loved sport, though was never very successful in it; but disliked the compulsion' (1937). An enthusiastic rower 'did not like to be pressured into sports I did not like' (1939). Almost a century after its introduction, compulsory sport is still singled out as something boys liked least about the school. Steven Kunstler (1975) objected in principle and also 'hated being forced to compete in a situation where I was entirely devoid of skills'.[172] A few 1979 fifth formers criticised compulsion in sport and homework.[173] And yet 'discovering running as a sport was a significant moment, which only happened because we were compelled to compete in the house cross-country race'.[174]

Although sport has remained officially compulsory, the rigour of its enforcement has varied. Under the later Littlejohn, at least one boarder recalls it as 'not compulsory'.

> After school sporting fanatics would rush down the Hill to their various activities, but ... I was content to walk down to the river, make friends with the draught horses of the groundsman, Bob Horne, and cast an occasional eye on colleagues doing their best to cripple each other on the Ovals. ... on two occasions I was requested to wield a cricket bat and kick a football in case of hidden potential but, thankfully, none was found.[175]

Under Gilray, 'officially, two afternoons of sport a week was compulsory but only token compliance was required'.[176] It also varied according to the boy, for two Gilray boys report quite different experiences, one complaining that not even congenital knee problems saved him from sport, whilst the other 'used much cunning in evading it, but I suspect that both masters and prefects helped by looking the other way, recognising that I was happy and successful as a "swot" and that forcing sport upon me would have made me wretchedly unhappy.' Under Selby Smith a bookish boy could similarly eschew sport.

For most boys in the twentieth century, playing sport became a part of their experience at Scotch. 'The hours spent in blazing sun or clammy mud on the oval. The dank smell of the boat shed. The whisper of feet behind us on the track (it is only the man *behind* us that a well-schooled memory recalls).'[177]

Scotch has always aimed to shape boys' character. Sport became one way of doing so. It teaches endurance, self-discipline and courage, virtues easily translated to other realms of human endeavour. It teaches social behaviours like co-operation, punctuality and self-denial. It teaches boys modesty when winners and resilience when losers. It can channel the drive to win into friendly rivalry governed by concepts of sportsmanship.

Over a hundred years ago Scotch and its boys struck a bargain. The school would allow the boys to play more sport and the boys would allow the school to depict sport as a moral activity. Morrison came to this bargain reluctantly but Littlejohn seized it and made sport compulsory, Selby Smith made widespread sport a reality, and Healey, Roff and Donaldson made it near universal.

Yet like wild grains sprouting beside fields of domesticated wheat, the old games of the boys still bloom. Marbles, tops, hoops, yo-yos, croquet, and skipping, for example, require dexterity, good hand-eye co-ordination, and have fixed rules—have, in short, the same trappings as established sports, and include moral practices, imposed without umpires, such as obedience to the rules and taking one's turn. Because they are not institutionalised they come and go (and are disdainfully dismissed as crazes). Because they are untamed, the school gives them little value. We smile at the thought of a Scotch–Wesley marbles match, or an interschool yo-yo trophy; they give us an insight into how Morrison saw inter-school cricket or football. Littlejohn encouraged games as well as sport. For example, he built fives courts. But the school does not welcome the games that boys play among themselves, for these games can serve only the boys' pleasure rather than be harnessed to an educative purpose. Fives ceased to be linked with tennis after 1912. When Scotch demolished the Fives Courts in 1991 to build the Lithgow Centre, it did not replace them, and the General House Committee banned yo-yos as dangerous and decried their competitiveness as 'friction between groups of boys'![178]

FIVES, LEDGES AND DOWNBALL

Fives is a game like squash but played with the hand.

A similar game in the 1940s and 1950s was Ledges. On the Hill it was played

in the red paved courtyard with its concrete dividing lines. The ledge was on the wall of the downstairs washroom & lavatories & one advanced a line if one hit the ledge & the tennis ball bounced up to catch it three times—then advance or go back on the return—to win the contest. Was it one v one? I wasn't bad at it—I had a good eye. This game was not played at Recess—not enough time.[179]

'Bill Morris [entered in 1944] did court in 10. …The possible is 9.'[180]

Downball was 'a game played between 2 or more players … The aim was with a tennis ball pat the ball down with an open hand. The ball would first hit the ground and then like the game squash each player would take it in turn to pat the ball until one was missed or an error made. First to win 15 would win. I think that's how it was played' (1985).[181]

Outside the tuckshop, 1978. Boys eat while standing, either alone or in huddles, or watching two cadets (one in a kilt) play downball.

Within a decade of its foundation, the character of Scotch was clear. The moral and intellectual values of the Classics and Presbyterianism formed firm reference points for all attitudes and actions. On these bases, Scotch prepared young men for life in the world outside. Scotch meant its Old Boys to be characterised by diligence, honesty, obedience to authority, and a common classical cultural awareness. Further special vocational training would, of course, be needed as well.[182]

Morrison's curriculum and buildings have long gone, but the school continues his approach to the question of how to teach character.

5

THE BOSS

1904–1933

At his first Assembly, William Still Littlejohn read from Joshua i.1–9. 'After the death of Moses ... the Lord said to Joshua ... As I was with Moses, so I will be with thee; I will not fail thee nor forsake thee. Be strong and of a good courage.'[1] Morrison was dead, and now they had another leader.

With Littlejohn we reach a time when photographs show people more as themselves rather than as concentrating on sitting still. The photographs, paintings, and etchings of Littlejohn catch something of what people said about him. Warm, genial, courteous, sympathetic, intelligent, humorous, he commanded respect with a natural dignity rather than imposing it by fear or threat;[2] 'the air of command sat naturally and was worn with good humour'. 'He caned seldom and with reluctance, and was notably clement to maladjusted boys threatened with expulsion.' His portrait shows him 'in one of his most typical moods; quizzical, rather urbane, perhaps in the midst of a good story, but still studying his listener, sizing him up and trying to assess him'.[3] He almost looks diffident, but in this we are misled, for his

William Littlejohn, third Principal, 1904–33.

nickname was *The Boss*, and his Old Boys called him that for the rest of their lives. Or they called him *Bill* or *Ginger Bill*, but by the 1920s there was no red left in his hair. His accent was Scots, and when he warmed to his work his Doric became more noticeable.

Scotch appointed him from New Zealand, where he had long taught. A Scotsman, aged 44, he was educated at Aberdeen Grammar School and, like Morrison, at Aberdeen University. He 'often said he was a Christian first and a Presbyterian second'.[4] He believed that 'Everything is an idea of God. That desk is an idea of God. You are an idea of God. I am an idea of God.'[5]

To select him, the Church enlarged Council, mostly with clergy. Council advertised locally but prepared to appoint commissioners in Scotland if need be. A sub-committee under the Chairman, the Rev. Dr Alexander Marshall, chose three of

MOTHER AND SON

I was beside myself with excitement and as an avid reader of that schoolboy magazine, *The Magnet*, I conjured up wild dreams of a school like Greyfriars with fellow students of the calibre of Harry Wharton & Co, guided by that ageless form Master, Mr Quelch. There would be feasts in the dormitory and I might even meet Billy Bunter! Naturally, out of the three boarding Houses (Leighwood, McMeckan, and School) I chose the latter because in *The Magnet* that was the most popular.

And so it came about that one afternoon early in February, 1929, in company with my mother, I was seated in the study of the then Mr W.S. Littlejohn in School House. My mouth was dry, hands moist, and my new suit, long trousers and all, hung awkwardly on my skinny frame. I was both petrified and speechless.

Opposite me, behind a huge table, sat what I thought to be an equally huge man with short-cropped white hair wearing rimless glasses behind which were the most beautiful of blue eyes. A neatly cropped white beard matched pearly white teeth through which breath was sucked with appropriate noises. This was the famed Principal of Scotch College and he was gazing at my previous school reports with what I thought to be some amazement as he sucked and smiled. My mother sprang to my defence.

"He likes reading, Mr Littlejohn, and as you can see he always passed in History and English." (The reports showed visibly that I had failed in every other subject.)

The smile left the Principal's face and he gazed intently into my very soul. Then … "He looks intelligent enough to me!"

In all my fourteen years I had never experienced such a surprise. I blushed profusely, helplessly twisted my fingers and stared unseeingly at my new shoes. Even my mother appeared shaken as she gazed at me with a new look in her eyes.

George Bremner (1932)[6]

the 32 applicants, and Council selected Littlejohn by preferential ballot. They then brought him over for an interview, and recommended the church appoint him for five years. Council did all this within three months of Morrison's death. Littlejohn took office at the start of 1904.

The arrival of a new chief executive officer is always a matter of moment in any organisation. Established pecking orders are ruptured, priorities are cast into doubt and a period of uncertainty is inevitable. This happened at Scotch only six times in the twentieth century and several themes repeat themselves: a tussle between Principal and Council, an increased turnover of staff (including the departure of the Vice-Principal left over from the previous reign, and the dismissal of another staff member), changes among senior staff, and an increase in the number of staff positions. All this occurs alongside the new directions in practice and policy.

TAKING THE HELM

At the start of each Principal's term, he and Council often wrestle for control (in 1905–09 Council intruded upon staff appointments). It ends not with victory for one or the other, but with the reaffirmation of both. Principal and Council are two different kinds of power and authority within the school, each with different attributes and domains, each needing the other, each testing the other's strength, each needing to be as powerful as possible, each holding the other in check, so a strong Principal is likely to generate a strong Council, and a strong Council enables the school to have a strong Principal, while simultaneously holding him in check. By 1908 Council was leaving key issues to Littlejohn, a sign he had won their trust.

In Littlejohn's 29-year reign Council had only two chairmen, Marshall, 1897–1919, minister of Scots Church, Collins Street, Melbourne, and Sir John MacFarland, 1919–34, Chancellor of the University. MacFarland and Littlejohn lunched every Sunday, and went on summer fishing trips. 'The Boss got on very well with his Council, but his Council would be very chary of trying to make any decision of which the Boss did not approve.'[7]

Littlejohn's opening problems paralleled Morrison's half a century before. Scotch was run down financially, with shrunken enrolments. He had to meet quite basic needs—new linen, crockery and cutlery, more desks and lockers, apparatus for the new Chemistry and Physics labs, and a kerosene heater for the Prep School Room. To recoup these outlays he introduced a user-pays approach for sport and cadets, and brought in various economies. He annulled all Morrison's fee concessions, apparently deeming them excessive. He held the fee for older boys at five guineas a term, 20 guineas a year.

Morrison had grown wealthy on no salary and most of the profit. Council reversed that arrangement now, and paid Littlejohn part salary, part commission: £600 p.a. with board and residence for him and his family and a bonus of 12.5% of the net annual profit. Enrolments picked up. He enrolled several Chinese, and students in their late teens and early twenties. In 1907 Scotch ran at a profit, and Littlejohn's 12.5% brought him £213.

In managing the school's economy, Littlejohn leant on his wife, Jean. She asked 'Do you want me to go into the social side or do the best I can for the school? I can do either, I can't do both', and it seemed best that she help the school.[8] In 1909 she became its salaried secretary. Council paid someone from the Church Office periodically to review the books. The school's Bursar 1923–34, John Berry, was her brother.

Scotch's standing rose when in 1904–05 an Old Boy was Australia's fourth Prime Minister, Sir George Reid, who was welcome at Old Boy dinners while still only 'that obscure and much abused person the Leader of the Opposition'.[9] As Premier of New South Wales, he had created a non-political civil service and introduced a land tax to break up large estates. Although ambiguous about federation, in the end he breathed new life into the federation movement in the 1890s, ensuring a Convention that was elected rather than appointed. 'This made federation both possible and genuine, founding it on the acknowledged need of the ordinary man, not on the compromises of politicians.'[10] Far from taking pride in Reid, Scotch has forgotten him utterly. In 1981 *Great Scot* assured its readers that 'Scotch cannot yet lay claim to an Australian Prime Minister'.[11] In 1906, Scotch's first Rhodes Scholar, John Seitz (Dux 1900, staff 1910–15, OSCA President 1952), further enhanced Scotch's cachet. Scotch has had 26 Rhodes Scholars. For a while its count was inaccurate, since that of Hugh Ward (1902), in 1911, was in New South Wales. Few schools have so many Rhodes Scholars that they lose track of them.

Sir George Reid (1858), fourth Prime Minister of Australia, 1904–05.

Littlejohn's arrival brought the rapid departure of six of the ten full-time staff. Council expected no less and had bluntly told the staff, between Littlejohn's appointment and his arrival, that they would have to apply to him 'if they desired re-engagement'.[12] (Six years earlier, Wesley's Council dismissed all the staff when it appointed a new Headmaster.)

The high staff turnover precipitated by a new Principal comes from many factors. Some staff are inspired to emulate the Principal and seek promotion elsewhere. Others decide they cannot work under the new regime. Others take the hint that the new Principal cannot work with them. At least one has to be asked to leave. Most dismissals of staff occur in a Principal's early years—thus Roff (Principal 1975–81) at once had to settle 'irreconcilable differences within the Music School'.[13] Conversely, Council is always amenable when a new Principal asks it to increase the number of staff. Littlejohn persuaded Council to create new teaching and non-teaching positions.[14]

A key way in which a new Principal shifts the direction of the school is by appointing the senior staff. When Alexander Morrison died, the staff included his brother Robert and Robert's son, Donald (1885). Donald resigned before Littlejohn took office, and Littlejohn moved swiftly against Robert, asking Council to halve his salary 'owing to the pressure of the financial position'.[15] The lower amount then continued as an allowance until Robert's death in 1908 (when Council described him as Vice-Principal emeritus). This was all very awkward. Council dithered about how much to pay him and spent a month drafting a letter telling him what they were doing to him. They relieved him of his duties but recorded their 'high appreciation' of his long service and loyalty.[16] Robert sent them his thanks, a gentleman to the last, and much loved. The Old Boys presented a portrait of him that in 1904 hung in No. 1 (the Assembly Room) beside that of his brother. Both portraits are now lost. Almost 400 Old Boys signed a farewell address to him, 'once their Preceptor, always their Friend, free from the spirit of self-seeking, ever willing to offer wise counsels and eager to stretch out a helping hand'.

Did the Old Boys disapprove of how Littlejohn and Council treated Robert Morrison? Littlejohn's later apotheosis has blotted out adverse responses to his early, pushy years of rapid change. It was at this time that the Old Boys, perhaps spurred by Robert's forced retirement, asked for seats on Council (which contained no Old Boys). In response, Council proposed that the 'Old Collegians' should chose two of their number by postal ballot, to be approved by Council and appointed (as were all members of Council) by the church. The returning officer was the Secretary of the Old Scotch Collegians' Club, where Robert ('Bobe') in retirement held court daily. The winners were (Sir) James McCay and Donald Morrison, renominated in 1908. Elections were irregular. Later there were four Old Boy representatives.

After Robert Morrison left, Ingram became 'head teacher' until 1908 when he went home to Scotland to die in 'the land of brown heath and shaggy wood'.[17] Instead, he recovered and in 1912 became Vice-Principal. The role was limited, for Littlejohn was 'an administrative dynamo driven by evangelical Scots fervour',[18] and he held 'in his own hand every thread of the administration and, as the school grew in numbers, shouldering a burden before which most men would have flinched'.[19]

'A GOOD TERM'S WORK'

Littlejohn made Scotch the largest school in the British Empire.[20] He doubled its size to 600 at East Melbourne and doubled it again at Hawthorn. Morrison's constant readjustment of class membership gave way to a more rigid structure, still based on ability, as boys were placed in classes for a whole year in a system eventually called streaming. This removed slower boys from classroom contact with faster boys.

Littlejohn had a passion for teaching, and it is said he could walk into any class and take over the lesson. He did not change the central syllabus, already shaped by university entrance requirements. He continued Morrison's aim of training boys going into business but brought this up to date with shorthand and typing, and with Sloyd Woodwork, which develops hand-eye skills and physical co-ordination, and is useful for boys destined for industry or engineering. 'My ashtrays—made of teak—kept disintegrating. I made so many mistakes they just got chiselled smaller and smaller until they joined the wood chips and sawdust!'[21] Littlejohn expected that demand would make the Sloyd appliances self-funding. Sloyd, smelling of wood shavings and varnish, always appealed to boys whose interests were practical. Campbell Watson (1947) was angry when his parents insisted on Latin instead.[22]

Because Scotch aims to educate the whole man, it has developed ways of recording this on paper. During the twentieth century Scotch has told parents ever more about their sons. This grew from small beginnings. Morrison for most of his reign issued no reports, until in his last years he gave out a tiny folded card recording merely each subject and the mark attained.

Morrison experimented to the last with how to extend the assessment system to cover all boys rather than only the most clever. This led him to a dual system of assessing both performance and effort. How to do this has remained a problem. Morrison measured boys' performance against the class average. Later he introduced a third element: a judgement of N, P, or W ('Not Pass', 'Pass' or 'Well'). For these there was 'no fixed standard … and in arriving at a decision the difficulty of the Examination, and the capacity of the boy are in every instance taken into account'.[23] This system tackled the weakness of providing the class average, which is that about half the class must fall below it. The judgement measured the boy himself. A poor scholar who worked hard could earn a good mark. Indeed, two boys with the same mark might receive different judgements.

Littlejohn expanded this into written reports. These addressed a boy's academic position or went beyond it to make personal comments about his conduct in class, about his personality in superficial ways, and about his character. There was room for brief comments from each subject master and the form master. In George Bremner's first term report in 1929 his form master's 'solitary comment of "Shocking" stood out like a lighthouse'.[24] There was a space for comments on three attributes: Conduct, Diligence and Progress.

After the teachers made their entries, Ingram encapsulated them in a succinct note, and then Littlejohn commented on every report, every term. His comments were often no more than an obvious summary which, though bland, assured boy and parents that *The Boss* knew just where this boy was: 'Very fine record except at one point', 'A—Excellent. Up to average in nine out of ten', or '7th in Form'.[25] At other times, Littlejohn's comments were more interventionist: 'He is falling off; I view with disfavour his Eng. & Geog. especially', or 'C—Good. One failure but he has too many fifties'.[26] Littlejohn saw no point in making objective comments, devoid of personality. Quite the reverse: 'An admirable report. Especially am I pleased to see his Arith. so good. He is a good boy and a good scholar.'[27]

There were six sets of exams, two per term, with a final end-of-year reckoning. Littlejohn followed the whole year's work, for example welcoming Bruce Cameron's (1928) first term's results—'A. Excellent' and 'A fine record'—then regretting his fall in second term—'B. Very good' and 'His bad result in Geometry has cast him out of the "A" grade'—and urging him on—'Very good, but I want to see the "A" again', which he achieved in 1927 as dux of the form when the red ink splashed in *The Boss's* large and legible hand: 'Congratulations'.[28]

The Preparatory School Headmaster, 'Jimmy' Jamieson sometimes made terse judgements (he said Hallam Thorpe (1925) was 'as garrulous as a barber'[29]), but often inclined to lengthy homilies. Thus of Norman Heron (1918) he wrote: 'Norman has done a good term's work and taken a good position in the form. He needs to make the most of life and not fritter away his time with things that after all are only of secondary importance.'[30] Norman was aged nine. Of ten-year-old Alec Buchanan (1919), Jamieson wrote:

> Alec has done very well, but is still, in many respects, very careless. He has a tendency to hurry through his work—speed without accuracy is useless, in fact, positively harmful. In this world it's often better not to be too quick. He is inclined to neglect 'trifles': he must not. 'Trifles make perfection', and perfection is no trifle.[31]

Leslie Galvin (entered 1903), later Deputy Premier of Victoria, proudly framed this report:

> We are glad to note an improvement in the manner and work of this boy, though at one period he went perilously near to establishing a record for the worst behaviour we've had in the Preparatory school. By continual checking we have kept him within bounds, and we trust he'll save his next master the necessity for this constant surveillance. There is distinct good in the boy, and when the stratum of indolence, disobedience and other failings has been further cleared away by his own efforts, his good points will be seen to greater advantage. He must endeavour to be more tidy in his habits, abstain from reading the illustrated penny pamphlet, get rid of the raucous roystering manner, cultivate a gentle manner of speech and then we shall see in him a boy of quite a different type. The longer these faults remain with him, the more ineradicable will they become.[32]

James Jamieson, Head of the Preparatory School, 1905–22.

Littlejohn's early appointment of Jamieson to run the Preparatory School seems to have recreated it as a separate part of the school, which it has remained and which frees it to have its own curriculum. In the absence of any statement of Jamieson's educational goals, we might note in the boys' reports that the pre-printed list of subjects appears in the following order: Scripture, writing, drawing, arithmetic, reading, recitation, spelling, dictation, composition, grammar, geography, history, French, science, home

THE AERONAUTICAL CLUB

The Aeronautical Club began in 1911, following the first flight over the English Channel. With 30 boys (one-tenth of the school) it set out to construct a two-seat glider. Later ambitions were safer. Jim Olifent (1938) designed and built a model aircraft, powered by a rubber band.

By rubbing glycerine on the rubber strands … we could get it to stretch to twice as many turns. On some planes, as the rubber driving the propeller came to a stop, the propeller and rubber strands were so loosened that they came unhooked, and fell to the ground, thus allowing the plane to carry on gliding without the extra weight. This was a ploy we used … in competitions for staying aloft for the longest time.

In 1954, the Model Aero Club ran competitions where two boys each tried to cut a streamer trailing from the other's model. In 1963, the club had 70 aircraft and held flying days on Friday afternoons. One of the planes caught fire three times but the spectators enjoyed its plight. Max Holyman (1937) was Australia's first licensed helicopter pilot.

exercise, plus (below the line) physical training, conduct, diligence, progress. If we assume that this order has meaning—follows Jamieson's chain of thought as he drew it up for the printer—then we can see that first came Scripture. Then came a clump of basic skills: to write and draw, to add, subtract, multiply and divide, to read and read aloud, to spell and to write what a boy hears or wants to write. Then came another clump, this time of knowledge rather than skills: grammar, geography, history, French, science, and then homework, and finally the physical and moral virtues.

Healey (Principal 1964–75) made reports' tone more caring, and by 2000 they have become careful, even bland, so as to give neither offence nor grounds for litigation. Donaldson finds that to read and sign every boy's report is impracticable and sees only one report for each boy each year.

LEADERS OF MEN

Littlejohn was a generation younger than Morrison, and his aims reflected what had changed in education since Morrison attended school in the 1840s. The nineteenth-century English Public Schools were revitalised (famously at Rugby School under Thomas Arnold). Littlejohn was eager to copy them, and found Scottish academies old-fashioned. Where Morrison had grudgingly accepted sport, Littlejohn at once made sport compulsory and brought in other Arnoldian devices. In particular, he put a more formal reliance on the boys, and he emphasised school spirit and widened it to embrace the Old Boys.

In 1904 he created prefects (chosen by the boys in the early years). There were thirteen, joined in 1922 by Probationer Prefects. Littlejohn had faith in and respect for the boys and believed in their 'inherent goodness'. He 'trusted the boys into trustworthiness'.[33] Their duties were to enforce the school rules, to put down practices that lowered the tone of the school, to check acts that might not come under the masters' eye (such as bullying, profane and improper language, or smoking), and to model 'a high ideal of conduct and duty'.[34] In choosing prefects Littlejohn had three criteria: interest in all the school's activities, unimpeachable character, and power to influence fellow students. Decades later, when he made Archie Glenn a prefect, it was 'in consideration of his fine character, his capacity for leadership and his devoted service to the school'.[35]

Morrison knew younger boys would ape older boys. Littlejohn formalised this by nominating which older boys to copy. The prefects were 'more than a police force, they are guides and examples'.[36] The prefect system capitalises on teenage boys' propensity for hero worship. This is less talked about today. Perhaps we post-Freudians worry that intensity between boys has sexual overtones, whereas an Edwardian like Archie Anderson, a prefect in 1909 and later Chairman of Council, could chat about this love between boys unabashed, even to that acme of respectability the Junior School Mothers' Association, telling them it was a natural part of boyhood. Each boy, as he deals with his fellows, will shun a few and mingle with most, and 'some few he will learn to admire, to emulate, and to love as I think only boys can love their heroes'.[37] He returned to this theme when launching the 1962 Building Appeal:

Scotch has never lacked for boys whose scholastic achievements have stimulated their fellows to greater effort; whose example has clearly indicated the difference between a sportsman and a mere athlete; whose integrity has demanded the allegiance & emulation of their fellows. Of such were our heroes & God help the boy who goes through school without having some hero whom he can strive to emulate. It is the memory of such boys, of masters of similar mould, that unite us all as Scotch boys.[38]

This powerful force within teenage boys is a central tool which educationists like the early principals of Scotch were eager to use. For Bob Wade (1949), 'the School Captains of the day—"Scotty" McLeish [Captain 1948], Bill Philip [Captain 1947, OSCA President 1974] etc. ... exerted a terrific influence on most of us—Hero worship is a very important factor in growing up.'[39] Tim Downing (Captain 1999) recalls that 'when you were at Year 7 or Year 8 ... looking up at the prefects, you ... thought "Wow". They set such an example. ... it's something to aspire to, to be that kind of person'.[40] Older boys— bigger, faster, higher, stronger, with more muscles better co-ordinated—embody so much of what younger boys want to be. 'His power,' recalls David Brand (1972); 'It was an aesthetic experience watching John Hendrie [1971] soaring for a mark. It was fantastic watching him play football. I was thrilled the whole time. You could just feel him doing it. He took one of the greatest marks I've ever seen.'[41] Seeing Frank Scott (Vice-Captain 1933) in action on the track and on the football field 'was athletic poetry in motion'.[42]

Prefects have mostly been sportsmen, but included non-sportsmen like Alec Lyne, much to his surprise.[43] Chris Adam was equally surprised to become Captain in 1981, as 'a rank outsider who didn't study sciences or maths, didn't play cricket and was not aiming to be a medical student'.[44] Others felt that to become a prefect was a great compliment, 'gaining the respect of my peers at such a young age',[45] and 'a wonderful thrill to be selected'.[46] 'Making

Athletic poetry in motion. Frank Scott (Vice-Captain) at the Combined Sports in 1933. He appears on the school's Honour Boards six times for his prowess in various fields.

Probationer … I was not a natural leader, and wished I was, this thin white enamel rim around the cap badge meant a lot to me'.[47] 'House Captain gave me immense pleasure.'[48] Such an office brought 'ego, social standing, / Schoolboy glory, glance commanding' but also 'the tragic kiss / Of realised ambitions'.[49]

Even so, Geoff Bolger (1949), although a house prefect, considered his best achievement was something else: 'Being able to shoot a .303 rifle at cadet camp as I am left-handed and to move the bolt is extremely difficult as the rifles are made for right-handers'.[50]

Prefects' privileges were their room, their badge and their exemption from detentions and punishments. They also had the privilege of power. At its most formal, in a Prefects' Meeting, they judged and punished fellow students. The Captain chaired the meeting and administered the strokes (cuts) of the cane. The meeting also imposed lesser penalties like detentions or warnings. Boys could appeal to the Principal, but rarely did so, and Principals usually ratified the sentence. Prefects' Meetings lasted until around 1970. Throughout that time they penalised smoking, swearing, leaving school in school hours, and wearing uniform incorrectly. In the 1930s, at least, they intruded into the academic areas, punishing boys who copied others' work or allowed work to be copied. Even boys smoking in their own homes, or in mufti, or on a country railway station, were caned. A

Scotch boy was a Scotch boy anywhere, and there was no such thing as a private life. A prefect recalls:

> Given our inexperience (and possible blood lust), I think that the Prefects' meetings were conducted in a fair and reasonably balanced way, allowing for the usual assumption that 'if you weren't guilty, you wouldn't have been here in the first place!!' If found 'guilty' (and most were), the penalty was discussed and agreed by all the prefects before the guilty party was advised [1956].

In 1956, as the strokes were administered, prefects sometimes gave a score out of 10 for what the stroke earned. They signalled it by holding up fingers out of sight of the victim. A recipient writes of 'the whistle of the cane and the biting pain after the first stroke. You felt the second one also, but after that the pain numbed the remainder.'[51] When Brian Taylor (Captain 1928) caned a boy for smoking, 'the offender's trousers burst into flames. Some wax matches had ignited in his pocket.'[52]

The creation of the prefect system formalised leadership as one of Scotch's goals. Boys could practise at being leaders and learn from their mistakes. Littlejohn thought it 'will train them to rise to further responsibilities afterwards'.[53] What leadership means has varied. The oldest view was that leaders are born naturally, and thus the selection of prefects merely recognised what nature had ordained. The early prefects were an exalted few. By the 1930s, Scotch was explicit that it aimed to produce leaders, to fit a boy for 'his share in the activities in a modern democracy … In short, not merely to be one of the ruled, but one of the ruling, if the call or the opportunity should come'.[54] Soon, being a ruler meant not so much having leadership skills as having intellectual breadth. So in 1950 the Secretary of the Applied Science Club talked about educating 'the leaders of tomorrow'—by exposing them to up-to-date knowledge.[55]

Leadership at Scotch has meant many things. It has always meant enforcing rules. It meant asserting authority, including the prefects' own authority (in cases where boys were caned solely for challenging a prefect). It meant shouldering responsibility to be caring—for the princes of the people to be shepherds of the people, said Healey following Homer (and drawing on classical rather than Christian notions of leadership). It meant leading by example, which in turn meant not asking boys to do something one would not do oneself. Matt Spargo (Captain 1998) confessed that in cadets he repeatedly avoided the tunnel—a pitch-dark maze of mud underground, which he found unbearably claustrophobic—until promoted to a rank that meant he could not 'pike out'. So he clambered in. Other boys 'would have had similar experiences as they achieved things that were seemingly impossible. This is what Scotch offers; this is what Scotch gives.'[56] Responsibility meant self-discovery. 'Those who have it in them to lead learn early the bitter-sweet taste of responsibility. Those who cannot with steady hand carry the full cup of pre-eminence and get swell-headed, learnt, from the candid speech of their fellows, that they must not think they are anything but just blokes. If they are wise at all they learn this lesson before they leave school.'[57]

The only training in leadership was by example. 'Padre Macneil in his capacity as Scoutmaster ... set an example of fair leadership which I tried to emulate in relations with my own staff.'[58] Littlejohn's leadership style forms part of many an Old Boy tale—for instance, that a rebuke is as educative as any stronger penalty—and we can see how his pupils pondered on his exercise of authority and power, and learnt from it. He was just but fair, firm but kind, loudly authoritative. Healey 'emphasized that it is the example, advice and encouragement, which a Senior Boy can give, that will be more effective than the punishment which is used as a last resort'.[59]

As Scotch grew, the Principal's chance of exercising a personal influence shrank. It shrank further when Healey gave responsibility to the majority of final-year boys. Healey therefore wrote guides for Housemasters. Far from recognising a few born leaders, Healey saw Scotch's role as training leaders. Leadership became one more skill to be taught, and anyone could learn it when properly instructed. Healey anticipated that

> Most boys who pass through this school will become leaders: it is not that the school has as its object the production of leaders; but that it is natural that a school of such eminence, drawing its pupils from the sources from which it does so, cannot but produce people who will, most of them, be leaders at some level. To be a leader, one must learn first of all to be a good follower, a good member of a team, or of a committee, or of whatever group one is attending. To enlarge the opportunities, with some chance of permanence of groups, is a sound educational object.[60]

An Old Boy judges that 'Scotch develops initiative and integrity but I am not certain that leadership development is so successful. Political leaders like Cain and Kennett seem to owe little to Scotch. And school leaders of the 1930's did not become outstanding leaders in the war of 1939–45' (1936). The school has never surveyed its accuracy rate in selecting leaders. To the extent that knighthoods reflect achievement (67 Old Boys have been knighted), being Captain of the school was a poor predictor (only Sir Laurence Muir, Captain 1942, OSCA President 1970, Foundation President 1973–74). Being Dux was a better predictor. Six Duxes have been knighted—Sir James McCay (1880), Sir John Monash (1881), Sir Thomas Cherry (1914), Sir Ian Wark (Dux 1915 and 1916), Sir Ian McLennan (1927, OSCA President 1961), and Sir Zelman Cowen (1935)—and Leifchild Jones (1878) became Lord Rhayader. The 1768 prefects have produced another 12 knights. Of course, Captains and prefects are chosen not only for Littlejohn's three criteria of involvement, character and leadership, but for a fourth as well: compatibility with the school. They must be law-abiding boys. The school as an institution would be disrupted by appointing a rebel as Captain, and yet to the extent that rebelliousness is linked with creativity, there are Old Boys of later achievements who could probably never have been sanctioned as leaders by Scotch.

Littlejohn's original concept of prefects still lives. In 1998, the boys at the top of the Junior School in Grade 6 began the year by learning about 'responsibilities, privileges, leadership and role models'.[61]

COLOURS, UNIFORM, SONGS: MARKETING THE SCHOOL

The them-and-us of interschool sport aroused excitement and a sense of school solidarity. Morrison was ambiguous. He discouraged scrapping with boys from other schools, although 'If you must fight then make sure that you win'. Littlejohn set out to entrench the school's difference from other schools, and pride in itself, by outward signs (school colours, badges and uniform), by a vehicle of discourse within the school (the *Collegian*), by circuses (he saw to the celebration of the school's 60th anniversary and started Foundation Day Concerts), and by drawing the Old Boys into the life of the school (he fostered the creation of the Old Scotch Collegians' Association).

Before Littlejohn, Scotch boys wore what their mothers provided. School uniform began with a cap. Cap badges were cloth or metal. An arcane system of coloured metals and enamels conveyed a boy's status and achievements. Boys also wore straw hats called deckers or boaters.

> And then a straw hat may denote a
> Scotch Collegian in a boater.
> A few will give this hat a try
> To help them catch the female eye,
> For in the past the decker fashion
> Has helped to stir up girlish passion,
> And then, O golly, how they've gloated
> Over those who were unboatered.
>
> *Robin Stewardson (1955)*[62]

Photographs show us the kinds of clothes worn: waistcoats, collars turned up or down, Eton collars, suits of a range of colours and varied watch-chains. Such a variety contrasts with later more democratic but actually more regimented times. Suit coats were usually unbuttoned, and ties (of any pattern) could be worn with the knot an inch or two below the top shirt button, or could be bow-ties (last seen worn by John Paton (Vice-Captain 1920, Captain of Boats) in the 1921 *Collegian*). Once into their teens and out of knickerbockers, boys dressed as adults, wearing the same items as the staff (both groups wore the clothes of gentlemen), in contrast to the schoolboy clothes of the modern uniform. An older boy and a young master

Scotch College Exhibition and Scholarship winners, 1912.

Back row (from left): A.E. Kelso, J.P. Adam, J.S. Green, J.W.A. Agnew

Front row (from left): J. Whitaker, A.G.B. Fisher, J.A. Troup

Before modern regimentation, a gentleman dressed as he wished. Note the variety of cloth, collars and suitcoat cuts. Before the advent of the wristwatch, pocket watches were attached to a chain through a waistcoat buttonhole.

side by side today are instantly distinguishable, but looked the same in 1910.

Boys in photographs sat in whatever position was comfortable, rather than being arranged identically. On honour boards their names or initials appeared, presumably as each boy preferred. Individuality was allowed in those days.

The first school colours, by 1880, were blue and white, the colours of Scotland. Cardinal replaced white about 1885 or 1887, and in 1906 Littlejohn added gold. Since then the school colours have remained cardinal, gold and blue.

In the Great War, Australia's flying ace of aces was Robert Little (1915) with 47 kills. He flew cardinal, gold and blue streamers behind his plane. Littlejohn later linked the colours to beauty, goodness and truth.[63] Miss Goodenough echoed this in 1959[64] and Robin Williams (staff 1960–96) on retiring presented the new west wing of the Junior School with three coloured plaques each firmly labelled. The colours may resist being tied down in this way. Colours have many meanings, and Scotch carries the cardinal, gold and blue into scenes of physical struggle which (unlike beauty, goodness and truth) can be ugly, painful and feinting. In the war-cry 'We're fighting for the cardinal, gold, and blue', the colours are not thought of separately, but together, as the cardnlgoldnblue, an abstract entity, a totem.

Caps at first were plain cardinal, but Littlejohn in 1907–08 introduced horizontal concentric circles of gold and blue (p. IX). Later caps had coloured triangles radiating from the top, and finally reverted to plain cardinal with a gold and blue braid round the edge. A 1956 description of a football match called Scotch 'The Cardinals',[65] but this never caught on (for the word's chief meaning was Catholic in the still-sectarian 1950s), and from the 1980s the name Cardinal was taken up by the rowing auxiliary, the Cardinal Club, and the Cardinal Pavilion.

Scotch let its 50th anniversary in 1901 pass quietly but celebrated its 60th vigorously, indeed ecstatically. Littlejohn helped engender this but was overseas on sick leave for most of 1911. The main impetus came from the Old Boys. After a dinner in the Town Hall, 600 dinner-shirted gentlemen, to the air of 'The Cock o' the North' played by hired pipers, marched in fours up Bourke Street to the Exhibition Building where they joined the boys for the first Foundation Day Concert.

The Concert itself and the school's major songs were the most lasting legacies of this Diamond Jubilee, and were the work of George Wood. He had taught at Scotch before. Littlejohn ran a competition for a school song, hoping for something like 'Scots wha' hae wi' Wallace bled', and when Wood entered Littlejohn invited him back as Senior English and History Master.

Singing would have been a human activity aeons before anything else Scotch teaches. The singer co-ordinates body and mind in the midst of the pleasure of a communal activity that works better the more the participants co-operate. Many boys since 1911 have found this concert the highlight of their time at Scotch, even if only as a 'drone'.[66]

Singing the Messiah in the Melbourne Town Hall especially the Hallelujah chorus … such mighty joy [1945].[67]

the school spirit at the annual school concert, as we roared out those songs, was pure gold [1945].[68]

the sheer joy of singing in the Choir … the feeling that you had when you were singing flat out, en masse is the most tangible memory—I can still hear it and feel it, much more than any of my classroom memories [1964].[69]

The concert since 1911 has varied in form. Early concerts included sports prize-giving, or ran over two nights, one night for parents and the other for Old Boys. It has always needed Melbourne's largest venues. At the start, the boys played none of the music and sang few of the songs, but it was the songs that reverberated for the rest of the century.

First that night came 'The Diamond Jubilee Song' which changed in 1913 to 'The Foundation Day Song' ('Foundation Day again is here, Hurrah! Hurrah!' to the tune of 'When Johnny Comes Marching Home Again'). At first this song summarised the current year—'Our numbers grow from year to year, Hurrah! / We'll greet six hundred with a cheer, Hurrah!', or in 1914 'The Empire calls her sons to arms, Hurrah!' In the 1920s it was only an encore song, but in 1929 returned with the Anthem to the top of the programme. After time had nicked his 135th notch, Dick Shirrefs (staff 1950–90) dropped it in 1987 when the concert moved to early August.

The second song was the 'College Song' or 'School Song' ('We are Scotch Collegians All', to the tune 'Tramp, tramp, tramp, the boys are marching'[70]). The 1932 and 1933 Foundation Day Concert programmes said that Wood wrote the words in 1908. By 1930 it had settled down to the present four verses, which are on Scotch itself, cricket, rowing and Old Boys. An academic element was long ago decently buried:

> Well worked Scotch the Profs. are calling,
> See them putting up the score:
> First-class Honours not a few,
> Prizes, Exhibitions, too,
> There's no height in life to which we dare not soar.

A verse on the crest also died: 'And to battle with our might / In pursuit of truth and right / Is expected of the cardinal, gold and blue'. So did an athletic verse, with chorus 'Well run, Scotch! the boys are calling'.[71] More surprisingly, a football verse and chorus failed to survive, despite attempts to find words that would take root, such as verses beginning: 'When the days are growing short, / And we strip for winter sport, …'[72] Three different football choruses were tried. They allowed for Scotch being behind in the score:[73]

> 'Buck in Scotch' the boys are calling,
> How the game delights their souls !
> They have scored a bit ahead,
> But the Scotch are far from dead,
> Be alive and kicking, brothers, kicking goals.

or in front: 'Though you've got the bigger score, / Don't be bashful, get some more; / Be alive and kicking, brothers, kicking goals.'

There was also a warrior verse: [74]

> Fathers who wi' Wallace bled
> And whom Bruce has often led,

Taught us how to fight for glorious liberty:
And with courage just as high,
We're prepared to do or die
That our land, beloved Australia, may be free.

Chorus
Fall in Scotch! the bugle's sounding,
All there when there's work to do;
Should a foe our land attack,
There will be no holding back
By the boys who wear the cardinal, gold and blue.

The easy rhythm and rollicking tune of this song have always welcomed new verses to suit the occasion. Greatly popular in the second half of this century, the *School Song* did not at first win a regular place at the Concert and in the 1930s was often omitted from the programme or demoted to an encore song.

The third boys' song in 1911 was the lugubrious *College Anthem*, 'Hail thou best of schools and dearest'. George Wood wrote the words, and perhaps the music too. The *Anthem* has been sung at almost every concert.

First in all our hearts we place thee,
Deeds of ours shall ne'er disgrace thee
Staunch if ever troubles face thee
We will love thee all our days.

A middle verse, 'On thy playgrounds we have striven', disappeared during the 1950s.

The *School Song* and the *College Anthem* sit nowadays at opposite ends of the Concert, the *Anthem*, 'nobly' sung and unavoidable comes early, whilst the *Song* helps race the concert to an exciting end.

Fourthly, the boys sang 'Boot the leather', to the tune of 'Green grow the rashes O' with its dragging bagpipe-like accompaniment. The 1933 Foundation Day Concert programme attributed the words to Wood.

When nights are long and days are short,
    And wintry grows the weather O,
We welcome in the king of sports,
    And chase the bounding leather O.

with a chorus of 'Scotch boot the leather, O'.

Finally in 1911, the boys sang 'The Scotch mixture' to the tune of 'The man who broke the bank at Monte Carlo'.

The staff in 1911
Standing (from left):
  E. Riley, G.F. Sharp,
  W.W. Briggs, J.A.
  Seitz, T.G.
  Howden,
  unidentified, J.E.
  Jones, J.W. 'Jonah'
  Whyte, J.F.M.
  Haydon, G. Wood,
  James 'Jemmy'
  Jamieson (Prep),
  R.H. Weddell
Seated (from left):
  T.D. Kay, C.E.
  Sandford,
  unidentified, Frank
  Shew, W.S.
  Littlejohn, J. Hall,
  W.R. 'Tort'
  Jamieson, J. Nance

You may hear a lot of the wily Scot
    And his independent air
    But when trumpets start to blare,
    You may bet your life he's there.
Only give us a gun, and then start the fun,
And we'll make the fiercest foemen run,
As our fathers did with other foes before us.

Chorus
Oh, fighting for the cardinal, gold and blue
    The cardinal, gold and blue,
    The cardinal, gold and blue,
Oh, fighting for the cardinal, gold and blue
We'll carve our way to glory.

Oh, the wily Scot, when he starts to swot,
    At his work is more than fair
    And the Profs they all declare
    That he shows a genius rare.
Only give us a pen and we'll show you then
What a number of wonderful things we ken
As many as our fathers knew before us.

'The Scotch Mixture' ceased at the Concert, but continued into the 1980s at OSCA dinners.

At the second Foundation Day Concert, in 1912, they sang 'Forty Years On', 'one of the great communal songs: part hymn, part battle cry, part poetic dedication'.[75] Scotch took it from Harrow. It is pitched at the Old Boys, with 'Visions of boyhood' and 'Echoes of dreamland'.

> When we look back and forgetfully wonder
> What we were like in our work and our play …
> Forty years on, growing older and older,
> Shorter in wind as in memory long,
> Feeble of foot and rheumatic of shoulder,
> What will it help you that once you were strong?

But if youthful suppleness is beyond recall, youthful idealism can still reinvigorate.

> God gives us goals to guard or beleaguer,
> Games to play out (whether earnest or fun),
> Fights for the fearless and goals for the eager,
> Twenty, and thirty, and forty years on.

It was usually an encore piece and had a place on the programme only a few times before the centenary Foundation Day Concert in 1951, but then became more regular. Logie-Smith cut its four verses down to two, though the words of the lost verses still spring to older Old Boys' lips: 'O ! the great days, in the distance enchanted …'.

The fourth Concert, in 1914, sang 'A Boating Song' by J. D. Burns,[76] to the ragtime tune 'On the Mississippi'.

> Sometimes in your dreams you'll hear a deepening roar …
> Scenes long past will rise up to meet you.
>> Shut your eyes,
>> All will rise,
> Now you can see the whole scene before you …

> Twenty strokes will take her home so plug along,
> Breath is coming short and quick but hearts are strong,
>> One stroke more,
>> Then the Roar …

It competed with the Eton 'Boating Song', which at one of Sir Arthur Robinson's (1887) annual dinners for the crew was sung as

> Wesley may be more clever
>> Grammar may make more row
> But we'll swing together
>> Steady from stroke to bow.[77]

From 1925 to 1931 the Scotch boating song was only an encore item at the Concerts, and Gilray is said to have frowned on it,[78] but since the 1930s its syncopated exuberance and orgasmic climax have won it a permanent popularity. In the programme it inched from being 'A boating song' (1938), to 'Boating Song' (1939), to 'The boating song' (1943). 'Its musical range is modest, and it can be sung or yelled,' as it builds to a crescendo of speed and volume.[79] Parallel bawdy texts were 'sung lustily at rehearsals' but not at the Concert itself.[80]

In the 1920s Scotch became self-conscious about its songs, for the best were not really its own. In the years after the Great War boys wrote an earnest succession of songs for the annual late Private W. L. Colclough (1911) Song Prize. The winning songs were sung at the Foundation Day Concert in the 1920s and 1930s, but none caught on. As this outpouring began, OSCA in 1920 launched a competition for a College Song. 'Something stirring, with all the spirit of a great public school ... a fitting rival to the famous "Forty Years On".'[81] Substantial prizes notwithstanding, 'the songs submitted were not of a sufficient level to ensure permanence'.[82] The last whimper of such hopes was the short-lived Junior School Hymn composed by Miss Elizabeth Pike (staff 1947–54?) around 1950. A song competition is being held for 2001.

The songs went with the boys when they left school. At the Foundation Day Concerts of the early 1940s, the Old Boys used to stand up after the show in the Melbourne Town Hall and repeatedly bellow out the 'Boating Song'. 'This rendition was supported by the school with Froggy Orton [staff 1920–53] mounting the stage (after much exhorting) to direct'.[83] The songs are the only shared experience common to all Scotch Collegians. Even the greatest events and personalities are unknown to different generations, so that there is no universal connecting reference point, whereas the following parody (from a 1950s meeting of the Scotch Lodge) is as amusing to a nonagenarian as to a current boy:

> There are men in Church and State, men a trifle overweight,
>> They've a wistful look in unimpassioned eyes,
> For to win the grudging praise of the boys of nowadays
>> Is the hardest thing an Old Boy ever tries.

(The original reads:

> There are men of Church and State, men of influence, men of
>> weight,

Who regard us with a keen but loving eye.
And to win the honest praise of the Boys of former days,
Is a hope that makes our youthful hearts beat high.)

Or an Old Boy and current parent, on receiving his son's latest term fees, might ponder the unintentional pun in the *College Anthem*, which proclaims Scotch 'the best of schools and dearest'.

OLD BOYS

Littlejohn could have resisted the Old Boys' increased say over the school. They were not, after all, his Old Boys, but Morrison's, plus a few Lawsonites. If *The Boss* wanted Old Boys' attention or respect he would have to earn it, and would have to deal with them as adults not boys. Each new principal faces the same challenge. Littlejohn never hesitated.

He flattered them as 'the school's great cloud of witnesses',[84] and welcomed their occasional endowment of prizes. We can watch their role gaining clarity by the emergence of a single term—Old Boys—whereas in 1904 when Littlejohn arrived Scotch called them variously *Old Boys*, *old students* or *Old Collegians*, and these terms might appear in inverted commas, a sign of hesitancy or a way of flagging the term as novel or not customary.

Littlejohn created the *Scotch Collegian* in 1904. It intended to knit together 'the brotherhood of Collegians Past and Present' and had an ample Old Boys' column.[85] The *Collegian*, presumably under his impetus and

An anniversary celebration. About 450 members of the Old Scotch Collegians' Association attended a dinner in celebration of the 80th anniversary of the school.

At the head table (from left): Sir John MacFarland, Chancellor of the University of Melbourne; Sir Arthur Robinson, President of the Association; Dr W.S. Littlejohn, Headmaster of Scotch College; Major-General J.H. Bruche, Chief of the General Staff, Commonwealth Military Forces

that of George Wood, firmly asked the Old Boys for money, and firmly pushed them into coherence as a group, solidifying their organisations and helping each other find jobs through an Old Scotch Employment Bureau.[86] An Old Boys' tie and blazer appeared.[87]

'When I commenced practice as a Solicitor', writes an Old Boy of 1949, 'I was surprised to find that my "old school tie" was my passport to both clients and opportunities.' Being an Old Scotch Boy 'definitely opened certain doors for me. For example, I'm sure it helped me get a job … when both my prospective boss and his boss were Old Scotch Boys! This of course was never stated' (1965).[88] 'The fact I was a student at Scotch helped my being appointed to a job' (1927).[89] At one interview, 'the Chairman of a very large financial institution … only looked up after I advised that I was an old Scotch boy' (1953).[90] 'The Scotch network is strong and beneficial at times' (1986).[91]

> You mix … with well-grounded and well-educated boys to start with and you make contact with the households your friends come from [with] men who have made a certain amount of a mark in the world, … that sort of atmosphere, those sort of people, and it means that you're less gauche in dealing with such people in life. It makes it easier for them to become leading citizens themselves [1909].[92]

The organisational locus of Old Boy life was the Old Scotch Collegians' Club, one of Melbourne's gentlemen's clubs. Formed in 1895 under the presidency of Sir George Baillie, Bart. (1875), by 1913 it had around 700 members. In 1907 it raised money through a concert to improve the Cricket Ground, alerted to the need by the new Old Boys on Council, which had just approved an engineer's report for the work signed *Jno Monash*.[93] But the club had two drawbacks. First, the licensing laws forbade members aged less than 21. To engage recent school-leavers, the Old Scotch Collegians' Junior Association was formed in 1908, its first president being Bowden (Captain 1906–07).

Secondly, the Club offered little to men in other clubs or outside Melbourne. It could never speak for all Old Boys—the committee to organise the 1911 Diamond Jubilee had two representatives from the club and two other men 'to represent Old Boys generally'.[94] After the Jubilee, the *Collegian* called repeatedly for an Old Scotch Collegians' Association open to all Old Boys. The OSCA was formed in 1913 at a meeting prompted by Old Boys in Hamilton led by W. H. Melville (1879, OSCA President 1916) and with Wood and Seitz as secretaries—these three men were effectively its founders.[95] There were 296 members, and the President was Shew (1867), a teacher since 1870. Since boys of one generation might not know those of another, it was easier to have a master as president, and Donald Morrison had played a similar pivotal role in the club.

Sibling rivalry, strong among boys, also happens among organisations.

The club opposed the association's formation,[96] and might have tried to strangle it at birth. That this did not happen was due partly to their overlapping membership. Henry Cohen (1889, OSCA President 1921–22), for example, held office in both bodies. The club faded with other gentlemen's clubs and in 1934 became The Public Schools' Club, open to Old Boys of any Public School. When in the 1970s OSCA was in its turn challenged by the upstart Scotch Association, OSCA managed, like the club before it, not to feel so threatened as to attack, and tried instead to co-operate. In this way the club paid Scotch one last service.

In 1919 the Old Boys persuaded the school to conduct an annual medical inspection. Dr Frank Hobill Cole (1881, OSCA President 1918–20) became school Medical Officer. (His first report detailed defective teeth, eyes, ears, noses, tonsils and feet, and found 2% of boys had curvature of the spine and 4% varicose veins.[97]) He was succeeded by Littlejohn's son, Euan (1911) (who believed he could identify left-handers by their eyebrows meeting in the middle[98]) and later by *his* son, Bill (Captain 1939) in 1964–87.

The brief period 1904–13 saw the start of Old Boy seats on Council, an Old Scotch Collegians' Association, an Old Boys' column in the *Collegian*, and the start of Foundation Day Concerts. All this drew the Old Boys into the life of the school. Fortuitously, this happened just before the Great War broke out in 1914. The emotional need to commemorate the war dead became focused on the school as much as elsewhere, generating the energy and money to finance an entirely new school at Hawthorn, which the Old Boys built as a war memorial for their dead.

The Great War

J. D. Burns wrote:

For England

The bugles of England were blowing o'er the sea,
As they had called a thousand years, calling now to me;
They woke me from dreaming in the dawning of the day,
The bugles of England—and how could I stay?

The banners of England, unfurled across the sea,
Floating out upon the wind, were beckoning to me;
Storm-rent and battle-torn, smoke-stained and grey,
The banners of England—and how could I stay?

O, England, I heard the cry of those that died for thee,
Sounding like an organ-voice across the winter sea;
They lived and died for England, and gladly went their way;
England, O England, how could *I* stay?

Vice-Captain in 1914, Burns died in 1915 at Gallipoli. Harvey Nicholson

During the two world wars, money for prizes went to fund the wars, so prize-winners received only a certificate. This certificate from 1917 combines Scottish thistles with Australian wattle.

(Captain 1936, OSCA President 1967) judged this poem as 'possibly the greatest event in the history of the first century of the School'.[99] On Anzac Day 1929, Littlejohn faltered as he mentioned Burns's name, and then the clear treble voice of a chosen boy sang the soul-stirring words of 'For England' and a new boy, George Bremner, found 'The bugles of England … calling now to me. I am not ashamed to say that tears sprang to my eyes and, at that moment, the Motto of the School "Deo Patriae Litteris" became alive and I vowed to do better. I became a Scotch Collegian.'[100]

Boyd Thomson (Editor of the *Collegian* 1912) more sombrely, and more aware of the issues for which he fought, wrote (although he had left school):

To the Mother School

Mother, thy blessing! the time has come
    To follow the rest of thy stalwart sons
Forth, to the sound of the rolling drum,
    So soon to be lost in the roar of guns,

Where the banner of Britain to glory runs.
Mother, thy blessing! the time has come.

Mother, thy blessing! before we go
    Leaving all that is dear to heart—
Love of the home and the fireside glow,
    Love of music and delicate art—
    With these and more it is hard to part;
Mother, thy blessing! before we go.

Mother, thy blessing! for life was sweet,
    Sweet with the love of a thousand things,
And every hour that sped so fleet
    Flung a flood of joy, as the morning flings
    The light of life from its radiant wings.
Mother, thy blessing! for life was sweet.

Mother, thy blessing! we went for thee;
    'Twas little to give, but much to lose;
But how could we think of thee else than free,
    While supple of sinews and strong of thews?
    How could we falter, or worse—refuse?
Mother, thy blessing! we went for thee.

Mother! our brothers have gone before:
    They call—they call us to join the fray.
And shadows of faces that are no more,
    The faces we loved so, cold and gray,
    Cry loud for vengeance; how can we stay?
Mother! our brothers have gone before.

Mother, thy blessing! and then, good-bye!
    Would you wish for your sons a happier aim
Than that a man go forth to die
    For a faith that is more than an empty name,
    For a faith that burns like a scorching flame?
Mother, thy blessing! and so—good-bye!

Thomson died in action in 1916. The headstone on his grave uses this poem.

Scotch supported the war fiercely. It favoured conscription in the referendums.[101] Littlejohn added *Patriæ*—For the Fatherland—to the school motto in 1914. (Bellicose fervour thus propelled a significant step, for to alter the motto from *Deo et Litteris* to *Deo Patriæ Litteris* was to drive a secular wedge between God and Learning, between Church and School. This disrupted the old Presbyterian ideal of church and school being inextricably linked, and introduced a more modern conception of the school as rooted within society.)

The senior Australian commander was an Old Boy, Monash. Scotch commemorated 205 war dead, equivalent to over two years' valedicts (although one is a teacher, George Wood, and two or three others appear not to have been Old Boys). Half of them died in the first eight months at Gallipoli. The dead included two Captains of the School, William Knox (1904) and Stan Neale (1912).

For the war dead, the school at Hawthorn built a hall 'designed to be their Valhalla, consecrated to their memory'.[102] For almost two decades the Dramatic Society under Vivian Hill (staff 1922–44) raised money, first for stained glass windows and then for a list of dead, unveiled by the Governor in 1936. Underneath, ran a line from Bunyan's *Pilgrim's Progress*: 'And so they passed over, and all the trumpets sounded for them on the other side'.

> Every Anzac Day in the 1930s Bumpy [Ingram, Vice-Principal] used to read an alphabetical list of the former students who had been killed in WWI—a pathetically long list. He always broke down before he finished the reading and we boys would predict whether he would manage to reach the memorable name "Snowball" [entered 1907] before doing so. We had a typical irreverent attitude towards this sign of Bumpy's humanity and the enormous tragedy which it reflected, but his humanity did penetrate our external crust and emotionally affected most of us. I know that it helped to make me a confirmed pacifist until I changed my mind about World War II in 1941.[103]

Courage was expected. Brian Taylor (Captain 1928) was in a car accident while the guest of a friend's family. He was sitting beside a girl and he instantly threw himself in front of her to shield her. One of his prefects, Ross Campbell, 'wondered if I would have behaved so well. Would I have shrunk in panic behind the girl, especially if she was a big girl?'[104]

Much is made of those who died in the two wars. More difficult to talk about was the fact that those who came back had killed (or tried to). Gilray and Macneil won the Military Cross. In World War II, Wilbur Courtis (staff 1961–79) won the Distinguished Flying Cross. Alec Fraser spoke of cheering when an enemy sniper was shot. (Fraser had a good preacher's ear for the arresting story.) Their experiences set these men far apart from Morrison and Littlejohn. From the 1920s to 1985 the staff was dominated by men who while they had not made the supreme sacrifice, had made that other sacrifice: a deliberate decision to break the Sixth Commandment. The effect on these men must have shaped the rest of their lives—and shaped the school. As the Cold War dragged on, these men felt a need to toughen their boys in readiness for fearful demands. A nineteenth-century master like Shew used to mark papers whilst sitting in the sun on the ground in the playground. For all their free use of corporal punishment, those nineteenth-century teachers were in a way more gentle, more affectionate towards the boys, than the teachers whom the twentieth century assaulted so barbarously.

Houses

The house system appeared only halfway through Scotch's life, in 1917. It has been a system in search of a purpose. The school has endlessly tinkered with it, using it as a vector for sport competition, music competition, pastoral care, and tutor groups. Houses' size and names have changed often.

Littlejohn used the Houses to institutionalise internal sport, because Scotch contained more sportsmen than could play in the few inter-school teams. Previously, competitions within the school had drawn on tangible existing divisions, for example between the Top and Bottom Storeys, between boarders and day-boys, and between classes, which regularly competed in sport, debating and singing. The first Houses were North and South (depending on boys' home address) and the Boarders.

The Houses won boys' loyalty, but never put down deep roots: when it was decided that this sesquicentenary history would be accompanied by lists of memorable achievements, no-one suggested compiling a list of cock houses. Nevertheless, whilst the boarders had their own house, named first School House and later Littlejohn, it won their hearts as the vehicle for the boarders' rivalry with day-boys.

Mainly, other loyalties were stronger, the larger loyalty to the school and the smaller, more immediate loyalties a boy feels to his classmates and year group, or to his particular sports or activities. To counter this, the school would have had to use its imagination. Teenage boys group into tribes and sub-tribes. An anthropological approach might have built Houses with totems and taboos, secret rituals and rites of passage. These need not have been nefarious. As the Houses had colours they could also have had emblems, as the scouts named their patrols after Australian animals. The Houses' nicknames seem strangely tame. Monash were the Ashes, Gilray were the Rays (but this never developed into either stingrays or the death rays found in boys' comics). Taboos might have generated solidarity without harm: the boys of one house would never eat liquorice, say, or always drank Passiona. Allocation to Houses was by the first letter of boys' surnames, which could have generated cabalistic words. In 1965 Morrison House's letters made AELMOQU and Monash's BHJNT. Or boys could have been

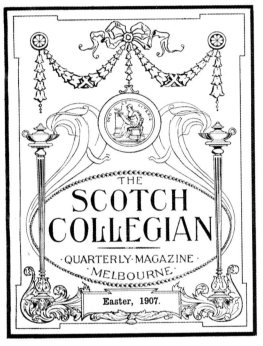

Collegian cover, Easter 1907. The school crest at this time was the seated figure at the pillar of faith, reading from the book of learning and lit by the lamp of hope. The motto is simply 'Deo et Literis': for God and learning.

allocated by home suburb so that House membership built on real factors in a boy's life.

SOCIETIES AND CLUBS

Extra-curricular activities scarcely existed for the first half of Scotch's life. Morrison's Scotch had few non-sporting activities—some walking in the holidays, some debating—and Littlejohn did not at first change this much. Boys learnt singing, dancing and the piano. He set up the Christian Union, and revived a school magazine and debating.

These few activities waxed and waned in the twentieth century's first decade. Soon, Littlejohn faced a change in the market in which the school operated. Some non-church private schools were gaining in permanence, like Caulfield Grammar, owned by Walter Buntine (1885). Also, the state

The Debating Society in 1904 resolved that Japanese military success over Russia posed no threat to Australia. For many decades Scotch reported the debates. They constitute a survey in their own right of  the issues thought to be topical—in 1913 votes for women, British power, chivalry, boarding vs day-boy life, too much attention to sport—and of arguments thought to be relevant.

DEBATING SOCIETY

government began its own secondary schools, University High School, whose Principal in 1915–41 was Matthew Sharman (Dux 1894), and Melbourne High School. The church schools persuaded the government not to build secondary schools in the eastern suburbs. There, until 1954, boys wishing to go to university had to study at church schools.

Many of these boys came to Scotch on government scholarships, such as Sir James McCay, Sir Ronald East (1917) and Arthur Burns (Captain 1940). Scotch welcomed scholarship boys. 'They knew they had to make their own way and they went to Scotch to learn',[105] so they stimulated their fellows and ensured fine academic marks for the school. 'The injection of very able boys into the school undoubtedly is of benefit to all.'[106]

To qualify to keep the scholarship boys, and to be exempt from the government's public examinations, Scotch submitted to government inspection of its teaching. (The Chief Inspector of Schools was Martin Hansen (1889), later Victoria's Director of Education. In the 1930s–40s Seitz also held these two offices.) In 1912 the state government set up the Schools' Board to control examinations and inspect schools. Although the government's appearance in secondary education put limits on Scotch, it also confirmed its leading position, for Littlejohn sat on the Board from its inception.

Until then, it had been enough for Scotch to be a secondary school, one

Alexander Morrison, second Principal 1857–1903, was later elevated into an Old
Testament patriarch. This painting, done after his death by a painter who had not
known him (the eyes are the wrong blue), is a copy of an earlier portrait and
shows little of the affability for which his boys loved him.

Council in 1989. As in eighteenth-century portraits, the source of their glory is displayed in the background. The Memorial Hall's unsightly organ box is concealed by the shadow line running along its top in this photograph by John Ingham (1969).

Back row, from left: Ralph Morris (1952), Neil Roberts, James Stewart, Robert Gillies, Philippa Barber, Andrew Gleadow (1966), Brian Randall (1952), Neil Gray, Hugh Falconer (1951), Werner Brodbeck.

Front row, from left: John Richards (1950), Michael Robinson (1955), Gordon Donaldson, Bruce Lithgow (1946), Rev. Norman Pritchard, Rev. Robert Humphreys, Barrie Orme (1951).

In 1920 the prefects held a competition for a new shield combining the existing crest with St Andrew's cross, but the result breached heraldic rules by letting metal touch metal and colour touch colour.

The Scotch College coat-of-arms.

Colin Gilray, fourth Principal 1934–53.

of the few in Victoria. The emergence of high schools charging no fees, full of bright boys because entrance was by competitive examination, offered the possibility in Melbourne of what was already the case in Sydney, where state-owned schools like Fort Street held their own against the independent schools. Melbourne's church-owned schools therefore needed to offer something not found in high schools. Moral education, of course, was a selling point, and so were extra-curricular activities. By the 1930s, a boy coming into Scotch from the state system appreciated the range of activities available.

W. R. 'Tort' Jamieson (staff 1909–48) was Senior Science Master from 1909. His nickname was variously attributed to his long pointed nose that made him look like a retort (1914).[107] Or to his abnormally large Adam's apple which, whenever he used the word *retort* 'put on a most extraordinary performance. Once seen never forgotten. From then on a *retort* was always referred to as a *round bottom flask* which of course caused a riot in the classroom' (1938).

> Who could forget 'the long and the short of it', the tall elegant 'Tort'
> Jamieson (the senior Chemistry master) with his coloured pocket
> handkerchieves and his Latin aphorisms (*mutatis mutandis*) and contrast him
> with the squat and rather scruffy Teddy Kay [staff 1914–45], his opposite
> number in Physics, with his quick temper and almost instant remorse ('I wish
> I hadn't hit that boy').[108]

Jamieson started the Museum in 1911 and in 1914 the Science Club which ran lectures, excursions and a library. The Dramatic Club, one of the school's great fundraisers, began in 1916. The Literary Club began in 1920. Orton organised 'an orchestra to supply the instrumental music at the Concerts and the Dramatic Entertainment'.[109] In the 1920s activities bloomed because of a new approach. Instead of staff launching activities that were morally improving or educational, boys set up organisations for their own interests. Instead of doing what was good for them, boys did what they wanted to do, in the Camera, Chess, Wireless and Philatelic Clubs.

The rise of these activities outside the classroom and playing fields was, said Littlejohn in 1926, the 'most remarkable feature in the modern development of school life'.[110] But his generic name for them was 'the social side'.[111] He saw Drama as merely a way to use 'surplus energy'.[112] Because the activities came from the boys, not the school, no philosophy underlay their emergence, beyond Littlejohn's openness in allowing them to occur. The earliest rationale for activities came from Ingram: that education should fit a man not only for work but also for leisure.[113] This idea of educating boys for leisure seems a new development, a twentieth-century matter.

Healey wanted to 'identify the boy who has no success and find out … what he would like to do if the school could provide him with opportunities to develop his special interest'.[114] 'How can we enable each boy to discover his own distinctive gift?', asked Davis McCaughey (Council 1953–80).[115] Yet one boy's teacher mused: 'He must have ability in *some* area but it is well concealed. Completely disorganised, has been the butt of many jibes because of his dithering and unspectacular progress.'[116]

The activities felt like 'a wonderful breadth of things that you could do'.[117] Their number at first was few, but sports were few, too, as there were only seven: athletics, cricket, football, rowing, shooting, swimming and tennis. In the next half-century, activities and clubs continued to supplement education (as with computers or biology clubs), branched out into physical activities not taken up by the school competitively (like weightlifting, scuba diving or horse-riding), and launched quite new kinds of activities (like scouts). By 1987, the school had clubs whose very meaning might not have been clear back in the 1920s, like the Remote-Controlled Car, Junior Computer and Stock Exchange Clubs.

Scotch's aim of teaching character thus acquired a new vector. Taught

SCOUTS

David Penington (1947) found

scouting was *very* fulfilling in that it encouraged independence and self-reliance, and it introduced me to a life-long love of 'the bush'—very important to a boy brought up in the city. There was a mystique about camping out under the stars and about the fellowship of the Troop around a roaring camp fire, singing and acting in groups. There was a real team spirit in the Patrols as they sought to work together in achieving a fine camp site, or cutting timber to make camp furniture. There were challenges to achieve in a variety of areas which touched on hobbies or introduced people to new hobbies. Everyone could do something useful and get support and recognition. Overnight hikes in deep bush, armed

with a compass and a map were another real challenge, as were many other opportunities to learn 'bush craft'. Relationships with older boys in the Scout Troop as well as with masters had real depth as they could be built on whilst away on camps. Ideals were often discussed as were the realities of life. It was, in my time, very different from the tight discipline, regimentation and conventional milieu of the Cadets.[118]

The Rev. Rowan Macneil, the chaplain, founded the Scotch scouts in 1926. He had fought at Gallipoli and in France, winning the Military Cross and Bar, and then became opposed to war. He hoped to dispel the fears that lead peoples to fight each other, and his prayers called on Scotch to 'do away with all race prejudice' (1931).[119] 'Purge us from false ideas of our own superiority, and … Help us … to change our thoughts of so-called foreigners to that of over-seas brothers' (1934).[120] 'In scouting he found a particularly congenial atmosphere, its informality, its friendliness, its wide range of outdoor activities, its emphasis on modest service, and so many of the Christian virtues—in all of these he felt perfectly at home.'[121] The presence of cadets at Scotch allowed scouts to emphasise Baden-Powell's less martial side, and so gave boys an alternative to cadets' warlike mien.

Many boys loved the Scouts. The following comments span decades.

I like outdoor life and extending myself with camping and other activities without the strict discipline of the Cadets. I made lasting friendships from within the Scout group. This became my 'peer group' rather than classmates which at Scotch tended to change each year [1941].[122]

So different from the confines and discipline of school life. One has to remember that fifty years ago Scotch was run as a clone of an English Public School. Caning by students was the norm. (I avoided this by sheer cunning.) Masters, in most cases were inflicted with the 'Do as I say Boy!' syndrome. Scouting on the other hand was much more of a two-way street, where … one got a chance to have a say, even if it was only to ask questions which were answered without ridicule [1947].[123]

It introduced me to, and taught me some proficiency in practical skills at which I was not naturally adept. The patrol system taught co-operation, appreciation of others' abilities and tolerance of

others' shortcomings and so it encouraged self-confidence to attempt everything [1961].

Scouting was just about everything to me … and provided an outlet for my interests and abilities, and an alternative to study [1963].[124]

Scout camps opened boys to new experiences, whether having to defecate amidst mud in a hole in the ground, or lying awake at night in the tent 'for a couple of hours swapping dirty jokes, most of which were a real ear-opener to me … There were no grown-ups there to stop us saying whatever we wished' [1970].[125]

Scouts encouraged improvisation, like garter-tabs made of red litmus paper.

Scouts took boys into the bush. They won badges for bird watching (no taking of eggs) and insect collecting, and in 1939 Paul Radford said that more important than collecting was 'Ecology, which is the study of where the insects, etc., are found and their foods, and Life Histories, i.e. the development of the insect from the egg stage to the adult'.[126] (Another early sign of Scotch's interest in environmentalism appeared in 1951, when the Junior Science Laboratory had a display on ecology, covering sand dunes, salt marsh, and heathland. Sir Colin McKenzie (1893) energetically espoused the conservation of Australian fauna and in 1920 had begun what is now the Healesville Sanctuary.)

One of the scoutmasters, 'Bower had a great love for the outdoors, and for the Australian Bush, so different from his native German forests. He was particularly interested in trees and flowers' and taught scouts the various eucalypts and acacias. 'He was a keen bush walker, and encour-

'Building a scaffolding to the moon'. Scouts, 1975.

aged exploration of the areas adjacent to Elliott Lodge. … he introduced many city-dwelling Scouts into the joys of the bush, and the range of natural phenomena' (1954).[127] Doug Callister (1949) recalls scouts

> sitting round a camp fire with him talking out the world's problems. However idealistic or hare-brained our thoughts were, he listened patiently, puffing his pipe under the stars, the glow of the coals showing us an attentive face and occasionally hearing an appreciative chuckle. His tolerance with us … He would encourage, without interference, the scheme to electrify the Lodge, the beginning of the Senior Scouts, and the running of two Scout Revues to raise funds [1949].[128]

Elliott Lodge was named after Major-General 'Pompey' Elliott who gave the land to the school. His son Neil (1930) was killed in 1939 as a patrol officer in New Guinea. The lodge was built in the 1920s by the boys, burned down in the 1939 fires, rebuilt in the 1940s, with electricity, water, and a wood stove, and steadily rebuilt and renovated since then.

In 1961 on Wilson's Promontory, a snake bit Colin Thomson (1964) on the hand when he gripped a bush to steady himself. Ian McIntosh (1960) administered first aid while another member of the party ran four miles over Little Oberon and along the beach to fetch a doctor from Tidal River. Thomson was carried back by stretcher and recovered quickly.

At Christmas 1956, scout hikers at Wilson's Promontory included Peter Motteram (1961), just 13, and Andrew Kemp (1960), 4 feet 10 inches (147 cm), 'who are believed to be the youngest and smallest people respectively ever to have hiked to the Lighthouse at the southernmost tip of mainland Australia'.[129] In 1965, the Rev. David Webster, a scoutmaster, conducted 'what we believe is the most southerly held communion service … two miles north of the southernmost point'.[130]

In 1977 there were 400 Scotch scouts, almost equal with cadets' 420 and more than double Social Services' 185.[131] In 1954 and again in 1981 they numbered 230.[132] In 2000 there are just 40, mirroring scouting's decline in Australia generally.

Roy Nichols (1926) was twice chairman of the World Scout Conference.

first through Christianity and the Classics, then through sport, character now reached boys through activities. They broadened a boy in knowledge and experience. They were run by the boys. They brought boys and staff together in situations less rigid than the classroom. Littlejohn hoped that in clubs, masters would be boys' 'guide, philosopher and friend'.[133] This was still the view 50 years later: a boy is 'most likely to choose as the master to talk to, the one with whom he gets on well, so school must open as many avenues as possible for boys to meet staff'.[134] 'The best pastoral care came from the accidental contacts which were made between master and boys'. Activity-focused clubs 'were ideally suited for the many natural opportunities for informal relationships', just as was the case in cadets and scouts. By contrast, 'it was rare that personal friendships sprang from communal meetings' like houses.[135]

THE DEPRESSION

The world-wide financial collapse after 1929 made Littlejohn's final years reminiscent of Morrison's. The Principal was an old man now nearing death in office, as was the Chairman of Council, MacFarland. Their response was no more than a determination to keep going.

Collapsing family finances meant that 'dozens and dozens of boys left suddenly' (1941).[136] Throughout the 1930s there were families where 'it was a struggle for our parents to pay for our education' (1935)[137] and families who had to truncate their sons' time at Scotch (1933),[138] creating Old Boys who still regret not achieving their goals at Scotch or not going on to university.

> Money was scarce so I had to go to work at 14 years of age [1933].[139]

> My one year was very brief. My father and grandfather had both gone to Scotch, but there was not enough money for me, although I had been booked in at birth [1941].[140]

> I would have liked to have gone back in 1937 to be a school leader, and completed an Honours year, but the Great Depression had taken a toll on the family's finances and the decision was made that I should join the work force [1936].[141]

> Family finances were needed for other children's education' [1943].[142]

Sir John MacFarland, Chairman of Council 1919–34—a man of few words, mostly verbs, in the use of which he favoured the imperative.

Among those who stayed, there was not enough money for coaching (1932)[143] or excursions (1935).[144] 'I never had any pocket money. The comparative affluence of others was a source of envy' (1940). Many 'families sacrificed a lot to keep us at the school right through the Great Depression. We all wore patched clothing and re-soled shoes' (1936).[145] Wealthier families faced a different dilemma, and 'kept their duller progeny in school as long as possible to avoid having them unemployed and hanging around the house' [1940].[146]

Old Boys from the 1920s to the 1950s are willing to be frank about their families' hard times, and give the lie to the view that all Scotch boys were well-heeled.

> At the end of 1923 my father died, so had to leave and start working [1923].[147]

> I could not relax ... We were always worried about the cost of fees. ... I met MLC and Merton Hall girls socially, but most social life was at Church. I could not afford much social life with 'public' school peers. ... I am glad I went to Scotch. My parents deserve great praise for their great sacrifice. [They] borrowed on our home to send my brother and I to Scotch [1951].[148]

> Due to financial constraints I was forced to leave at year 11 [1952].[149]

> My mother was a self-employed dressmaker working long hours at her shop in Brunswick. ... By May 1949 I learned that my mother had not paid my 3rd term fees for 1948 nor my 1st term fees for 1949. I don't know now whether I felt a sense of embarrassment, of shame, or a sense of obligation to relieve my mother of the strain of keeping me at Scotch, but in any event I chose to leave the school and entered the workforce. I can't remember my mother's reaction [1949].

> I left at the end of 2nd Term in my final year as my father died on that day and I considered that I should enter the family business. Always regret that I didn't finish [1949].[150]

> My parents had already sacrificed a lot to send me to Scotch and I felt it unfair to stay any longer [1952].

Outside Scotch, financial devastation caused widespread despair and political unrest. There was even talk of armed attempts to seize government. It was in these years that Monash rejected overtures from former soldiers that he impose an emergency government. (Later, one night in 1948, Fleming feared that a communist attack on the school was so imminent that he issued boarding-house prefects with rifles from the cadet armoury.[151])

RICH MAN, POOR MAN

The Depression exaggerated the social divisions among the boys. Boys often came from families who lacked the means to pay school fees, or who found the means only by making sacrifices. Whilst it is hard to discern social class from a father's occupation, few school teachers can have been wealthy—thus the fathers of Sir Arthur Dean (1910) and Sir Harold Dew (1908). A commercial clerk, master mariner, painter, pastry-cook or warehouseman seem even less likely—thus the fathers of Leslie Galvin, Sir William Philip (1908), George Christie (1935), Herbert Buchanan (1915) and Alfred Jacobs (1915), to name only men distinguished enough to appear in the *Australian Dictionary of Biography*.[152]

Old Boys talk about class from the 1920s onwards.

Scotch kept me humble. Many times I wore my brothers cast-offs![153]

My sweater is darned and so are my socks.[154]

I could never afford recess and lunchtime prices [at the tuckshop].[155]

I felt inadequate and in a different social status.

I often felt I was from the wrong side of town.

I encountered [a] certain snobbishness … We lived on the West Side (Sunshine, my father was a Chemist there) and there were occasions when we were (whether really or imagined) regarded as second-class citizens by those of the East Side.[156]

Being made to feel socially inferior by more privileged fellow students.

My father was an itinerant. … At Scotch I immediately felt uncomfortable and 'out of place'.

A majority attended only 'by the sacrifice and forethought of their parents. There was no feeling at all that this was a school for "rich kids"'.[157]

Boys coped with these feelings in different ways. One felt that at least 'it taught me how to mix comfortably with the highest in the land'.[158] Another 'enjoyed Scouting, more than any other activity. I suppose this was because I had come from a comparatively humble background (and felt, incorrectly, disadvantaged) but Scouting, for which I had a flair, enabled me to maintain a degree of equality with those I otherwise considered my superiors.'

Other boys experienced class more as a matter of behaviour: 'We were much more aware of "class" when I was a boy. Class was like a string which was useful as a lead by which a boy could be led. (Puppy training). We learnt to say please and thankyou and to ask for first-class tickets at the railway booking office as a matter of course.'[159] Some did not really notice class much at all: 'We were I suppose all from a privileged socio-economic group and were insulated from the tough real world. It was not until I went to Melbourne University that I came into contact with my generation who had not been to Public Schools.'[160] Some found it only outside the school: 'While at Scotch, I learnt something more of life by working as a labourer in local factories (Sunshine Potteries, H. V. McKay Farm Machinery, ARC Engineering Company) and on a farm, during the greater part (approximately two-thirds) of all term and end of year holidays'.[161]

This lack of class awareness meant that the 1950s *Collegians* felt no ambiguity in referring to 'Young readers of the upper classes',[162] or in calling an Old Boy footballer 'one of the best left-wingers in the state'.[163] Yet class was built into the school. Teachers received salaries but groundsmen received wages. The *Collegian* called teachers by their surnames but wages staff by diminutives, as when the 1954 tennis notes thanked 'Mr Hill' and 'Hughie' (Harold Hill, staff 1942–75; Hugh Aitken, curator 1937–74).[164] Such distinctions were approved by the hymn that ran: The rich man in his castle, / The poor man at his gate, / God made them high and lowly, / He ordered their estate.[165] (In 1958 the boy delivering the boarding houses' morning newspapers received at the kitchen a cup of soup in winter and an apple in summer.[166]) Arithmetic examinations asked about partnerships, or rent or began: 'An investor sells £2400 of $3\frac{7}{8}$% S.E.C. inscribed stock at $98\frac{1}{4}$% …'.[167]

Boys' social advantages were one more aspect of the *noblesse oblige* they owed to those less privileged. Socially, boys' class was shown by the girls they went out with, mostly from St Catherine's, Firbank, Lauriston, Ruyton, PLC or MLC, and by the suburbs in which they lived. 'I think there was a narrowness in social background/attitudes at Scotch which needed to be balanced out by broad life experiences with a range of people from different backgrounds in adult life. I am surprised at how many Old Boys live within about a 5 km radius of the school many years down the track' (1975).[168] Yet a 1960s survey found that Scotch and Wesley drew from a greater variety of suburbs than other independent schools.[169] A generation later, in 2000, six postcodes account for half the school, covering Hawthorn, Auburn, Glenferrie, Camberwell, Kew, Kooyong, Malvern, Gardiner, Glen Iris, Toorak and Heyington.

Because private schools charge fees beyond the reach of the basic wage, and because sending a boy to school deprives his family of the money he would earn,

the socioeconomic status of Scotch students was clearly from the affluent

LITTLEJOHN AND THE THREADBARE TALE

A friend of mine, an Old Boy, quite late in the Boss's regime had dinner with him one evening. After the meal they were sitting in the study smoking when there came a knock at the door and a boarder entered. He wanted a late pass or permission for a night out with friends, or some such concession, and the tale he told in support of his request was so obviously a tale, and so threadbare with use, that my friend marvelled at his effrontery and pitied his lack of originality, and constantly expected a refusal, even an outburst of pedagogic wrath. To his great surprise the Boss listened with close attention, meditated a moment, and then graciously granted the request. My friend was quite touched for he felt the old man must be failing, losing his sureness of touch. With scarcely concealed jubilation, not unmixed with surprise, the boarder withdrew and, as the door closed behind him, the Boss caught my friend's eye, threw back his head, and burst into a great guffaw of laughter.[170]

MEN OF INFLUENCE, MEN OF WEIGHT

Scotch continued to excel in many fields, not all of them trumpeted. Five members of class 7C in 1934 are said to have been later convicted of murder. Otherwise, Sir Frank Clarke (1896) held high commercial and political office. Edgar Ritchie (1888) was the engineer in charge of Melbourne's water supply in 1908–36, constructing its major dams and aqueducts. Ernest Kendall (1895) was Chief Veterinary Officer 1926–38. Sir Hugh Denison (1878), the newspaper magnate, largely financed Mawson's 1910 expedition to Antarctica, and won the Melbourne Cup and the Caulfield Cup twice. Sir Francis Rolland (1895) was Headmaster of Geelong College in 1920–45. Sir Stephen Morell (1887), a brewer and proprietor of Young and Jackson's hotel, was twice Lord Mayor of Melbourne, in 1926–28. (Morell favoured a unified Greater Melbourne Council, 'but was ideologically unable to support the adult suffrage necessary for reform'.[171]) Sir Hayden Starke sat on the High Court of Australia in 1920–50. Sir Harry Lawson (1891) was Premier 1918–24. (He entered politics aged only 24 when he defeated Sir James McCay (1880) for Castlemaine. At least once he rode to Melbourne by bicycle.) Sir John Latham (1893, OSCA President 1953) a tinsmith's son who attended Scotch on a scholarship, became Deputy Prime Minister, Attorney-General, and Minister for External Affairs in 1934, and was Chief Justice of Australia 1935–52.

Sir John Latham, Deputy Prime Minister in 1934 and Chief Justice of Australia in 1935, here as a university student playing lacrosse.

end of the spectrum, as it is now. Although there were a few students from less fortunate backgrounds, I recall often being reminded that the school taught students from 'all walks of life'. This may have been so but it was hardly representative. I would not have expected the school to change the way it is but it could at least be honest.[172]

Scotch is not an elitist school academically, for it sets no entrance tests as hurdles. Whilst this confirms that entrance is primarily by ability to pay, it does also have educational implications. For example, in 1974, when the

Commonwealth Education Minister, Kim Beazley Senior, was concerned about maintaining standards for the brightest pupils, Healey assured him that schools like Scotch showed 'that it was not necessary to segregate pupils into schools where only the brightest specialists would be concentrated'.[173]

In 1933 Littlejohn announced his retirement for the end of year, but influenza forestalled it. 'His wonderful constitution and the ordered simplicity of his life caused us to believe that he would soon shake off the effects of this illness. The attack was, however, of a desperate character, and grave complications developed. The unremitting attention of his family and medical advisers was ineffective.'[174]

His coffin lay in state in the Memorial Hall, draped with the college flag and on it his trencher. Prefects and senior boys stood on watch until a full memorial service, after which his coffin left for a public service at Scots Church.

One of Littlejohn's Old Boys, Graham McInnes (1930) wrote later of the school's amalgam of Scottish, English and Australian.

Littlejohn leaves Scotch for the last time.

Scots was the religious tone, the moral fervour, the insistence upon examinations and above all exam results as the eye through which even the most bulky camel could enter the Kingdom of Heaven. English was the emphasis on innumerable societies—debating clubs, dramatic societies, camera clubs, science clubs, stamp collecting clubs, the orchestra—with their passionate amateurism. English too was the emphasis on games; but the overwhelming importance attached to them and the prowess attained in them were both indubitably Australian. Moreover, though the school itself was located in a city of almost one million inhabitants, it could not escape from its hinterland; and the grey brooding bush, the deep sunny skies and the enigmatic wariness of the Australian landscape gurgled and flowed around the school buildings and permeated us all.[175]

Littlejohn made Scotch the largest school in Australia, indeed in the British Empire, with around 1300 students. He appointed distinguished teachers but kept administration firmly in his own grasp. He stamped his personality upon the school—a driving ambition, a questing intelligence tied to assessing and commenting upon academic outcomes, and a hearty religious belief more Christian than Presbyterian and yet dourly Scottish in tone and trappings. When he began, to follow Morrison must have seemed an impossible task; by the time he died thirty years later he had created his own legend.

6

TO HAWTHORN

From 1916 to 1926 Scotch gradually moved from East Melbourne to Hawthorn, from one hectare to 25. The site is impressive and Scotch has thrived there, although in the face of a disconcerting variety of problems.

The small East Melbourne site limited the school's size, and Morrison's enrolment averaged 300. Littlejohn doubled this by 1913 and soon Scotch claimed to be the largest school in Victoria. He built classrooms, rented nearby rooms, and in 1915 decanted the Preparatory School into a primary school he bought, called Parkville High School. (Since this school was co-educational, its 90 girls must be counted as attending Scotch. Charles Meckiff (1967) has *both* parents as Old Scotch Collegians.)

Scotch faced a future fragmented on various sites. It could have stopped expanding (Littlejohn's opponents said a large school lost its sense of community), but Littlejohn believed that a large school provided more variety of experience and facilities. Most Old Boys knew how pokey Scotch was and in 1911 a deputation led by William Cattanach (1880), President of the Old Scotch Collegians' Club, persuaded Council to seek a larger site. (Cattanach, Chairman of the State Rivers and Water Supply Commission 1915–32, 'was acutely cross-eyed and this certainly disturbed any who might argue with him'.[1])

Council found an unsubdivided area in the suburbs, the Hawthorn Glen estate. Scotch took this name

The rustic charm of Gardiner's Creek around 1921 with Glen House above the treetops. The school moved here from cramped inner Melbourne at this time.

119

to heart at first. As late as the 1950s the school's racing eight was called *The Glen*, and the whole property was called Hawthorn Glen, or the Glen, by Old Boys, to whom 'Scotch College' still conjured up East Melbourne, but this usage died out. There was no ambiguity later when Council named the new sports complex the Glenn Centre after Sir Archibald Glenn.

Littlejohn attributed the Hawthorn idea to Dr Alexander Marshall, Chairman of Council.[2] In bringing it to fruition, Littlejohn credited Sir Arthur Robinson's insistence on the school's claims upon Old Boys. Sir Clive Steele (1910, OSCA President 1946, Chairman of Council 1950–54) said of Robinson that 'it was due to his foresight, energy and enthusiasm that we owe this School site to-day'.[3] Robinson was a lawyer, closely associated with his brothers (of the Collins House Group, Anglo-Australian financiers with extensive interests in mining and metallurgical operations). He held several Victorian cabinet posts in the 1920s. Supported by Duncan Love and Dr Hobill Cole, he led the fundraising to buy the land and erect buildings, and emerged as a moving force in the school's affairs. He was President of OSCA for 20 years (1923–43) and Chairman of Council for eleven (1934–45). His passion for Scotch was such that he converted to Presbyterianism.

Sir Arthur Robinson (1887), Chairman of Council 1934–45. President of the Old Boys for 20 years, this forceful man was a visionary who yet attended to details as small as rewashering taps. Such was his love of Scotch that he converted to Presbyterianism.

NEW GROUNDS

Hawthorn offered what Littlejohn modestly called 'Ample space for all purposes for all time'.[4] The site was at the confluence of the Yarra River and Gardiner's Creek, open pasture 'dominated by a pine-clad hill rising steeply to a bluff crowned by one of those mid-Victorian Gothick palazzi so dear to the wealthy merchants of Melbourne in the 1870s and 1880s'.[5] Along the watercourses stood ancient river red gums. Littlejohn, after asphalt Eastern Hill, was delighted to fall asleep with the sough of the wind in the trees, and awake to the singing of birds.[6] Room abounded for buildings and ovals, and even a shooting range, all within a few minutes' walk. Scotch became self-sufficient, and in the 1930s it caned boys for leaving the grounds during school hours, whereas at Eastern Hill boys lunched in the city and frequented its busy arcades. Even in the 1920s, boys exercised that freedom at Hawthorn with lunchtime strolls to Glenferrie Station, Malvern Town Hall and Tooronga's gasometer. Scotch bought Hawthorn Glen in 1915.

Work on the grounds began almost at once. The Main Oval had to be carved into the hillside on three-quarters of its circumference and built up on the other quarter with surplus soil and rock from building work. The Junior School oval also had to be made level on a slope. Scotch needed a thousand loads of soil from the city council's roadmaking, or a thousand loads of road sweepings, as topdressing. Water had to be laid on.

'The grounds they call ovals are really quite round.'[7] Ovals are contradictory things. They have to be flat and yet drain well, and it took decades to get this right. The Junior School oval drained badly until the 1990s, when Scotch covered the old surface with 2 metres of sand (no more mud-covered boys). The Lower Oval, as its name shows, lay on the flood plain, as did the Meares Oval, named after Robert C. Meares who in 1927 bore the cost of forming it. The Lower was named after W. H. Melville who paid for its formation, but this name never prevailed against the oval's characteristic smell of mud conveyed so accurately by the word 'Lower'. After a generation, in 1949, the three big ovals (Main, Meares, and Lower) all needed attention. Draining poorly, in winter they gave off a noticeable sour smell. They were regraded, treated for weeds, resown, and rolled henceforth with a spiked roller. The Main Oval's poor drainage was traced to 'a layer of clay some way down'.[8] After another generation, in 1976, the Meares was unusable. Further improvements included ten concrete practice wickets with a synthetic surface. Between the Lower and Meares Ovals, the Hockey Oval was created in 1956–58, and still had drainage problems in 1975–77.

Tasting the Forties

Apart from absorbing
My first flavours of architecture
From the warm orange chapel
Carved into its hill,

School is the Lower Oval,
Its trodden white grasses
Against the river gums

And fluttering cabbage-whites:
Or the ache of morning fingers
In winter's transient white

As I lurked out fairly wide
On half-forward flank
Or slid up into the pocket
To shark another goal.

Chris Wallace-Crabbe (1950)

Ovals have to be subject to many booted feet, but can be covered only with grass. Scotch has therefore tried various grasses. It sowed the Junior School

Oval, for example, in 1939 with 'winter' grasses from F. H. Brunning and in 1991 with a strong deep-rooted turf grass bought expensively from Turf Grass Technology.

At the centre of most ovals was the wicket. For play on Saturday it had to be watered during the week, then watered, cut, and rolled on Fridays. It took two hours of rolling to produce even a reasonably firm wicket. Preparation for a Public School game on the Main Oval required three days.

All these ovals made the smell of freshly cut grass part of the school (with a concomitant increase in hayfever). The first mower was a gift from Melville. To pull it, Scotch bought a horse, harness, and rollers. In the 1930s 'Old Charlie' kept the ovals in mint condition for cricket and athletics with an antique horse-drawn mower made up from 'bits and pieces mostly of old farm machinery. There was a fair bit of fencing wire holding it together. Scotch spent steadily on repairs, new parts and new mowers, economising where possible with second-hand equipment. Sheds for the mowers and harness were beside the

A 1940s view across the horse paddock (between the Lower and Meares ovals) towards the Heyington railway bridge. The horses drew the mowers.

swimming pool. Scotch either owned horses, or arranged with a cartage contractor, giving him grazing rights in return for use of his horses, but the type of horse available proved unsatisfactory. One horse had served in the army, and when Alan Malcolm (1942), practising the bugle, blew the cavalry charge, this horse took off, damaging the mower.[9]

The technology rose a notch in 1949 when Scotch bought a motor mower, and in 1950 Hugh Aitken, Curator, and Ewen Davidson (1927, staff 1932–73, Director of Physical Education 1938–64), were allowed to replace the horses with a Ferguson tractor.

Mechanization[10]

Hughie Aitken my jo, Hughie,
    When first we were acquent,
A' ploddin' horse ye were ravin'
    Your bonnie brow was rent.
But noo your brow is braw, Hugh,
    Wi' tractor fine to mow
Doon grassy swathes an' careless knaves,
    Hughie Aitken, my jo.

Thenceforth Council rode the whirlwind. Over the decades it bought a special mower to prepare wickets, a motor roller and a rotary mower, a new tractor with a rear-mounted rotary mower, a triple mower, a rider mower, and an attachment for vacuum cleaning leaves. Only when 'Johnny' Miles (staff 1954–76), the master in charge of cricket, wanted a motorised roller, did Council briefly hesitate, and then only for safety reasons.

In 1936 Scotch began to plant trees, paid for by Dramatic Society profits, and by OSCA, which planned a Coronation Avenue. One money-raiser was a Radio-Telephone Bridge Evening: 40 hosts held bridge parties and phoned 3UZ with the names and scores of the highest-scoring lady and gentleman. Planting began with the avenue of elms along the Monash Drive, whilst on the hillside many straggling pines were replaced with trees of attractive foliage. Most new trees were native, 'in the hope that an appreciation of the merits and beauties of some of the best Australian trees may be developed in many of the boys'.[11] The smell of eucalypts became part of Scotch, especially after rain. (It was another decade before Claude Monteath (Director of Music 1948–58) introduced Australian composers in the Foundation Day Concert: Alfred Hill, Dorian le Gallienne, Iris de Cairos-Rego, and Enid Petrie. In 1952 the Collegian carried a photograph of the school taken through some gum trees.[12]) Native plants also helped make stink bombs 'by crushing wattle seeds in tins, spitting on them and letting the mixture stew for a while and then opening the tins in class'.[13]

The trees attracted birds. In 1953 Scotch welcomed over 65 species, including some that seem unlikely, such as Fuscous Honeyeater, Yellow-tufted Honeyeater, Nightjar, Native Hen, White-Winged Triller and Blue-Winged Parrot.[14] Pigeons nested in the air vents of upper storey rooms, where their chirping and fluttering were distracting.

In 1941 A. O. Barrett offered to plant a wood of English trees. Oaks, elms, beeches, chestnuts, rowans and ashes would 'form a delightful balance to the preponderantly native trees' elsewhere in the grounds.[15] Barrett planted the nearby levee bank with willows, poplars and binding grasses. The Barrett Copse was completed in 1945 and a notice was erected testifying to the 'generosity of Mr A. O. Barrett, an Old Melburnian'.[16] After naming a man's school no more need be said about him. By the 1960s the copse's well-grown trees and long grass gave shelter for boys to smoke, or loll. In 1978 it shrank as the New Oval expanded. It is still the part of the grounds that is most wild. In 'Summer on baking hot days we played … up, down and around the bushes and "jungle" of the copse and the slopes bordering the soccer oval … and we would leave … the end of each lunch time hot, sweaty and smelling of the plants, grass and weeds' (1996).[17]

The early ovals were created by Bob Horne the Elder, groundsman since 1895 who died in 1929 whilst rolling a wicket. He laid out the grounds, and Hugh Aitken fleshed them out. Healey attributed to Aitken 'almost all the landscaping and orderliness of the grounds. … He has kept himself up to date in his knowledge of trees and shrubs, mechanisation and grasses. His cricket pitches are among the best in the world.'[18] During

the 1950s he steadily planted trees and shrubs and replaced old or diseased trees, mainly wattles.

The grounds are a joy. Their spaciousness allows a variety of different environments 'including the river and creek frontage, the levee bank and the copse. These areas gave space away from the buildings at recess and lunch times' (1967)[19] and 'room to grow, room to be with friends …

A view from the Hill around 1925, looking down to the new school. The few trees are mostly pines. The buildings were red and white ('blood and bandages', said Sir Clive Steele) before they were reclad to match the chapel. On the left is the Science Block, later the Junior Block.

room to be alone' (1939). Strangely, there are few seats. In 1967 Hec Ingram (1926) paid to erect seats (from the demolished Grey Smith Stand of the Melbourne Cricket Ground) around the Main Oval.

NEW BUILDINGS

As the first ovals took shape in 1919, Robinson, after raising money from the Old Boys to buy the land, set out to persuade them to contribute £50 000 or more for buildings (1700 times the annual fees). The whole new school was represented as a war memorial. His committee (half Council and half Old Boys) consulted the architect, Henry Kemp. They decided that the plateau would contain only the boarders, and they adopted Kemp's sketch plan for the main building down on Morrison Avenue, with a Memorial Hall in front, Science buildings at the side, and Gymnasium and Swimming Bath at the back. It is possible that Kemp favoured erecting the main school buildings 'on the rising ground nearest to Glenferrie Road and just below the plateau', but this site was 'liable to be isolated by flood water'.[20] If the school had been built on the sloping hillside it might have resembled an Italian town, in a cascade of terraces and ramparts. Below, all the flat land would have been playing fields.

For the second time in its life Scotch moved to Melbourne's outskirts. As before, it felt like an isolated, even rural, area and the new classrooms seemed large and bare. The surroundings seemed less homely, but more scholastic. The first building was probably a groundsman's shed, moved from the Yarra Park cricket ground.

In 1916, 40 Junior School boys began in Hawthorn Glen under Arthur

Waller (Junior School Headmaster 1916–45). Ron Ballantyne (1922) was the first day-boy to arrive on the first day, and raised the school flag there for the first time.[21] On 5 March 1920 Sir John Monash laid a foundation-stone for the Senior School in honour of those who had served in the Great War. Buried in the wall behind the stone are said to be the names of the boys enrolled in 1920.[22] Numbers at Hawthorn rose each year, as senior boys and finally boarders arrived, swelling the total muster to around 1300. Whether the mice that lived at Eastern Hill[23] managed to come, too, we cannot tell. If not, that was a loss, for they may have been there for many generations.

Scotch began at Hawthorn with the Junior School in 1916, here photographed during that year in front of Glen House. The child in front has not yet been breeched.

Council expended a large sum to accommodate boarders at Hawthorn. It remodelled Glen House for the domestic staff, a laundry and a sick-bay. It built two new houses, School and McMeckan, both the gift of Anthony Mackie, his brother and sisters, in memory of their uncle, Captain James McMeckan. Each accommodated sixty boys and resident staff, and had three sleep-out balconies. A 'temporary' dining hall seated 250 boys, and its modern kitchens used electricity, steam and gas. It hosted the Old Boys' reunions in 1926 and 1928, to show them what they had built.

Arthur Waller, Junior School Headmaster 1916–45, in 1938. In 1916 Waller began the first classes at Hawthorn.

Deo patriae, litteris—
For God's sake don't litter Australia

Boys are untidy creatures. 'We are a free country and we can throw what we like where we like and feel proud of it.'[24] Scotch leaders try to set an example. Archie Anderson (1909) recalled Littlejohn,

in all the dignity of trencher-board and billowing gown, come sailing across from the Office towards his own house. As he passed the rubbish-tin he halted, stooped to pick up a banana skin which some careless luncher had thrown in the general direction of the tin, dropped it neatly inside and sailed on again like some stately galleon, his dignity unimpaired. A lesser man, and one of more brittle dignity, might have told the yardman to pick it up.[25]

A boy from a quarter-century later, Hal Oxley (1933), recounts that Littlejohn

complained several times about the paper left around the main oval after lunch. This lunch time, with hundreds of boys sitting around the oval, he came down the steps from the hill, gathered up his gown and walked around the oval picking up papers and putting them into his gown. We all sat silently as we watched the man we loved clean up our mess. After that the boys themselves attended "efficiently" to those who scattered paper.[26]

In 1999 Tim Downing the School Captain stooped to pick up rubbish in the quadrangle while embarrassed 14-year-olds wished they were somewhere else. To teach by example is mankind's oldest way.

Of all the spring and summer flowers which decorate our school grounds, what are lovelier or more widely distributed than the bright blossoms of the Litter family? They vary in colour from the gay reds, purples and oranges of the chocolate wrappings to the more delicate and familiar hues of the cigarette carton. And few will have failed to notice the humble toffee papers peeping out from among the daisies and roses. ... and who has not seen the fish and chips bag lying empty on the grass, the subtle grey grease stains dappling its surface and giving off a friendly smell of whale oil and candle grease in the fresher specimen?[27]

Down on the flat land was the main school. Compared to Eastern Hill's hodge-podge of rooms built during half a century and connected by odd staircases, Kemp made Hawthorn a coherent, cloistered, inward-focused set of classrooms. The design allowed Littlejohn when he stood in the quadrangle to see most of the school at a glance. He would stand there at the end of recess and lunchtime, an awesome figure in gown and mortarboard, and the moment the bell ceased ringing this son of a watchmaker would shout 'You Boy' at those still scuttling to their classes, which automatically meant a detention after school. 'To avoid being caught we used to crawl on our hands hidden by the upstairs balustrade and were often joined by some Masters who were similarly late'.[28] Thus 'many a future soldier learnt the art of concealment under fire!'[29]

The quadrangle was the school's crossroads, and repeated attempts have been made to render it hospitable, with seating, shade and water. Early seats were repeatedly broken and eventually not replaced, despite the hope of Monash House first formers' (Year 7s) in 1975 for a place to eat lunch on windy days. A grander plan in 1979 proposed eating areas where staff and students could mix. From 1997 a circular bench round the central tree (a weeping Scottish elm) offered a shaded charm. There are small drinking fountains, and in the middle of the west wall is a disproportionately large one, out of order for decades, a memorial to Lionel Robinson (1881). In his grief for his

The quadrangle under construction in the early 1920s. When it was completed, Littlejohn could stand in the centre and see most of his school at a glance, while boys running late to class stooped low behind the balustrades.

brother, Sir Arthur's judgement was clouded. The monument's scale would have allowed it to be a full fountain, which might have added a pleasant sound and cooled the quadrangle's asphalt paths and hot red brick.

On the quadrangle's eastern side looms the Memorial Hall. Higher than the two-storey main building, it seats over a thousand boys. It glows with light from tall windows on three sides, and from a great rose high on the west wall, the full glory of which, from the afternoon sun, is rarely seen. On the honour boards gilt names glisten on polished wood. Their grandeur hides the human muddles that put initials first on some boards but last on others, and the squabbles that limited the number of initials to three, even when a short-surnamed Stroke of the Crew like P. E. M. L. Philp had enough room for all.

It has a spire (or flèche) to attract lightning, and scares everyone when it does.[30] To repair the spire in the 1920s F. E. Raven (staff 1905–37), the foreman carpenter, had to lay a ladder on the steep roof and then scale an almost vertical ladder, while the boys watched open-mouthed.[31] In 1977 Scotch bought an extension ladder.

Acoustically the hall is extremely reverberant. 'Choirs rather like it, and if you're playing something very washy on strings, it can sound quite nice.' The echo is useful also 'when things are a little under-rehearsed and everything bounces round and you don't hear too many details!'[32]

Buying a thousand chairs took time. OSCA annually urged Old Boys to 'instal a chair, bearing your name' for 2 guineas.[33] Boys are not gentle to furniture. By 1948 the school owned 674 incomplete chairs. Repairs were costly, and in 1939 the Finance Committee decided to replace the chairs gradually with benches from Messrs Thear and Sons, who built the pews in the chapel and Mackie Hall. The war postponed this until 1948. The Finance

Committee took the matter seriously enough to visit Scotch twice and inspect the chairs.

When the benches were installed, there was no longer room for the whole school (though one might think that boys in pews could be packed closer than on chairs), so in 1949 Forms IV and V (at that date Years 7 and 8) began Junior Assembly in Mackie Hall under their Group Master, 'Cakey' Adams (nicknamed from Adams cakes). They liked this and regretted its end, but Selby Smith wanted the whole school to assemble together and proposed a gallery for the Memorial Hall. It was financed by the World War II Memorial Fund built up from the boys' fortnightly collections, which thereafter went to the Hospitals Appeal. For a month in 1954 assembly was held in the quadrangle while the gallery went up, then the whole school once again assembled, although it was a near-run thing in the gallery, with only six places to spare.

Because the whole school was built as a war memorial, early plans called the hall the Great Hall, but it became the Memorial Hall. By 1965 *Satura* could call it the memorial hall, without capitals, and by 2000 it was often just 'mem hall', suggesting that the words no longer had a meaning but were just a name.

It was the school building most likely to be portrayed, later joined by the chapel. Dudley Wood's watercolour of it graced the *Collegian*'s front cover in 1953–63 (see p. XI). It draws Old Boys back today, because its interior is essentially unchanged, and it has what Aaron Abell (1991) calls 'a familiar musty smell ... not a smell smell, more just like an *old* smell, ... an old wood smell'.[34]

As it grew sublime, it shed mundane uses. At first it hosted weddings— starting with that of Douglas Bain (1917, staff 1922, Chairman of Council 1959–63)—and routine meetings—of Lawson House or the Camera Club committee. It held inter-house music competitions in the 1950s and today. Yet it seemed sacrilegious when Healey began examinations there (where they continued until the Glenn Centre upper gymnasium was built). To allow the benches to be moved in and out, every second bench was left unbolted, and in the 1970s and 1980s Assembly was distracted as the boys in the fixed rows pushed the loose benches in front of them forwards, whilst the boys sitting on them pushed back. The alternative, said Healey, was to remove pews and substitute stackable light seats. 'But to treat the Memorial Hall as an all purpose Hall may not be seemly'.[35] The hall was also used for large occasions, like a fundraising audio-visual presentation in 1974, and in 1988 for gala dinners to raise funds and commemorate OSCA's 75th year, with 'Visions of Boyhood' presented by Campbell McComas (1970) and The Good for Business Theatre Company.

Beside the quadrangle was the Science Block. Its lecture theatres were steeply tiered semi-circles that enabled boys to watch what the master did on his bench. Most boys associate it with who taught them there, like 'Ossie' or 'Okka' Ferres (staff 1946–69, Senior Physics Master 1947–69). 'Short, dumpy statured Okka would peer over his glasses to keep an eye on the class. If ever he became embarrassed or angry, his face would turn as red as a beetroot.'[36]

The move to Hawthorn meant that many boys had to travel to school by public transport. Journeys were longer than to a city location, especially for boys living in Sunshine or Heidelberg or if several connections had to be made—Bill Gleadell (1966) used bus, train, and tram.[37] A benefit of commuting was that boys thrown together every day became friends. By train boys came on the Darling line to Heyington, a single track before 1926,[38] and then crossed the creek over a plank.[39] For Patrick McCaughey,

> The train moved from one dreary
> Scene to the next, from one backyard
> To the next. Each indifferently the same …
> … slum yards …
> The grimy patched-up washing, the stripped-down bike …
> The Edwardian iron hangs gloomily here.[40]

An electric tramline ran along Glenferrie Road—

> Trams rumble through a street
> Stained with stale beer, smelling of baked beans.[41]

Among local lads, Gordon Hill (1923) rode to school on horseback.

The school's buildings sprawl around the Main Oval. Soon Council dreamt of a school on the top of the Hill, in a great cloistered quadrangle (see map p. 251). An outline can be partially discerned by the buildings along the edge of the plateau overlooking the Junior School. One wing of Arthur Robinson House, the Shergold Building, the former maids' quarters, and the hospital are generally aligned, and were to be joined by cloisters. Another line, at right angles, comprises the other wing of Arthur Robinson House and the dining hall. As well as the Hill's present buildings, Council's plans included two more boarding houses and a dining hall, all linked by cloisters, and a clock tower visible from far down the Yarra.

Such plans show a vision of the school now lost: that soon after arriving in Hawthorn Council intended to shift the school's architectural centre away from the down-to-earth teaching quadrangle and up the Hill to a high-towered boarding establishment. This probably echoed a view influenced by English Public Schools that the great Public School was a boarding school, and it also reflected Gilray's view that the boarding houses were the essence of the school. This dream flickered on after World War II, as Council planned cloisters from Arthur Robinson House to the staff quarters, and died only when Healey firmly told Council that, for reasons of cost, all building must be modern.

The plan emerged in 1934 when Council approved building the hospital subject to a plan for the whole plateau, so designed that each unit could be erected independently 'as demand or circumstances permitted'.[42] The plan shunned Glen House. John Scarborough, the school architect, deplored the cost of its upkeep, and proposed to demolish it once he built the hospital and female staff quarters. It was therefore allowed to fall into disrepair, and in 1942 was knocked down as an air raid precaution measure (it was said to be a fire danger to nearby buildings). This is one of Scotch's mistakes. Taste changes and if The Glen stood today it might be a lovingly-renovated show

A view of the Hill, graced by Glen House, from the Main Oval in 1935. Wesley won the match by 7 wickets.

piece. The Glen was visible from the main oval, and its survival might have meant keeping that vista alive, instead of allowing trees to screen the Hill from the day school.

RIVER AND CREEK

As Scotch developed the Hawthorn site, however, its drawbacks also emerged. Storm water from the plateau scoured pathways, necessitating drains and channels. But the main drawback proved to be not the site itself, but its boundaries. A key function of any organism is maintaining its outer skin. In East Melbourne Scotch had to struggle with its neighbours, and now it had to do so at Hawthorn.

To the east, Glenferrie Road ran up a steep cutting from which rocks fell in 1942 and 1954. Experts recommended removing all creepers, to prevent moisture from lodging in cliff pockets. Scotch wondered if it should insure against injury to pedestrians, but instead pinned responsibility on the City of Hawthorn, which had made the cutting and promised The Glen's original owner 'to maintain the cutting in perpetuity'.[43] Across Glenferrie Road, neighbours complained about trees growing too high, or about unsightly washing on clotheslines!

To the north, the empty streets filled with houses, and Scotch had to placate neighbours in Callantina Road who were horrified as Arthur Robinson House loomed over them. The school planted trees to screen it.

The 1934 flood lapped at the steps of the Memorial Hall. Looking east, the Junior School Oval is in the left centre of the picture.

To the west and south lay the watery boundaries of the Yarra River and Gardiner's Creek. Here, very large problems claimed time and money more years than not. To have a river frontage was charming. Ian Phipps (1952) treasured 'the walks along the creek and river banks at lunchtime with a few close friends'[44] and John Cumming (1967) 'enjoyed ... the pleasant environment of the Yarra River, the gum trees along the levy [sic] bank and the greenery in general'.[45]

Water came into the school's life as never before. A boy at East Melbourne never went to the Yarra except for the Head of the River races. Now boys swam in the river, where one diver soon died from hitting his head on a log, Ellerslie Clayton (1924), son of 'Reggie' Clayton (staff 1919–40). The Melbourne and Metropolitan Board of Works (MMBW) belatedly made the river safe near the school, much to the delight of John Collins (1927) watching them blast snags and drag out stumps.[46] Boys were forbidden to bathe in the river unless they could swim 50 yards and were accompanied by a master. To avoid the river's dangers, Sir John MacFarland gave £1000 towards a swimming bath, dug by the boys. It brought Scotch the distinctive smell of chlorine.

The river had its own micro-environment. It exuded a smell of wet soil and faint decay,[47] and 'was more heavily polluted in 1950 than now'.[48] In the mornings, fog wavered over the sodden playing fields as the sun tried to creep through.[49] The river brought the world to the boarders. Bill Norris (1945) trawled it for golf balls: 'went down river and got 1 ball. I have 26 now',[50] and found a 'dead dog with rope around its neck tied tight'.[51] David Taylor (1949) recalls shouts of 'body in the river', with everybody racing down to see the corpse.[52]

River and creek also brought floods. Scotch sat on the flood plain, and built dykes ever higher and installed pumps ever stronger, and struggled against outsiders who damaged these systems.

The creek regularly flooded the grounds, and it did so with growing velocity as Melbourne outer settlement deforested its headwaters. (Council learnt this from its consulting engineer in 1939, Clive Steele, whose reports here, as on the Glenferrie Road cutting, were expert but without longwindedness, and no doubt paved his way to the Chairmanship of Council in 1950.) The 1934 flood was vast. Glenferrie Road flooded at Gardiner's Creek, and boys who came by tram from the south 'were excused attendance until the flood receded'.[53] The Main Oval lay several feet deep and debris deposited there included a wooden shed and an upright piano. Water lapped the steps of the Memorial Hall. The boatshed set off like an ark down the river, with the boats still inside. It floated quite well until the Heyington railway bridge. 'The shed was undecided as to which arch it should take and, in the meantime, was smashed on the pylon.'[54]

The cost of new boats, boatshed and staging, tennis courts repaired, pump and motor overhauled, carried the damage to several thousand pounds. Like all floods, it curtailed sport and lunchtime activities and made work for staff, and the mud stank all through the school. The new boatshed was built of ferro-concrete (which Monash had pioneered) and was designed to withstand the violence of the Yarra in flood.

To prevent further flooding, the MMBW proposed to widen, deepen, and straighten Gardiner's Creek upstream from its junction with the river. Scotch was alarmed that this would cut into the school's land, but fell silent once its surveyors found that the creek's course had altered since the school bought the property, chiefly to its advantage.

In 1942 the school raised a levee bank along the creek, the only capital work done in that year of national emergency as the Japanese swept south. To stop the levee bank eroding, Scotch planted kikuya grass, and, on the advice of the State Forest Commission, willows and acacias. This levee would not hold back a flood of the 1934 scale, but 'should provide ample protection' against ordinary wet winters.[55] Instead, flooding continued. In 1946 the creek flooded the Lower and Meares Ovals. In 1952 'there was a continuous sheet of water from Glenferrie Road to the Boulevard, covering completely the New, Rugby, Lower and Meares Ovals'.[56] In 1956 the scouts launched their new canoe—on the Meares Oval. 'Scotch has not anything to show more bare, … Good grief, the very classrooms seem to seep'.[57]

Selby Smith was phlegmatic about a flood in 1959, welcoming its useful silt. As floods continued into the 1970s, Roff decided their frequency was unacceptable and in 1976 raised the levee bank a metre, 'to the height that only a once in a lifetime flood can get in'.[58] Roff achieved this 'at no cost because a builder working [in] Hawthorn was overjoyed only to haul the earth he was removing half a mile instead of 20 miles'.[59]

The levee bank, though it stopped water getting in, also stopped it getting out. To enable the ovals to rid themselves of rainwater, flap valves in the bank let the water out but not in. These closed when the river was up, so Scotch installed two large sumps and pumps on the outskirts of the Lower and Meares Ovals.

Where once the grounds sloped to the creek, from 1942 the levee bank cut the creek off from the school visually, and the space between bank and creek became an out-of-sight area where the school's writ did not quite run. Sexual trysts took place there, heterosexual—'There was a Merton Hall girl who used to meet boys down by the river for dalliance'[60]—and homosexual.[61] That boys smoked there was so well known as to be a subject for humour. 'Some senior boys, for some unaccounted reason, wish Mr Christie [1935, staff 1951–66] would refrain from his lunch-time strolls along the mossy banks of the pellucid Yarra.'[62] The concept of secrets-that-are-in-fact-known seems contradictory. But healthy organisations need grey areas that lie both within and outside, for this creates a place for play and for imagination. Scotch's outstanding example of this is the persistent belief that there are tunnels under the Main Oval. Buried in the very heart of the school, beneath its most sacred soil, these constitute a secret place indeed. Access is said to be through the chapel crypt. Official denials of the tunnels' existence only confirm the rumours. Apart from tracing the tunnels back to war-time slit trenches, one may also postulate psychological origins: boys' desire to kill off rules and scrutiny, or boys' dreams of plunging into tunnels.

Finally, Scotch had to deal with people reluctant to acknowledge the creek as a boundary. The MMBW threw a bridge across the creek and was promptly asked to take it down. (Similar structures included the cadets' flying fox and a scout bridge across the Yarra—half a dozen crossed but one school officer fell in.) The SEC ran underground cables through a corner on Gardiner's Creek. The school made no claim for compensation, perhaps because the SEC's founding fathers included Robinson, Monash, Sir Harry Lawson, and Hyman Herman (1890) who as geologist and engineer campaigned for the use of brown coal and researched briquetting. Later the SEC marched catenary towers along a new easement in 1964. Scotch spent two decades fighting for compensation. Each side produced widely different valuations (the SEC offered $2000 and Scotch asked for $44 000). The matter lapsed because of the freeway until in 1979 Scotch won $38 597, with costs, plus as much again in interest calculated back to 1964. None of this was paid, however, while the ownership of the school was under litigation. Only in 1982 did Scotch at last receive $94 929 as final settlement.

By 1950 Scotch had been at Hawthorn for a generation. The trees were sprouting, and the buildings looked less raw. In that year Harvey Nicholson (Captain 1936) entered Council, the first Old Boy to do so who had known no other Scotch but at Hawthorn.

7

IN SEARCH OF
A NEW IDENTITY

1920–1950

Surgeons. A generation apart, carving on a windowsill from Eastern Hill: J.S. Paton (1893), Member of the Royal College of Surgeons, and served in the Boer War; F.W. Fay (1911) fought in World War I and afterwards became a Fellow of the Royal Australian College of Surgeons. The two men became friends in later life.

The move from Eastern Hill to Hawthorn left a scar on the school's memory. For boys and staff the loss was profound, 'a great grief'.[1] Even in 2000, a few Old Boys' schooldays lie back in the early 1920s at East Melbourne, but the Scotch community at large has for a long time neither known nor cared that Scotch once lived elsewhere.

Does this matter? It means there is a lack. We cannot say 'This is Morrison's study' or 'Look, here's John Monash's name carved in the bluestone',[2] or 'This is the tree my great-grandfather climbed' (the old pines on the Hill record the names and dates of generations of agile boarders). Half the school's life has no physical existence. The Hawthorn buildings are all twentieth-century and lack a historical depth to match the school's age. There is no sandstone arch or Edwardian flourish, as adds a touch of bygone age to some corner of many a poorer school.

What meaning might this rootlessness have? An *absence* is not immediately obvious and provokes little thought.

Has it lessened Old Boys' attachment to the school? The 'old school buildings meant quite a lot' whilst the new school's buildings 'meant nothing as far as I was concerned.'[3] Many did not connect to the new place unless they sent their sons there. Perhaps this showed itself financially. In the 1960s the average Scotch Old Boy gave less to his school than did the Old Boys of other schools.[4] Perhaps Scotch Old Boys had always been less generous (though their numbers ensured that their combined generosity was lavish), or perhaps this dip in support followed the amputation in the life of the school, as the pre-1920 generation reached donor age.

Of course, the school would slowly have shed its physical history anyhow. Junior School furniture, carved with initials, went in 1938 when the classroom furniture was replaced.

As well as replacing one physical reality with another, Scotch changed its mental map, changed the very way it talked about itself. Take, for example, a poem about Scotch at Eastern Hill, which contains four things that soon were no longer said:

> Climbeth the ivy still around her?
>> Grey are her walls, and broad her towers?
> Standeth she still as when we found her,
>> High on the hill that is yours and ours?[5]

At Hawthorn, Scotch is neither grey, nor with towers, nor high on a hill, nor has it let ivy stay long. The classic photographs of Scotch at Hawthorn are of ivy-free, red buildings without towers, viewed across flat land. There is no echo of Eastern Hill's verticality (imposed by so small a site) with its three-storey buildings and prominent towers. East Melbourne poetry celebrated the building because that is all there was, on one hectare of land, whilst Hawthorn poetry is as likely to celebrate the physical environment, like the Yarra at sunset: 'Lost is the last long light on the hills, / The last quick light where the water spills'.[6] To fill the gap between these two images of the school, Scotch hunted for new ways of representing itself. It tried to find words or music that would be uniquely Scotch, it threw up a succession of visual images that mostly lodged in no-one's memory, and it rejigged its architectural style, all in the hope of transcending the dissonance within a red brick school whose Old Boys pined for grey. Scotch's songs today still avoid any description of the school as a physical entity.

SYMBOLS

Scotch has not much gone in for symbols. The staff wear gowns, but nowadays only in Assembly. The cricketer at the crease, the footballer taking a high mark—in its visual representations of itself Scotch prefers pictures of action, not symbols or metaphors. For a brief moment this was not so. A few years either side of turning 80 years old in 1931 Scotch introduced the visual symbols which still most widely say what the school stands for: the coat-of-arms, the Memorial Hall windows, the blazer and the chapel.

The coat-of-arms is the white cross on a blue background which is today Scotch's most distinctive and ubiquitous emblem, appearing on stationery, clothing, cufflinks, crockery, car stickers, golf-balls and so on.

About 1860, school prizes bore a Scotch thistle in flower. It is the traditional emblem of Scotland—said to have been adopted when invading Danes gave away their position by yelping when they trod on thistles. Scotch has always used it as a straightforward way of affirming the school's Scottishness. Each generation shaped it afresh, like the *art nouveau* thistles in the 1914 *Collegian*. It surrounds the chapel doors and in 1999 was contemplated as the device on the tie of the 1858 Club, the football auxiliary. From 1861 to 1924 Scotch used a toga-clad 'young man reading the Book of Life by the Light of Hope placed on the Pillar of Faith'.[7] In the 1980s it reappeared in a stained glass window in the Junior School. By 1914 Scotch began to play with this imagery, using the lamp by itself and when war came the reader put on a uniform and marched off to fight (see pp. 107 and 135).

School coat-of-arms outside the Art Building.

Despite this living and versatile tradition, in 1920 the prefects held a competition for a new shield, incorporating both the reader and the Scottish Cross of St Andrew. The result (see p. III) breached heraldic rules, and in 1924 Council adopted a heraldically correct coat-of-arms designed by Sir Edward Mackenzie Mackenzie at the behest of Sir Arthur Robinson (see p. III). Alan Moorehead regretted the departure of the sage, and wondered 'Was he too pagan?'[8]

Its basic feature is the diagonal white cross on a blue background. This is the flag of Scotland, St Andrew's Cross, and in Victoria its main use is by Scotch College. Each of the four spaces created by the cross contains an object. Two of these are instantly clear in meaning to any Australian, the Southern Cross (asserting the school's antipodean location), and the crown (asserting loyalty to the sovereign and, more generally, loyalty to legitimate government).

The two other symbols are more of a problem. One is a torch, indeed the torch of learning, but most people will think first of the Olympic Games, which has captured this emblem since Sir Edward's day. The final, bottom, item is a Greek, oared, sailing ship of the kind used by Ulysses or Jason, and not uncommon in Scottish heraldry. Heraldically it is called a lymphad. In Scotch's arms the oars are in use and the sails furled, so it is rowing into the wind. Thus it stands for enterprise and perseverance, said Littlejohn,[9] and Sir Edward meant us to think of a 'bold spirit of adventure' which recalls the writing of Ossian, the ancient Scottish poet: 'Tales of the times of old; / The deeds of days of other years'. But few boys at Scotch have ever felt moved or emboldened by their lymphad. Even in a school in the thrall of nautical heroism in the annual Head of the River (or Scotch-at-Cowes flotilla, the boarders' yachting on Albert Park Lake, or the Sailing Club), the lymphad still looks cumbersome and uninspiring. Indeed, since Ossian is now deemed a fraud of the Ern Malley variety, we may say that Sir Edward missed his mark here. The meaning can, of course, be explained, but we live in an age when advertising and symbols have to speak for themselves.

The shield is usually vair-shaped. From time to time the school toys with a square shape (see p. 383).

The crest, above the coat-of-arms, is a gold burning bush. Moses met a burning bush, and although it was alight it was not consumed (Exodus iii.2). The Presbyterian Church has this bush as its emblem, and the motto, *Nec tamen consumebatur* (And yet it was not consumed) alludes to the faith of its martyrs burnt at the stake during the Reformation. Like the lymphad, this is an arresting symbol once its story is known, but its meaning is not otherwise immediately clear. Scotch has compounded this by sometimes using a stylised version as at the top of the chapel tower where no-one knows what it is. The bush encircled by the school motto was the cap badge for 40 years (from 1926 until caps were abolished). The caps reintroduced in the 1990s carried the coat-of-arms. The bush reappeared as the emblem of the school's 150th anniversary. Among the boys, it lives most vigorously in the chant 'Burning bush, burning red, / Kick the [inhabitants of another school] in the head'.

Architects like John Scarborough and Garry Martin set it high in sandstone cartouches on school buildings, most recently on the Randall Building in 2000. It appears in full colour on two buildings, gazing out over the Main Oval, but both are insecure. One is over the main entrance to Mackie Hall and will move to the Forbes Academy. The other on the Art School was made by Peter Farrer (1975) when still at school, with support from his father, the General House Committee, and the art master, Donald Cameron (1943, staff 1972–77). It will eventually be relocated if its present site is covered by a false roof designed to give that building the same high sloping roof as its neighbours.

When Scotch became an incorporated company in 1980, it was, oddly, not its own master heraldically, for the arms could not be altered without the consent of the Presbyterian Church. In 1994 the church transferred this armorial ownership to the school.

The other utterly familiar visual images of the school are the stained-glass windows in the Memorial Hall (see pp. VIII and IX), designed and executed by Messrs Mathieson and Gibson (William Mathieson entered in 1913). Lady Somers, wife of the Governor, unveiled them on Armistice Day 1930, for they pay homage to the Old Boys who fell in the Great War. In 1925 Littlejohn and some senior boys had decided the Memorial Hall needed a specific war memorial. The Dramatic Society under Vivian Hill each year raised the money.

There are six windows, containing six large male figures surrounded by a host of smaller items. There are the coats-of-arms of the Australian States and Commonwealth, of the school, Scotland and the King, linked with emblems of peace and victory. Above are doves bearing scrolls inscribed with the twelve fruits of the Holy Spirit: Faith, Meekness, Patience, Long-suffering, Gentleness, Chastity, Goodness, Temperance, Peace, Modesty, Love and Joy. All of these have been enjoined on Scotch boys, some by sports coaches and some not.

The main figures are St Andrew, patron Saint of Scotland (and thus of the school so far as it has a patron saint); St Martin, whose feast day is 11 November (Armistice Day); and St Michael and St George, the patron saints of soldiers. Since the Presbyterian Church has not much truck with saints or feast days, these figures are intriguing as drawing on a wider Christian heritage. What is frankly extraordinary, however, is that the two central figures are pagan: King Arthur and Sir Galahad. They are said to 'typify the Moral and Spiritual Virtues of Soldiers'.[10] Perhaps because of their non-Presbyterian, non-Biblical associations, these windows are never drawn on. No preacher ever alludes to them, no homily ever puts words to the pictures.

Visually, the figures are less exotic. They slouch. Their swords are drawn but are not raised for battle. A Pre-Raphaelite influence makes them all of one ethnic group, with golden hair. Their armour looks too light, hugs too closely as though made of aluminium. Ultimately, these heroic figures are dull and therefore unmemorable. Boys face them for years, but neither current boys nor Old Boys can recall them. Among the mass of symbols in the windows only St George's shield really stands out during Assembly, as the morning sun gives the windows their full glory.

These six figures are also the school's major representation of the male body. At Scotch the established arts of bodily representation are absent, apart from portraits and a bust of Monash in the principal's office. Although it is a boys' school, and memorialises boys' physical achievements as the records carry its boys higher, faster and further, Scotch has been reluctant to celebrate the male body, probably for fear that the boys would damage anything in the grounds and for fear that anything that explicitly admired the male body might smack of homosexuality. (Of course, where the school and Presbyterianism fear to tread, boys will seek their own graven images, like collecting pictures of football heroes. Bill Norris (1945) bought newspapers 'for my footy scrapbooks. I pasted the photos in at Prep.'[11])

The eastern windows in the Memorial Hall are the most splendid of Scotch's visual representations of what it stands for. In this they fail. They do succeed, however, in helping to create an ambience, for in entering the Memorial Hall people feel awe.

In the chapel, built in 1936, the first three stained glass windows, presented between 1940 and 1950, were private memorials. They commemorated Sir Arthur Robinson; his late first wife, Annie Summers Robinson; and George Aitken (1882), a leading pastoralist and woolbroker, and the member of Council who secured Scotch the Mackie Bequest. These windows represent religious themes, rather than aspects of the school. Aitken's window portrays the Road to Emmaus. Like the burning bush, this tells of an encounter with God who is not immediately recognised, as two travellers on the road walk with another without realising it is the resurrected Jesus. (Many Old Boys say that while they were at Scotch they never realised how good a teacher was, or how good Scotch was.)

Two other successful emblems of Scotch to appear in the 1930s were items of clothing: the blazer and a newly designed Old School Tie.

The blazer (see p. IX) was vertically striped in 1908–16, and plain from 1917. In 1932 Littlejohn designed the striped blazer still worn today. Importantly, he changed the meaning of cardinal, technically a deep scarlet. Until then, cardinal was the plum or claret colour that continued in use for the cap. It tended to turn brown with age. Littlejohn now adopted a more brilliant red. He modelled the blazer himself by wearing it to the 1932 Preparatory School sports.

In 1935 the OSCA *Yearbook* explained that OSCA 'has adopted a new tie of distinctive design consisting of narrow cardinal, gold and blue stripes, upon a dark blue background, the stripes being set off from the background by a thin silver line. This attractive tie may be worn with practically any coloured suit.'[12] It was available only at Henry Buck's.

In 1932 Littlejohn designed a new blazer and modelled it himself at the Preparatory School Sports.

AN ARCHITECTURAL STYLE

Scotch also tried to develop a distinctive architectural appearance. The earliest buildings (the Junior School, the Senior School quadrangle and School and McMeckan Houses), were designed by Kemp and were all of a kind, in red and white (see p. V). The bricks were red, smooth and tuck-pointed, and the spacious cloisters and open-bedroom balconies had cream, plastered, wide, pointed arches, whilst the upper walls beneath the gables were rough-cast render. The roofs were tiled in red. Everything alluded to the cardinal in the school's colours. As a style it was not excessively institutional, and looked as though it might belong also to a wealthy, wide-verandahed, Queen-Anne style home in nearby Hawthorn.

In the 1930s a new architect appeared, John Scarborough of Scarborough, Robertson and Love. After the chapel, he built Mackie Hall, the Monash Gates and Lodge, and the second wave of building on the Hill (Arthur Robinson House, the hospital, the domestic staff quarters, and the Sub-Primary, now the Shergold Building). Scarborough preferred a rougher brick called Rippletex, more orange-pink than red, and instead of Kemp's flat expanses of brick, Scarborough delighted in bricks' versatility, even running them into curves, quite at odds with their rectangular shape, so that many of his buildings have turrets (see p. V). He also liked tiny balconied windows. The style was called Collegiate Gothic,[13] though it is perhaps more of a suburban Chambord.

Just as all this contrasted with the style of his predecessor, so Scarborough's successors in turn abandoned *his* style, and Scotch now has several uncoordinated styles. Scarborough's influence has, however, remained predominant through his masterpiece, the chapel (see p. VI).

The Scotch chapel watches on the hillside overlooking the Main Oval. It floats serenely at a point where various forces meet, where the steep hill intersects with the flat plane of the main grounds, where the wooded hillside becomes the green lawn of the oval, where the straight Monash Drive bends. There are no other buildings nearby. Littlejohn chose the site shortly before he died, and asked Robinson to turn the first sod. The site's high visibility deliberately symbolises for Donaldson 'the centrality of the Christian message in the ethos of Scotch College'.[14] When it was opened, the clergy felt obliged to remind us that 'not in architectural design lay its perfection, but in the greatness of the benefit derived',[15] but everyone else saw that it was an architectural triumph.

Scarborough became its architect by winning an OSCA competition judged by Percy Meldrum, a Melbourne architect. The design drew on Albi Cathedral, a fifteenth-century Gothic structure in southern France: 'general simplicity of line, concentration of ornamental detail and a tendency towards loftiness in proportion being salient characteristics. Consideration of cost necessitated the use of brick', but they were bricks of pleasing texture and colour.

> The exterior of the building depends almost entirely on proportion, massing, and the effects obtained by faceting the wall faces, resulting in a constant change of light and shade. Ornament is entirely confined to the traceried window heads and door surrounds; and this concentration of detail with its contrasting plain surfaces forms a keynote which is retained throughout the scheme.[16]

Inside, 'the light tone of its fine Manchurian Oak panelling imbues it with a young and ageless quality'.[17] The west front is asymmetric because the building is on a hillside, and Scarborough wanted to give it the appearance of being prevented from sliding down the hill, hence the staking effect of the stair tower, and the buttressing of the south porch and vestry.

Scarborough's partner Kirkland Robertson (1926, staff 1935–36) said later, in singing Scarborough's praise, that

> the most distinctive and original feature of the Chapel is the undulating effect of the side walls. Normally a gothic structure is distinguished by buttresses projecting at right angles to the side walls, as on the Memorial Hall. By this

device the thickness of the walls, and therefore the amount of stone in them could be reduced, so the buttresses provided a necessary resistance to the overturning of the walls because of the enormous outward thrust of the heavy stone vaulting, or the thrust of the roof framing. The Littlejohn Chapel has no stone vaulting nor any roof thrust, because the roof is very light, and the roof trusses quite inert, so neither buttresses nor tie rods (as in the Memorial Hall) are needed in the Chapel. The need for such buttressing as exists is only to resist wind load.

Charlie Macmillan, the old Scots foreman bricklayer [found that] the walls he was building were not walls at all, but a series of complicated piers separating the windows. ... Yet if ever a man built a memorial to himself it was bricklayer Charlie Macmillan, for we gave him a most involved problem to build in brickwork, which he solved with the greatest credit to himself and to our great satisfaction. Yet there is one flaw in the building, a dimensional error at the N.E. corner, probably the general foreman's fault, but you'll never find it.[18]

The Littlejohn Memorial Chapel in 1970. The architect, John Scarborough, based it on the cathedral at Albi, in southern France. Despite this, it is unmistakably modern.

The chapel used 300 000 ordinary bricks and 120 000 hand-made bricks in 200 different shapes. The fundraisers hit upon the idea of donors paying five shillings a brick. The appeal committee represented both OSCA and the Old Scotch Collegians' Club. By January 1935 they had raised half the estimated cost, and still had not raised enough when the tender was let to T. and R. Cockram. Built in the Great Depression, it was an act of financial defiance. At its consecration, the President of OSCA presented it to the school, and the Moderator received it on behalf of the school. The presence in the chapel of an organ marked Scotch's last break from its Free Church founders, who referred contemptuously to this instrument as a 'kist o' whistles'.[19]

The chapel brought out the clergy's architectural metaphors. At its dedication William Marshall (1902) preached on 'So the house of the Lord was perfected', and they sang 'The Church's one foundation is Jesus Christ her Lord'. They sang 'Christ is made the sure foundation' in 1986 at the chapel's 50th anniversary, when Norman Pritchard preached 'Jesus-Christ himself being the chief corner stone' (Ephesians ii.20).

The Rev. Robert McDonald (1944) supposes

that all of us, especially in formative years try to marry the less understandable (spiritual) with the supposedly understood (everyday life in the material). Most seem to give up and I in no way found religion at all attractive. The more 'normal' aspects of Scotch did not provide me with answers (eg 'Cakey' Adams' classes added nothing here, nor attendance once or twice to a lunch-time Crusader Union group), but Scotch did provide the Chapel; a distinctive focal point which suggested there are answers to the mystery. Otherwise why would the school build it? In other words, God *must* be real. The *School* is saying so! I take it that the Chapel impressed that in my mind. Thus, it stands where it is as a 'silent' witness and will always add its own message to all the other learning the school may impress upon the minds of boys.[20]

Architecturally, the chapel's long-term effect was unexpected: Council and Scarborough set out to make everything else look like it. Its brick was to be used in all later buildings, and put as a facade on existing buildings. This began at once, in 1936, when Scarborough proposed work inside the Science Block on the Biology Laboratory, for £1630, and outside a brick veneer, for £1160, two-thirds of the cost of the necessary work and a high cost for mere appearance. Council deferred reconditioning the laboratory, but went ahead with making the external walls 'conform with architecture of the Chapel'.[21] Sir Arthur Robinson then quickly veneered the main building's east and south external walls, raising additional funds to do so. At the same time the new brick was used to build the hospital and Arthur Robinson House.

When building resumed after the war, Scotch intended to veneer the Junior School and the north face of the Senior School. The Chairman of Council, Sir Clive Steele, dismissed the old red brick and white rough-cast as 'blood and bandage' architecture.[22] Scotch ordered 80 000 more Rippletex bricks, but delays ensued, and in 1965 a further brick shortage delayed work on an upper storey for McMeckan House prep room. Worse, Scarborough now discovered that 'Future supplies of these bricks may be difficult to obtain'.[23] For its manufacture, the Eureka Brick and Terra Cotta Tile Company of Ballarat had to reserve one kiln, and this was uneconomical. Already the bricks' cost was rising, and for the hidden west wall of the kiosk Scarborough used a pinky buff 'Rocktex' brick, at half the price. In 1970 Healey cut the costs of the new dining hall with 'a less expensive brick of similar appearance to Ripple-Tex'.[24]

Major-General Sir Clive Steele (1910 Captain of Boats), Chairman of Council 1950–54.

Since then Scotch has matched the earlier bricks as best it can. The Lithgow Centre has bricks of the same texture, but the colour is less pink and more tawny. Plans in the 1960s to veneer the school's north wall on Morrison Street came to nothing. In 1999 the nearby new administrative building, sitting close also to the red brick Memorial Hall, was done in smooth red brick also, apparently ending the long reign of tapestry brick, which is, however, to reappear in the Forbes Building.

Another Scarborough creation was the Monash Lodge, the cottage at the lower Glenferrie Road entrance, which shows him at his most charming and domestic. It replaced the groundsman's hut displaced by the hospital, and was at first occupied by the caretaker and then by boarding-house masters. Alongside, OSCA erected the Monash Gates to commemorate the great man's example. 'He had no special facilities for easy success,' said Sir Arthur Robinson. 'He had to carve his own way.'[25] Handsome iron gates hang on typical Scarborough curved brick walls. The gates bear a row of wrought-iron symbols illustrating aspects of Monash's career. They are part of the school's efforts to develop ways of representing itself. Mysterious and a challenge to schoolboy curiosity, in 1956 *Satura* doubted if any reader could say what the symbols represented. Beside the gates, a rain shelter promised by the Hawthorn City Council in 1973 remains unbuilt.

Gates and a lodge were also planned, as a World War II memorial, at the Morrison Street entrance, astride cloisters running from the Music School to the Memorial Hall. Other projects gained priority and this was just as well, for the proposed arched gateway was not much larger than that needed for a 1940s Morris Minor. Thus a vision of gateways and gate-houses died away. Perhaps it was too medieval. Perhaps it will be revived when Morrison Street is fully absorbed into the school grounds and a new gateway appears, more grand than the cyclone wire gates of the last half-century.

A war memorial planned in 1947 for the Morrison Street entrance. The arched gateway could accommodate no vehicle larger than a Morris Minor.

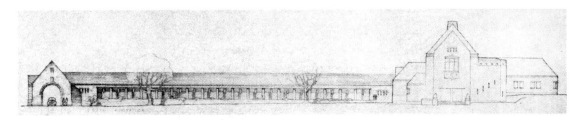

Forty Years On
(For A. G. Serle)

Elegantly unpresbyterian,
Preoccupied with style,
The slim chapel soaring in orange brick
Continues to boast
Its oddly affecting gargoyles.

The music school where I sweated in the greasepaint
Of Sir Thomas Erpingham
Still tucks itself away
Into the Hill's green armpit
Meticulously
'Arts-and-crafts revival.

But it was always trees
That stirred my deepest blood
And made me what I am—
The noble river redgums,
Plump elms and lifting pines
A valley plumfull of landscape and pibroch.

A valley in which the dented willow
Went chunk, chunk, chunk
To offbreak bowling all
The shadelong afternoon of adolescence,
The cream, swaying figures marked out by our talismanic trinity
Of cardinal, gold and blue.

Chris Wallace-Crabbe (1950)

PICTURES AND PEN-PICTURES

As well as symbolically, Scotch also displayed more prosaic representations of what it stood for. In 1925 OSCA commissioned a portrait of the then principal, Littlejohn, by W. B. McInnes. Not to be outdone, the Old Scotch Collegians' Club in 1926 commissioned from McInnes a portrait of Shew (who had retired in 1921 after 52 years on the staff). Other Old Boys then had George Bell paint a portrait of Alexander Morrison, by copying Walton's 1889 portrait of him at Ormond College; this, too, was hung in the Memorial Hall. Sir John MacFarland's portrait by Percy White followed in 1927.

Until the 1960s the Hall long contained a photograph of Monash, who laid the Hall's foundation stone. Archie Anderson called it 'the Monash Hall'.[26] Monash's photograph was certainly there in the apse in 1960 along with photographs of three sovereigns (George V, George VI and Elizabeth II).

As the school searched for ways to represent itself to itself, written portraits also began to emerge, as people at last published their memoirs. They painted Scotch as full of sexually charged adolescents, run by domineeringly religious Scotsmen, and staffed by splendidly eccentric teachers. Walter Turner (1901), the poet and critic, set the pattern in 1935 with his whimsical *Blow for Balloons*. *Fiddlers of Drummond* by Arthur Davies (1924, staff [?]–1941) was allegedly fictitious but based on Scotch. (Hal Porter, who fashioned his public persona on that of Davies,[27] described Davies's teaching as 'keeping swine quiet enough to hear the pearls drop'.[28]) *Road to Gundagai, Humping my Bluey* and *Goodbye Melbourne Town*[29] all by Graham McInnes (1930), *Luck's a Fortune*,[30] by David McNicoll (Editor of the *Collegian* 1932), *An Urge to Laugh*, by Ross Campbell (Editor of the *Collegian* 1928) and *Screw Loose*, by Peter Blazey (1957) all rejoice in affectionate mockery. Even Blazey, who begins by declaring that Scotch constituted 'a healthy object of hatred: few things can give life more focus', soon confesses how his heart beats faster as he remembers the school songs.[31]

A more serious vein of autobiography appears in *A Late Education* by Alan Moorehead (1926), a journalist, *An Australian Son* by Gordon Matthews (1969), a diplomat, and *Things to Be Remembered* by Sir Archibald Glenn (1929), an industrialist,[32] and in three works by women: *Three-quarters of a century* by Eliza Mitchell and *Family Fresco* by Nancy Adams, Morrison's daughter and grand-daughter, and Elizabeth Pike's *New Every Morning*.[33]

The year before Turner's *Blow for Balloons,* Scotch's first biography appeared, by Alec Pratt (Editor of the *Collegian* 1922): *Littlejohn: The story of a great headmaster*.[34] A widening circle of biographies includes Serle's *Gilray*,[35] and biographies of Old Boys like the soldier Monash (also by Serle), the lawyer and Governor Sir Henry Winneke (1925),[36] the educationalist and Fabian, David Monash Bennett (1942), Monash's grandson,[37] and the 'red barrister', Ted Laurie (Captain 1930).[38] Janet McCalman's collective biography, *Journeyings*, includes Scotch boys.[39]

SCOTCH FAMILIES

In 1875, one of the new boys was Robert Andrew Ramsay (1888), son of the Hon. Robert Ramsay (entered 1852). This is the earliest known appearance at Scotch of a son of an Old Boy. Whoever the first son of an Old Boy was, we may imagine that his initial day at his new school was, as for all new boys, confusing—as he tried to work out what to do and where to go—and physically uncomfortable—'1st day the seams of my shirt were prickly and the shoes uncomfortable' (1990);[40] 'the stiff collar and tie felt like they were strangling me' (1991).[41]

The arrival of the first son of an Old Boy changed the school forever. From that day, Scotch grew another exoskeleton, and no longer depended for its survival entirely on the church. From then on, when the school struck trouble and needed money or people who would put themselves out, it could rely on the continuity of the families that walked with it down the decades.

A generation later, the first grandson arrived, perhaps Westmore Stephens (Captain 1911), grandson of Henry Langlands (entered 1851). His descent was noted at the time, and Scotch found that it liked tracing this sort of connection. From 1914, as the Old Boys created OSCA, so the *Collegian* identified which boys were sons and grandsons of Old Boys. To do so was extraordinary, for it singled these boys out from their peers. By

1975 the possibilities ran up to five generations. Andrew (1985) and Tim (1986) Maxwell were the sons, grandsons, great-grandsons and great-great-grandsons of Old Boys. Three other boys, Bill (1976) and Richard (1980) Fleming and Richard McNaughton (1978), laid claim to be great-great-grandsons of Lawsonites.

Elizabeth Baird, c. 1950. This happy Scottish woman, one of a family of Bairds at the school, sold the tuckshop's leftover food to the boarders after school at bargain prices.

For all this, the school has kept no accurate or sustained records of Old Boys' descendants. The *Collegian*'s lists, which ceased in 1985, were only as reliable as families' memories, and often omitted Junior School entrants. There is evidence that the proportion of Old Boys' descendants peaked around 1970, at almost half the school. Otherwise we have only snapshots. In 1924, for example, 11% of the school were sons or grandsons of Old Boys.[42] In the early 1930s around 10% were the sons of Old Boys,[43] in 1993, 28%,[44] and in 2000, 21%.

Boys know their status. Tom Lane (staff 1997–98) when teaching Classical Civilisation split his class into groups to illustrate the subject. Boys with earlier relatives at Scotch became patricians, and the rest were plebs. Each boy knew to which group he belonged.

Such multi-generational affiliations led the school to talk about 'Scotch families'. The families that boys know most are staff families. A teacher, Moses Thomas, had his son Walter at Scotch as early as 1857. The Junior School Headmaster Arthur Waller was known as 'Dog' (on the cockney rhyming analogy of Waller, collar, dog-collar).[45] His son was therefore known as 'Pup': Sir Keith (1931, Head of the Department of Foreign Affairs 1970–74). In 1970 the prefects included a son, grandson and great-grandson of Scotch's Principals.[46] The Baird family provided two caretakers, Jim (staff 1930–77) and Gavin (staff 1940s–50s). Their sister Elizabeth Baird worked at the tuckshop for 26 years till 1955. 'This happy Scots woman',[47] 'a darling, always smiling'[48] kept many boarders alive by reopening the tuckshop in the evenings and selling the left-overs at bargain prices.

At some point reality blurs with myth. *The School Song* contains the words 'As our fathers and our brothers used to do', and thereby implies that all boys are sons of Old Boys. The boys to whom it did not apply sang it without embarrassment, indeed without disbelief.

'My father's got Nelson's telescope,' boasted Johnny. 'That's nothing,' answered Willie, 'my father's got Adam's apple'.[49]

In celebrating its families in the *Collegian*'s lists and photographs, and in *Great Scot*, Scotch drew the final lesson from its move to Hawthorn—that the essence of the school was not its land or buildings, which it had abandoned, but its people. In a way, there is no such thing as Scotch College. There are only Scotch Collegians.

FATHERS AND SONS

That fathers send their sons to the school they went to is part of the wider relationship that exists between fathers and sons. A man who enjoyed Scotch understandably wants his son to have the same experience. Oddly, many men who were unhappy at Scotch also send their sons there.

John and Graeme Blanch, father and son, were both Captains of the school.

Perhaps they want Scotch to work out this time? It is often the burden of children to succeed in the things their parents failed at.

It is also often the task of children to realise their parents' dreams. One of a father's most powerful hopes is that his boy will grow up to be like him. When a son repeats his father's achievements there is a great sense of the rightness of things. John (1938, OSCA President 1964–65) and Graeme (1969) Blanch were both School Captains. So were Bill (1939) and his son Euan (1970) Littlejohn. In 1974 the premiership-winning First XVIII was captained by Tim Ashton, son of Peter Ashton, who captained the winning team in 1939. The cox of the 1965–67 Crews was Richard Smith (1967), son of Frank H. Smith (1939) cox of the 1939 Crew, and grandson of Frank P. Smith (1911), cox of the 1911 Crew. Scotch likes to tell such tales. It greets sons of Old Boys with a wash of expectations, and even aged five a new boy is hailed with 'hopes that he will surpass his father in both cricket and football'.[50]

Many sons flourished by following their fathers— 'my father (a renowned classicist) said if I tried Greek I would love it. He was not wrong!'[51] Many sons did something they disliked because their fathers wanted it, like boxing: 'we did what our fathers wanted',[52] 'my father … insisted that I learnt to box so that I could "look after myself".' A boy who liked Mathematics least of his subjects did it 'because my Father was so good at it and I was not!! I liked it better in later life. Also I was a lazy little sod and wouldn't work at it' (1950). Other boys rebelled. 'I regret not having been more active in sports [but] my father (and to a fair extent my mother) was sports-mad, which probably turned me off.'[53]

Leonard Kemp (1927) found 'coming to the same school as one's father has a meaning. It was important.'[54] Noel Ramsey (1941) 'enjoyed being a 3rd generation attending Scotch'.[55] But for Ross Hyams (1980),

sometimes I felt it had negative connotations in that I felt I had to "Live up" to whatever standard that had been set by others… It did, however, make you feel you belonged to the school and … that Scotch had an old tradition, which had been shared by most of the male members of my extended family, certainly provided a sense of belonging to the school.[56]

As Littlejohn warned, a father 'is apt to [think] that where he himself prospered, so must his boy also, and contrariwise, that what he has found irksome and uncongenial must prove the same to his son. He may be pardoned for sometimes overlooking the fact that not seldom the son takes after the mother.'[57] Tapp warned of shoving fathers' achievements at sons. Staff tried to be aware of the pressure on sons, noticing that 'Father pushes him hard & Chris responds to good effect' (Grade 7) or that 'Father appears to be particularly hard regarding standard of work. Hamish is an average achiever— excessive family pressure to achieve. Talented elder brother' and 'Hamish has average ability, but appears to be losing self-confidence as father continuously criticizes spelling, etc.' (Grade 5).

Fathers in turn were under pressure from sons, although Ingram felt sure that 'Boys, of course, are never, and were never so good as their fathers, and never will be! But I will make so bold as to say that despite all the critics one hears, the [modern] product is better educated and better equipped for life than ever his father was!'[58]

Fathers' reputations deserved protection. Old Boys playing cricket against each other on Old Boys' Day 1946 were assured that 'for those of us with sons at the school, every effort will be made to preserve the illusion that we were once cricketers of merit'. The umpire would treat appeals against fathers of present boys 'with studied neglect'.[59] Yet in a Junior School versus Fathers match about 1946 Don McClean (1952) bowled '5 fathers in a row',[60] an oedipal achievement.

8

THE BLUE
1934–1953

How does a shy man manage a thousand boys? By a clear, firm austerity. Colin Macdonald Gilray was a Rhodes Scholar and an All Black, with a Rugby Blue and a Military Cross, an accumulation that speaks of his intelligence and courage. Physically, he 'was indeed a grand figure. His whole body had been laid out regardless of cost, with plenty of face and eyebrow, and a monumental slab of trunk.'[1] As he strode along the corridors, boys shrank out of the way, and if he saw a boy 'bokkering'* a smaller boy, he gave the bully the same treatment.[2] They called him 'The Blue'. This is variously attributed to ginger hair, a five o'clock shadow (hence Bluebeard) or his university blue. Always neatly dressed, in winter he wore spats to keep his feet warm.

He was near fifty years old when he came to Scotch, an age when a man decides to make one last jump or settle where he is. Born in Scotland, he migrated to New Zealand aged five. He attended the universities of Otago and Oxford, was a schoolmaster in England and practised law in New Zealand. For the 12 years from 1922 he was Headmaster of John McGlashan College, Dunedin.

After the ebullient Littlejohn, Gilray was formal and reserved, his intelligence and kindness 'largely obscured by ... an innate shyness'.[3] During the war, Neville Hurst's mother,

> used a small wheeled vehicle, about half a metre high, for shopping (no cars). It was ideally proportioned to strike an adult just behind the knees, causing loss of balance and some pain. ... by the entrance to the Glenferrie Station, she encountered Mr Gilray in this way. He showed his true breeding by raising his hat and apologising for obstructing her progress. I was very mortified to learn that my mother had so assaulted my Headmaster and expected to hear more of it—which of course I never did.[4]

In writing of the Gilray years it is easy to forget the grey, shy Gilray and write instead of others more flamboyant or who seem more active. Yet those staff held their positions and enjoyed their freedom because Gilray wanted it so.

CIVILISING INFLUENCES

Gilray broadened life for 'those whose interests lay outside the mainstream sporting and academic activities.'[5] There were various lunchtime clubs and

*Bokker: forcibly to strike the biceps with a knuckle.

an increasing emphasis on music, art and drama. For plays and concerts Scotch built Mackie Hall. When it opened, 'Scotch came of age'.[6]

Since its foundation, Scotch has steadily expanded its repertoire, starting firstly with secondary education, then adding, secondly, sport under Morrison and, thirdly, extra-curricular activities under Littlejohn. Gilray's uplifting of music, art and drama brought into play an even stronger group of activities, later called co-curricular. Music, art and drama are ancient human activities which we enjoy in their own right, but which can be treated as school subjects. Scotch harnesses boys' enjoyment in the service of teaching skills and self-discipline, as well as the subject itself.

Music

Gilray appointed a full-time head of music, John Bishop (Director of Music 1937–47), later Professor of Music and founder of the Adelaide Festival. Old Boys call him 'incomparable',[7] 'indelible',[8] and 'a fantastic teacher'.[9] Through his 'genius … a completely new, wonderful Day of the Arts dawned at Scotch'.[10] Before Bishop, Scotch had well-intentioned men like Wood and Orton.[11] A few boys always did well, but George Bremner's (1932) lessons were perhaps more typical: 'Mr Fyshe [staff 1925–39] was a pleasant rotund man wearing an obvious hair piece which he continually shuffled around on top of his head. … When it came time to sit for the exam I declined the honour as it was not a compulsory subject. The relief was mutual.'[12]

Initially Bishop provoked antagonism with his long and 'fluffed up' hair, his garish dress and supercilious manner.[13] In a few years he changed the prevailing attitude to music,[14] giving it a place where none had been before, fostering talented musicians and broadening the knowledge of ordinary boys.[15] 'I can thank [him for] a love of music although I play no instrument.'[16]

He worked through existing institutions. Foundation Day Concerts were transformed. Previously, vocal items predominated, mainly from 19th-century operas. Bishop reached back to Mozart and Handel and forward to Grieg and Holst, and living composers like Britten, Bliss, T.F. Dunhill, Ireland and Vaughan Williams. (His successors continued this. Claude Monteath introduced Borodin, Bruch, Delibes, Khatchaturian, Falla and a richer vein of older composers, like Bach, first performed at the 1950 Concert. John Ferguson (Director since 1991) in 1996 presented only twentieth-century items, most younger than the Concert itself.) Bishop developed the school orchestra, helped by Violet Woolcock (staff 1936–60) as violinist, and he had boys perform as instrumental soloists.

Bishop demanded that even the Concert's mass singing was done well. He 'cancelled a song because we couldn't sing it well enough at the practice'.[17] At the rehearsals in the Memorial Hall, as he grew hotter he 'stripped off—bit by bit down to his singlet. The school roared as each item came off.'[18] One time 'he ran the length of the hall and "king-hit" a boy he suspected of playing cards during the rehearsal'.[19] 'The best bit of teaching

I saw at Scotch was the skill of John Bishop in getting the whole school to do what he wanted.'[20]

Bishop's greatest achievement was to reposition music within the school, by having it treated as a sport. The inter-house sports standards competition expanded to include music standards. (How did he persuade them!) Playing a piece of music earned cock-house points. Like a sport, Music had a Captain, first appointed in 1939.

Gilray also built a Music School. Attached to Mackie Hall, physically separate from the Senior School, it acquired a character of its own. (Brass rehearsals had 'the attractive smell of brass polish'.[21]) This sub-school expanded music's prestige and popularity under Bishop and his successors, men suffused with music. Claude Monteath (Director 1948–58), when his car malfunctioned, told the mechanic it sounded like an open diapason on low D flat. A succession of forceful directors positioned themselves within the school's mainstream— George Logie-Smith (Director 1959–78) trained footballers, and Dick Shirrefs (Director 1987–90) commanded the cadet corps. Louise Vay provided administrative stability for over 25 years, from Logie-Smith to Ferguson, whom she called 'the boy'. Logie-Smith made music the first discipline to have its own parents' auxiliary.

Logie-Smith, combining theatricality and musicality, made instrumental music widespread. To instrumentalists like Issy Spivakovsky (staff 1937–65, violin) and Eveline Limb (staff 1937–73, piano) he added others like one of Scotch's most distinguished musicians Roy Shepherd (1923, staff 1975–85, piano), Leslie Barklamb (staff 1960–77, flute), Henri Touzeau (staff 1969–93, cello), and Mack Jost (staff 1975–99, piano).

A 1968 example of Scotch's combination of music and sport. George Logie-Smith, Director of Music and in 1968 coach of the winning First XVIII, conducts the football ensemble.

Back row (from left): David Orr, Don Symington, John McCulloch, Munro Walker, Steve Lilley, Andrew Scott, Dave Robinson, Rob Wilson, Graeme Blanch, Andrew Oliver.

Front row (from left): Richard Eager, Rodger Morton, Doug Patrick, John McKeand, Dave Pascoe (sousaphone), Athol Smith (Captain), Tony Clark, Geoff Cumming.

The team won every match and meets annually for dinner.

By 2000 there were a dozen permanent staff and 40 part-time. In the Junior School, where the exemplary Peter Chapman long taught (1947–82), by the 1970s Tapp made music compulsory like sport, to ensure exposure to it. Shirrefs established a Year 2 string programme under Angie Robertson (staff 1988–), and Ferguson had Robert Wakely (staff 1996–) develop a Suzuki-based programme in the Junior School.

In the Senior School, in Forms I–II (Years 7–8), obligatory weekly music classes taught boys how to read music, and every boy had one term of free compulsory tuition in an orchestral instrument. Older boys took music if they wished. By 1965, one boy in three learnt an instrument; one in two if we include class instrumental tuition. By 2000, this meant over 700 elective lessons per week.

Spreading beyond the Foundation Day Concert, an annual May Concert began in 1970 (the year of the orchestra's first overseas tour), and a Middle School Concert in 1987 for younger boys, and Ferguson added others. These concerts gave a platform for the ensembles and small orchestra groups that emerged since the 1960s to which boys learning an instrument were required to belong. There, 'rather than just have a lesson in a room, boys learnt to play with other people and how ensembles work and how to respond to conductors'.[22] Ferguson has increased the number of ensembles and has systematised them so that boys progress through them as skills develop. Thus wind ensembles now progress from Junior, through ensembles named after Ted Joyner (staff 1986–90) (Years 7–8) and George Dreyfus (composer, bassoonist and sometime staff member) (Years 9–10), then to Symphonic Wind. 'The result is that Dreyfus plays the sort of repertoire that Symphonic played years ago, and Symphonic plays repertoire that could not have been dreamed of.'[23]

Composition was less well developed. Julian Duband (1980) did not feel encouraged, but Gareth de Korte (1994) did.[24] In 1972 orchestra practice won precedence over other activities on Friday afternoon, even over sport. Increasingly boys' compositions were performed at the Foundation Day Concert, like a fanfare by Warwick Stengards (1979), now in Europe conducting opera, and Lynden Roberts's (Captain 1988) 'Idyll' for four instruments.

Music has produced a number of distinguished musicians (like Ian Munro (1980), a leading classical pianist), but its greater achievement is that it became an integral part of the school, something not necessarily sissy. Scotch delighted in boys like Morris Barr (1939), who was in the First XVIII, the Crew, and Athletics team, and vocal soloist in several Foundation Day concerts. By century's end such a combination is unexceptional. Music's ubiquity means that whereas in the 1950s a boy might be called a 'muso', by the 1990s there are no such labels because all kinds of personalities have musical talents.[25] The innate capacity of humans to respond to the language of music, whether melodic or rhythmic, can be nurtured or quashed. Scotch has for generations tried nurturing.

In 2000, music at Scotch is unique because every boy participates, and because parents pay for music lessons whilst expecting school fees to cover lessons in other activities, like art, drama or sport.

Music serves several different ends, with different emphases over time. It trains some boys to play an instrument well, and exposes all boys to some instrument. It trains boys' taste and ability to listen to music. It develops co-ordination. Ferguson appeals to research showing that mathematical and spatial awareness, at primary school level particularly, is 'colossally' enhanced in people who learn instruments.[26] Scotch's immersion in music matches its commitment to science and output of engineers. Perhaps this helps explain why a school strong in mathematics will also develop a strong music school.

Walter Chang, 1982.

Art

Scotch had always taught drawing. At least 'it didn't require much homework'.[27] Artists had emerged, like Charles Richardson (said to have entered in 1862), who exhibited at the Royal Academy and was President of the Victorian Artists Society. When Gilray changed the name from Drawing to Art he hoped for a wider canvas, and soon Murray Griffin (1919, Art Master 1936–37) as well as teaching drawing wanted to teach art appreciation, using a projector in a dedicated studio. The Finance Committee decided the timetable did not allow for a second room solely for art. So Francis Roy Thompson (staff 1937–46), the distinguished Australian artist, began lunchtime talks, continued into the 1950s by Oscar Helms (1927, staff 1936–71; called 'Oscar' by the boys and 'Bill' by fellow teachers) and Frank Paton (1924, staff 1947–71). They spoke, for instance, on the Heidelberg School or the history of Melbourne architecture. No doubt they hoped to reach boys who were interested but not enrolled in art. Mike Reid (1958) praises the excellent introduction Paton gave him to the work of modern artists like Gauguin and the architect Frank Lloyd Wright.[28] Reproductions of artists such as Turner or Murillo hung in classrooms from at least 1910, but were rarely elucidated.

A picture of an old boot, by J.G. Liddell, published in the 1948 *Collegian.*

Art was not regarded as a serious subject for study. It consisted of 'still life' drawing, art-history and gouache painting on paper, only in the classroom. Drawing was its essence. At Bruce Pettigrew's first lesson with John Shirlow (said to have entered 1883, Drawing Master 1926–36), 'the task was to draw a jug and he told us to draw an ellipse for the top as the first step. He was horrified to find that I had drawn the two axes. "That's no way to draw an ellipse" and with one stroke he drew a perfect ellipse.'[29] An old cadet boot, dirty, wrinkled and well-worn, had to be drawn from various perspectives for weeks on end. Later, the gentle Paton chided Reid that 'Ellipses don't have corners'.[30] Into the 1960s, the elaborately over-dressed[31] Helms taught Art 'formally and with little imagination';[32] 'too 2-dimensional … No use of oils allowed or experimentation.'[33] Yet Helms inspired other boys, and outside the curriculum he encouraged the Art Club where boys modelled clay and made lino cuts, or went to see French paintings at the National Gallery, where Jeffrey Hawes (1953) wrestled with nudes ('very unshapely and graceful curves were missing') or Picasso (who 'lost all sense of proportion but not colour').[34]

Donald Cameron, designer of Australia's first Christmas postage stamp, widened the range and scope of art activities and techniques, and taught in a more orderly and sequential way. He 'gives us an assignment to do each week and then gives us a demonstration at the end which leads on to the next week's assignment. We are starting off with a simple outdoor sketch.'[35]

His successors were the eccentric and student-focused Rick Rowton (staff 1977–84) and the long-suffering Kim Hornby (staff 1985–92), who combined professionalism with an easy manner. Under these two men many difficult boys found a haven and meaning in the Art rooms. Art's changing nature means that the current head, Chris Taylor (staff 1993–), has expertise both in formal art and in modern technological and computer processes.

Unlike music, art's leading teachers have been outside the main activities and lacked the principal's ear. But it is now done by 620 boys, and their work is regularly displayed at the Lithgow Centre's fountain and in the Principal's ante-chamber. The Junior School had an artist in residence from 1977 and developed art to include photography, ceramics, silkscreen printing and sculpting. Older boys there could even distinguish between impressionists and expressionists.

Scotch's artists include Robert Wade, Harold Hattam (1931), and Philip Wischer (1984), as well as cartoonists Peter Nicholson (1964), Ward O'Neill (1969) and John Howcroft (1952) who drew the *Life. Be In It* cartoons.

Drama

Gilray also transformed drama. Mackie Hall brought the smell of greasepaint to Scotch, with backstage excitement and the 'magic of the curtain opening'.[36] Farces to entertain audiences gave way to serious plays meant to challenge performers and audiences. Shakespeare arrived. In the 1940s Lyne began his long direction of school plays, driving acting and production standards upwards. Harrison's 1970 production of Arthur Miller's *The Crucible* was 'the best school production' Healey had ever seen.[37]

The school plays brought various benefits. Learning to act equips a boy for the stage of life. It is 'invaluable for the development of poise and

personality so essential for the modern business or professional man'.[38]
Ancillary skills developed, too—as boys, Brian Randall (1952, OSCA
President 1981, Foundation President 1990–93) managed ticket sales and
Hugh McK. Wilson (1965, Finance Manager 1991–)
was the play's business manager.

Mackie Hall was outgrown. David Paul's inaugural
Middle School Play, *The Insect Play*, was the last held
there—'we had to fan the switchboard when the
dimmers were in operation'.[39] In 1968 Harrison's
production of *An Italian Straw Hat* was performed
elsewhere, and thereafter plays were presented in
outside venues, although during 1976–85 some
performances were in the new Science Lecture Theatre,
whilst Mackie Hall was surrendered to the Music
School.

Music, art and drama became part of the curriculum
as well as being extra-curricular. Drawing had long been
a subject that awarded marks. Music had an external
system of assessment into which Scotch boys soon
moved. Drama entered the curriculum later, in 1970,
with five periods a week for part of the year in Form I
(Year 7) and some for Form II. This was different from
putting on plays, insisted the first drama master,

A poster advertising
Scotch boys singing
on a drama tour of
Tasmania in 1935.

Harrison in 1974. Drama educated the emotions, the imagination and the
body, filling out a curriculum otherwise directed at developing only the
intellect. Drama allowed role playing, 'stepping into someone else's shoes'
and so extended the pupil's imaginative sympathies. It developed self-
confidence, improved oral communication, made the pupil more aware of
his body and his senses, and gave opportunities for working in a group.
Harrison therefore had the Dramatic Society disbanded and introduced a
structure parallel to music, with himself as Director of Drama.[40]

Drama was expanded with the Middle School Plays. Initially boys only
(1968) and then with St Catherine's (1969) and from 1970 with Ruyton. Ken
Mappin (staff 1969–87) started a second senior play continued by Colin Black
(staff 1980–87, Vice-Principal 1986–87), Stephen Ritchie (staff 1979– , Head
of Drama 1985– , Chairman of Common Room Association 1995–2000),
and David Mustafa (staff 1995–). School plays varied from a farce like *Arsenic
and Old Lace* to *Macbeth*, from Sophocles to Stoppard, and included musicals
as varied as *Hello Dolly* and *Whistle Down the Wind*. Plays have not been
especially tied to the syllabus and have leant towards large casts, with plenty
of scope for both the main actors and the smaller parts. By the 1980s, drama,
music and dance were intertwined in the Junior School, whilst in the Senior
School new courses were introduced for older boys.

Gordon Fisher (Captain 1941), summarising what he gained from Scotch, includes the phrase 'appreciation of the arts'.[41] No-one seems to have said this before Gilray. In 1989 Donaldson listed boys' aesthetic development as a routine part of the school's work.[42] Thus the school brought in an educational reform because it saw it as good, rather than in response to parental demand.

There is a shifting balance between curriculum, sport, extra-curricular activities and co-curricular activities. 'During the 30s and 40s all the newspapers devoted pages to school sport in a way that would seem incredible to the present generation.'[43] Some boys have always felt that sport was overemphasised at the expense of academic work, whether in the school's culture or in the choice of prefects. Other boys have felt the reverse, that too much emphasis went on academic matters. Since Gilray, a third group have felt that not enough emphasis was given to activities such as music. Scotch has long tried to bridge this rivalry. An 1897 prize had 'the express intention of encouraging boys to give an equal amount of attention to study and to athletics'.[44] Ashley Tucker (1992) was delighted at winning a prize 'for being the highest student on the academic list whilst being in a sporting team.'[45] Wei Ch'ng (1985) welcomed how 'Scotch encouraged a better all round attitude rather than just books or sport. It's given me a general grounding from physics to football.'[46]

THE LIBRARY

To underpin his enhancement of cultural activities, Gilray made Kirby librarian, secured endowments and built a new library on the top floor of the new Mackie Hall. The Library moved there in 1939 from Room 35, fumigating the books on the way.

The old Library was neither large nor continuously funded. In 1904 it held 300 books, and in 1934 only 3000. By 1953, Kirby had doubled it to

7000, and doubled acquisitions from 100 to 200 books per year. On his appointment in 1935 Kirby found the library uncatalogued, and run by a committee of well-meaning senior boys. Kirby catalogued the books, introducing the Dewey decimal system of classification. In 1949 Gilray gave him time to instruct junior forms on how to use the library, with a resultant rise in junior borrowers. He used the committee to institute a large-scale borrowing system.
Losses of books were 'not unduly high'.[47]

Half way through the century, most books borrowed were fiction. Geoff Serle (1940) read Kipling, *Chums*, the *Boys' Own Paper* 'and all the other literary effusions celebrating the British Empire and the English public schools'.[48] In the Junior School in the late 1940s Biggles boomed. From 1950 the library repeatedly claimed to detect less interest in him. 'Boys of eleven no longer have the intimate knowledge of the far-flung campaigns of World War II, with which the miraculous exploits of Biggles were so often connected.'[49] In 1957 boys in grades 5 to 7 were still constantly enquiring for sensational and sanguineous literature in the form of war stories. Biggles now seems to be considered to be a little tame! Owing to the multiplicity of these obtainable in inexpensive paper-cover editions, their inclusion in the Library seems unnecessary. What the Library and the class teacher should aim for is to provide examples of all types of adventure so that children are led to appreciate as wide a view of literature as possible.[50]

In the early 1950s, also, Enid Blyton was much in demand, 'especially among boys of eight and nine, who at one time rarely entered the Library'.[51] At least, so the librarians comforted themselves, W. E. Johns and Blyton wrote in a literary kind of English. In 1954, a frequent question in the Library was 'Are there any Space books in to-day?'—and this before Sputnik. Space books included the stories about Kemlo, a boy who could breathe in space, and works by A. E. van Vogt.[52] John Buchan was popular. Older boys read Mickey Spillane and Westerns.[53]

A survey of Scotch library-users' favourite books in 1956 found only the 18-year-olds showed variety.[54] The list was headed by the *Dam Busters*, *Reach for the Sky*, *Biggles*, *The Cruel Sea* and *The White Rabbit*. The school library pointed out that it had many better and more interesting books than the narrow selection the boys chose. Some boys already knew that, of course; a future professor of history devoured Orwell, Macaulay and *Dissent*.[55]

Satura

In 1936 the boys set up a permanent newspaper. The *Collegian*, in its early days so chatty, had become an increasingly formal journal of record and carried much Old Boy news. *Satura*'s frequency and newspaper format allowed it to carry debates and have fun.

Vol. 28   Friday, March 8, 1963   No. 1

Earlier newspapers lasted only briefly, like *The Thistle* or *Ragtimes* (a name that somehow slipped past the censor, for though it refers to music it was also slang for a woman's period). *Umpah, the Voice of School House* in 1922 was professionally laid out and printed. *Quisquiliae* in 1936 was handwritten, duplicated in purple by spirit copying (later Fordigraph), and bound in brown paper. The Junior School's typed and roneoed *Scotch Broth … Proceeds for Red Cross* revelled in schoolboy puns:

> Two soldiers entered a café and the following conversation took place.
> Soldiers: We want Turkey served in Greece.
> Waiter: Sorry, but I can't Servia.
> Soldiers: Well get the Bosphorus.
> The Boss: I don't want to Russia, but you can't Roumania.
> The Soldiers: Well, we'll have to go Hungary.

Scout Scoops in 1938–39 was typed and roneoed, with a yellow cover. Derek Sawer and Zelman Cowen brought out *Libertas* in 1935, but it fell at its second issue when Sawer wrote an article on Karl Marx and the censor suggested an article on Shakespeare instead.

Satura was part of this journalistic upwelling. Sawer and Jimmy Ochiltree started it 'because it was fun, not from great foresight'. It was their second attempt, the first one having been 'a rather messy affair involving duplicators'. This time they used professional printers whom they paid by selling advertisements.

> By the end of the year, *Satura* had a room for its editorial offices, a few wounds resulting from encounters with the Common Rooms (Masters and Prefects), a proper scorn, as befitted newspapermen, of the 'Collegian' people, an overweening pride and a sad mess in its business affairs … Revenue lagged behind costs, and time and time again we cut classes to bustle about selling more advertisements … Had it not been for the great forbearance of all forms of Authority at the school we would never have gone beyond two issues.[56]

Later advertisements were from boys with things to sell, which contravened Morrison's ban on 'buying, selling, or exchanging of books or any other articles'.[57] Capitalism had come to Scotch's internal life. Later, *Satura* was funded by a levy on fees.

Satura flourished as a newspaper for several decades. Complaints or suggestions were referred to appropriate staff, and the editors prided themselves that 'many of the changes witnessed around the school have originated' in letters to *Satura*.[58]

Its appearance improved as did newspaper technology. Council in 1965 awarded the editors an annual prize. The *Collegian* dismissed it as 'a rag of no great worth', 'And now it's getting fat and fattera / A truly torrid journal *Satura*'.[59] The gulf between the two publications was apparent in their format and style and even in their personnel, for few boys have edited both.

The censor was the Vice-Principal. Bond denied that he dictated content, and saw his role variously as a safeguard against libel, as protecting Scotch's interests, and as maintaining standards of good taste.[60] Humour was the most common area of dispute. If Cecil Campbell (staff 1933–67, Vice-Principal 1964–67; called 'Cammie' by his colleagues and 'Bats' by the boys) could not see the point of a joke, he censored it on the grounds that it was probably obscene. Andrew Kemp was 'mystified' over Fleming's reasons for 'scrubbing' many good jokes 'and many (what appeared to me) perfectly harmless letters'.[61]

Editing *Satura* was always exciting. James Simpson (1971) recalls 'all-night paste-up sessions; drives to the *Age* office in school hours; dealing with everyone from "Chesty" Bond (censor) to wild and zany contributors.

In short, being allowed an intellectual and managerial freedom.'[62] A staffer found that 'Satura was probably a defining moment, and a recognition that I could join and lead exciting, creative, slightly subversive activities and an influential part of an emerging positive sense of self'.[63]

The older newspaper tradition revived in the 1960s when Chris Johnson (1968) and Hugh Duncan (1968) wrote and duplicated an oppositional magazine called Saturated.[64] Class newspapers appeared, like 1A's Chronicle, 1B's Grapevine and 2 Russian's Bolshevik.

During the late 1980s, with the advent of desktop typesetting and printers that were better than dot-matrix, production moved into the hands of the boys. Satura lost its professional appearance and became an in-house publication on A4 sheets. Presumably this also reduced costs. Perhaps that was also why it became less frequent. That in turn made it harder to carry debates, although its editors believed that 'Now that the G.H.C. is defunct, Satura should be the clothes line of school boy opinion'.[65] From 1989 Satura ran items of current interest on topics outside the school (international affairs for example). It tries to strike a balance between reporting and entertaining. Today, crosswords combine with articles that show how far acceptable taste has changed over Satura's 65 years. Topics range from girlfriends to farting. (The latter is a subject on which teenage boys deploy a repertoire of taxonomy, from silent 'fluffing' (1941)[66] to 'SBD: Silent but Deadly' (1968, 1990).[67] In the 1960s, there was an 'etiquette if someone farted … audibly in company other boys were entitled to give you a single punch on the arm, unless you got in first by saying "Vince"; if you did this, you were immune to the penalty. It was quite common at one time to hear boys fart brazenly in company, and utter the magic word "Vince" almost simultaneously; and there wasn't a thing anyone else could do about it under the rules, which of course no-one ever questioned.'[68])

SOCIAL CONSCIENCE

At least two of Gilray's appointments were decidedly left-wing, as he guided Scotch along the road to becoming caring.[69]

Steve Yarnold (chaplain 1935–44) 'rarely wore a dog collar'.[70] He linked Christianity, politics, scholarship and a social conscience. 'He never bashed our brains with Scripture and codified morality yet he was able to guide pubescent boys. Just how I find hard to say; he was the opposite of a dogmatist.'[71] Rather, he 'questioned belief and faith, which he said should never be undertaken without the requirement of critical, rational and honest enquiry first and foremost, before drawing any conclusions'.[72] He 'approached Christianity not from a personal salvation point of view but rather the application of Christian principles to life here on earth.'[73] 'I suspect that the language which Yarnold used was affected by a Marxist view of history. He had a reputation of being "pink". But we were all so right-wing, and those who were not kept quiet about it.'[74] 'During the war, of course,

Marxist Russia was our ally'.[75] He was kindly, too, and if a boy looked lonely Yarnold 'without being too obvious offered words which were of comfort'.[76] He was, in sum, 'quite the most remarkably sincere and credible clergyman I have ever known'.[77]

Yarnold, supported by Scholes, helped make Social Services activities a regular part of school life. 'Camps for underprivileged children, staffed by teachers and schoolboys, were held in the late 30s and continued on in the 40s. A boys' club at the Fisherman's Bend housing estate was staffed by Scotch boys on one night a week'[78] and from 1940 Scotch boys served at National Fitness Camps at Cowes for boys from the poorer inner suburbs.[79] (Archdeacon George Lamble (1892) also worked in inner Melbourne, as 'a father to the fatherless and father-forsaken', heading the Mission of St James and St John, and helping unmarried mothers and girls with venereal disease.[80])

Eric 'Ric' Marshall (staff 1922–56), although he had a degree in English at a time when not all staff had degrees, never taught above the lowest secondary levels. He could

control them and keep them happy while driving in the small amount of knowledge they seemed able to absorb. The boys all loved him and no

RUGBY UNION

Even a small man can bring down a large man: 'take them low and lock their legs, and they simply cannot run!'[81]

Rugby Union football began at Scotch in the 1930s, favoured by Gilray (who had played for New Zealand and for Scotland) and the new chaplain, Yarnold. After one Scotch defeat Gilray visited Yarnold in his study and 'expostulated "The trouble, Yarnold, is that they don't tackle low enough … They should tackle like this", and with that he hurled himself across the room, bringing the startled Chaplain to the ground!'[82]

Rugby appealed to boys like Ken Fraser (1941) who found that playing Australian Rules meant that 'one could find oneself stuck in a back pocket or somewhere, with nothing to do for the greater part of the game, all the action being up the other end of the ground. With Rugby, on the other hand, the team moved as a whole up and down the ground, and you were "in it" all the time.'[83] David Thomson (1941) came from an isolated country farm; he had never played Australian rules and would have had no chance of getting in one of its teams.[84]

As few other schools played rugby, Scotch usually played against teams who were older and larger, or from interstate— exotic opponents such as naval and army cadets and Sydney Grammar. 'Paul Radford was habitually on the side-lines, racing up and down shouting encouragement and advice. Unfortunately, as he was a French Master, we were never too sure if he was yelling "Feet" to dribbling forwards, or "Vite" to tardy backs.'[85]

Rugby, 1980.

In the 1940s, ten-a-side rugby was a quarter sport in the inter-house competition. The season started a week after football, so that those not selected for football could turn to this, but even so in 1942 and 1945 there were not enough players for a full inter-house competition. In 1944, however, 65 players were available, and rather than house competition played a club competition outside the school. George Mullenger (staff 1935–65), coached rugby for 30 years.

There were only two rugby teams in 1952, and four in 1957, when the First XV were the best side since the war. In 1958 nearly 100 boys played Rugby. In 1959 it became a minor and then a full sport with 13 not 15 a side.

In the early 1960s Scotch regularly fielded five teams, but in the 1970s Rugby 'probably lost out more than any other sport to soccer'.[86] The 1972 1st XV won all their matches, no school crossing their line

for a try throughout the whole season. In 1980 Rugby started to grow again in numbers, possibly because the 1st XV coach was a Grade 6 teacher, Harry Weston (staff 1979–85), and so recruiting was good.[87] From 1984 to 1991 Scotch did not lose a single competition game at First XV level in Victoria, due to the very strong coaching by 'Jack' Dzenis (staff 1984–90). In the 1990s, Ewen McKenzie (1977), Andrew Heath (1987) and Richard Harry (1980) all became Wallabies, remarkable for boys from a Victorian school.

In the 1990s the Master-in-Charge of Rugby, also Head of English, published a news-sheet full of gripping evocations of the game. For example: 'The newly discovered try-scoring machine Peter Short [1999] … With his lanky gait, he is deceptively fast, and also very determined; on several occasions he simply kept running with a couple of tacklers grimly fastened around him, until either they fell off, or he was able to unload the ball.'[88] Key words in writing about rugby seem to be *fearless, courage, pace, power, speed*, and one finds phrases like *searing run*.[89] Even verse appeared:

There was action at St Kevin's for the word had
    got around
        That the card'nal, gold and blue were on
        their way
To seek revenge and glory on St Kevin's own
    home ground
        And make the match a Scotch red-letter day.

For since that dreaded final from the game a
    year before
        When the hopes and aspirations took a fall
There had been a secret building of the team to
    make the score
        A sound reflection of the boot and ball.

wonder as he understood them so well and knew how to treat them. How he could stand this drudgery for over twenty years is hard to imagine. Perhaps it was because he was so deeply involved in good works in his free time. ... A really great humanitarian, never fully recognised at Scotch.[90]

During the war, he and his wife Alma, called 'Grannie', befriended Asian seamen stranded in a country with a White Australia Policy. Later they founded the East-West Committee, described in Marshall's book, *It Pays To Be White*. Alma has her own entry in the *Australian Dictionary of Biography*. At least one parent, however, 'was not impressed with young minds being subjected to Marshall's political philosophy and anti-British sentiment'.[91] His humour ran to Spoonerisms like 'Carrick, you have tasted the last worm'.[92]

RIVALRY
Ranks and trappings

For most of the century a debate raged between those who wished to restrict the use of school and house colours and those who wished colours to be awarded more widely. Males enjoy badges of achievement. Boy Scouts accumulate them and cadets splash themselves with insignia. Caps and blazer pockets proclaim the domain of a boy's glory with letters (Aths, XVIII or XI) or devices (crossed oars). As in heraldry, arcane debates take place. Could First and Second teams players wear school colours on white sweaters? Or could only cricketers do so, because they take the field in those sweaters? Colours were a visible sign of achievement. Bill Pugh (1951) 'regretted not getting any colours, even house, ... though I really tried'.[93]

> making the 1sts Volleyball team in 1994 and receiving my playing top, knowing that very few got to play in a firsts team of any sort. A great honour.[94]

> Full Colours—being able to proudly display the candy coat with Basketball full colour along with 5 house sports [1985].

Colours were the outward sign of two hierarchies. They indicated the difference between sport played against other schools (by Scotch's best players) and sport played merely within Scotch between Houses.

Colours indicated, secondly, the relative importance of sports, because in the inter-house competition some sports won more points than others. Cricket, football, athletics and rowing were the chief APS sports, and when Scotch created inter-house competition in 1917 these four were deemed to be major, whilst swimming and tennis were minor. A win in a minor sport earned only half the points of a major sport in the competition for cock house. As Australian society took up new sports, their adherents wanted them included in the Scotch system and promoted to major sports status as their numbers grew. Thus in 1959 rugby and hockey joined tennis and basketball in edging up the ladder. Yet elevation was no mere bureaucratic process, for those above kicked at the climbers below. As late as 1981 there were boys who opposed colours for any but cricket, football, athletics and rowing. It cheapened colours to give them to rugby, tennis or hockey.[95] As for golf, badminton, squash, skiing, table tennis, volleyball and weight-lifting—even if played for the school the participants should receive second colours only.[96] Volleyball rose from nothing in 1975 to school colours in 1982 but, also in 1982, the General House Committee (GHC) refused school colours for winter tennis.

After Bishop's incongruous success in having music classified as a sport, indeed as a major sport, other activities took the same route (always against fierce opposition) by becoming house sports, first as quarter sports (where victory earned a mere quarter of a major sport's points), then half or minor sports, and then full or major sports. In the 1950s chess and debating became quarter sports, and in 1957 debating rose to half sport. (When Houses tried to use Chess Club equipment, which the club had bought itself, 'Club members were enraged and regarded the forced House competition as ludicrous and intrusive'.[97] In the long run, the club ceased to exist and chess became either a House activity or was played casually in the Library.)

Alongside disputing *which* activities to reward, came another argument about the activities' *nature*. Should not Scotch reward boys who put in hours of hard work, like umpires ('the man in white does the most work on the ground', he runs all the match, and gets no praise, nor even a piece of orange at half time[98]) or House music captains? Clubs could honour their officials with various emblems, although at this the editors of *Satura* protested: 'There is a limit'.[99]

Music colours for outstanding musicians began in 1979. In 1981 came colours for boys in senior plays, actors and backstage, who were said to put in as much time as boys training for the First Crew. Fearing the cheapening effect of widespread colours, Shugg suggested them only for outstanding boys. Chris Adam concurred, pointing out that he had no school colours although he was School Captain.[100] But 'outstanding' could only mean 'outstanding at sport', as John Buttery (1981) found when he failed to persuade the GHC to allow chess colours for Steve Solomon, Australian Junior Chess Champion. Chris Barnett (1983) argued that a chess player needs just as much practice, concentration, skill and dedication as any footballer.[101] They were told it would get out of hand.[102] Eventually colours expanded beyond players, to services and drama, and even for being a rugby official (like the 1999 Dux, Adam Sher). Few blazers now lack full colours, once a rarity. In the 1990s it was thought that blazer pockets should also display duxes of forms and of subjects, but colours remain only for the co-curriculum.

How should the school honour achievement? Should it value some activities over others? Should it value effortless ability over hard-won skill? Should there be many awards or a few god-like figures? Should sport and non-sport share the same system? These issues seem still alive, but much has changed.

The new twelve-house system in 1989 was co-ordinated by Richard Kleine, a mathematics teacher, who joked that he would allocate colours by points,

> one or more points for any given activity (ie $x > 1$, where x = the no. of points you get). To receive your colours you must amass a sum total equalling the integral number 12. Multiply this for every year you are from sixth form.
>
> (Let y = your form level.
>
> Let z = points you must get
>
> $\therefore z = 12(6 - y)$ QED)
>
> … Still confused so are we. All that we can suggest is that you do heaps of sport, and pass maths.[103]

The Group system: Five good men

As Morrison had academic departments, and Littlejohn created Houses, so Gilray introduced the Group system. Each age-group in the Senior School had a Group Master (from 1997 called a Head of Year). The two lowest age-groups shared the one Group Master. Gilray thus handled the whole Senior School through five men, as a colonel manages his regiment through the company commanders. A Group Master became knowledgeable about his group's problems and choices (curricular, developmental, age-related).

David Bradshaw (1924), Junior School Headmaster 1945–53.

From 1935 Scotch thus placed each boy in a matrix of three systems. The Group ran horizontally, for membership was determined by age and a boy rose through each Group. The House ran vertically, and a boy stayed in it as he moved up the school, for membership was determined by surname and stayed constant. The Department ran vertically, too, as boys progressed through successive years of French or Physics, but no boy studied in all disciplines, whereas Groups and Houses embraced every boy.

This new hierarchy challenged the authority of the staff who had previously ranked highest, the Senior Subject Masters, of whom only Will 'Hoppy' Waller (staff 1924–51), of English, became a Group Master.

Gilray's new system was an institutional response to Littlejohn's creation of a large school. It added a new way in which the school watched and controlled each boy, and yet the old ways remained, too. Growing organisms and organisations are alike in becoming increasingly complex, because new developments are added to, rather than replace, the solutions to older problems.

THE FINANCE COMMITTEE

How does a shy man manage Sir Arthur Robinson? That forceful leader, a visionary who yet attended to details, became Chairman of Council in 1934 on the resignation of Sir John MacFarland. Sir John was a man of few words, mostly verbs, in the employment of which he did not shun the use of the imperative.[104] As Chairman, however, his policy was 'to interfere as little as possible with the principal in the conduct of affairs, and he had found that policy very successful',[105] whereas Sir Arthur dominated. Robinson and Gilray began at the same time, and they worked together well. Under them, until the war intervened, Scotch boomed.

In 1934 Council set up under Sir Arthur a Finance Committee (from 1951 the Executive and Finance Committee). This entailed a large shift in power from Principal to Council, for the Committee met monthly and exercised far more control over day-to-day matters than Council had ever done. Such a step was taken as Littlejohn left and Gilray arrived, so it reflected on neither. It was precipitated by a need to deal with overdue fees (running riot in the Depression), and the Committee spent its early years pushing up

A SMALL STORY OF 'BILLY' BLENKIRON (1925, STAFF 1942–72)

The penalty for most infringements in Billy's class was the calculation of "12,345 cubed, and prove by long division" which my computer tells me runs to 13 digits, so it was a real incentive, especially as you had to get it correct! Lex Leslie received this penalty so many times that he kept a master copy, so that he just had to copy it out each time, which still took a *long* time.

Billy was renowned for never letting anyone off when homework was not presented—except once...

As he was collecting the homework he came to Altson.

"Where is your homework, boy?"

"Well Sir, it was like this. After football practice last night, Malcolm took my bag home by mistake."

No comment from Billy.

When he gets to Malcolm, "Where is your homework, boy?"

"Well Sir, it was like this. After football practice last night, Altson took my bag home by mistake."

"Ah", said Billy, "You could have done each other's homework."

"Oh, but Sir", they both chorused, "That would not be right—to do another boy's homework!"

There was the flicker of a smile on Billy's face, and he let them off.

Bill Meyer (1947)[106]

Two kinds of power and authority, 1938: Colin Gilray, Principal, and Sir Arthur Robinson, Chairman of Council.

income (by enforcing the fees), and driving down costs (for example, by competitive tendering for meat and vegetable supplies). Its detailed examination of the school's life extended to mattress repairs and even to re-washering taps. This illustrates Sir Arthur's dedication, and reminds us that there were no other committees to which such matters could go instead.

Managing detailed costs led to preparing cost estimates for 1935 and 1936 and to limiting expenditure until the Committee could lower the school's debt to the church. The Committee's financial responsibilities thus led it into a wider, executive role. This in turn led it into becoming a policy committee as it drew Council's attention to central issues, and made recommendations on them. It slid from being a money committee towards being a leadership group.

In 1937 it jettisoned its earlier goal of never allowing debt to rise, and instead urged a 'temporary increase' in debt to fund a building programme.[107] Within five years of its creation, by the outbreak of war at the end of 1939,

> the whole appearance of the School property has been revolutionised, its equipment brought to a high pitch and amenities provided which ... are not excelled by any Public School in the State. The permanent improvements include the Hospital, Staff quarters, Monash Lodge, Arthur Robinson House, new wing to the Science Block, fencing of the whole property, etc. To these must be added the Littlejohn Memorial Chapel, the total cost of which was provided by subscription; and the Mackie Hall about 75% of its total cost being met by the gifts from the Trustees of the Estate of the late Miss Helen Mackie.[108]

The Committee comprised the same four men for its first eleven years (over half of Gilray's headmastership): Robinson (1887), Chairman; Bremner Lewis (1895), Vice-Chairman; Oliver Addison (a parent); and Robert Mathieson. Gilray attended, too, but his role is obscure, which is typical of this reserved man.

'IN A HEALTHY BODY'

The hospital brought a few more women into the school's life, increasing the range of mother figures. Sister Stephanie Power (staff 1942–72) was 'kind and gentle'. Sister Molly Irving (staff 1938–72, widow of George 'Phantom' Irving, staff 1915–37), the first matron, was 'big and strong and made her points known' (1954), and was 'one of those women who just

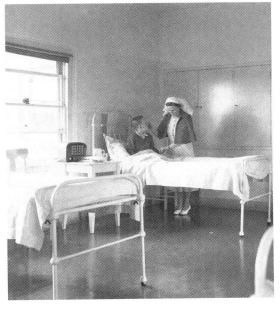

The neat modern lines of Scarborough's hospital, kept shipshape by Sister Power, produce a sparse effect, offset by the luxury of a modern wireless receiver (1951).

have a way with teenage boys. Boarders thought they could confide in her and rely on her advice.'[109] She was clearly the client of an SP bookmaker; boys in the hospital on a Saturday afternoon listened to the races with her and rejoiced in her occasional win. If she had a good day there might be something special for dessert in the evening (1955).

In 1919 the world-wide influenza epidemic had closed the school for a month, curtailed boarders' leave and kept whole classes away sick. The most serious health problem to hit Scotch in its 150 years was poliomyelitis (infantile paralysis). A disease most prevalent in the first half of the 20th century, it tended to strike children less than ten years old. At its worst it brought death or permanent paralysis (usually of the lower limbs). As the only major disease that targeted school-age children, its epidemics terrified the school. Doctors believed polio was spread by contact, so in late 1949 and early 1950 Scotch cancelled the Foundation Day Concert and cadet camp, closed the pool and kept boarders in. Parents took one boy away from school altogether. In 1956 Selby Smith co-operated with health authorities in a large scale experiment designed to discover the optimum dosage of Salk anti-polio vaccine for Australian children. (After American vaccinations spread polio by mistake, many Australians shrank from vaccinating their children.) Over 1200 Scotch boys were vaccinated and 300 gave blood samples for the necessary tests. Selby Smith saw it as a contribution to the community at large. In 1957 almost everyone in the Junior School underwent blood tests and inoculation against tuberculosis.

Until the early 1950s Scotch had repeated epidemics of measles, mumps and scarlet fever. These and other conditions like an infected ear would often keep boys away from school for longer periods than boys miss now, and many boys felt they never caught up on the missed schooling. In the fifty-year window of public health that has followed the discovery of antibiotics, the main health problem has been Melbourne's annual winter bout of flu and colds. Severity has varied. In 1974 a quarter of the staff and students were absent. Colin Davey (1944, staff 1948)

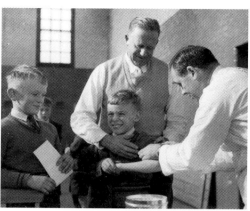

taught physical education and he must have been good because he later played football for Collingwood. He made us play football in the rain and this was bad. It was so bad that there was talk amongst the boys about us dying from inflicted influenza. We were going to be buried on a Saturday because funerals cost more on Saturdays and Mr Davey would have to pay! Serve him right![110]

In 1955 Scotch helped to re-establish public confidence in the Salk polio vaccine, here administered by Dr Percival Bazeley, Director of the Commonwealth Serum Laboratories. 'Ginna' Davidson comforts Don Beaurepaire, while Alister Edwards looks on.

WORLD WAR II

In 1939, Scotch's philatelists noted that a Dantzig stamp was reprinted with a new watermark of swastikas.[111] Hitler was on the move.

When war broke out, Scotch did what it could. Masters taught Mathematics and Physics evening classes to the RAAF. The boys made camouflage nets or knitted unexpectedly good scarves and jumpers for soldiers, and funded a motorised Field Dressing Station, costing £600, 15 times annual fees. The Rev. Eric Owen (1921), by contrast, was a pacifist. (He later sat on Council.)

As in World War I, Council suspended unfunded prizes and donated the money to a War Effort Fund. Scotch allowed fee concessions for the sons of Old Boys in uniform, and soon for the sons of anyone in uniform. One-fifth of the staff enlisted[112] and if this disadvantaged them financially, Scotch made up the difference. Replacement staff tended to be elderly (most young men were in uniform) but included, for example, a distinguished geologist, Dr George Pritchard (1888, staff 1940–46), and two escapees from Hitler's Germany, Herbert Bower and Dr Bernard Mendel. (That Gilray hired these two men while Australia was at war with Germany gives us his measure.) Bower's nickname was 'Vot' or 'Vottis' (from his pronunciation of 'What is'). Roger Hughes (1969), who found him a good teacher, once asked his advice and he 'replied with his German accent "Use the marvellous theorem". Again I toiled but I could not work out what the marvellous theorem was. Then it dawned on me—DeMoivre's Theorem.'[113]

There were widespread shortages of food, labour, building material and fuel. Asphalt paths fell apart, classrooms went unheated and the Scotch Lodge abandoned Masonic dress (full tails) due to clothes rationing. Butter was rationed, and boarders 'would print six lines on the top of the slab and then cut equally six pieces'.[114] 'Doc' Pritchard had a war-time vegetable garden, and working there with him was what Malcolm McKenzie (1947) liked most about Scotch.[115] (How to generate such close and satisfying contact between staff and boys is the school's perennial problem.)

To assist the war effort boys volunteered for summer camps to chop wood, pick fruit or harvest chicory and flax. In organising and entraining these boys, Arthur Mitchell cut his teeth for Scotch-at-Cowes.

At first, Foundation Day Concerts sang Burns's 'For England' and British patriotic songs. In 1941 the mood turned Australian, with 'Waltzing Matilda' and Margaret Sutherland's 'Land Of Ours'. (Her father, George Sutherland (entered 1870) had in 1901 published *Twentieth Century Inventions: A Forecast*.) In 1943–44 songs honoured the American and Russian allies.

On the Radio Club's initiative, gramophone records were made of the 1940 Foundation Day Concert, to raise money for the War Effort Fund. Radio station 3DB recorded some of the 1947 Concert, Bishop's last.

In 1942 the Japanese bombed Darwin. To prepare for bombs on Melbourne, Scotch held air raid drills, and the boys dug slit trenches and pasted muslin on the windows to stop flying glass. The glue was 'some kind of shellac lacquer and, there being no rubber gloves, it was a particularly messy job'.[116] Boys also learnt unarmed defence.[117] An urgent public meeting of parents debated whether to evacuate the school at once or wait till the government ordered it, by which time transport would be hard to come by and the reserved site might be lost to someone else.

Refugees fleeing from the Japanese were mainly Chinese or Dutch like Pieter Marseille (1947) who brought his own way of playing marbles. 'I fired the marbles with my middle finger and not with the thumb like the Aussies. It was more accurate and sometimes other kids came over to have a look.'[118]

In contrast to the school's warlike mood in World War I, this time Scotch talked more about how Old Boy casualties obliged boys to become worthy citizens. Yarnold, who was 'always available for a discussion (and argument) and constantly introduced us to literature and current writing on the topics of the day ... helped us set up the Senior Assembly (our own Parliament) to discuss in a democratic forum any issue of concern'.[119] It comprised students in the three final years of schooling. At first concerned with fundraising for the war effort, under the leadership of the 'brilliant'[120] Arthur Burns (Captain 1940) it 'evolved into a forum with democratic ideals raising such issues as the running of the House system, compulsory sport, the extension of the school playing fields and ... holiday camps for the disadvantaged'.[121] (Burns later became a foremost scholar on superpower rivalry.) They developed 'a strong interest in social service and in community welfare issues. ... It was a period of idealism.'[122] They encouraged students to be more caring within and without the school community and to have some say in the policies and running of the school.[123] 'War-time Scotch brought forth a period of idealism and social awareness. Boys at a young age showed an amazing willingness to serve—we were galvanised by the war effort on the one hand and the intellectual and social challenges posed by teachers such as Steve Yarnold, John Bishop, Francis Thompson and Colin Gilray.'[124]

Wesley College's buildings were commandeered by the US army, and Scotch offered Wesley a home. In the mornings Scotch used the classrooms whilst Wesley played sport, dug trenches, made camouflage netting, took art appreciation, etc., and vice versa in the afternoons. This worked well, perhaps helped by Wesley's Headmaster being Neil MacNeil (1911). Scotch even barracked for Wesley against other schools. John Philip (1944) thrived on Wesley's library, well stocked with modern writing.[125] To help Scotch accommodate Wesley, the army built two single-storey timber buildings near the Morrison Street gates, and the green grandstand with dressing room, showers and lockers underneath.[126]

Officers of Cadets, c. 1950.
Standing (from left): Harold Blenkiron, Stuart Sayers, Keith Elliott, 'Bill' Helms, Ron Bond (seventh Vice-Principal, 1968–85).
Seated (from left): Charles Boyes, Ewen Davidson, Frank Fleming (fifth Vice-Principal, 1956–63), Frank Nankervis.

At least 314 Old Boys died. The grimmest thing in Alec Hilliard's time at Scotch was to hear the weekly reading of Old Boy casualty lists.[127] John Jones remembers 'saying goodbye to boys in uniform and perhaps only some months later Mr Gilray would announce that so-and-so was missing in action or killed'.[128]

After World War I, the War Memorial Fund paid to build the new school at Hawthorn, but the similar Fund after World War II raised scarcely enough to build a memorial of names, until the McKay brothers made up the balance. The wars were different, and this second war did not evoke the same passionate feelings. It was somehow a more real war, fought in home waters, impinging directly

MEN OF INFLUENCE, MEN OF WEIGHT

Sir Neil Fairley (1908) in 1942 was the first Old Boy to become a Fellow of the Royal Society, whilst in one class in 1941 were three future Fellows, Richard Dalitz (Dux 1941), John Philip (1944) and Alan Head (1942).

W. S. Robinson (1890), Sir Arthur's brother, an industrialist and mining magnate, was the 'first Australian to become one of the world's greatest financiers'.[129] From a base in London he helped shape Australia's, and to some extent Britain's, economy in the 20th century. He was godfather—and more—to the Australian base metals industry, the Commonwealth Aircraft Corporation and to Australian aluminium smelting. From 1926–47 he was Managing Director of Zinc Corporation (now part of Rio Tinto, the largest mining company in the world), and its president until 1951 when he was succeeded by his son, Lyell Robinson (1915). In World War II W. S. played such a key role that, when he declined all honours, Winston Churchill presented Scotch a Bible printed by the great 18th-century printer Baskerville.

Cecil McKay (Captain 1918–19, Deputy Chairman of Council 1950–56), Managing Director of H. V. McKay Massey Harris, led the engineering industry against the unions and helped set up the Institute of Public Affairs, of which Charles Kemp (1929) was Director 1948–76, and father of two Liberal ministers, David (Dux 1959) and Rod (1963) Kemp.

Sir George Knox (1901) was an effective and impartial speaker of the Victorian Parliament. Sir Walter Murdoch (1891), literary scholar and friend of Deakin, became Professor of English in Western Australia where Murdoch University is named after him (Scotch is the only Australian school with universities named after two Old Boys—Monash and Murdoch). Ian Maxwell (1919) became Professor of English at Melbourne University, 1946–68, followed by Chris Wallace-Crabbe (1950). Norman Harris (1906) was Chairman of the Victorian Railways in 1940–50. He proposed an underground railway for Melbourne, and the Harris blue trains in the 1950s were named after him. Sir James Kennedy (1897) was president of the Congregational Union in 1940–41.

Hugh Pennefather (entered 1908) became a leading wool-classer. He believed that sheep-breeding was a total concept and classed many famous merino studs and flocks. When asked what he looked for in a ram, he replied 'Lust'.[130]

on civilians through rationing and the threat of invasion. The heroic poetry of the first war did not recur, and the more matter-of-fact attitude extended even to funds for memorials.

For the Memorial Hall, Scarborough could not obtain or match the tiles of the 1914–18 War Memorial. Instead he put the new Honour Roll on the western, opposite, wall, on three large sandstone panels, designed to appear as one memorial. The format is the same, a simple list of names without ranks or decorations. Otherwise, this second monument differs from the first in several ways. Whereas the dead of the Great War float on high, a little lower than the saints, the dead of the second war, who might have been put at the same level on their wall, are pushed, by the newly built gallery, down to eye-level, so that boys look at the dead Old Boys man-to-man without having to crane their necks. And whilst the first war names are now hard to read, black letters on mottled stone, the stone this time is a plain grey on which the chiselled gilt names are all too legible and personal— BLOM, E. D. O. ... STEEL, J. H. ... In the chapel, World War II is commemorated in its western window, replacing the original amber panes. As the window is invisible from outside and is behind the congregation inside, it is little known. A single large theme might have worked better than the many small symbols.

None of this occurred until the 1950s, because the war, for long after it ended, threw a shadow of shortages and rationing over Gilray's final years.

Gilray transformed Scotch. He did so by the remarkable financial and architectural achievements of his early years, by acquiring prints and an impressive gramophone collection, and by appointing outstanding people. Bishop and Monteath (music), Helms, Paton and Francis Thompson (art), and Arthur Davies and Alec Lyne (drama) 'introduced aesthetic and cultural standards not previously a feature of Scotch. Watching these passionate teachers (and artists) win the hearts and minds of the boys was a highlight of my school days,' says Laurie Muir (Captain 1942).[131] Yarnold (chaplain), Ric Marshal, and Gilray himself, similarly inspired boys' social conscience. Given Gilray's 'seemingly conservative outlook, that fact that he was prepared to appoint people unusual in dress, appearance and views was really amazing'.[132] In a Senior School with about 40 teachers, the impact of each appointment was greater than today.

Gilray pervades what was achieved, although he himself seems sometimes in the background (just as Scotch's new music and drama complex in 2001 is not named after him). The Old Boys of his time retain a truer picture of him, as a dominating presence, and they are jealous of his reputation. 'I often feel', muses Brett Harvey (1950), 'that Gilray was never given full credit for his efforts at Scotch. He was a very fine and strong man.'[133]

9

SELBY SMITH

1953–1964

R ichard Selby Smith as headmaster looks deceptively effortless. His brisk, intelligent touch made all that he tackled seem straightforward, and his light discipline concealed that he ran a tight ship. He was blessed with few external troubles. He improved staffing and buildings, and launched the school into professionally run fundraising whilst soothing church opposition to receiving the funds that Prime Minister Menzies poured into education. He left the curriculum alone, but the education that staff provided as individuals was broadened by his deliberate appointment of masters from many backgrounds.

For a school just past its centenary, Scotch was strangely innocent in the appointment of headmasters. Scotland chose Lawson and Morrison, and the Council that chose Littlejohn was specially enlarged. Only with Gilray had Council made the decision itself. Precedent was slight. So at Gilray's retirement Council's first response was to ask Edinburgh to find the replacement. Upon reflection, Council advertised, in Britain, Australia and New Zealand.

The salary was £2000 annually (twenty times annual fees), with house and keep provided and superannuation on a contributory basis. For the first time the headmaster would earn merely a flat salary, without a bonus if he made a profit. Presumably this change followed from Council's own control of the budget since it had set up the Finance Committee. Applicants should be aged under 40, with an honours degree, and be a communicant Protestant, preferably Presbyterian.

A sub-committee, advised by Gilray, winnowed the applications to four Australasians and two Britons, but could agree no further. From Britain, the Moderator of the Church of Scotland (who had visited Scotch recently on its centenary) reported favourably on Selby Smith. Council held a preferential vote. Selby Smith won a majority on the first count.

Aged 38, he was Deputy Chief Education Officer in Warwickshire,

Richard Selby Smith, fifth Principal 1953–64.

responsible for all schools. Educated at Rugby (where he was school captain), Oxford and Harvard, he had studied and taught in the United States, which was unusual for an Englishman of that time. In World War II he enlisted as an ordinary seaman and after service at sea and on the Naval Staff was finally a lieutenant-commander. He was the first Englishman to be Principal, and the first Principal not to bear the name of a King of Scotland. He belonged to the Public School tradition of duty and challenge, but he stood outside the school's Scottish Presbyterian austerity.

He arrived by sea in 1953 with his wife, Rachel, and their two sons, Christopher (Dux 1959, Captain 1960) and Peter (Dux 1965), then aged ten and five. The ship was met by senior Council members, the Moderator and Gilray. It was the first time a Principal had met his predecessor. This was the last time the school acquired a principal without having met him first, and we may imagine the mutual shock. Selby Smith was a youthful, brown-eyed six-footer (1.83 m), 'English in manner and rather gentlemanly.'[1] He spoke rapidly with a clipped English accent, and his surprisingly large eyebrows took a vivacious part in the conversation, as did his wide and flashing smile. He had great charm. From his arrival Scotch stopped hyphenating his name.

At his installation, the Vice-Chairman of Council, the Rev. Alan Watson of Toorak, referring to the previous Headmasters, suggested that

> you do not seek to imitate them, but to imitate their spirit; not to do as they did, but to do your work in your own way, emulating their motives for service and devotion to duty. We want you to be yourself. We want you to bring your own personal contribution, and to feel perfectly free … to exercise in a bold and resolute fashion those abilities which your training and experience have given you.[2]

It was what Scotch would like to say to every new boy.

On 1 May he took Assembly. Littlejohn's portrait gazed straight at him from the west wall opposite (before gallery or War Memorial were built there) and Selby Smith thought, 'I'd better get this right!' Without antipodean contacts (Littlejohn and Gilray had at least known New Zealand), he toured Victoria. He saw where his boarders came from. Old Boys gave him 'spontaneous loyalty and goodwill',[3] and had the fun of introducing a Pom to Australia. He chased emus by car, hunted kangaroo and watched shearing. In 1954 he dined with OSCA's Sydney branch.

Within the school, he probably had to overcome reactions to his youth. Principals had been aged over 50 for most of the past 80 years. 'There was some relaxation in manner as befitted the times and his wife was charming to us boarders—and we weren't used to much charm. Being the post-war period, many Edwardian attitudes were changing and Selby Smith seemed to epitomise these changes.'[4]

At first, Council asserted its authority in small ways such as disapproving a minor expenditure. A lesser man might have grown cautious and started to submit all sorts of things for approval before he acted. Selby Smith kept taking action, and soon won Council over.

His reports at Council meetings were of such breadth and clarity that they were preserved, which was new. They drew Council into the school's daily life. He managed his Council very skilfully, recalls Davis McCaughey (Council 1953–80): Council, 'when you looked at it round the table, was full of good will towards the headmaster but unlikely to be easily moved to make many changes'. Selby Smith's reports often raised matters for action, but often also sought merely 'to inform the council. And he would encourage them to discuss it with him and ask questions. … He was so good at inserting into people's minds a fresh understanding of the school and what had to be done in response to that, and then letting the seed grow.'[5] His memoranda focused Council's discussions with a clear statement of problems and possible solutions. When, on State Aid to Church Schools, Council adopted his advice 'as an expression of its own opinion', no stronger endorsement was possible.

BUILDINGS AND FINANCES

In his first few years, Selby Smith moved both slowly and fast. He judged that the school ran well, and that he could take a while to learn its ways and its role within Victoria. He kept Bowden on for a few years as Vice-Principal. Not having been a headmaster before, he was prepared to find his way carefully. As an experienced educational administrator, however, he acted confidently in that domain. Almost at once he proposed a list of building improvements, with estimated costs and likely sources of funding. He had the impetus of being a new principal, and the energy of a man in his thirties replacing a sexagenarian, and he galvanised Council, which had baulked only a few years before at a new building for the Junior School, into a whole programme of building.

This first round of buildings, in the 1950s, attended to pressing needs, and was funded by money to hand. The Junior School gained a two-storey Sub-primary. To avoid cutting into the junior oval or the stand of gums at the Callantina Road gate, it went on the Hill where Arthur Robinson House had zig-zagged wartime air raid trenches. Building costs were soaring (500% since 1939), and rose further when foundations had to go deep because the edge of the Hill proved to be merely shale fillings taken from the Glenferrie Road cutting and used for terracing Hawthorn Glen's grounds fifty years before. The space vacated by the Sub-primary, under Arthur Robinson House, became the Junior School art and craft room, which Tapp (Selby Smith's new appointment as Junior School Headmaster) had made his first priority. The school staff under Arthur May did the work, from plans drawn up by Miss Marion Scott (Junior School Art Mistress 1946–62). Parents raised money for the furniture. Scott encouraged parents to see art as something for all boys.

Garth Tapp (1939), Junior School Headmaster 1954–77, in 1970.

An organ for the Memorial Hall was bought at less than cost price, a thought to warm Scottish hearts. It had been built for Wellington College, NZ, which had difficulty installing it. It was dedicated in 1955 with the 1939–45 War Memorial. It was vast (946 pipes), and had 'fire and brilliance'.[6] With 'a great selection of stops' it was 'lovely to play—quite gentle keyboard actions (electric)', although there was some time delay.[7] Scotch dispensed with the hall's Erard grand piano.

The pipes loomed into the hall. 'I always wondered what would happen if the pipe-box would crash to the ground. I never wanted to sit underneath it!'[8] The bellows and engine went in a new brick structure bulging on the outside wall. This was one of Scotch's rare acts of vandalism. The bulge's functional square shape clashed with the building's vertical lines, and its Rippletex bricks clashed in colour and texture with the Hall's smooth red bricks. On the less-seen northern wall, the visual damage would have been limited. On the southern wall, it thrust crassly into the school's greatest panorama, the wide sweep of buildings around the Main Oval. Pictures of that vista, ruined, ceased to appear, and photographs of the Memorial Hall had to be taken from a north-east angle to hide the wart on its south. Presumably neither Council nor Scarborough saw anything amiss. Tastes change. Healey, for example, thought the Memorial Hall ugly. But since there was no plan to demolish the Hall or clad it in new brick, it is odd that Scarborough could not see the need to preserve its appearance, at least on its Main Oval side.

Eventually, the bulge constituted a challenge. In a 1989 painting, Robert Wade (1949) blurred the blemish out of existence. John Ingham (1969) (see p. II) and Christian Bromley (1998) photographed it when the shadow-line of the setting sun ran along the top of the bulge.[9] Ben Shearer (Head of Junior School Art 1980–94) squiggled the bulge into inoffensiveness in the sketch of the Hall used by the Foundation and on lists of valedicts. A new organ is planned for 2001, and a new façade for the bulge.

New administrative offices appeared outside the quadrangle's north-east corner. Emboldened by all this building, the teachers in 1953 suggested extensions to their common room, then in the south-east corner of the quadrangle. Amenities were primitive. Lyne (staff 1942–74) recalls:

* Robert Wilson, a Scottish mathematics teacher, the boys nicknamed 'Nutty' because he pronounced 'Nothing' as 'Nutting'.

Winter heating was provided by about four water radiators and a hot plate under the south windows where half a dozen privileged members would stand. The tables were large enough for six men but only large enough to accommodate their six brief cases so lunches were eaten from the tops of the cases or with the cases cluttering the narrow passage ways between the chairs. Long-time members—Billie Wilson [staff 1911–56; his name was Robert; the boys called him 'Nutty'*], Bosh Bowden, Alan Ross [1922–60] and Bill Adams—had desks under the east windows—with drawers! The rest of the staff had one locker each no larger than those provided for the boys. The pegs along the west wall were quite inadequate for the gowns and winter overcoats and umbrellas, which resulted in a morning scramble through a mass of black cloth and perhaps as a final resort to someone else's gown when yours could not be found. In one corner ... was the entry to the single toilet and urinal. Next to it was a sink with a cold water tap. One tiny felt notice-board was crowded with little pieces of paper. Those who wanted a cup of tea at recess or lunch time had to journey to the diagonally opposite corner of the quad where we could use a tiny screened off corner of the tuckshop to pour the tea from an urn on a bench. There was scarcely room to move and many a cup of tea was spilled over a neighbour. Periodically the voice of Miss Kniebusch [staff 1926 (?)–56] would boom over the partition, and the noise of the boys in the queue, with the words: "You masters, be quiet in there, you're making too much noise". Then it was a rush back through the hurrying mass of boys to pick up books and not be late for class. ... At some time a gas ring must have been put in next to the sink, because we always had to ensure that someone with a spare period put the kettle on. One of the early C.R.A. [Common Room Association] requests was for an urn to replace the kettle. This meant we didn't have to go to the tuckshop but we still had to provide each his own cup—stored away in the locker when not in use. Some were never washed properly—how could they be without facilities?—and became as brown inside as the tea itself. Carrying the cups of tea (no saucers) was almost as dangerous as it had been in the tuckshop as we moved among desks, chairs, cases and fellow masters.[10]

The Masters' Common Room c.1950. George Mullenger (white) plays Don Walker.
Watching (from left): Albert Orton, Ken Luke, Alan Ross, Henry Bowden (fourth Vice-Principal 1935–56), Harry Fry, Harold Blenkiron, 'Cammie' Campbell (sixth Vice-Principal 1964–67), P.R. D'Abbs

Meetings had to be elsewhere, in a classroom, adult frames jammed into boy-sized desks. Around 1950 when 'we were very short of staff lockers, someone dared to saw the padlocks off two lockers which seemed to be currently unused—one had belonged to Kelso [staff 1923–42] who had died at least twelve years earlier, and the other to Bienvenu [staff 1917–40] who died in 1940!'[11]

The architect consulted the masters through the Principal, and used a plan drawn by Bill Helms. The extensions were completed in 1955 and included a new quiet room. 'This was a great asset as it really was impossible to do any work or any corrections in the old room—there were always a few men who carried on a loud conversation—or sang. For years (or was it only months?) Alan Ross sang or whistled continuously: *How much is that doggy in the window?*'[12]

The common room was for teachers only. The Bursar never went there. When Healey asked if he could come, they assured him he was welcome at any time, so he often went there, and enjoyed it.

In 1954–55 a new Biology curriculum led Scotch to enlarge laboratory facilities. The maintenance staff built a new Matriculation Biology Laboratory between the cadets' QM Store and the fives courts. The old Biology Laboratory then became a new Junior Chemistry Laboratory. The old Junior Chemistry Laboratory then became a balance room for the Senior Chemistry Laboratory. (As each change prepares for the next, we are reminded of Selby Smith's wartime service on an aircraft carrier with the task of guiding aircraft in the right order to their target.) The stench of formalin still permeated the laboratories, as did the 'terrible smell' from the bunsen burners' coal-gas fumes. Later came the smell of gas released when 1 cent or 5 cent coins were immersed in beakers of nitric acid during lunch breaks.[13]

One other building had great consequences: the Scout Hut. It was built in 1957 so the scouts could store everything in one place. To fund it, scouts and their parents raised money in the traditional ways (a dance, bottle drives, stalls selling to Saturday sports players), and by staging 'Cardinal Follies' in the Mackie Hall. What they could not raise they borrowed from Council. The architect and builder gave their services free. The hut soon acquired the itchy smell of dust, and of creosote baking from the walls in hot sunlight. It was named after Rowan Macneil, the Scotch scouts' founder. Lady Baden-Powell opened it, the Rev. Frank Rolland dedicated it and the chairman of Council received it on behalf of the school. (That tripartite ritual is common to Scotch, and at other times there is also a donor, as when OSCA donates a portrait—or a chapel.)

Lady Baden-Powell opens the 1st Hawthorn Troop's Scout Hall in 1957.

This small hut unleashed Scotch's modern fundraising. To make donations tax-deductible Scotch registered a Scotch College Building Fund with the Taxation Department. Significantly, the fund was held by the school, not by the church.

DESKS

School and boy intersect at the desk, not just in the learning process but in a war of physical attrition. Furniture for boys has to be sturdy. Boys rise to this challenge. Scotch was always buying new desks.

To spare the desks, Littlejohn set up a board in the gym with a space for each boy to carve his name, but by the 1940s the desks were stained and scarred, and smelt of stale wood. These old cast-iron frame desks were replaced by new tubular steel tables and chairs, which appeared in the 1960s in the Junior School and in the New Geography Room. The school put this off for as long as it could in the 1950s and 1960s by having the carpenters make wooden desks. 'The type is old-fashioned somewhat in design but opportunities for the boys to dismantle them during class have been reduced.'[14] Even so, boys of the 1960s sat at old dilapidated desks so deeply engraved with the names of past pupils that they were hard to write on.

Single and double desks came in and out of fashion. Littlejohn favoured single desks. Perhaps they put each boy more on his own resources? In 1946 two-boy desks were used to seat three boys when the class was large. Later wooden desks were single and could be used 'as foot propelled dodgem cars (c.f. Fred Flintstone), with satisfying thunking noises whenever an impact occurred. The most furniture induced decibels I recall was when 3 or 4 of these desks were stacked vertically in a classroom then toppled. These old desks were progressively replaced with new steel desks and chairs around 1972.'[15]

A recurring fad, at least from 1918 to the 1960s, was Push Penny. Using small coins,

> Combatants usually started with their coins in diagonally opposite corners of the table. … the object was to knock the opponent's coin off the playing surface, without having your own coin ricochet off as well. Poorly aimed shots might strike obliquely and self destructively career off onto the floor. There were different hand techniques, flicking the index finger being the most common. Some specialists used the middle finger, braced between the two adjacent fingers. I hazily think there was another variation where wooden rulers were used, a bit like a billiard cue.
>
> Bigger desks such as the teachers' tables were used… I think this activity used to wax & wane, there being repeated epidemics a few years apart among new cohorts of students. When the new laminated desks were introduced about 1972, these provided a superior surface (smooth & flat) for push penny, but had the shortcoming that they were not long surfaces like teachers' tables.[16]

The cadets carried their rifles on public transport, with the bolts in! To store these weapons and other equipment, Scotch built a wooden Cadet Hut. It soon gained its characteristic smell of webbing, oil, leather and mustiness, and its characteristic sound of pipers practising where the uniforms were stored, as they deadened the noise. The army agreed to pay an annual sum towards the hut's cost, but failed to do so. Scotch first deployed its Chairman, a major-general (Sir Clive Steele), and then, on (Sir)

Henry Winneke's advice, sued the army. The army surrendered and paid up. It is a tale that illustrates Scotch's doggedness in dealing with external bureaucracies, repeated with the SEC and the freeway. One cannot help noticing, also, the difference between the methods of the cadets and the scouts in funding their new huts, the cadets from the government with a drain on Council's time and the scouts by their own efforts with no fuss. Baden-Powell would have approved.

The financial base for the rest of the building programme was laid down in the late 1940s and early 1950s, when the school began planned budgeting. At its centenary in 1951 Scotch was a relatively small business, with an annual budget of £113 000 (1100 times annual fees). The day-to-day accounts were well-kept and properly audited, but the management had little grasp of the underlying financial position. For example, in 1950 Council ordered architect's drawings for David Bradshaw's proposed Junior School extensions. Yet Council gave no prior thought to funding what it had asked for, was nonplussed by the cost and, indeed, did not know how much money it possessed. Almost childlike, Council asked the church how much money the school had, and whether it was enough. The amount held in trust funds by the church was soon ascertained, but Council needed also to know the school's running costs.

Thursday afternoon outside the Masters' Common Room in the early 1950s. The rifle hanging on the coat hook has its bolt in, which means it is a functioning weapon.

To ascertain these, in the late 1940s the new men running the Finance Committee pushed the Bursar towards producing the kind of documents later regarded as routine: cost estimates, a budget, comparative statements of receipts and payments, and annual estimates of profit and loss. In 1949 he included depreciation. Council members could examine these reports in his office, but from 1954 Council had them sent out to them. Winneke moved this (and perhaps he was also behind the increased pressure on the Bursar to have the 1953 accounts audited by June 1954!). To increase the accounts' usefulness, the Committee urged various steps. Items should be calculated the same way each year. Keith Wilson (1927, OSCA President 1962–63), who joined the Executive and Finance Committee in 1956, advised the Bursar on presenting the accounts. From 1958 the balance sheet included the investments that the church held in trust for the school. Before then, Council had not had routine knowledge even of large sums like the Cattanach and Mackie Bequests.

In 1956 the school plunged suddenly into a deficit of £5600. There was an 'unsatisfactory delay' before Council found out, and to prevent its being caught out again Council appointed 'a male accountant', Lindsay Locket. Male accountants perhaps had a higher order of training than female bookkeepers. Council also adopted Wilson's suggestion of an audit not annually but each term. Some of the disaster reflected on the bursar, Ken Field (Bursar 1953–85), but he had the excuse of being new.

One reason why Council wished accurately to know what it earned and spent was that it aimed to run at a surplus. In 1947 it decided to make an annual profit of £5000, to be used for building. This policy fell apart because of uncertain accounts and Korean War inflation, and in 1956 Council resolved instead always to make a surplus of 5% of gross income. Henceforth fees rose as required to meet that target. As a policy it was made public when fundraising began in the 1960s. The surplus went chiefly to erect buildings and to expand staffing. Since the surplus was raised from current parents, the money spent on staff and on building-related debt reduction benefited their boys, but the money spent on new buildings benefited only future boys.

Selby Smith completed much of his building without incurring debt, by emptying most of Scotch's piggy-banks, like the tuckshop profits (accumulated under its astute manager Miss 'Topsy' Kniebusch), and the Special Reserve set up to pay masters' pensions but no longer needed for this purpose because Selby Smith had had Scotch set up a superannuation scheme. The £10 000 War Memorial Fund paid for the Memorial Hall's new organ and gallery. The new Junior School building, however, was financed by borrowing £45 000 from the church. Scotch paid this off with a steady £3000 a year from its annual surplus, even when this turned the surplus into a loss.

Until that debt was reduced, Selby Smith began two lesser streams of work: replacing temporary buildings and renovating. He renovated several laboratories, and began a rolling programme of classroom renovation, redecorating several each year 'in rather lighter colours'. Healey continued this, and the income from the Endowment Fund was large enough to cover the cost. In 1981 Scotch accepted that classroom upgrading was a continuous cycle; when completed 'it will have been more than 10 years since its beginning, so it will need to start again.'[17]

Using the 5% annual surplus, Selby Smith undertook a steady succession of projects. He made the Junior School Cub Hut usable as a gymnasium (1958), so that indoor Physical Education became possible. He extended the Music School (1960), and built a New Geography Room above the tuckshop (1961). He began the gradual conversion of some classrooms into specialist rooms for subjects like History, Economics, and Modern Languages.

In 1959 Selby Smith launched Scotch on modern fundraising. He proposed four major projects: an Art and Craft Block; a new gym and pavilion; a new dining room, kitchen and maids' quarters on the Hill; and in the Junior School a new hall, library and changing rooms. As these would be 'very expensive', he suggested 'a full-scale appeal',[18] assuring Council

THE LINE OF HUNGRY BELLIES

The tuckshop itself was

far too small. It is not possible to serve the boys, at lunch time, as quickly as is desirable. In spite of a good deal of thought as to the best ways to form queues, and to keep them moving, and much help from the Probationers, it is a constant source of petty irritation, [yet] the position of the building is such that it is impossible to extend it; nor does it seem possible to make any really worth-while improvements within its present area.[19]

Arthur Davies, a teacher, saw the restrictions as character-building. The lunch bell unleashed a

headlong skirmish for positions ... The line of hungry bellies pressed slowly nearer to the counter, where saliva started in great gushes at the coloured piles of napoleons, lamingtons, cream slices, éclairs, sugared buns, chocolate biscuits, cream cakes, tarts, pies, and pasties. ... At home it is hard to get all

the elbowing, smashing, and tearing that honest enjoyment of food demands. It takes appetite away, to sit more or less still and quiet at a table to eat. In their wise direction of the school [the Headmaster and Council] had remembered that small boys must be allowed some natural freedom, and therefore ... In a practical and common-sense fashion [the boys] simply fought in a line until they could stuff themselves with whatever pastry and sweetened soda-water they could afford. This kept them from softness, and preserved the great Saxon tradition of tearing beef and sousing mead before and after battle.[20]

Selby Smith made what improvements he could, but in 1967 the queues took a quarter of an hour (and over half an hour on Mondays) and a future professor of economics suggested some efficiencies of production and distribution: that orders could be put in earlier and picked up by a class representative five minutes before end of fourth period.[21]

that overseas school appeals run with professional advice always succeeded.

In 1959 Scotch had only three main funds, all young: the Endowment Fund, the scout hut Building Fund, and the new Pension Fund.

OSCA had begun the Endowment Fund in 1953 as a Million Pound Endowment Fund. It did not achieve its aims. It certainly never raised a million pounds, and it stumbled through various difficulties associated with tax-deductibility and life insurance policies (its most common kind of donation). Such policies made the Endowment Fund a long-term project, and the money in hand amounted in 1960 to only £11 000 and in 1965 to £15 000. Even so, the school learnt much about fundraising, which gave a sureness of touch to the successful Buildings Appeal of the 1960s.

To the anger of its creators, Selby Smith blocked a further Endowment Fund appeal in 1960. Douglas Bain, Chairman of Council 1959–63, concurred, as this fund lacked specific goals to use as selling points. Instead,

Selby Smith persuaded Council to launch an appeal for capital funds with the Wells Organisation as consultants. Selby Smith then left on sabbatical leave, whereupon Bain promptly had Council put the Appeal instead in the hands of Donald L. Chipp and Company. In 1963, when the appeal changed into a follow-up phase, Selby Smith had the National Fund Raising Counsel take over.

The campaign was chaired by Bill King (1920), and aimed at raising £250 000 (1250 times annual fees). With belated approval from the church, it was launched in 1962 by Sir Arthur Rylah, not an Old Boy but Deputy Premier, and raised £225 800, of which only 5% went on costs. Although short of its target, it laid the groundwork for later appeals. It doubled the number of Old Boys on the mailing list to 9500. It revealed the commitment of various groups to the school: unexpectedly, parents gave more than Old Boys. (Parents were three times more likely to donate, and made larger donations.) A complex fundraising structure deployed teams and individuals armed with brochures, newsletters and a manual. The money went into an account held by the school. In 1962, on the strength of the appeal, Council obtained church permission to mortgage the Hawthorn site for an overdraft of £200 000 to be used for building.

The appeal also accelerated a change in Scotch's self-image. It came to see itself less as a self-contained world inhabited only by masters and boys, and more as the focus of a wider community. To the needs of that community Scotch now paid more attention. It built new ladies' toilets. The scoreboard had to be legible to squinting Old Boys, so a new one was built in 1962. It was operated by boys: 'I was responsible for this for about 2 years. I liked organising things and numbers, and this combined the two' (1968).

The appeal funded Selby Smith's final round of building. It involved his usual successive decanting from one part of the school to another. A new scoreboard graced a new Senior Pavilion finished in 1963, which allowed the demolition of the old pavilion.[22] That old pavilion was 'one of the most attractive buildings in the School', said a campaigner for its preservation, but the editors of *Satura* replied: 'You must be kidding, it was only a temporary construction'.[23] On its site, between the Changing Rooms and the Main Oval sprang up a new Art and Science Block, finished in 1965, with Art teaching rooms and storage upstairs, and new Geology and Biology laboratories downstairs. Box-like and functional, it smacks of the 1960s, and its exposed rooftop plumbing recalls the Pompidou Centre. The Senior Art Studio and the Museum were then freed to become advanced laboratories.

Douglas Bain (1917), Chairman of Council 1959–63.

The new Junior School Block (1963) contained a gym, library, remedial classroom, music room, toilets and tuckshop, and was named after J. Ross Montgomery (1910), who donated £100 000.

Another £50 000, from Irene Longmore, was for a library to commemorate her late husband, Carlisle Francis Longmore. He had entered Scotch in 1897, almost 70 years earlier—a long lead-time for a return on an investment, but possible for an established institution. Selby Smith built the Longmore Library north of the Memorial Hall. Keith Darling (Librarian 1958–89) wanted to move the library from Mackie Hall where it was remote from the main school. Since Logie-Smith had his eyes on Mackie Hall for music, their interests converged. Even before the Longmore, Darling introduced library periods, extended library hours and allowed borrowing. He even lent reference books, pleased to see any book in use.

On the Longmore's ground floor was a new Masters' Common Room— a large well-lit work room, a separate lounge with tables and chairs, and a kitchen with facilities to heat food. There was a small quiet room, a conference room, a small interview room, adequate (male) toilets and hanging space for gowns and coats—'in fact all the things we had lacked before'. A large sheltered entrance gave boys easy access to the staff. Unfortunately, 'Selby Smith was adamant that the staff would never be any larger,' whereas Healey, arriving before the building was completed, at once had the masters' desks made smaller so as to fit more in, though staff still 'felt like kings … We even had Mrs. Moyle to pour our tea and coffee and wash the cups!'[24] Healey believed the new accommodation fostered a friendliness between young and old on the staff that was not present when he arrived.[25]

Amidst all his building, Selby Smith scarcely mentioned his own accommodation. Only after he resigned did he feel free to push this firmly, and a house for the Principal was finished under Healey. The church at first refused permission, saying it was too costly, but it was paid for almost entirely by the £30 000 bequest from William Cattanach, though the building was not named after him. The school thought of Cattanach's bequest as its own money and had regarded church approval as a formality, but in the church's eyes the school owned nothing, for it all belonged to the church.

STATE AID

In 1956, as costs soared, the church asked its schools to comment on receiving government aid. Selby Smith, an Anglican who had worked for the English state-funded education system, did not share the Presbyterians' apprehensions. They feared government interference, but he reminded them that the government already monitored church schools (to ensure standards), and already subsidised church schools (for example, by allowing tax-deductions for fees and donations). He urged the church to campaign to increase those benefits. As for direct grants, the Free Church had accepted

EXTINCTIONS

Scotch's ever-widening range of activities has also seen some extinctions. Quoits, for instance, and inter-school shooting as a sport.

'Tort' Jamieson founded the Museum in 1911. Boys donated rocks and minerals, shells, reptiles in spirits, and nulla-nullas, woomeras, spear-heads, stone axes, hair string and microliths. By 1950 it had Roman coins, items from Egyptian tombs, and native items from New Britain. More educationally, the rock display helped Geology students, and the collection of 2500 shells was classified by the Waratah Club. Boys' fascination with weapons meant that swords, pistols, rifles, or a muzzle-loading musket drew an average of 50 boys each lunchtime. Mrs Aeneas Gunn, author of *We of the Never-Never*, donated a fine collection of Australiana in 1930.

The Museum was run by boys. The handful on the 1950 committee enjoyed the club-room and brewed coffee on the bunsen burner. 'Museum work was grudgingly conceded to be an alternative to Cadets or Scouts so on Thursday Afternoons I didn't have to go to "The Bludgers' Room".'[26] 'Among the rich assortment of mere curios in the Museum there were some items of genuine historical or scientific value but we had no adequate training or supervision and despite some quite energetic and well-meaning attempts to provide educational & attractive displays the collections were not properly cared for and fell into disorder' (1950).

In 1954 Selby Smith partially disbanded the Museum 'owing to the increased need of classrooms for the science subjects'.[27] The rocks went to the Geography Room and articles from the school's history went to the Library. The Biology Club took over the work of classifying birds' nests and eggs. In 1961 the Museum was converted to a Senior Chemistry Teaching Room.

Its contents, says Lyne, went 'to the husband of someone who had worked for Mr Selby Smith, and who was starting a museum in West Gippsland. Cammie Campbell was very annoyed as he had had supervision of it for many years, boys being actual curators, most of whom had taken great pride in the collection ... much of which had been given to the school in good faith.' Lyne and Campbell salvaged a few things and when Lyne retired he gave the egg collection to Provan, and the large collection of Aboriginal weapons and artefacts to an Aboriginal group in Sydney which was setting up its own collection.[28]

In 1993 Sir Thomas Ramsay (1924, Managing Director then Chairman of Kiwi Polish Company 1956–80) bequeathed Scotch his impressive Australiana library and collection, generating discussion as to how to use this gift in the life of the school. It includes complete original sets of Gould's *Birds, Mammals* and *Macropods*, a 'stick' barometer owned by Captain James Cook, and the prosecutor's brief in the trial of Ned Kelly in 1880, including witness statements with annotations made in the courtroom, shorthand notes and additional affidavits.

them for Scotch in the 1850s, and he advised Council to look seriously at any government offer. Council adopted his memorandum 'as the expression of its own opinion,'[29] as well they might, for it was a joy to read, succinct and practical.

In 1964 the church allowed its schools to receive government grants directed at a precise goal: to improve science facilities to meet a national shortage of qualified scientists. Scotch built a new senior Science Block (by 2000 called the General or Junior Science Block). It was opened in 1967 by (significantly) the Commonwealth Minister for Education. Its laboratories continued the quadrangle's south wall out towards the river, above the 1934 flood level. Underneath, an anonymous donor had funded manual craftrooms. Healey believed that science's theoretical aspects were more easily grasped when accompanied by practical experience. He hoped Scotch could have scientific machine- and model-making, and also pottery, printing, painting and sculpture, to let boys 'be creative in spare time as well as in class-time'.[30]

Scotch's fear of conforming to government requirements implied that Scotch's standards were higher. In 1971 Scotch learnt its library was *below* Commonwealth standards. It had to increase its library allocation to $7500 and, embarrassed, for the first time it drew up a Library budget, providing for an unskilled assistant and for buying videotape equipment.

Receiving state aid drew the independent schools openly into the political process. They had to argue publicly that as well as government money going to government schools it should go to independent schools (because these took pressure off government schools). They had to argue that their grants should be increased, and certainly not decreased.

Scotch risks looking selfish in such arguments. This is particularly so at those times when governments cut funding for the state education system but, at any time, Scotch looks more amply endowed than most other schools. Scotch expects its boys and Old Boys to make sacrifices for the common good; that Scotch itself should do so is another matter.

STAFFING

Scotch's class sizes have been remarkably stable. Morrison's 300 boys were taught in classes of about 25–30. Gilray's were the same or larger. Selby Smith aimed for a class size that was economically practicable yet educationally desirable. He lowered the Senior School staff–student ratio from 25:1 to 20:1. Final-year class size fell from 32 to 23, though classes varied considerably. He noted that wealthy American schools in the 1930s had reduced senior classes to 12 but had since restored them to 24, because larger groups produced a vigour and liveliness lacking in the smaller ones.

At the lower levels a homogeneous group of able boys can be taught effectively so long as it does not exceed thirty or thirty-two, but groups of slower learners, or groups which include wide ranges of ability or achievement must be a good deal smaller. Our plan, therefore, was to allow our fastest groups to rise to 34 …, and to put a limit of 24 on the slowest forms in each age-group.[31]

(In 2000, official class size in Year 7 is 26; in Years 8–11, 24–25 and in final year, 20–22.)

Selby Smith increased the number of teachers by 11. He also introduced laboratory assistants for Physics, Chemistry and Biology. In the humanities, part-time, married women typed notes and examination papers, kept records and corrected boys' work in co-operation with teachers.

By 1973, there were two support staff for every three teachers. As well as 99 teaching staff (including librarians) in the entire school there were 60 other staff: 15 administrative and 15 maintenance staff, 12 grounds staff, eight cleaners, four laboratory assistants, three assistant librarians, a hospital sister, a craft assistant and an audio-visual assistant. In Darling's 31 years as Librarian, the staff rose from one to nine. In 2000, the teacher–supporter ratio remains the same, though quite new areas have appeared (like computers), and others have been outsourced (like cleaning and catering). The welfare area has increased from one chaplain, and the OSCA and Foundation staff has also grown.

Frank Nankervis, Senior Economics Master 1938–71, Senior Master 1959–71, Acting Vice-Principal 1963.

As for how teachers taught, Selby Smith believed that good teachers 'should be given the utmost freedom to conduct their classes in their own way, and be treated as truly professional people: and I believe, too, that the knowledge that they will be treated in this way if they join the staff of a particular school will be a great attraction to them to do so'.[32]

Selby Smith soon appointed his own Vice-Principal, Fleming, and created a new position of Senior Master to which he appointed Harry Fry (staff 1939–59; the boys called him 'Jimmy'), the Senior Chemistry Master. Fleming's skills lay with the Old Boys and parents whilst Fry attended to detailed organisation. When Fry died prematurely, Frank Nankervis (Senior Economics Master 1938–71) replaced him.

The chief concern of a headmaster, said Selby Smith, is to recruit and retain teachers of quality as scholars and as human beings, and who are prepared to sacrifice their own personal inclinations in the interest of their pupils.[33] Conditions of service therefore had to be attractive. Gilray had countenanced no such thing. He disapproved of government measures to train teachers, perceiving 'a danger that this may … attract some who have no real call for it'.[34] Selby Smith, by contrast, improved salaries and superannuation. He pushed Council to keep salaries in line with other schools. Before Selby Smith, salaries at Scotch (though they compared well with those in other schools) were meagre. To supplement them 'in the 40s, and for many years before', a number of masters like Bienvenu, Kirby, and Vivian Hill taught in the coaching college Moscrop and Donald in the city

founded years before by Charles Moscrop (staff 1915–37).[35] A few masters
made money from writing text-books. Robert 'Nutty' Wilson and Alan
'Stonk' Ross became the joint authority in mathematics, and one of them
told Lyne 'that he had made £32 000 out of his book. And that was in the
'40s! … 'Forty-five' [Clayton] must have made a mint out of his books, too'.[36]
Text-books were set for every subject, and a book might be recommended
in every state and have an assured market.

Pensions were inadequate, which obliged old men to keep teaching, 'all
these quaint old men [with] their bleak assured atrophy'.[37] Their final years
were often not very effective: 'He had not given much instruction for some
time. However, no child could sit under him without receiving that
imperishable sense of … tradition which is a finer thing than mere academic
learning.'[38] So teachers who, 'to put it kindly, had reached their use-by dates'
lingered on perhaps because Gilray was 'too kind to give them a push'.[39] In
1954 a debating topic was 'That compulsory death at 65 would be beneficial
to Australia'. Selby Smith won Council's permission to compel retirement
at 65. Geelong College set up the Combined School Superannuation Fund,
which Scotch soon joined. (The state Government declined to make it a
joint scheme, although no subsidy was required.) Benefits included
provisions for sick leave and permanent disability.

The Cart Horse

He was old
And tied to his post by humble servitude
But he blinked and nodded at me passing
And I smiled, and nodded a greeting back at him.
And it was like old friends, but never met before—
And looking back he was gazing after me.[40]

A. McD. Taylor (1958)

Just before Selby Smith arrived, the automatic seniority of the older
males was for the first time challenged, politely. Until 1952 the staff

was a completely unstructured body of individuals, each doing his own
thing. If any member had a matter which he wished to raise, he would call a
meeting at lunch time which he then proceeded to chair. … Such meetings
were rare occurrences … If any resolution was passed, there was bound to be
another meeting within a few days to rescind the motion. No minutes were
kept.

Thus Lyne, who between Gilray's announcement of his retirement and
Selby Smith's arrival seized the moment to persuade his colleagues to set
up a Common Room Association, despite opposition from those who asked
'if we thought we were going to tell the headmaster how to run his school'.

The association aimed to make more effective the staff contribution to the general working of the school; to help shape policy on staff welfare; and to elect the Common Room's representatives to the Victorian Assistant Masters' Association. (Lyne was the representative because Wilson asked him to be.) The CRA's first chairman was Fry whilst Lyne became Secretary for the next 20 years. Support for the association came from younger staff and, crucially, from Bowden, Vice-Principal. Other senior men preferred to deal directly with the Headmaster, and scorned Fry because of his Education Department background. The next year Fry did not wish to continue and Robert Wilson agreed to stand—but only if no-one else was nominated. 'So began the tradition that the senior member of the staff by age, i.e. the next to retire, should be the chairman of the C.R.A.' Wilson was then followed by, in turn, Messrs Adams, Ross, Clayton, Campbell, Mark Stump (staff 1947–68), Alec Fraser, Frank Stuckey (1924, staff 1957–71), Paton, Ferres, Don Walker (staff 1945–69), Harold Blenkiron (1925, staff 1942–72), Nankervis, Davidson, Wally Butler (staff 1962–75) and Lyne. Some, like Ross, felt little obligation, when meeting the Principal, to support the Association's line.

Alec 'Tiger' Lyne: Dux 1928, staff 1942–74, Senior Geography Master, Drama Master, founder of the Common Room Association.

> However the chief opponents of the C.R.A. progressively retired … and it became established practice that matters affecting the staff should be raised at C.R.A. meetings and not dealt with personally with the authorities. Mr Selby Smith expressed his pleasure at having an organised staff with whom to deal. Both he and more especially Mr Healey came to refer matters to the C.R.A. for its opinion.[41]

Meanwhile, the association's succession of young and able secretaries were often the coming men: Lyne, Shugg, David Hosking (staff 1970–94, Senior Economics Master 1972–87, Vice-Principal 1987–94), Roger Slade (staff 1976– , Senior Master—Curriculum [later called Dean of Studies] 1991–), Steve Kong (1968, staff 1980– , Senior Master—Students [later called Dean of Students] 1990–).

Since at least 1919 staff had drawn support from a professional body, the Incorporated Association of Secondary Teachers of Victoria (from 1922 the Incorporated Association of Registered Teachers of Victoria). Its foundation in 1904 was helped by Martin Hansen (1889), who in 1907 was Acting Headmaster of Wesley. It argued for better salaries and training. Scotch teachers like Wilson and Lyne were among its presidents, and Bowden long sat on its Council which sent him to the Schools Board. The association persuaded the independent schools to create a Teachers' Training Institution, later Mercer House. In 1957–58 Scotch hosted a fundraising fair for it and seconded Tapp there for a year.

As specialist teachers' organisations appeared, Scotch teachers presided over several: Commercial, Geography, History, Indonesian, Mathematical and Science. In 1992, 15 Junior School staff were office-bearers in professional associations related to their teaching areas.

Selby Smith thought it 'of great importance to recruit men and women of widely differing backgrounds, so that pupils, in their daily contact with them, could have the enriching experience which such variety can provide'. Avoiding Old Boys who had been away only long enough to complete a degree or their teacher training, he 'tried consciously to recruit new staff from overseas, and from other States, to find some who had themselves been pupils of independent schools, and some who had been educated in the State system; and also to attract out of industry or commerce men whose experience there could … fit them for teaching'.[42] Leon Bates (1939, staff 1960–87) had worked in industry as a research chemist. Wilbur Courtis, once a railway clerk, had won distinction in the war and then took a degree and taught in a high school. Frank Stuckey, aged over 50, brought a background mixture of China (where he was born and partly raised), science, economics and business. Like Gilray, Selby Smith was not disconcerted by men who were unconventional. Colin Scott had worked as a labourer and was almost certainly a Communist. He coached the First XVIII, and was good at teaching Mathematics even to boys who found it hard.

Selby Smith appointed some young men, because boys need teachers 'still young enough in our eyes, as 17- and 18-year-olds, that we could empathise with'.[43] To keep them, Selby Smith wanted Scotch to have enough well-paid senior posts so that those who decided to make their career in one institution might have reasonable prospects of promotion, as they would certainly have in the large state education service.

Selby Smith encouraged teachers' professional development. The tribal elders were generalists, some of whom had developed skills in specialist areas on the job, but the late 1940s were a watershed for the teaching profession as young men appeared with degrees in education and special subjects. In 1950 Gilray employed Dugald MacLeish, B.Sc. (1943, staff 1950–54, 1960–78) part-time while he studied to be a teacher. Until then, only a master like Dr Mendel, both academically minded and inspired by a different scholarly tradition, had seriously advanced his qualifications, writing a B.Ed. thesis on education in India. In the Junior School the impressive Miss Elizabeth Pike, B.A., Dip.Ed. worked towards a B.Ed. and left in 1954 to be a headmistress. In 1957–59, Robin Rowlands (1931, staff 1936–66) gained a Ph.D. in Education at the London School of Economics, taking two years' long-service leave and leave without pay. In 1953, 34 out of the 43 Senior School teachers had a degree. In 1973, most had them.

Selby Smith sent staff to conferences. His own educational experience had shown him how stimulating such contacts could be. This increased as travel costs fell. Healey in 1973 sent 14 Junior School teachers interstate to the Junior School Headmasters' Association of Australia Biennial Conference and Refresher School. This benefited the teachers and enriched the conferences.

RELIGIOUS AND ETHNIC MINORITIES

Selby Smith also widened Scotch's religious and ethnic composition.

The Presbyterian Church owed its origins to breakaway Catholics and regarded Rome as a foe. 'Cakey' Adams's Religious Instruction classes in the 1960s were often 'a tirade against Roman Catholicism', but 'it didn't seem to me at the time that my Catholic friends personified evil in the way that Cakey indicated' (1963). Scotch has always had Catholics. Morrison enrolled them from his arrival, and later hired at least one as a teacher, J. P. McCabe-Doyle, an old Xaverian. At Morrison's funeral, his friend the Rector of Xavier honoured him by adding Xavier's boys to the Scotch boys following the hearse. George Anderson (1932) recalls 'We were nearly all white Anglo-Saxon Protestants. There were a few Roman Catholics, whose spiritual needs were attended to by a visiting priest.'[44] Sister Irving at the Hospital was Catholic. Selby Smith engaged Dr Joseph Jordens (staff 1959–61) as a teacher. A Belgian with a first-class honours degree in languages, he 'spoke French, German, English just like a native', and Selby Smith thought: 'we really can't pass this chap up'. Selby Smith knew that 'of course there were Presbyterian ministers on the Council who weren't very enthusiastic about this kind of thing happening', so he raised it in his regular pre-Council meeting with the chairman, Anderson.

> I said to Archie 'Although I normally just mention the people I have appointed, I think I'd better explain this one, because it might not please some people'. And Archie said 'Good idea'. ... So I simply explained to the Council that I had appointed this man and the reasons why I had done it and I wanted them to know that he was a member of the Catholic Church. And Archie Anderson just smiled at me and said 'I think we are most grateful to the Principal for explaining this particular case because after all it is his authority to appoint people and we shouldn't really have any hesitation about backing what he does but it is so nice of him to explain in such full detail'. Full stop. That was it! He didn't give these what we might call slightly bigoted religious people a chance at all. And isn't it wonderful to have that kind of support, you see, and intelligent support![45]

Another Catholic followed, Frank West (staff 1964–69), Secretary of the Victorian Society for Crippled Children, and brother of the novelist Morris West. Healey appointed Kevin Purcell (staff 1973–84), and the presence of Catholic teachers now is routine and unnoticed. The number of Catholic students rose steadily and the 1995 intake contained more

Catholics than Presbyterians, 21 to 18. In 1999 it was uncontroversial, if known at all, that the School Captain, Tim Downing, was a Catholic.

Scotch's most famous minority is the Jews, who were present from the start. They included Monash and Sir Zelman Cowen. Both were Dux, as were Henry Cohen (1889), John Helmer (1962) and Adam Sher (1999). No School Captain has been Jewish. Gordon Fisher (Captain 1941) noted 'that very few Jewish boys were appointed prefects or probationers'.[46]

Anti-Semitism lies deep in European culture and so appears within the Presbyterian Church. The Rev. John Ewing told his Toorak Presbyterian congregation in 1886 that unscrupulous greed was 'the evil characteristic of the … needy-looking little Jew'.[47] Morrison held no such views. He welcomed Jews to Scotch, put Hebrew on the curriculum, and in 1884 presided at an evening lecture on the Talmud by the Rev. Mr Meyers. Under Littlejohn and Gilray, a Jewish boy found 'considerable latitude and respect extended to religious minorities … and our attendance at Prayers and Scripture was optional' (1936). This was put to practical use in the Junior School, where Jewish boys not at Assembly monitored latecomers.[48] Many Jewish boys flourished at Scotch, and served it thereafter, not least Sir Edward Cohen (1930). Henry Cohen (1889) was President of OSCA 1921–22, and his son Colin Keon-Cohen (1925) in 1982 made one of the largest bequests the school had yet received.

During and after World War II, bullying as a whole increased and so did anti-Semitism. There was 'a strong anti-Jewish undercurrent, led by a number of irresponsible individuals whose activities made life miserable for most Jews at the School. [One Jewish boy found] his days at Scotch represented the most unhappy period of his life' (1946).[49] Immediately after the war David Grounds (1946) 'saw anti-Semitism practised before my eyes for the first time. … Many boys from wealthy families, and particularly those boarders from the squattocracy did not hesitate to make comments about "bloody Yids" in their hearing'.[50] David Taylor (1949), in boarding and day school, witnessed Jewish boys 'persecuted and sometimes physically attacked by other boys'. Taylor 'was amazed the matter did not come to the attention of the school authorities',[51] and Jim Kelso (1947) also wonders at masters' inaction and wishes now 'that I had taken a more active part in crushing this anti-Semitism rather than just being a bystander'.[52] Fights occurred.[53] Monash had already dispelled the myth of the unpugnacious Jew, and Alan Hartman (1970) smelt 'The stench of a blood nose as I punched [——] for calling me a Jew Boy'.[54]

From this same period there are gentiles who recall no anti-semitism. Ian Phipps (1952) delighted in his Jewish friends—'I attended their Friday night services and learnt a lot about Judaism. The Headmaster taught Old Testament Scripture in Matriculation and most Jews attended and this helped as we had a shared religious beginning which he stressed.'[55] Gilray, who had close Jewish friends, stopped a boy of German parentage distributing

Nazi propaganda in the 1930s. During the war, when 'there developed a very nasty persecution of some of the Jewish boys', Gilray addressed Assembly, 'demanding that those responsible apologise to the victims, and pointing to the Roll of Honour said that those names were there because people wanted to stamp out such persecution. He was absolutely magnificent, and his strength and compassion were unforgettable.'[56]

Since Gilray, both these strands have continued—a low level of anti-Semitism sternly opposed by the Principals and other staff like 'Gunner' Owen.[57] In the 1950s boys sang 'Adieu adieu, my friend, adieu adieu'.[58] In the 1960s Hartman found Scotch 'over-endowed with misogynous anti-Semitic snobs who were not very accepting of a short un-athletic Jewish scholarship boy who lived in Carlton'.[59] The most hurtful aspect of anti-Semitism was when a Jewish boy found that 'Many of my "friends" joined in. This period made me extremely aware of the difficulties suffered by minority groups … I carry this scar to today' (1955). On the other hand, Steven Kunstler (1975) 'encountered very little anti-Semitism and then from 1 or 2 ignorant students only'; 'my Jewish birth and "non-practising" stance on matters religious was never criticised or commented upon by teaching staff'.[60] A Jewish boy thought Healey 'did a marvellous job by speaking out at morning assembly at least twice, and the boys who were causing trouble kept their mouths shut' (1968). Healey also took the lead in inviting the Headmaster of Mount Scopus School to join the Headmasters' Conference. Yet, strangely, at an official level Healey's Scotch became less tolerant of Jews. A Group Master publicly told Hartman to sing the hymns in Assembly—'I stammered that I was Jewish, sir. But to no avail. "You will still sing my lad!" '[61]—and Kunstler 'had to attend Chapel and say prayers and sing hymns as a condition of being at the school', which he found quite acceptable.[62] Similarly, religious education under Healey was made 'an essential part of the curriculum',[63] which every boy had to attend.[64] Donaldson made attendance at Christian Education compulsory, and required all boarders to attend chapel—one Muslim boarder returned to being a day-boy to avoid this.

Scotch's other visible minority has been the Chinese. Cheok Hong Cheong (1874) became a Christian missionary to, and leader of, the Chinese community in Melbourne. James Cheong (1888) became a priest at St Peter's, Eastern Hill. Ling Ah Mouy (1885) won a French prize, and 'was cheered enough to make the old rafters tremble … good chap'.[65] (Morrison's nephew, Ernest, had a career in China and was known as 'Chinese' Morrison. His biography was written by Cyril Pearl (1917) journalist, author and raconteur.) At the centenary, a congratulatory cable from Hong Kong Old Boys included Chinese names, and at the Sydney Dinner the four Kaw brothers attended and it 'was said no Old Scotch function would be complete without a Chinese representation'.[66]

But the White Australia Policy shaped boys' views, and in a Leaving

(Year 11) English discussion in 1946 Australian and Chinese boys agreed that no respectable member of either race could marry into the other. At the time an Anglo-Celt like John Green (1947) did not see such an exchange as racist. Rather, it affirmed China's equality as an ancient culture and led to 'a much broader outlook, perhaps a certain moral sense of fairness'.[67] As the White Australia Policy faded in the 1960s, the number of Asian boys increased. In 1964 E. P. Wong was the only Asian in Year 12. In 2000 there are eight (whilst twice that number have Asian names but are Australian-born). In 1972 Stan Brown (staff 1954–83) made John Hoe (1972) Captain of School House. He was also Captain of Swimming, with Victor Ho (1972) as Vice-Captain. In the early 1980s Wei Ch'ng (*Collegian* Editor 1985) recalls

quite a bit of racial prejudice. In my junior school years the boys had always known me since prep. ... at Scotch there were very few Chinese above me (Charles and John Su and Eugene Wan [1983]). As I went into the senior school there seemed to be an increasing number of Asians in the boarding house and the boarders from the country seemed to delight in tormenting them for being different. However I was still one of the first Chinese and due to the other three more senior boys being quite timid and my refusal to be abused it did become a daily battle of taunts between my friends (all European) and the boarders. It wasn't so much that it hurt me, but I always believe in standing up for myself, and I think even that has made me a better person.[68]

At century's end, a Year 3 class corresponded with Yusuke Murakami (1936) in Japan, Kazuma Naito (1989) was the widely liked Captain of Forbes, and his brother Teruma Naito (1995) was—50 years after the war—Regimental Sergeant-Major of the cadets and 1995 Perelberg winner. E. P. Wong and David Yu (a parent) are Trustees of the Foundation.

Selby Smith widened Scotch's outlook also through American Field Scholarships, whereby Scotch gave an annual free place to an American teenager, whilst a Scotch boy went to America. In 1959 Selby Smith admitted as a boarder 'the first native New Hebridean boy to attempt a full secondary education'. Kalpokor Kalsakau (1964) became Finance Minister of Vanuatu.

Racist opinions still occur, especially on the Hill which speaks for rural Australia. But in the school at large in 2000, even a cursory glance shows many clumps of racially mixed boys in play or talk, and also more racially homogeneous clumps.

At Scotch, boys 'learned to live together ... all sorts and conditions of us ... And that living together taught us toleration'.[69] 'It gave me an acceptance of people, and the ability to see the good in people'.[70] Tolerance was one of the best things learnt at Scotch, said the 1955 *Collegian*, 'because Scotch does not try to mould all the students on its roll into one stereotyped character',[71] but this was always warring with teenagers' peer pressure to

conform and with the school's demand for school spirit. 'We learned that injustice of some degree is inseparably connected with human affairs, and that taught us not to moan overmuch.'[72]

SOCIAL SERVICE

Scotch boys' outlook was broadened in a different way by bringing them into contact with Australians of other classes and needs. From the 1920s, the boys supported the church's mission school in Korea. Now, charity went to fellow citizens; and not through donations but through personal service. We have already seen how Yarnold stimulated social service, and at least from the 1940s some boys who were not scouts or cadets on Thursday afternoons worked for charity organisations, gardening or shopping for the elderly. In the 1950s, boys occasionally gardened at children's homes, and at Cowes boys chopped, mowed, painted and cleaned for pensioners.

In 1961 Ken Evans (1948, Senior Mathematics Master 1961–87, Senior Master 1988–90) set out to bring boys regularly into contact with the less privileged, and to give boys a chance of a coherent and sustained response. Evans organised 20 Form V (Year 11) boys who were neither cadets nor scouts. Every Thursday, for at least an hour, boys encountered 'the reality

Rowers' barbecue lunch on the river bank in 1960. In those days a non-Caucasian such as Kal Kalsakau (1964) was uncommon.

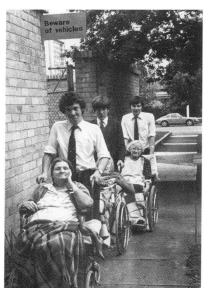

Beware of vehicles.
Social Services in
1983.

of the actual needs and the difficulties of elderly citizens and of the handicapped'.[73] Boys helped children, young adults and the elderly, widows and orphans, the deaf, blind and 'crippled'.

Social Service had low status compared to cadets and scouts, and perhaps still does. It seemed a bit 'sissy'. 'There was pressure to join the cadets. I resisted and joined the social services group. Although what we did was quite useful, any member of this group was typecast by the admin. as not showing much potential.'[74] By 1979, 226 boys took part in 35 different centres, including manning three after-school play centres every weekday—one of them in the Junior School. Organising their work in small groups proved more effective than allocating it by house (Monash the Blind, Lawson-MacFarland the Aboriginal Education Incentive Scholarship Fund) which was tried in 1968 but discarded. Healey hoped that voluntary social services would become habit-forming.

The boys benefited, too. It was 'a tremendously powerful emotional and educational experience'.[75] It meant a different kind of meeting together and fostered leadership skills. Boys grew close to the people they helped. One lad voluntarily spent Good Friday straightening a pensioner's garden, and planted seedlings bought with his own pocket money. Bill Shattock (1979) found he 'often stayed a lot longer than I needed to and took a real interest in the kids'.[76] Other boys found visiting the elderly was depressing, or disgusting—'picking up a sock in a nursing home to find it sodden with urine'[77]—and wondered if they achieved anything. Yet even at the Lady Herring Spastic Centre, 'although it's pretty nerve wracking—some of them are in pretty bad shape—I feel as though I'm doing something … we play dominos or draughts or clean wheelchairs etc.'[78] or on a weekend camp 'we shower them, feed them, play with them etc.'[79]

In 1976 under Roff and a new Master-in-Charge, Geoff 'Wildcat' Walker (staff 1971–90, with his 'paisley long-sleeved shirts worn underneath a beige short-sleeved safari suit'[80] and 'his wicked sense of humour and abundant delight in the ridiculous'[81]), the work became more politically aware, expanding to include the socially and economically disadvantaged. Expanding beyond Thursdays, Social Service established links with children in the Richmond high-rise Housing Commission Estate. Each afternoon a few boys looked after children who lived there. One week in the August 1976 holidays 25 boys looked after 150 of them. They came by bus for the day, played games, were fed, and did pottery and painting. Boys led camps at Cowes for them,[82] or Aboriginal children, or children from Gowerville Primary School (from single-parent families or wards of state, none had had a seaside holiday[83]). In 1999, 250 boys gave between one and 3 hours a week for 25 weeks, amounting to 10 000 hours of community work.

In 1973 parents, with Mrs Betty Cox as first President, formed the Social Service Parents' Auxiliary, chiefly to organise the boys' transport each week.

SPORT

Melbourne hosted the 1956 Olympic Games. Three Old Boys competed: Bob Grant (1953, staff 1960–86, Chief Coach of Athletics 1964–86) in javelin, David Boykett (1952, staff 1963–96) in rowing, and Graham Drane (1933) in yachting. ('Ginner' Davidson was earlier twice selected to represent Australia as a high-jumper and sprinter, but chose not to burden his family with the expense. His father was the Presbyterian minister at Hawthorn.) Herb Engel (1915, staff 1921–56) became Olympic Equipment Manager in 1956. Scotch gave him leave on full pay until he was paid by the Games Committee.

The Main Oval and its dressing room became a reserve ground for Olympic hockey. Scotch charged no fee: the Games Committee top-dressed the oval to a first-class condition. Olympic soccer training used another oval. Boys watched the training, and played cricket against the British athletes—Scotch's first international match. England won by one run. During the Games the school had the afternoons off.

The long-term effect was to invigorate field games: discus, javelin, pole vault, hammer throwing, and hop, step and jump. Australia's poor performance in these was attributed to their not being school sports, and letters to *Satura* called for their introduction. So as not to cut areas of turf from the Main Oval, Scotch built nearby it a long-jump pit, a high jump, and a weight putt area. Inaccurate shot-putting soon hurt nearby trees. The discus and javelin can be dangerous. When a javelin injured Mike Reid (1958) it 'caused quite a bad infection' because it was covered with the sticky turf from the ovals which had a real farmyard smell, 'and one had to be careful that scratches received when playing footy did not go too septic'.[84]

Selby Smith doubled the number of boys regularly playing sport. When he left there were '44 teams in the Senior School—24 Australian Rules (each with umpires and reserves), 6 Rugby Football, 8 Hockey and 6 Basketball teams, while some boys were rowing, playing tennis, or running in Cross-Country races'.[85] Critics grumbled at declining attendances at major Public School matches, a decline said to indicate a fall in school spirit but as likely to reflect the rise of new sports at the expense of cricket and football. But it is true that Selby Smith saw little value in compelling boys 'to watch games

Javelin-throwing around 1975. One long-term effect of the 1956 Melbourne Olympics was to invigorate field games such as the javelin and pole vaulting. Australia's poor performance in these was attributed to their not being school sports. But javelins were dangerous, and are no longer thrown at Scotch.

which others play; occasionally perhaps, it is good for the whole school to watch their team in some important match, since a worthwhile sense of community and companionship may arise from the shared experience'. Selby Smith's *laissez-faire* outlook extended to playing sport. 'Very rarely was a boy compelled to play a particular game; rather, as wide a variety of games as possible was made available, in the hope that almost every boy who was fit enough to do so would choose one or the other, and might be able, from a varied selection, to find one which he could play well enough to find enjoyment in it.'[86]

Widespread sport also shifted attention from watching to playing. Saturday sport marks a profound difference between an earlier Scotch and the Scotch of the last 50 years. A boy focused now not only on the Firsts, but also on his own hard-fought games that usually went unsung. David Brand (1972) wrote home that 'The oval was the worst I have ever seen. In some parts your boot would sink about 4 inches into the mud. ... Everybody got covered. Unfortunately when we finished, the showers were cold. ... it was quite rough sometimes. Due to somebodies [sic] elbow, I have a sore tongue, when I got hit in the jaw and bit it.'[87]

> Wesley ... had hundreds of really big kids. We didn't think we had a hope. ... Once in the 3rd quarter and twice in the 4th, I combined well with a handball and drove us into attack (If I may say so myself). ... The first time was on our half forward flank. A team mate was tackled but managed to handpass to our half forward flanker. I came streaking through like a flash of lightning, received the handball booted it up into the forward pocket. Unfortunately a Wesley kid marked it. At 3/4 time the coach said that it was the only piece of good dry weather footy that he had seen. In the last quarter, ...the same half forward handballed it across to me. I had to run towards a pack of Wesley ruckmen to kick it with my left foot. I got a sore backside into the bargain (such a hero). I thought it would have only gone about 10–15 yards but when I got up, I was just in time to see a Wesley ruckman punch it away right on the goal line. It had gone dead centre, 30 yards. I couldn't believe it. ... I hope I don't sound as though I'm bragging but the significance of it all is that people are finally looking for people on their own or people who are backing up. ... The scores were Scotch 3.4 (22) & Wesley 1.6 (12).[88]

Societies and clubs

Selby Smith presided over the widening participation of boys in school activities that pleased them.

In 1955 Arthur Mitchell began an annual summer holiday camp at Cowes. Unlike compulsory cadet or scout camps, at Cowes 'you were there because you wanted to be' and that shaped its nature.[89] The camp was run entirely by a committee of boys—'a more haloed and talented fraternity you will not find'—who provided its entertainment, administered 'justice', and by

THE WARATAH CLUB

The Waratah Club, later the Biology Club, began in 1954 for boys interested in Natural History. Members of the old Museum Committee and some Senior Biology boys formed the Committee. Woolcock and Stan Brown were the Vice-Presidents.

It had six sections. The experimental group under Roger Fry bred mice for coat colours, and sold excess stock to junior boys as 'a profitable sideline'.[90] At the club's Mouse Exhibition in the Mercer House Fair, several mice spoilt the show by going to sleep under the wheels. In 1956 the club earned £30 by selling birds bred at the school, and in 1957 sold budgerigars to raise money to buy larger birds. They sold the Indian Ring-neck Parrot, because it kept escaping by burrowing.

The flora group planted 80 plants and two other groups on insects and birds recorded what these plants attracted.

School holidays made keeping live creatures problematic. The sea-life section made its own sea-water, but over Easter 1955 the aerator failed and all the creatures died. In other holidays mouse and bird numbers fell as many killed each other. Holidays interrupted daily watering and feeding, especially since most of the members who took a special interest in this were boarders. Perhaps they were country boys used to animals? Perhaps they needed some acceptable way of showing care and affection?

In the 1960s, under the Senior Biology Master, 'Wacky' Thomas (staff 1957–87), members worked mainly in four groups: mice (experimental breeding), fish (two large tanks, one sea-water, one fresh), plant life (raising trees for the new 170 acres of bush bought adjacent to Elliott Lodge). The bird group had 40 birds in eight cages; 'One interesting bird has no feathers because it was bred when its parents were moulting' suggested a Lamarckian rather than Darwinian approach.

means of daily chores kept the camp running smoothly. This gave boys 'a chance of leadership which often the school (being so large) cannot give'.[91] It was 'a place where men are born' because there, more than anywhere, they were supported as young men rather than being taken care of like little boys. They had more freedom than at other camps or school endeavours, 'and in the main that freedom was appreciated more than it was abused'. But there were embarrassing moments, as when members of Council visited a rain-sodden camp in January 1983 and heard this grace before lunch: 'Thanks for the food. Now pull your finger out and give us some good weather. Amen.'[92]

A quarter-century after Mitchell's first makeshift camps, Scotch-at-Cowes had tented accommodation for 96 campers and 20 Committee Members, and various permanent buildings. 'Committee Members have regular life-saving drill, and all beach activities are rigidly controlled. A doctor is available at all times.'[93]

In the 1920s, small parties of boys went skiing. By 1936 Scotch had a Ski Club.[94] A boy exulted in 'the unique thrill of sliding effortlessly down a mountain slope, the wind in his face and freedom in his heart'.[95] From 1956 the club built a ski hut, funded by parents and an interest-free loan from Council. Members built the hut on a block in Box Hill then re-erected it on Mount Buller, steadily improving it over the years. In 1958 Scotch won all the Schoolboy Championships of Victoria. Later lodges rose elsewhere. The club's members included mothers, fathers and sisters. Because of this, OSCA declined to affiliate it and, when the club incorporated itself, Council

reluctantly denied it the use of 'Scotch College' in its name. It became the Koomerang Ski Club.

Scotch had an astronomy club from the 1940s. Sputnik boosted interest, as did a telescope donated by D. J. G. Strang for which Scotch built an observatory in 1960, in its day a strikingly modern achievement.

New clubs mushroomed: the Riding Club (1952), Waratah Club (1954), Geography Club (1955), Handiwork Club (wood, metals, and leather, 1956), Radio Club (1956), Fencing (1957), Young Farmers (1957), Gould League of Bird Lovers (Junior School, 1957), Rifle Club (1958), Constitutional Club (1963) and Weightlifting Club (1963).

Such clubs give us a glimpse into the world of the boys. To boyish minds, one other significant moment occurred under Selby Smith, for 1961 seen upside down still read 1961, the first time this had happened since 1881 and the last time until 6009.

REMEDIAL TEACHING

One aspect of Selby Smith's gentler and broader vision of education was that Scotch began remedial teaching. Old Boys back to the 1920s who describe themselves as slow learners found that 'The bright and outspoken students were favoured and the timid, lacking in confidence were neglected' (1929).[96] 'Masters who taught the brains as we called them were often impatient with us "duffers" who could not grasp their message at one go' (1936).[97] 'It was a tragedy there was no remedial help. The brilliant succeeded, but the rest of us had a really hard struggle' (1951).[98] As late as 1984 there was a 'Lack of help for people who struggled'.[99] A few masters stood outside this pattern. 'Ric' Marshall 'especially cared for those boys who found academic work difficult.'[100] 'He had lots of patience with the dregs, and made it interesting, with many non-educational stories' (1952).[101] Spencer Sayers (staff 1937–79), too, 'would always find time for the slow learners' (1945).[102] In 1958 Tapp appointed a remedial teacher in the Junior School, the melodiously named Miss Ursula Tyrell-Gill (staff 1959–70), for whose work no fee was charged. She also helped lower forms in the Senior School. In 1962 Tapp made her full-time, and the Senior School hired its own part-time remedial teacher, Mrs Winifred Beale (staff 1962–71). Rae Brown (staff 1974–80), Stan Brown's wife, began as a part-timer and the job grew like Topsy. Even when full-time she had no superannuation and was not a member of the Common Room, a comment both on its entirely male composition and also of the low rank of remedial teaching. Scotch also supported well-disposed masters, paying for David Burt (staff 1955–63) and Don Macmillan (staff 1959–87) to take courses in remedial teaching. Roff and Wirth greatly developed this area, and its (usually female) practitioners dealt with pastoral as well as academic problems.

Its changes of names—from remedial education, to Special Education, to Educational Support Unit—suggest both a discipline trying to define itself, and a social transformation of the problem it hoped to tackle.

In 1963 Selby Smith resigned to become the first Professor of Education at Monash University, though he stayed until Easter 1964 to see the school year successfully commenced. He had been trying to leave for some years, but this was not generally known and his departure was a shock, especially to those who thought a headmaster of Scotch should stay for the rest of his life.

Selby Smith came to Scotch from being an educational administrator and left it to become a professor of education. Both facets show in his headmastership at Scotch. He improved the school's finances, buildings and staff conditions. He broadened the staff's character and brought a mood to the school where new things were possible, great and small. Being Principal of Scotch was just one of his achievements, and not the greatest. As an old

TELEVISION

'TV is not replacing radio half as fast as it is replacing homework.'[103]

Television began in Melbourne in 1956, for the Olympic Games. The first face to be broadcast was that of Geoff Corke (1950) who hosted a GTV-9 test transmission from Mt Dandenong on 27 September 1956. He became King Corky in *The Tarax Show*. 'Uncle Doug' Elliot (1931) was the jovial spruiker of *World of Sport*.

Before television arrived, it was possible to argue in a debate that people would not want to see films in their own homes, but television quickly became part of Australian domestic life. Boys built sets at the Applied Science Club, the Junior School bought a set to receive lessons screened by ABV-2, and the tuckshop financed 'a television receiver' for the hospital. One lunchtime in 1969, boys watched man's first walk on the moon on television sets in the chemistry laboratory, the library or the Prefects' Room. Educationally, Healey was unconvinced that television would replace teachers, but wanted new buildings designed so that television could be installed if required.

man his talk was most energetic when about the war, which was, as for so many men of the first half of the century, perhaps the transforming event in his life.

Selby Smith is the last principal of whom it is said that he seemed to know every boy at the school personally. Whatever this says of him as a man, it speaks also of his times. He was not distracted from the boys by permanent fundraising, he dealt little with governments, and there were few Scotch organisations whose meetings he had to attend. All that organisational complexity was about to arrive.

MEN OF INFLUENCE, MEN OF WEIGHT

In 1954 Gilray became Deputy Chancellor of the University of Melbourne. 'Scotch take over University', ran the *Sun News-Pictorial* headline, for the Vice-Chancellor was Sir George Paton (1920) and the Chancellor was Sir Arthur Dean (1910), who sat on the Supreme Court in 1949–65. Paton's successor, Sir David Derham (1937) had founded the Monash University Law School. A later Vice-Chancellor was David Penington (1947).

In 1958 Sir Francis Rolland (1895), the Presbyterian Moderator-General, was the first Australian minister of religion to be knighted. Sir Gilbert Chandler (1919) was Minister of Agriculture in 1955–73. Sir Thomas Cherry (Dux 1914) became a Fellow of the Royal Society. Thomas Lowe (1926) was Director of the Baker Medical Research Institute 1949–74.

During the 1950s, Alfred Jacobs (1915) was honorary secretary of the Narrogin Native Welfare committee in Western Australia which lobbied for better conditions, for land and fishing and mining rights, and for citizenship for Aborigines.

David McNicoll (1932) was Editor in Chief of Australian Consolidated Press 1953–72. Geoff Goding (1934) established the Bouverie Clinic and was a significant figure in family therapy. 'Jimmy' in the ABC's *Argonauts* was John Ewart (1944), later a film actor.

10

HAWTHORN AS A PLACE FOR A SCHOOL
1950–2000

In the second half of the twentieth century Scotch discovered that its move to Hawthorn had tumbled it into a bed of nettles. The school found itself engaged in a running battle with the local parish, in skirmishes with neighbours, and in wars against traffic, powerlines and a freeway across the ovals.

EAST: ROAD SAFETY

On the school's eastern boundary, Glenferrie Road became lethal. During the 1940s cars killed several boys. Scotch pressed the City of Hawthorn for better signs, and considered a cattle pit at the Monash Gates to stop boys running through. In 1952 the death of a boarder chasing a ball brought action. A meeting of Junior School parents was astonished that the school had not yet asked for traffic lights at the corner of Glenferrie and Callantina Roads. David Bradshaw, the Junior School Headmaster, put a male teacher on duty there before school.

Map of Hawthorn.

The City installed traffic lights in 1952 (Scotch offered to pay half the cost). Boys activated the lights by pressing a button. On the steep hill in Glenferrie Road, elderly cars, with weak hand-brakes and engines, found it difficult to stop and restart. Sometimes it seemed almost as if the boys deliberately turned the lights red at the worst possible moment.[1] Cars travelling in Callantina Road activated the lights when they ran over a rubber strip. 'After school we had great fun jumping on the strip to stop the traffic in busy Glenferrie Road, much to the displeasure of drivers who had to wait for the non-existent traffic in Callantina Road.'[2]

At the Monash Gates, Council declared the tram stop across Glenferrie Road out of bounds (as it still is) to stop boys running across the road. The gates were also put out of bounds and side tracks were built. This is a pity. The handsome gates are marred by the tracks' wired runs. Worse, only fifteen years after their construction, the gates were effectively banished from Scotch's cognisance, because few people now walk past them, and their mysterious symbols excite no curiosity.

The parish

Between 1950 and 1970 the school had several tough fights with the local parish. The relationship between parish and school always risked instability, for the school was subordinate to the parish in church law but was larger in membership, wealth and reputation. That divergence widened as the school grew and parishioners dwindled.

The parish's small role in the school's life was plain at the induction of Selby Smith in 1953. The parish Session Clerk, Maxwell Bradshaw (1928), found himself excluded from the official party of dignitaries (Council, OSCA and higher echelons of the church). This reflected the reality of power in the school, for it lay with Council and, in the church, with the state General Assembly which appointed that council. The parish's only power was to control religious matters within its boundaries, namely, the administration of the sacraments (baptism and communion), the conduct of other ceremonies such as marriage, Sabbath observance and the approval of public worship. The parish now began to exercise these powers more rigorously.

Apart from Sabbath observance—the parish told boarders to stop playing football on Sundays—the rule-tightening impinged not on the boys (already baptised; not yet marrying) but on the Old Boys who wanted to come back to the chapel to marry, to baptise their children and to take communion.

Scotch had always intended weddings and baptisms at its chapel. As soon as Old Boys started raising money to build at Hawthorn, they wanted a chapel, both for boarders and also to be 'available to Old Boys for weddings, christenings and other services'.[3] This is how it was described during fundraising,[4] and how it was in practice, for the first wedding and christening happened within a week of the chapel's dedication. Thereafter OSCA's *Yearbook* routinely reminded Old Boys of Littlejohn's hope that 'Old Boys should be married in the School Chapel and have their children baptized there. Accordingly the Chapel is available for Old Boys for weddings and christenings.'[5] Littlejohn envisaged the chapel as a focal point of the Scotch community. OSCA wished to draw Old Boys into the school's daily life and sought to increase the number of weddings and christenings in the chapel.

Marriage

Weddings happened at Scotch already, in the Memorial Hall, and moved to the chapel in 1936. The setting was inspiring, the groom could consecrate his manhood where once he was a boy, and as Old Boys became less likely to attend a parish church the chapel offered them the opportunity to be married by the chaplain, a clergyman they knew. Of all the things Campbell Watson (1942) did at Scotch, the most enjoyable was 'My marriage at

Littlejohn Chapel'.[6] Throughout the 1950s even the briefest note of weddings filled a page in each *Collegian*. The parish Kirk Session viewed this with misgiving. Many couples wished to be married by a non-Presbyterian clergyman, but the parish insisted that weddings 'must be conducted by a Presbyterian minister who may, if he wishes, invite a minister of another denomination to assist him'. The Presbyterian clergy on Council concurred.[7]

An aerial view of Scotch College in 1956, taken by Sabre Air Snaps. The copse (centre top) is scarcely grown. The horse paddock (middle right) separates the Lower and Meares ovals (top and bottom right). The quadrangle (centre) has the temporary wartime Wesley buildings running along the roadside to the north, while to the west is the round, dark water of the Settling Pool.

The number of weddings in the chapel declined, perhaps because of these restrictions. In the 1960s there were over 100 weddings a year; in the 1970s the number halved. In the 1980s they averaged 70 a year, and now 45 a year.

When Scotch became incorporated in 1980, the Memorandum of Association stipulated that weddings had to be in accordance with the forms of the Presbyterian Church unless either partner was a confirmed member of another Protestant church.[8]

Baptism

Matters were more troubled when the Presbyterians were divided, that is, when the clergy on Council disagreed with the parish. This happened in 1961 when Scotch had a brawl with the parish over baptism.

Underlying the clash were two quite different views of what was done in the chapel. The school saw that baptism and communion kept Old Boys in touch with the school and honoured the promise made in raising the money to build the chapel. The parish saw the chapel as a sub-unit within the parish and subject to proper Presbyterian practice. The chapel was certainly intended as a place for baptisms. It has a baptismal font, graced by a small but striking stained glass window, the gift of the architects. In the 1950s, an Old Boy in Port Moresby, Bill Mather (1944), delayed christening his son until he returned to Australia so it could be done in the chapel.[9]

In 1961 the parish tightened its control of baptism in the chapel. This followed a decision on the conduct of baptisms in school chapels by the General Assembly in 1960. However, none of the Presbyterian clergy on Council supported the parish view except the parish minister himself, the Rev. Robert Swanton. The issue hinged on who performed the baptism. Parents often wanted it done by a minister whom they knew, but Bradshaw, as parish Session Clerk, said baptism could be done only by the Hawthorn Parish minister or the parents' parish minister.[10] In the Presbyterian Church baptism makes a child a member of a congregation, which baptism in a chapel does not achieve. The Kirk Session insisted, therefore, that at least one parent be a communicant Presbyterian whose parish minister should consent to the baptism. 'This was to avoid the situation where people who had ceased to be actively involved in churches brought their infants to the school to be "done".'[11]

The focus of the dispute was the parish's new form, which parents had to fill in. Bain, Chairman of Council, and Fleming, Acting Principal, made unsuccessful representations to the parish.[12] Council then resolved that it

> views with grave concern the deplorable consequences that the form of
> application for baptism in the … Chapel might have on Old Boys, and
> courteously requests that the Hawthorn Kirk Session [insert] a paragraph
> affording the parents an opportunity of expressing a wish as to the officiating
> minister. The resolution was passed with the Reverend R. Swanton recording
> his dissent.[13]

The Kirk Session replied that such an insertion 'could not possibly be justified'. Two members of the Session, Fleming and Tapp, declared that they 'had been unaware that a Session Meeting had been called'. Worse, Fleming believed that a conspiracy was afoot, because 'notice of that meeting had been given at the evening service only at the Hawthorn church, when both he and Mr Tapp had been attending, as usual, the evening service with the Boarders in the School Chapel'. The Session, nevertheless, had authority in this matter, and the Chairman had to tell the Old Boys the new rules.[14]

Christenings vanished overnight. In the 1950s they annually filled a column and a half of the *Collegian*. From March 1961 there were only five a year.

The dispute rankled with both sides. The parish insisted it was merely enforcing church rules, whereas the school saw a complete overturning of previous policy. A further restriction came in 1967 when the General Assembly pronounced that a child could be baptised only when its parish assumed pastoral responsibility and when the parents promised to assist the parish. Baptisms ceased altogether.

This new approach upset many Scotch families. Bruce (1945) and Ronda Symon married in the chapel in 1954. (She became President of the Scotch Association in 1979 and he President of OSCA in 1994.) They baptised their first three sons in the chapel but in 1963 their pleas to baptise their fourth son fell on deaf ears.[15] The very first baby baptised in the chapel was Michael Paton (1953, born in 1935), yet his son was baptised there by the Rev. Alec Fraser in 1966 only 'after one hell of a row' with the parish.[16] Much had changed in a single generation.

Holy Communion

In the same year that baptism became controversial, so did communion. Push came to shove. The parish arraigned Fleming. At Council, one version of the minutes had to be sticky-taped over another, and a motion of dissent challenged the Chair.

Unlike weddings and baptisms, with many separate requests from individuals, Scotch's communion services were long-standing and routine, at Easter and at year's end. Also, the Old Boys held a communion service annually and it was over this that Fleming came to grief. The service had begun in the centenary year, when the organisers included Bradshaw, which shows that the parish had no objection in principle and that it was in the details that problems arose.

Communion could be conducted at Scotch only with parish approval and only by the parish minister.[17] Each year OSCA's Communion Sub-Committee applied to the parish for permission. In 1961 this letter was returned unanswered and without comment. Bradshaw, we may conjecture, intended the school itself to make the application, and waited for this to happen. Fleming, however, knowing OSCA's letter was 'the usual practice', did not grasp that Bradshaw, in handing the letter back, meant that he had not taken official cognisance of it. 'I am afraid it never entered my head', Fleming wrote later, 'that there could be any objection to an ordained minister taking a Communion'.[18] It was only when Fleming went to finalise the arrangements that Swanton 'informed me that these were illegal and that the matter would have to be reported to Presbytery'.[19] Abruptly Fleming was tarred with breaching church law. His hasty apologies failed to placate

Swanton or the Session, and he was obliged to explain himself in writing to Presbytery. The Session felt it acted leniently by merely reporting him rather than laying charges against him,[20] but it left Fleming distressed and humiliated, and it aroused surprise and outrage in Old Boys.

Fleming was dumbfounded. He could not deny the charge, but he was 'disturbed and bewildered by the attitude and methods adopted by my own Minister and Session Clerk', whom he found 'cold and uncompromising'.

> I thought I would receive every help and encouragement … in what is, for me, a most difficult year, when I am acting for our Principal. … Surely, when it became clear that I was not carrying out the procedures required by Church Law … it should have been obvious that either I was deliberately defying [them], or else I was under a serious misapprehension as to what was required. I cannot understand why a phone-call, or a friendly word of advice, or even of reproach was not given. I cannot help concluding … that I have seriously misjudged the men with whom I was dealing.[21]

Neither he nor Tapp attended the Kirk Session meeting that indicted him because it was held at the same time as the Sunday evening chapel service. Accusations flew. Fleming complained that the Session handled the matter in a 'ruthless and completely unsympathetic manner'.[22] The Session naturally resented these 'aspersions [as] utterly unjustified in fact and most improper'.[23] The school had become embroiled in what has always been the most dangerous kind of dispute for Scotch, one between Presbyterians, in this case between members of a Kirk Session.

It was a mismatch between two personal styles. Fleming experienced Bradshaw as legalistic, dispassionate, and lacking in Christian brotherhood to his fellow parish elder, while Bradshaw described Fleming as confused and inaccurate. Fleming and Bradshaw, the bluff soldier and the canny lawyer; the Acting Principal, good at delegating and not interested in details, and the Procurator, quietly legal and, having chosen his ground, able to wait and watch events unfold. Whatever their personal animosity, a deeper issue was that of differing primary loyalties. Fleming assumed that the parish should attend to the needs of the school whilst Bradshaw believed the reverse.

It was no small matter to compel an apology from the Acting Principal of Scotch College, who is a significant figure in the Scotch community, in the church and in Melbourne society—the trams and traffic stopped in Glenferrie Road for Fleming's funeral as the pipe band at the slow march escorted the coffin out of the Monash Gates. It was no small matter to impugn 'Faf': a much-loved teacher of generations of boys, coach of the winning 1952 First XVIII, a familiar and reassuringly solid figure. He had spent his life at Scotch apart from World War II (when imprisoned by the Japanese), and his year as Acting Principal was the climax of his career, but it brought him travail. He died two years later.

What cooled the dispute over communion was (as with baptism) the general decline in Old Boys' religious observance. Numbers fell steadily, and in 1975 OSCA discontinued it.

The organisational rift between parish and school now became explicit. Fleming resigned as an elder and so did Tapp, and no senior Scotch staff ever sat on the Hawthorn Session again. A new phase opened. The school began fastidiously to consult with the parish on all religious ceremonies, and the parish began ever tighter controls. The Old Boys' and Parents' Service had been held annually for forty years, but in 1961 the Session gave it only qualified approval.

The parish's handling of religious rites vexed Scotch. As he handed over to Healey in 1964, Selby Smith confided his hope of escape by changing the parish boundaries, a plan endorsed by Healey,[24] but no doubt a long and complicated undertaking with no guarantee of success. (The Session knew of this 'agitation' to remove its 'lawful authority' over Scotch, but insisted that this in no way influenced its treatment of the school.[25])

The public nature of the breach—the parish in formal protest, Fleming in formal disgrace—meant that people with another objection felt less obliged to suffer in silence. Dissatisfaction with the Rev. Robert Swanton began to be aired.

Place of worship for boarders

In the struggle between parish and school, the parish seemed to hold all the cards. When Healey arrived, he took the offensive, playing to the parish's major weakness with an ace that could not be trumped. He moved the boarders away from the Hawthorn Presbyterian Church to the Toorak Presbyterian Church. A long estrangement became a rupture.

Boarders had attended the Hawthorn Church since Scotch moved there. In 1929

> Best suits were donned and we lined up in the Prep room for inspection by 'Bill' [Littlejohn] and the issue of our sixpence for collection. In relation to the latter, one quickly learnt the art of tapping the plate and pocketing the sixpence, but care had to be taken that the collection in the plate looked substantial before performing the sleight-of-hand.[26]

The Hawthorn parish grew inappropriate for boarders' worship because it 'had been in decline since the first world war. That reflected in part the change in the character of the neighbourhood.'[27] The small numbers were masked by the presence of boarders from Scotch, Methodist Ladies' College and Stratherne Presbyterian Girls' School. (A similar demographic fate befell Scotch's local Anglican church, All Saints', Kooyong, which in 1975 was 'an elderly and dwindling parish'.[28]) A more particular problem was the minister at Hawthorn since 1942, Swanton. The boys called him *Cactus* and his church the *Cactotorium*,[29] for they found him dry and prickly. A tall and learned man, his virtues did not include an ability to engage boys. In any case he did not have to do so, for they attended by order of the school.

Alan MacQuarrie's (1939) greatest dislike at Scotch was going there. 'We had to put sixpence in the plate from our limited pocket money and listen to a sermon we did not understand. It did little for my future religious activities.'[30] Boys' dislike was not a lack of Christianity. Philip Pullar (1957) greatly enjoyed Sunday evening chapel but his least favourite activity was going to the Hawthorn Presbyterian Church.[31]

Swanton was also conservative. This had two aspects. First, socially he might have helped his young parishioners meet each other. Instead, the MLC, Stratherne and Scotch boarders sat apart.[32] (Scotch abetted this rigidity. At the first service of the year the Littlejohn House Captain arranged the Scotch seating—usually the 1st form at the front and the 6th at the back—and seated himself and the other House Captains about halfway down but to the right of the boys and just in front of Mr Owen.) Secondly, Swanton stressed the Bible's literal meaning. In this Bill Sides (1964) compared him unfavourably with the school chaplain, Alec Fraser. For example,

Rescuing the 'O.J. Addison' from floodwater on 10 November 1954. From left: Peter Rowland, Peter Newman (obscured), Tom Hyslop, Bob Ewing, John Osborne, Russell Frater (Captain of the School 1956), Hugh Learmonth, Alastair Nicholson, Nigel Cooper, Hugh Dick.

> Alec explained biblical creation by telling us how Adam and Eve was a story made up by ancients to explain something they didn't understand. At Hawthorn we were told they were the first man and woman and that was the start of mankind! Boys could relate to Alec's approach which helped them understand and adopt the ethics and lore of Christianity.[33]

Healey at once learnt that parents, boys and staff had a 'general lack of satisfaction' with the services at Hawthorn,[34] and at once saw it first-hand when he attended. As an educator who wrestled with methods of seizing and holding boys' attention, and as a Christian who knew what boys should be taught, Healey was dismayed. Others began to act. In 1966, Swanton's derision of Jews led to a walk-out by a boarding-house master, Dick Briggs (1958, staff 1964–68, 1993–), and some boys.

In 1965 Council decided that McCaughey (Vice-Chairman), Keith McK. Wilson and Healey should meet Swanton and the Kirk Session 'to discuss the situation'.[35] The meeting cannot have met Healey's concerns, for in 1966 he obtained Council's support to move the boarders' Sunday worship to Toorak. Before Council reached that decision, Swanton raised a point of order, which Glenn over-ruled. Swanton then moved dissent from the Chair, the only time this has happened on the Scotch Council. The motion provoked only an awkward silence because no-one would second it. Eventually, Sir James Forrest (Council 1959–71) did so, 'pro forma'. Then 'The motion that the Chairman's ruling be disapproved was put to the meeting and lost, the only person voting in favour … being the Reverend R. Swanton'. Unabashed, 'He requested that his dissent be recorded'. Glenn then put the motion approving Healey's intention to move the boarders to Toorak, which was carried. Again 'The Rev. R. Swanton requested that his dissent to the motion be recorded'.[36] Council's meetings were usually convivial, with decisions reached by consensus, and the events of that evening must have been embarrassing.

So Healey exercised his right to choose boarders' place of worship. At the risk of hyperbole, we could surmise that some members of Council took satisfaction in applying this church rule *against* the parish which they saw as having over a decade stunted the school's customs, harried Fleming to his death and treated Council itself like a group of wayward boys.

Healey now began the process of moving the boys, and Council authorised him to engage the services of a solicitor, Swanton again dissenting. Nothing more happened. Perhaps Healey tried once more to make it work at Hawthorn. In 1969 Swanton was replaced by the Rev. Donald Simpson. He preached long sermons (one was 34 minutes). A boarder with a choice went to the Church of England service which was 'boring as usual', but an hour shorter, 'so it seems that C of E is still best'.[37] In 1970 Healey asked Simpson and the Session to consider special Sunday services for young people, shorter and at 9.30 a.m. This was rejected, and Healey at last moved the Presbyterian boarders to Toorak, having consulted Council and in particular the clergy on Council (McCaughey, the Rev. Gordon Powell (1929), the Rev. Max Griffiths and the Rev. Donald Macrae (1930)). Healey acted, as he told the Presbytery of Melbourne North, only after 'serious consideration over a very lengthy period'.[38]

'Today I went to the Preso Church. It was really good.'[39] Toorak gave the Presbyterian boarders a warm welcome, parishioners even inviting them home to lunch. The 'younger boarders had "Sunday Focus" instead of having to sit through a full-length service aimed primarily at adults.'[40] When the Toorak parish later joined the Uniting Church the Scotch boarders continued to attend, although Hawthorn hoped for their return when the Presbyterian Church won Scotch in 1980, and again when Donaldson arrived in 1983.

In any case, Healey soon diminished the importance of the parish church by reducing compulsory attendance at Toorak or All Saints to once a month. He made 'the main regular service for boarders our evening Chapel'.[41] Boarders' chapel was a formal affair with boys sitting in allocated seats so that prefects could check absentees without calling the roll. There were six boys per row '(the head doesn't like seven in one row) and leave some spaces for new boys and rejects from the choir.'[42] Chapel began at 7 p.m., which obliged boys on leave to be back by then. Also, 'the hit parade was played on radio from 6.30–7 pm. It was good timing to hear the No. 1 hit and, with a real turn of speed, get from the boarding house to the Chapel in less than 1 minute.'[43] George Bremner (1932) found Macneil's Sunday evening services for boarders 'an inspiring hour of peace and tranquillity … the usual closing hymn "The Day Thou Gavest Lord is Ended" sung with so much gusto and feeling. It was here that I first reached for the stars and felt the presence of a Supreme Being.'[44]

The number of Presbyterian boarders declined. In the early 1970s, 20 boys were confirmed each year, but no more than 10 in 1974–75, and then a further drop as most Presbyterians joined the Uniting Church. In 1982 the number of confirmations was 'disappointingly small'.[45] Now there is none.

This succession of religious disputes coloured the way Scotch reacted when in 1977 the school was allocated to the ongoing Presbyterian Church, among whose leaders were members of the Hawthorn Kirk Session.

SOUTH: THE FREEWAY

The thorn in the side of the Hawthorn site became clear in the 1960s when Melbourne's traffic problems led to the construction of freeways. In inner Melbourne the only continuous belts of land not already built on were the water courses, so a freeway arched along Gardiner's Creek. Idyllic, isolated Scotch found itself abutting noise, movement and malodours. In the 1960s Scotch tried to stop this, failed, and then tried to push the route elsewhere. At the same time, it tried to limit it to four lanes. In the 1990s Scotch tried to stop it being widened to six lanes, failed, and tried to push some of the

The tranquil junction of the River Yarra and Gardiner's Creek in 1935. In the centre of the picture is the Scotch boat-launching ramp, above which an SEC catenary tower hints at the desecration to come.

widening on to St Kevin's and to ensure that good soundproofing barriers were erected.

At first, the threat seemed slight. In 1954 the freeway was planned to pass along Gardiner's Creek. Scotch's objection to the acquisition of school land was disallowed in 1957. The Melbourne and Metropolitan Board of Works (MMBW) assured Selby Smith 'that the proposed Highway would not encroach on any of the playing fields, but would adjoin the Lower Oval on the Southern boundary'.[46] 'At no point did it come on to the School's side of the levee bank .... the Board were emphatic that the proposal did not involve any of the area used for playing fields'.[47] The MMBW's chief planner was Edwin Borrie (1911). He retired in 1959.

In 1960 the Bursar happened to hear that an entirely new route might be considered. A junior engineer contemplated a route right across the Meares, Hockey and Rugby Ovals and the Lower Ovals, such that 'they could no longer be used for their present purposes; nor is there any other

The scene from the Chapel roof around 1962. 'The freeway will pass behind the central electric power pylon and will cut the left corner of the Rugby Pitch to join Glenferrie Road on the left.'

land available on the school site which could be utilised in place of that which would be lost'.[48] Selby Smith at once visited the Board, which assured him that this was merely a possible alternative route. Since the new route made sense (it was shorter), Scotch firmly registered its opposition.

Scotch argued that its ovals were thoroughly used—on Saturdays four successive matches were commonplace—and by schools other than Scotch. For example, the Victorian Junior Rugby Union ran a seven-a-side competition that included several high schools. 'If this is not held at Scotch, it could not be held at all, as it is not possible to get facilities anywhere else for such a competition.'[49]

But 'it is the assault on the tranquillity and beauty of the place that is far more grievous and far less easy to explain, to prove and to assert, by contrast with public utility'.[50] The levee bank 20 years after its construction was a green walk among well-grown trees, with the smell of blackberries when they were in season. It gave boys seclusion for a quiet cigarette, or to eat lunch while strolling along the bank beside river and creek.[51] 'Beauty', said Healey,

> is easily and often destroyed: … These grounds and buildings have been planned with foresight: no one could have expected a road to be driven through this area. It may be said that the road and the noise of its traffic will be far from the teaching installations of the school. But such an argument forgets the educative influence of natural beauty, of grounds in which there is room not only for athletic sports and games, but also for other activities and, just as important, for the gentler and contemplative moments in a young person's life. In modern education we try hard to get young people out into the country, so that they can receive that benefit which our lovely country can bestow. It is paradoxical to see the foresight of our fathers ruined by the proposal to remove the countryside from our midst.[52]

In 1965 Ken Gifford (1939, OSCA President 1972) overruled doubters and advised Council to appeal, and Council asked him to act for it, with Alan Lobban (1930, Council 1971–80) as solicitor. Clifford Menhennitt (1929) represented OSCA. Council adopted Gifford's ideas for a press release and a brochure to explain to MPs why the school wanted the freeway re-routed. Afterwards, Council specifically thanked Gifford, Lobban and Ray Northrop for their expert, unremitting work.

The school had four aims: Firstly, to change the freeway's route, either moving it well south to run above the railway (an existing transport corridor), or pushing it across the creek on to the school on the other side, St Kevin's. In this Scotch was unsuccessful. Secondly, if the route did follow the creek and come on to Scotch land, then to make it follow the line of the creek and not encroach on playing fields. Thirdly and fourthly, to keep the freeway narrow (with four lanes rather than six) and low. In 1966 the Minister concerned, Hamer, limited the freeway to four lanes, only 12 feet (3.7 m) high. It would not diminish the ovals, and would take only 3 acres on the line of Gardiner's Creek.

An aerial view (see p. VII) shows the freeway swerving round Scotch instead of taking the direct route across the ovals. Scotch's clout is manifest. Yet Scotch could not push the freeway any further south. Scotch had met the limitations of its power. Perhaps most frustratingly, Scotch's Old Boy politicians were not very useful, because they did not wish to be seen overtly to influence public policy to favour their school.

Three issues now remained: compensation, the physical disturbance of the freeway's construction, and (long-term) preventing public access to the land beneath the freeway.

Scotch had to allow access through the school to the freeway construction site, but retained access to the boatsheds and launching ramps, and prevented the contractor cutting down school trees to allow large equipment to manoeuvre. The lower ovals became unusable, because the contractor breached the levee bank, which let in floods in January (2.4 m deep), March and April 1970. The ovals could not shed this water or rain-water, because the contractor repeatedly blocked the outlet-valves, and the contractor's temporary access route prevented the ovals from draining. 'Some kids were swimming in the assault course and some other kids were actually sailing a yacht on Lake Meares!'[53]

The contractor, McDougall–Ireland, offered less than $3000 in full settlement for restoration of the school grounds, but Scotch insisted that the MMBW restore the grounds to the situation they were in before construction began. Once the ovals were dry again they had to be scraped of silt, then harrowed and re-sown, and sloped to the main peripheral drainage ditch. A drainage pipe already laid by the MMBW, had to be re-laid 'so as to lead downwards to the drainage ditch (instead of up-hill as at present!)'.[54]

In compensation for loss of land, Scotch received land to its north,[55] both the unmade western end of Morrison Street and the land along the river as far north as Hambledon Road. Scotch wanted this land zoned the same as the school, that is, the same as the land that had been lost. The MMBW, however, proposed to restrict its use to recreational purposes, and Hamer believed it 'should be preserved forever against being covered with buildings'.[56] Not that Hamer was handing over a rural idyll, for the river bank was eroded in places, and the school had to clear up and replant the whole river bank from the creek to Hambledon Road. Further, Scotch opposed any right of public access through its land, for instance at the end of Morrison Street, whereas the Board proposed a 5 feet-wide path along the northern boundary of Scotch's new land.

When the MMBW acquired land for the freeway, Council tried to impose a condition on its use: to prevent the general public having access. Council wanted to protect the school's boundary with the creek, but its conception of this area changed over time. At first Council wanted a safety fence (still with thoughts that a road endangered boys), but once the freeway was built Council realised there was no need for a fence and that the space near and under the freeway, though marred by pylons, was still a grassy creek-side. No fence, however, meant that 'motor bike riders and other undesirables' could enter Scotch along the creek from Glenferrie Road. Horses were 'ridden over our cricket pitches and *at* our groundsmen',[57] and there was gun-fire along the creek and drunks in the copse. Scotch asked for a wire fence for 150 yards (140 m) from Glenferrie Road along the creek, which did reduce vandalism in the grounds.

Trees were planted to screen the freeway. Other trees were already mature and needed care. Gums near the Boat Shed were lopped to save them from the decaying effect of mistletoe. Elms on the walk to Mackie Hall past the grass tennis courts were dying from beetle infestation and had to be cut down in 1981. That same year the new Council ordered an Arboreal Master Plan for the next 25 years. In 1983, after prolonged drought, the Scotch Association began to help maintain the school's treescape. Tree-planting days continued to occur into the 1990s. In 1992, auxiliaries helped plant 500 trees.

Scotch dealt with the freeway as best it could. It helped to limit it to four lanes and to route it along the school boundary; it received compensatory land in the form of the western end of Morrison Street and the riparian land north of there up to Hambledon Road; it survived the construction of the freeway—loss of trees and repeated flooding of the lower ovals once the levee banks were breached—and it made sure the MMBW paid for the re-landscaping.

North: Morrison Street

From 1957, the year it failed to stop the freeway on its south flank, Scotch crept northward. It outflanked Morrison Street and then slowly absorbed it.

First, on the north of the river-side end of Morrison Street, Nicholson, a Council member who lived nearby, noted that the City of Hawthorn owned 0.1 hectare. Council bought it in 1959, and installed tennis courts named after Nicholson. In 1963 Council tried to buy from the City the land north of those courts extending to Hambledon Road. The City would sell only with many conditions including public access to the river, and the use of the land only as open space. Scotch withdrew its offer, and later obtained this land as freeway compensation.

In 1959, two houses in Morrison Street were for sale, but Council took no action. Then in 1960 Council 'resolved that every effort be made to acquire property in this street'.[58] This key change in policy has no explanation in the minutes and perhaps occurred without much debate for Council members seemed not to remember it, and repeated the decision in 1966, again without prior discussion. Perhaps it grew out of the loss of land to the freeway, and was either to make up for the lost land or to link with the land wanted in compensation? Soon, to secure a vacant block in Morrison Street, the Bursar was 'instructed to take any steps he considered necessary'.[59] This new and vigorous policy did not extend to Hambledon or Callantina Roads, where Council felt it should pay no more than market value. But such properties have more value to Scotch than to anyone else, for the school can only expand into the immediately neighbouring streets. In 1961 and 1966 Council snapped up 7 and 8 Morrison Street for around $13 000 each (26 times annual fees).

Cricket match, Main Oval 1976. Tony Miles is about to take a wicket. The recently built freeway sits high in the background; its light reduced the usefulness of the observatory; noise pollution troubled classrooms; and, visually, the looming freeway spoilt Scotch's feel of parkland.

In 1962 Morrison Street counter-attacked. Solicitors for Mrs 'Paddy' Dorum, on the corner of Fordholm Road and Morrison Street, drew attention 'to the disturbance of the peace and quiet of her home by reason of the sounds emanating from the Music School'.[60] Mr Dorum was a writer who required 'complete peace'.[61] (He was, also, the piano accompanist at the 1939–41 Foundation Day Concerts.)

Scotch addressed the problem in several ways. It reduced brass instrument practice in the early morning. It brought in some portable soundproofing and acoustical architects. Logie-Smith, however, warned 'that the more effective sound absorption is, the further one gets from an ideal or even acceptable standard of acoustics from the point of view of instruction'.[62]

Council sent Selby Smith 'to interview Mrs Dorum with a view to a property exchange in the area',[63] a suggestion she naturally rejected. Also, Scotch sent the Principal and the Bursar, on advice from Scotch's solicitor, Keith Ness (1924, President of OSCA 1959), a member of Council, to interview the Dorums' neighbours and 'to obtain written statements from them'.[64] Ness meanwhile noted that Scotch had some time ago offered to buy Mrs Dorum's property and that she was not prepared to sell. Now Ness would have a title search done to ascertain what she paid when she bought it. Scotch was not used to dealing with neighbours who spoke their mind, and its response was heavy-handed, but it met its match in

Mrs Dorum, 'a lady of somewhat combative character, industrious in asserting what she regards to be her rights'.[65]

The Music School was dismayed that the constructive activities of hundreds of people were subordinated to the desires of one person, and felt she 'should have known what Music Schools were like when she chose to live next door to one'.[66] But the noise level had risen, for Logie-Smith's increased instrumental tuition 'had made it necessary to use rooms adjacent to Mackie Hall but not soundproofed', and boys studying in the library (then nearby on the upper floor of Mackie Hall) had also complained. Scotch had only begun to think about soundproofing rooms.

Mrs Dorum's neighbours all said they suffered no discomfort or annoyance at Scotch's noise, but the matter was not to be resolved by a local vote but by the law, and at law Scotch's advice was that Mrs Dorum had a case, and might win, so Scotch had to placate her as best it could. In the long run relations with Mrs Dorum became amicable. She sold her house to Scotch, retaining the right to dwell there while she lived, and she supported the school's closure of Morrison Street.

By 1970 Scotch owned nearly half the houses in Morrison Street. Council hesitated to buy one in 1975, but thereafter took such purchases in its stride. Because Scotch bought the houses one by one, some were rented to masters, but Donaldson saw them as essentially part of the school grounds, and reserved them for staff with a particular need to live at the school, for example having duties in the boarding houses. From 1981, Council concentrated on buying houses in Morrison Street, and sold most of the half-dozen other houses in nearby streets. To expedite this, in 1985 Scotch asked Morrison Street's four remaining private owners to approach Scotch first when they wished to sell. In 1992 Scotch owned all properties in Morrison Street.

From at least 1968 Council intended acquiring the Morrison Street roadway itself, in order to close it off. In 1992 Scotch acquired the western end of the roadway for $310 000. As with the freeway, Scotch found that Old Boys in high office were the least able to help, and the final decision to sell Morrison Street to the school was taken not under either of the Old Boy Premiers, Cain or Kennett, but under the premiership in between, that of Joan Kirner. By 2000, Scotch owned Morrison Street right up to Fordholm Road. Owning Morrison Street gives the school room to expand. When it does so it will impose its own imprint on what was once a street of houses, and there may come a time when it will no longer be clear where the older pattern of land usage lay, just as we can no longer detect that the main school buildings replaced an older building and its driveway.

OVALS, ROADS AND WATERWAYS

A wider circle of threats and opportunities lay just across the school's surrounding roads and waterways.

In 1969 Scotch expanded eastwards across Glenferrie Road. It asked the

Malvern City Council for winter occupancy of the two rugby and two hockey ovals there. The school would share these facilities with the Old Scotch Rugby and Hockey Clubs.

This revived the problem of traffic danger to boys crossing Glenferrie Road. The only safe way was to go under it, along the creek, but the creek was often up after rain. Mullenger House proposed a suspended footbridge under Gardiner's Creek Bridge, but the General House Committee declined to endorse this, as it would be expensive and would let outsiders enter the grounds. Instead Scotch asked the City for a pedestrian crossing and lights at the Monash gates or even a footbridge, but the City did a traffic survey and declined to act.

The older traffic danger continued. In 1978 James Crowther (aged 14) died after being hit by a car near the school. In 1977 Junior School boys surveyed average traffic 8–8.45 a.m. at Callantina Road and found 346 boys alighting from southbound trams and 34 cars travelling through amber or red lights.

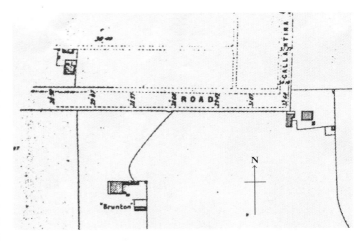

An old sketch map of the present location of the Senior School, shows the junction of what is now Fordholm (then called Callantina) Road and Morrison Road and the house named Brunton near the present Memorial Hall.

To the north-east, in 1968 a developer planned an eight- or nine-storey block of flats at the corner of Glenferrie and Callantina Roads, diagonally opposite Scotch. Scotch objected on grounds of increased traffic and danger to pupils. Gifford successfully put the school's case before the MMBW and the Town and Planning Appeals Tribunal, with supportive attendance from the Junior School Mothers' Association. The building was disallowed as being out of harmony with the area.

To the south, across Gardiner's Creek, the Kooyong Tennis Stadium was in 1973 used for 'pop music' concerts which forced the school to employ additional uniformed guards, whilst staff patrolled the grounds to control trespassers. Council acquainted the Lawn Tennis Association 'with the magnitude of unauthorised entry, damage to fences and cases of sexual exposure and indecency that have occurred on the College property at the time of these promotions'.[67]

To the west, just across the Yarra River in the Bartlett Reserve, Channel 9 proposed in 1991 to establish a heliport, but failed to get approval.

RATES

Scotch used to pay Hawthorn municipal rates like any other landowner, and the rates steadily increased as Scotch put up new buildings. Sometimes a dispute arose about the amount levied. In 1952 the High Court exempted the Salvation Army from municipal rates. This unleashed requests for similar exemptions. In 1958 the City of Hawthorn exempted Scotch, which instead made the City an *ex gratia* payment, thereby saving £1500.

Arguably, municipalities need rates from all landowners, and in 1966 the Statute Law Revision Committee looked at this question. Council asked the church to represent the school's view in this matter, but also engaged Gifford as counsel. (In these small ways we see the school becoming less sure about church support and more self-reliant.) Gifford suggested that, far from depriving municipalities of rates, the presence of schools elevated surrounding values.[68] Scotch produced evidence of this from a sworn valuer. (In 2000, nearby properties sell themselves as being on 'the Scotch Hill'.)

A second argument against independent schools paying rates was that it would ruin those schools and then the government would have to provide more government schools. The City valued Scotch at $1 500 000. If it levied rates, they 'would be immense and, indeed, annihilating'.[69] Of course, rather than go bankrupt the schools would increase their fees, but the schools had no wish to make narrower the social base of their pupils, as could be seen from their scholarships and fee concessions. Schools also allowed use of their grounds to outsiders. Scotch stopped describing its annual *ex gratia* payment as 'in lieu of rates'[70] and in 1969 began an annual gavotte in which Hawthorn asked for a payment *in lieu of rates*, and Scotch made the payment as *a contribution to the upkeep of the City*. Had Scotch not been exempt, the rates due would have been eight times what it paid.

SOUTH: THE BIKE PATH

In 1983 the school once again defended itself against people using the land between its grounds and the creek. This time it was a freeway for bicycles. Hawthorn and Malvern City Councils planned a bike route along Gardiner's Creek to connect with the Yarra Bicycle Path by a bridge over the Yarra immediately north of the freeway. The path would run along the levee bank. This was the school's land, and riders would have easy access to the rest of the school unless Scotch erected a fence, thereby curtailing its own access to the levee bank. Council denounced the whole idea as 'a threat to the School's occupancy of its own grounds',[71] and refused to grant right of way, suggesting that the path go south of the creek. To mobilise support, the school called a meeting of Scotch Family residents in Hawthorn. In 1992 the path was slung under the freeway.

The problem had widened in 1985 when the MMBW published a Lower Yarra River Concept and Development Plan, which proposed new legislation regulating the use of the river and its environs and amending the zoning regulations on land adjoining the Yarra. The school hired solicitors versed in town planning to combat 'this major threat to the School's independence'.[72] The MMBW soothingly replied that its proposals did not affect privately owned property and agreed to say so in the plan.

SOUTH: THE FREEWAY AGAIN!

Scotch's success in limiting the freeway to four lanes was always only temporary. Increased traffic meant that eventually the freeway was widened to six lanes. Scotch had two major concerns. First, it lost up to 11 metres of land along its southern boundary. Critically, the Lower Oval was no longer large enough to provide two cricket pitches, effectively depriving the school of one oval.

Secondly, Scotch argued that the noise standards applied by Victorian authorities were inadequate for educational and residential environments, and although the Environmental Impact Review panel supported this view, the government ruled that the generally applied noise standard of 63dB(A)L10 over an 18-hour period should apply at Scotch. Then, in 'extensive negotiations, lasting over two years', Scotch argued for 5-metre sound barriers, higher than those proposed by VicRoads.[73] Scotch would pay the additional cost out of the money received in land acquisition compensation. Scotch's architect Garry Martin designed a barrier with colour and texture that would make it less of an eyesore. Where the barrier loomed most closely over the ovals it was transparent, to lessen the imposition.

All this took a great deal of time and energy by the Chairman of Council, Principal, Bursar, and other officers, as well as a great deal of money paying professional representatives.

In dealing with the freeway Scotch, like any landowner, concentrated on its own interests. There was no talk of sacrifices for the common good, so often a part of Scotch's discourse. This is understandable. A road across most of the ovals, with visual and acoustic intrusion on all the key buildings, was a mortal threat that had to be resisted fully. Other boundary threats, however, were not mortal yet evoked the same fiercely protective response. Scotch risked looking selfish—and knew that it risked this—but still defended itself without compromise against all intrusions and complaints. Whatever 'school spirit' means to boys in their teens, in Scotch's adults it emerges as a resolute determination to let nothing hurt the school at all, to brook no interference. Scotch is tenacious in protecting its property and its right to use that property freely, now and in the future.

As a property-owner, Scotch is at its least heroic. It resisted complaints (Mrs Dorum), refused to make concessions to community wishes (freeway, bike path) and declined to pay any more to the public purse than it had to (rates).

TO MOVE OR NOT TO MOVE?

Scotch has spent only half its life at Hawthorn, but it has invested much money and emotion there and will probably stay. Nevertheless, in 1946 Gilray floated the idea of moving the Junior School away from the main property, and in 1954 Nicholson wanted a second Junior School in North Balwyn. In 1976 Council toyed with 'Long range plans' to relocate the Junior School Sub-Primary to a nearby property where a Kindergarten could also be developed. From the 1980s, Scotch's planning has repeatedly assumed that it will remain in Hawthorn.

In floods and freeway traffic, Scotch has chosen to stay where it is, with all the benefits of having the whole school on a single site.

11

SCOTCH REINVENTS ITSELF

1950–1975

After its centenary Scotch at last came to terms with having moved to Hawthorn, discovered new ways of presenting itself, and broadened the very meaning of who belonged to the Scotch community.

INVENTING A TRADITION OF SCOTTISHNESS

In the second half of the 20th century Scotch College invented a new tradition. Bagpipes skirled on formal occasions, the cadets sported kilts, Balmorals and Glengarries, and Old Boys dined on haggis and *a wee birdie cookit wi' tatties*. In 1945 none of this existed.

How and why did Scotch invent its Scottish tradition? Scotch is unique among Melbourne's Public Schools in having an ethnic affiliation. The Scots' College was not matched by Irish or Welsh Colleges, and only in this century has there been a Jewish college.

The school's Scottishness has had several phases. At first it was simply true: its founders were Scotsmen, and so were many early teachers. So we saw its boys called 'the Scotsmen' at the first football match in 1858. The 1883 crew consisted entirely of red-heads, a fine Celtic display. All this was peripheral to the main task, and the syllabus contained nothing particularly Scottish. The boys studied Shakespeare and Milton, but not Burns or Sir Walter Scott.

The Scots accent was long present. Around 1900, a new boy 'was at least a month at the school before he could understand more than one word in ten spoken by Dr Morrison and most of the other masters'.[1] In 1929 Ingram's Highland burr was not immediately intelligible when first heard, so a new boy had to consult 'neighbours familiar with foreign languages'.[2] This tale confirms both Ingram's accent and its relative uncommonness by that time. Obituaries of Littlejohn in 1934 mentioned his accent, whilst those of Morrison, thirty years earlier, had not. After 1950 the Scots accent was heard mainly from people appointed before 1950 and who lingered on—Fraser, the chaplain, Elizabeth Baird in the tuckshop 1930–55, Hughie Aitken and Bill Mundie, groundsmen for 30 years, or Wal Fowler (staff 1929–71), 'a quiet gentle Scot' whose demeanour, gait and speech were all unhurried. Graham McInnes (1930) remembered the senior staff as Scottish dominies 'whose accent stuck to them for life. Unlike our English masters

223

whose crisp upper-middle-class voices soon became overlaid by the open sunny Australian accent, the Dominies' voices remained locked in craggy glottal fastnesses for the whole of their lives.'[3]

The formal link with Scotland attenuated and then broke. In the 1914–18 war J. D. Burns wrote the 'Bugles of *England* are calling', and the Scots-born Littlejohn, consoling the parent of a dead Old Boy, quoted a poem about 'lives for honour & for England given'.[4] As late as 1952, needing a new principal, turning to Scotland was Council's first reaction, but only its first.

In the first half of the 20th century, Scotch's Scottishness lay largely disused. The great old Burns poem and song 'Scots wha' hae wi' Wallace bled' died out, and has not revived, despite the film *Braveheart* which made Wallace once again a well-known hero. 'Auld Lang Syne' was sung from at least 1909 at Old Boy dinners because it was popular, not because it was Scottish. Boys played golf because they enjoyed it, though it was fun to call it the Scottish national game. In the 1920s boys called their newspapers the *Thistle* and *Oorsels*. The Scots tradition was one of several at the school: available but not predominant.

THE SCOTTISH NATIONAL GAME

'Golf is a game in which one places a ball one & a half inches in diameter upon another ball 8000 miles in diameter. The object of the game is to hit the smaller ball'.[5]

Bert Dupin (1927) learnt golf during vacation from one of the masters, a Scot. Some masters had constructed a few golf holes, with the first tee 'down a fairly steep slope immediately behind School House'.[6] In the 1940s boarders after school 'went down for a hit at the "Scottish National game" on the Rugby oval'.[7] Littlejohn and Gilray were golfers, and in the 1960s Healey would hit his way round the ovals in the evening after the boys had gone.

Golf's popularity grew—the 1950 prefects and probationers included several players—and in 1954 there was a Scotch College Golf Championship won by Michael Winneke. In 1956 there were six trophies to be won. Handicaps were on the Calloway system as used by the Victorian Golf Association for all schoolboy events. 'It is based on your worst holes.'[8]

The competition was not played at the school, and this long delayed golf's becoming a school sport. A 1971 attempt to set up a golf club foundered for lack of a place to play. In 1976–77 it became a school sport, and later an inter-school sport, though not an APS sport.

Michael Clayton (1974) has become an internationally notable golfer. Tom Crow (Captain 1950) won the Australian Amateur Championship and represented Australia in the World Amateur Cup.

Since most boys do not continue the sports they play at Scotch, perhaps it should teach the sports that middle-aged men play? Robert Swann's (1960) main regret about Scotch was 'Not getting involved in … golf because a good grounding in golf would be an asset in later life.'[9]

The link with Scotland was wheeled out only on formal occasions. To celebrate the school's centenary came the Moderator of the Church of Scotland, the first time a man holding this office had travelled overseas. Many speechmakers appealed to Scottish characteristics like thrift, hard work, egalitarianism and a belief in education. In the school's 75th year David York Syme (1892, OSCA President 1949) said that 'One of the characteristics of the Scottish race was a true democracy in deed and spirit, and at Scotch College no distinctions were made. Snobbery has never been allowed to creep into the life of the school.'[10] In the centenary year Sir John Latham (Chief Justice of Australia, Scotch's most distinguished living Old Boy), said that 'the Scottish way of life values three things in particular: Intelligence—we must use our brains to develop them … ; Industry—rewards come as the result of work, not of luck, and we must do everything to our best; Self-respect—we must have nothing of which we are ashamed'. In that same year the *Collegian*'s editors rhapsodised the Scots' 'deeply religious nature … rigidly strong personal convictions, and an equally profound respect for education'.[11]

This habit of appealing to Scottish national characteristics had problems. Firstly, its impact diminished as Australians' knowledge of Scotland faded. Secondly, these virtues of 'our race' were pitched at an audience who were told that they or their forebears came from Scotland,[12] although this was not the case even when Scotch began. At Speech Day in 1935 the Governor, Lord Huntingfield, praised the school which 'equips you to play the distinguished part which Scotsmen have played since time immemorial'. Perhaps someone took this up with him, for the next year at Scotch his lordship conceded that not all 'of those who are educated at Scotch College have any claims to be connected by descent with Scotland, but if you are being educated in a college which is being called by the name of Scotland you must take the responsibility which attaches to that position. … that the Scottish nation has been distinct above all others in its thirst for knowledge'.[13] Nowadays one appeals to the Scottishness of the founders rather than to Scottishness in the present Scotch Family (though this is still welcomed when noticed). Thirdly, tying the school to the myths of another country ran the risk of an untidy involvement with that country's own identity struggles. Alongside the picture of the Lowland Scots as dour, thrifty, hard-working, religious, canny and down-to-earth there is another quite different picture of the Highland Celts: emotional, poetic, imaginative and impractical, with a red-headed impulsiveness and flaming temper.

By 1950, organisations having an explicit connection with Scotland were in decline. The Victorian Scottish Regiment was disbanded and the Caledonian Society was in the hands of its creditors. At the school, Scotsmen and Scottish practices were uncommon. The literal meaning of the school's name was no longer noticed in day-to-day usage, any more than one expected Fleming to be from Flanders.

Scotch's release from any real Scottishness, however, freed the school to reinvent its Scottishness by focusing on certain elements: pipes, kilts, haggis and mock Scots wording in menus. (This echoes the invention of these traditions in Scotland in the eighteenth century.[14]) At Scotch, it began in the centenary year, 1951. The *Collegian* parodied Burns to celebrate the head groundsman's new tractor, 'Hughie Aitken my jo',[15] and to describe the cross-country runner's stitch 'Tearin' my breast wi' bitter pang'.[16] More seriously, at the Centenary's Foundation Day Concert the vice-regal party was led in by pipes, and the boys sang many traditional Scottish songs— an evocative medley of landscape, love-song and war-making—orchestrated by Claude Monteath, Director of Music. The programme called this item 'Our Scottish Ancestry', asserting a biological as well as a cultural connection. The House choral competition that year included other Scottish songs. Monteath repeated his arrangement of Scottish songs in later Foundation Day Concerts in the 1950s.

Bagpipe drones reach skyward. In the last 50 years bagpipes have become an integral part of Scotch's life. They are often heard at practice and are deeply moving at ceremonies.

Of all Scotland's claims on the school, music had lingered longest. The first Foundation Day Concert in 1911 contained nothing Scottish, but later concerts had Scottish songs and airs, and from 1925 two Scottish songs became customary until tastes changed in the 1960s. Meanwhile the songs became part of the boys' cultural heritage, and occasionally they glimpsed the strength of those ties, as when at Ingram's last Speech Night the school sang to him before he went home to Scotland:

Ance mair, ance mair where Gadie rins
  Where Gadie rins, where Gadie rins,
O let me dee where Gadie rins
  At the back of Binachie.

Ingram wept.[17]

Bagpipes came late. Perhaps this was because to play them is a 'futile [and] vicious circle … All the air you blow into them in one breath you squeeze out of them the next. The only reward you obtain is the most inhuman screeching.'[18] In 1933 Littlejohn would have loved a pipe band 'to play on ceremonial occasions and to lead the school Cadet corps on a march-out' but the school could not afford the cost of uniforms, instruments and instruction.[19] The issue arose that year when the Victorian Scottish Regiment regained permission to wear the kilt and embarked on an expensive project to do so. Because they were affiliated with the Gordon Highlanders, they wore the Gordon tartan. In 1946, after World War II, the Regiment's Colonel,

Tom Cook (whose son, Geoff, had just left Scotch), gave Scotch ten sets of pipes, six guard pattern side-drums, two tenor drums, and one bass drum. Gilray asked Donald 'Danny' MacPherson (staff 1946–58) to start up the Scotch pipe band. Gordon tartan kilts were purchased, and soon they could play 'The Skye Boat Song', 'Blue Bells' and the 42nd March, even with a few grace notes. On Thursdays before the band's practice MacPherson would spend two hours tuning and adjusting all the pipes. 'He cut, pulled, wet, sliced and even chewed those reeds to make them go. ... when he had his teeth pulled out in 1950, he was at a considerable disadvantage, being unable to set his pipes as well as previously.'[20]

Fleming secured the band an annual equipment grant, and with money from the Melbourne Scots and OSCA the school imported from Scotland wide black leather belts, sporrans, socks and flashes, Balmorals or tam o' shanters, and twelve sets of pipes.[21] David D. Lindsay, a parent who lived in India, presented the skin of a leopard (which he shot himself) for the base drummer. The band added impressively to the school's public face, accompanying the Cadet Guard at the opening of State Parliament in 1955.

As Director of Music, Logie-Smith loathed bagpipes played indoors and would not have them at the Foundation Day Concert,[22] but his successor, Chris Latham (Director of Music 1978–85), put two pipers on the balcony at the 1978 Concert, Tim Swain (1978) and Andrew Carnegie (1978), and soon there was a pipes and drums item on the programme. Pipes became a distinctive way of marking school occasions. Two pipers played as guests arrived at a Junior School Mothers' Association function in 1981. In 1977 the Junior School was summoned to Assembly by a rostered piper. The pipes are now an integral part of Scotch's life, often heard at practice, and deeply moving at ceremonies, perhaps most of all during the annual Tattoo when a lone piper plays on the chapel steps in the gloaming.

When Bond took command of the cadets only the Pipe Band and Guard were kilted, but Bond told Selby Smith he wanted to end this sartorial discrimination and kilt the whole unit. Selby Smith said, 'Crumbs!' Macpherson's pupil and successor, Pipe-Major Bill Brown (staff 1959–75, in the mornings he was a Physics Laboratory assistant) acquired the kilts through his innumerable connections and, as a tailor, also mended them. The newly formed Cadet Mothers' Auxiliary raised money by selling refreshments to Saturday sportsplayers. The unit was fully kilted in 1962. One boy dreaded wearing his kilt to school 'while walking past MLC and getting whistled at by the girls' (1975). Only after 50 years did *Satura* risk a joke about wearing nothing under the kilt.[23] The military band set up in 1959 wore a scarlet jacket and tartan trews.

Twice, boys have worn kilts as an ordinary item of apparel, Alec Pratt (1922) in 1916 and Bill (1939) and David (1944) Low in 1936.[24] Whilst not laid down as uniform, Scotch would be hard pressed to forbid boys from wearing a kilt, but even in the rebellious 1960s no-one did so. Perhaps the

A practising bagpiper was walking up and down his street, when a neighbour complained he was making an awful row, so he took off his shoes and continued to practise barefoot. (*Satura*, 10 Feb. 1956, p. 2)

link with cadets robbed it of any rebel effect.

'Wheest noo! while oor ain Meenister asks the blessing', began the menu of the 1954 OSCA annual dinner, organised by John Baker (1926). 'The serious work o' the nicht noo starts, so tuck in yer table hankie.' The menu included 'Gundy wi' snaw o' Ben Nevis on it' and ended with coffee 'A heathenish drink, but uisge-beatha improves it'. Three years earlier, the Old Boys' Centenary Dinner in 1951 ate seafood cocktail, tomato soup, whiting meuniere, roast chicken and bacon, and cauliflower au gratin. There was no tradition of Scottish dishes, though we search back to the annual dinner of the Society of the Old Scotch Collegians at Gunsler's Café in 1880.

From 1954 the mock Scots menu instantly became traditional at the OSCA annual dinner. At the 1955 dinner the official party was led in by pipers, and the haggis arrived escorted by kilted cadet officers with swords drawn. The 'Bill o' fare' included a detailed explanation of haggis. The menus for decades from the 1970s all had exactly the same style, beginning 'Ye can set him a chair tae the tableside and gi' him a bite tae eat.' Dishes included 'Roastit spring chookie' and 'apple pastie, wi' clorty cream'. The salmon came *wi' awld Reekie sauce*, and the Aberdeen cockerel *wi' Ayrshire tatties, neeps, an' Kail*. All this was fun. It was, however, directed at entertaining Australians rather than reviving Scottish usage, and although it was said that OSCA's President had 'to learn a wee drap of Gaelic for the occasion',[25] OSCA probably neither knew nor cared that wee and drap are Scots not Gaelic.

A new tradition is invented. *Wheest noo, at an Old Boys' Annual Dinner around 1980 while Ross Campbell (Pipe Major from 1976) pipes in the haggis, which is escorted, with swords drawn, by John Graham and Fred Rovner.*

In 1985 the Junior School Parents' Association decided to sell shortbread. Other aspects of Scottishness were not taken up. Keith Wilson suggested celebrating St Andrews Day (30 November),[26] but it falls too late in the academic year. No Gaelic or Scots word survives in the war-cries. A 1917 chant ending 'Ready to do or die. (Hooch-aye)'[27] had by 1958 become 'Ready to do or die—hi, hi!'[28] No word or phrase endures from all the Scotsmen who taught at the school. Even in recent decades, with Australia's revived interest in ethnic roots, Gaelic has not gathered even a small club of enthusiasts. Sword dancing and the eightsome reel are ignored. Perhaps they seem sissy, although the Victorian Scottish Regiment danced them, and there are ways of making them sound manly: Jim Bryce (1937), who married Gilray's daughter, Ruth, took joy in Highland dancing, and was said to show the fruits of that exercise later, in the spring of his step on the tennis court. Nor does Scotch have caber-tossing, although that would certainly be manly.

Scotch could develop its own tartan, but replacing the existing kilts would be expensive, and the Gordon tartan is rare enough in Melbourne. In matters of curriculum, Scotch has not used its influence in educational circles to add Burns or Scottish history to the syllabus. Jacobitism had a revival around 1900, and a Scottish school might have given it some flicker of recognition. Not even the accession of each new Stuart Pretender has been celebrated, even in fun. Robert the Bruce's encounter with the spider has had only a few echoes. The 1913 First XVIII, for example: 'Like the spider, oft they failed, / But at last their grot prevailed'.[29]

In 1998 the School Captain, Matt Spargo, urged boys to attend the Head of the River by drawing on Wallace's pre-battle speech in *Braveheart*—'dying in your beds, many years from now, would you be willing to trade all the days from this day to that, for one chance, just *one chance* to come back to the Barwon and tell our enemies that they may cheer against us, but they'll never harm the cardinal, gold and blue'.[30]

After 50 years the school has developed a Scottishness quite disconnected from Scotland. The songs that began the revival are no longer sung, and the present Director of Music, Ferguson, grimaces at the thought. Few boys or staff would know even the titles, or recognise 'Flow Gently Sweet Afton' as Scottish.

Indeed, in the midst of the revival, in 1963, Scotch abandoned being *the* Scotch College, and became simply Scotch College.[31]

COMPLETING THE MOVE TO HAWTHORN

It took a generation for Scotch to come to terms with having moved to Hawthorn. It happened with a rush in the years immediately after the 1951 centenary, at the same time as the new enthusiasm for things Scottish.

Scotch became able to represent itself with images of Hawthorn rather than East Melbourne. In 1953 the *Collegian* made the Memorial Hall its new front cover, designed by art master, Frank Paton (see p. XI). Next, new half-titles displayed the interior of the Memorial Hall and cloisters.

In 1953 Council decided to meet at the school (in the Principal's residence) instead of at the main Presbyterian Assembly Hall. The decision was taken twice, which suggests some resistance or uncertainty. Meeting at Scotch was both an acceptance of where Scotch now lived and a step away from dependence on the church. In 1959 Council's minute-taker, the church's Secretary, G. D. McKinnon, asked to hand over to the Bursar, Ken Field, who was soon 'Racking his brains to record and report / What he thinks they think that they ought to have thought!'[32]

While Council moved in, John Gardiner moved out. As sometimes happens when people buy old houses, they are tempted to claim its family portraits as their own. Hawthorn Glen was linked with Gardiner, an early Melbourne pioneer, and Scotch rather adopted him. It named a house after him, and gave land for a memorial cairn near the Monash Gates. In the decade 1944–54 Scotch shook loose, demolishing Hawthorn Glen and renaming Gardiner House after Gilray. Two small memorials to the Head family, local pioneers, are tucked away near the boatshed, but form no part of the school's mythology.

Other ghosts were also laid to rest. At the end of 1925, East Melbourne closed. In farewell, 700 Old Boys from every decade back to the 1850s filled No. 1 and overflowed into the quadrangle. Scotch sold the property to a Presbyterian charity, which later built St Andrew's Hospital there. In 1959 St Andrew's demolished Scotch's old buildings and gave Scotch a quantity of bluestone from No. 1, which made a forecourt to the Memorial Hall's Foundation Stone. A plaque there exhorts us to 'Look unto the rock whence ye are hewn' (Isaiah li.1), but it is not clear which is the stone from East Melbourne. *Satura* errs in saying it is the paving stone,[33] which is sandstone. The East Melbourne stone was used, too, for the new barbecue near the boatshed, for crews rowing on Saturday.

In 1975 further demolitions threatened an East Melbourne building classified by the National Trust, whose citation linked it with Scotch. The school, however, declined to raise any objection. Scotch had had no connection with the building for decades, said Council, and could make no financial commitment to preserve this link with its past.

THE OLD BOYS

In 1954 the OSCA Council also started to meet at Scotch (in the Masters' Common Room), moving from the Public Schools' Club.

As Australian society recovered momentum after World War II, OSCA asserted itself. There was a church rule on appointing to Council four members nominated by the Old Scotch Collegians. In 1956, to secure its position, OSCA wanted this changed so that the nominations came from the Old Scotch Collegians' *Association*. This brought the rule into line with practice. It also prevented Old Boys choosing their representatives in some other way, such as a postal ballot as was originally the case.

OSCA in 1956 also asked Sir William Dargie, seven times winner of the Archibald Prize, to paint a portrait of Bowden, recently retired after two decades as Vice-Principal. Apart from Robert Morrison's lost portrait, no other Vice-Principal had been painted. Bowden was also a leading Old Boy. He had helped create OSCA and was about to be its President. He kicked 21 goals against Xavier in 1907, a record that stood for decades. Captain of the School and of Football 1906–07 and Captain of Cricket 1905–07, his name appears seven times on the Honour Boards in the Memorial Hall, more often than any other, a pre-eminence that has lasted now for almost a hundred years. Alex Sloan (Captain and Dux 1924, staff 1933–45) and Frank Scott (Vice-Captain 1933) each appears six times.

As Acting Principal while Gilray was overseas, Bowden was the first Old Boy to be in charge of the school.

OSCA further strengthened itself by obtaining permanent accommodation. Until then it lived in the office of whoever was secretary. In 1958 Bowden suggested Scotch give OSCA a room at the school and a member of staff as secretary. Selby Smith agreed, and freed Davidson.

In the 1950s OSCA resumed its role as the school's long-term planner. Council administered the finances and managed the buildings and staffing, but its focus was annual. It was OSCA that in 1953 proposed setting up an Endowment Fund. They had to push to get action. They politely asked for Council's views. Council appointed a sub-committee. A month later OSCA was more forthright, and proposed that Council appoint three representatives to meet three from OSCA. Council acquiesced, but its main item of business was selecting the prize-giver for Speech Day. (The clergy on Council wanted it done by a cleric, feeling that prize presenters had become too secular.) One cannot help contrasting the narrow focus of Council with the vision and energy of the Old Boys, cannot help noting who is exercising leadership. Confident and independent, OSCA acted as Council's equal. The relationship between Council and OSCA is a dynamic one and in the 1950s the balance tilted in favour of OSCA whilst Council faltered slightly. This is natural: over 150 years the school as a whole will have its ups and downs, and its major component parts will have theirs.

H. Bremner Lewis (1895), Chairman of Council 1945–47.

During the two decades 1943–63, Council's chair fell several times into uncertain hands. After half a century with only three chairmen, it now had five in 20 years. Sir Arthur Robinson died in office in 1945, an old man. His successor, H. Bremner Lewis, was an old man who soon resigned and died. A younger man, James Aitken (Captain 1920), soon died in office, having struggled in his last years. Another old man, Sir Clive Steele, soon said he wanted to retire, but even when he stopped attending, Council deferred replacing him, which left Anderson, the Deputy Chairman, as Acting Chairman for much of 1954. When Anderson at last became Chairman, Council dawdled in filling the Deputy Chairmanship (customarily the successor-in-waiting), and then did as Anderson wanted and chose Douglas Bain over Henry Winneke. Winneke then resigned from Council (and as a consolation prize became successively Chief Justice and the first Australian-born Governor of Victoria). Bain was a devoted and hard-working servant of the school, though Winneke might have been a better chairman.

At much the same time, the Executive and Finance Committee stumbled in managing its own business, when it failed to notice until it lacked a quorum that many of its members were overseas. At this point Anderson decided to act. (He felt awkward in doing so, explaining that 'When presiding at Council Meetings I feel that the need for impartiality as Chairman makes it difficult for me to express an opinion on matters which come up. But I feel, also, that it is part of my duty as Chairman to set before you the conclusion I have reached in this important matter.'[34] The dilemma between these different models of leadership—helping people realise their potential or telling people what to do—recurs at lower levels of the school.)

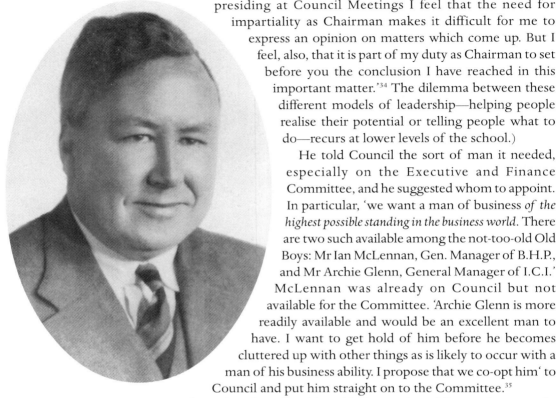

He told Council the sort of man it needed, especially on the Executive and Finance Committee, and he suggested whom to appoint. In particular, 'we want a man of business *of the highest possible standing in the business world*. There are two such available among the not-too-old Old Boys: Mr Ian McLennan, Gen. Manager of B.H.P., and Mr Archie Glenn, General Manager of I.C.I.' McLennan was already on Council but not available for the Committee. 'Archie Glenn is more readily available and would be an excellent man to have. I want to get hold of him before he becomes cluttered up with other things as is likely to occur with a man of his business ability. I propose that we co-opt him' to Council and put him straight on to the Committee.[35]

James Aitken (Captain 1920), Chairman of Council 1947–50. Though he fell ill, and died in office, he began the improvement of staff superannuation.

Council was sharply woken. Two elderly members fell upon their swords, and Keith Wilson and Glenn were soon on the Executive and Finance Committee. To keep the Committee fresh, Council resolved to rotate its members. From 1959 the three elected members each had three-year terms, one retiring each year and eligible for re-election. The Committee when strengthened was a different kind of problem for Council, as some members objected to its taking too much power financially, but Council as a whole backed its committee and, formalising matters, delegated certain financial decisions to it.

THE LADIES' AUXILIARIES

During its first hundred years Scotch took the view that parents should be neither seen nor heard. They were met at the beginning and at the end. They were met while deciding what school their boy would go to (Graham McInnes's English mother chose Scotch after hearing the 'devastating' accent of the Junior School headmaster at Melbourne Grammar), and they were

met at prize-giving. Otherwise their task was to entrust their sons to the school and step respectfully into the background. Morrison limited his availability to parents to two hours a week, and at other times by appointment.[36] Many parents found this entirely satisfactory. On George Bremner's (1932) first day, his father 'vanished. Having left school at the age of 12 he viewed the teaching fraternity with suspicion and to be kept at a distance'.[37]

In the second half of the twentieth century the school began annual parents' meetings. There, it replicated the classroom mode: it sat the parents down and lectured them, and later, as teaching changed, showed them audio-visual material. David Bradshaw of the Junior School led the way, addressing a meeting of 250 parents in 1952. By 1954 these meetings were annual. In the Senior School Healey inaugurated an annual meeting of parents. All masters had to attend, short of 'grave domestic inconvenience or ill-effect on health'.[38] After supper, parents of each year-level met separately with masters, no doubt to talk about their sons. The meetings had to serve

Council in 1956, after it decided that a group photo of Council should be taken every four years.

Standing (from left): Harvey Nicholson (Captain 1936), Vic Nilsen (1926), Bill McKendrick (1925), Archie Glenn (1929), Sir Ian Clunies-Ross, Keith Ness (1924), Rev. Donald Macrae (1930), Rev. William Marshall (1902), Keith McK. Wilson (1927)

Seated (from left): Dr Colin Macdonald (1913), David York Syme (1892), Douglas Bain (1917), Dr Archie Anderson (1909, Chairman), Richard Selby Smith (Principal), Rev. Dr Alan Watson, Major Stuart Love (1901), Rev. Robert Foyster (1899, the church's observer)

Absent: Rev. Professor Davis McCaughey, Ian McLennan (Dux, 1927), Rev. Robert Swanton.

Of Council's 18 members (Selby Smith and Foyster were not members), 14 were Old Boys, of whom eight were past or future Presidents of OSCA.

as both a general parents' meeting and also as a parent-teacher night.

Healey told parents what he thought they should know about matters of educational or school policy. He felt he discerned their response ('It seemed to me that there remains a strong desire that our standards be maintained'[39]), but the structure limited feedback from the floor. In 1970 nearly 1000 parents were present. To make the experience reciprocal, Healey encouraged parents to communicate with him and the staff—a far cry from the attitude of senior staff in the 1940s, who had openly said: 'We must not let parents around the school'.[40] Healey also told parents the school's financial position. This dispelled any myth of vast wealth. He published it in the annual *Newsletter* he initiated in 1966, and he encouraged the creation of *Great Scot*, OSCA's newspaper, which went also to parents.

Less passively, parents began to do things around the school. During World War II, Junior School cubs' parents worked on improving the grounds and built the cub hut.

The oldest parent body with a continuous existence is the Junior School Parents' Association, founded in 1935 as the Junior School Mothers' Association. Its focus was practical and localised. In 1938 it hoped for hot water in showers, and in 1952 was more successful in shaming Council into ensuring traffic lights at the Callantina Road corner. Over time it asked for cotton summer socks instead of woollen, better tuckshop food, and sex education. Throughout the 1950s and 1960s it held regular lunchtime meetings for mothers, and evening meetings for all parents. The guest speaker was sometimes a Junior School art or music teacher, and the committee's organisation was thorough, allocating members to bring milk, shortbread, and sandwiches or asparagus rolls; 'borrow three teapots from the Scout Hall and the thermos urn from the Boarding School; extra cups from the church Hall; extra chairs from the School. Mr Tapp agreed to hire two maids for washing up. Four members will lend bridge tables, and three heaters. Bring flowers'.[41] The evening meetings succumbed to television and then from 1975 re-emerged to accommodate the rising number of working mothers (65% of mothers in 1981).

The Association's aims changed over time. By 1971 it had thrown 100 coffee parties for the mothers of each class. At that time it called itself 'a point of contact for parents and the school'[42] and eschewed fundraising, but by the 1980s it was raising money for equipment and teaching aids, through, for example, a Ladies' Tennis Day. (Contact with the school moved to small regular meetings arranged by Don Wirth (Junior School Headmaster 1977–86) in his office.)

In the 1950s two more groups of parents coalesced into permanent organisations.

In 1956, scouts' parents borrowed money from Council for the new scout hut, and then continued in existence as a body to pay off that loan. The niche they (and later the Scout Mothers' Auxiliary) occupied was unnamed clothing. Unwanted clothing went to a Boys' Home.

In 1959 at the instigation of Dr and Mrs W. P. Heslop, parents of boys who went to Scotch-at-Cowes formed 'a Parents' Auxiliary to raise money for equipment and amenities for the camps'. Cowes needed, said Stan Brown, the commandant, stoves, a piano, a dinghy, septic tanks, trestle tables, a table tennis table and a portrait of Elizabeth II. The inaugural meeting in Mackie Hall was attended by 130 parents with another 70 apologising. The auxiliary soon acquired those trappings of a permanent body, a minute book and a constitution. Its committee comprised the parents of the committee of boys who ran the camps, with power to co-opt other parents. From 1960 working parties went to Cowes in the off-season. In May 1961 a party of masters, parents and boys installed a septic tank system and new water tanks. In 1963 ten work-weekends forged 'a magnificent spirit of friendship amongst the parents'.[43]

To pay for these improvements, the auxiliary's ladies' group held an annual round of fundraising: a dinner dance, a buffet dinner and a wine and cheese tasting. Their chronicle of each year's events built up an accumulated practical wisdom. In running a coffee stall, for instance, 'you need a number of cartons & shoe boxes to hold sugar stirrers, barbeque tickets, roster name tags, and containers to stand the paper cups in so coffee powder can be put in cups early without blowing over. The wind caused a lot of trouble in all the above items.'[44] In 1970 they changed to paper plates, which were adequate for out-of-doors and put an end to washing up and repacking.

These three auxiliaries were hardworking, creative and long-lived. Slowly they became part of the school's life, and the school became involved in what they did.

A younger auxiliary was the Cadet Ladies' Auxiliary, which raised money by selling meals and drinks to teams playing on Saturdays. Dismayed to see them endure the rigours of winter under an awning, Healey had a kiosk built. 'Their efforts are most noble, paying a great deal of the cost of keeping the Cadet Corps' uniform in fine condition' and establishing a bursary to help the parents of cadets in financial need.[45]

Healey tried to draw the mothers, as he did their sons, away from self-interest (raising money only for their own children) towards social responsibility, by asking them to raise money for Rossbourne House, a nearby school for slow learners. They did this from 1970 at the House Sports Day, and in 1971 raised $1000. Auxiliaries also took on wider responsibility for the school. In 1969 two auxiliaries raised money for bursaries to help deserving boys. In 2000, the auxiliaries raise money only for Scotch.

In 1975 the first woman entered Council, Cecily Tulloch. Daughter of Sir Arthur Dean (1910), she had four sons at Scotch, and had been President of the Junior School Mothers' Association 1964–65 and served on the Music and Scotch-at-Cowes Auxiliaries. Her female successors on Council have also held office in the same Association: Ann Price, Philippa Barber, Pam Marshall and Jill Spargo.

Until the 1970s the auxiliaries were female in membership. Healey called them 'the Ladies' Auxiliaries'.[46] Through them, mothers gained a place in the school. They established their credibility also with 5000 'woman-hours' of clerical and typing work in the 1962 Building Appeal, whose Chairman sang their praise. In the last few decades of the century they deliberately attracted fathers and removed the word *Mothers* from their titles.

In 1968 the four auxiliaries began working together. They organised morning coffee receptions for new Senior School parents. Healey was delighted and made the receptions an annual fixture. In 1972 the auxiliaries cut costs through a shared catering pool of dinner plates and stainless steel jugs. They published a joint yellow sheet to parents. Such a resource network drew the school into involvement. Field, the Bursar, offered the school's support and in 1978 took on what the auxiliaries had once managed themselves, like buying crockery, cutlery, trays, and jugs.

Field helped the auxiliaries work better but Healey transformed them. The auxiliaries did not embrace all parents' interests, and their representatives met jointly only to plan the year's activities. In 1971 Healey proposed 'an over-all Parents' Association', to be called the Scotch College Association.[47]

THE SCOTCH ASSOCIATION: HEALEY'S UMBRELLA

The Scotch Family Association is the formal umbrella body of the Scotch community. It drew the auxiliaries into a confederation. It gave parents, at last, a formal role in the school.

The idea of the Scotch Family is variously attributed to Field or Healey. Donaldson, in his conciliatory way, credited them both: that Field first voiced it and that Healey took it forward.[48] To 'draw together the various organisations that together comprise the Scotch Family', Healey set up the Scotch Association.[49] He modelled it on the Melbourne Grammar and Tintern Associations, and intended it to lift the auxiliaries into a body that could support Scotch about the freeway or state aid.[50] Scotch parents needed their own public voice 'now that education is becoming such a political football'.[51] It would also help co-ordinate fundraising.

It met first in 1972. Representatives came from all five auxiliaries (Junior School Mothers, Scouts, Scotch-at-Cowes, Cadets and Music), the Koomerang Ski Club and the two Staff Common Rooms (Junior School and Senior). (Sir) Laurence Muir (Captain 1942) was its first Chairman. Since then, membership has expanded in several ways. Representatives came from new auxiliaries, from new bodies like the Foundation, and from new constituencies like the parents of boys in each year.

The Association took up explicitly political tasks, like objecting to the reduction of the allowable tax deduction for education expenses. At first it

Lost vista: a view of Mackie Hall from the Main Building's upper cloisters. Scarborough's Collegiate Gothic style flaunted rounded turrets.

Below: The Junior School in 2000 still displayed the school's original red and white of bricks and rough-cast render.

Master plan in 1989:
what might have
been.

Below: French-
derived architecture
seen behind a gum
tree.

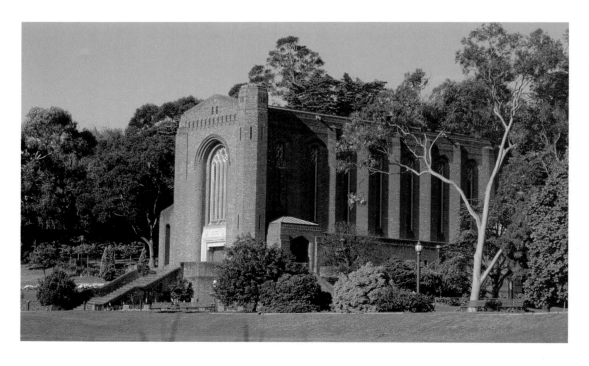

An aerial view of the freeway shows it swerving around Scotch instead of taking the direct route across the ovals. Scotch's clout is manifest. Yet Scotch could not push the freeway any further south. Scotch had met the limits of its power.

Assembly in the
Memorial Hall, 1995.

View across the
Meares Oval in 2000.

lobbied MPs only when Council asked it to, but later did so on its own initiative. It also broadened parents' knowledge of the school.

At first called the Scotch Association, it became the Scotch Family Association in 1987. (In tandem, *Great Scot* changed from being *Newspaper of the Old Scotch Collegians' Association* to *The Scotch Family Magazine*.) The phrase 'Scotch Family' was in the air. Healey used it in the 1960s, often in inverted commas to mark its newness. The House Sports Day, which he toyed with calling Community Day, he eventually called the Scotch Family Day. That name took at least a decade to catch on. The Day was held on the weekend nearest the Foundation Day Concert (itself on the Friday nearest 6 October), and these two events drew together the widest participation of boys, staff, Old Boys, parents and friends. It took 20 years to shed the inverted commas around the words Scotch Family, but their disappearance after 1984 signals that the phrase had become an ordinary part of Scotch's discourse. A year or two later the Association changed its name to Scotch Family Association.

The word *family* also began to be used to describe eating and teaching situations: the new Dining Room provided 'family style service'[52] and there was a family grouping model in the classroom.[53] Perhaps as Australian families became looser structures, the word 'family' was also under reconsideration.

The usefulness of the idea of a Scotch Family was its simplicity. It did away with cumbersome titles like Parents and Old Boys. Also, involvement in the school extended to whole families, literally. The parents' working bees at Cowes deployed children, too, and were soon called family work parties[54] at 'The Family Work Day'.[55] In 1982 Henry McLachlan (staff 1974–84), its commandant, described Scotch-at-Cowes as 'a family group … developing strong family bonds',[56] not the most obvious characteristic of camps that gave boys holidays *away* from their parents.

Parental involvement strengthened through another change that occurred at this time. Boys began to attend Scotch for longer. Only a minority of boys ever attended the Junior School, which in 1970 had only two classes for each age-group. For much of the twentieth century, boys arrived at the Senior School in two waves, in what are now Years 7 and 9. The Year 7 influx of two classes comprised boys who attended primary school elsewhere (and then merged in Year 8 with two classes of boys coming from the Junior School). In Year 9 two further classes-full (called Removes) of new boys arrived, many of them scholarship boys from state schools where Year 8 was the highest year. Effectively, Scotch was a finishing school, providing higher education, a route to university and useful social connections. By 1972, boys were more likely to arrive younger. In that year, Scotch had four Year 7 classes, whilst the reduced intake of Year 9 entrants no longer entered Removes but were distributed among existing classes. In 2000, 90% of boys enter the Senior School in Year 7, which comprises eight or nine classes. Only boarders arrive in any numbers in Year 9.

The pattern of enrolment is shown by Mishura's computerised database of all known Scotch Collegians, with 32 000 entries. The graph on page XII shows new intake of all age groups as a percentage of total new intake. Several age groups have been the largest group of entrants. In the school's first ten years, the chart's jumble reflects both the lack of fully accurate records for the Lawson period before 1857 and also the unsettled demographics of a new colony. From the late 1860s, a clear set of long-term trends emerges. For 70 years, the 14- and 15-year-olds seesawed as the largest group of entrants. Then for the last 60 years, since the 1930s, the entrants' age fell (so that the largest group was often 12-year-olds), and rose again (so that today and for the last 20 years the largest group has been 13-year-olds).

THE SCOTCH COLLEGE FOUNDATION: SERIOUS
FUNDRAISING

Scotch Family Day, 1983. Ted Hellier conducts the Show Band, which largely overlapped with the Cadet Unit's Military Band.

Healey considered the Scotch Foundation his proudest achievement.[57] In 1973 Muir presided over its creation, recommending this over one more building appeal. It is a permanent trust fund, a permanent fundraising body and 'the treasury of the school'.[58] It is run by a Board of Trustees, who in certain key areas can take initiatives only with the prior approval of Council. Since 1986 the Board may retain half its annual income to accumulate. From 1976 the Foundation had an executive officer, Dick Durance (1976–80) and

then Peter Crook (staff 1967–). Some members are bodies, for example, the Old Scotch Tennis Club.

Members rank according to their generosity. The most senior level was Trustee until 1981 when that of Life Governor (appointed by Council) was introduced for gifts of over $100 000. But as the Foundation grew up, it preferred to confer its own honours, and since 1996 bestowed membership of the Forbes Society on donors of over $150 000, of whom (in 2000) there are fifteen.

In 1979 the Foundation's cumulative fundraising passed $1 000 000, 'the first Foundation in Australian Schools to reach that figure'.[59] In 1993 it received $1 000 000 that year alone. During the 1990s the Foundation underwrote all Scotch's building programme, and the school no longer borrowed for this purpose. Its original aim was also to raise funds for scholarships and fee concessions for deserving boys. This aim has less tangible results than a new building, and has been less sustained, but the amount donated is rising steadily.

Sibling rivalry?

OSCA was long the school's sole outside body and fundraiser. It might have resented the newcomers, might even have tried to strangle them at birth. It so happened that OSCA was undergoing a phase of self-doubt caused by declining membership, which in 1970 fell below 4000 (out of 19 000 Old Boys). Fewer boys joined as they left school. Back in 1959 the majority of boys leaving school joined, but the baby-boomers were less enthusiastic. In 1968 only half joined, and in 1970 only a quarter. 'Some people', says an Old Boy of 1969, 'find it very difficult to leave Scotch behind. I enjoyed and was enriched by my time at Scotch, but I've kind of moved on from there in the past three decades. It's the school I once went to—that's all. The attitudes it shaped in me then have undergone many revisions since. All that I have met is a part of me—not just the Scotch part of my experience'.

The Launceston branch disbanded in 1969 for want of numbers. The Old Scotch Rugby Club's players were mostly not Old Boys, and in 1971 it changed its name to Hawthorn Rugby Club and disaffiliated from OSCA. The Old Scotch Football Club, under the determined presidency of Leigh McGregor (1956), falling in numbers and facing relegation to C Grade, altered its constitution in 1975 so as to be able to field non-Old Boys.

To help OSCA, from 1973 Scotch met its running costs and helped maintain its records, because the school benefited from OSCA's work. A Secretary (later Executive Director) was appointed, part-time—Frank Crawford (1925) from 1973—and full-time Tapp from 1978 and from 1988 Leigh McGregor. In 1975 membership of OSCA became automatic, funded no longer by a membership fee but by making an initial charge at a boy's entry to the school. Nowadays a voluntary life membership charge appears on a boy's last account, and most parents pay it.

OSCA also lifted its profile. From 1971, under the guidance of Robert McKay (1962), it published *Great Scot*, which took over the Old Boy aspects of the *Collegian*. Costs were defrayed by carrying advertisements. OSCA had long deplored the cost of buying and mailing the bulky *Collegian*. At first *Great Scot* was a monochrome tabloid-size newspaper but became a colourful A4 magazine. OSCA also reached out beyond Old Boys, by inviting fathers who were not Old Boys to luncheons. From the 1980s mothers also attended.

'WE ARE SCOTCH COLLEGIANS ALL'

Who are the Scotchies? The answer to this question has changed in the last 50 years. A century ago, the early *Collegians* contained photographs of boys, distinguished Old Boys and Principals. Teachers appeared with sporting teams but rarely in their own right (and then only on their death or retirement). Fifty years ago, around 1950, things were much the same. *Collegians* began with pictures of prefects and other leaders. A few photographs appeared of staff and distinguished Old Boys. 'Scotch College' meant chiefly the boys and by extension the Old Boys. In 1998 the *Collegian* began with pictures of Council and of the whole staff in colour, whilst prefects and school officers had only small black and white photos. A shift had taken place in the meaning of the words 'Scotch College' to embrace a community larger than the boys.

12
THE HILL

The Boarders' Hill is 400 million years older than most of the school. Its yellow rock (Silurian Dargile) is exposed on Glenferrie Road and in the railway cutting at Heyington, and can be seen in the bowels of the Lithgow Building.

The Hill's steep drop to the Main Oval was cut by the ancient Yarra probably, and Scotch sits at the eastern edge of that old valley. In the last million years, volcanoes to Melbourne's west poured out lava that filled the valley right up to its edge. After the lava cooled and rain fell, the water cut into the join where the old and new rock formations met, so the Yarra now runs along that geological contact. (Today the lava's black basalt is just across the Yarra from Scotch.) For a while, the Gardiner's Creek valley became a long, narrow lake that filled up with silt, sand and gravel dropped by the water in the lake. Scotch's ovals stand on that silt, and on the flood plain of the new, narrow Yarra valley.

Geologically, Mackie Hall (where the Forbes Academy will stand) straddles solid rock and sediment. It sits half on the Hill, with foundations at a normal depth, and half on the lacustrine silt in the cutting of an old stream, with brick pillars descending through 9 metres of sediment before reaching solid rock. The building is so delicately poised that the consulting engineer would allow not one brick to be touched when the drama master, Lyne, wanted to remedy Mackie Hall's inadequate stage—small to start with, it had no wings, nor space to cross from side to side behind the scenery backdrop. The school's other buildings sit more securely. Only in 1934 have flood waters lapped the Memorial Hall, for the school sits on a terrace of Silurian rock above the lower flood plain.

High on their ancient Hill, the boarders are Scotch's oldest sub-culture. A hundred years ago, boarders' attitude to the day-boys

was snobbery, complete. *We* were the school and the day-boys were just things that came and learnt and then went away. … When he'd finished the day's work, he went home and played with one of his hobbies or read or went with cobbers in the street on a dam expedition or something like that. His life was home, and the school was just where he got his education. For us, Scotch was home and it was our life altogether and we felt that way towards the scabbies. Of course that was mutual, we called them scabbies and they called us scabbies, but we knew quite well who were the scabbies.[1]

Boarders since at least the 1920s have called the day-boys 'da(y)gos'. A day-boy walking alone along the Monash Drive could be frightened of the boarders, who attacked 'from their vantage points on the hill particularly at weekends' swooping like 'Highland Scots, always with group advantage' (1939).

Among themselves, the boarders have rivalries between their three houses, McMeckan, School, and Arthur Robinson. The sewing machine in Arthur Robinson belonged to its matron, Miss Bews (staff 1930–55). When she retired Scotch bought a new Singer portable electric machine and soon had to buy one for McMeckan, too.

An earlier boarding house, Leighwood, in Glenferrie Road, was sold after Arthur Robinson House was built. A boy of another house recalls Leighwood's 'All for one and one for all' attitude. Anyone criticising Leighwood 'was in for BIG TROUBLE'.[2]

'ONE BIG FAMILY AND PLENTY TO DO'

The timeless problems of boarders' life are predictable: homesickness and food. Homesickness could move boys to tears. 'Several boys ran away, to be returned by the police if they hadn't made it to their homes.'[3] It was worse at the start of term after holidays. 'It's already getting me down in the dumps. There are so many stupid trivial rules which are so restricting and depressing. … I wish I was back with you or I wish I was a dayboy or something. I just wish I wasn't here.'[4] Then began the count-down to escape. 'Only two months to go.'[5]

As well as missing home itself, a boy missed mundane daily life. 'Gee I wish I was home with you. You have so much fun visiting people and going shopping.'[6] Even a dreaded visit to the dentist at least let a boy 'look through all the book shops, poster shops and the stamp shop in Collins Street. I just browse

School House, on the Boarders' Hill. In the early decades, boys slept out on the upper balconies.

around. I haven't bought anything yet but I'm considering buying a poster with birthday money. Don't worry; it's not a rude one.'[7]

Younger boys missed parental affection. An unhappy 13-year-old discovered that 'House masters never spoke to boys with the fondness or encouragement parents do'. Indeed, he felt he never received reassurance or encouragement. The exception was 'Herman the German' Bower, who did offer help and encouragement to boys during nightly prep, but 'confined it to maths which was his main forte. He lived in the house at Monash gates so was seen in the boarding house at best only a couple of days a week for an hour or two' (1964).[8] Yet at the same time Don Macmillan in School House found helping students with their homework very stimulating.

At meals the older boys dished out the food and 'smaller or younger boys were often not allowed to get enough food' (1951).[9] In the dormitories, boys shared or traded apples or had night-time feasts like caraway seed cake (1928).[10] They caught pigeons on the window ledges and cooked them for supper over tiny spirit stoves (1949).[11] They cooked toast on upturned radiators (1949).[12] Mrs Littlejohn banned tomato sauce because it heated the blood. This prohibition had the opposite effect to that intended. The more forward boarders, before going to romantic assignations at the Malvern picture theatre, would take a furtive swig of Rosella (1928).[13]

In 1934 John Pullar and Wilton Rail kept a daily record of the food. They found weevils in the porridge, flies in the butter, and hairs in the custard. The food was often cold and often insufficient. The salmon dish was cold and congealed 'to the extent that the plate could be turned upside down and none of its contents fall off …. Meat was like dogs' meat (or perhaps a dog would shudder).' 'The mince meat seems to act as a hypnotising agent, in so far as its sight turns every one limp.' 'The tea was a cold one, and so was the night.'

Sleepless Boarder

Soft dripping silence....

Minutes ticking by....

Down the hall …
Clock breathes out 'One'
Soft, whispering 'One'.

Stale smell of steak,
We had that steak for tea
Off chipped, blue plates—
"Willow pattern, dear."
Horrid smell,
Stale steak, staler beer,
Mixed with smelly cabbage water,
Slimy beans,
And tasteless greens.
Hateful tea! …

Out the back,
Way out back
Near refuse tins

The cistern groans
And rumbles,
Water mumbles
In some pipes,
Pauses... then down a thousand flights of sound
It mumbles, rumbles, tumbles down—
Cascades of sound diluted water ...
Water gurgling down the pipes.
Down a hundred thousand flights
Of C flat minor cadences,
Takes the wearied mind away
To some sweet haven, some clear pool
Of silver water, sweet and cool....

Geoff Shillinglaw (School Captain 1953)[14]

The old Boarders' Dining Hall.

Beyond the lonely, hungry, restless boarder, it becomes hard to generalise. The nature of boarding—isolated and inward-looking—intensified both its joys and tribulations. Boarders live at the school for a '24 hour day 7 day week'.[15] 'There is a major difference for day-boys—who have families to discuss the day's school events. Not so the imprisoned boarder.'[16] 'Scotch

had to substitute for a home, mum, dad and family.'[17] This fired an intensity of experience unknown elsewhere at the school, and fired greater disparities within that experience. The majority of boarders actively enjoyed themselves or at least muddled through. A small number had a quite awful time. This divergence of experience makes for a contradictory history, though of course boys living side by side at home can have quite different experiences, too.

As well as its hermetic intensity, boarders' culture has other distinctive features. It is unique within the school. Compared with the day school, it tends to be more conservative. Boarders have been less socially diverse than day-boys, and less tolerant of diversity. Boarders have come mainly from rural Australia, and to the extent that rural Australians are more politically and socially conservative than others, so are the boarders. Within this closed, tight-knit, conservative culture boys lived their lives.

Many boarders have enjoyed themselves. Bert Dupin (1927) found a

complete absence of bullying of the juniors by the older boys. We had our own dormitory at the end of the House but used the same washing areas etc &, even in the mornings which were obviously rushed, the older boys were always helpful & protective towards the youngsters. Probably an aspect of Australian culture as well as an indication of good morale at Scotch.[18]

John Brown (1933) recalls 'my days as a boarder at Scotch College as being some of the happiest days of my life, with the opportunity it offered of mixing with a wide range of personalities in a community situation. This enabled me to be, as a citizen in later life, more tolerant of the quirks of friends, neighbours and business acquaintances.'[19] Alexander Campbell's diaries in 1927–29 detail a happy life as a boarder, with occasional fights and creeping off to 'the flicks', and no sign of bullying or fagging. Bill Norris's diaries in 1942–45 detail a daily life of much happiness and companionship. 'Being a boarder in Arthur Robinson House' is what Trevor Steer (1955) enjoyed most about Scotch; 'boarders sporting teams at all levels were deadly serious affairs. I don't think I ever tried harder at anything than those football and cricket matches (harder than the 6 years of VFL with Collingwood)'.[20] 'I just loved it. It was one of the happiest times of my life' (1944).[21] 'Being a boarder in Arthur Rob. It was one big family and we always had plenty to do' (1960).

Douglas Aitchison (1945) writes:

Life in the Boarding school in the '30s was hard because great emphasis was placed on things physical. It was believed that to develop a boy into 'a man' he must be able to display physical courage. Initiation was carried out, some of which was in the area of bastardisation, bullying was not uncommon, caning for breaking of the rules was not uncommon, and so you quickly learned to adapt and to fend for yourself. Meals whilst wholesome were not exciting, accommodation was basic and discipline was pretty well enforced. Great emphasis was placed on sporting participation and should you have the ability to perform well in this area life was a lot more pleasant. ... The system seemed to breed self-reliance—after all if you could come through the trials and tribulations you felt you could handle most things. At the same time a spirit of comradeship was developed. 'Adversity maketh friends of us all.' We really came to believe we were better than the day boys, we believed we were tougher and of course were more aggressive, further there was a bonding between boarders called House spirit.[22]

In the 1950s 'The rules were rigid, the discipline harsh. I was present when a 15-year-old boy ... was caned on the bare buttocks by an 18-year-old ... a nice bloke who I met years later ... 6 strokes—so hard the skin split and bled. He had bruising for 6 weeks—His sin?—he rang home from the public phone. He remained bitter for decades.' Thus James Lawson (1952) who found the Scotch boarding experience 'sadistic, bullying and profoundly anti-Christian. ... many of my era have kept our vows—I have never been to a Christian church service for nearly 50 years.'[23] This is the risk a church runs in owning a school: that boys will judge the church by the school instead of by the gospel message.

Makeshift swimming pool. The Settling Pool was where water from the River Yarra dropped its silt before watering the grounds. The gymnasium is behind.

But others experienced the discipline differently:

> The discipline of the Boarding House gave you the courage to face adversity. It was very black and white, but you knew exactly where you stood. Many institutions in later life have fallen very short by comparison. ... Andrew Peacock [Vice-Captain 1957] ... and I decided to go for a swim in the school pool one hot night. ... as we were sneaking in the back door FAF [Fleming] intercepted us, & asked us what we were doing. Andrew said 'Been for a swim Sir'.
>
> 'Own up, Cop it, Get on with it', FAF was heard to say some time later. 'Ask a boy a straight question and get a straight answer. Great stuff' [1955].[24]

James Edward Tierney (Royal Humane Medal for Saving Lives at Sea) was gym instructor 1920–35.

In the 1960s one boarder found the Hill 'was basically a hostile place for a young lad. Any activity not involving sport or study was frowned on. … House prefects, not staff, basically ran the boarding house and they were bound by inflexible rules. This meant that there was never any spontaneity or change in the nightly ritual.'[25]

Without enough adult supervision, the boarding-house prefects might develop 'pet hates, always picking on the same kids'. This set up a pattern whereby boys became resentful and thus subject to further caning for insubordination. An ordinary boy might be caned six or ten times, and some boys were caned dozens of times. For boys whose punishment at home up till then had been the odd slap, caning came as a shock. So did the physical sequelae. David Brand (1972) drew colour illustrations of his bruises as they bloomed and faded over several weeks.[26]

Punishment requires record-keeping, like the Lines Book of Peter Anderson (1974, Captain of McMeckan House). The crimes therein warranted 73 725 lines and give us glimpses of boarders' life. Boys received lines for lateness; for cooking toast; for talking (in prep, in chapel, during prayers, during grace and after lights out); for being bare-footed, or in shoes, or slippers, at the wrong time or place; for stealing; for bullying and for 'malicious', 'spiteful' or 'consistent knocking'; for fighting and bed-wrecking; for pissing out windows; for projecting a missile in the refectory, for throwing food and blowing pepper; for 'not undoing buttons on washing'; for 'active insurrection in showers', for 'disobedience & undermining the system', and for 'playing with Frogs! In Chapel!'

Of the 1970s, Al Thomson (1977) recalls:

> The school was our whole life, for better or worse. We were bound by its values and regulations, by its peer group pressures and bonds, much more than the boys who came and went each day. Food, home-sickness, prep and lights out, caning and gating, bullying and exclusions, a fierce loyalty to our house and to fellow boarders ('rurals') against day boys ('day-gos') which exploded on the sports field (and which was ironically/paradoxically a reason for our very great pride when [we] won the inter-house debating competition in 1977—boarders were not expected to be able to think)—these were themes which dominated our adolescence. … We were a minority with a strong sense of identity and difference, predominantly shaped by Australian male rural culture which most of the boys brought with them and reinvented in an extraordinary, insulated microcosm, and which was both a source of support and affirmation and site of exclusion and victimisation, especially for those who were, or seemed to be different. I lived on the cusp, sometimes relishing the fraternity, sometimes lonely, eventually wanting different opportunities and being lucky enough to find them.[27]

Teenage boys put great emphasis on conformity. Bill Baxter (1964) 'felt somewhat oppressed and harassed as a boarder because I did not fit the norm'.[28] Thomson remembers in 1972 'arriving as an 11-year-old and seeing my older brother getting a hard time because he was "different" and consciously determining to "fit in" as much as possible to gain acceptance. Being good at sport helped gain acceptance'.

> A couple of fellow boarders … were terribly victimised because they were slightly effeminate (in one case) and assertively camp (in another case). The rural standards of the boarding houses were pretty tough and unrelenting. Very macho and yet also terrified of affection or emotionality, cruel and even barbaric to anyone who was different. I realised this very quickly and decided that survival was a priority. I did survive, but I don't think it did a lot for my emotional development in the long term. I would say that the experience of boarders was very different to that of day boys, where sub-cultures were more possible.[29]

In 2000, 'prefects may issue lines and get boys to do menial tasks about the House but always under the watchful eye and supervision of the House staff. They are in no way allowed to physically interfere with any boy', and breaches of the school's policies against bullying are severely punished.[30]

'NEW BOYS PRACTICE'

In 1929 George Bremner entered School House. 'New boys under the cold shower!' at the first morning's ablutions; the allocation of a nickname ('Marie') which he immediately loathed but soon took great pride in; dragging a roller round the oval; singing, with a mug of salt and water for those whose efforts were not appreciated—all this culminated in the gymnasium where new boys ran between lines of boys armed with tightly rolled towels wetted at the ends. 'A half hearted attempt was made to force us up the ceiling ropes, but Jim Tierney [the gym instructor 1920–35] put a stop to that with a few well-chosen oaths.' The presence of a staff member shows the school sanctioned the event and restrained it. A welcome was also generously extended to the new Housemaster, Mr Thompson ('Thommo') who had his bed 'short-sheeted plus a liberal application of tooth-paste here and there'. 'Bunny' Lappin, the Housemaster 'nearly wore his cane out whacking both innocent and guilty'. At the end of the year, the new boys were 'blackened', 'being stripped down on the locker room table and liberally blackened with boot polish'. Bremner describes blackening as 'a harmless exercise reminding us that we were still new boys. The half hour under the hot showers was well worth the temporary inconvenience.' He adds: 'At no stage did we virgins look upon initiation ... and allied "tortures" as bullying in any shape or form. In this day and age it would probably be called "bastardisation", but we didn't call it anything. We just accepted it and carried on even if at times spirits were temporarily lowered.' Another boy only slightly later in the 1930s felt that initiations provided 'a licence for bullying and was very traumatic for less prepared or sensitive people [and] had a very bad effect on the performances of students in their first year'.[31]

In the 1940s, when the level of bullying in the day-school was high, for the boarders things were even worse. Few boys living at home had their bed 'suspended with ropes, across the back courtyard, high up ... and when [——] saw his bed, he burst into tears'.[32]

New boys had to be fags, 'doing menial chores' like carrying books,[33] 'we acted as 14-year-old (and younger) servants to final year (18 year plus) boys. This included cleaning their shoes, preparing food, tidying their rooms. This was enforced by beating with coat hangers and running shoes'.[34] Also, 'We had to have a "School spirit"—which meant knowing boating and school songs—word perfect. Failure meant more beatings and "tanning". Tanning meant being covered fully (naked—total skin including genitals) with boot polish then having to wash it off with tomatoes under a cold shower (this took 4 plus hours)',[35] 'enacted to the jeers and cheers of colleagues'.[36]

Around 1950 there was an effort to wipe out 'New Boys Practice',[37] 'because, at times it became a little dangerous and, probably, could have been seen as emotionally destabilising'.[38] David Shave in 1951 'was one of the last two boarders to be tanned. I guess I must have been too cheeky.'[39]

Fagging was also forbidden. Yet John Spence (1964) recalls, 'At any time, the shout of "New Boy" caused all first-year boys within earshot to run to the senior who called, who would then assign jobs, ranging from polishing boots to making coffee or a few laps of the Oval'.[40] Fleming, Housemaster of Arthur Robinson from 1946, allowed initiation of new boys to re-appear, until this was in turn reversed when Owen took over. In the 1970s tanning was an occasional part of bullying rather than institutionalised. In 1985, renewed fagging had to be 'stamped out'.[41]

In 1990 a Year 7 boy was 'beaten nightly'.

> I must admit, being beaten regularly was fairly awful. The Year 12 boys had the authority to hand out lines; 'I must not … etc' but instead used physical violence to enforce their authority. I spent the first year in the boarding house pleading not to have to stay at Scotch. Eventually, two of us 'dobbed' despite the threatened consequences but this did little to alleviate the problem. The major threat was from the Year 8 boys, who were near the bottom of the pecking order but still had us to release their aggression on. … when we were in Year 8, we decided not to pass the violence on down the line, and this carried through the years below us. As we moved through the years, we were able to stop bullying when it arose in younger year levels.

He feels proud of this, and believes that 'now the younger kids are barely touched'. On past evidence, new waves of repression seem likely; the peaks each time are less severe.

The wide, wide world

Max Paton (1926) describes a life almost incomprehensible to the modern boy: 'No library, no music, no tv, no wireless except crystal set for morse code from ships at sea. Limited exit permits—Spartan existence.'[42] The after-school activity was sport,[43] but when Owen became Senior Boarding Housemaster in 1964, he said 'Sport is no longer enough: in any case they get plenty of that. … we can no longer rest satisfied with giving each boy a bed, a seat at a dining table, and a desk. This is his home, and boys of today need more of the variety that a home offers.' Also, boarders were older than they used to be. A social trend against sending boys away to board too young had combined with another trend to keep boys at school longer. Arthur Robinson 'now has no third-formers [Year 9s] and about twenty sixth-formers [Year 12s]. If we do not provide these young men with a worthwhile existence, they are going to seek relaxation in less desirable ways.' Boarders gained weekend use of the old craftroom under the Hospital, and a craft teacher in residence. Owen welcomed

> the variety of articles they turn out—canoes, auto-trays, fruit bowls, and a host of other things. The lathe is never idle. … We have also managed to get … metal work equipment—lathe, grinders and buffers, drill press, anvil,

forge, oxy-acetyline [sic] welding outfit, stocks and dies, and all the other paraphenalia [sic] for fitting and turning and for metal beating. …. In addition we hope to erect a brick oven and make a wheel for pottery.[44]

(Owen's spelling suggests that his magic as Senior English Master sprang from his ideas.)

Owen made outings more routine. Geoff Donaldson (1930, Chairman of Woodside Petroleum 1956–84) gave Fleming, his brother-in-law, a boat on Albert Park Lake for the boys, and Owen created a fleet, partly built at Scotch. In 1965 they had ten boats at the lake's Yacht Club, and more than forty boys learnt to sail. They were free to do this at weekends so long as they met their commitments to school teams. In 1978 the boarders had six Mirror dinghies on the lake in constant use at weekends. (Scotch sold the boats in the 1990s to MLC Marshmead.)

Further afield, Fleming took boarders on trips to his home at Olinda. Owen persuaded Jack Kollosche (1956) to donate a small second-hand bus, to be driven by a master or reliable Old Boy, to take boarders 'canoeing up the Yarra, hiking at Healesville with the Scout Hut as their base, down to Cowes, or surfing and golfing at Point Lonsdale'. In 1972 Keith Andrews, a parent, offered to lease land for a boarders' camp at a nominal rent. On a

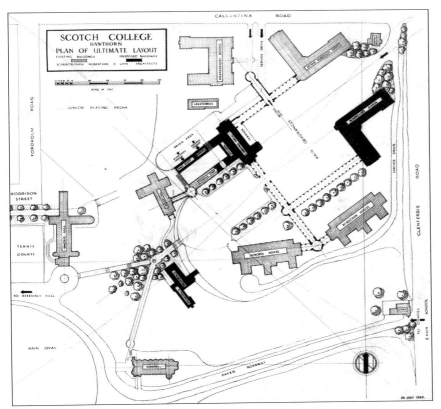

Scotch College Hawthorn, Plan of Ultimate Layout. In this vision of Scotch's future in 1939, Scarborough planned a great quadrangle on the hilltop.

timbered hill in rugged terrain overlooking Lake Eildon, parties under Owen built a hut with structural advice from Ken Bethell (1937, OSCA President 1978) and support from Hec Ingram, who brought an old church to the site. Don Bartlett (1962) supervised building what became Owen Lodge, with 12 bunks and porta-gas refrigeration, cooking, and lighting. In 1977, work parties went there 'almost every weekend extending the lodge and clearing an area for a small pine plantation'.[45] 'We had a fantastic time up there.'[46] In 1999 Scotch bought the property from the Andrews.

Boarders today lead less isolated lives. Using the telephone is routine, giving regular contact with people they care about, as do fax and email. Senior boys can pay visits and receive visitors, even girls, although not in their rooms. Weekend leave is unrestricted if with family, and is also possible for two weekends per term with others. Owen Lodge often hosts 20 boarders on a weekend, particularly in the snow season. Boarders also reach out to the outside world in unexpected ways—like strawberry topping bombs, or the fruit bazooka in 1997 that shot oranges at the neighbours across Glenferrie Road.

RUNNING AT A LOSS

In 1946 Scotch began a decades-long policy of running the boarding houses at a loss. The loss that first year was small, but Council's response was to subsidise the boarders, whilst seeking economies if possible. The next year squeaked into profit, but as inflation soared in the early 1950s so did the boarding loss. It was over £3000 in 1953 and 1956, over £5000 in 1952, and over £9000 in 1965. These were substantial sums (30–50 times annual fees). Council raised boarding fees but never enough to make a profit. Rather, Council was content when the loss was reduced, and throughout the 1960s and into the 1970s the loss was so routine as to be often written into the budget in advance.

Moreover, these losses were based on a policy that boarding fees were to be kept low enough to cover 'costs' only, whilst the overheads were spread among all boys. Thus the school's accounting systems, in reckoning boarding house expenditure, omitted 'salaries of Housemasters, rent, rates, interest on cost, and repair and maintenance wages on buildings and gardens, etc.'[47] Also, the boarders lived rent-free. Selby Smith calculated that to charge boarders the cost of the buildings would add £100 to each boy's annual fee and that by not doing so the school was effectively subsidising the boarders by this amount.

Among the acknowledged costs, half went on staff: cleaning, maintenance, kitchen, laundry, mending, nursing sisters, house matrons, coke-boiler staff. This cost was exacerbated by rising wages and salaries, and by the irregular but lengthy hours necessarily worked in school boarding houses. The introduction of the 40-hour week after World War II did not fit with a residential organisation where boys had to be fed morning and

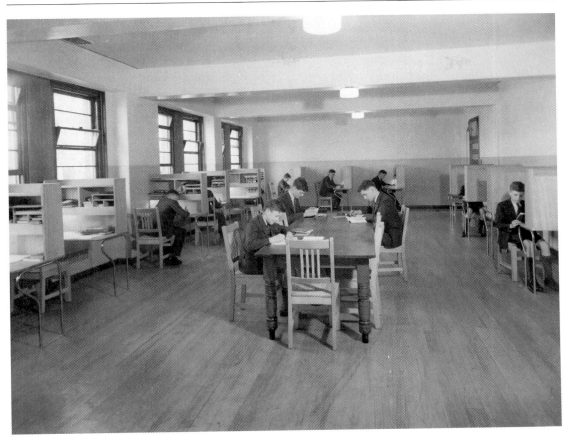

evening, outside a 9 a.m.–5 p.m. day. Similarly, the episodic nature of school terms made it uneconomical to employ laundry and kitchen staff for the whole year, and yet the school found it difficult to let out the laundry contract, as no outside contractor would guarantee to pick up and deliver regularly on the same day each week. (A week's laundry in 1947 per boy was 2–3 shirts, 3 collars, 2–3 singlets, 1 pair pyjamas, 1 sheet, 3 pairs of socks, 7 handkerchiefs, and 3 trunks.)

In 1961 Council looked at the problem (perhaps because Scotch was launching a building appeal), but only for long enough to side-step it. After a 'prolonged and careful discussion', Council shifted boarding costs to the main school budget. This had some justice. For example, the school should carry 'the cost of maintaining the Principal's household and the cost of catering for visiting sports teams and Speech Day entertaining'.[48] Bain, Chairman of Council, however, said the school should pay for paving the roads on the Hill, although most boys and staff never went there and day-boys were forbidden to do so. Even this sleight of hand plugged the deficits only briefly.

In 1965, as a larger-than-ever loss loomed, and no further accounting

The Prep Room in Arthur Robinson House in 1963. The turned legs of the central table contrast with Scarborough's more modern 1930s design of rooms and furniture with metal Bauhaus table legs.

solutions were possible, Council was told that the boarding costs were due to increased wage rates for domestic staff, coupled with rising food prices and maintenance costs—that is, that the boarding houses were expensive to run. This was Healey's first full year, and he acted decisively. From February 1966 Nationwide Food Services ran the Dining Room. This quickly lowered the domestic staff wages bill (by getting rid of those staff), as well as bringing a better standard of catering. A cost per meal of 22.5 cents lowered the standard as meat costs rose. Council thought this was undesirable, and raised expenditure per meal to 24 cents. At least such a decision could now be an informed one.

Boarding fees were about the same as at Melbourne Grammar and Wesley: lower than the Geelong schools, but much higher than at most newer Public Schools. Nationwide checked rather than reversed losses, for 'no substantial improvement could be expected in board finance'. The loss for 1966 threatened to be $21 000, and more in the next year. Boarding fees now reached $300 per term. In 1967 Council at last decided that 'the cost of the boarding establishment must be borne by the fees charged'.[49] The budgeted aim became to break even or make a very nominal surplus. Fees rose, yet for 1967 Council was in its usual position of congratulating itself that the boarding deficit was lower than budgeted! Healey repeated this argument in his annual newsletter, but at least, for the first time, the school acknowledged publicly that it subsidised boarders.

Why were the boarders indulged for so long? Scotch is mainly a day-boy school and it should not ask the day-boys' parents to subsidise the boarders' parents. This was the practical position, advanced by the Rev. Dr Alan Watson, Vice-Chairman of Council,[50] for here the clergy had their feet on the ground whilst businessmen and educationists grew illogical and sentimental.

Gilray said that the school had a duty to keep the boarding houses, even at a loss, as they allowed boys to come to Scotch who would not otherwise obtain a secondary education.[51] This was true for boys from country areas without adequate high schools in those days. Even so, the boarding house loss subsidised a particular group, largely non-Melburnians, and there were other groups who might equally have benefited from such a subsidy. For example, boys from Melbourne's western suburbs were few, and the train from Coburg in 1944 carried a mere handful: Richard Reyment and the sons of the local doctor and the local milk contractor.

The application of Gilray's argument was that the school helped a particular group of landowners and regional professionals. Unlike the parents of Coburg these parents actively wanted to send their boys to Scotch and were often Old Boys themselves, so the subsidy seemed more natural. Selby Smith had 'a few city boys in the boarding houses ... either because the mother or father is dead, or because the parents are temporarily overseas [as] diplomats, missionaries, and service men. ... But we give preference to the country boys.' Less than half of them were farmers' sons and the others were 'the sons of business or professional men whose homes are in the country or in country towns … this surely will always be so, and is, I think, natural and proper.'[52]

Beneath the question of who should be subsidised lay the question of why the school should keep boarding houses at all. Gilray said Scotch's tradition centred on the community life of the boarders.[53] To most boys such a statement would have seemed incomprehensible. The Hill was out of bounds, and the life there something unknown but thought to be narrow. Gilray's view may not even have reflected the boarders' view of their life, since they preferred to stress that the life on the Hill was superior or unique, rather than central. Gilray's statement does throw light on his own view of the Hill, where he lived, where his domestic and official life merged, and where he clearly found the school's soul, with its orderly, bell-rung rituals and worship. Anderson (Chairman of Council 1954–59) knew that 'the boarders were, are & always will be the backbone of the School. They *are* the school.'[54] The 1985 Captain of Littlejohn (then the boarders' house) agreed: 'the boarders are the elite group of the school'.[55] If so, the boarding loss was a necessary expense.

Arguments like those of Gilray and Anderson prevailed in the 1940s, and continued to do so for a generation. But no public statement was made that the boarding houses ran at a loss, and one must assume that this was hidden from the majority of parents because the Council suspected that it would have been unacceptable. Even today, the day school subsidises the Hill, for example by lessening the teaching load of the Dean and the three Heads of Houses.

DINING IN STYLE

Council's particular attachment to the Hill emerged also in building the new dining hall. Council as a body inspected the site, and as well as the usual artist's perspective Council required colour photographs with the building superimposed, and even a model, with detachable portions. All this far exceeded what had happened with any other building. Was it that the Hill was the heart of the school? Was it a collective memory of Council's vandalism in knocking down the Glen? Council behaved similarly when placing a collection box in the chapel—it was the symbolic buildings, rather than the ones to do with education, that engaged them.

Although 'it was the Council's wish that the Dining Room be … the focal and commanding point in the Hill',[56] cost kept this fantasy unrealised. Instead, Healey set about giving the boarders an up-to-date kitchen and a dignified and attractive dining hall. In use from the third term 1971, cafeteria-style service was for breakfast and luncheon 'with the family style service being retained for the evening meal. The facilities were excellent and economies had been possible particularly in the employment of domestic staff.'[57]

'The Hill'

The custom of referring to the boarders' hill slowly entered official parlance. From 1967 Healey referred to 'The Hill' in inverted commas.[58] The new House system of 1989 intermingled the boarders and day-boys amongst all the Houses. Littlejohn was no longer the boarders' House. Many boarders were dismayed, but it helped boarders make more friends among day-boys, and reduced the Hill's insularity. Instead a boarder was appointed as Captain of the Hill, starting with Andrew Kelly (1989). The 1998 Captain called its denizens 'the Hillmen'.[59] Littlejohn House had come and gone as the vehicle of boarder particularity, but the boarders' unique lifestyle means that they will always feel separate, and closely knit, and that the school must always attend to institutionalising the boarders' conception of themselves.

From 1997 there has been a Dean of Boarding, Nick Browne (staff 1989– 2000), then Doug Galbraith (staff 1977–). Free from administrative pressure, his task was to improve the boarding experience.

Long cultural cycles about privacy have meant the boarders were three or four to a room in the 1870s and in dormitories in the 1930s and today are back to three or four, with partitioning for privacy. Since the 1960s, Year 12 boys have increasingly had rooms of their own (see p. XIV).

Things change. Once, one of the three boarding houses, McMeckan, contained only Junior School boys, but by the early 1960s there were no Junior School boarders at all, and Selby Smith and Healey gave McMeckan House the same range of boys as the other houses. Today's changes in boarders' enrolments will surely reshape the Hill's culture. In 1991, 80% of boarders came from the rural sector. In 2000, a quarter of boarders are Asian. From 2001, Scotch will also have weekly boarders who are expected to be Melburnians (from families where both parents have busy professional jobs).

The vision of the current Dean of Boarding, Galbraith, is of the Hill as a cosmopolitan and exciting place where older boys care for younger, and where privacy is balanced with 'the great strengths of living together in a community which only sharing provides'.[60]

13
_____

GROWING UP: SEX AND CONVERSATION

Of all the developments boys undergo at Scotch, the transformations of puberty are the most powerful and long-lasting. Pulse-rate, blood-pressure, blood composition, respiration, and metabolism accelerate or decelerate. The stomach lengthens and the adolescent finds it hard to be filled up at a meal. The face lengthens, losing its infant look and perhaps complexion too. Hair sprouts. Lengthening vocal cords change the voice. On the sporting field, hormones increase muscle tone and make boys faster and stronger. Boys who make this change early stand out in sport. Being caught up in these changes physically, and dealing with them socially and mentally, make up a great part, perhaps the greatest part, of any Scotch boy's life.

Sexually, a new life begins. David McNicoll (1932) rhapsodised about 'the magical world of masturbation, ... that awesome sensation ... an ecstatic flash ... brilliant enjoyment'.[1] In communal settings, boys showed off in front of each other, even in classrooms (1929, 1944, 1981),[2] although as sex education 'watching boys masturbate in the tents at Scotch at Cowes [was] not particularly helpful' (1964).[3] Other boys grew modest. 'Regarding showering in the change rooms, I would not do it until I was in Year 11. I was too shy and as I lived near the school I would walk home in my sports stuff. Many guys did not shower until later years' (1958).[4]

Most boys developed a great interest in girls. In the 1930s could Scotch boys go out with girls? 'Are you kidding? We led a closeted male-dominated existence. Social outings were confined to holiday times' (1937). 'Teenage dating was far less common than today' (1936).

The school long thought girls were none of its business. 'School activities were for boys alone' (1929). For boarders, the 'Boarding house dance and dancing classes were the limited social contact with girls' (1946). Whether or not boys met girls thus depended on life outside Scotch. Families might be as cautious as the school. Don Symington (1968) 'socialised very little... because my mother would not allow me to attend dancing classes. She thought I would fail my exams.'[5] Boys themselves also held back. Ralph Pickford (1936) 'as a shy person ... took little part in social matters and was quite frankly terrified of the opposite sex.'[6] Mike Reid (1958) had acne and became self conscious and diffident and 'just about withdrew entirely from the social scene; this was quite common'.[7]

Throughout the 20th century there were Scotch boys who had 'no contact with girls. … the first I met was after leaving school' (1926).[8] 'No idea about the opposite sex' (1953).[9] 'I had very little social contact with girls before I went to the university' (1948).[10] '1st year Uni [was] the first time I really had good female friends' (1995).

A boy's fate often depended on whether he or his friends had female relatives near his own age. 'I was one of a family of five boys, and I was shy. As Scotch was an all-boy school I had literally never met a girl of my own age when I left it at the age of 17. When I did "discover" girls I was naturally annoyed that I had not done so earlier' (1945). 'Always rather shy in the company of females, since I had no sister' (1949).[11] Graham Carrick (1935), however, had 'a sister at PLC 18 months younger than me, we had mutual friends at school dances strictly chaperoned, birthday gatherings etc.'[12] Don Hare (1929) 'had 4 lovely girl cousins and Jim Beatton (my best school mate) had 4 beautiful sisters. We called ourselves "Les Beaux Esprits". Our group had some great parties at each other's homes and … happy days playing tennis … horse riding etc.'[13] David Sharpe (1949) learnt dancing only because 'I promised the sister of a friend of mine at Scotch, to accompany her to her school dance'.[14]

Otherwise, 'attending a single sex school, without any sex education, (and … without brothers or sisters close in age) left me with little contact with or knowledge of the opposite sex. I found that attending church and

Sunday School helped to rectify this by providing a setting for meeting and getting to know girls' (1950).[15] The advantage of meeting at church was that a boy did not look too eager. He was at church, and so meeting girls could be represented as a pleasant bonus. Public transport had the same sweet advantage, that a boy did not have to explain why he was there. In the 1930s 'Social activities related mainly on 64 tram to Balaclava Junction with M.L.C. girls' (1939). In the 1940s 'Certain tram stops were popular meeting places and one collected badges of girls schools under the lapel of one's school coat' (1948). 'Romance of a kind blossomed in the trains on the way to and from school, when we fraternised with the girls' (1944, 1943, 1966).[16] On a few train lines, tunnels gave the opportunity for a stolen kiss, although *Satura* lamented Australian tunnels' shortness.[17] Wei Ch'ng (1985) felt nervous about girls and welcomed Kooyong station, which 'being a meeting place for many female schools became an education in itself'.[18]

Another cover for meeting girls was social sport, like tennis and hockey in the 1930s. Prefects were particularly trusted to be able to mix with girls.

The 1932 prefects played hockey against St Catherine's. The 1967 prefects had a pleasant afternoon's tennis with St Catherine's prefects until Hamish Ewing's serve 'hit his partner on the back of the neck and put a dampener on the whole event'.[19]

DANCING AND DATING
Dancing class

A more intimate activity was dancing class. These 'were a Very Big Thing' (1947),[20] 'Our first awkward relationships with girls. My first love' (1958).[21] Scotch began teaching dancing in Morrison's day and continued for boarders under Littlejohn, taught in the gym with an annual competition for the Captain of the Floor. Dancing smacked of sin—Presbyterians were not allowed to dance on church premises until the late 1940s—but a gentleman had to dance, and each dance had its own steps which had to be learnt in advance. In the 1920s, there were lessons at the school, and at dancing schools. Participants wore cotton gloves.

In the 1940s and 1950s, just across Glenferrie Road, in Kennon Hall, the redoubtable Miss Katey Lascelles ran much-frequented classes, which underlined social graces, and provided a very formal setting for boys to meet girls. She regularly sent assistants to patrol the grounds to discourage extra-mural activities. Mrs Nell Challingsworth conducted classes locally. Hans and Alice Meyer ran the Meyer School of Movement and Language. Although refugees from Hitler's Germany, during the war they were interned, separately, and their property confiscated. They became citizens in 1946. He was honorary Venezuelan Consul, 'immaculately dressed with a monocle and a dark red carnation in his button hole'. Barrie Johns (1955) began there in Year 11, although 'more pretentious boys … started in Year 10.' 'One attraction of this dancing school was the "Five Ways" milk bar at the Junction. It was a good place to take your partner for a milkshake. This had to be fairly quick because your partner was inevitably collected by her parents within half an hour of the lesson concluding.'[22]

Wherever they were, classes started awkwardly.

The first Friday night … We were going to kill the fairer sex. Seven o'clock arrived but we weren't in any real hurry to enter. We were certain that some class mate had not arrived. Eventually … we had to enter the hall because all the girls had [arrived]. We entered and immediately went to the end of the hall opposite the end where the girls were sitting. 'Take your partners for the first dance!' Not a movement! Eventually Mr and Mrs Meyer went to each end of the hall and made two circles. You danced with the girl standing opposite you. … it was a Miss Mansell from PLC and years later we met and recalled the hell of the first night. Nobody changed partners that night!' [1955].[23]

Thirty years later, at PLC or Merton Hall, 'when we all arrived … the girls were as nervous as all of us boys. We stood at one end of the hall and the girls stood at the other. After one boy made a move to speak everyone else would join in' (1986).[24]

Andrew Bales (1988) remembers

> dancing classes with Merton Hall. A couple of the girls in the group weren't too bad! We would line up opposite one and another, boys one side, girls the other. This was always a frantic start to the night. A quick head count along the row of girls and some shuffling on your side meant you met the right partner once joining to dance. I learnt pretty quickly not to count the girls like sheep, in 2's or 3's (as I had done on the family farm). This often led to mistakes.[25]

Andrew Mackay (1970) 'always got the "bags". They had braces/pimples etc. I thought I was a handsome young man but obviously I wasn't.'[26] Once the dancing began, the most extraordinary thing about it was that 'at a dance one could not only meet girls but, up to a point, touch them' (1928).[27] 'You Beaut,' wrote Geoff Mayor (1949) in his diary, 'Started Dancing. Whacko.'[28] *Hip contact!* That was the instruction given by both the Meyers. It became a comment which brought many a smile to my lips when in later life I again encountered ladies I had first met as young girls at Meyer's' (1955).[29] 'Many of us had trouble with erections at dancing class and had to dance side on to our partners' (1958).[30] Often the dancing was learnt badly. 'My toe was rarely light and never fantastic.'[31] This hardly mattered if boys were there chiefly to touch the girls.

As the end approached, 'There was great competition to "book" the last dance, always Goodnight Sweetheart played from a record, with who you thought was your "sweetheart". If one was lucky, the night's climax was holding hands while walking to the tram stop where we boarders were committed to split and return to quarters' (1952).[32] 'Boys who had girl friends who were day girls could walk them home, go for a milk shake and so on', but Bill Meyer's (1947) 'first great love' was a Lauriston boarder. After the dancing class there, 'in order to have a cuddle … a certain amount of skill was required. She would leave a selection of "smalls" outside on the line, so that she had to go out to bring them in.'[33]

Dancing class could be 'a wonderful start to social interaction' (1945),[34] a social springboard where John Goldsmith (1951) met girls 'who asked me to parties'.[35] The Meyers' classes 'were a rite of passage' (1954). 'For many boys at Scotch in the 1950's there was a huge social division between girls and boys. … and it was possible for a boy to have had very little contact with girls outside his own family. The Meyer Dancing Class enabled this contact to take place, and for boys to develop some social graces' (1954).[36]

Some boys found dancing class 'an enormous strain, probably due to a lack of experience at mixing with girls' (1967).[37] 'Dancing class was very awkward' (1976), 'dreadful' (1964), 'appalling' (1969), 'Fumbling and awkward. ... the girls all seemed much larger' (1977)[38] (as indeed they sometimes were, for the spurt of growth that comes at the start of puberty for girls comes later for boys). 'During dancing class, I had braces on my teeth, zero confidence and no idea how to communicate with women (talking to them would have been a good idea!)' (1975).

The School Dance

The lessons' climax was the School Dance. Before the Dance, 'in the usual fashion of boys great discussion was held as to which girl to take' (1954).[39] 'It was always a tremendous challenge to (a) find a girl to ask to the school dance and (b) ask her. ... but that was partly my own fault, since there were many "Don Juans" amongst my peers' (1967).[40] Dances make one's social situation very public: in 1956 rumours spread that top cadets were having trouble getting partners for the dance. Once the 'date' was organised 'my mother had graciously invited some of my friends and their partners for a pre-dance lemonade. I am very serious about the "lemonade", I can't remember any talk about alcohol being consumed at any time around a school dance' (1955).[41]

> The School Dance was the real star in the social firmament of a testosterone-riddled Year 11 student who had just encountered, and not very successfully, the demands of shaving. You really had to be seen at this event. A dinner suit would really be impressive. An older cousin, in Sydney, had a white tuxedo, this would really "kill"! It took a lot of forward planning to have this charismatic jacket delivered to Melbourne for the necessary date. ... The night arrived and so had my white tuxedo. My partner's father delivered his daughter; so did the partner of another friend. My desires for the white tuxedo had remained constant but not the keenness for my partner. It was the 'other lady' who was now my heart's delight and it proved to be a rather stressful evening. Life was not meant to be easy when you are sixteen! [1955].[42]

Tuxedos and fickleness also occurred elsewhere.

> Tuxedo has charms for the fair
> And I've plenty of that and to spare,
>   And a father's old rejects
>   When sported by prefects
> Can give quite a glamorous air.
>   A fact that I counted upon
>   When I first put this dinner suit on.

But though with my figure it's graced,
And the bow-tie is tied without haste,
  The female heart's warmer
  For a *school*-tied fifth former,
And the dinner suit's all gone to waste …
  I didn't anticipate that
  When I first put this dinner suit on.

Robin Stewardson (1955)[43]

The dance 'was to be the first occasion on which I could demonstrate my dancing skills. We had learned the Foxtrot and the Modern Waltz. The really big arrow in my quiver was the Samba. There was a very long Barn Dance and I didn't know this complicated set dance. It was a good night but I was very disappointed that the Samba did not feature' (1955).[44]

After the dance I 'had to take home to East Malvern my partner at the boarders dance—no train home—station master lent me his bike to return to Scotch & climb sewage pipes in McMeckan House—returned bike on Sat morning' (1936).[45]

OPEN WINDOWS

On a Drama tour of Tasmania in 1935. From left: Les Hancock (who died eight years later in the war), 'Chick' Evans and Jack Scholes.

For several generations, dancing classes and the School Dance were the highlights of the social calendar. Otherwise, in the 1930s 'All my social outings were family/church related. I had little Scotch outings.' During World War II, 'apart from dancing lessons … and the school dance I cannot remember any mixed social activities'.[46] 'The war and the immediate post-war years left little money and opportunity.' The social field in the 1940s was a closeknit affair of the schools centred in Kew and Hawthorn.

After the war, social possibilities broadened. Although there were very few school social activities, there were Saturday night dances at Ormond Hall and the Power House, a rowing shed on Albert Park Lake, which 'was a social and sporting club founded and run by people who … had attended the Lord Somers Camp. It was very well run and as a result well supported by parents as a venue to which daughters could enjoy in good surrounds a social evening with the boy of their choice'.[47]

Sometimes boarders were absent illegally. The buildings on the Hill were easy to slip in and out of. One of the young teachers in 1946 had only come to Melbourne to be near his fiancée and his few free nights were spent at her mother's place,

taking on nutritional fuel, and these nights usually ended up about 1.00 a.m when I would badly bark and bruise my legs as I climbed through Arthur Robinson House downstairs prep windows. In those days no one in authority thought of issuing young masters with a front door key, on the simple assumption that one was not expected to have any desire to go out when not on duty. I strongly suspect that Chick Williams [1946] the House Captain, each night took a deliberate and delicious delight in locking all bar one of the prep windows, leaving me with a baffling nocturnal conundrum 'Which window will be open tonight?' After a few months of this, I was finally forced to say … 'You really will have to marry me, for I have no more skin left on my shins!' So, we were married.[48]

Ron Bond, for it was he, was later Vice-Principal.

'For some devilment, at night,' David Shave (1952) and others 'snuck out of the dorm, by door or window, after lights out and had a midnight swim or, if really game, walked to one of the nearby girls' schools in the hope there were sleepless girls. This ruse never worked.'[49] Keith Thom (1951) would go 'AWOL' in the dead of night, which had 'a fugitive quality which I found enjoyable'.[50] Forty years later Aaron Abell (1991) found that

> During form 6 [Year 12] these outings were very easy, because being in School or McMeckan House the form 6 rooms were out in the 'back-block'. So, any after-hours activities were easy to organise through the bottom exit door. Although you had to be careful with the door or you could be locked out and not be able to get back in, but we fixed that by leaving my window open which just happened to be on the ground floor. The steep descent and ascent to the bottom gate on Glenferrie Road, was usually very quick and quiet so that we would not be seen. From there we were usually picked up in a car of some people we knew outside of school, and went to … usually a pub or bar somewhere. This didn't take place every week, but maybe once a month.[51]

The boarders held a dance from the 1930s, and in the 1940s–60s an At Home. The Dining Hall in 1956 was festooned in Cardinal, Gold and Blue and also in Black and White, the colours of Littlejohn House which then was exclusively the boarders' House. Since many boarders knew no girls, they had blind dates, allocated by size and form—details in advance to Mrs Owen, Mrs Healey or Mrs Brown. Mrs Northwood in the early 1970s matched boys and girls by height. Outside the dance Mr Owen stipulated a bright light 'so that there will be no confusion after the dance, when parents are looking for their daughters' (1968).[52]

LOVE AND SEX

Sooner or later meeting a girl led to a boy's first kiss.

> One afternoon all the other passengers got out two stations before Heidelberg, and for the first time Mary and I were alone. I knew I would be

ashamed if I failed to make some use of this opportunity. As the train pulled out of the last station before ours, I slid my arm behind her neck. To my relief she did not draw away. She turned her face slightly towards me, the grey eyes closed, and I kissed her. … the moments of emotion in the train that introduced me to a new stage of life [1928].[53]

As kissing was one stage, so there were others, in ascending order of intimacy, and boys gave each step a score. This word is used by Old Boys from the 1950s to the 1970s. 'We were told to respect girls but nobody did. The game was to "score" as high as possible on a list from 1 to 10. Whatever you "scored" you always added a couple more points to impress' (1954).[54] 'Those things probably weren't talked about other than "schoolyard banter" about "scoring" etc. etc. But we probably never really knew whether anyone actually did! In short, girls and things sexual remained a frustrating delightful mystery' (1965).[55]

The effect of scoring was that girls were not people to get to know, they were to score off. 'That was what Scotch unwittingly taught me about girls. They were to con' (1965).[56] 'We (I) did not learn much at school about treating women as "equals", not just as items to kiss!' (1969).[57] Misogyny was fairly strong at least into the 1970s, and Al Thomson (1977) felt that 'what I did learn mostly needed to be unlearnt. I was lucky to meet some assertive women at University (mostly ex PLC girls and feminists) who helped me to think very differently about women—as females, equals, minds, not just bodies to be scored'.[58] Back in the 1920s girls were objectified by being called janes. Someone who 'rowed in the school eight was doing a line with a jane at the Methodist Ladies College'.[59]

The highest score was for sexual intercourse. 'Sexual intercourse,' wrote David McNicoll (1932),

came in about my third or fourth year at boarding school. The recipient of my favors was a not unattractive prostitute in Little Lonsdale Street. A team of about six of us had set out to indulge, headed by a senior boy whom we looked up to with awe because he had had a woman on three occasions before. How old hat it now seems, … But the mid and late-twenties were the days of furtive fumbling in motor-cars, and in the back rows of cinemas. To own a French letter made you something of a celebrity. There was plenty of bold talk, plenty of bogus claims. But those were the days of terrified girls, prepared to go a long way, but not all the way. At least, not with 15 and 16-year-olds. In my last two years at school I found things different.[60]

A decade later, Ken Fraser (1941) reports that

we revelled in mixed birthday parties, where occasionally the more craftily venturesome might escape the vigilance of parent-hosts, and lure a girl into the garden. But whilst their hormones might definitely be functioning, I am sure most boys—and girls—of the age would get to a stage where, through ignorance, reticence, or downright cowardice, they would not be given free rein; descriptions of conquests would almost certainly be hyperbolical. Of course, in that less liberal age, the endured, compulsory scripture lessons might also have taken their toll on some confused young minds.[61]

Another boy recalls, 'Had some contact with girls during my school years— taking them to dances, the Royal Show—attending mixed tennis parties and dancing classes ... It was all pretty innocent and low key, with no heavy petting—just the occasional chaste "peck" ' (1941).[62] A member of the class of 1948 'can recall only 2 boys in Year 12 who had experienced sex while still at school'. 'Most of the time I was sexually frustrated and found it hard to control' (1951).[63] 'School-boys are much interested in the mystery of feminine beauty and attractions. ... every date was hysterical, some more than others. In my case, most thankfully, all encounters with the opposite gender left the mystery comfortably intact' (1944).[64]

The 1940s and 1950s were still 'long before the "Sexual Revolution", and at the time the only effective contraception known to women was a firm "No" ' (1944).[65] 'There were only condoms to come between you and the girl friend's pregnancy—unspeakable topic!' (1945).[66] 'A friend ... was paralysed with fear for a fortnight because the French Letter broke' (1943).[67]

> After school we would look for condoms (we called them frangers or french letters) on the ovals across the road from Monash Gates where couples used to park at night. I often used to find them on my way to school. We also read with interest the graffiti in the toilets of the Sports Pavilion ... in Gardiner Road only about 200 m from the school gates [1958].[68]

Old Boys of the 1990s say that scoring no longer carries a points system, and that 'scoring' a girl implies sexual intercourse.

Sexual attraction led not only to scoring but also to love. Its flashes are flashes of fire, says the Song of Solomon (viii.6), and it brings jealousy as bitter as the grave. Walter Turner (1901) wrote

> He now looked with different eyes at ... Lottie, a dark slender good-looking young woman of about twenty-three to whom he was merely a boy but, perhaps, an interesting and charming boy of sixteen or seventeen ... and they spent almost every day riding together. ... One beautiful hot day when Henry had helped her to mount and was about to get on his own horse a puff of wind blew her skirt right above her knees and a pang of ecstasy shot through him as he saw above her boots her beautifully shaped stockinged leg and white lace-edged linen. Looking down at him she caught his eyes and smiled mockingly as she drew her skirt back over her boots. Henry mounted

but rode in a dream … in a delirium of love. …

Presently the road broadened into open country and Lottie with a touch of her whip galloped away. Henry though not an experienced rider, for he rode only on his holidays, followed her. A mad exhilaration rushed through his veins as he recklessly abandoned himself to the very real danger of being thrown off. But to be dashed to pieces before her eyes was not enough. Could he have been ground into a dust of atoms innumerable as the stars and spread like a Milky Way for her to walk upon so that the infinitude of his being should quiver under her steps like the sea rippling under the moonlight

he would have been content. … Incommunicable agony of desire … thus did you make your first appearance in the life of Henry, …

As they rode back the waning bush had already started on its lifelong recession from Henry's mind. He no longer felt, saw and heard every throb of its hot quivering life. Other images, other sensations attracted his attention. He did not know it but this was to be his last contact with the natural life of his boyhood's country. Boyhood and the bush were fast vanishing together. At that moment he was like a pool over which a storm has swept.[69]

Geoff Storey reaches the point of no return in the outdoor swimming pool in 1976.

Like scoring, love had its degrees. Bruce Andrews (1944) 'advanced through the usual stages of "puppy love" first with a Lauriston girl, with all its desperate yearnings, exaggerated joys and sorrows, and total sexual frustration which I gather were the norms as Australian middle-class boys achieved sexual awareness'.[70] Gordon Powell (1929) 'admired Gwen Gilchrist from afar—a PLC girl. When it came to the Scotch dance in the Kooyong Tennis Club in 1929 I invited her to be my partner. … Recently we celebrated our Diamond Wedding.'[71] David Ashton (1965) 'wasn't ever really in love with any girl during my time at Scotch, so I didn't go through any great trauma in that respect—in hindsight, that was probably good, as I wasn't diverted from study or sport'.[72]

Each boy passes through at least some of all this, but at his own pace and in his own order. Even boys of the same age will be strung out like a cross-country race. Some boys fall in love early, some late. Some masturbate early, some never. Some boys, whether in the 1940s or 1980s, were 'more occupied with sport' (1946, 1986).[73] 'Sport, bikes, dogs, adventures were our life. Females were something our mother evidently was!' (1933).[74] Several

Old Boys see themselves as having been a 'late maturer' (1949)[75] or 'late developer' (1963).[76] 'I was a very late starter in showing interest in dates but was comfortable talking with girls' (1943). Indeed, the boy less sexually interested in girls was more able to get to know them as people.

Younger boys listened and watched 'on Saturday night, when the lads would go off to dancing at Tintern & other girls' schools'; then 'the boys would talk about the girls on a Sunday' (1945).[77] 'I had no dealings with janes, but I looked at them with growing interest. The amatory phase of life was on the horizon, though still only a cloud no bigger than a man's gland' (1928).[78]

Some of the sex and loving was with other boys. This might mean no more than having 'special friends at the school, with vaguely homosexual overtones' (1944).[79] Not all the sexual activity between boys meant that they were homosexuals. Not all the homosexuals were sexually active. One Jonathan knew his David's daily timetable and arranged his own route between classes to glimpse his adored. He recorded each sighting in his diary with a brief dash, with an additional mark if, bliss, they actually spoke a few words. This went on for two years with the other boy quite unaware.

Attitudes were harsh. A boy of 1940 was told that if he was propositioned by a homosexual to 'Hit him between the eyes and run for your life' (1941). In the 1960s, 'Any boys who were a little different, ... even just a little "softer and more feminine" were treated with scant care and ... were very much on the outer. The school ... had little way of dealing well with this' (1968).[80] By 1980 a boy could sound more tolerant. 'I really wish Scotch had been co-ed. I was really into girls but only socialized with them on weekends ... Rather than this I seemed to attract other boys, being the quiet sensitive type of guy. I would have preferred girls flirting with me than other guys!' (1980). Homosexual behaviour has remained very covert. Of the 750 Year 12 boys in 1998, 1999 and 2000, not one was publicly out. Peer pressure is probably even heavier at a single-sex school, whose boys are sensitive to catcalls of poofery. A gay student enjoyed being in the school play because it meant he 'learnt to act—a very useful thing for ... a gay man!' (1979).[81]

> I was unbelievably naive at the time and confess that I enjoyed the group culture of 'the boys' more than I did the company of 'girls'. We were not in any way homosexually inclined (well most of us), we were just unready for a fully mixed society and I don't think this did us any lasting harm. We gradually extended our circles to include 'the girls', experimented with pairing off, and eventually became fully paid up members of the heterosexual society [1947].

TALKING ABOUT SEX

Boys are deeply interested in their bodily changes and urgent needs. 'Sex was of course discussed ... amongst ourselves all the time!' (1952),[82] 'the inevitable talk among the boys' (1945),[83] comparing experiences and comparing body parts, a natural way of making sure they are all right. Sexual jokes abounded since humour relies on incongruity and ambiguity, both eminently applicable to sex. Many sexual jokes hinge on a *double entendre*. A collection of 'Notes written by fellow boarders during Prep, after tea, in School House, passed to each other, collected by Bill Norris' are full of sexual content.

Never was so little known about a topic of such interest: 'the way one learned these things then was from one's peers, and what a marvellously cock-eyed and misinformed view they imparted, with all the usual smuttiness and innuendo' (1944),[84] 'the usual badinage' (1945),[85] 'rumour and speculation in the dressing sheds and down along the river bank' (1950), 'in the Dorm after Lights Out' (1947),[86] 'the wonderful poetry on the backs of the dunny doors' (1946). 'Did we really suffer as a result—I doubt it' (1947).[87]

Not all boys joined in 'the to me distasteful coarse sexual references of teenage boys' (1951).[88] 'I did not like the way many of my contemporaries at school spoke about the girls they knew ... as fields for sexual exploitation' (1948).[89]

If any other topic had evoked such incessant chatter the teachers would have seized upon it, but though there was 'no shortage of discussion amongst students' there was 'very little discussion from the teachers' (1940).[90] 'I remember no teaching or guidance about this area of life' (1951).[91]

The challenge facing the school has been to find ways of talking to the boys about sex.

We might expect that since its foundation the school has grown steadily more open about such matters, but this is not the case. Scotch in the 1800s was comfortable with the idea that men were attracted to women. The 1860 Bible exam required boys to study the Song of Solomon, which lovingly catalogues each detail of a girl's body—thighs like jewels, breasts like young deer, neck like a tower of ivory, eyes like fishpools—and even contemplated tasting its fruit: 'Thy stature is like to a palm tree, and thy breasts to clusters of grapes. / I said, I will go up to the palm tree, I will take hold of the boughs ...'[92]

The early school magazine in 1878 described Sports Day 'with the vision of fair ladies still haunting our eyes',[93] and in 1905 recounted courtships:

> 'Twas at a dance
> I met by chance,
> Two sisters, fair and sprightly;
> I cast a glance,
> They looked askance,
> And danced mazourkas lightly.

Then smiling I,
Upon the sly,
Winked love-smit at the elder;
Hypnotic sigh,
Mesmeric eye,
Immediately felled her

Alexander Rentoul (1906)[94]

The 1920 *Collegian* even ventured a risqué joke: Why is love like photography? Because they both need a dark room to develop in.

Men of those days may have felt constrained about how explicitly to talk about sexual attraction to women, but they had no hesitation in celebrating its existence. Later, the 1978 *Collegian*, say, gave no hint that boys have any sexual urges at all. Somehow the pleasure of sexual attraction has become unmentionable in the school's publications. Today's *Collegian* offers photos of boys and their partners at school dances, but still finds it hard to mention in words—to talk about—this central aspect of boys' lives. (Exceptions occur, like the 1987 *Collegian*'s piece on the embarrassment and panic of asking a girl out.)

Similarly, older generations were frank about the male anatomy's vulnerability, sympathising with divers who 'came in sudden and painful contact with the water abdominally'.[95] This would now be thought rude.

Early *Collegians* were open about puberty's manifestations. The rise and fall of a boil was faithfully reported. The *Collegian* mocked boys growing moustaches, and was interested in boys starting to shave. Alexander Rentoul (1906) penned an 'Ode to My First Shave'. Older boarders shaved with dexterous sweeps surrounded by gaping novices. Jokes about shaving could be printed into the 1960s. A boy who claims to have been shaving since last year invites the reply: 'Yes, and cut yourself both times'.[96]

Talking sex in class: Religion

Discussing sex in class has all the pitfalls of any lesson when boys have a wide range of familiarity with the subject. Boys with older siblings were advantaged. Nevertheless, Ken Foletta, still attending a co-educational state school whilst his elder brother was at Scotch, found that 'as far as sex was concerned (and that's not having girlfriends or being social with women, I mean just having sex), ... I had overtaken him' (1964).[97] In any one class boys are in various stages of puberty and of sexual knowledge or experience. A class of 13–14-year-old boys may range from boys yet to masturbate through to a few who have already had sexual intercourse.

It is only from the 1920s that we have any record of what Scotch said to its boys about sex. Scotch has spoken with more than one voice, in particular the chaplain and the biology teacher.

The early chaplains taught a trinity of fear, manners and cleanliness.

Macneil was chaplain 1925–34. ' "Boys," he said grimly, "I am going to tell you today of the evils of self-abuse." He left us in no doubt that anyone who fell into the sin of Onan was doomed, and his nose would probably drop off.' In condemning masturbation, he impinged also upon another of life's turning points, going into long trousers—what Ross Campbell (1928) called 'assuming the trousers of manhood'. 'They had ample pockets at the sides, but one was discouraged from putting one's hands in them for any length of time. Otherwise one came under suspicion of "playing pocket billiards" ' (1928).[98]

Other than fear, Macneil taught 'very little, and what we did learn was of very little value' (1936).[99] Sexual matters were taboo. Sex education was seen as the responsibility of parents not schools, so Macneil's aim was a more general morality. He taught right and wrong, either in the negative terms of the Bible's *Thou shalt nots*, or by asserting the vague but principled view that a boy should 'behave as a gentleman' (1948).[100] Standards applicable to all aspects of life applied also in sexual situations. 'It was automatic … that good manners, pride in oneself and honesty etc. came naturally' (1944).[101] 'Politeness and good manners meant a lot to girls in those days' (1949).[102] 'Self-discipline and balance in all things, good Christian ethics and respect' (1934).[103] 'We learned that girls could be and were wonderful and genuine companions. In those days sex was not a part of our fun' (1929).[104]

Boys walking into the quadrangle past the Memorial Hall in 1931: includes John Forsyth Ross, Roy Paton, Jack Evans, Sinclair Mosley, Duncan Fraser Smith, Ken McKay. In the background is the Hill.

Cleanliness is next to godliness. If a motor-car 'has a speck of dirt in its carburettor it ceases to go. In just the same way, if we have something in our lives that hinders our witness for Christ, then we cease to be able to work for Him.'[105] A prayer of Macneil's confesses that 'We come to Thee conscious that we are unclean, and that we dwell in the midst of a people of unclean lips. O Lord, cleanse us, we pray'.[106] Healey wanted boys to live lives that were 'clean'.[107]

Implicitly Scotch conveyed to boys the message that women should be avoided. It did this by its 'single-sex environment and the lack of any organised/encouraged mixing of the sexes. Social outings had to be individual and usually originated from activities outside school although maybe involving fellow pupils' (1952). Boys made of this what they could: that women, and sexual feelings for women, were best ignored? were dangerous? were beyond the school's ability to help with?

Sometimes Macneil never reached the topic at all. He was going through the Ten Commandments and approaching the Seventh, 'Thou shalt not commit adultery', when Ken Bethell 'asked a question about the 6th and he never reached the 7th. The boys never forgave me! That was the extent (nil) of sexual learning the rest was innuendo and guess work' (1937).[108] At other times Macneil was more purposefully educational. In 1928 he

> announced that he would give a series of lessons on sex. He was going to call a spade a spade or rather 'a bloody shovel'. We looked forward to the lessons with keen anticipation, but there was nothing we didn't know, and there were no spicy bits. Yet on the whole I am sure the series did good in bringing sex out into the open and making it a subject you could discuss without embarrassment [1929].[109]

He 'cleared up the usual schoolboy misunderstandings' (1936).[110] But it 'should have been discussion not just lecture' (1935).[111] 'Class seemed to enlarge if word got around that one of his talks was on, he wasn't happy about that' (1936).[112] 'Boys who sniggered were obliged to leave' (1929).[113] He 'looked as though he had drawn the short straw on sexual matters and wanted to get his little talk over with quickly' (1934).[114] 'I learnt about sex in the usual way, peer education. ... the chaplain, didn't add much to that' (1936).

'In Christianity a man can only have one wife. This is called Monotony.' (*Satura*, 9 Apr. 1965, p. 13)

Macneil's successors as chaplain, Yarnold (1935–44) and Fraser (1945–67) were even less forthcoming. 'Sexual matters were barely discussed—Steve Yarnold gave superficial useless guidance' (1947),[115] and Fraser mouthed religious dogma which was 'totally useless' and more rigid than what came from home and the local church (1954).[116] If the role of the school was to reinforce standards, Keith Thom (1951) found this 'so iron clad with restriction that it had to be disregarded'.[117] But another boy says of Fraser: 'I'm not particularly religious but I liked his earthiness. I remember his advice "The trouble starts when some people finally realise that 85% of married life is spent *out* of bed".' (1964). (Fraser was a good preacher, using his Scots accent to effect and illustrating his sermons with apt stories. He was 'a sophisticated—perhaps even a "worldly" prelate' (1952),[118] and to the boys' great interest he bought a new car each year.) The Headmasters echoed the chaplains. 'Littlejohn gave us a filth lecture at night prayers' (1929).[119] Selby Smith, Polonius-like, gave a 'headmaster's speech to the departing 6th formers, he told us to be aware of 3 things in life—alcohol, fast cars, and fast women. One at a time was ok, but never 2 or 3 at the same time' (1963). 'He implored us to remain chaste until marriage. My girlfriend thought this was amusing' (1959). Tapp lauded 'purity' (1964)[120] and told Junior School boys that Jesus as a boy was not interested in sex (an unhelpful model for boys just reaching puberty).

Two 1967 boys summarise the situation: 'Scotch was a male-dominated insular society shrouded in tradition and espousing conservative moral values that were out of sync. with society at that time' (1967).[121] Scotch

> gave an introduction to the social & sexual morals of *my parents' generation* & this did prove a useful benchmark—to be left behind rather than followed. Of course, a paradigm shift was under way in the '60s, though I was scarcely aware of this at the time. It was better to be confronted with this paradigm shift with some guidelines than totally without [1967].[122]

A striding 'Faf' Fleming leads the staff back from the chapel after Selby Smith's inauguration. To his right are Frank Nankervis, Laurie Christie and Alec Lyne. In the next row are (from left) Violet Woolcock, Gordon Owen, Bernard Mendel, Laurie Provan and Don Walker.

Talking sex in class: Secular

Meanwhile an alternative and secular education sprang up. It so happened that from the 1920s to the 1950s the Biology teachers were women.

> The biology teacher, Mrs Ada a'Beckett, was a grey-haired, handsome woman with unusual prestige. Her name suggested saintly connections and her son Ted was captain of the Melbourne Grammar School cricket team. We called her Ada, but only behind her back. She had a commanding personality, and discoursed on ovaries and testes with a bland confidence that kept the most prurient pupils quiet. Ada's cool treatment of such topics made a healthy contrast to the horrific talks by the school chaplain [1928].[123]

A'Beckett's successor was Violet Woolcock. 'In an era when open discussion on sexual matters was rare, she brought a very sensible and informative atmosphere into the classroom—demystifying the subject lucidly yet directly' (1950).[124] She was 'the only woman teacher in the Senior School and regarded by the male teachers as rather intrusive. But her own strong but warm personality, her great sense of humour, the gender difference and the subject matter all lent themselves to the breaking down of many stereotyped attitudes, traditional barriers and taboos' (1950). Her humour allowed her repeatedly to end the lesson by saying 'You can down tools now boys', at which everyone laughed riotously while 'Miss W. sat there pokerface and asked us what the joke was' (1959). 'What organ quadruples in size when excited? We were all wrong, it's the *Iris!*' (1958).[125] 'I remember her advice to keep ourselves chaste. The class immediately chose to reinterpret this as *chased* and she joined in the general hilarity' (1950). She said she had played the violin in a New Orleans brothel, but she was no libertine. Rather than discourage the use of condoms she had advice: 'Remember boys, there's a dud in every pack' (1958).[126] 'Boys, when you get that sort of feeling run around the oval and have a cold shower' (1952).[127]

Many Old Boys mention her with affection, as their only source of knowledge. Others chafed at her 'circling the perimeter of hard information' (1958).[128] She dispensed 'very clinical and biologically accurate information … but that seemed to be confined to frogs, dogfish and rabbits and [had] very little relation to the complexity of human activities in these areas' (1944).[129] She 'gave us an outline of Biology; but … You worked it out for yourself as Adam and Eve did' (1952).[130]

Elsewhere, 'Nutty' Wilson in General Science taught the basic anatomy of penis and testicles. Other boys learnt from adults they knew. To a 1940s boarder, the matron 'explained more to me than teachers' (1940).[131] The news from Biology and Science sped to other boys (1950).[132] Yet even education about the 'plumbing' was not always satisfactory: Tapp left David Dyson (1961) thinking that 'penis' referred to his navel.[133]

Outside Bible and Biology, sex lurked everywhere. In Ancient History 'we laughed … when a passage referred to Alcibiades being persued by lovers of both sexes' (1952).[134] The French master, Kirby, was one day

> going over the nouns that form the plural by adding 'x', like *genoux* (knees) and *joujoux* (toys). He quoted a sentence to help us remember them. 'You get down on your *genoux* to play with your *joujoux*,' he said. The ribald members of the class … roared with laughter. From then on they spoke frequently of Mr Kirby playing with his *joujoux* [1928].[135]

In the 1950s,

> I think we had either a lecture or film at cadet camp about the dreaded VD— snigger, snigger, etc., but nothing serious and mature like the kids get today.

And there was no discussion with the teachers (including the chaplain)—or parents, for that matter—on this important subject. It really was a matter of peer group education and boasting! I guess you could say that the peer pressure was for it (if you can get away with it with the 'right' girl) and the social mores (teachers and parents) called for abstinence. This was a dilemma for the conscientious—a restraint which I was glad to throw off the day I threw away my school (prefect's) cap! ... Scotch certainly did *not* prepare me for the onslaught of actually dealing with girls in the way which university offered, so it was easy for many of us to put Sex 1A a little ahead of most other subjects [1956].

Scotch goes a'wooing

With reticent chaplains and sex education restricted to Biology, many Scotch boys learnt nothing,[136] or 'Very little'[137] in the forty years between 1926 and 1967, during the chaplaincies of Macneil, Yarnold and Fraser. 'It was as if girls did not exist' (1954). The little that boys learnt was 'as useful as a condom bought at a seconds shop' (1968).[138] Scotch boys emerged like Ian Picken (1937): 'prim, proper and Presbyterian at home and abroad. ... I became a company commander in W.W.2 with 200 troops under command at age 23—I realized just how very *green* I was.'[139]

Until the 1960s this was how most people thought it should be: 'sexual matters were firmly parental, not school, responsibility' (1948).[140] This could work well: 'Luckily my mother and father had advanced ideas for the times ... Hence, I was in a position to speak knowingly amongst my peers "behind the bike shed" when sexual topics came up' (1949).[141] In other homes sexual matters were as taboo as they were at school (1948).[142] Or parents left all aspects of a boy's education to the experts (1963).[143] Ian Phipps's father, 'a Doctor in general practice, presumed I received my sexual education at school and never referred to it!' (1952).[144]

By the 1960s, towards the end of Fraser's chaplaincy, Old Boys sound exasperated—'The sexual education at school was pathetic. Aunty Vie [Woolcock] told us about catching VD off toilet seats and I learned about the gestation of a frog' (1962)[145]—whereas Old Boys of earlier generations sound as though they expected no more. The pressure for change was growing.

From the 1950s boys' lives centred less on local organisations and more on the school. Parties 'were usually organised at family homes of friends at school—parents supervised' (1963).[146] Many school dances sprang up, like Boat Race, Cadet, Scout and Ski Club Dances. At the Cadet Dance to dance in a kilt was an 'interesting' experience (1975).[147] This dance was discontinued in 1958 because it ran at a loss, but reappeared in the 1970s. The ski dance in 1962—*Collegians Jazz Band with Mr Bruce Moore* (staff 1958–64)—was held in the gymnasium, which 'was good—sneaking out and having a smoke and a pash in the scout hall on top of a pile of tarps or tents' (1965).[148]

At the Cadet Dance—

She: What's the difference between dancing and marching?

He: I don't know.

She: I didn't think you did. Let's sit down.

(*Satura*, 9 Apr 1965, p.12.)

SMOKING

Smoking, like sex, was an adult behaviour forbidden to boys.

Adult men smoked as a matter of course for most of the 20th century. Christie (staff 1951–66; nicknamed 'the Count' as in the Count of Monte Cristo) 'couldn't go a whole period without going out on the balcony for a fag' (1967), and boys knew firsthand 'the absolute fog of tobacco smoke in the masters common room at lunch time' (1948).[149] 'Several masters smoked and had very stained fingers; one could really smell them when they were close by, particularly when they sat next to one. It was not offensive; in fact it was one of the smells I associated with mature adults' (1958).[150]

Boys smoked too, amongst the pines on the hillside, at the river, on the 'Boarders' Picnic. 'Went to Emerald. Had 2 weeds' (1943),[151] or any 'place away from the prefects to grab a quick couple of puffs' (1982).[152] Jokes in *Satura* and the *Collegian* hinged on knowing that Scotch boys smoked. The gentle 'Tiger' Lyne noticed that on one Geography excursion 'there was a little group who always finished their lunch in time to go for a walk along the road. We knew quite well what their purpose was, but they never let us see them smoking, which was considerate of them.'[153]

Scotch forbade boys smoking because 'it ill-becomes a schoolboy', as Fleming put it whilst Acting-Principal in 1961. Also, he added, a boy smokes 'because his mates do. What weakness of character this shows. We do not want this in Scotch Collegians.'[154] Fleming thereby attacked the same psychological process which in sport was lauded as 'team spirit'.

In the 1970s, Field, the Bursar, found that English Public Schools 'inevitably' provided smoking areas for senior boys.[155] Rod Tasker (1978) made an emotional plea for a sixth-form smoking room, arguing that smoking helped to reduce anxiety and tension.[156] By the time this might have become socially acceptable, the health arguments against smoking had appeared and led to the entire school becoming a no-smoking area in 1992.

Such details are a brief chronicle of a change in social habits spread over a century. We could trace the same for, say, spitting, now similarly decried as disgusting or unhealthy but once an acceptable habit, with cuspidors a sensible item of furniture.

What is startling about smoking is that when Scotch caught boy smokers it punished them savagely. Between at least 1936 and 1971, School Captains routinely gave smokers four to six strokes of the cane. At some stages it made no difference if the offence was committed in Geelong, or out of uniform, or in a private house, or that a boy's parents allowed him to smoke, or even whether he was actually smoking—in 1964 a boy received three strokes 'for carrying cigarettes'.[157] Six strokes was a heavier penalty than given to boys who stole, lied, cheated, bullied, or brought explosives to school.

How are we to explain the particular punitive fervour that smoking aroused? Did smoking touch some nerve of the school authorities? Did it spark some deep anxiety? Does the prohibitive and punitive approach to smoking parallel the school's approach to sex? Perhaps Scotch had some fear of boys' appetites in general, or of any behaviour that made a boy look less able to say 'I am the captain of my soul'.

The Prefects and Probationers Dance also began in the 1950s. 'I met my wife of 34 years at the Pres & Pros dance' (1955).[158] Dances for Forms V and VI (Years 11 and 12) were proposed in 1956–57, but a letter in *Satura* warned they would 'lower the moral tone of the school'.[159] Campaigners for a Form VI dance in 1970 were told it would have to be under school rules, that is, without smoking and alcohol, and with adequate lighting and adults, which dampened enthusiasm. At last in 1977 there was a Sixth-Form Dinner-Dance.

So many dances diminished attendance at the main School Dance, which in 1972 barely broke even. Perhaps financial restraint explains why the 1974 Dance dispensed with 'electronic' musicians and hired a conventional band, which Healey welcomed as 'a blow for freedom from noise'. A subsidiary, but 'mod' band, was provided free by one of the prefects, Harry Goddard (1974), but that, too, was quieter.[160] From the 1950s, dances had become more disturbing to staff and parents:

> Rock 'n' roll
> Cacophony,—
> Beat and rhythm;
> Shaking floors,
> Banging doors,
> Uncouth roars,
> Broken laws,
> Beat and rhythm.
> Swirl and swing;
> All of them craving,
> Some of them waving,
> None behaving;
> It all inflaming
> That irresistible urge that sets the young ones rolling,
> Sets the ball a'rolling,
> Sets the rock 'n' rolling.

Chris Stewardson (1962)[161]

'Rock 'n' Roll Hits Scotch' ran *Satura*'s page-one headline in 1956. 'School Dance a Great Success', with George Watson's band. The music was subversive not only because it was loud, but also because it overturned the old order: where once boys and girls had to learn to dance like adults, now they had their own music. Despite Healey's derision, there were boys who exulted in the music, and who found it a more important consideration than their partner (1968).[162] In 1978 the band was Sidewinder, dressed in red like true Scotch Collegians.[163] This band included, on electric violin, Richard Lee (entered 1967), who also played in Dragon. 'Other old Scotch pop musicians of note include keyboardist Ian Clyne (1963) of the Loved Ones and guitarist Rob MacKenzie (1965) of the avante garde MacKenzie Theory.'[164]

Scotch was equally flat-footed as boys began actually to talk about sex publicly. *Satura* in 1956 mentioned prefects' sex lives, at least by saying they had none (apparently an acceptable way of raising the subject). David Cowper (1956) claimed to be uninterested in the fair sex, whilst of Peter Yunghanns 'We hear he is a woman-hater—but personally we think he is very much of a dark horse'.[165] Such gossip was not new. In the 1920s Ross Campbell was said to be 'carrying on a secret amour on the banks of the Yarra at Heidelberg. Although untrue the story was flattering and I did not discourage it' (1928).[166] What was new in the 1950s was that it appeared in print.

Others resisted this trend. In 1941 one boy asked the Captain to do something about a Probationer who regularly seduced women and was known as 'a pretty fast worker'.[167] In the 1950s Scotch's 'two evangelical groups', Crusaders and the Australian Student Christian Movement, 'adopted a strict interpretation of what was then the conventional attitude towards premarital sex—in fact, any sexual experience outside marriage' (1956). As a Presbyterian institution, Scotch's outlook was equally conservative.

Used and Abused, 1983. From left: Fenton Long, Mark Lipscombe, Michael Martin, Lachie Fraser-Smith (drums), Duncan Fraser-Smith, Bruce Bartley.

But from the 1960s Scotch realised that its task of framing boys' character must extend to sex. The school began to introduce its boys to girls, to manage this encounter, and to train boys not only about sex's anatomy and morality but also about its social side.

In 1960 Scotch began joint activities with girls' schools. Few measures have been so universally welcomed, and so useful. A workaday interaction with girls gave boys the possibility of getting to know girls as people, though there was no lessening of lust and love. Joint activity began for practical reasons, to supply sopranos and contraltos. The new Director of Music, Logie-Smith, put on the *Messiah* in 1960 with MLC, and in 1961 did so again and at Easter organised the *St Matthew Passion*, with St Catherine's in the Memorial Hall. This powerfully enhanced Easter. Yet these were 'hardly a social event as very little interaction occurred. It was thus very easy to only have male company until one left school' (1972).

In 1965 Scotch and PLC presented *HMS Pinafore*. Dick Dead-eye, the spoil-sport, had to be 'a coarse and ugly character' and Logie-Smith decided that Jeff Kennett would be 'suitable'.[168]

Later, girls acted in school plays. In 1950 it was enough to inflame the imaginations of final-year boys that Philip Sargeant (1950), who had played Henry V in the Scotch production, was asked to re-enact the betrothal scene opposite 'a real girl' from St Catherine's. In 1968 the Drama master, Ian Harrison, put on *An Italian Straw Hat* with St Catherine's girls in the female roles. To 'the smell of greasepaint at the back of Mackie Hall' was added 'the intoxicating smell of teenage girls' perfume' (1970).[169] That same year, Scotch boys played the male roles in the St Catherine's play. Joint plays became routine, with Ruyton and St Catherine's, and sometimes with distant PLC. Perhaps joint ventures in drama came later than in music because they involved closer contact between girls and boys over a longer period of time, during rehearsals, and this aroused staff fears. Yet the closeness meant that boys could 'develop relationships with girls beyond the desire for "unseemly" activity which seems to have struck me quite early!' (1975).[170] Plays 'were a great opportunity to mix with the opposite sex (often with great trepidation!)' (1975).[171] One actor started dating girls through school plays and 'fell hopelessly in love with the lead girl in my last year—unrequited' (1977).[172] Thirty years later, plays are still 'a good way to meet the opposite sex' (1996).[173]

From the mid-1960s sixth-form boarders entertained boarders from girls' schools. They danced, played table-tennis and billiards, and listened to records. It forced boys to mix and to develop a sense of responsibility as host to a group rather than to a single girl. From 1972 the Captain of Littlejohn (the boarders' House) organised these 'socials'—a variety of sports on a Sunday afternoon, after which the senior girls stayed for dinner, chapel and a discussion. Littlejohn Captains compiled advice for their successors, especially on socials, 'by far the worst and most time-consuming part of being house captain'.[174] They learnt to have as many socials as possible in first term, so that in second term the girls would reciprocate. It was best to assemble the boys before the start, rather than let them wander in: 'this helps a good start which either makes or breaks the social'.[175] In 1984, however, a social for older boys 'was disastrous. Halfway through the night many of the boys left the social and … girls were left on their own.'[176] The choice was always between doing something active like sport, at which boys could look at the girls, and something that involved actually talking to the girls.

The girls' schools concerned were Merton Hall, Tintern, PLC, St Catherine's and MLC, because they had boarders and were of similar social class to Scotch. In 1996 'it was and still is a small social group'. Inevitably girls became objectified by school. In 1947 'Lauriston was No. 1, Tintern No. 2 and St Cath's no where! PLC was even lower, but they held crazy whist evenings from time to time and, as Boarders, anywhere that offered free food was ok.'[177] In 1978 'the Korowa girls were gorgeous, classy, witty and down to earth as well. St Catherine's were downright scary (so mature, beautiful and wealthy). Lauriston were scary because they knew far more about sex than we did. MLC were too common although everyone could find someone there. PLC were snooty.'[178] Girls objectified boys, too. 'Some girls were attracted to the fact one went to Scotch but in reality this meant very little for personal confidence etc.' (1965).[179] The School Dance continued to be the social event of the year, and Scotch boys modestly believed that 'The girls felt they had "Arrived" when invited. It was the event' (1967).

The kinds of activities with girls expanded. In 1978 Scotch and PLC students went on a five-day kayaking and hiking trip on the Buffalo River. Shugg, as Russian teacher, led Scotch boys and MacRobertson High School girls on a three-week trip to Russia.

In the last 50 years, as before, there were boys who 'didn't know any girls' (1964). 'Little contact with girls in any situation whilst at school' (1975).[180] Even in the 1990s it is still possible for a boarder to lack female friends until university: 'only 2 Saturday nights out a term didn't help. We really couldn't go to parties or any other nighttime events' (1995). There's the rub. 'The school (especially boarding) tries to show that it adequately covers this area of life and yet you could forget it if you actually wanted to go out with someone. Unfortunately socials are not where you meet girls in the real world' (1995).[181]

Sex education

As well as managing boys' meetings with girls, the school tried to talk to the boys about sex. The problem, as ever, was how to do so in classes containing a wide range of sexual experience and knowledge. In *experience*, as the century advanced, boys sound as if they were more sexually active. Probably this was so, or perhaps younger Old Boys are franker. We can be more sure that boys' *knowledge* grew. Boys were more likely than their fathers to read sex education books, and there was enough knowledge of body parts' names for a burst of hilarity in Form III Science when one boy gave 'vagina' its Latin pronunciation of 'wagg-eena' (1964).[182] Outside the school, also, sex was talked about increasingly widely, even in the most respectable places, as local churches ran 'father and son' programmes (1963).[183]

Just as Scotch at last contemplated a co-ordinated sex education programme, customer demand changed. Boys still wanted to know about bodies, but they also wanted to know how to relate to women, a necessary thing to teach in a school that excluded girls. 'The single sex situation [meant] I was badly prepared for relations with girls/women. Separating this aspect of socialising from other development is odd to say the least' (1963).[184] Scotch was a conservative male environment, and someone who was 'one of 3 boys in an all-boys school' felt 'socially inept when it came to girls … Mine was a very "blokey" education'. 'I really wish I'd done the plays with the girls school, dancing class or something because Scotch taught you nothing re girls. … The social skills you were taught were very "macho" ie leadership, survival in groups, teamwork via scouts and sports etc.' (1978).[185] Boys became more likely to use dancing classes not to score but to make friendships that endured (1952, 1991, 1996).[186]

Scotch did not teach social skills, or group dynamics. Psychology was taught in Year 11 only as late as 2000. If anything, Scotch long fostered eccentric students and masters. Manners were no longer enough social skills.

Girls were all different. There was the small and very funny and clever girl met at the social at Korowa—'Roger said, "Gee you're a card". She said, "Hmm, I'd like to deal with you!".' Or there were two quite different girls met at dancing class: one 'is really great fun but hasn't got a particularly good personality and the other … I thought we were just very good friends, more like brother and sister. We have good talks but she really isn't very attractive to me or as much fun as the other. She was apparently in tears afterwards which makes it difficult for me.'[187] Having girlfriends was complicated, and boys had to wrestle with how to start relationships— 'I don't know what's going to come from it. … She seems interested enough and I certainly am'—and with how to end them— 'Sunday … I'll tell her then. I would have thought that she'd got the hint by now but I haven't been unkind or anything. I feel that if I do it now we'll … still be able to remain good friends. I don't know whether it works that way but I hope it does.'[188]

The need for both sexual and social education was taken up by the Rev. Archie Crow. Once chaplain in his own right, from 1968, Crow introduced a new subject, Religion-In-Life, which aimed at developing Christian values and conduct in the context of boys' lives, and covered a range of social issues. His training allowed sex to be part of a programme, rather than a one-off topic. He addressed issues frankly, advising abstinence and self-restraint. 'Sex education fairly good' (1976)[189] says an Old Boy—at last. 'I

Colin Black (ninth Vice-Principal 1986–87) takes the cast of *My Fair Lady* through their paces, 1983.

remember Archie Crow asking us to anonymously put in written questions to him in a fourth form class [Year 10] and he then attempted to answer them. Of course he got some rather funny questions but took it all very well and managed to reply frankly and honestly!' (1976).[190] 'Sex lessons with dear old Arch …with a form of sniggering unruly testosterone packed boys' (1975).[191] Crow screened Health Department films, one of which, without his planning it, showed a woman masturbating. The reaction was smutty, but also a mixture of aroused, embarrassed and awed. 'I don't believe many of the boys actually knew girls might masturbate too. Archie Crow didn't flinch or move or comment during the whole film, what's more not one word was spoken by him after the film. He just got back to talking on another subject like nothing had just happened' (1985). Crow's course was a balanced one, for the chaplains did not want sex education and religious instruction to become synonymous, as there were other religious matters that needed attention: the Bible, grace and the numinous.

In 1975, the General House Committee proposed 'a co-ordinated sex education program'. It imagined an improved Religion-In-Life course, though it acknowledged that 'Different levels of knowledge and the all-male situation make it difficult to plan a suitable course'.[192] An Old Boy of that time thinks 'it should have been a biology type of class and included in the curriculum. That way it may have been taken a little more seriously' (1973).[193] Another argues that 'sex education should not have been taught in Science or Religious classes at all' but in a second-form (Year 8) 'course known as "Human studies" or something like that which covered all aspects of human relations—communication, sociology, psychology and sexuality. However, such a course would not be taught by a minister of religion' (1980).[194] Boys welcomed a more positive attitude to sexuality, that 'sex was like putting your finger into a warm orange' (1971).[195]

Sexuality was taught elsewhere, here and there. Robbie Torrick (staff 1968–88) taught sexual reproduction (via rabbits!) to Form II (Year 8) Science, covering it 'in 23 long and embarrassing minutes' (1982).[196] Dick Briggs in 1965 included sex education in Science. Leaving the moral aspects to the chaplain, Briggs covered basic anatomy and physiology, masturbation (does no physical damage), and contraception. Healey first heard about this on the golf course when a parent praised it.

Healey accepted the need to teach such things, but felt uncomfortable about them, which set the mood for the school. Healey frowned on any physical expression of affection. 'Kissing and embracing at parties' he discouraged as 'bad manners'.[197] At a School Dance one boy

had very blond hair. Towards the end of the dance, many couples ended up in rather warm embraces (despite having been repeatedly told that 'public displays of affection are in poor taste and a cause of embarrassment to others'). I was no exception, except that my hair made me stand out in the crowd. Col Healey focused his distaste for such 'displays' on me, asking me to attend his office for a dressing down first thing next school day. He wrote to my parents and so forth [1970].

'Unclasp', Healy would tell dancers. Under Roff, by contrast, the *Collegian* was allowed to mention, albeit in a piece of fiction, that boys read pornography and might 'leave the best bits for bed'.[198]

In 1985 the Rev. Graham Bradbeer became chaplain and under him boys complain 'Useful? Not much! Without the country boys to teach you a thing or two about how to handle the women this aspect would have been non-existent' (1995).[199]

> Apart from a topic on Reproduction in year 8, I recall one session, I think it was in year 9 ...when we did go through some issues about safe sex etc. During one of our classes one day, Mr Anderson [staff 1987–] (... a great person and teacher) took the class and talked about safe sex issues and how to put on a condom. I can vaguely recall this only because: 1. He did such a good job of teaching us something about a difficult topic. 2. The session was so out of the blue and uncharacteristic of the school that I can still remember the shock of a teacher talking about sex! ... one session on this topic in 6 years of high school is not enough and a pretty lame attempt at preventing deaths from unsafe sex. It's the only topic we ever covered in one class—why couldn't we have done the same with Trigonometry! [1995].[200]

Other boys felt they 'didn't learn a great deal about these matters, so you learned by yourself' (1991).[201] 'Our sex education classes did not involve education on STDs'; 'we had sex education in year 8, but ... the school did not condone sex before marriage ... it was a taboo subject' (1991). It is still possible for a boy leaving in 2000 to say that he had had, in the previous six years, only half an hour's sex education.[202]

These memories are at odds with Bradbeer's aim to teach safe sex (which means both that he covers the details of sex and also that he accepts the reality that boys will have sex before marriage). He resolved also that no Scotch Old Boy should die of AIDS through ignorance of how it is contracted. Bradbeer began day-long seminars on sex in conjunction with girls' schools. At first this occurred within General Studies and when this ceased Scotch lost a 'well-contexted' sex education course. Sex education in 2000 appears in Years 7–12 as part of Christian Education and Social Education. It can appear also in health education, and is taken up at appropriate moments by other teachers. Much depends on teachers' comfort with facilitating such discussions.

Too young to know?

The age at which Australian boys reach puberty may have fallen by three years during the 20th century. It is said to start one-third of a year earlier every decade, perhaps linked to better nutrition.[203] Over the century, the average weight of the First Crew increased by 20%, from about 73 kg (11.5 stone) in 1909 to 88 kg (13.8 stone) in 2000. The earlier onset of puberty makes adolescence longer. The school preferred not to notice that younger boys had sexual urges. Yet even in the 1930s 'at 15 years you are fast coming to grips with adulthood' (1933).[204] In the 1960s a boy in Year 8 (aged 12) had 'to pay for a new desk top after I carved my girlfriend's name in the desk top' (1967).

In tackling this demographical shift, the school faced two practical questions: at what age should it teach sex education, and down to what level should it involve boys in social activity?

Younger boys pushed to be part of social activities. In the 1960s, boys in Form IV (Year 10) protested at their exclusion from the Boat Race Dance. The trumpet-playing Geology teacher 'Slugger' Moore 'played at some great dances in some funny halls around the suburbs while 4th form Scotch boys groped and pashed 4th form MLC, St Cath's and Lauriston girls. We were all so sophisticated' (1964).[205]

At the Boarders' Dance Mrs Healey discouraged blind dates for boys below Form IV, and though the 1968 Dance allowed Form III blind dates, this was for economic reasons.[206] They tried it again in 1972:

> because we had a very expensive Band and we were short on money ... This proved to be a real mess. Boys were arranging blind dates for the 3rd formers (only 3 could get their own girls) and their girls were being incorrectly invited and their mothers were upset. ... So please take my word for it and forget about the 3rd formers. If you get into financial troubles the school will come to your aid.[207]

But soon Ian Shimmin (1977) believed that Socials were 'just as important for the younger boys as for the sixth formers',[208] and Graham Hearn (1980) wrote: 'make sure that the younger boys and not just 6th formers have them. I had a problem last year as the third formers wanted to have a social but the girls schools didn't have the numbers'.[209] By the late 1970s the socials included fourth formers and 1984 saw a separate social for the Forms III and IV (Years 9 and 10).

In 1986 'a young second former organised a social'.[210]

> Early ripe, early rotten! I went off with a bang at the 2nd form dance held at Corowa and had a brief telephone romance. However, I then was forced into hibernation while I waited for puberty to arrive (and waited, and waited ...). By the time that finally occurred, I was busy in 5th and 6th form so nothing really happened beyond very brief encounters until uni. [1984].

Bruce Whittaker argued in 1976 that sex-education should be done earlier than Form III,[211] and Ross Hyams (1980) concurs.[212]

The idea that boys past puberty might be interested in sex spread even to the Junior School. In 1978 the Mothers' Association asked the Headmaster, Wirth, to introduce sex-education for Year 7 boys, especially as it was already available to the Year 7 boys in the Senior School. Wirth was dismayed. He did 'not want to rush into anything which may prove to be unsuitable',[213] and passed the problem to the chaplain. In 1983 Wirth pushed the question back at the mothers, asking what they wanted taught. 'After some discussion it was agreed that enquiries be made about suitable films to be shown in the evenings for parents and boys on a voluntary basis.'[214] Wirth thus declined to give leadership in this area, relegated it to a voluntary basis, and neglected the family-based educational approach he so encouraged in teaching computers. In 1984 Wirth thought the school should perhaps have someone on staff who was trained. 'Sex Education type books must not be put directly into library [but first] must be read by staff & perhaps parents.'[215] By this stage the new Principal had told Wirth 'that any parent wishing the school to teach sex education must make an appointment personally with Dr Donaldson himself',[216] who held that sexual relationships 'should be avoided outside marriage'.[217] Graham Nowacki (Junior School Headmaster 1986–98) believed that sex and relationship education were both essential parts of the school programme and encouraged teachers to answer questions openly and honestly at any time. Boys in Years 5 and 6 learnt from a humorous *Bodyowner's Manual* about 'what changes your body would go through ... at that stage of your life'; 'I found that quite useful' (2000).[218]

Pole vaulting. Don Allinson clears the bar, 1978.

Wirth was more effective in increasing boys' socialisation with girls. He agreed to a production of *The Mikado* with 'a bevy of beauty from Morris Hall, the Junior School of M.C.E.G.G.S. ... This production will provide an opportunity to explore aspects of Japanese culture during term two.'[219] It would also allow boys to explore the culture of girls, but to say so was perhaps too controversial.

'A VERY CONSIDERATE GUY'

The Sixth- and Fifth-Form Dinner Dances began in the early 1990s. They were intended to be more socially educational than the old School Dance. Instead of merely a band and supper, the formal dinner-dance had tutors attending with their partners. Anne Colman or Peter Joyce (1956, Foundation President 1996–2001) told the boys about etiquette, ranging from the invitation, to picking up partners from home, to formally introducing partners to members of staff. In teaching such social skills, Scotch was doing what parents once did. Formal attire like tuxedos emphasised the tone of the evening.

In the last quarter-century, boys and parents have asked Scotch to provide sex education, a complete reversal of how things were only two generations earlier. No doubt change will continue. In 1988 AIDS seminars for sixth formers, and another for parents, were organised through the Scotch Association, another example of parents being more willing than the school to tackle sexual issues.

Fifty years ago, most Scotch boys who knew girls met them through local organisations rather than knew them as a part of their lives with their schoolmates. As recently as fifteen years ago a Scotch boy might have 'very little idea about the opposite sex when I arrived at Uni. … I don't think it has really bothered me in the long term, although I was quite awkward in my early days there' (1984). By the early 1990s a Scotch boy might have a social life in which school and girls intertwined. 'We had a few parties toward the end of Year 12 and about six of my mates liked this girl but she liked me and I didn't want a bar of her. This caused plenty of classroom comments from both parties!!' (1992).[220]

Nowadays the School Captain, even in Assembly, mentions girlfriends and pick-up lines. The whole training schedule of the First VIII was said to be organised around the girlfriend of one of the Crew; 'She is obviously a very important part in his life. Their eighteen-month anniversary is coming up this week.' The Stroke of the Crew was 'a very considerate guy when it comes to women; last year he kissed one girl and her best friend on the same night'.[221] Many Scotch boys now have active social lives that routinely include girls. What this means probably varies from boy to boy. It may be 'superficial … based around looks and appearance' (1996),[222] and a way of furthering a boy's 'own ego and standing within the social scheme', whilst even 'those that had girlfriends were perhaps forced to moderate between (real) feelings that they held for girls, and tough talk of looks, etc' (1999).[223] 'During teenage years, boys' and girls' relationships are based around appearance. This is what society encourages and this is perpetuated by being in a single-sex school where there are no members of the opposite sex with which one might learn to establish more healthy relationships' (1995).[224]

Teaching about sex, and about human relations more generally, continues, taught by chaplains and other staff. The latest phase, discussed below in Chapter 21, notes the school's new policy of teaching harm minimisation, which accepts that some boys will be sexually active and should be taught about sexually transmitted diseases and condoms.

14

HEALEY

1964–1975

'Whom have I hurt? What artists have I broken?—No, don't write or telephone to tell me; I can guess; … But this must be the shadow on any headmaster's mind.'[1] Thus Colin Healey in his retirement. Most boys of his time will be surprised to find him in such a mood, surprised to find anything but Healey as they remember him: fierce, forceful, unbending, conservative.

Colin Healey, sixth Principal 1964–75. His gaze is paralleled by that of W.L. Bowles's bust of Sir John Monash.

To talk of Colin Oswald Healey, Scotch's sixth Principal (and second Colin), is to talk in contrasts. He seemed so different from Selby Smith that people postulate a Council policy of alternating principals between liberal and conservative. They say Healey was brought in to fix up the mess left by his predecessor. In fact, Selby Smith recommended Healey, and Healey himself found little sign of decline. Healey had slightly more premierships in the big four sports (athletics, cricket, football and rowing), but he did not agree that sport and exam results were the only way to judge a school, and welcomed its achievements in music, drama, and art.

Industriously, he thought and wrote about most of the issues facing the school in the second half of the twentieth century.

Healey's appointment was uncontroversial. Scotch advertised in the English-speaking world, for a communicant member of a Protestant church, academically qualified and preferably under 45 years old. The salary was £5000, with superannuation levied at 5% plus 7.5% paid by the school. There were 21 applicants, but Council's sub-committee (Glenn, McCaughey, the Rev. William Marshall (1902), Sir Ian McLennan (Dux 1927) and Tom Scott (1922)) recommended that Council invite Healey, who had not applied but who had been sounded out. An Englishman, with an Athletics Blue from Oxford, for the past 13 years he had been Headmaster of non-denominational Sydney Grammar, which he had revived, and was current Chairman of the Headmasters' Conference.

You boy!

How shall we talk about Healey's shouting? To leave it to the end is to avoid what his contemporaries most instantly remember about him—Healey at a crowded sports afternoon bellowing 'You boy!' at a lad who dropped some litter. Healey standing on a chair in the common room, striking his fist into the palm of his hand and shouting at the masters 'I will be obeyed'.[2] 'His rages were legendary.'[3] Healey screaming at a child who had strayed on to the Main Oval or 'tearing strips off' a parent.[4] The shouting was the manifestation of a general quick-temperedness. Even Healey thought he sometimes went too far, for instance at Sydney Grammar rescuing 'a boy who had been hung up on clothes-hooks by his braces. I was so angry that I pinned a great lout, much larger than I, against the wall, with my hand round his throat. Of course I shouldn't have done so.'[5]

Scotch echoed with his shouts of 'You boy!' Monosyllabic words ending in vowel-sounds, like *You* and *boy*, 'can be vocalised much louder than words ending in consonants, where your mouth has to shut to complete the word, which impairs the shock wave'.[6] The power of his voice froze boys from across the quadrangle (1972). As an experienced teacher, Healey was least provoked when boys set out to inflame him deliberately, for example by releasing chooks in Assembly (with many a loud *b-gairk*!) which he handled with aplomb.[7]

Boys and staff who turned to Healey in need found him kind and helpful. When Gordon Matthews (1969) complained about bullying, Healey's response was prompt and compassionate. In contrast with his helpfulness in private and personal situations, he was not very approachable in public. Small boys who tried to talk to him were likely to be greeted with a rebuke about their uniform, at which point they turned away.[8]

Healey insisted he should be addressed as 'Sir' or 'Headmaster'. When Baxter Holly (Senior English Master 1967–84), once publicly called him 'Mr Healey' the equally public rebuke was: 'Holly, that is disrespectful and very State-Schoolish'.[9] He always called staff by their surnames (famously calling the Librarian 'Darling' in front of visiting dignitaries) which was not rude, as boys of the time usually called each other by their surnames.

The following is said to catch him well:

Healey's was a sincere, strictly principled, straightforward character seeking to express itself through an exceedingly complex personality. The result was that there sometimes appeared in him tensions and contradictions that some found disconcerting. He was deeply considerate of people and intensely loyal to them: at the same time (being, as he once said, 'choleric and peevish') he could be impulsive and tactless. He possessed an absolute sense of fairness but through hastiness was sometimes unjust. But whenever he was aware of having been so he would be at pains to seek out the person—be it the most senior or the youngest member of staff, the highest ranking or most lowly boy—and would apologise ... Healey's relentless following through of issues to their ultimate resolution, however painful that might be to himself or others, had in it a streak of ruthlessness, but at the same time was deeply reassuring to his staff, who knew that here was a man who would never back away. The staff and boys of a school look first to a headmaster for consistency and strength: it gives them a sense of security and confidence. And if the strength happens to be linked to a volatile and fiery temperament, well so be it.[10]

In his own mind what saved him from the worst consequences of his failings was that 'In all my work ... my wife Margaret has been the mainspring of my life. ... her importance is implicit in the whole story. Perhaps her greatest contribution has been her simple and uncomplicated friendliness and sweetness to everyone.'[11]

Healey's achievements left his mark on the school long after his personality was forgotten, for he was a thoughtful and creative leader. The manner of that leadership was often at odds with the calm reasonableness we meet in his writing.

TAKING THE HELM

Healey took office in mid-1964, and if he and Council jostled for position it was soon over. No principal has arrived with such authority already established. When he at once acted independently, Council meekly acquiesced. Also, they were quickly thrown together by an external threat, when the church stopped Council building Healey the new house it had promised him (see pp. 184 and 385).

Healey soon took that other common act of incoming principals, when he dismissed a teacher who 'ruled by fear of physical punishment'[12] ('he used to hit me regularly with a metre ruler'[13]). 'His language was disgraceful' and, worse, he referred to other masters by their nicknames.[14] Healey gave him a term's salary in lieu of notice.

Of another master, Selby Smith told Healey that he 'is an extraordinarily nice and gentle person, but is probably the least effective teacher in the School. I have often wondered whether I ought to try to find another post for him, but I have always come back to the conclusion that he is such a nice person that we should retain him in the School.'[15] Healey kept him.

The Senior Art Master, Helms, presented a more difficult problem. Healey demanded 'a quickening of spirit on the part of his department. Art is no good without élan; there are always obstacles to be overcome and it does not sound as if he has tried.' Healey considered appointing someone over him. Selby Smith 'agree[d] with all that you say. I have spoken frankly to Mr Helms'.[16] Yet one of Helms's students attests to his 'very profound effect on my life [and] what I am today'.[17] Later, Donaldson had a similar experience over Rowton. It seems to be difficult for Principals to make fully accurate assessments of Art masters. Perhaps it is the nature of the discipline. Even so, one cannot help compare the Art and Music Departments at this time, as Art languished and Music became mainstream.

Helms retired in 1971, succeeded by a former student, Donald Cameron, who presented Scotch with a portrait of Helms in homage. (Cameron also had a portrait of Helms's predecessor, Shirlow, and Shirlow's etching press.) Cameron later painted the official portrait of Healey. 'I had always considered him a remote, aloof figure until he visited my studio home on Saturday mornings for sittings. My wife would make scones and I felt he dropped his mask and relaxed.'[18]

Healey brought about the present abundance of portraits in the Memorial Hall. In 1951 the walls bore just four portraits: two Principals (Morrison and Littlejohn), a Chairman of Council (MacFarland) and a beloved teacher (Shew). Gilray (painted by Ernest Buckmaster) appeared in 1951, and Bowden (by Sir William Dargie) in 1956. None had an identifying label; one was meant to know who they were. In 1963 the Executive and Finance Committee ruled that only Principals should hang there. Healey soon had this reversed, to admit OSCA's gift of a portrait of Fleming by Dargie, who also painted Selby Smith. The Hall, said Healey, had 'plenty of room for many generations to come'.[19] Council agreed, and Fleming was followed by his successors as Vice-Principal, Campbell (by Bruce Fletcher, art teacher), 'Mick' Eggleston (1947, staff 1958–87, painted by Cameron from photographs), and Bond (by Paul Fitzgerald). (Fine photographic portraits of later Vice-Principals, Black and Hosking, however, have been

The Longmore Library and Masters' Common Room, opened in 1965. Its brisk international modern lines contrast pleasingly with the older architecture. In 1998, it was demolished apart from the steel frame, around which the Randall Building was erected.

hung elsewhere than the Hall.) Fleming's predecessors also appeared: Ingram (by Dargie) and Robert Morrison (by Barbara McManus). MacFarland has been joined by Glenn (by Wes Walters) whilst Fitzgerald's portrait of Bruce Lithgow (1946, Chairman of Council 1981–91) graces the Lithgow Centre. Healey was joined by Roff (by Ron Crawford) and Donaldson (by Fitzgerald). Also, Barbara McManus painted Lawson and Forbes from earlier pictures. In 1963, Scotch bought Percy White's portrait of Monash, also now in the Memorial Hall.

Overall, Healey found the staff impressive, with distinguished Senior Subject Masters heading industrious departments. Ferres in Physics was a legend (as were his Fourth XVIII, the Iron Men). Logie-Smith in Music, Nankervis in Economics and Lyne in Geography were distinguished outside the school. New men, like Ken Evans in Mathematics and Webster in History, continued those departments' leading place in Victorian education. Since there was then a teacher shortage in Victoria (and perhaps there is always a shortage of good teachers), the staff reflected credit on Selby Smith. 'Ken Evans (Maths) was a patient and kind man who encouraged his students to believe in themselves and that they could achieve anything they wanted to. "Ocker" Ferres (Physics) was inspirational in a different way—by his sheer enthusiasm for his subject which almost literally bubbled over' (1965).

As Scotch was running well, Healey might have relaxed and coasted through his final decade at the peak of his profession. He did no such thing. He set out to make a good thing better. There was little of Selby Smith's that he reversed, other than some building priorities. Rather, he looked at areas such as teaching and pastoral matters, and the loss-making boarding establishment, that were not Selby Smith's focus, and he also swept Scotch forward into quite new ways of thinking about itself.

He soon challenged the staff in a variety of ways about how they worked. Healey was an enthusiastic communicator. He often circulated roneoed documents which modestly invited improvements. Before his appointment, when Glenn and McCaughey flew to Sydney to ask him if he was available, Healey warned them that he did not have a first-class mind and would therefore be slower than Selby Smith in reaching decisions. McCaughey wonders whether 'one consequence of that difference which he himself defined was that he found it more difficult to make up his mind and did so sometimes more conventionally. Whereas you always felt that Dick's decisions were fresh, and were very quick.'[20] If Healey did wrestle with things, he often put this to good use by setting it down on paper. His proposals to reform the House system, for example, went through several versions. This revealed what underlay his ideas. As befits an educator, he believed that 'Given the opportunity to speak to people, one can persuade them'.[21]

He applied this approach to parents, too, and wrote to them regularly (as did Tapp), sharing his thoughts and drawing parents into the school's life.

'To give praise when deserved and appropriate'

Scotch kept ever more records on its boys. At a classroom level the survival of this information is haphazard, but it gives a marvellous snapshot. Next to boys' names in a 1970s class are comments like: 'Has a go', 'More reliable, working very well', 'Quietly purposeful', 'Charming—good worker', 'excellent', 'erratic behaviour', 'lazy—unreliable, needs to be stood on with *two* feet', 'a pleasure to teach', 'tries hard', 'has achieved very little', 'more settled', 'vastly improved in approach & effort', 'a trier—very pleasant', 'very good mechanically', 'enjoys a challenge', 'improving', 'enjoys a chat but top flight', 'pleasant & reliable—paternal', 'an excellent year's work', 'erratic—needs to be watched with all three of one's eyes', 'a battler, obtaining more success'.[22] There are several sets of criteria here, showing us the many levels at which teachers interact with their pupils, measuring some by how hard they try, others by how settled they are, by their personality, by what they are like to teach, by how well they do, by whether they improve, or by where their skills lie.

Another teacher found the same boys 'easily distracted', 'great improver', 'a real trier', 'excellent in every way', 'in too much of a hurry', 'can be a disturbing influence', 'hard to "read" ' (this was the boy who needed to be stood on with two feet), 'conscientious', 'works well', 'still flighty', 'excellent results', 'fooled around', 'works well for me', 'off the air most of the time' (the boy who has to be watched with three eyes), 'tries hard', and 'excellent'.[23] This last was the battler with more success, reminding us how different teachers notice different things.

For of course different teachers experience boys differently. 'A thorough nuisance in class & inclined toward larrikinism out of it' (Remove, 1954), was described next year as 'A pleasant lad—not polished but straightforward … I venture to say that he is quite sensitive' (Intermediate, 1955). Another boy's teachers found him 'surly & unpleasant' (Remove, 1951) and 'a lout' (VII, 1952), but his 1953 teacher wrote 'It is true that he can be surly & loutish; but he is a boy who needs responsibility & without it he is lost. … His physical appearance is against him.'

These comments are from the blue cards. From 1917 these were the school's permanent personal record of each boy. They listed his subjects and marks, his extra-curricular activities, and under Gilray contained teachers' comments.

The information varied according to pre-printed categories. Littlejohn's cards asked for a judgement of Moral Qualities but sagely allocated only 2 square centimetres of space, which were rarely filled. Gilray's design invited comments on Conduct, Diligence, Ability or Special Aptitude. Under Selby Smith the cards asked for a letter ('A = Superior, B = Normal, C = Poor') under the headings of Initiative, Determination, Reliability, Diligence, and Helpfulness. We may take these as Selby Smith's summary of the school's key aims. From Selby Smith onwards the cards recorded 'circumstances affecting home life or health', and the results of standard tests (IQ, Otis Test Higher C, ACER, etc.) and thoroughly recorded extra-curricular activity. From Healey onwards the cards carried a photograph. From Roff they recorded his place in the family (for example, second eldest) and number of siblings. Donaldson urged 'as much detail as possible …, for this will build up a picture of the boy for those members of staff who perhaps do not know him well and yet have occasion to help, advise or discipline him. Entries on the Blue Cards are … very confidential.'[24]

The cards allowed an overview, and showed trends: 'seems to be a loner' (Form II, 1977), was followed by 'has been more involved this year' (Form III, 1978), 'A capable boy who does not rely on others' (Form IV, 1979), and 'Well involved' (Form V, 1980). Such cumulative pictures depended on what went before, so that Rowlands' laconic comment that a boy 'Has developed' must be read in the light of the previous form-master's view that he 'Shows signs of developing criminal proclivities'. Often the pen-sketches are striking:

> Enviably and delightfully unaffected by life or classroom inclination—a very friendly, happy and stable boy—who hasn't much to offer and is rather naive for his age. Untidy and disorganized. A likeable boy who will happily plod along. [Grade 5, 1966]

> Confident without being "cocky". [Form II, 1984]

> Well in charge of his destiny. I find him delightful but some may see his confidence as arrogance. [Form III, 1985]

> Cheerful as ever but not very popular. This does not seem to worry him at all. Energetic individualist. [Form V, 1987]

Other comments show a master lightening the tedium of filling in the cards, as when Provan wrote that a boy 'Seems to feel that his image would be affected by any impression of diligent work' (Form III, 1970). Or Blenkiron's enigmatic comment: 'Dull. Plays cricket.'

All these comments, at times so personal or idiosyncratic, had to be squeezed into a third, formal document, the school's reports to parents. Healey, that tireless improver, drew up a guide for staff on how to write reports.[25] 'What is the object of a report? Surely it is to state what the boy has achieved, to indicate how he can do better, and to give praise when it is deserved or advisable.' He redesigned the form with more room for comments. He urged 'constructive advice' rather than condemnation. 'We should remember that both parents and boys are more sensitive than we sometimes realise.' He advocated 'praise of the conscientious, widely occupied boy, who may at present not get the commendation which he deserves, just because he is not outstanding in any particular activity or subject'.

Teachers should avoid criticism of other departments or activities. 'Remarks such as "Football has interfered with his work" are best … worded more tactfully, e.g., "His interest in football is admirable, but he has still to learn how work can be given its full time even during the football season".' Staff should not make unnecessary use of Christian name or nickname ('Stick to it, Kim—you'll win through'). Ever the teacher himself, Healey told staff to 'Have a dictionary by you and watch your grammar'. He deplored 'Faults of diction or style, such as "disinterested" where one means "uninterested"; "may" when one should write "might" '.

A good report was one that tackled the central questions about a boy. What are his strong points and weaknesses? Is there a difference between his learning work and his written work, between oral work and written composition, between homework and class-work? Has he done some particularly good piece of work? Is he confident, co-operative, diffident, isolated, mildly inattentive, or listless, defiantly inattentive and restless, ebullient or just plainly rude? Does he learn methodically or does he just try to learn without 'handling' his subject, without using pen and paper to help?

Finally, Healey ruled that 'A boy should be allowed to see his report before it goes to his parents, and he should be allowed to ask what is meant by any comment and to question the accuracy of a mark'.

Lyne judged that 'after several years of persuasion by the Head I think all members of staff eventually acquired the skills and found the time to write thoughtful and helpful comments'.[26]

Rowing, like cross country, took boys outside the school. Further down the Yarra, the South-eastern Freeway bulges over the river, reminding us that Scotch was not alone in dealing with this side effect of Melbourne's growth.

ENRICHING THE CURRICULUM

Selby Smith did not touch the curriculum, although he appointed distinguished teachers, and by updating laboratories he facilitated the new Science syllabus. He was flexible with boys who wanted practical farm knowledge rather than scholastic learning, arranging for boys to attend classes at Swinburne Institute of Technology or the Burnley Horticultural College.

Healey was more interventionist. He monitored departments' performance in external exams, and when English fell short he goaded it into action. English had suffered as Christie fell ill in middle age with rheumatoid arthritis, and only partly revived when Owen succeeded him. Owen's English Literature notes were legendary, but he was less interested in the basic English that was the compulsory final-year subject, and he was nearing retirement. Healey then brought in the youthful Holly.

Healey also tackled the curriculum's overall shape, and we must reach back to the school's beginnings to match his innovations. Like Morrison, he asked himself what secular knowledge and skills a boy needed for a successful career. He brought in General Studies and Legal Studies. He introduced Russian, the first new language since Morrison's day. Butler taught it, having learned it from a Korean guard while a prisoner of war of the Japanese.[27] (Butler was witty, intelligent, and a brilliant teacher. Of a late-comer to a French class, he asked in one breath without change of tone: 'Ah, vous êtes en retard monsieur why are yer late bloke?'). As Russian's enrolment remained low, it disappeared in the early 1990s, along with Latin, to admit Chinese.

Healey wanted Scotch to teach 'an Asian language and preferably one that involves a great literature and history'.[28] Unable to find anyone to teach Chinese, he turned to Indonesian, taught by the Assistant Chaplain, Crow, who led the development of Indonesian in secondary education, and who in 1969 first took boys overseas, to South-East Asia. In 1970 the School Orchestra and Choral Group toured South-East Asia. Healey believed this fostered good-will and understanding between young Australians and Asians.[29] By 2000, tours to Asia are routine. Junior School parents had wanted an Asian language since 1964. Tapp wanted to teach it in 20-minute spells, largely with tape-recorders. 'Very few children will go on to study a language in depth, but many could find some fluency useful in connection with either business or travel … Australia is geographically part of Asia, and … Britain's entry into the European Common Market is likely to bring us into closer contact with Asian markets.'[30] Most masters knew little of Asia other than as soldiers and prisoners of war. David 'Poon' Fraser (staff 1961–66) had worked for a British banking company in Asia.

Scotch was unable to retain the Indonesian 'Hendy' Hendrata (staff 1970–74), and in the 1980s results in Indonesian were below average and the subject was under threat, but it revived and flourished. In 2000, with 320 boys, Indonesian ranks after French (400), but before German (260) and Chinese (240). Healey's innovation has taken root.

New bodies, new pathways

Healey when he arrived was 'most surprised at 1st to find out how "paternalistic" Scotch was. This died hard & one had to change it slowly.'[31] Whilst he remained authoritarian in small matters, in larger ones he thickened Scotch's organisational structure, thereby reducing the Principal's power. Most famously he oversaw the birth of the Scotch Association and the Scotch Foundation (see pp. 238–9). He encouraged the Common Room Association's interest in educational matters (see pp. 319–30). He began the move from large Houses to small.

Houses

Healey tackled the House system twice, in 1965 and again in 1970. What changed in between was his emphasis. In 1965 he aimed to create more posts of responsibility for sixth formers (Year 12s). He reserved the five House Captaincies for boys who held no other leading positions, and he created a new position, that of House Prefect. He split each of the four day-boy Houses (Gilray, Lawson–MacFarland, Monash and Morrison) into Divisions of sixty boys. Each Division at first spanned all ages, then from 1970 contained boys of the same age. It had a House-master and six prefects. Including the boarding Houses, this gave over 100 sixth formers some responsibility. Healey urged Housemasters to train leaders.[32]

Healey's widened responsibility for sixth formers fortuitously prepared the school for an abrupt demographic change about to occur. Since Morrison's day, many boys who had completed the final school year returned to school, whether to prepare better for university or to broaden themselves. This core of older boys usually provided the Captain and

prefects. The 1955 Captain, Mike Winneke, was in his third year. Several Captains held office for two years. During the 1970s the practice declined (51 boys returned in 1970, 33 in 1971, and only four in 1986). By 1981 the hardest thing about coming back to be Captain was the loss of friends. In 1979 Monash House proposed that the School Captain could be a first-year sixth former. Donaldson prefers a repeating boy, more mature and with his place at university secured. Today no boy returns except the boy asked to be Captain. Unblemished by peers, he is ever more god-like.

With House Prefects, Healey introduced a new democratic element: they were elected by all but new boys. 'When the system is reasonably well established the Principal may undertake to select the School Officers from those elected to office within Houses and Divisions. This will, I hope, give the School a feeling that it is partly responsible for choosing its own officers.'[33] Not all boys welcomed democracy. Geoff Wemyss (Captain 1972) worried that boys might merely vote for their friends.[34] But in 1971 Healey appointed the day-House Captains and Vice-Captains 'after elections. Indeed no day-boy becomes a School Prefect or a House Prefect except after a process of election. On the whole the electors are acting with increasing responsibility. This, too, is a valuable educational process.'[35]

Healey's second motive for creating Divisions was to enhance the House system's care of individuals. The Houses were large, but in a smaller Division the master could get to know boys, especially as a boy would belong to the same Division every year. This pastoral approach reversed the original relationship between House and boy. Houses were created for boys to serve, and it required a significant shift for Houses to find out how to serve boys. For a House really to attend to its members would require almost a reinvention of why Houses existed. 'Johnny' Miles, coach of the First XI though he was, suggested Houses abandon the idea of competition.[36] Or Houses could compete in new ways, for example by each adopting a charity, although collections stayed by form as this was easier to organise. Sport, too, was now re-described as a way to 'develop better staff–student relationships'.[37] A new emphasis on the teacher–boy relationship outside class permeated the school.

In 1971 Healey wanted Council to ask itself: Do we care enough for each individual boy? Are we *seen*, by boys and parents, to care? Do our boys care for others?[38] One boy from Healey's day recalls 'The absence of pastoral care was enormous, you swam or sank'. Scotch's size—under Healey the Senior School rose from 1100 to 1200 boys—meant it was possible for a significant number of boys not to be known by any teacher. Healey did not solve the problem, but he did make Scotch look squarely at it. For as McCaughey said, 'we should not waste time shedding tears about the size of Scotch. We cannot do anything about that. In any case, modern society is large.'[39]

The School needed to assume that boys might not take the initiative. 'I spent that year in quiet desperation knowing maths was quickly getting away from me.'[40] As a Group Master, Keith Elliott found that his greatest difficulty was in getting boys to come forward with their problems. 'Parents often raise matters which boys could have brought up themselves.'[41] The question for the school is: why did the boys not speak up?

Healey's fostering pastoral care parallels the end of caning by the School Captains, thus ending the official sanction of violence among the boys.

General House Committee

Before Healey, Scotch gave boys a long-standing and active involvement in the executive side (prefects and probationers) but no legislative role. Healey introduced an elective element in choosing these executives, and he oversaw the introduction of the Staff / Sixth Form Seminars and a new General House Committee.

In the Junior School, successive headmasters from David Bradshaw on have created parliaments (variously named) with members elected by each class. There, boys learnt meeting procedures, imbibed 'the democratic process' and mutual responsibility,[42] and gained some 'ownership of issues around the school—especially with discipline issues at break times'.[43]

In 1970 Healey created a quasi-parliament in the Senior School. It was 'a forum for presenting suggestions'[44] to Healey, and could discuss 'any facet of school life'.[45] A single meeting in July 1972, for example, dealt with the Masters' Common Room microphone, seating in Assembly and use of classrooms during lunch hour. Healey saw it as a safety valve. It met at least twice a term. It published its decisions.

It was called the General House Committee (GHC). Matters came up from Divisions through their House Committee. ('The feeling among Gilray boys was that service in the tuckshop was too slow.'[46]) As a creative conservative, Healey adapted the existing House system into a conduit for discussion of school issues. Opinions and suggestions flowed up, and decisions and minutes cascaded down. Also, Healey grafted this new system on to what existed already. The GHC went back to 1917 as an inter-house committee managing the then only inter-house matter, sport. That function now went to the GHC Sports Committee.

The new GHC's composition varied over the ensuing years. At first it comprised 20 members and at the end 40. It tried to keep membership low, for 'otherwise a lot of the frankness and honesty would be lost',[47] but succumbed to the clamour of constituencies. It had to spread representation among (a) the Houses, (b) students and staff, and (c) older boys and younger. Under Healey there were five Houses and under Roff six, each sending Housemasters and leading boys. The Houses contained Divisions (under Healey) or minor houses (under Roff), which sent staff and students by rotation. Principal, Vice-Principal, Captain and Vice-Captain sat in their own

The General House Committee in 1973.

right. It became even more unwieldy with the addition of its own office-bearers. It had a chairman (Healey had chaired but Roff preferred a student elected as chairman), a secretary and an executive to follow GHC decisions through to implementation. Finally, people attended to speak to proposals. Seating so many made for an over-large committee. To keep numbers down, the various constituencies were rotated, depriving the committee of a continuous membership.

In 1979 the GHC decided that its important decisions needed a two-thirds majority. Decisions to refer matters elsewhere in the school (like raising scarves with the Uniform Committee) needed only a simple majority. Ten years after its inception, the GHC was developing as a political arena with its own stamp and sophistication.

Much about the GHC is impressive. It ran for almost two decades. It discussed most aspects of the school, including curriculum. As a representative body in a democratic country, it taught at least some boys about elections, representation and meeting procedure. But it never took root. Year after year Healey, Roff, concerned masters like Shugg, and the committee itself, repeatedly revamped its membership or tried to improve its communication with the school. The fantasy was that if only people knew more about it they would become interested. The reality was that the GHC never seized boys' imaginations because it had no power. Scotch stresses achievement, results, leadership, and the daily exercise of authority.

DRINKING FOUNTAINS

For thirty years, from the 1950s to the 1980s, the boys complained that the school's drinking fountains were few in number and weak in water pressure. The low pressure made drinking slow and led to queues. Letters to *Satura* and motions at the GHC achieved little, and even allowed staff to dismiss the democratic experiment of the GHC by sniping that all the boys were interested in was drinking fountains. (Staff had their own water supply.)

The boys' problem was a practical one. Their only other sources of liquid were washroom taps (unhygienic and with poor water pressure) and the tuckshop. Drink-vending-machine companies long refused to install them after the first machine in 1956 was found to be full of 'filed-down half-pennies, washers, etc.'[48] The tuckshop sold drinks, but a boy who was thirsty had to join the queues of those who were hungry, and after around 1970 boys in the lower forms ordered their lunch by class and were not allowed into the tuckshop until the second half of lunchtime. The school's largest concession was in 1956 when to the existing two fountains it added three more. 'The power of the Press' exulted *Satura*. One of the new fountains commemorated Wesley's time at Scotch (Chapter 8).

The school's problem was that the pipes supplying the fountains were old. Even so, not to replace them for thirty years suggests a sustained policy of not taking the matter seriously.

Scotch trains its boys to be leading decision-makers, and the GHC, a mere consultative body, was not the sort of body they would waste their time on as adults. If one decision per year had been binding on the school, the dynamics would have been quite different.

Senior Masters' Committee

Healey set up a Senior Masters' Committee, later the Heads of Department Committee. Healey chaired it but tried not to lead it too strongly, in order to unleash members' talent. 'I found at Scotch that my predecessor having had so brilliant a mind, the senior masters when I called them to meetings ... tended to sit round, rather like the ring of stones at Stonehenge, and wait for the headmaster's directions, instead of proffering their own ideas, though they had plenty.'[49] They spoke more after he set up the committee.

It dealt with a wide range of items: Assembly, teaching, assessment, pastoral, room use, Duke of Edinburgh's Award, the Hansen report (see Chapter 15) and matters originating in the GHC or in the Common Room Association (CRA) Education Committee. It included the Vice-Principal, Senior Master, Chaplain, Librarian, Senior Subject Masters and Group Masters. This made the Senior Subject Masters responsible not just for their own departments but involved them in a shared responsibility for the school. A sort of cabinet solidarity developed. This was a far cry from Littlejohn's day, when the Senior History Master, '45' Clayton, might go a whole year without a conversation with the Principal.[50]

The committee also provided an arena for the struggle between departments. Senior Subject Masters must face in all directions at once: down to manage their staff, up to preserve and increase departmental funding, and sideways to elbow other departments aside, though of course there are more elegant ways of putting this. Any Senior Subject Master worth his salt had a passion for his subject. Ken Evans extolled the 'great need to think in a mathematical way about all aspects of the human condition', so that mathematics may become the 'central integrative discipline in our society'.[51] Teachers care about education, and sometimes debates were heated. In 1990, Syd Boydell [1954, staff 1976–82, 1988–] 'disagreed strongly' with the Mathematics Department's point of view, so much so that at the next meeting 'Dr Boydell apologised for what he regarded as his "immoderate language" at the previous meeting'.[52]

Healey drew departments together. He herded the Science departments (Chemistry, Physics and General Science) by appointing the tactful Mappin as co-ordinator in 1969.[53] Mappin's task was to streamline use of materials, equipment and laboratory assistants, to 'secure a just sense of purposefulness in these three departments', and to speak for Scotch at 'the rapidly proliferating meetings of all kinds connected with science and the reforms in examinations that are crowding in on us'.[54] Similarly, Healey made Butler overlord of Modern Languages.

Sixth-Form Common Room

In 1961 a letter to *Satura* proposed a Sixth-Form (Year 12) Common Room, to which the editors replied 'You're joking, of course'.[55] But soon Healey widened sixth formers' leadership role and enhanced their status with a Sixth-Form Club in the former Masters' Common Room in the quadrangle. Running costs were met by an annual subscription charged to boys' accounts. Each class was on duty for one week, washing up and drying, keeping urns filled, the room tidy, and coffee, sugar and milk supplied. The Common Room's Chairman became a person to deal with on final-year matters. It became a comfortably rowdy meeting place, where boys played cards, and inflicted the usual indignities, for instance when some 'n-butyl-whatever-it-was' unexpectedly broke over the heater. 'No one could go in there for two weeks without throwing up' (1975).

Roff found it 'well run and mostly well looked after'[56] and spent money improving it, hoping that this would promote 'a more civilized standard of behaviour.'[57] In 1980, however, he decided the room would always be too small for 200 sixth formers, and closed it down, converting it to rooms for the chaplain and others. The GHC appealed unsuccessfully for a new room, for example the old gymnasium, which they said could hardly be damaged much further.

To acknowledge the special place of boys in their final year, Healey told School Officers to treat them with courtesy. 'For instance, they should not be told to tidy up litter, unless it is obvious that they are themselves responsible for it. On the whole it is better not to award a punishment summarily to Sixth Formers, but to try to get their cooperation.' By the time a boy had reached Form VI or even Form V, he would be fairly set in his ways; and it had to be recognised that some older boys will be 'non-participants, however much we may regret it'.[58]

The Sixth-Form Common Room, 1978. On the wall, a naked woman has modestly turned her back to the boys.

Blazer and cap designs are dated by when they were first worn. From left: the 1899, worn by James O. Robertson (1907); the 1908, Colin McK. Skene (1922); the 1925, Eric Love (1929); the 1933, Frank W.W. Scott (1933).

Left: St Andrew and St Martin. Large panes of special 'streaky glass' were scored and cut according to the patterns of impurities in them to create the detailed pictures in the Memorial Hall windows.

Foundation Day Concert, 1988, in the Victorian Arts Centre's
concert hall, designed by Roy Grounds (1920).

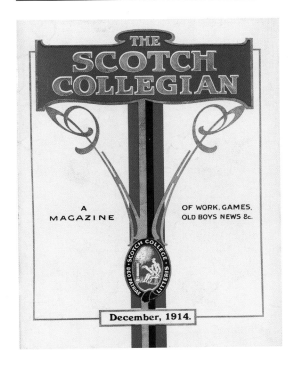

Collegian front covers: 1914; 1959 (with Dudley Wood's watercolour of the Memorial Hall); and 1983.

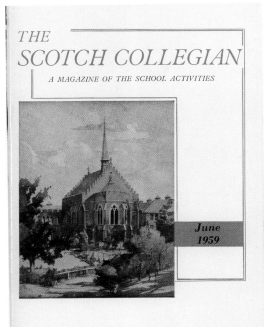

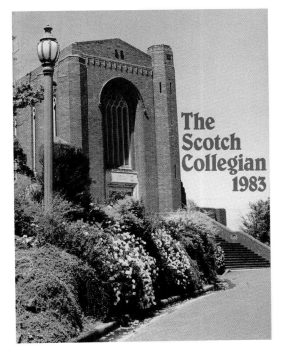

The chart shows the new intake of all age groups as a percentage of total new intake. The purchase of a preparatory school in 1915 disrupts, visually, what is otherwise a slow swing among the older age groups as the 17-year-old entrants almost disappear and 16-, 15- and 14-year-old entrants shrink before increasing numbers of 13- and 12-year-olds. Some features derive from the incompleteness of the data, particularly for 1976–77, where Junior School records have vanished.

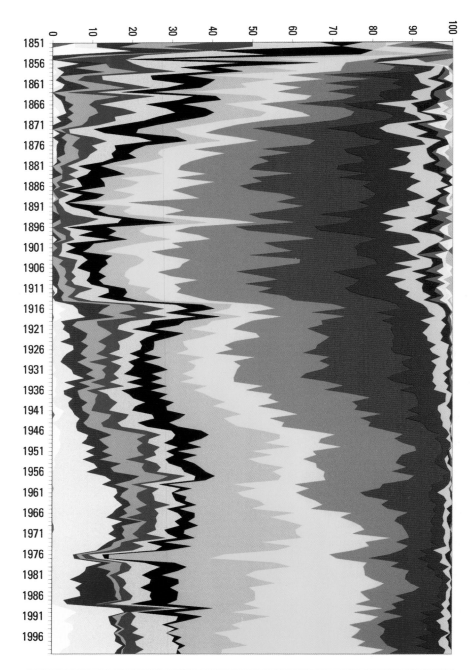

PLAYING CARDS AND GAMBLING

Even under Morrison whist was acceptable, and the 1936 *Satura* carried a bridge column. The 1919 *Collegian* mentions two-up. Since Scotch did not allow betting, it presumably forbade less intellectual card games but of course they happened. Bill Norris's 1944 diary records poker values,[59] and *Satura* in the 1960s suggested that a boy who was asked to write on the topic 'My First School' wrote about his first card school. On the Hill boys were caned for playing cards in the dormitory.[60] Card-playing and gambling in general reached the same point as smoking: we can see that they happened because they were the subject of jokes, and yet officially boys were punished for indulging. In 1961 a boy was caned for crimes including gambling, yet in 1963 *Satura* carried the following:

> Master: The amoeba has no permanent form.
> Pupil: Yeah … like a race-horse.[61]

Boys ran sweeps on the Melbourne Cup at least from the 1950s. One in 1971 was very mathematically sophisticated on advice from a statistically minded Old Boy, a high Treasury official. Auxiliaries raise money by raffles. But in 1998 a stop was quickly put to running the staff Melbourne Cup sweep by email, as this made it too official.

John Rothfield (1971), 'Dr Turf', made his name as a horse-racing tipster.

Under Donaldson, Year 12 boys developed a sartorial way of proclaiming their uniqueness. Among Year 12s 'it was quite popular to wear the white cricket jumper, even if you played cricket or not. We had "VCE – 1990" embroidered on the cricket jumper – I think they now wear a blue pullover'.[62]

Staff–student seminars

In 1971 the CRA Education Committee won Healey's approval for a voluntary staff day to discuss examinations and testing. Some sixth formers (Year 12s) would participate, as though they might know something about the school. Their presence nudged the agenda to include personal development and relationships within the school.

As the day approached, the organisers became anxious. Unsure as to how many staff would attend, they also worried about how many boys would come, or could be invited. Perhaps the 20 sixth formers who were interested would swamp the masters? Would the Head veto particular boys? If so, Ken Evans said this would negate the whole approach of contacting the boys. Keith Wilson (staff 1971–89) and Michael Achurch (staff 1964–79) worried that 'raggers' among the boys might treat the whole thing as a forum for 'heresies', but Mappin and David Paul (staff 1968– , Senior History Master 1971–88, Group Master/Head of Year 1989–98, Head of Social Education 1999–) said this was a 'Risk we have to take'.[63]

The day went well, with guest speakers in the morning and topics in the afternoon each presented by a senior master and a boy: 'The ethos of the school' by Archie Crow and James Simpson, 'The senior years at Scotch' by

David Paul and Stephen Digby, and 'Student–Staff relations' by Ken Evans and Bill Mountford. Of course, 'the 6th formers spoke very well'. More important, they 'very much appreciated the whole conference … and the opportunity to join with the staff in such a function'.[64] They found it 'a most important experience and one perhaps unique to Scotch'.[65]

The seminar at once became an annual event, run by the Senior Masters' Committee. By 1973 the presence of boys was so routine that Healey called it the staff/boys seminar. And he was at pains to ensure 'the presence of suitable intellectual leaders among the Sixth Formers and I suggest that we need 30 or 40 boys if they are to be effectively visible and present'.[66] Healey was never frightened of boys expressing their views. Boys were asked to 'be frank and feel prepared to make (i) Constructive criticism (ii) suggestions as to improvement'.[67]

The seminars dispelled any idea that all students were radical and all staff conservative. Take, for instance, Individualised Instruction or Learning, a teaching approach that allowed students to work at their own pace, draw on their own motivation, and often assess their own work. David Scott (1944, staff 1948–88, Senior Master 1972–77, Registrar 1977–88) felt that this was 'by no means the whole answer to the education of young people. It overlooks the problem of ordinary laziness' and the need to keep students 'closer to their needs in educational content covered'.[68] Rick Jefferies (1973) concurred: 'master supervision was necessary and too much emphasis on individual learning at too early an age was a bad thing'.[69] 'At the lower level students are too immature to work on their own. Hard study of grammar and vocabulary are essential in languages.'[70] John Simpson (1975) agreed also and sounds positively reactionary: 'It was the teacher's function to teach & the student's to learn'.[71]

National Council of Independent Schools

Outside the school, Healey encouraged new organisations. Scotch had long belonged to the Association of Independent Schools of Victoria, and supported setting up a National Council of Independent Schools. The NCIS began in 1970, chaired by Scotch's (Sir) Laurence Muir (Captain 1942), and looked at the question of government assistance to independent schools. The Headmasters' Conference argued that such assistance did not deprive state-funded schools of government aid.

Healey welcomed the NCIS. Until then, when governments wanted to know about private schools they still asked the churches, which did not speak with one voice and were not always fully informed. The Presbyterian Church did not gather from its secondary schools the 'complicated and detailed' information that government needed, and Healey considered it unfit to present the schools' needs to government.[72] Instead, Scotch was building its own lobbying system. This was one more way in which the school was growing away from the church.

The General Science
Building was opened
in 1967 by a federal
minister, a sign of a
whole new source of
funding.

Scotch supported the NCIS financially, and endorsed Roff's time-consuming involvement. From 1976 Scotch reached out to the Victorian Parents' Council, comprising parents from independent schools, non-denominational but mainly Catholic. When Defence of Government Schools (DOGS) fought government aid to church schools in the High Court in 1979, Scotch supported the NCIS case.

CHARACTER: ADVENTURE TRAINING

Developing character reached a new phase with the rise of outdoor activities. In 1971 Healey proposed an Adventure Training programme. It would 'help

THE A.P.T. CLUB

In the year of the first moon walk, 1969, Scotch boys decided to construct an 'Automatic Picture Transmission receiver' to collect pictures from orbiting weather satellites. It was to have been completed in a single year. Like a miniature CSIRO, the boys organised themselves into five divisions: Admin, Supply, Technical, Finance, and Secretary. There was a lot of trial and error. The receiver was 'most difficult to construct', said the Collegian, comprising such things as an integrator (designed and built by the boys), a receiver circuit (which had to be rebuilt due to poor workmanship) and an aerial (the first of which, of 65 pounds [30 kg] of aluminium tubing, was too heavy to be mounted).[73] The new aerial was the bane of the club's existence. During 1971–72, while the other components were perfected, funding for the aerial stalled the project, which the Collegian never reported as completed before dropping the APT from the list of clubs in 1976.

boys to overcome challenges, get to know each other and learn to live with each other, gain self-confidence, and develop leadership'.[74] It offered what was best in sport, cadets and scouts, without their competitiveness or regimentation.

It brought together the outdoor activities that had increasingly sprung up.

Canoeing began under Selby Smith in the senior scouts. They had a canvas canoe for some years and in 1962 bought fibreglass shells and added keels and seats, then went on a four-day trip up the Yarra. Each boy made his own paddle in the craft room. In 1965 senior scouts canoeing from Yarra Glen to Templestowe, suffered early spills in the boiling white water and lost a paddle, a seat, a bit of yellow fibre-glass, a hat and one sock.

In the 1963–64 summer holidays Macmillan led other masters and two senior scouts, John Piesse (1963) and Jim McMeckan (1962), on what became Scotch-in-the-Alps, or Scalps. It was organised by boys. The parties, by various routes of from about 70 to 110 miles (110 to 180 km), made their way to a base camp. Only one or two boys dropped out. Ian Picken (1965) was bitten by a snake, but 'his companions showed great resource and good sense, treated him promptly and effectively and conveyed him so speedily to civilization that the doctor, when reached, found that there was nothing left for him to do but to certify that the patient was fit to continue with the hike'. Selby Smith said boys

> learn to endure a good deal of fatigue, some discomfort, and even a dash of genuine risk; they learn, above all, to know themselves, to recognize their weaknesses by comparing them with the strengths and weaknesses of others, and to be tolerant of the peculiarities of those with whom they share these experiences so closely. In these days of an Australia which is largely suburban, many boys never experience these things unless their school can provide them.[75]

James Simpson (1971) remembers it as the best thing he did at Scotch—'walking incredible distances in astonishingly, unforgettably beautiful mountain landscapes, with an almost complete sense of solidarity, for 5 days.'[76]

In 1965 Achurch introduced rock-climbing, and oversaw the first 24-hour hike. The scouts arranged the hike, and non-scouts also took part. Hikers chose their own routes between 20 check-points. At some check-points half a dozen boys supplied constant hot food and drink. This freed hikers to carry simply torch, map, compass and emergency rations. It grew into a well-organised annual event. Sixty boys hiked, and forty boys manned check-points in 1969, and in 1993 a record 133 hiked. Coin-sized blisters proudly appeared in colour in the 1990 *Collegian*. From Roff's day, it has raised money for charity. A trophy now commemorates Andrew Kelso (1971), a keen 24-hour hiker, killed on Mt Cook in 1976. The hike tests strength and courage as much as any sport. It is competitive in that someone will travel the furthest, but it is also about each boy's competition with himself.

Healey's Adventure Training proposed that fourth formers (Year 10s) attend a compulsory course of several weeks during term run by a specially trained teacher in a rural setting close to a wilderness area. A permanent site would cost about $1.25 million, and a mobile one about $10 000. Council rejected it on financial grounds. It was one of the few matters on which Healey failed to carry Council. (In the long run, having no permanent outdoor centre allows Scotch to be innovative and to stage its outdoor events in public areas anywhere in the state for the cost of transport.)

At least one Council member, McCaughey, was unconvinced of Adventure training's importance. 'The first thing we exist for is the teaching of what is concerned with the class-room, the laboratory, the library. We cannot teach everything. The intellectual content of our teaching comes first' and was more important than being with the boys on a mountain top.[77] Opposition probably came also from Scotch's established outdoor activities, although Healey reassured them that Adventure Training would not replace them, but merely co-ordinate them and help their logistical and administrative problems.

Outdoor activities continued, though not part of a single programme. Ian Stapleton (1968), winner of the 1996 Perelberg Award, founded and built outdoor education projects for young people otherwise unlikely to use such facilities.

FUNDRAISING FULL-TIME

Fundraising appeals continued, but became closer together, indeed continuous. Healey urged Council to ignore pessimists and boldly intensify the campaign.[78] 'To make and improve high standards in a school', he said, 'one must have the money.'[79] A new intensive phase began in 1965 with a National Fund-Raising Counsel (NFRC) office in Mackie Hall. By 1968 the appeal had garnered promises of $900 000 and already received $600 000. A special edition of *Satura* dunned Old Boys, donors, and parents of current boys, and launched a new burst of Dine-and-dial evenings (forerunner of the 1990s phonathons). The appeal was chaired by Muir and extended under Lobban. Of Muir, Healey said, 'No words of thanks or praise can be enough'.[80] Muir agreed it was hard work:[81]

> A man knocked at the heavenly gate
> His face was scarred and old.
> He stood before the man of fate
> For admission to the fold.
>
> 'What have you done', St Peter asked,
> 'To gain admission here?'

'I've been a campaign chairman, Sir,
'For months and months this year'.

The pearly gates swung open wide,
St Peter touched the bell.
'Come in and choose your harp', he said,
'You've had your share of hell.'

Permanent fundraising required a permanent plan. The phrase 'master plan'
appeared in Council papers from 1965, though rarely. In 1970 Healey set up
a committee of teachers to consider future building and curriculum
development, and in 1971 he had Council set up its own committee to co-
ordinate future planning, but its name (Building Sub-Committee) shows a narrow gaze. Its reports to Council were few and it left no minutes. External pressure for planning came also from Canberra, which from 1970 asked for a Summary of Needs.

The targeted government grants that appeared in Selby Smith's time now became a permanent part of school finances. In 1971 the Commonwealth Department of Education and Science contributed to the alterations of the Physics and Chemistry laboratories in the General Science block, and thereafter towards building and equipping a new Senior Maths and Science Block. This ran northwards from the 1967 General Science

Rational and proud. Twenty-five years after it was built, the 1975 Maths–Sciences Building still provides a model for other schools' buildings. Healey encouraged strong staff input in its design.

block, and reached nearly to the Settling Pool. John Scarborough and Ken Atkins designed it in consultation with Mappin and Andrew Tait (staff 1970–83). Healey's encouragement of staff input into the design meant that the building was remarkable for its time and set the standard for a generation. When approved in 1973, it cost $750 000 (over 700 times annual fees), and the fact that Council decided to go ahead 'unanimously' suggests that debate had occurred.[82] Strikes and shortages of material slowed the building, which was opened in 1976. Many staff found it stark, but Council persevered with the architects' design. The external walls were Rippletex brick with natural-finish timber for the windows. On the large concrete expanses like the locker bays, the impress of rough sawn planks of random widths produced a pleasing texture, which masked the colour and surface blemishes of otherwise smooth concrete. By 1999 they were stained and slimy, and Ian Savage (staff 1976–84 and 1989– , Head of History 1989–90, Head of Year 1991–94, Vice-Principal 1995–) had the lockers on the ground floor removed.

Other renovations were more rudimentary. In 1970, students in adjoining classrooms (2 Russian and 2 German A) drilled through the plaster, mortar and brickwork of the intervening wall, using nails, a file and an umbrella. The hole enabled 'interchange of small fast-moving projectiles, and squirting of fluids.'[83]

After 1967 the state and Commonwealth Governments granted Independent schools a sum of money per student per year. Council used this to offset fee increases. The Governments' declared purpose was to keep independent school enrolment up and so keep pressure off government schools. It was cheaper to subsidise students at independent schools than to have them at government schools. Without such support, some independent schools could not maintain themselves. 'During the three-year period 1974–76, more than 60 non-government schools closed' including ten 'so-called "wealthy" schools'.[84]

These grants became a routine and significant source of income. By 1977 their cumulative value exceeded that of all Scotch's endowments and appeals since 1954. In 1971 grants made up 8% of the school's income; in 1990, 11.5% and in 2000, 8.3%. Presbyterian churchmen in 1971–72 tried strongly to have the church order its schools to refuse this government aid, and Healey lobbied hard to defeat them.

From Healey to Donaldson, principals welcomed the government money but wanted it calculated according to parental income, instead of by the school's wealth. Healey repeatedly argued in public that not all Scotch parents were wealthy. Not that they were poor, but there were parents who made financial sacrifices to send their boys to Scotch. Healey deliberately tried to enrol the sons of people of lower-income groups. In his last, 1975, budget the provision for concessions and scholarships was $253 000 (170 times annual fees), of which less than one-tenth came from endowments. The rest was funded by a self-denial of revenue, and thus was effectively borne by full-fee-paying parents. Out of 1600 boys, 600 (including younger brothers) did not pay full fees. Some boys would not have been at Scotch at all without Healey's help. (In 2000, income from endowments has risen to fund 40% of scholarships and concessions, and the self-denial of income is $751 000, of which $260 000 supports sons of staff and Presbyterian ministers.)

In 1971 Healey floated the idea of grouping Old Boys by year. In 1975 OSCA defined a boy's year as the year he reached, or would have reached, Form VI (Year 12). This was an important step conceptually, dividing Old

'My father was a building worker with his hands on a shovel each day. On school holidays I worked with him most of the time— sometimes country jobs sleeping in tents at night, replacing stumps under farm houses during the day. School was heaven' (1966).

Boys into groups that were administratively easy to determine and would function socially. In retrospect it seems simple. In 1975 the first 'Year' dinner was held, for the boys who left in 1965. In 1976 Scotch began holding 25-year reunion dinners. The Year structure also led to a new fundraising technique called Annual Giving, hatched by a Foundation subcommittee convened by Lithgow, which by 1997 reaped $175 000 a year. Publishing the number of each year's donors, and the amount raised, makes this an annual competition.

It is never too early to train a year group in philanthropy. Since 1986, each group while still in Year 12 makes a gift to the school. Aesthetically this has made Scotch more pleasing. Presbyterian and Scottish frugality had generated buildings that were unadorned. Decorative effects appeared only where they had a purpose, as in the chapel or the Memorial Hall. In their Year 12 gifts, however, the boys have indulged their school with portraits, mosaics, stained glass, a shady seat and an internal fountain.

Fundraising spawned and consolidated both the Scotch Foundation and the Scotch Association. Scotch's new organisational complexity was held together by stronger leadership from Council, under Glenn's long chairmanship (1963–81, entirely straddling the headmasterships of Healey and Roff). The balance of power between Council and its Executive and Finance Committee tilted in favour of the committee. Council hankered after a Presbyterian approach of rotating all its members through the

MEN OF INFLUENCE, MEN OF WEIGHT

Scotch's Old Boys continued to scale the heights. Professor Richard Downing (1932) became Chairman of the Australian Broadcasting Commission. Vice-Admiral Sir Alan McNicoll (1921) was Chief of the Naval Staff, 1965–68. Ian Beaurepaire (1940) was Lord Mayor of Melbourne 1965–66. Professor Geoffrey Sawer (1927) was President of the Australian Academy of Social Sciences 1972–75. In 1973 Sir David Zeidler (1935) succeeded Sir Archibald Glenn as Chairman of ICI.

Sir Henry Winneke (1925), Governor of Victoria, was son of another Henry Winneke (Dux 1892–93) and father of John Winneke (1956), footballer and in 1995 first President of the Victorian Court of Appeal (three of whose eight judges were Scotch Old Boys). Clifford Menhennitt (1929) joined the Supreme Court of Victoria in 1966. His 1969 ruling about the legality of abortion became known as the Menhennitt ruling.

Graham McInnes became Canadian ambassador to UNESCO. Sir William Philip (1908) was President of the Alfred Hospital Board in 1948–75. Patrick McCaughey (1960) became an art critic and gallery director.

In 1973 in Canberra Sir Frederick Wheeler (1928) was Permanent Head of the Treasury, Sir William Refshauge (1931) of Health, Sir Keith Waller (1931) of Foreign Affairs and Sir Lenox Hewitt (1933) of Minerals and Energy (and in 1975–80 Chairman of Qantas).

CROSS-COUNTRY RUNNING

Cross-country running scorns the expensive prepared surfaces used by other sports. 'I led by about 400 yards as we went down the muddy levee bank. I slipped over twice and was nearly caught by [the] pre-race favourite.'[85]

> I slip an' fa' in greasy mickle,
>   As round the bank the giglets kickle,
>   To see me loup,
> When ravin' mad I collect a nettle,
>   Slowly I droop.[86]

It appeals to boys who are not attracted to 'violent sports' like football.[87] It appeals to boys as individuals. It lets them 'excel by my own efforts, rather than relying on others'.[88] Peter Ashton, who won the 1964 Junior Cross-Country, trained for it by himself.[89] Above all, cross-country races favour courage and endurance rather than strength or size. In the Boarders' cross-country run in 1927 the young Bert Dupin

Cross-country races favour courage and endurance rather than strength or size. Raoul Stewardson (left) and Jason Digby in 1979.

came second although the boy who was first was years older and 40% taller.[90] The lightly built David Mason (Captain 1966) recalls that Healey first noticed him in a cross-country race coming in sixth but the first boarder.

In 1952, 500 boys finished and in 1956 it became part of the House Athletics competition, with cock-house points to each house's first six runners in both junior and senior races. It became a major sport in 1964, the year Healey arrived, and Scotch was premier in 1967, the year it became a full-colour sport with Robert McK. Wilson its first captain, through to 1969. After a decline, Slade revived it in 1976, doubling the regular runners to about 50 each week. The 1994 and 2000 teams won the triple crown of state titles, road relays, and APS premiership.

committee, with retiring members not immediately re-eligible, but in practice Council either neglected to enforce its own procedures in this regard or rendered them nugatory by surrendering the choice of committee members to the Chairman, or to the committee itself. Members with expertise thus stayed on the committee for as long as they were needed. Since the committee met every month, it made sense to empower it to take certain financial decisions.

When Healey left, the school's finances were solid indeed. The 1960s building appeals raised large sums of money, and the Endowment Fund had begun to earn a useful cash flow. The frequency of benefactions rose, and a new torrent of government money transformed the possibilities open to the school, although some Presbyterians still opposed receiving such aid. Even the boarding houses no longer made a loss. Perhaps the clearest sign of this financial well-being was that Council in 1968 abandoned its often-reaffirmed policy of budgeting for a 5% surplus on income, letting it drop to half that rate. They did this by deciding to take account of non-cash items, and so to budget for a surplus of 5% of total income, deducting from that the sum budgeted for depreciation. That was the formula, but the underlying cause is that they felt more financially secure. The effect was to lessen increases in fees. Fees still went up, to meet the constant increases in teachers' salaries as Scotch followed the State Teachers' Tribunal awards or the National Wage increases (inflation in 1975 leapt over 20%). But though the parents had to pay for such current cost increases, Scotch now halved its demand on the parents to generate a surplus. At the same time Council confidently increased the school's overdraft provision from $400 000 to $750 000, so as to manage cash flows when building the new Advanced Science Block.

Healey is remembered by his Old Boys as a disciplinarian. As we have seen, this was by no means the central focus of his activity, but before we can make any final judgement upon him—which comes at the end of the next chapter—we must look more closely at discipline and at the student movement of the 1960s which Healey so unexpectedly found himself facing.

15

THE TIMES
THEY ARE A'CHANGIN'

The 1960s and early 1970s began a time of questioning in Western society. In the United States Martin Luther King Jun. marched and in France students seized parts of Paris. Television brought all this to Melbourne. The Beatles, the Rolling Stones and Bob Dylan gave boys a new way to speak and move. The protest against Australian troops in Vietnam swelled into the 1970 moratoriums when tens of thousands of people sat down in Bourke Street. Melbourne's own Germaine Greer became an international champion of feminism. It seemed natural to question every idea and to challenge every authority.

This whirlwind of ideas blew established bodies from their accustomed courses. The Public Schools' Head Prefects' Meeting had discussed only sport for 50 years but in 1968 it addressed an educational matter. The Scotch College Common Room Association had kept to industrial and staffing issues, but in 1968 suffered some Young Turks to set up an Education Committee.

Even in sport, change was afoot. Between 1971 and 1976 soccer leapt from a summer sport to being Scotch's third largest winter sport, seriously challenging rugby's second place. Soccer fielded seven teams every Saturday. (In 1997 it fielded 13 teams, occupying 200 boys, the same as hockey.) Scotch did not welcome such changes. Volleyball had enthusiasts since the 1960s, and in 1975 they won all their matches. But when they tried to make volleyball a House sport in 1975–76, the sportsmaster, Bob Grant, said their numbers were too small.[1] In any case, House-sport policy 'was to provide more opportunity for boys to play the major sports,' and volleyball would take numbers away from these.[2] Cracknell, by contrast, argued volleyball's case: 'a good team sport with no special skills required ... most versatile in that either six or nine players can participate with the possibility of substitutes'.[3] By 1982 volleyball had school colours.

From the 1960s, in the *Collegian*'s original column, England, Esperanto and the Taj Mahal were joined by apartheid, Biafra and the treatment of Aborigines, whilst pieces on war shifted from the World Wars to Vietnam— 'So this was war ...'.[4]

Healey both welcomed and opposed the mood for change. He urged teachers to look at how and what they taught and he welcomed debate, but he insisted on maintaining standards, he opposed anything that smacked of left-wing politics, and he scoffed at 'progressives'.[5]

EDUCATION
Creativity and independent thought

Educationally, in some areas even the most basic tenets were overturned. Education had long leant towards getting things right: perfecting skills and mastering knowledge. Yet perhaps this stifled creativity? In Art, George Yule (1935) felt 'I had some ability and [Shirlow] killed it. For three years we drew a wash-up basin and a football—week after week. He said he was teaching us perspective.'[6] Now a new credo encouraged boys to express themselves no matter how, so long as they had ideas. Marion Scott (Junior School Art Mistress 1946–62) turned the old order on its head: instead of boys trying to understand the teacher, *she* tried to understand the boys. 'Let the child say what he wants to in the way he wants to' and gain 'confidence to express his own ideas without the fear of non-conformity'.[7] Her successor, Denny Evans (staff 1963–88), aimed to give full vent to boys' imagination in contrast to the formal teaching in other subjects.[8] Their Headmaster, Tapp, agreed: 'For the individual, creation, not the quality of creation, is the valuable point'.[9] In Senior School Art, boys welcomed how Helms left them to their own devices to see what they would come up with,[10] and Paton 'provided a wonderful outlet for creativity'.[11]

Junior School Art, Grade 5, 1960.

We put our clay in a big hat bag, or under a towel, or else blindfold our eyes with a handkerchief.

Then, using a ball of clay which can be held comfortably in two hands, we work with our fingers until we can 'see' the clay taking shape.

When do we look at it with our eyes?

When we like the feel of it, because we have discovered that a model which feels right will also look right.

Working like this calls for a degree of concentration and perceptions which one would not expect from younger grades.

His classes were like a masterclass. Yet valuing boys' creativity requires administrative attention, too, and when David Brand (1972) asked an art teacher for the previous year's work, the teacher said he had burnt it all 'just to get rid of it ... I was livid.'[12]

In English, Healey was torn between encouraging creativity and upholding standards. Masters 'could take examples of errors ... and deal with them orally in a later lesson'.[13] (Thus Harrison 'made me feel confident and intelligent, while quietly correcting me and maintaining me in HSC English.') Yet Healey also said: 'The teacher of scholarship must be ruthless. Failure to insist on excellence is in the long run failure in duty and misplaced kindness.'[14]

The idea of boys thinking independently had been in the air since the 1930s. In 1934 Henry Marshall, Editor of the *Collegian*, wrote about the phenomenon of the thinking schoolboy. Boys have always thought, he said. What was new was being allowed to *express* their thoughts, although Victorian die-hards saw this as impertinence. Gilray saw clear-thinking in rather defensive terms, 'to guard ... against propaganda',[15] but a Gilray boy praises 'Bishop who taught me to hold to one's standards even in the face of criticism'.[16] A Healey boy concurs: 'an education at Scotch helped one to develop confidence in forming one's own world view'.[17] Yet complaints about spoon-feeding continue to this day, revealed most recently in an AC Nielson survey.[18]

The curriculum made no room for independent thought, but '45' Clayton (Senior History Master 1925–63) was legendary for challenging boys to think. Although he wrote the text-book and sat on the Victorian Schools Examination Board, he believed boys were educated better by not sticking to the syllabus.[19] He let class discussion range where it would and then put ten minutes of syllabus-oriented dictation at the end. His pupils regularly gained excellent marks. 'His classes were always good fun. He encouraged us to think for ourselves.'[20] He welcomed views vigorously held. He recalled: 'There was a really hot argument one day in the room and I interjected with some remark and [the boy] was so excited he said "Oh rats, Sir!" I don't think anybody else said anything, I didn't say anything, that was the sort of atmosphere. I don't think anybody ever thought the place was out of control, it was a lot of fun.'[21] 'He would accept logical points of view even if he did not agree with them' (1939). He was fiercely right-wing,[22] and his rambling classroom discussions on the history of capitalism were conservative but they 'challenged us to think and produced several notable communists' (1947).

In Science it was easier to stay with the syllabus. 'Occar' Ferres, the 'flamboyant, but very enthusiastic'[23] Senior Physics Master, 'encouraged you to think and respected you if you ... enquired about some aspect of what you had been thinking about. This was regardless of whether you got an idea right or wrong, so long as you had shown a sound logical approach ... especially if you could think laterally and come up with an alternative approach to something' (1947).[24] He 'was transparent and honest. We learnt that it was ok for anyone (including Occar) to make a mistake. He was a real scientist, displayed genuine curiosity and discovered the truth together with us' (1951).[25] 'He actively encouraged hobby groups at lunchtimes, in particular the Radio Club' (1959).[26] 'David Scott (Year 11 Physics) was clear,

'45' CLAYTON

Clayton had an eye problem—a cricket ball hit him on the head when he was 12—and to correct it he wore very thick glasses and held his head at an angle. He was known as 'Forty-five' (because his head was on an angle of 45°) or 'Isaiah'—(because one *eye's 'igher* than the other).[27]

'45–Clayton would wander, unrelentingly up and down the aisles, imparting wisdom, and nipping inattention in the bud. I experienced his teaching as stimulating and uplifting'.[28] 'He practised the life of a Christian without preaching',[29] yet kept the boys entertained with jokes, such as

'What happened to the lady who bent down to tie her shoe lace too close to the aeroplane propeller? Answer: Disaster—(Dis-arsed-her) ...
'Another of Fort Clayton's jokes was a ditty:

The boy stood on the burning deck
He picked his nose like mad.
He rolled it into little balls
And flicked them at his Dad

Now what 16 year old school boy would not tune into a teacher like that?'[30] (Nowadays such a joke may appeal more to a younger boy? If so, we glimpse how puberty slipped earlier as the century went by.)

lucid, and related new or complex ideas to everyday experiences. He often sought feedback from students, and got whole-of-class participation in discussions' (1959).[31] 'Day after day I saw John Graham (Physics, HSC [staff 1970–87]) explain, show in experiment, derive the equations on the board—lose everybody—and go back until he had figured out where we were not understanding and had reminded us from where that particular term or equation had magically appeared on the board (1975).'

Science teaching can be authoritarian, yet these examples show how flexible a teacher could be. In any case, boys' tolerance for authoritarian teaching varied with age. In a 1977 survey, boys in their early teens preferred more authoritarian classroom teaching practices than older boys could easily tolerate. Boys in their second-last year at school particularly wanted closer staff–student relationships. Boys in their final year, under exam pressures, did not usually favour permissive teaching practices.

Younger boys have less-developed learning skills, conceptual abilities and motor skills. The school adjusts teaching methods and curriculum accordingly. Bond taught Latin to younger boys dogmatically. 'It was more of a series of intimidations rather than lessons' (1965). 'He was a fanatic for his subject—he was a tyrant—but successfully got away with it' (1950).[32] Teaching final-year boys, however, he made Greek History 'fun and interesting'. Thucydides' *History of the Peloponnesian War*

was better than *Boys' Own* as far as an adventure story, in some ways even more interesting than a Shakespearean tragedy as high moral values were set forth, overturned, reinstated. The good guys sometimes won and sometimes they lost. [Bond] handled the relatively small class as adults and brought interesting insight and anecdotes that made the whole episode live. … learning could be fun in itself as well as meeting the immediate academic goal [1964].[33]

Tapp told Junior School mothers in 1954 'not to think too much for their sons—let them think for themselves—and, if they forget, to take what is coming to them'.[34] To think was more important than being right or wrong. Even the Chaplain, Fraser, could take this stance. He 'stopped me reading the Bible in Divinity one day and asked the class the question "How do we know what Goldsmith is reading is true?" Nobody answered and he said shortly "We don't know—continue reading, Goldsmith!" ' (1951).[35]

New curricula

Under Healey, being encouraged to think moved from a bonus provided by outstanding masters and became a deliberate part of the school's work. Teaching moved away from rote learning. The exciting teachers were those who 'taught me that facts were nothing without a pattern to systematize them, but that the more facts one knew the more likely one was to detect

ONE BOY'S TEACHERS, 1977–1979

The best teachers were interactive. 'Buddy' Holly, in scenes which would preempt the film *The Dead Poets Society*, leapt around the class in a passion of poetry which captivated me. I still pull out the first poem he read out loud and with some mirth try and recapture that reading for my own benefit and those of my children. They think I am daft.

Others like Rick Rowton (Art) made tremendous impact because they listened to us and consulted us as they would a colleague. This was heady and mature stuff (which we did not always want of course) but it drew us in. Rick taught by asking us what we thought, what we had discovered, what we had unearthed in the library/Art Gallery/museum.

Others made an impact by being dazzlingly technical. Commerce Form IV comes to mind, listening to Galbraith unravel the ledgers made us shake our heads in wonder that he could make it make sense. That he could do it with such ease made me all the more resolved to get my own head around it. Sadly my results for that year tell a sorry story but the point was the teaching inspired me to do my best—not the fear of an ordinary result or the threatenings of parents who wanted to see some return on their investment in fees.

'Whacky' Thomas conducted some brilliant Biology classes through his technical mastery of the subject but also through a mix of engaging the students in the same way Rick did, along with some tart and sharp debating of points with students. You had to know your stuff if you were to take him on. Few did.

Bruce Lyman[36]

the significant pattern' (1961). If a subject was boring it could be because it was taught as 'a dull regime of facts',[37] or because 'I never passed beyond the stage of seeing it as a collection of unconnected facts' (1961).

To teach patterns as much as facts, in 1958 Rose Turnbull introduced the Cuisenaire method of Arithmetic. Its aim of teaching the relationships within mathematics appeared also in the New Mathematics, which arrived in the 1960s. It used set language to unify the various branches of mathematics. This was particularly important in the study of relations and functions which occur all the time in all branches of mathematics. In Algebra, emphasis changed from purely manipulative skills to include the idea of algebra structure. Some probability theory was introduced in the final years as a model for experiments where more than one result was possible. The once-mighty Pythagoras's theorem was mocked in the *Collegian*,[38] as Euclidean geometry in Forms I–IV (Years 7–10) gave way to transformational geometry in Form V as a means of obtaining a deeper understanding of geometry. Form V learnt matrices to describe these transformations. The structure of the algebra of matrices could thus be compared with the structure of the algebra of numbers.

Some of the teachers who taught the New Mathematics had never learnt its language before. Junior School teachers managed the unfamiliar content and teaching materials as best they could. Wirth believed 'the traumatic effects of this "ad hoc" approach to curriculum change' could still be felt fifteen years later.[39] In the Senior School, too, it shell-shocked one or two staff, and Ken Evans, Senior Mathematics Master, was grateful to Bower— a refugee from Hitler's Germany, he had survived greater changes than this—who 'used what is best in the new, but … moderated my idealistic enthusiasms'.[40]

Evans put the emphasis on 'understanding rather than rote-learning. Getting the right answer (without understanding) is no longer good enough'.[41]

The first satellite to orbit the earth, the Russian Sputnik in 1957, shocked the Americans into developing new secondary-school science-teaching programmes. Scotch took advantage of these. The US Physical Science Study Committee (PSSC) and the UK Nuffield Foundation developed courses to teach pupils to think like scientists. The Nuffield approach was that 'you can't just tell kids things … they actually have to have some evidence before believing something, so … the intention was to teach [what] was applicable to students' experience'.[42] Indeed, to teach *through* experience. Facts deferred to processes. Students learnt 'How' and 'Why' rather than 'State this law', and they learnt them by doing them in laboratories. Mappin, Head of Science, encouraged learning through investigatory practical laboratory work. Teaching methods relied more on students and less on the teacher.

In Physics, from 1963 teaching emphasis 'shifted from a collection of scientific facts to an understanding of concepts'.[43] The Physics courses in the final years relied heavily on practical work in the laboratory, made possible by the new Science Building and the technical expertise of Alex McCormick (staff 1963–78). Form V (Year 11) studied Energy (mechanics, optics, electricity and radioactivity). Boys even studied the dynamics of kicking a football. The Senior Physics Master, Tait, was also soccer coach. He predicted a generation of expert snooker players, devastating swing bowlers, and long-hitting golfers.[44]

In the 1980s the idea of training the whole population to think like scientists relaxed to a view that the citizenry should at least understand their environment better. Without a burdensome amount of mathematics and physics, they should grasp how things work. To this was added social responsibility in science: environmental issues like uranium mining or the ozone layer.

Chemistry changed, too. When 'Tort' Jamieson retired in 1949, Chemistry's main thrust was how to analyse and identify substances.[45]

> In the dry way, in the wet way,
> Testing for an unknown salt,
> A priori, fortiori
> In the customary way.
>
> *Chorus*
> Test for chloride, test for nitrate
> Test for sulphate, arsenate,
> 'Tisn't sulphide or hydroxide—
> Would it not make one irate !
>
> Sublimation, condensation
> Avogadro, Berthollet,
> Saturation, titration
> Dalton and Lavoisier.
>
> *Chorus*
> Oxidation, levigation
> Is it arsenic or lime?
> Perspiration, resignation,
> Try again another time!

Chemistry was 'recipe' chemistry, with a great deal of rote learning. From the late 1950s, the Chemical Bond approach invited boys to reason why certain things happened. Even later, still using understanding of bonding theory, there was a swing back to bench chemistry and an understanding of practical matters (simultaneously see it and grasp theory).

Under Rohan Braddy (Head of Chemistry 1988–2000)

we state what it is and investigate its properties. By generalising and theorising about the properties, we make 'guesses' as to the structure of the material. For example, show the Year 10s the green verdigris on the Mem hall spire, and then start to think about what is happening to the metal. Maybe a few practicals (even though this is an Americanism, I think it describes what we do better than 'experiments'). Later the kids will realise that the metal is losing electrons. From this, we can get a definition of oxidation. The underlying principle is that we should go from the known to the unknown and we attempt to do this wherever possible.[46]

(This attempt to replace rote learning with theory remained an issue for the rest of the century, because it crunched up against the fact that 'the course writers are different people from the course examiners'. The VCE Chemistry course from 1992 emphasised teaching concepts 'from within the students' frame of reference. Human skills/issues were to be a big part of this. Environmental, economic, social, technological issues were to be introduced wherever possible. However, the examiners continued to be the same people that had examined the old, rote-focussed course for the past 20 or so years. Hence the students are *taught* in a methodology kind of way, but *examined* in a rote way.'[47])

George Logie-Smith, Director of Music 1959–78, rehearsing for the Foundation Day Concert.

Language teaching, also, benefited from the Cold War. The United States' large standing army needed basic skills in foreign languages. Out of this came language laboratories, which applied the repetitious techniques of gun dismantling to language comprehension. If you say something often enough it will lodge somewhere. Noam Chomsky then debunked this, but grammar did not return to pride of place. Today, language teaching includes realistic communicative conversations (like talking about sport, or meeting someone). Grammar is explained as needed rather than taught in its own right. The new emphasis on learning to speak (for until the 1960s the emphasis had been on exposure to the culture) was driven, also, by the invention of the tape-recorder, as teachers saw its possibilities, and by the 1987 National Language Policy to teach languages that had a practical application.

In History, SHEP (Secondary History Education Project) gained a following because of its intellectual aspects, for it emphasised what is unique to history—the study of continuity and change over time—but in practice it trivialised history's content, for example studying packaging.[48]

Despite these changes within individual disciplines, Scotch as a whole never embraced any educational movement. An eclectic approach seemed to serve this complex organisation best.

Since each discipline's reform has its own story, we risk overlooking the broader patterns that link them. Language laboratories reduced the importance of grammar, but they did so at much the same time that English teachers also abandoned grammar, albeit for the different reason of encouraging creativity. In Mathematics, too, learning the times-tables came to seem less important, just as, at home, parental discipline became more liberal. Dr Spock seems the key. Feeding babies every four hours, and refusing to feed them at other times, gave way to feeding babies when they were hungry. At school, force-feeding pupils gave way to trying to stimulate boys' hunger and thirst for knowledge.

Side-by-side with reshaped educational content, educationalists considered the process of learning. Like a Spock baby, a boy could set his own goals and rate of consumption. Ken Evans introduced a British mathematics project that let students work at their own pace, from cards. The new doctrine of Individualised Instruction or Learning suggested staff think about each child's needs, rather than the needs of the class. Dispensing with classes 'breaks the lock-step of fast-, medium- and slow-learners going through the same topics at the same rate, and … being "passed" or "failed" on their ability to measure up to the normal distribution curve cut-off point'.[49] In a large school like Scotch, boys would work in small groups of similarly paced boys. It hinted at a return to Morrison's system of classes. Clearly this had implications for timetabling and class-size. Healey, however, believed that America was swinging away from such flexible timetabling and that it would be a pity if Australia, being five years behind, took it up just as it was waning there.[50]

Thinking about teaching and learning

From 1968, thinking about teaching became communal. Healey challenged the staff with his encyclical 'Questions for our consideration'. He pondered teachers' work and methods, and outlined issues that would occupy the school for the coming decades: ventilation of boys' grievances, team teaching, assessment, the Sixth Form and Assembly. He asked 'Can we find time for staff-discussions? Can we inform each other of experiments being made in our own school?'[51] Healey had the power to impose changes, but a wise principal knows that change takes better root if supported by the school. He preferred to raise issues and ask questions. Strategy aside, it was what a good teacher cannot help doing.

Two months after Healey's 'Questions', the Common Room Association, until then a social and industrial body, set up an Education Committee to look at matters of educational interest and significance. The Rev. David Webster became chairman and Alan Shugg secretary. The Committee's average age was around 40. Webster—quiet, incisive, with a mellifluous voice and a poker-faced wit—was Senior History Master. He taught about reform and revolution and knew how they went. So the Committee was careful not to push too hard. (History and Newton's Third Law of Motion said this would produce a counter-thrust.) Instead, it exposed staff to new ideas while murmuring that the Committee's views 'have no official standing'.[52] It sparked its own discussions with members' papers, outside educationists, and visits to other schools. It circulated Curriculum Advisory Board reports.

Its members saw it as several things at once. Crow saw it as an ideas group, Shugg as enabling self-education and Mappin as 'the *only* forum we have for hearing and discussing together views relevant to the school's function, our role as teachers, etc., on a semi-regular basis'. At large, 'we could prod, we could suggest, we could support'.[53]

Healey harnessed their energy, and referred matters to them. Yet reformers under an autocracy must move circumspectly, and when in 1971 the committee *notified* him of something rather than *consulting*, he sharply rebuked them as a group of 'young men'. The committee protested that this 'had implications of inexperience, lack of weight, etc.' and Healey agreed to withdraw this term as the Committee contained Group Masters and Heads of Departments. Indeed, once placated, Healey gave them tactical advice. He 'pointed out that Ed. Committee is often under attack by some senior men, however, he defends our rôle & wants us to continue to discuss, disseminate, report, & recommend. He suggested that to avoid "cruelling our pitch" we should be careful not to antagonise such men, & yet no need to "pussyfoot" around. Need for a middle course.'[54]

What should the Committee tackle first? To Healey's major themes it added pastoral care, ventilation of boys' grievances, staff–parent relationships, under-achievers, House system, inter-discipline communications, and group work. The Committee decided also to look at Scotch's educational objectives and assumptions. The Committee always faced a choice between formulating overall aims, or tackling particular problems. 'General opinion favoured the latter course'[55]—a practical Anglo-Celtic approach. Yet, as academically minded men, they saw that addressing curriculum development meant clarifying goals. They felt the need to

Home Time in the 1960s.

conceptualise the school's work, also, because so far in Australia most reform had been directed towards physical changes, like laboratories.

The Committee enabled teachers to share their teaching methods and educational models. David Scott, for example, in 1970 suggested a model of mental domains.[56] As well as the obvious cognitive domain, and the psycho-motor domain covering manual skills, the affective domain covered how boys felt about a subject. It could be measured by questions: 'Do you enjoy persevering with your maths homework until you get it right?'; 'In your conversation out of class do you enthuse about the concepts and processes you meet in maths?'; and 'Do you have a sense of excited achievement when you master a mathematical concept or process? ... Often/Rarely/Never'.[57] Teachers 'do attempt to establish or influence attitudes in our boys, and it is useless to have such aims unless one can in some way measure their attainment, even if that measure is intuitive'.[58]

Darling, as Librarian, was well placed for an overview, like an uncle living with a family. He found the boys unstimulated and, as they grew up, with lessening intellectual excitement at their work. He compared Scotch with government schools: Scotch final-year boys lacked intellectual curiosity, unlike boys of the same age and social class in Beaumaris High School. He told his brother teachers that their lessons were often boring, that brighter students were held back by being harnessed with other boys merely because they were the same age, and that teaching in fixed-length periods meant that boys were frustrated from following something through when it engaged them.[59]

The Committee accepted that even among its own members it would not always reach agreement, for example on assessment. By 1971 it feared it had gone too far in even-handedness and become merely a discussion group without effecting change. Under the chairmanship of Mappin it tried to germinate practical outcomes by organising staff–student seminars.

The Committee met every month or two at night in the Common Room or members' homes. It ceased in the late 1970s, having accomplished its purpose of making discussion about education a routine part of the school's life. It did not meet in 1976, for example, because staff went to a Scotch–Wesley Reading Group that discussed educational philosophies.

Members also took their broadened thinking outside the school. Mappin chaired the Victorian Universities and Schools Examination Board (VUSEB) Standing Committee for Chemistry, later the Chemistry Subject Committee of the Victorian Institute of Secondary Education (VISE). 'In these capacities he was largely responsible for two major revisions of the Chemistry course.'[60] Similarly, Evans sat on the Mathematics Standing Committee of Melbourne University's Schools Board in the late 1950s, later the VSEB, later the VISE, later the Victorian Curriculum and Advisory Board (VCAB). The very list indicates the constant changes in the regulatory environment in which the school has operated since the 1960s, averaging a new system every decade.

The new teaching ideas in the 1960s flowed on to libraries in the 1970s. Previously, the library sheltered a few bookish boys and final-year boys with spare periods. It played no part in teaching. Mark Stump (Senior Chemistry Master 1960–68) wanted no Chemistry books there. He taught from the text-book written by the examiners, and he did not want boys getting any other ideas.[61] Now, self-based learning required libraries to work alongside the classroom. The Longmore Library (1965) was one of the first school libraries in Australia with audio-visual facilities, like reel-to-reel tapes and long-playing records for loan, and later cassette-recorders. It also introduced a photocopier, 'a monstrous Xerox machine' that filled a small room and emitted black smoke when the paper jammed, 'much to the joy/consternation of the boys'.[62]

The Longmore was soon too small. Plans for another storey gave way to plans for a new library. Such plans stimulated thought about what a library should be. Darling in 1975 asserted the library's claim to 'take a more direct role in providing learning experiences within the school. The library staff should be more closely associated with syllabus planning and with the preparation of teaching materials.' The library was to be part of the learning experience and not just an aid. The Longmore lacked provision for small group activity, whereas 'Modern libraries', said Darling, 'plan for individual use, small group use (6–10 students) separated from the main work area, and large group use, using, in particular, A/V [audio-visual] facilities'.[63]

General Studies

'General Studies courses … are either *integratory*, attempting to tie together common strands which run through different subjects, or *compensatory*, providing for time to be spent studying and discussing important matters which do not at present form a part in the other subjects'.[64]

Dividing the curriculum into separate subjects was based on an unsound theory of knowledge, Webster told the Education Committee in 1968, citing a Curriculum Advisory Board report, and he suggested a more integrated curriculum, such as that tried at Moreland High School. 'Considerable discussion ensued.'[65] In 1969 the Committee proposed 'general courses available in both the "maths/science" and the "humanities" groups for the non-specialist pupil wanting to broaden his studies'.[66] John De Ravin (Captain 1974) said his studies had made him critically aware only in the narrow framework of the sciences, and he regretted his lack of cultural education.[67] Already, fifth formers (Year 11s) were obliged to do a science or a humanity outside the main trend of their courses, but the committee hoped for a more *general* subject than those currently available for this purpose. Form V seemed the right year because final-year boys were focused on university entrance. Also, fifth formers 'are often aware of, and argue for, contemporaneity at this stage of their mental and emotional development. First formers [Year 7s], however, are just as much at home with the Hittites.'[68]

General Studies appealed for several reasons. It offered teachers stimulation through integrating subjects and through team teaching. It offered the stimulation of 'Insight into present problems of society'.[69] It could be taught by topic. A topic such as 'The environment' might involve teachers of Geography, Geology, Biology, History and Social Studies. It could be taught by units, for example six units in different disciplines. It could be taught as a 'broadener',[70] in which case it would most likely have staff in its own right.

Most departments were intrigued. *Biology* could enhance understanding of the human body (drugs, antibiotics, disease, disorder, reproduction); genetics (family, race); and eco-systems (food webs, the environment, pollution, evolution, radiation). *Geography* mooted studies based locally, either Hawthorn and Richmond or the Gardiner's Creek basin (sequential land use through Aboriginal hunting, grazing, artists' colonies, market gardening, orcharding, to suburban sprawl), or on pollution, or on traffic. Study would include work in the field, teaching the geographer's method, namely 'to observe, to record, to explain'.[71] *Mathematics* was less imaginative, and could think only of statistics in survey methods, although probability, for instance, has applications to ethics, and to the risk-taking behaviour of young males. *Physics* posited (a) energy (solar, tidal, nuclear; their uses and limitations), (b) history of science, (c) development of some grand theory, like Newton's, or (d) science and the environment.

The Senior Physics Master, Scott, doubted parents would agree to subjects not leading to tertiary courses. Yet 'weaker pupils are not given enough rewarding experience in class' and he hoped that General Studies could reconcile what parents wanted for their children and what children who were low academic performers needed for their greater happiness.[72]

Healey supported General Studies as a way of educating for life. He wanted boys 'instructed in the historical development of the problems of race, war, political institutions and creeds, complications of industry, the growth of population, the need for conservation, the meaning of evolution'.[73] It might cover topics such as health, sex relations or living in cities.[74] It should familiarise boys with current affairs, some commercial, legal and economic facts and usages, and some important aspects of science.[75]

Healey's support was crucial because General Studies provoked what Eggleston briskly summarised as hostility, lack of cooperation, administrative problems and sheer ignorance.[76] Eggleston was Fifth Form Group Master. The academic argument against General Studies was that 96% of Scotch boys went on to further academic study. The practical argument was that of finding space in the timetable. Form V already had two compulsory subjects, English Expression and Religion-in-Life. The latter was inviolate and it was unwise to reduce English further, when the Scotch pass rate was only 62%, and the state rate 63%.

General Studies was approved by the Senior Masters' Committee, which Healey chaired, and was pushed along firmly by Eggleston, who admired a similar course he had seen in England. He hoped to have the course running by 1974.

It began at last in 1978, under Eggleston, as a non-examinable compensatory course for all Form V. Although it had handicaps (only two periods a week and not assessable), it had stature from being backed by leading staff, such as Michael Achurch, Phil Anthony (staff 1970–86, Group Master 1979–86), Ivo Beattie (staff 1973–98, Common Room Chairman 1987–89), Syd Boydell, Patricia Holdaway (staff 1977–) and David Paul. They met regularly as a body (a first for Scotch) and read widely, given time to do so when Roff secured another 1.5 teachers. The course used a recent book by Charles Birch (1935), *Confronting the Future*, and concentrated on three main issues, one per term: the energy crisis, multiculturalism, and freedom and control (which touched on the 'Law, Drugs (including Alcohol and Tobacco), and Road Safety'). Roff judged its start successful.[77] It used 'spectacularly high profile' outside speakers,[78] like John Halfpenny, Jeff Kennett and Dr Jim Cairns.

For the first time, the teaching staff as a body had shaped the curriculum and had reconsidered the view that teaching could occur only through discipline-based departments.

General Studies had its growing pains. The speaker session (students sometimes inattentive, topics too difficult, speakers not good for the age-bracket) was followed by a tutorial session (twelve tutor groups of about 20 boys). 'Humanities-trained staff generally found this easier than science-trained teachers. Yet we insisted on a cross-departmental team to cover the range of topics from political, social, environmental and technological areas.'[79]

It ended when the new Victorian Certificate of Education (VCE) course introduced compulsory Australian Studies. There was no room for General Studies. 'No point in complaining'; VCAB made it impossible by insisting on specific time allocations for subjects.[80] Scotch felt disquiet about the new course itself and about the destruction of the General Studies course, and tried to continue some of its curriculum under the new guise. Australian

The Junior School as seen from the Junior School Oval from the 1920s to the 1980s.

Studies later ceased to be compulsory and promptly disappeared (boys disliked it), but the structure of the VCE made it difficult to revive the General Studies course. (Perhaps the desire for such a course had lessened.)

The Junior School meanwhile toyed with the Integrated Day. This removed subject divisions and allowed children to be largely self-directing in their education. *Random* choice of activity created too much disturbance among the children, but this could be contained if all children worked at the same activity at the same time for at least part of the day. Also, Tapp insisted that each child spend a certain amount of time each day, or each week, on a particular activity, such as maths, reading, or art. Tapp was equally cautious about vertical or family groups, which grouped children in a range of ages, 'in the belief that this is a more natural atmosphere for development. … It seems to me to be a good social exercise to have younger children learning from older children in a school situation and to have the older confronted with the need and the opportunity for helping the younger.'[81] He restricted it to the Sub-Primary.

Competitiveness

Scotch has always been competitive. Morrison measured it against other schools, and stimulated competition internally. Many Scotch boys have always been naturally 'competitive and enjoyed winning' (1927, 1936),[82] and 'revelled in the competitive atmosphere' (1996, 1991, 1949).[83] 'There is a virtue in ambition, and those who win … value [it] all the more if they have won the honour by a fight' (1905).[84] 'Competition is part of life and that was well (and gently) taught at school' (1972).[85] 'One's self-confidence was continually challenged. It was a tough environment; probably tougher than the business world in some ways' (1972).[86] Scotch 'instilled a competitive edge and a strong desire to achieve' (1975).[87]

The pre-eminence of competitiveness was challenged strongly only once, in the 1960s and 1970s. At the annual staff–student seminars James Simpson said competitiveness was unChristian.[88] Other boys said Scotch motivated its boys by competitiveness,[89] with too much emphasis on winning rather than on participating,[90] so that 'instead of learning to *be*, we learnt competition'.[91] 'We are pushed to be tops in everything', said David Coote (1978). This 'lust for success' suited the top few well but not those of average ability.[92] 'We are taught to compete fiercely with each other', said James Neyland (1977). 'Success is the name of the game and everything else must come after it. Rather than enjoy and appreciate our fellows we must learn to compete with them in a cycle that will become our lifestyle.' 'In order to make the competition fair we are made supposedly equal. … our individuality is taken away and replaced with a certain degree of sameness. Rules, uniform and hair-length are small but important aspects of this.'[93]

One new boy had at his previous school been 'encouraged to enjoy and participate rather than focus on the competitive aspects of the game with the aim of "winning".' In Physical Education at Scotch, however, the teacher made it 'a competitive, aggressive and belittling experience. ... one boy who forgot his togs having to run round the oval in his underpants on a cold and frosty morning. ... the cars from the South-Eastern Freeway could see him in full view. I detested the competitive aspect of this school.'[94] Peter Howe (1980) is 'still weaning myself of a need to be successful at all costs'.[95]

The alternative was 'that work and sport ought to be the individual competing against himself ... as in the House Cross Country Races or the Decathlon'.[96] Scotch tended to emphasise the successful boy, whereas more emphasis needed to be given to the happy and sociable boy.[97]

It is probably not possible to resolve these competing claims of competitiveness and co-operation. Scotch wants its boys to be both successful and good citizens, tempering ambition with social responsibility whilst energising social responsibility with success.

Healey tried to find an acceptable way to talk about competition by talking instead about excellence. As an aim for the school it appeared in Council's minutes for the first time in 1973.[98] Healey spent a good deal of money explaining it. He talked, wrote, and used films and slides with taped commentaries. The 'pursuit of excellence'[99] became a new way for Scotch to talk about itself. One of Healey's Captains, Finlay Macrae (1967), believes that 'excellence with modesty' is 'the mark of an Old Scotch Collegian ... and can be seen across generations of old boys'.[100]

Assessment

Academically, competition focused on assessment. In the 1970s the teachers thoroughly explored assessment, led by Healey and the CRA Education Committee. Assessment lies near the heart of teaching, and will always be controversial. Different personalities and different disciplines diverge on why, how, how often, and when. Webster proposed working from first principles, by establishing aims and from them deriving practice. He stimulated an Education Committee submission to the staff that addressed the purpose, nature, and use of assessment.

The purposes were many, which clouded the discussion. Evaluation was said to be part of learning. It measured change. The boy finds out if he has absorbed knowledge, mastered an intellectual process, learnt a manipulative skill, or enjoys what once he did not. An unsuccessful boy may try again until he succeeds. This is at odds with a one-chance-only view of assessment, but it is how boys learn to ride a bike or bowl a leg break. Healey held that trying again was the best way for boys to learn English Expression. Webster proposed it more generally in a test of 15 items in 5 groups (note-making, recall, research, communication, and comprehension and application). Boys could repeat the test until they passed it. Some boys would take all year, others would pass by mid-year and thereafter 'can work through the remainder of the syllabus with appropriate assistance and supervision in accordance with their interests and abilities'.[101] Boys repeating would not be described as having failed.

Healey believed assessment was a good thing. Later, he quoted Donald Barr's *Who Pushed Humpty Dumpty?*: 'The need to verify one's competence is strong, deep and universal. Young children demand to be quizzed: "Ask me about such-and-such." Older children and adults play quiz games and solve puzzles. ... *Not* to be examined in a subject leaves the competent student frustrated.'[102]

For teachers, assessment was useful, to gauge the effectiveness of their teaching and course. The school used it to award prizes and to allocate boys to classes.

Scotch also debated about the *kind* of assessment. Healey when he arrived found Scotch spent 35 days a year on examining, and one of his first actions was to abolish the mid-term (or 'minor') examinations in second term. Thereafter he abolished examinations for Form I (Year 7) and curtailed them in Forms II–V. He did not think examinations were wrong, indeed they 'encouraged industry and self-denial, and were a test of character and virtue'.[103] But younger boys wasted time having so many.[104] Instead, he challenged staff to use well-designed tests built into normal teaching.[105] Webster, similarly, argued that tests in lower forms could be as short as ten minutes, and integrated among other incentives rather than as an incentive divorced from teaching.[106] Other critics of examinations, like two future Vice-Principals Eggleston and Hosking, thought them 'vastly over-rated, and that there was far too much emphasis on retention of knowledge, rather than interpretation and use of material',[107] which were not necessarily best tested by exam.[108] Boys complained that the examination system pushed them into studying just for examinations[109] and killed the love of learning.[110]

If examinations were to be educational, then feedback was as useful as a mark, but seldom happened, though the Senior Masters' Committee

In Battleships and Cruisers two opponents put their ships on a grid and shell the other's grid to locate his ships and sink them.

BATTLESHIPS AND CRUISERS

In the 1930s after examinations, 'Phantom' Irving read them Kipling, or recited the books of Jerome K. Jerome from memory.[111] The Physics master, Bienvenu,

spoke to his class. 'Those of you who want to read comics, go over to my left in the classroom. Those who want to do something useful, make to the right.' He produced from the cupboard a car generator, a starter motor, a cut-out relay, a spark coil, a distributor, a sectioned battery—and for a couple of weeks, took us right through the theory of automobile electrics. It was unforgettably absorbing and permanently valuable stuff.[112]

Around 1950 time was 'misused or wasted', reading Mickey Spillane and Westerns, or playing 'form cricket'.[113] Selby Smith tried to remedy this, but 'Battleships and cruisers' continued.

encouraged it. Today few teachers see examinations as educational. Examinations are to measure performance or position. Educational dialogue between teacher and pupil on any particular paper is curtailed by the ferocious deadlines on getting reports back to parents.

Gymnastics, 1951.

Boys bound for post-secondary education needed to sit external examinations to win entrance there, and so Scotch had to train boys in the necessary skills. Scotch could have taught them separately, but parental pressure pushed all pupils into the academic group. The presence of abler boys could stimulate others to achieve marks they would not otherwise have won. But other boys were condemned to endure classes that did not engage them, when their educative and personal needs would have been better met in other ways.

Examinations were also said to spur boys to work. Webster doubted this.

In so far as it is an incentive, it is an incentive to the *top 10%* of boys to produce *excellent exam results*. To about two-thirds of the remainder it is an incentive to be content with the *low* standard of 50% (except that the more cautious will aim at, say, 60% to be on the safe side) while, for those whom it has accustomed to 'failure' (about 20%), it is a *dis*incentive. That is to say, for the *majority* of boys (perhaps as many as 80%) it is *not* an incentive to do their *best*.

It tends to make all boys work to produce good *exam* results at three widely separated points of time rather than so as to achieve *a progressive and integrated mastery of the subject*.[114]

The structure of Scotch since Gilray is that boys climb disciplinary ladders that cut across age-based Groups (Years). Group Masters liked examinations for the firm data needed to judge a boy's work against the norm for his age, and to advise on subject choice. So Brown, Elliot and Spencer Sayers (staff 1937–79) said tests were too easy and the results too flattering.[115] Group Masters had each boy for one year only.

Masters in charge of disciplines preferred the opposite tack, anticipating training a boy for several years. They had less need of a clearcut authoritative assessment, and were more likely to want to integrate assessment as part of teaching. So they preferred continuous assessment to examinations, or perhaps no assessment at all.

Healey over-ruled the Group Masters and reduced the number of examinations, but left it to each Senior Subject Master to work out his own assessment, so long as 'adequate testing is done to provide information for Group-Masters and Parents'.[116] Ken Evans in Mathematics seized the chance to have no examinations in lower years. He hoped to avoid 'the negative attitudes of boys who judge themselves to be failures', to 'avoid interruption to the main flow of teaching, to avoid cramming and the worst forms of anxiety', and to 'use testing more diagnostically for the help and guidance of individual boys'.[117] Evans disapproved of the magical 50% pass: 'one boy's pass is another's failure'.[118] Even in tests, therefore, he did not reveal the marks.[119] Similarly, Briggs in teaching General Science to slower boys gave no marks, and preferred to encourage and praise.

(This contrasted with the very public way Shew handed out work 70 years earlier. 'Higgins. Not your best, therefore less than nine. Biggins. Well meant, but inadequate, therefore less than five. Jiggins. Oh! my poor boy! therefore less than three. Wiggins. An insult to me and a disgrace to the Class, therefore one.'[120])

Butler, in Modern Languages, found that teachers using audio-lingual methods wanted no examinations at least till Form IV (Year 10), whilst teachers using other methods wanted examinations. For Form V most felt the need of some examination to help make decisions about further study. If tests did replace examinations, time for marking them should be found in school hours.[121]

The Science Department mainly wanted to dispense with formal examinations until the final year. David Scott, a Group Master, 'disagreed with this, saying that boys liked the pressure of examinations' and that an examination at the end of Form V was 'a reliable guide … to indicate who should continue with Science'. Mappin, as head of Science, replied that tests should indicate this adequately.[122]

Ian Ling (staff 1964–75, Senior Chemistry Master 1969–75) suggested two marking systems, one to show a boy his achievement, the other to show where he fitted into the general pattern. Evans and Ling looked into how to do this. It recalled Morrison's approach of listing at least the top half of the class, but Healey was reluctant to have anything like a 'form order' or class list.[123] By 2000, Scotch re-adopted Morrison's device of awarding boys a mark for both Effort and Achievement. When four terms reappeared, rather than have four termly reports, there were two full reports at the end of each semester and at the end of Terms 1 and 3 a 'Progress Report' requiring less staff input. It seemed that what parents wanted to know was achievement and effort. The letter grades have no numerical basis.

Never before was there such a flowering of teacher discussion about assessment, nor was there again because from 1978 the new Victorian Institute of Secondary Education (VISE) reformed HSC (Year 12). The new system granted schools some freedom: schools chose one-third of the course's content (from a range of options) and school assessment counted for between 30% and 50% of the final assessment. Nevertheless, in the debate about education and assessment, the key decisions were now taken outside the school, at VISE and its successors.

Streaming

Startlingly, some teachers have discouraged *fast* learners—because they upset the class's progress by getting too far ahead. Fast runners or swimmers never had this problem, but Barrie Johns (1955) 'got the sand shoe from "Cliffy" Pledge [staff 1946–65, Acting Headmaster of Junior School 1958] … We had been learning the 11 times table. I quickly saw the pattern … I sped forwards and I was up to: "Seven elevens are seventy-seven!" The rest of the class was still on: "Five elevens are fifty-five!" … and I was punished for being out of step!'[124]

Sorting boys of the same age into classes according to academic ability seemed unavoidable to Selby Smith, though he wanted movement between levels to be relatively easy. Streaming began in Form II (Year 8). By Form IV

> the level of performance inevitably begins to show much greater variations: the longer the race, I suppose, the greater the distance between the first and the last. Our plan was to try progressively to enrich the course offered to the faster streams … and to lighten and simplify the load of the slower, so that they could cover the essential ground more slowly and, we hoped, more effectively and could aim at an objective such that success need not be beyond them. Thus the three fastest groups studied ten subjects, usually including two foreign languages; and, of these ten, their English comprised wider and more advanced reading.[125]

A boy's class was a very public pronouncement on his ability, and risked mortifying those in the lowest class (called 'Shell' from 1912 to 1953). 'I was almost numerically illiterate and sometimes got a mark less than 10. Each day in 1954 our first two periods were arithmetic and maths. Sheer hell. Master was Mr Blenkiron, if I kept quiet he seemed to accept my lack of knowledge.'[126] A boy demoted to a class like 2 French B in 1966 saw himself as among 'the dumboes, a lot of boarders who only wanted to go back to the farm, a few dumb (seriously) and a lot of misfits. [This] gave me a poor attitude and a chip on my shoulder at the tender age of 12!'[127]

Mr [David] Scott taught me mathematics in one of the 'struggling' second forms. One day he gave us a pep talk that we should not give up hope … that he had had a former student in that class once before who had gone on to become Dux of Mathematics. He set the challenge and I set about repeating that performance. Now I work as a mathematician. [1969]

What put boys into lower classes varied. One boy acknowledges himself as 'a dreamer and scholastically rather a slow learner—not dull but finding it hard to be articulate to all the knowledge and beauty that grew within me'; he gained his BA when aged 52.[128] Fisher (Captain 1941) judged that streaming was unfair to 'the less bright' as there were no facilities for technical-type training apart from carpentry.[129]

Healey tried to break out of this. He deplored streaming 'as destructive of harmony and devastatingly depressing for a good many boys'. He encouraged Bond, as timetabler, to develop flexibility.

Theoretically (but it does not really happen) a boy can be in a 'top' set for Maths and a 'bottom' set for English. Undoubtedly some separation of the very quick from the very slow is necessary. But … we must make sure that no clever boy is held back, and we must beware of allowing pupils to opt out of difficult courses or become resistant to tests or examination for selection.[130]

Under Roff and Donaldson the only streaming has been in Mathematics, generally two top classes, six to eight mainstream, and two small classes of students requiring additional help (boys and staff call it 'Veggie Maths'). Also, Roff approved Maths Camps with Monash University to stretch intelligent fourth formers (Year 10s). All other disciplines have classes of mixed ability. Sometimes artificial streaming is created by the timetable when a small group of boys choose to study two languages from Year 8 through to Year 10. As a group their subject choices mean that many of them appear in the same classes for other subjects (they tend to be able boys and therefore in the top mathematics classes).

INDIVIDUALITY AND CONFORMITY

Educationalists enthused about stimulating boys to think. Whether the boys were right or wrong was less important than that they questioned and puzzled. Inevitably boys also questioned about sex, clothes, hairstyle, smoking, music, and so on. Could the school cope with 1500 individualists? All too quickly Scotch found itself reminding boys that their intellectual skills were for the classroom only, and not for their own lives.

School spirit

The debate about individuality and conformity already existed within society at large, and had its own versions at Scotch. Littlejohn said Scotch aimed to 'help a boy to develop and express his personality, always subject … to the rights of others'.[131] The aim, said Peter Craw (*Collegian* Editor 1951), is 'the individual … the cultivation of his peculiar talents'.[132]

But what if a boy's individuality clashes with the school?

Ignoring the school's diversity, some sportsmen began to claim that to support them was synonymous with supporting the school, and that not to support them was disloyalty to the school. From the 1940s, boys who did not attend inter-school sport came under increasing criticism. Neither Selby Smith nor Healey put much value on compelling boys 'to watch games which others play',[133] but the leading boys were more sanguine. In 1953, to redress the small attendances, 'for the first time rolls were called at 4.30' but a stream of red caps went out the gate at 4.31.[134] In 1957 *Satura* bewailed the attendance at the First XI's match against Melbourne Grammar. *Satura* allowed no possibility that the boys who were absent had made a reasonable decision about the use of their time. They were either lazy or did not care about the school. They should attend because teams would do better if supported; because it would be enjoyable; because 'They are playing for you' so you owe them your gratitude; because otherwise the team gets nothing for their efforts; and because you are letting the school down in the eyes of the public.[135]

Please remove bags from shoulder, 1980.

This debate within the school revolves around what is called 'school spirit'. Healey hated the phrase,[136] but it cannot be escaped. The debate is an old one and unlikely to be settled. Ron Stott (1937) says that 'The ra-ra-ra school spirit thing was greatly overdone'.[137] Adrian Jones (1962) felt that 'Scotch made no allowances for those who did not fit the mould'.[138] But Russell Coutie (1932) declares that 'The spirit of Scotch College (not whisky) has been and will remain an important influence in my life as it would with any other boy who attended the school'.[139] Bruce Lyman (1979) describes attending major sporting events like the Head of the River or athletics: 'These were the priestly "high days" in the Scotch temple and not to be missed.'[140] Such enthusiastic tones continue today. Jed Macdonald (1996) 'enjoyed the feeling of belonging that is associated with being a Scotch Collegian. There was an incredible spirit running through the school, a certain camaraderie between students as well as teachers that I don't believe is matched in other schools.'[141]

The School Song may begin with the reassuring statement that 'We are Scotch Collegians all', but it moves at once to prescribe what this shall mean: 'and we rally at the call'. Boys must love the school and defend it, must fight and win. There is not much room here for the variety that exists among a thousand boys. The song mentions only sports, and indeed only team sports. Moreover, if each boy is to find his own way, the school must allow the possibility that some boys won't like Scotch. Yet there is no accepted way in which this diversity can be publicly processed.

In 1951, the centenary year, the *Collegian*'s editorial waxed lyrical about what Scotch had done for its boys and what they owed to it. The writer knew, however, that not all boys thought that way, and so he attempted to deal with those boys in two ways, although not so directly as to acknowledge that theirs was a position worthy of direct engagement. What he said was, first, that the loyal filial feelings were felt by all 'true Scotch Collegians'. A boy who did not love the school was, somehow, not actually a Scotch Collegian at all. Secondly, the editorial said that, 'sooner or later', Old Boys come to realise what they owe to the school. As a debating tactic this postpones indefinitely ever having to listen to anyone with reservations about the school: such a person has yet to reach the correct position. It is a position that many do reach. 'I now have more Scotch spirit than I had at school!', says David Sharpe (1949); 'while at Scotch I lacked much "School spirit". I wanted to be more independent than the school allowed.'[142]

In the 1990s the annual Perelberg Award for exemplary Scotch Spirit precipitated official definitions of that spirit, as embodying, said Donaldson, 'learning, participation, leadership, character, achievement and humility'.[143]

Discipline

From the start, Healey asserted discipline and called on parents to help him do so.[144] His *Guide to Scotch College* ensured parents knew the school rules and regulations. It covered religion, academic and extra-curricular organisation, customary annual events, and had appendices on school work, but its weight was disciplinary: rules in general, rules on attendance and

SCHOOL SPIRIT AT THE GENERAL HOUSE COMMITTEE IN 1982

James Garde said 'at the moment the school spirit is low and that singing school songs cannot enhance the spirit, but perhaps if the school could watch a football match it may be enhanced'. He moved compulsory attendance on Friday at home matches, of which there are only 3 or 4.

Andrew Wilson said forcing people to go to something they don't want to go to won't generate school spirit.

Mr Francis [staff 1962–89, Group Master 1984–89] wondered why Australian Rules alone is to be used to generate school spirit; why not soccer too?

Rob Fuller pointed out that Australian Rules is most popular.

Prakash Pillay replied that if it is so popular if should be able to generate its own support.

Defeated 12 to 10 with 7 abstentions.[145]

absence, rules on school uniform, and on parties and dances.

Healey's impetus at first was to assert control rather than to tackle revolt, for the revolt was still small. The disciplinary views of Scotch's leading boys were conservative. In 1960 *Satura* told boys they were subject to discipline not just at school but everywhere except in their own homes, whether or not they were in uniform.[146] The Public School Head Prefects claimed control over their boys' smoking or drinking even when at private parties.[147] In 1963 Scotch caned a fifth former (Year 11) for smoking away from the school and not in school clothes. Most caning in the early 1960s was for smoking for which four strokes was the usual penalty. This was heavier than Nicholson's caning back in 1936. The aim was both to punish and to change behaviour. A recidivist smoker was condemned to six strokes and 'Told by School Capt. some pertinent factors about School life & we hope was brought around to our way of thinking'.[148]

The prefects' claim to rule boys' lives outside school, and their savage punishment of ordinary social behaviour like smoking, began in the 1960s to be questioned. Doug Eager (Captain 1963) increasingly caned boys for disrespect to school officers.[149] A letter in *Satura*, entitled 'Pres and Queues', mocked school officers' privilege in the tuckshop to go to the head of the line.[150] Charles Ream (1964), an American, told a Prefects' Meeting 'he disagreed with the prefect system anyway'.[151]

A thoughtful Captain like David Mason (1966) believed that the Prefects' Meeting would be accepted if 'it functions with the right intentions and in the right spirit'. The prefects must be dignified, and refrain from sarcasm or jokes in the presence of the offender. Nor should they take 'any delight in the actual infliction of the corporal punishment [which] itself is not the most important thing; it is the interrogation and reprimanding before the punishment that often has the most effect; and, in some cases, it is not necessary to use the cane at all'.[152] Among the prefects, doubts grew. John McCaughey (1964) refused to be party to a caning, and Hamish Ewing (1967), present at one, was horrified. Finlay Macrae (Captain 1967) feels he caned 'rather gingerly'.[153] Andy Mackay's boarding house captain 'was trying to hit my backside but I bet he couldn't hit a par 3 to save himself. I had cuts at the back of my knees and along my back by the time he finished.'[154] The 1968–69 Captains, John Field and Graeme Blanch, caned no-one, but caning resumed in 1970 and 1971.

Caning by staff ended in 1988 with the departure of Campbell Stewart (Year 8 Group Master 1984–88). On the Hill, caning ceased around 1990. Long before, the Prefects' Meetings had expired. There was none in 1973 or 1974, for 'All smokers and the like were dealt with by the School Captain and the prefect(s) concerned'.[155] The last meeting, in 1975, dealt with a culprit who had disobeyed a prefect and thrown a dead pigeon in his face. He 'pleaded guilty … but said he did not aim at the prefect's face. This was thought to be not very important.' He received a Saturday detention.[156]

'An army marches on its stomach'—Napoleon.

Steven Russell demonstrates bush cooking. Cadets, 1982.

In 1964 prefects had caned less harshly (the only boys who received more than three strokes had hitch-hiked or brought firearms or explosives to school), and only 13 cases came before a Prefects' Meeting, compared to 49 in 1963. Instead, alternative punishments were tried. Rowan McIndoe (1964), for example, set an essay. In the following years, however, John 'Mon' Thomson and Mason (both boarders) tightly enforced dress and discipline 'right from the beginning of the year; this makes it far easier to maintain a high standard throughout the year'.[157] The number of charges rose again.

During the 1960s new ideas crept into the thinking even of the prefects. They punished boys for crimes not previously recorded, like setting a poor example to younger boys. They caned boys for having too many detentions. They punished boys for insolence to masters (one boy shouted 'Bill' through a ventilator into a classroom). Previously masters had looked after themselves. In 1967 a boy was caned for 'Using foul and obscene language to St. Kevin's boys over Gardiner's Creek'. He denied his swearing was obscene, and in any case it happened 'under provocation from St. Kevin's boys. Stated that he was trying to stand up for Scotch. Attitude throughout meeting was somewhat impertinent'; 4 strokes.[158]

From 1961 the prefects discerned a new crime: General Attitude,[159] or GA. In Australian law a state of mind is not usually in itself an offence, and though Prefects' Meetings punished boys for GA, they usually spelt out its manifestations in the culprit's dress (about which rules did exist) or apathy in activities like sport or choir, or lack of respect. In this way the prefects addressed both the behaviour and its meaning. In this the prefects walked alongside Healey, whose obsession about apparently petty details can be understood as defending not those details but what they stood for.

Leadership

Scotch saw itself as training leaders.[160] The disappearance of prefects' power to impose caning was part of a wider shift in perceptions of leadership, away from leadership imposed by fear and punishment, and towards a leadership of persuasion and example, leadership modes that Scotch boys might eventually exercise out in industry or commerce or the professions, where caning is often not employed. Prefects learnt to lead, rather than drive. Healey challenged them to develop the 'faculty of persuasion and tact' rather than rely on punishment or the threat of it. 'The exercise of power ... turns out to be far more difficult than is at first realised. The [boy] who really takes this experience seriously [will find] it will stand him in good stead later in life.'[161] This changing concept of leadership shows on the honour boards. Rowing displayed the Stroke of the Crew up to 1993, and thereafter the Captain of Boats (as the Champion had become Captain of Athletics in 1932). That is, it changed from the best player, as it were, to the best leader. Similarly, the Captain of Music is a role model (punctual and neat) and, like a middle manager, he channels student opinion to the Director.[162]

Hair

Hair and clothes in human societies always have meanings in the eyes of wearers and beholders.

Boys' hair has always worried Scotch. In the 1862 list of required articles for boarders, five of the 30 items related to hair: brush and comb bag, small-tooth comb, pocket comb, large comb, hair brush.[163]

Healey was viscerally opposed to long hair. Behind him in the Memorial Hall's stained glass windows the long-haired saints and knights watched in vain. Sir Archibald Glenn, Chairman of Council, wore his hair over his ears because youth's fashions influence adults. The bursar, visiting English Public Schools, found 'long hair, often shoulder-length, is commonplace'.[164] But Healey insisted that hair must not cover ears nor extend below the top of the collar. 'Side-whiskers must not come below the point where the lower part of the ear joins the face, and the whiskers must not be bushy or splayed'[165] nor slope forward.[166] 'Excessively long and excessively short hair are not in keeping with the standards of Scotch College.'[167]

Boys thus faced two challenges: how to keep their hair long, and how to hide it. A boarder like David Brand (1972) took any opportunity to avoid a hair cut. 'With a bit of luck I might escape haircuts tomorrow ... I haven't had a proper haircut ... since just after Easter. I thinned the sides out a bit after May and a kid tidied up the back a bit today but that's all. It makes things much happier for me.'[168] In September, just back from holiday with his parents, 'The first thing that happened at school was that I was kicked out just before assembly and told to go up the street and have a haircut! I couldn't believe it. This was really putting hair before school work especially as I could have had it done that night when the barber came to school.'[169] When his hair grew long again, he concealed it by walking with his head thrust forward (which lifted the hair off the collar), or draped the hair round either side of his head and tucked it under his ears, with a little Brylcream to hold it there.[170] Other boys held their hair above the collar with hairpins (*Satura* had warned that long hair was effeminate![171]) and in the washrooms before Assembly there was great crush before the mirrors as boys arranged their hair.[172]

Even the prefects were not whole-heartedly disapproving, and never charged anyone with long hair, although several boys arraigned for other reasons were told to get their hair cut. It was the masters a boy had to avoid, especially the masters he liked (who would pause and chat). Thus Healey mocked his own hopes that the house Divisions would give each boy a teacher 'who can be regarded as his friend and supporter, who can be relied on to be loyal'.[173] (Similarly, Healey urged masters to 'seize opportunities to sit and gossip with boys when the weather is pleasant and you can perhaps sit on a seat in the grounds'.[174]) Healey's policy on hair risked Scotch's relationship with its boys. Richard Sicree, third-ranking student in 1971, 'Refused to cut hair for prize-giving'.[175] Gordon Matthews (1969) on his last day was brusquely sent out to get his hair cut. He felt so rejected he did not go back for the final ceremony.[176]

Healey's reason for opposing long hair was not one of taste, but that 'this school is expected to uphold certain standards which include moderation as to fashions and fads'.[177]

Uniform

As with hair, uniform became a battle-ground. This was not always so. A gentleman chose his own clothes, and Scotch long took the view that private sartorial taste was none of its business. At some stage the school turned this into an issue. Morrison would not have dreamt of laying down what socks boys could wear, but Healey said they should be 'Prestalene Melange Grey (666) or light grey Terylene and Wool Classweave fabric (quality 8530, colour 407)'.[178] Duncan Reid's (1967) only personal contacts with Healey were the '2 or 3 ... occasions when I was told off about some minor misdemeanour (hair too long, wrong coloured socks!!)'.[179]

Scotch wants its boys to look neat and well-dressed. In enforcing this, it may chain itself to particular fashions. As men's suitcoats swung from double- to single-breasted, Healey enforced the old style, whilst boys argued that single-breasted suits were not only more fashionable, but cheaper. Nowadays the school does not become involved.

Whole items of attire come in and out of approval. Scarves sound unexceptionable, but whilst in the 1950s a cardinal, gold and blue scarf warmed a cyclist leaving home at 7.30 am, under Roff they were banned, and under Donaldson controversial (forbidden but longed for). Braces come

Wearing golf socks— because they had 18 holes in them.[180]

and go in fashion. In the 1950s Miss Kniebusch in the tuckshop would not serve 'boys displaying their braces .... One hot day I inadvertently left my suit coat in the classroom. ... [She]waited until I reached the head of the queue before pointing out the error of my ways.'[181]

Some of the disputes about clothing seem odd. Long-sleeved football sweaters were enforced by Public School Headmasters until the 1990s. The footballers themselves pined for sleeveless sweaters, as worn by professional footballers. (The headmasters' response can thus be seen as part of their broader wish to keep schoolboy sport amateur. It is for this reason that they have set their faces against sporting scholarships although academic and, say, music scholarships are routine.)

On Saturdays, boys in blazers had to wear grey slacks. Flares like Elvis Presley's gave way to a very narrow cut, the drainpipe. Healey therefore imposed a minimum diameter.[182] A letter in *Satura* asked the school to relax its insistence on grey. 'Some very pleasing and subtle shades are now available in men's slacks', whereas 'grey slacks faded from men's fashion about five years ago'.[183] These debates were conducted with a mutual incomprehension. A donnish headmaster in middle age might not notice that what he wore was five years out of fashion, but to a teenage boy five years was his whole lifetime since puberty.

The No. 69 tram in 1983.

Within months of arriving, Healey staked out his position. The uniform was not a matter of clothing, but of pride. 'Pride in correct uniform' would

'inculcate pride in the school'.[184] So the prefects in 1966 caned a boy for 'wearing school uniform improperly in a public place, and thereby lowering the name of the school'.[185] The two worst improprieties were 'Cap off, coat undone'.[186] These were entirely generation-specific, as most generations of Scotch boys have worn neither caps nor buttoned-up coats. The *Collegian*'s first photograph of Littlejohn and its most recent photograph of Council are alike in sporting unbuttoned coats. Yet Healey enforced these matters of mid-twentieth-century taste as though the fate of the school depended on them, insisting that 'open and flapping jackets … are marks of contempt for the school'.[187] (Humans use clothes as social indicators, but the indicators are always changing. For example, suits, despised as conservative in the 1960s, are now somehow radical whilst 'the sports group are straight into the shorts whenever possible and long socks in summer.'[188])

If parents demurred, far from bowing to their right to clothe their own children as they saw fit, Healey set out to pull the parents into line. He told them that what boys wore reflected on the home,[189] and he told them that they embarrassed the school if they had their own opinion or 'individual custom' on disciplinary matters.[190] Meanwhile, Kenneth Pirrie (1950) designed new fashions for the swinging sixties.

In response to Healey's rules, the boys launched a two-pronged attack on the school uniform. They sought to vary the rules, and they sought to create uniform-free zones.

Varying the rules meant adding or subtracting items of clothing. To Healey, removing was anathema but adding was acceptable. He allowed waistcoats, which went on sale at the official outfitters, and are presumably still legal.

The cap was a focus of resentment, for it perched uneasily on long hair. The APS Head Prefects' opinion swung from retaining caps in 1965 to abolishing them in 1968. What persuaded Healey was being with a serious and responsible Captain when they met an archbishop inside his own cathedral and the boy did not lift his cap.[191] Healey realised that the whole etiquette of male hat-wearing was gone. In 1968 he assured Council that caps were obsolescent. (In the 1990s caps returned, though in a new, American shape and in the bright red of the blazer. Their revival derived from a new concern for sun protection. Sport-oriented boys ('jocks') wear them most, so that they are a symbol of one of the school's sub-cultures.)

Ties, Healey ruled, 'must be tied in such a way that the knot is big enough to cover the button at the throat, that is, at least 1¼ inches wide at a point 2 inches below the knot, and that the broader part is over the narrower'.[192] He said this because the fashion for narrow ties led boys to arrange the narrow end on top and tuck the broad end inside their shirt. Ties had to be worn at all times, and the prefects enforced this.

When caps disappeared they took with them the signs of rank or achievement they displayed, and much of this was transferred to new ties designed by Healey with senior staff and boys. Enhancing the status of the tie proved to be a sound decision, for ties revived as an item of men's clothing. Soon there were calls for a tie for each form. Art students designed a Scotch-at-Cowes tie. Under Donaldson, at certain times of year boys may take them off whilst at school. Boys often remove their ties while commuting.

Summer uniform provoked another battle. In 1963 a boy hot from wearing his suit in summer proposed a khaki shirt, shorts and long socks, tie and boater. *Satura* scoffed and the authorities said 'No'.[193] In 1969, 'after two hot summers',[194] Healey conceded an optional summer uniform—shorts and long socks—which Council approved after viewing it 'on selected boys'.[195] Shorts had to be Prestalene Melange or Terylene and Wool Classweave.[196] The new fabrics meant the end of a characteristic smell: 'the dank drying of woollen suits and cadet uniforms in classrooms in the first periods as students dried out after a wet walk to school'.[197] Shorts go in and out of fashion: by 1974, long summer pants were suggested, whilst under Roff, wearing shorts became so popular that some boys wanted to do so all year, and a long squabble broke out on whether summer uniform could be optional or dependent on dates set by the school.

As well as trying to alter the uniform, boys also tried to designate times or places where uniform did not have to be worn. Wearing uniform to dances aroused boys' deep dismay in the 1960s. The GHC found an argument that got below Healey's guard (that final-year boys' suits looked shabby) and persuaded him to allow a non-school conventional dark suit to be worn by day-boy sixth formers (Year 12s) in 1971. In 1972 this extended to fifth formers, and in 1974 to fourth formers, overcoming fears of 'extravagant and exotic dress' and of competition among boys which would be expensive for their parents.[198] By 1976, a similar campaign advocated not just dark suits but also sober-coloured suits. By 1982, wearing casual 'jacket, collar and tie' to the School Dance was carried at the GHC 21 votes to 7. In the 1990s, tastes swung fully in the other direction and boys at the Year 11 and 12 Dinner Dances rejoiced in dinner suits.

A parallel campaign challenged the rule that boarders had to wear school uniform when going out. Healey allowed them to 'wear casual clothes at barbecues or other parties where uniform is obviously unsuitable but they must wear their uniform to and from the venue of the party'.[199] Nowadays there is no such requirement.

So Healey rode out the storm. His rigour was balanced by a conceptual openness that allowed him to abolish caps and to introduce a summer uniform. He even asked Council and the Junior School Mothers' Association if they wanted a school uniform at all. Both said yes.

The tide of student revolt subsided. Roff was as adamant about the uniform as Healey, but had to fight less. Only a few boys protested at dictatorial rules on shoes and hair.[200] Attempts continued to create uniform-free zones, such as excursions and Saturday sport. When Roff set up a

Uniform Committee, complaints were so few that it met only twice in two years. Far from complaining, the student body itself resisted further change. It was the GHC under Roff and Donaldson that blocked wearing casual clothes to school plays, or to examinations, or for boarders 'to go down the street in'.[201] A Plain Clothes Day would let boys wear casual clothes every now and then. It had supporters from 1970 to 1984, but in 1979 not even the GHC could be persuaded. Casual clothes 'would help boys to express their personality in an easy and obvious way', but the GHC thought there were other ways of expressing personality.[202]

The great unwashed

Because Healey did not like their taste, he failed to notice that boys were paying more attention to grooming themselves. An example of this is soap. Before Healey, even sturdy soap-dispensers in a washroom were quickly stolen or damaged.[203] Scotch continued on its smelly way. The sporting change-rooms exuded in winter a 'steamy slightly mouldy smell',[204] 'on a wet dark evening after football training ... a mixture of B.O., and mustiness from boys' wet and damp sports clothes rotting away in their lockers'.[205]

> Grey towels hung on the pegs, malodorous and stiff with mud. Football boots, jock-straps and torn sweaters mouldered in the bottom of lockers from one winter term to the next, and unventilated steam from the showers redistilled the heavy stink of sweat and crept through everything. It seemed strange ... that this foetid place should be called a pavilion when, at morning assembly, we had been asked to envision *The King, all glorious above— pavilioned in splendour.*[206]

Soon after Healey left, the GHC heard calls for better supply of soap in showers and toilets. The Bursar recounted the constant vandalism to soap dispensers and how bars of soap were thrown around and soon vanished. The prefects on duty in the changing rooms to prevent theft protested that the smell was unbearable, and asked for odour eaters there. Boys' increased olfactory sensitivity means that today boys smell of shampoo and soap in a way unknown to their fathers. It is a far cry from when Mrs Littlejohn herself manufactured the boarders' soap as an economy measure.

Boys' new concern for themselves affected what they ate. The Junior School Mothers' Association in 1958 had tuckshop cakes changed from sweet pastries to something plainer and more wholesome. Sweets were limited to plain chocolate, barley sugar, and ice cream. In the Senior School under Healey, boys asked for fresh fruit. Mrs Luckie, the manageress, protested that she sold what experience showed the boys would buy. Fruit 'has been tried in past years, but very little was sold'.[207] By 1975 the complaint was about the price of the fruit. Sweets were withdrawn in 1976 after the GHC doubted they were healthy or good for teeth.

Healey arrived at Scotch 19 years after the end of World War II. The baby-boomers now filled the school. As they had passed through the Junior School six years earlier, Miss Goodenough found 'that aims have not changed so much in her time but that … Today there is more freedom and children are more independent.'[208] Boys wanted a wider range of stimulation, and at Scotch-at-Cowes, for example, Stan Brown in 1969 found that, although they had previously been keen on games and camp life, 'this did not satisfy them now', and the camp needed rethinking, with perhaps more boating and sailing, or 'overnight camping away from site'.[209] Owen addressed the same restlessness among the boarders. Healey's world-view was older. He believed in obedience for its own sake. In 'the enforcement of rules it was important, particularly for sixth form boys [Year 12s], to learn to respect the authority of masters and the School Council'.[210] The content of a rule was ultimately secondary. Principal and boys were at odds.

ASSEMBLY

In 1968 Healey asked 'If daily assembly is irksome and, in its religious element, meaningless, what changes could we make?'[211] In doing so he allowed discussion on perhaps Scotch's oldest tradition. Since Morrison read prayers in No. 1 at Eastern Hill, Scotch's day had begun with an act of consecration of the day's work. At Hawthorn the procedure seemed timeless.

> The bell rings out in the morning air. We all begin to straggle into the Assembly hall. … younger ones in the front, graduating to Matrics in the back. Much noise. Suddenly a chord strikes, loud and clear. Froggy (Mr A. R. Orton) is at the piano. We all stand. There is a hush.
>
> Through the back doors come gowned familiar figures of the staff, led by the Head, Mr C. M. Gilray, known as 'The Blue'. We stand in awe of his presence.
>
> On to the platform they come. …
>
> The Head initiates the doxology: 'Now to the King of Heaven, your cheerful—voices—raise'.
>
> The prefect announces the Reading. It is from Amos, the Blue's favourite book. … He stumbles over the words.
>
> Then Alec Fraser leads in prayer and, in his Scottish accent, exhorts us to be grateful and mindful of 'Our lot being cast in so goodly a heritage'.
>
> A hymn is announced. We grasp the old Presbyterian Hymn Book. Today, the tune is wrong! …. Doesn't fit the words. But we sing them anyway. The Blue glares at our grinning faces! We sit down. A bit noisy. 'Silence' he thunders.
>
> We hear the announcements of the day, some praise, some blame.
>
> We stand. The Blue leaves, staff follows, and we are dismissed for class. … Another day begins at Scotch in the late 1940s.[212]

The hall reeked with 'the fusty, active, aggressive smells of male puberty as we were all jammed together for morning assembly',[213] a 'mix of sweaty bodies from lads who had run from train and tram to make it in time, to the rather antique smell of the Presbyterian Hymn books'.[214]

Into the 1970s boys sat by form, the Year 12s in a block down the middle, the Year 11s down the sides, and 'there was a tribal kind of feel to the school. All the staff were on the stage although Spencer Sayers used to sit with his Year 10 boys up on the balcony'. 'There were some robust assemblies. ... they sang louder' than today,[215] 'the soaring, magnificent sound of 1000 boys singing their hearts out as we smashed through a hymn'.[216]

Younger boys liked Assembly more than older ones.[217] Opinions of Assembly always varied. If one boy in the 1930s found it 'a grand start to the day',[218] another deplored the 'awful hymns',[219] whilst yet another, though he found it 'routinely tedious', conceded that it was 'enlivened when the chosen hymn was "Onward Christian Soldiers" or, better still, "For Those in Peril on the Sea"; rendered by 800 vigorous voices these were inspiring even to an unbeliever'.[220] Healey thought

> that Blake's Jerusalem was an absurd hymn to ask Australian boys to sing, with its declaration that they would not rest until they had 'built Jerusalem in England's green and pleasant land' ... but I was astonished at the verve with which the Scotch boys sang it. However, they assured me that they liked the tune, and as for the words, well—they didn't bother about the meaning.[221]

The Memorial Hall, looking towards the great west window. Dick Shirrefs exhorts musicians at a Foundation Day Concert practice, 1983. At the organ (centre right) stands Chris Latham, Director of Music.

When Roff changed the seating so that boys sat in Houses, the volume of singing was less, as it was the now-dispersed older boys whose force had given the lead to everyone else. In 1979 Gilray House complained that 'members of staff who were obviously not singing did not inspire boys to sing'. Perhaps the keen singers among the staff could sit towards the front of the stage. The truth of the claim was challenged.

> Mr Achurch made it clear that he thought his contribution in assembly was more than significant and the School Captain, who sits immediately in front of Mr Achurch in assembly, verified this claim. ... Mr Achurch also issued a challenge to any boy game enough to try to out-sing him. The net upshot of the suggestion is that Mr Achurch will endeavour to sing even more loudly in assembly than at present.[222]

The Rev. Ken Melville (1948, Assistant Chaplain 1968–75) thought Assembly was 'outdated, boring, unnecessarily repetitious, and irrelevant to many boys', and as a religious experience was invalid because it was compulsory. It 'was a style of service designed for 19th century Scotsmen who were already committed'. Modern boys 'might be more touched by watching a good religious drama'.[223] Crow, the chaplain, discovered that the doxology and Lord's Prayer were meaningless through repetition. Crow worked with the tools he had. He wove the Bible readings, hymns and prayers into themes. He wanted to preserve the religious component in Assembly, but resisted the idea that Assembly was the only religious part of the day, and hoped staff would take up moral issues in any class whenever they arose.[224]

The Vietnam War

In 1965 the Menzies government sent conscript troops to Vietnam. On the dual questions of conscription and warfare, Healey argued that democracies must sometimes have conscription and that Christians in an imperfect world might sometimes resort to force.[225] Within the church he rebutted criticism of cadets.[226] Healey opposed communism but allowed David Paul in history to use Mao Tse-tung's *Little Red Book*, so long as it had a context, and let Darling in the Library display any material on the war so long as it covered both sides.

Among the boys, most were probably of an age or political persuasion not to be troubled. As one boy found, Scotch was 'very much the pillar of conservative society ... The conservatism comes from the aura pervaded from such things as OSCA, the church and the plethora of ex military officers as masters' (1972). But Duncan Reid (1967) grew alarmed at Australia's involvement in Vietnam, found cadets distasteful, and decided in 1966 'that I could never vote Liberal'. Inspired by his fifth-form English master he bought the *Communist Manifesto* from the International Bookshop.[227] Senator Ivor Greenwood (1944) and Arthur Calwell put their opposing views on the war to final-year boys. On the anti-war moratorium marches, Scotch attendees included Keith Macartney (Dux 1921),[228] Colin Christie (staff 1970–), then a young teacher, and some Scotch boys,[229] like Geoffrey Love (1971). Healey said boys could attend with written permission from their parents. David Scott feels 'pretty certain that a few boys went but probably not according to this Healey formula'.[230] Alan Hartman (1970) tried to organise an anti-Vietnam War protest group at the school in 1968, and 'was caned for some other minor disciplinary infraction at about the same time ... the first and only time I was caned in my entire 6 years at Scotch'.[231] He also

tried to organise a chapter of the SDS (Students for a Democratic Society) at Scotch ... on the same lines as any other club .... My proposal was met with total opposition—not surprisingly— since the SDS was ... supposed to be 'subversive'. ... Healey's reaction was to call my parents in

for an interview—or rather my father—since he refused to speak to my mother about the matter. (This really riled my mother who was a staunch feminist ...). Healey explained that there could not be any political activity at the school—and told my father that I was in danger of being seduced by the communists. All this just made him look ridiculous in my eyes—and in the eyes of my family and friends.[232]

As in previous wars, OSCA and the school sent Christmas parcels to serving Old Boys, of whom the school knew of six in 1969, and one in 1971. Bruce Pigott (1963) was killed there as a journalist.

THE HANSEN REPORT

Hair, clothes, Assembly and Vietnam all challenged Healey's ordered world. Other signs of student rebellion surfaced in end-of-year pranks. Ric Birch (1961), director of ceremonies for the Los Angeles, Barcelona and Sydney Olympics, was expelled for his part in painting masters' seats in Assembly with diluted varnish and for using petrol on the quadrangle lawn to spell out 'the four letter word starting with F. ... We all went home tired but happy.' The next morning, grounds staff replaced the dead turf, and the four-letter word stood out in bright green.[233] A 1972 writer described Healey on the lawn using weedkiller.

Major-General Sir Alan Ramsay returns the salute from Cadet-Under-Officer Neil Lucas, while Lieutenant-Colonel Bond watches proudly at the 1964 Remembrance Day Parade. The Military Band wore its scarlet jackets for the first time.

Healey's instinct was to reject rebellion, but as a thoughtful man he tried to understand it. McCaughey agreed with

> taking contemporary 'youth culture' seriously: students frequently, like poets and artists, state imaginatively—in advance of their time, and sometimes in an exaggerated form—positions with which in the end we all have to come to terms. The 'awareness' of the articulate young, as of artists of all sorts, is perhaps more sensitive than that given to the rest of us.[234]

In 1971 Healey commissioned Dr Ian Hansen, who that year published a scholarly study of Scotch and five other independent schools, to 'survey and report on the seriousness or otherwise of the restlessness of the boys in class and out, their relationship with masters, and the problem of Group Behaviour'. Hansen spent time at Scotch teaching and observing. Before he reported, Healey judged that the crisis had passed.

> Nowadays there are bound to be some obvious 'progressives' for whom school is always wrong but … I find that the majority of boys are keen on their work, their sport and their cultural activities, and enjoy them. Dr I. Hansen will be submitting his report to me soon … I fancy that there will be nothing very startling in it but that it will contain some useful suggestions.[235]

Hansen's recommendations were thus undercut in advance as Healey distanced himself from them, and undercut further when Healey soon retired. The report was never published, though Healey announced some of its findings. Some Hansen recommendations nevertheless bore fruit. He advised Scotch to become less formal. Scotch amended its classroom renovation cycle to include removing the raised dais carrying the master's desk, and laying carpet. Slowly, whiteboards replaced blackboards.

Hansen recommended the further informality of using boys' Christian names.[236] Morrison called Monash 'My dear Monash',[237] and later principals usually called staff and boys by their surnames, just as boys called each other by surnames. In 1970, the idea had to be laboured that senior boarders might call new boys by Christian name. Teachers began to use boys' forenames only slowly. A rare teacher like Ken Evans used them in the late 1960s. In the 1960s and 1970s, a few staff occasionally used a boy's forename on his blue card, a quite new development. In 1980, in his final year, all the teachers but David Paul called Hyams by his surname.[238] In 2000, staff use boys' forenames. Boys still often call each other by surname, perhaps especially around Year 9—perhaps part of becoming a man. In the 1970s some boys wanted teachers called by forenames, too,[239] but Scotch has not countenanced this at all, apart from isolated cases, such as Rowton's preference to be called 'Rick' not 'Sir'. In 2000, the *Collegian* prints only staff's initials.

CHALK AND TALK

For most of the twentieth century, even in scientific disciplines, the process of teaching stood back from technology. 'Mostly it was chalk and talk' (1956). Teachers filled blackboards with prose, diagrams, or calculations, which the boys had to copy and which perhaps lodged in the mind as they went through. Blackboards became works of art with coloured chalk and models of good handwriting. Bond's handwriting was beautiful. Creative teachers rotated subjects through different parts of the blackboard. Some parts changed daily, and others remained for some time, protected from other teachers by a polite 'Please leave'. As befitted its central role, the blackboard occupied a whole wall. At the start of the year it was 'as newly washed as the inquisitive twitterers who stared at it'.[240] Alexander Campbell 'got 4 cuts from the Boss for drawing a spider's web on the blackboard'.[241]

From 1977, whiteboards replaced blackboards. So Scotch abandoned 'the smell of chalk dust floating in the air, especially on warm summer days', and the sight of 'The afternoon sun filtering in winter through the old window panes ... and shafting across myriads of beams and motes of chalk dust'.[242]

The student rebelliousness of the 1960s now looks rather tame. Drugs were few, and violence against people or oneself was slight. At the time, it broke new ground, and older teachers had little in their past to help them make sense of it.

HEALEY RESIGNS

Healey was appointed until 1976 when he turned 65. In 1971 he began to tell Council how difficult was his job (and the job of the senior masters).[243] He suggested Council consider 'what sort of headmaster they want to follow me? ... I am now sixty.'[244] This was the meeting where Council declined to set up Adventure Training. Something in Healey's mood sapped Council's preparedness to underwrite a new and expensive scheme. Council thereby contributed to that atmosphere, for Healey's defeat was a public one.

In 1972 Healey organised a Special Council meeting 'to consider the function, purpose and "mores" of the school'. The agenda raised little more than school uniform and pastoral care. Suitable senior masters attended and the proceedings were tape-recorded. This 'was probably the first occasion there has been a philosophical discussion at Council level on the purpose of the school'.[245] The main outcome was Healey's gratitude that it was held.

In 1972 he told Council 'at some length ... the problems that face the Principal [and senior staff] in the daily life of the school'[246]—this after Hansen's report. The world of the 1970s had changed since he had reigned supreme at Sydney Grammar School during the 1950s, and at first at Scotch. Roff judged Healey's reaction to the student rebellion as unique in that I don't think anybody else was able to sustain that to quite the same extent. ... it must have taken an incredible personal toll. I think he was a very kind man masquerading as a martinet. He would rarely present the

human face to those he was dealing with, feeling that it was ... important not to show any weakness .... But ... control was more evident than care. I think that must have been a personal conflict with Colin, because I think he thought that both were important.[247]

Under this burden, or some other, Healey was starting to struggle. It was the struggle of an intelligent and courageous man, so there is something admirable about it.

The end came swiftly. In January 1973 he anticipated remaining until 1976.[248] In March 1973 Glenn told him to take a holiday.[249] In June 1973 he said he would like to retire at the end of 1974.[250] He felt tired, say the staff to whom he talked about this decision. His last report to Council thanked them

for their understanding generosity in this matter of my retirement, which I know is early, and the provision for my pension. I cannot really explain how great a comfort this provision is to my wife and myself—and to those of my children old enough to be anxious for us. I hope that I seem to be remaining vigorous in your service to the last, which is the reason why I wanted to retire before the limit of age was reached.[251]

Scotch talks of the Memorial Hall as its timeless and unchanging epicentre, but the chairs and the tester of Queensland maple over the pulpit are now a surprise.

As Healey shrank, Bond grew. Healey had made him Vice-Principal in 1968 and began to speak of 'Mr Bond and I'.[252] Bond, says Michael Edwards (1970), was

an imposing-looking figure with sandy-coloured hair neatly parted and combed and Brylcreemed, with eyes that could pierce into you relentlessly, with very fierce-looking eyebrows which could frown formidably, and with a magisterial voice that could be doom-laden when he chose it to be, or at other times sardonically humorous in a strangely attractive manner. I think he had quite a good sense of humour, actually. ... He had such an awesome and fearful image in my mind that, because I didn't know what his first name was (just his initial), I couldn't imagine what it might be; it didn't seem possible that such a man could have any kind of ordinary Christian name at all. [Yet] somehow I confided to him something that was troubling me, and found him unexpectedly kind and caring, quite sensitive. I found him a strange paradox.[253]

Bond was personally forceful and in the classroom would brook no challenge. Yet he was reticent, too, in his shy way. As Acting Principal he never sat in the Principal's chair in Assembly and he often signed himself merely as Vice-Principal. After he had been Acting Principal in 1969 Council asked him to keep attending Council meetings (as Vice-Principals have since then). Already powerful, Bond was again Acting Principal in 1975 between Healey and Roff, during which time Bond scrupulously consulted Roff on appointments.

Captains' advice to their successors was not public, so Healey's Captains wrote what they actually thought. To Mason (1966) Healey was my 'most valuable asset. ... an extremely friendly, tolerant and understanding man who was always ready to listen to new ideas, and always willing to do all he could to help you with nasty problems that arose.'[254] 'Ask the Head's advice on all matters', wrote John 'Mon' Thomson (Captain 1965), 'he is a good listener and always willing to try a new idea if it is wise ... he is a terrific bloke, tolerant, friendly and just.'[255]

Colin Healey was a small man and slightly built. If his presence filled a room it was by force of personality, by the fierce sense of command that he exuded. His sport was cross-country running, which gives victory not for strength or height or musculature but for endurance. The cross-country runner is measured against others for a place, of course, but the real struggle is with himself, to keep going through the pain.

16

ROFF

1975–1981

Men make themselves but they do so in circumstances not of their own choosing. Marx's apophthegm catches much about the brief reign of Scotch's seventh principal, Philip Anthony Vere Roff. Roff's drive carried him into office and into conflict with many people, which he accepted as the cost of his vigorous insistence on change. He might have weathered the opposition except that Scotch, for external reasons, now ran into the major institutional crisis of its existence, which toppled the council that appointed him.

Philip Roff, seventh Principal 1975–81.

The selection committee comprised Glenn and McCaughey (Chairman and Deputy-Chairman of Council), Muir (Captain 1942) and Philip (Captain 1947). They sought 'a young Australian with high academic qualifications and one who is progressive and innovative'.[1] Half the 93 applications were American and nine Australian. The committee interviewed five. Roff was a Rhodes Scholar, a rower and Headmaster of Scotch College, Adelaide. He was educated at Launceston Church Grammar School. His first degree was in engineering. Aged 35, he was near half the age of the departing Healey. Council hailed him as 'a man of intellectual capacity, educational experience, strength of conviction, vigour, character and personality'.[2]

Like Littlejohn, Roff arrived at a run. At his first Council meeting, in July 1975, he delivered a sustained critique of the school, and although Council welcomed his youthful confidence after Healey's self-doubt, it cannot have felt entirely comfortable when told that the buildings were 'bare bones and that is all'.[3] Yet Council was happy to indulge him, delighted at having appointed the school's first Australian-born Principal.

Roff was a thoughtful man and when asked a question he would … pause before answering. He seemed to be weighing up what to say (if anything), but the effect could be disconcerting, even intimidating. If the question itself was risky, then the silence swelled in meaning. So when

R. A. I. Grant (staff 1972–79) asked Roff at his first staff meeting what he would like to be called—was it as 'Sir', or 'Headmaster', or 'Mr Roff' or 'Philip'—then Roff sat in a lengthening silence, as people squirmed and wondered whether he was offended, until he at last replied that people might call him whatever they felt comfortable with. They used all four.

SAY WHAT YOU WANT: TIMETABLING

The staff soon saw how Roff worked, at an all-day discussion on timetabling. The issues were period length and rotation. The day had seven periods of four different lengths, from 50 minutes in first period to 35 minutes in seventh period. Bond, when Acting Principal, had suggested a day of six 50-minute periods, to bring uniformity.

Was there an ideal period length? Languages preferred shorter periods more frequently, whilst History for senior classes preferred longer periods, even if less often. There was some support for eight 35-minute periods, not unmanageable if one had a double of 70 minutes. Drama, Art and Physical Education preferred doubles anyhow. Short periods were particularly impractical on Thursdays, when all periods were trimmed so the school could end early for cadets, scouts and social service.

The impact of Thursdays always hit the same subjects, because Scotch taught the same subject each day at the same time. R. H. Clayton thought this was enviable, as it bred a serene predictability and was simple to administer.[4] Yet it was boring for students and staff. Subjects with only one class a week (like Music, Art, Physical Education or Religious Instruction) suffered if stuck on Thursday or at either end of the week, where they lost Mondays to public holidays and Fridays to the looming excitement of the weekend. Bond's proposal allowed a rotating timetable (English in first period on Monday, second period on Tuesday and so on), adding variety to the day. A 'Jumbled timetable' would give even more variety.

Discussions on timetabling always become political, as departmental heads jostle to increase their portion. The timetable in 1975 generated vigorous discussion, mostly critical. Roff, however, said timetabling 'was predominantly a technical process. What was needed was for people to make their bids, to state openly and selfishly what they wanted and for a mock-up to be done.' He was happy to hear issues aired but then wanted a decision. 'Don't start by considering *difficulties*. Start with what you want.'[5] Roff's whole manifesto is encapsulated here perhaps? His crash-through-or-crash approach matched that of the then Prime Minister, Whitlam, who was heading towards a collision.

Soon Scotch adopted a day of six 50-minute periods, on a six-day cycle which kept out of step with the week, thereby rescuing subjects from being moored to one day. The last word on timetabling could go to Ken Evans, who found 'no proven relation between amount a boy learns & time he spends with his teacher'.[6]

NEW LIFE FOR OLD IDEAS: THE GLENN CENTRE

Roff puffed new life into old ideas. The gym was built in 1922 for 700 students, and could accommodate only 20 boys with safety at one time. For decades Selby Smith and Healey earmarked it for improvement or relocation, usually in conjunction with building a new tuckshop. Roff said he thought Physical Education needed more than 'lip service'.[7] He gave priority to a new Physical Education complex, later named the Glenn Centre after Sir Archibald Glenn.

Roff was an eloquent advocate. 'We all have a body and are capable of learning many things physically. It is vital that this aspect of learning is not ignored. Our health has a great bearing on our happiness and in most cases our health is related to our physical condition.'[8] Also, a reasonable standard of fitness renders boys more able to think clearly, work efficiently and be more stable emotionally. To achieve such ends, sport was not enough. It gave boys exercise, and many boys liked it, but 90% gave it up when they left school. 'A good physical education programme (as well as developing physical co-ordination, strength and skills) should promote an interest in lifelong health and exercise.'[9]

The minimum time required to achieve these objectives was three periods per week per boy. That meant accommodating up to five classes (150 boys) at a time. Classes could be held out of doors, of course—most were—but if the weather was inclement 'the only possible activity is to go for a run—again very healthy, but not doing much to achieve the objectives of a Physical Education programme'.[10] Even before the new centre, Roff increased the time devoted to Physical Education. In 1978 'For the first time for many years 5th form [Year 11] students have a significant amount of P.E.'[11]

An under-15 tennis player going for a smash, 1980.

The first steps towards the PE building were taken in what became the routine for all new buildings. The Foundation started a drive focused on the new building, Council chose an architect, Ken Atkins, and a consultant to manage the planning and construction. It was to go on the site of the existing pool and would contain a new covered pool, a large multipurpose area, a remedial gym, squash courts, storage and staff space, and a visitors' changing room. The pool would be heated—'worst thing: Swimming—particularly in the old outdoor pool on bloody cold days'. 'I remember being made to swim under 50° F [10° C] and Dave Boykett just saying it was good for character.'[12]

Construction of the Centre meant Scotch had no pool in the 1981–82 summer. Even without a home pool the swimming team won the Victorian Amateur Swimming Association (VASA) All Schools' Championship for the fifth successive year—then a record. The team trained in Strathcona's and St Catherine's pools. Many boys might have enjoyed this.

The cost was estimated at $1.9 million in July 1976 prices (for Council to specify the month shows how rapid inflation was). It was a huge sum (1100 times annual fees), and 'Members of the Council stressed the dire need to freeze the design details at the point of tender' and to avoid cost overruns.[13] The Foundation was optimistic about raising funds, and Council formally approved the project in March 1977. The National Bank in May 1977 agreed to allow credit of $2.5 million, with the customary condition of church approval.

In May 1977 the schism, as we shall see, brought it all to a stop. The school's ownership fell into doubt and rendered it unable to borrow money.

As well as wanting a Physical Education building, Roff saw a general lack of space. Scotch needed more room to accommodate existing classes

THE GRAND SLAM

In 1978 Scotch won the Grand Slam, carrying off the four major Public School premierships of athletics, cricket, football and rowing. It had only been done once, in 1931 by Melbourne Grammar, before the APS expanded to 11 schools. Peter Thompson (Captain 1978) set it as the school's target in a rousing speech at the year's first Assembly, and urged the school on through a succession of exhilarating triumphs, each of which raised the stakes for the next. As he said at the end: 'There were no easy wins this year. Each time, Scotch won by extremely narrow margins: a few inches, a few runs, a few points. When skills are so closely matched, the difference between victory and defeat is the "will-to-win", drawn from the feeling of each individual, striving not just for himself, but for the team and the school.'[14]

First, the cricketers (R. A. I. Grant coach, Michael Polkinghorne Captain) won the premiership over Brighton Grammar in a series of narrow victories, one of them by only one wicket. (Polkinghorne took 28 wickets including a memorable 8 for 10 against St Kevin's.) Next, the crew (David Boykett coach, Iain Belôt Captain) won the Head of the River by a metre from Melbourne Grammar. The footballers (Mick Eggleston coach, Anthony Wallis Captain) tied with Xavier for the premiership after defeating Melbourne Grammar by two points in the last match of the season, as Peter Sharp took a defensive mark on the goal line at the final siren. The athletes (P. N. 'Jock' Thomson (staff 1962–82) coach, James Sartain Captain) won the Combined Sports by 15.5 points from Haileybury with a sustained team effort, winning only three of the 35 events. Scotch also won the premierships in hockey, rugby and soccer.

Even as the old sports reached this pinnacle, new sports were arriving. Lawn bowls became a House sport in 1976. Billiards, cycling and golf were considered.

adequately, and room to diversify. Growing departments like Art and Biology would soon be 'bursting at the seams'. 'None of the non-Maths Science subjects have a really adequate classroom set-up.'

Roff wanted everything to have a space of its own, whether an academic department or a boys' activity. The maintenance staff developed various departmental teaching areas for Languages, Drama, History, Religion-in-Life and Economics/Accounting/Commerce, but the schism in 1977 brought this to an end. In 1981 'the whole of the Art teaching in the Senior School takes place in two reasonably sized and one small classroom. This limits very much both the range of activities and the number of boys able to take Art at certain levels.'[15]

'The students in the Senior School lack space for indoor recreation, eating and meeting.' On wet days, especially, the boys had nowhere to go; the libraries were overcrowded, and there were no lunchtime club-rooms. After first favouring the Sixth Form Common Room, Roff thought 'a better scheme in the long term may be to arrange such spaces on a House basis'.[16]

FRESH THOUGHTS
Cowes

Roff had an ability to look at things afresh. Cowes impressed him. But whereas Cowes saw itself as a summer holiday camp, he saw that with all-weather accommodation it could be used for class camps at any time of the year and could be a ready inducement for such activities to take place. Accommodation in two blocks would allow both sexes to attend. Council helped the auxiliary financially. The school bought a weatherboard cottage from Kew Cottages and moved it to Cowes. It became the Archers. The bunks were made at the school and installed by fathers, with the cost borne by the school.

In 21 of the 28 weeks from October 1977 to April 1978 the campsite was used by Scotch and other organisations. For instance, Junior School boys went there for Geography lessons. The Cowes auxiliary asked users to contribute towards costs, especially if they left the camp untidy. Steadily the camp shifted out of the parents' hands. It was the school that installed sewerage in 1984.

Planning

Some of Roff's ideas were completely new. In 1975 he advocated a Development Plan for capital works priorities, and persuaded the Executive and Finance Committee to set up a Development Committee. Chaired by a member of Council, Marshall Addison (1934, OSCA President 1966), it included Bib Stillwell (1946), Chairman of the Foundation. Presumably the Foundation's fundraising would be more vigorous for projects about which it was consulted. Addison's prompt report covered likely developments over the next decade, and estimated costs. A Development Committee (Finance) under Lithgow prepared a cash flow estimate for the decade, estimating inflation at 10% to 15% annually.[17] Roff summarised both reports, and combined them with his own outline of the next ten years. Council could thus examine 'the total concept of the ten year plan, the co-ordination of the integral parts of the plan, and the financial implications'.[18]

To make planning routine, Roff twice pushed Council into appointing a permanent Development Committee, chairing it himself the second time, to crystallise plans for Council and monitor their implementation. For the Principal to chair a committee of Council was unprecedented, and an acknowledgement both of Roff's leadership in the school's adoption of planned development and also of his stature in Council's eyes. A Development Officer was appointed to manage planning and also to administer the Foundation, thereby co-ordinating planning and fundraising.

Once again Council appointed two committees, Development (to review and update the plan annually) and Budget (to analyse each year's budget, set priorities and tie the budget to the Development Plan). The two committees had the same convener, Jim Leslie, and almost the same members, useful for co-ordinating their work, but not useful for developing a committee system that involved the whole Council.

Ever since Roff, Council has continued the practice of long-term plans.

Maintenance staff

Roff decided that the maintenance staff's work should be governed by efficiency rather than cost-saving. Previously, the priority had been to save money. Outside contractors were avoided, and renovations had to be juggled with routine maintenance. Work on the School House downstairs bathroom took eight weeks 'because the men are constantly being called away by other demands of the school'. Roff preferred to give large tasks to outsiders even though that cost more. The alternative was to expand the staff, but

Start of the 200 metre race at Family Day, c. 1978.

Roff was reluctant to do so 'because the greater the number of men here the greater the chance of union interference'. Roff valued Scotch's 'good small crew of maintenance people who cover a range of specialties and do work of a good standard. We are a union-free school and the men are quite willing to work outside their specialty when necessary.'[19]

This atmosphere was nurtured by the families on the non-teaching staff over generations—the Hornes, Ravens and Bairds—but changed as the workforce changed. In 1982 Bond reported that 'union representatives penetrated the school and as a result of their pressure our maintenance personnel have been obliged to join unions.'[20] Scotch sounded reluctant, yet it had already produced trade unionists of its own, like James Dunn (1904), a labor MLA and foundation member of the Wonthaggi Coal Miners' Union.

Co-education

Bowden House meeting, 1980. Tony Bladon (left), Scott Bennett and Patricia Holdaway. She had the robust qualities needed when female teachers at Scotch were rare.

Another new direction was co-education. The Geelong church schools adopted it in the 1970s (mainly, it is said, to boost enrolments). Roff's wish to make Scotch co-educational was tempered by his perception that so major a change could be done only slowly.[21] No need to rush into it, he announced; 'There was, after all, a tradition of good single-sex schools'.[22]

The simplest way of becoming co-educational was by merger, and Clyde, a girls' boarding school, its numbers tumbling with the rural economy, asked if Scotch would amalgamate. Scotch declined. This was in early 1975, a few months before Roff took office. Another option was to exchange students. In 1974 boys wanted to go as exchange students to a girls' school in order,

they said, to 'see the way girls study'. Healey agreed.[23] Or Scotch could train girls (Don Macmillan trained some Lauriston athletes at Scotch) or allow girls into its classes. Littlejohn's daughter Jean had studied there, though not enrolled. In 1969 Healey agreed to accommodate in Form V (Year 11) Physics one girl from Stratherne Girls' School which was closing. Roff repeated this when four senior St Catherine's girls studied Mathematics. In 2000 one girl is attending some Year 12 classes.

Roff had more freedom to redress the gender imbalance among staff, and he appointed Patricia Holdaway to teach English, the first female teacher in the Senior School since Woolcock died 20 years before (although Darling had had female library assistants, such as Agnes Gregory). She received superannuation as a matter of course, whereas earlier female staff like Misses Woolcock, Scott and Olive Turner (staff 1920–46) had battled in the 1940s for superannuation on the same footing as the men, £5 a week at age 65.

Holdaway's pupils liked her: 'she treated us as people rather than students only. She was interesting and interested. She provided a much needed female influence in a very much male-dominated school.'[24] Roff told her he saw her as paving the way for becoming a co-educational school. To Council he praised her 'considerable experience' and 'the robust qualities necessary to be a woman member of staff in a largely male common room'.[25] In less than ten years Donaldson could talk in a routine way about attracting men and women to Scotch.[26]

Roff believed

> that the total man (woman) must be educated—his physical, intellectual, social and emotional aspects, his moral outlook—and ... one of the basic problems [is] whether it is better to achieve this by educating the sexes together or by educating them apart. One of the most powerful factors in society is the influence of male on female and female on male. An important task is to consider whether this influence ought to be used in education or deliberately excluded from it as detrimental.[27]

Co-education's effects were academic and social. On the academic side, Roff said, research showed boys did better whilst to girls it made little difference. Socially, boys were less boisterous and rude, and girls less 'catty'. There was a greater tendency for boys and girls to see each other as *people*; and opportunity existed for richer, less superficial discussion of important topics. The employment environment into which the boys would go was becoming one in which both sexes would be present, and the boy would be advantaged who was used to dealing in a day-to-day way with female colleagues. Roff dismissed fears of promiscuity.[28]

Roff's view, finally, was that if Scotch remained a school for boys only, this must not be merely as a rejection of co-education but that Scotch should develop a rationale for itself as a boys' school.[29]

At various staff–student seminars, a few boys spoke in support of co-education and none against, but the numbers were small. Similarly, when Old Boys, reflecting on their own times, mention co-education, it is usually to wish that they had had it,[30] as 'more healthy'[31] and 'more balanced'. 'I would have behaved better.'[32] To be educated at a single-sex school 'actively mis-educated me about life itself'.[33] Mixing with women at university 'was like a breath of fresh air, after being at a single-sex school'.[34] 'I regret not having had the opportunity to meet more girls while at school. For me, the orientation week of first year Uni was an explosion of "catch-up" adolescence that ultimately made me more at ease with girls. … many Scotch boys have [difficulty] in stepping beyond the single-sex domain of school.'[35] *Satura* had canvassed co-education in 1968: boys would be more used to girls and would not, when they saw them, act like lions at feeding time.[36]

Only old Old Boys seem to oppose it: 'probably saved us from much needless stress and confusion' (1947), 'distraction, disturbance to academic careers and the occasional sad pregnancy' (1945).[37] Another man has doubts too:

> I spent 2 years at a co ed. high school before coming to Scotch. I was not a brilliant student & being laughed at by the opposite sex when asking the Teacher what probably seemed a simple question I found very difficult. On the other hand, being given a 'raspberry' by a room full of guys didn't worry me anywhere near as much. As a result I'm sure I learned a lot more [1964].

Co-education vanished with Roff. Council's master plans now routinely reaffirm that Scotch will remain single-sex. Separately, Scotch has developed, as Roff suggested, positive reasons for remaining a boys' school. In 1992, when the issue was alive at Melbourne Grammar, Donaldson cited research findings 'that boys and girls benefit from the separation of social and academic concerns'.[38]

LOCAL CONNECTIONS

In 1981 Roff said that scouts in future would take entrants only in Form III (Year 9). This brought scouts into line with cadets, but another reason for the change was 'that a boy could profit from maintaining an association with his local troop in those early years'.[39] Boys need to feel they belong, and 'the school's society does not exclude participation in all other societies' (as Healey put it).[40] Thus Healey and Roff wrestled with Scotch's tendency to challenge other loyalties.

Many boys valued their local connections. Socially 'Most of my development … came from the home and local areas and local church and other groups which was quite different to the school rigidity'.[41] At the Sunshine Presbyterian Church in 1950 Ian Teague was involved in Sunday School, choir, Presbyterian Fellowship Association, kindergarten teaching and tennis club.[42] Local tennis and church youth groups were where boys interacted with girls.[43] A boy in the 1960s was happily active in a local scout troop but 'the school forced me to leave the local scout group. I was very bitter about this.' Many Junior School parents, in 1983, 'are strongly opposed to Saturday morning competition as … it would prevent their sons playing in their local teams'.[44] Nowacki therefore strengthened weekday sport.

Roff also hoped to link Scotch with its own local community. He wanted to offer facilities to outsiders, which the church also favoured. He wanted the PE Centre open for community use in the evening and at weekends, and contacted the Hawthorn City Council Recreation Officer. By the time the centre opened, however, Roff had gone and Scotch delayed its wider use till it was run in, and then extended it only to the Scotch family—and on a user-pays basis. Few used it. Nowadays, the Language Centre runs language and cookery classes for outsiders. Roff also applied for Scotch to become a centre for adult and further education. He expected to cover all costs. The scheme could not obtain funding because there was already enough adult education in the area. Meanwhile Cameron began evening art and woodwork classes for the Scotch Association.

DEMOCRACY

As Healey had found Selby Smith's legacy autocratic, so Roff found Healey's—

> the lack of involvement of most staff members in the development of policy for the school, the centralization of influence in a few pairs of hands, the tension … between staff and boys. The role of the Principal fitted in with these observations. The Principal was expected to decide policy and issue it. The staff member and boy were expected to obey without question. The way in which policy was changed was through personal influence on the Principal. Precedent was strong, however, and many a staff member has been dissuaded by his colleagues from making a suggestion or querying a policy on the grounds, mainly untested, that he would not get anywhere.

Probably the last Principal who felt at home in such a role expectation, Roff thought, was Littlejohn, whose successors 'have had this institutional pressure brought to bear on them, have resisted it in certain ways and have succumbed in others. This sort of pressure is inevitable in a large fairly conservative institution. Some of the outcomes of these role expectations for Principal, for staff and for boys are not particularly helpful when one is trying to equip boys to face an uncertain world.'[45] Roff hoped to make constructive changes. He widened staff involvement in making policy. Staff sat on committees and attended Council and its Development Committee. Staff helped shape policy on continuing professional education (courses, conferences and study leave), and helped design the Glenn Centre.

Critics felt that after hearing staff views Roff made the decision he intended to make all along. This would certainly have happened at times, as Roff both pushed the staff to become involved and pushed on with his own programme. Short-term and administrative decisions seemed more difficult to delay for consultation, but at the policy level in 1978 Roff set out deliberately to increase staff input. Instead of two staff meetings a term, staff met once a fortnight.

> Mere frequency of meeting was not sufficient however. Members of staff had to become more involved in the meetings. Instead of the Principal constructing the agenda three staff members were elected to form a Staff Business Committee [chaired by Jock Herbert (staff 1978–81)] ... to arrange agenda for staff meetings, to see that actions arising from staff meetings and authorised by the Principal are carried out within a reasonable time.

'Naturally in the early days of the Committee's functioning there is still some cynicism about its likely achievements. ... The overall purpose is to encourage a more open approach in tackling problems.'[46] Herbert, a former Principal of Scotch College Launceston, was Roff's agent in leading a number of change programmes. Younger teachers welcomed these chances to be heard and to develop their grasp of issues facing the school.

Selby Smith had met a Common Room Association scarcely born, and Healey met one yet to look beyond issues of staffing. Roff on his arrival met an active body thinking about educational issues. In 1979, the Association stopped choosing as chairman a teacher about to retire and instead chose men to hold office for some years and thus provide a sustained and purposeful leadership. After Roff, the Staff Business Committee disappeared and the chief influence in staff meetings was again the CRA.

Swimmers, 1976.

Roff continued Healey's Senior Masters' Committee, which also began to be called the Heads of Department meetings. They focused first on the timetable, and would review academic directions.

Roff strengthened the link between staff and Council. He passed staff views on to Council (for instance, on the retention of HSC), which was not something his predecessors had done. The peak of Roff's democratisation of the school's processes was that from June 1981 Council invited staff observers for a trial period of twelve months. The observers were usually Mappin and Stephan Costa (staff 1977–88), representing the Senior School and Junior School Common Rooms, of which they were chairmen.[47] After a year, and with Roff gone, Council ended the experiment. Perhaps Council had enough on its hands with its own internal tensions. Perhaps Council could not see what use it could make of teachers. As intelligent men committed to education, Mappin and Costa were interested in a great deal of Council's business. Instead, Lithgow, Chairman of Council, depicted them as interested only in staff matters like superannuation and study leave.[48]

Character
Responsibility for the boys
Roff thought the boys were not involved enough 'in those aspects of running the school which are within their competence. This is a matter on which it does not pay to move too quickly, but I would hope to build up this involvement over the years.'[49] He invited teachers to ask themselves if staff made too much of the running.[50] Euan Walmsley (staff 1974–86) agreed, and wanted to hear boys' views on their participation in the school.[51] Roff continued Healey's elective element in choosing School Officers. Each Minor House voted to choose which of its sixth-formers (Year 12s) would be candidates—votes were weighted, older boys' votes counting more—then all fifth and sixth formers voted, marking up to ten names. The Principal then took advice from Housemasters and the Form VI Group Master. Those selected were asked to talk it over with their parents. 'Becoming a school prefect … was something I really valued, as part of it involved a poll of the boys' (1982). Once, it was the honour of being chosen by the Head; now there was a shift in authority models, as the democratic idea took root that authority comes from below.

The Staff/Sixth Form Seminar continued in strength; 175 people attended in 1978. Boys felt that staff–student relationships improved after this seminar so from 1978 it was held earlier in the year to let them enjoy the fruits for longer. This left room in September for a new body, the Staff/Fifth Form Seminars. They had the same format and were integrated into the new Form V General Studies Course, where the third-term topic of Freedom and Control was applied by the seminar to Scotch. Both seminars died by Bond's regency in 1982. They were repetitious for staff, who 'had to sit through a whole day of the same complaints and similar observations from students year after year'.[52] Instead, the day became used for staff 'in-servicing' and development.

Roff continued Healey's consultative system of House meetings and the General House Committee. For example, a drama festival proposed at the GHC (and opposed by Harrison, the drama master) was dropped through lack of support at House meetings. Such plebiscites weakened the GHC's chance of being a parliament. Bond pushed this further, when Acting Principal, by wanting nothing at GHC until discussed in Houses.[53]

Roff saw the GHC as encouraging boys' viewpoints. At the lack of interest in the GHC, he proposed even wider discussion by setting up Student

Advisory Councils of Form Captains, but the idea languished. In 1979 one-third of fifth formers (Year 11s) wanted more student participation in school management. The other two-thirds were uninterested in the school politically, preferring that it prepare them for later life, which preparation they equated with success at HSC.

Roff's enthusiasm for the GHC derived from the fact that he did not see himself as training boys in democracy but, more educationally, as developing their creativity, skills and competence. Roff believed there were, basically, two types of achievement, competitive achievement and creative achievement. He feared that the former swamped the latter, whereas both must have a place. Educationally, children needed to develop decision-making capacities, and this was done best 'by requiring people to make decisions which are within their capability'. 'It is quite damaging to require a boy to make a decision which he is incompetent to make. The other day', Roff told the Junior School Mothers' Association,

> I offered a scholarship to a boy and the parents told me in the interview that they were going to get the boy [in Year 6] to make the decision as to whether to accept or not. What possible basis can this boy have for making a decision at that stage other than the knowledge of his present school at its present level? On the other hand there are many decisions which quite young children can reasonably make and for which they can accept the consequences. They ought to be encouraged to do so.

Crucially, Roff 'would not extend decision making with young children and even with most teenagers to include allowing them to opt out for this denies them experience and to take this course would be an abrogation of responsibility on the part of a school'.[54]

Boys' control over their activities varied. They had less control where expertise or authority had to prevail, in music or drama, or in the *Collegian*. But *Satura* had more freedom (Bond censored it line by line but mainly on aesthetic grounds[55]), and many clubs allowed boys initiative. The clubs' pattern varied, sometimes due to historical accident. Chess was run by the boys ('Cheesey' Walker's generous legacy), whilst House debating was largely run by masters (in the spirit of '45' Clayton). At the Scotch-at-Cowes annual general meeting in 1979, a quarter of those present were boys.

In 1980 Herbert found 'the student body is involved, frank and open, and yet friendly and respectful towards each other and the staff … [and] displays a standard of corporate and individual discipline'.[56] 'Campus co-operation', reported one group at the 1979 Staff/Fifth Form seminar, 'is best served by self-government by the pupils of the pupils'.[57] Scotch managed to achieve this quite often in its executive arm, where boys led other boys, and the number of prefects and House prefects expanded. Only when Scotch tried institutions that looked like parliaments did the unfavourable contrast with real democracy become unbridgeable. Roff judged in retrospect: 'I don't think Scotch was very good at looking at things from a student's point of view. It was pretty good at looking at things from the adult point of view.'[58]

Leadership and outdoor activities

Aside from leadership in running the school, Roff also encouraged boys' leadership and decision-making skills whenever possible. Whilst Littlejohn sounds as though he thought leaders were born, Roff thought leaders could be trained. That took place mostly in extra-curricular activities, and Roff expanded these in all directions. He oversaw the introduction of a fourth Thursday activity and the development of a formal outdoor programme.

When Roff left, boys were engaged in camping, hiking, cycling, rockclimbing and abseiling, horse-riding, boating, skiing and snow activities, skin diving and scuba diving.[59]

Within cadets and scouts, new activities emerged. The senior scouts were renamed Venturers in 1974 (the Sea Scouts became Sea Venturers) and expanded into horse-riding. This was helped by the flexibility of the scouting system of badges for skill or knowledge. In 1978 the Venturers camped at Joker's Flat, north of Omeo, concentrating on kayaking and rock-climbing. In 1978 three Sea Venturer groups in the summer vacation went skiing, snorkelling and sailing at Portsea; fencing, shearing and swimming along the Murray; and surfing and bushwalking on King Island. Twenty years later the Sea Scouts' camps in David Boykett's garden at Portsea 'were always tremendous fun. He and Mr Baillieu would take us sailing (with Bob Lachal [staff 1993–]) or surfing at Quarantine. Participation was always voluntary and we all truly appreciated freedom to do as we pleased, whether it be boating or swimming or relaxing on the beach' (1996).

Cadets had long encouraged ancillary skills (radio, first-aid and music),

Leadership. Cadets in 1982. Cadet-Under-Officer Nolan gestures commandingly.

although bush skills were taught less formally, but by 1971 it too moved towards activities similar to the scouts, like canoeing.

A new Thursday activity appeared in 1980, the St John Ambulance Cadet division, 'the first one established at a school anywhere in Australia'. It began through the drive of Vaughan Smith (staff 1976–82), who also ran first-aid courses for staff. The 20 members put their training to use at school sporting fixtures, Victorian Football League (VFL) matches and Cadet Camp. The new activity was at first belittled but grew in stature and in the number of adherents. In 1982–83 numbers doubled, and it acquired a parents' auxiliary, a good indicator that it would survive. At century's end, however, Scotch severed ties with St John and trained boys in first-aid and especially sports first-aid.

Roff also increased the stature and enhanced the organisation of outdoor activities, which became a programme in its own right, separate from scouts and cadets. Bushwalking and hiking, which in the nineteenth century had predated scouts, recovered their independence. It was a change that had been in the air for decades, indicated in the 1950s by the Horse-riding and Ski Clubs. Boydell attended a course in outdoor education in the Welsh mountains in 1978, and in 1980 he and John Francis led an outdoor activities programme for Form II (Year 8). Training on Thursday afternoons culminated in an overnight training camp and a three-day camp. 'There is no doubt that this programme will raise the general level of camping ability before a boy's entry into Cadets.'[60]

Boydell hoped to impart what he himself had gained from such activities: 'A certain reflection on myself that wasn't possible in civilised and comfortable city life. We are put under considerable physical strain, so we have to draw on physical resources that we weren't necessarily aware that we had.'[61]

The House system

Roff continued but reshaped Scotch's internal organisations, the Houses.

The most straightforward reshaping was the creation in 1976 of a sixth House. The existing five Houses comprised four day-boy Houses, each with about 270 boys, and the boarders' House (Littlejohn) with 151 boys. Littlejohn made up for its smallness by its fierce House spirit, but the imbalance limited inter-house sport to the number of teams Littlejohn could field. To allow more boys a game, Roff reduced the average size of day-boy Houses to 210 by creating a new House. Council warmly adopted his suggestion to name it after Selby Smith.

Allocation to Selby Smith House was alphabetical according to a boy's surname. To avoid taking boys already in Houses, Selby Smith also contained many new boys, so 'there was no cohesion, camaraderie etc., etc. and we did our level best to see it self destruct'.[62] As no division of surnames consistently gave five equal groups of day-boys, Scotch soon ceased allocating boys to Houses by surname, except that boys could choose to belong to the same House as their father or some other male relative. In advocating this, the GHC appealed to the concept of Scotch families.[63]

Roff's creation of Selby Smith House was an essentially conservative step, tied to the twin ideas that Houses' main activity was sporting and that boarders should have their own House. More radically, he reshaped Houses' internal structure. Healey's day-house Divisions had gained solidity, each with its own meetings and leading boy. Roff renamed them as Minor Houses. His motives for doing so were the same as Healey's—leadership opportunities and increased pastoral care—but Roff wanted the older boys to provide the care. Healey's Divisions contained boys all of the same age; all a House's sixth formers formed one Division. This was referred to as dividing a House *horizontally*. It reinforced what already happened at school, where 'You simply didn't have anything to do with boys of different forms!'[64] Roff divided Houses *vertically*, so that each Minor House contained boys of all ages. This deliberately replicated what happens in families, where siblings of various ages live together. Minor House activities obliged senior boys to get to know and help younger boys. 'There is nothing quite so alienating to a young man than to be given no responsibility … the Minor House organization will go a long way towards overcoming this.'[65] Roff welcomed evidence of senior boys looking after younger ones, as mutually beneficial. Assembly was held only on Mondays, Wednesdays and Fridays, and Houses met on the other two mornings. The Lawson-MacFarland captain reported that younger boys felt more involved.[66] An Old Boy from the 1960s is struck by the present ease and friendliness between senior and younger boys.

Littlejohn was already divided into the three boarding Houses. Each day House now also split into three Minor Houses. Selby Smith House led the way in 1977, under Tait, and by 1979 the dawdling Monash was last, after a wholesale replacement of its Housemasters.

The Senior School thus had 18 Minor Houses spread among six Major Houses (five day-boy and one boarding). Roff imposed the Minor Houses to develop a 'house system of pastoral care'.[67] Each Minor House had 'about 70 boys covering the range from I to VI form. In turn each of these is divided into three tutor groups of 20–25 boys again spanning I to VI form. Each of the 9 tutor groups in each Day House has a member of staff responsible for it.'[68] 'With boys remaining in the same Minor House for up to six years it is possible for the Housemaster and his tutors to get to know the boys' and the parents.[69] But one Old Boy recalls no sign of a pastoral system; 'the only thing the House system appeared to do was entrench the concept of sporting rivalry and sporting achievement'.[70]

Roff believed that the Minor Houses' smallness made them easier to identify with. Identification would come through the traditional means of competition and leadership. 'Tennis, Swimming, Debating, Cross-Country and Athletics were run on Minor House lines.'[71] Even so, inter-house music

MINOR HOUSES' NAMES

The new Houses' names did not aspire to capture the boys' imagination, for they were all named after teachers, a commodity of which the boys were not in short supply. Roff decided to use staff's names as a political measure to sweeten the new system for resistant

Ross House meeting, 1980, with David Paul (left) and Robert Newton.

older staff. 'I felt it wouldn't make a great deal of difference in the long term what they were called ... The alternative I guess would've been Scottish clans or something like that.'[72] The former long-serving, legendary, teachers now honoured were: Helms, Jamieson and Ross in Gilray; Mullenger, Nankervis and Robert Wilson in Lawson–MacFarland; Bowden, Boyes and Orton in Monash; Adams, Fleming and Wood in Morrison; and Ingram, Shew and Whyte in Selby Smith.

Such names mark a departure from previous House names. Scotch had named Houses after Chairmen of Council (MacFarland and Arthur Robinson, so why not Marshall or Glenn?). Scotch had named a House after its then most famous son, Monash, so why not Cowen, Reid or Latham (respectively, Governor-General, Prime Minister and Chief Justice)?

Other Old Boys had become household names, like the cricketers McDonald or Cowper. Or Gerald Paterson (1913) who won the Wimbledon singles title in 1919 and 1922 and, with Suzanne Lenglen, the mixed doubles title in 1920; a big man, he used 'strength rather than touch to become one of Australia's first power players'; from 1935 he was managing director of Spalding. In football, Bill Morris (1938) won the Brownlow Medal.

Other names might have celebrated Old Boys' contributions to music (Graeme Bell (1930) the Father of Australian Jazz), literature (Walter Turner), or art (Charles Richardson).

Scotch might have held up for boys' emulation its first Rhodes Scholar (Seitz), first premier of Victoria (Shiels), first Olympic medallist (David Boykett), or even its anarchists (John Andrews, 1881) or communists (Esmonde Higgins, Dux 1913, or Ted Laurie, Captain 1930).

Scotch has bred adventurers like Robert Hall (1886), an ornithologist who went to Siberia for specimens and eggs of birds that migrate to Australia in summer. It would probably be going too far to name a House for Jack McLaren, who ran away from

Scotch in 1900 and carried a swag for a year, sailed as a cabin boy on a windjammer, and in 1902–11 'engaged in various romantic occupations in tropical places', exploits recounted in his *Blood on the Deck* (London, 1931).[73]

Finally, Scotch might have commemorated Hugh Syme (1922, later General Manager of the Melbourne *Age*). Australia's most highly decorated sailor in World War II, he won his medals not for blood-heat valour but for defusing mines, a task that required all Scotch's aimed-for spiritual courage and intellectual rigour.[74]

Such men, held up as models, might inspire or surprise. They would show that Scotch boys can have lives of distinction and variety. They would illustrate that any boy may flourish if he lets himself find what he is good at. To celebrate only men who spent their lives inside Scotch, however dutifully, offers boys an example too narrow and unchallenging.

Worse still, the names were meaningless as boys had only a hazy idea of who these old men were. One Old Boy (1989) of Fleming House, when asked what he knew about Fleming, responded only with a hawking sound in the throat. Another (1980) felt that 'We were never going to shout "C'mon Orton!" in an athletics competition, in place of "C'mon Monash!" It inspired no pride, as we all had a pretty good understanding of who Sir John Monash was, but who the hell was Orton?'[75]

competitions were abandoned in 1976 (though revived in 1987 for choral work) and a 1978 suggestion for inter-house drama competitions lapsed. The inter-house domain no longer seemed intrinsic to developing boys' creativity.

Little attempt was made to bind boys to their new Houses by symbolic or psychological means. The tribal, totemic energy of teenage boys received but a brief nod when Roff permitted Minor Houses to fly banners on House Sports Day, as suggested at the GHC by Richard Bangs (1981), to the dismay of 'Jock' Thomson, who foresaw problems if one house tried to capture another's.[76] In 1998, the Junior School's Campbell House designed 'a fantastic new banner', developed a new war cry, and called themselves the Campbell Crocs.[77]

Two contradictory movements now broke out, over whether House spirit belonged to the Major or Minor Houses. It was argued that Minor Houses lessened 'house patriotism' for Major Houses, although Minor Houses in the same Major House never played against each other. In Assembly the new custom that each Minor House sat together provoked a GHC motion to restore sitting in forms. Sitting in Minor Houses was intended to stir House spirit, and link housemasters and boys. But at least sitting by forms had mixed boarders with day-boys. Slowly, however, the new Houses gained a place, and the old, Major Houses faded.

In the Junior School, Wirth ran a separate system. Its four Houses were named after Waller and David Bradshaw (the Junior School's first two Headmasters at Hawthorn), and Healey and Campbell (the recent Principal and Vice-Principal). Laurie MacLennan (staff 1958, 1965–91, Junior School Deputy Headmaster 1980–91) organised them into small Pastoral-Care Groups, soon called Tutor Groups, under a member of staff. They were structured vertically with 15 or 20 boys from Grades 3 to 7. One day per cycle each Pastoral-Care Group met 'before school and again at lunch time for various activities designed to encourage intra-group understanding and co-operation'. Soon, the oldest boys in each group were 'encouraged to perform some duties of responsibility with respect to the younger boys and even lead the discussions in each group as often as possible.'[78]

HAIR, CLOTHES AND IDENTITY

Roff stood less on his dignity than Healey did. Ian Mackenzie (1982), who found his style co-operative rather than authoritarian, ran a cartoon strip in *Satura* called 'The Nice Adventures of Wombat & Budgie' that depicted

Roff as a character called 'Peanut Head'. 'Given the way we chose to portray him, he could have put a stop to it. But he didn't and in not doing so taught me a lot about the responsible use of authority.'[79]

On hair, Roff reaffirmed Healey. In response to hopes that hair could be long if it was neat, he replied that 'The word "neat" can be interpreted in too many different ways by different persons to be useful in this regard'. He maintained Healey's rule, which was 'explicit and not dependent on personal opinion'.[80] Also, a relaxation of hair rules 'would result in a loss of public respect'.[81] Roff also held Healey's line on clothes, but differed from Healey in the way he talked about it. Roff emphasised practical matters: that a uniform enabled a large school to see who belonged to it, and enabled boys to identify with the school. Healey's talk of 'pride' and 'contempt' he replaced with a less fiery, older view: that certain ways of dressing are, simply, 'ungentlemanly'.[82]

Donald Wirth, Junior School Headmaster 1977–85. The figure on the table is a smurf.

In practice Roff continued Healey's opposition to change, even when the attire in question was as gentlemanly as scarves, and he continued Healey's ban on mufti at dances, on the grounds of cost. Otherwise the disputes moved from the uniform worn in class to the uniform worn in sports—tracksuits, sweaters and so on.

Boys whose journey of self-discovery involved adjusting some of their external trappings, like hair or clothes, clashed with a regime which also held these things to be important. Boys whose journey was otherwise found Scotch an easy place for 'being myself'.[83]

GOALS
The Evaluation

Roff's unique act was to submit the school to an outside evaluation. Using a packaged American model, first came self-evaluation, when for nine months Scotch prepared a report on every aspect of the school. Then a visiting committee assessed the report's accuracy. Since Roff chose the committee, he could influence its leanings. The school's response to this process was wary but not deeply so. Staff who opposed it strongly kept their own counsel.

During the schism Roff was determined to prevent Scotch becoming an organisation on hold. He challenged the school to look at the small matters 'often overlooked when major building is taking place', and to look at how effectively the school was running.[84] At a time when the school was under siege, it could focus on itself and what it did well.

It began in 1978, co-ordinated by the ubiquitous Herbert. Throughout the Scotch community people assessed what they were doing and how it might be improved. The visiting committee came for a few days in July 1979 and reported in August, but Council's attention was elsewhere, as the schism reached its climax, and no formal outcome ensued. Like the Hansen Report, its impact was blunted by the departure of the Principal who commissioned it. The new Principal, Donaldson, made no reference to the Evaluation.

In preparing the report, Roff found that whereas Americans focused on management Australians focused on curriculum. This meant outcomes often occurred in the process of writing, as departments pondered what they were doing[85] and developed an understanding of issues confronting a school.

The school defines its goals

As part of incorporating itself in 1980, the school had to state its aims. It helped to have done so already in the Evaluation. McCaughey in *Great Scot* tied the aims that emerged from the Evaluation with the aims the school proposed to have as a corporation.[86]

Various goals had long been preached in many a speech and report, but there was no single, agreed-upon set. Agreement might even be problematic: Ling in 1974 imagined that different groups (parents, boys, teachers or employers) had different expectations.[87]

Roff grasped this thistle. In 1976 he declared that 'the definition of objectives is a very important task for any school which does not want either to drift or to be straining in too many directions at once. It would probably be true to say that the process of defining the objectives is more important than the end result. It is a process which ought to be undertaken quite regularly probably at four or five year intervals.'[88] He appointed a working group to identify areas of staff agreement and disagreement, and to 'take the plunge and … spell out as a group what they think the objectives should be'.[89] This report drew responses from 'individual staff members and groups'. Roff tied it all into a second draft and invited further responses from staff again, from Council, boys in final year, the Scotch Association and the church.

In 1976 he persuaded Council that Scotch should have 'a clear and articulate statement' of its aims.[90] Until then, one of its members believes, 'I don't think Council had a philosophy of education or anything else. They just loved the school and wanted to keep it the way it was and to strengthen it in every possible way'.[91] Anderson (Chairman 1954–59) said Council never examined its views on the aims of the school. 'Not audibly.'[92]

STAFF
Hierarchy

All new principals manage to increase the size of the staff, but few have done so as fast as Roff. In 1976 he told Council of pressures on the staff, and Council at once authorised four additional teachers. In 1977 Council approved an additional two to help General Studies, and in 1978 six more, because enrolments had increased; because Roff showed that Scotch's staffing level was poor compared with other Victorian schools (government and non-government) and with Schools Commission targets; and because Heads of Department needed time to undertake proper planning and supervision within their departments. Thus he added a dozen staff in his first three years. Indulged by Council, the opposition to Roff lay not above him but immediately below.

Roff's drive for change inevitably brought him into conflict with the existing hierarchy: the Vice-Principal, Bond, and the five Group Masters, David Scott, Eggleston, Sayers, Elliott and Stan Brown. Even the youngest was almost a decade older than Roff. They had taught at Scotch for between 17 and 38 years. Two of them were of that older generation of teachers that had no university degree. Three of them were ex-servicemen. As a group, these six men were of a different generation and background from Roff. Moreover, Scotch has always appointed Group Masters from inside the school (apart from Cam Stewart in 1984). This made for a conservative phalanx of leading staff, whose opposition to Roff seemed disloyal to at least one young teacher. Perhaps the exception was the youngest, Eggleston, an Old Boy, successful coach of the First XVIII, and a strong-minded and determined man. As the leading star in his generation of staff, he was a future Vice-Principal.

In contrast to the conservative Group Masters, Roff found support from several disciplinary heads: Holly (English), Tait (Physics), Crook (Chemistry) and Latham (Music, with whose bouncy bonhomie—'Jolly good, jolly good'—Roff had replaced Logie-Smith).

Gravely, there was a gulf at the very top between Roff and his Vice-Principal, Bond. Roff was aged 37 to Bond's 52, and was eager to bring in new ideas. Bond was dismayed at tinkering with the smooth systems he had helped frame over the decades, as Form V Group Master, Acting Senior Latin Master, Officer Commanding the Cadet Unit, and Vice-Principal. He had been at the school his entire professional life. In particular he favoured the Group Master system, up through which he had risen, whereby the school was organised by age group, whereas Roff was more interested in replicating family-like structures, linking boys of different ages. Bond and Healey had worked well together. Between Roff and Bond their differences in age and perspective were not lightened by the spark of friendship. Under Roff, Bond always 'felt that the skids were under him'.[93]

In solving the uneasy working relationship between Principal and Vice-Principal, Scotch had no precedent to guide it. Scotch's Vice-Principals had been long-tenured, and if Roff was the seventh Principal, Bond was only the seventh Vice-Principal. Every other Principal has had a Vice-Principal he could work with, but Roff did not. Littlejohn speedily ejected the aged Robert Morrison. Ingram was due to retire as Gilray arrived; and Bowden was due to retire as Selby Smith arrived. Fleming died in office and Selby Smith, aware of his own itchy feet, appointed Campbell who was due to retire in a few years, thus enabling Healey to appoint his own man. Healey appointed Bond, and when Healey left, Bond was not due to retire for more than ten years.

Of course, Bond might have left before then to become Principal of another school, as many senior Scotch masters do. But he had hesitated

Brian Woolacott discusses Archimedes with Baxter Holly at the House swimming trials in the Swimming Centre, 1981. Both were in Adams House.

(and the most tempting possibility arose when he was Acting Principal and felt he could not consider it) and the time to move passed as he grew older. In any case, the pull of Scotch was strong.

> Several times I was tempted and almost lured away, but it was in 1965, the year of the great march by our senior cadets to Puckapunyal that I solidified my resolve to stay on at Scotch.
>
> I was standing at the top of the long road which leads down into Puckapunyal camp. Quite a few Regulars were also there, slightly sceptical at the thought of mere boys having marched in full battle order, with weapons, rations and sleeping gear, the 100 or so kms up from Melbourne. Everyone knew of their imminent arrival, for Bill Brown's pipers and drummers, who had accompanied them all the way, could be heard coming closer and closer—it was just like an extract from a Kipling yarn—and then quite dramatically over the rise came that company of 100 boys in column of route, three perfectly straight lines, rifles at the slope. Not a single boy had dropped out in those two very long days. The Regs came, saw, and departed in respectful silence. That day I said to myself 'You fellows will do me'.[94]

In 1977 Roff thought the differences between Bond and himself were so wide that he would have to ask Bond to leave. He discussed this at length with Sir Brian Hone, under whom he had taught at Melbourne Grammar, and with Glenn. Glenn's advice was to persevere a bit longer and soon it became too late, for the schism broke out in May 1977 and thereafter the forced departure of a Vice-Principal would have been too controversial when Scotch needed uncomplicated support. So Roff and Bond had to work together as best they could, no doubt at a cost to each of them and to the school.

Roff now replaced or moved sideways some of the next most senior men. He first secured Council's agreement that older staff who relinquished positions of responsibility and suffered a consequent loss of salary would keep their super benefits at a higher scale.

David Scott was Senior Master, Form VI Group Master, and Head of Science. Roff relieved him of all three roles. Eggleston became Senior Master (and Acting Vice-Principal when Bond was overseas), Tait became Form VI Group Master, and Mappin took overall responsibility for Science. (Roff had wanted to appoint the quick and intellectual Mappin to this in 1976 but had bowed to Bond's preference for Scott.[95]) At the same time Roff appointed Bates as Form III Group Master, replacing Elliott. Elliott's wife had died three weeks earlier, so Roff's action was seen as insensitive. Other changes came more routinely as men reached retirement age.

NEW POSITIONS

Roff appointed Scott to the newly created position of Registrar, to handle admissions for both Junior and Senior Schools. This allowed a unified enrolment policy, and relieved the Principal and the Junior School Headmaster of a time-consuming burden about which they had complained since Selby Smith. A Registrar's office was built and the Principal's assistant secretary became the Registrar's secretary. Though seen as demoted, Scott grasped the possibilities of the Registrar's position and built it into an effective operation.

As well as the Registrar, Roff created three other new positions: Marshal, Curriculum Co-ordinator, and Counsellor.

Theft was endemic in 1978 and in the next year Roff appointed a School Marshal, Joe Challoner (staff 1979–82). The Marshal took on policing previously done by teaching staff and prefects. He helped Group Masters check on absent boys by ringing their parents unless they had contacted the school. He ensured boys' lockers had locks, which cut theft dramatically. He became a clearing house for lost property. He supported school officers in their duties. The concept was 'seriously criticised. ... The boys felt that a supervisory official with high profile as a school policeman has been appointed.' Difficulties occurred when prefects attempted to mediate between the marshal and a boy. 'Students feel that the presence of a marshal reinforces a law-and-order mentality' and distanced pupils from teachers and prefects.[96] His role seemed unclear.[97]

Bond asked Challoner to leave in 1982. Norm Bain, appointed in 1984 as Property Officer, is the Marshal's successor. He 'sneaked up on us in camouflage gear and busted us—(like a covert Vietnam operation behind enemy lines!)' (1996). Opinions on him vary from his being 'the School's unsung hero, ... Strict but fair and funny',[98] to disapproval of a non-teacher having disciplinary powers.

The Curriculum Co-ordinator chaired the Heads of Departments and had overall responsibility for curriculum development and in-service education of the teaching staff. As the Victorian Institute of Secondary Education authorised schools to develop their own curricula, Scotch needed someone to back up departments in this, and to co-ordinate their work so as to achieve a desirable curriculum balance, rather than one determined by historical accident. Roff appointed the Scottish-born Colin Black in 1980. He brought coherence and persuaded departments used to acting alone that it was worth co-operating to some extent. He was particularly well-placed because as well as teaching English he was knowledgeable about Mathematics and Science.

After Black became Vice-Principal, the co-ordinating role was seen as important enough to continue. In 1987 Ken Evans became Senior Master, Curriculum, responsible for the Senior School academic programme, followed in 1991 by Dr Roger Slade. In 1989 the Junior School also appointed a Director of Studies, Mrs Betty Fuller (staff 1979–96).

Roff also brought to fruition the appointment of a school Counsellor. Of the 1960s, one boy's keenest regret was the 'lack of counselling support which of course reflected the era'.[99] In the early 1970s, both Healey and the GHC favoured having a counsellor. Healey acknowledged the limits on the chaplain's usefulness, as 'he is regarded as a member of the teaching staff [and] some boys are sceptical of the Christian approach'.[100] 'Independent Counsellor' is how the GHC described the position in 1974.[101] It had to be somebody the boys could relate to, preferably a woman.[102] The matters boys thought boys would discuss with a counsellor were family problems, careers, master–boy relationships and how to approach 'problem' boys.[103] When Tapp caught five boys stealing, he preferred to remedy rather than punish and felt that 'At such times, the availability of a counsellor would be of help, particularly when parental reaction gives little hope of a sensible and satisfactory follow-up being made at home'.[104]

In 1980 David Freeman, a practising psychologist with experience in independent schools, was appointed, as a consultant rather than as a member of staff. He was to provide personal counselling to boys and families, and to support and educate staff in pastoral care. Small groups of housemasters met with him regularly. In the Junior School he impressed Wirth with his expertise in test interpretation and in follow-up parent-interview sessions. He referred boys to specialists when further advice was needed.

As Scotch dipped its toe into mental health, John Cade (1928, grandson of Joseph Cade who enrolled in 1851, grandfather of Tom Cade, Captain in 2000) was becoming famous during the 1970s for his discovery that manic-

Computer Club 1978. Standing (from left): Hugh Leslie, Paul Dodd and Bill Borrie. Seated: Andrew Carra. A notice reads: 'Pictures must NOT be drawn on the line printer'.

depressive disorders could be treated with lithium, which was cheap, naturally occurring and widely available. To ensure its safeness he tested it first on himself. Modestly, in his book, *Mending the Mind* (1979), he discussed the use of lithium treatment without mentioning his own part in it. From the number of human lives directly touched by his work, he is Scotch's greatest Old Boy. Even by 1985, it was reckoned that Cade's discovery had saved the world $US17.5 billion in medical costs.[105] He was a contemporary of Sir Jock Frew (1929), cardiologist, and Sir Benjamin Rank (1928), plastic surgeon, and steps to knight Cade were cut short by his death.[106]

No sooner had Roff left than Bond discontinued the Counsellor position. He preferred to see counselling done by Christians. In appointing someone to teach Religion-In-Life, Bond thought 'it would be useful if any such staff appointed in the future had formal qualifications in counselling'.[107] Since then, counselling has been done by the chaplains, by Heads of Year, by the teachers boys choose to approach and by the school's Educational Support Unit, which became a de facto counselling service, helping boys with 'emotional or behavioural problems' and, implicitly, alcohol problems. Today few staff have counselling qualifications, and counselling is in practice privatised, staff referring boys to known practitioners outside the school.

Alexander Morrison was his own registrar, marshal, curriculum co-ordinator and counsellor. Each of the many things done by the early principals has been devolved on to a specialist. Enrolment, discipline, curriculum and advice all once seemed to be inextricably part of the Principal's work. Littlejohn began to disassemble this by appointing a chaplain in 1916. Roff accelerated and formalised this. In 2000, the people carrying out most of these functions formed a Senior School executive: the Dean of Students, the Dean of Studies, the Heads of the Upper and Middle Schools and the Director of Educational Development and Research, with the Vice-Principal in the chair.

John Cade (1928), left, discoverer of the therapeutic effect of lithium, and a brother. Their father allowed his sons to choose which school they went to.

REFORM AND RESISTANCE

Scotch's appointments lagged slightly behind the beat of Australian society, and so during the swinging sixties it had as Principal the conservative Healey, and then it brought in an enthusiast for change, Roff, as the demand for change receded. There were therefore areas where Roff not so much introduced change as held the line against a return to the starting point. Roff was particularly aware of this in curriculum, where each educational development is championed, opposed, and compromised, as in Hegel's endless cycle of thesis, antithesis, synthesis.

Mathematics, Roff believed,[108] used to be taught everywhere with

> little appeal to the imagination, little in the way of excitement, much emphasis on learning processes—getting the right answer was the prime aim, rarely was there any consideration of whether the technique or process was useful. As one progressed through school and beyond, the philosophy did not change. The mathematics became more difficult, but one was still learning unrelated processes rather than attempting to understand the basic coherence of the subject.

To rectify this, the 'new maths' had appeared after 1959, but it

> became too popular and wholesale replacement of syllabuses took place. This was particularly so in Australia in the late '60's and early '70's. As a nation we have an extraordinary penchant for not allowing people any choice. This is exactly what happened in mathematics. Instead of having a range of math syllabuses co-existing, the original ones were tipped out and a combination of the new ones put in.

Staff had to teach it even if their own understanding was shaky.

By the mid-1970s there were cries to revert to the 'old maths', but to do so would mean teachers had learnt nothing in the previous 15 years. Roff wanted to use the best of both approaches:

> unless a child has a grasp of basic mathematical processes such as addition and multiplication and a few others he is not numerate enough actually to do any mathematics even if his potential understanding of concepts is good. ... These processes and knowledge must form the basis of any mathematical programme in the sense that they must be known. They are not an end in themselves—they are rather the tools of the trade. As a person progresses in his mathematics his repertoire of tools must increase so that at each level he can do the mathematics required.

But they are only a means to an end and, as the 'new maths' suggested, should not be allowed to dominate. (In 2000, Year 7 boys must know their times-tables, and must not use calculators.)

He saw the same pattern in English. Once, the emphasis was on techniques of written expression, on descriptive rather than creative writing. Then the emphasis swung towards encouraging creativity. 'Again things went too far and it was discovered that children were not being properly equipped with the tools of expression—both written and verbal', and that there was a 'significant decline in reading standards'. Again, Roff wanted to rectify but not to return to the 'good old days'. 'Reading skills and skills of spelling and written expression are basic, and must form the foundation of the study of our language, but they're tools not ends in themselves. On this foundation must be built both imaginative and descriptive uses of language.'[109]

In what Scotch taught, Roff saw a bias towards Mathematics and Sciences which meant that some other departments under-valued themselves. 'There are very good reasons for boys to study Maths and Science as long as possible, but every subject must develop some bite.'[110] He saw Healey's achievement in 'the resurgence of English as a welcome beginning of the return of balance'.[111] A sixth former, Andrew Rubins (1976), also deplored the excessive specialisation in Science courses.[112]

Roff was more than a balancer, and wanted to set new directions. 'The study of foreign languages tails off too much in the upper forms. In Australia

ENGLISH

In the 1940s, one English master

knew that there could be no brave new world unless it were full of accurate parsers. He knew that the only possible pleasure to be got from reading Shakespeare (apart from a vague sense of discharging a national duty) came when you spotted the ethic datives, and predicative uses of the gerund. He had been able to parse every word in *Antony and Cleopatra* when he was twelve, and knew that he was a better man for it. It would not be his fault if his pupils could not do the same. They learnt to respect his gerunds, complements, and datives, although they feared and could not understand them. People who pretended to enjoy poetry they simply despised. Grammar at least was disagreeable work. It was moral and hard, like speaking the truth, and no doubt pleasing to God. Literature except as parsing, was bunk.[113]

Rex 'Saucy' Saunders (staff 1971–83) was 'an inspirational teacher' and Colin Black got 'the best out of you by involving you in his enthusiasm for language' (1985).[114]

Scott Crozier (staff 1979–87) 'had an ability to get people who may have had only an average skill in the discipline he was teaching, and enthuse them about the subject and help them to reach greater levels of proficiency' (1981).[115]

In 1996, a boy immersed in the sciences won his best mark in English, whose Head, Watkinson, 'nurtured my love for English that probably would have vanished as I became swamped with studies that took me further and further towards the sciences ... Through his teachings he has given me the potential to, occasionally, leave the bare facts of life, and to stop, and think.'[116]

'English isn't always a hands on class but Laurie [Malcolm, staff 1988–94] made it one especially during the Novels. ... the teachers really included the whole class in a full discussion (and it did remain orderly), and I think this is what stimulated ideas and thought, and ultimately made us remember what we had been taught' (1991).[117]

Peter Robinson (staff 1978–83) 'managed to fascinate a group of adolescents, struggling to determine how much of Diana they could actually see through that summer dress, with the works of Dickens ... Chaucer, Hardy and Steinbeck. At no time were we made to feel like "students," we were more his crew' (1982).[118]

MEN OF INFLUENCE, MEN OF WEIGHT

Roff's brief reign saw Sir Keith Macpherson (1937) become Chairman of the Herald and Weekly Times. Craig Kimberley (1959) set up Just Jeans. 'Bib' Stillwell (1946), racing champion and car-dealer, became president of Gates Learjet Corporation. In Canberra, Whitlam's dismissal was proclaimed on the steps of Parliament House by the Governor-General's secretary, Sir David Smith (1951), earning him the epithet from Whitlam of Kerr's cur.

of all places the study of a foreign language should be virtually mandatory.'[119] The foreign language the school favoured was Italian. The GHC suggested it in the late 1970s, preferring a European language to Indonesian. The school doubted Italian would be economic, though it offered to run a lunchtime conversation course; 30 boys showed interest. Such a Morrisonian system of optional extra subjects was no longer appropriate. Scotch already made many claims on boys' lunchtimes, and to teach a subject out of hours rendered it second-class.

The Junior School Mothers' Association had told Healey as soon as they met him that a language should be taught there. Roff's appointee, Wirth, agreed, because 'the younger the child, the easier it is for him to assimilate new ways, ideas and language, and yet we delay their first language contact until Year Eight'.[120] He and Shugg, head of the Senior School language department, decided on the employment of a teacher of Italian, with adequate primary school training, who could develop a language/social studies course which would teach this language in a cultural setting, initially to Years Three and Four. The children would be encouraged to develop contacts with members of ethnic groups, schools etc. The Italo-Australian Education Foundation has promised help through one of its Directors, Mr Bini, who is a Scotch parent.[121]

Sir Zelman Cowen (Dux 1935), Governor-General of Australia 1977–82.

But the newly incorporated Council baulked at Italian. (Perhaps learning the language of Catholicism was too much for Presbyterian sensibilities.) And though this Council had boldly embarked upon many costly enterprises without referring them to committees, in this case it set up a sub-committee and adopted its recommendation that the Junior School have a multi-cultural awareness programme instead of a language course.[122] This did not address the need for a language; in 1991 the Junior School began teaching German at Grade 4, and Council made no comment, treating the matter as one for the Principal.

Roff held office for six and a half years, which is not even as long as many boys are at Scotch. After the first two years the school could not borrow money, and in the last year and a half Roff publicly lacked the full support of Council. Yet the breadth and depth of what he did is impressive, a testament to his energy and purposefulness. Some of his achievements are now mundane aspects of the school: long-term planning, Council's committee system, female teachers, the Glenn Centre and widened sport and outdoor programmes, pastorally focused small Houses and a curriculum co-ordinator.

17

SCHISM

1977–1980

In 1977 Scotch was reminded that it did not control its own destiny. It found, too, that its increased sense of itself as a community of people counted for nothing in the eyes of the Presbyterian Church, which insisted that Scotch be treated merely as property for the purposes of an Act of Parliament for church union. It was a bitter pill to swallow, and Scotch gagged and spluttered.

The Presbyterian Church appointed the school Council, and the school's property was vested in the Presbyterian Church of Victoria Trusts Corporation upon trust for educational purposes in connection with the Presbyterian Church. On 3 May 1977, as the Presbyterians split in two, the Property Commission of the Presbyterian Church in Australia gave the school to the smaller and more conservative group of Presbyterians that emerged from the split. Scotch had no say in this decision. The school was handed over like a sack of potatoes, Roff told a staff meeting, without consultation.

The Presbyterians split when most of them united with the Methodists and Congregationalists to form the Uniting Church in Australia. The existence of a minority wishing to continue as Presbyterians raised the question of what property they should retain. There was a precise precedent. When the Free Church that founded Scotch united with other Presbyterian churches to form the Presbyterian Church of Victoria in 1859, it brought Scotch in its entirety to the new church, although some parishes remained outside the union. In 1861 this continuing Free Church laid claim to a fourth part of Scotch's property, but was unsuccessful. If applied in the 1970s, that precedent would have given Scotch to the Uniting Church. This majority-takes-all approach had been adopted recently by the Presbyterian Church in Canada. Presbyterians there who had remained outside that union were left with no property at all, which had led to bitterness.

A quite opposite precedent occurred back in Scotland in 1900, when two Presbyterian churches merged. About 30 Free Church ministers, most of them in the Highlands and Islands, refused to accept the union. Popularly known as the 'Wee Frees', they launched a vehement campaign for the church buildings and funds which, they said, those agreeing to the union had forfeited. The dispute provoked violent scenes and at one stage a warship had to be sent to calm tempers in Lewis, but eventually the few Wee Frees obtained the property and funds of two thousand parishes. The judgement of the law being so far from reality, the British government overturned it with legislation in 1905 that gave the disputed property and funds to the majority.[1]

Aware of such precedents, Australian Presbyterians in the 1970s decided that the continuing Presbyterians would own some property. Any parish where one-third of members voted against union would keep its church and manse. Of church property overall, the continuing church would have in Victoria one boys' school and one girls' school. There was no definition of these schools' size or importance. Allocation would be done by a Property Commission, which was not required to explain its decision or to consider submissions. Thus, as Davis McCaughey later mused, whilst the smallest congregation in the outback had a say on whether or not to go into union, enormous institutions with a great weight of tradition and commitment behind them had no say at all.[2] All this was approved by the church and then enacted by all Australian State Parliaments. Scotch later complained about this legislation, but it was drafted with the assistance of the churches, not least from the Presbyterian Church's own Procurator, F. Maxwell Bradshaw (1928).

With these issues settled in advance, the Presbyterian Church then voted for union, by referendum in 1973 and by resolution of the General Assembly on 1 May 1974.

Union took place on 22 June 1977. By then the Property Commission had done its task. It comprised three Presbyterians from those joining the Uniting Church, three continuing Presbyterians, and three non-Presbyterians: two Anglicans, Kenneth Handley, QC, advocate for the archdiocese of Sydney, and Brigadier Ian Hunter from Queensland, and a Baptist, Geoffrey Stevens, a Melbourne chartered accountant. They received little thanks for their work. Hunter and Stevens, wrote David McNicoll in the *Bulletin*, do not 'appear on the surface to have particular qualifications for a task of such magnitude and intricacy'.[3] Glenn later confronted Hunter personally, and ticked off Handley for having 'done a dirty day's work'.[4] Scotch and the Presbyterian Ladies' College (PLC) went to the continuing church by a 5–4 vote.[5] The three Presbyterians and three Uniting Church men voted according to their church. Stevens voted to allocate Scotch to the Uniting Church whilst Handley and Hunter allocated it to the continuing church.[6]

One of the continuing Presbyterians' appointees was Maxwell Bradshaw. His membership was challenged in the courts by the Presbyterians heading towards union, who secured a judgement against him in 1975, but Bradshaw appealed and was reseated. Bill Philip (Captain 1947) described him as 'the greatest advocate for directing Scotch to the Continuing Church'.[7] Mr Justice Northrop, Chairman of PLC's Council and Bradshaw's successor as Procurator, says it was Bradshaw who persuaded the church that legislation was necessary and who shaped the substance of that legislation.[8] McNicoll judged that

Bradshaw 'is, without any doubt, the motivating force in the spirited fight being put up by the Continuers to retain Scotch College and PLC'.[9]

The greatest advocate and motivating force? Perhaps we might pause to look more closely at Bradshaw, who played a central role in Scotch's destiny.

Bradshaw did what all Scotch boys are encouraged to do: he had a goal (to keep Scotch Presbyterian), and he pursued it with all his might and intelligence. He probably planned it in advance, and though some see that as duplicitous, it is how Monash won his battles. When Bradshaw helped draft the 1971 legislation on church union he probably did so with his later moves in mind, although to accuse him of sleight of hand is to forget that this draft had to pass many eyes in church and parliament before it became law. If he laid a successful ambush, that is an option open to the numerically weaker party, and the antipathy he aroused is a measure of his success. He sat on the Property Commission and influenced its decisions. He dared to dream what most people would not have thought possible, what no-one even thought to guard against.

Why did he do all this? In the absence of any explanation by him, we must conjecture. Perhaps some of it was very personal. Back in 1953, at Selby Smith's installation, he felt slighted. Although Session Clerk of the parish in which Scotch lay, he was shuffled into unimportant seats, without enough of a role to warrant putting on his gown, which instead he carried all day on his arm, whilst other men took places of honour.[10] He would also have been dismayed that in Selby Smith Scotch had appointed an Anglican. Perhaps, too, he resented Selby Smith's triumph over his cousin, David Bradshaw, the Junior School's Headmaster, who had also applied for the Principalship?

To these possible personal motives we may add other more public streams of motivation. He cannot have approved when Healey took Scotch's boarders away from his Hawthorn parish church. Bradshaw had little interest in ecumenicalism and was deeply immersed in Presbyterianism. His book on the early Presbyterian churches in Victoria, *Scottish Seceders* (1947), lovingly traced their intricate negotiations and used warlike words such as *tactics, plot, plotting, danger* and *chink in the armour*. When in 1974 the Presbyterian opponents to church union walked out of the church's General Assembly and reconvened elsewhere, Bradshaw among them, to proclaim that they were the true Presbyterian Church of Victoria, he at least knew that he was re-enacting a scene from Presbyterian history. As he said of earlier men doing the same thing in 1859: 'There were ample Presbyterian precedents as to what to do next, and … both sides by their actions next morning indicated more than a passing acquaintance with such information.'[11]

Bradshaw feared that the Old Boys threatened to undermine Presbyterian influence over Scotch. Healey had found among churchmen a feeling that Council contained too many businessmen and too many Old Boys.[12]

Bradshaw—stocky, wealthy, secretive—made a fine target and offered a tempting way of summarising the movement to preserve Scotch in the Presbyterian Church. The continuing Presbyterians, similarly, at times explained the opposition to them as due to McCaughey or Alec Fraser.[13] A dispute of such bitterness will have had deeper causes than a few leading figures. Yet leaders they were.

COUNCIL NAPPING

At the heart of Bradshaw's success lay surprise. When the Property Commission awarded Scotch to the continuing Presbyterian Church in 1977, the school was thunderstruck. Scotch did not expect this outcome and had made no preparation for it. The whole matter of church union scarcely appeared in Council's minutes from 1972 to 1976. Any discussion was mostly about financial technicalities. Most of Scotch's money was held in church trust funds and Homer Fraser threatened Scotch that if it went into union it would lose all its funds.

Council was caught napping. How did it not see what was coming? Council had decided unanimously in 1975 that Scotch should belong to the

Junior School swimming sports in the early 1980s in the outdoor pool paid for by Sir John MacFarland and dug by the boys in the 1920s. The pool was replaced in the 1980s. The building on the upper right was the Science Block and then the Form I and II Block.

Uniting Church and apparently believed that its wish was the reality. A school less proud or less powerful might have taken more care. Council ranked in talent and prestige with most companies' boards of directors, boasting some of Australia's most eminent businessmen. Recent or current members included Sir James Forrest, Senior Partner of Hedderwicks Fookes & Alston and Chairman of the National Bank and Alcoa; Sir Ian McLennan, General Manager and then Chairman of BHP 1950–77 when he became Chairman of ANZ Bank; Sir Ian Clunies-Ross; and Sir Laurence Muir. Tom Scott (1922) was Assistant General Manager of National Mutual, and Jim Fletcher Assistant General Manager of Colonial Life Assurance. McCaughey was Master of Ormond College and later Governor of Victoria. Jim Leslie was Chairman of Mobil and Qantas. Such men were accustomed to exercising power and to having their wishes met. They had influence with the highest in the land. They were likely, though mistaken, to dismiss Bradshaw as an irritating busybody from the local parish.

Healey as soon as he arrived in 1964 had suggested that Scotch become incorporated as a public company.[14] Scotch toyed with this in 1971 to avoid being fought over by the two groups of Presbyterians, but did not pursue it. (Incorporation would not have made Scotch untouchable, but without it Scotch presented less complication.) It was mooted again in 1974, but only as something to be kept 'under review'.[15] Lyne had 'thought for many years that the schools should be independent'.[16]

Council anticipated that church union, far from posing a threat, would usher in greater independence. For when the Presbyterian Church asked its schools what church they wished to be associated with—all chose the Uniting Church—it asked also how the schools would like to see their relationship with the church. Scotch's answer to this intriguing question was that, when the church was ready, Scotch would like to be incorporated under an act of parliament. That the church had asked such a question implied it was amenable. The idea was in the air—and that is why Council did not hurry.

Council was caught unawares also because it 'believed from its contact with the church that there was little likelihood of the school being allocated to the Continuing Church'.[17] Unfortunately for Council, its contacts were chiefly with Presbyterians favouring union, such as McCaughey, first President of the Uniting Church, and Macrae, Moderator in 1974–75. In retrospect, such Presbyterians may have been too closely involved in campaigning for union, or may have wanted union too dearly, to see the possible repercussions on the school. It was an Anglican, Healey, who feared the Property Commission but McCaughey rebuked him: 'It is inconceivable that [the] Commission would act either hastily or without due regard to the history, tradition or wishes of the institution concerned. … I am sorry to say that I think your fears about the negotiators and of the commissioners who are unknown to you, are unworthy.' McCaughey believed also in 'the strength of the Presbyterian tradition of granting freedom to its institutions to do their work in their own way. ... Scotch will continue to enjoy that high degree of freedom in the future'.[18] McCaughey later came to the view that in the face of 'the very clever footwork by Maxwell Bradshaw ... some of us were simply naive and blind in not seeing this. So schools were given no say at all in what their fate would be.'[19]

Council's very freedom blinded it to the fact that legally it had no independence. Legally it was appointed by the church.

Although Council was merely a church committee, it was an ancient and sturdy one, with a broad and often expert membership, sure of its own judgement, and when not sure, confidently seeking the best available advice. (Even in minor matters it went to the top, asking the ABC about tape-recorders and the CSIRO about the boats' landing stage.) Whilst paying respect to the church, Council felt it knew best. For example, in the mid-1960s the church's Board of Investment and Finance declined to approve building a house for the Principal. The Board was firmly visited and it at once retracted, issuing a long explanation of why it now approved what it had previously disapproved, which Council merely 'noted'. All Council wanted was the go-ahead and it was not really interested in the Board's views. Council valued its independence.

Within the church, the perceived extravagance of the Principal's house was attributed to Council's containing too many businessmen and not enough clergy. At the General Assembly in 1966, therefore, an attempt was made to unseat half the Council. Each year half Council retired, and Council itself nominated who should be appointed. When members wished to continue, it nominated them for re-election, and when vacancies arose Council suggested who should fill them. In practice both church and Council had long made this a routine procedure. Each year, the church appointed the people suggested by Council, which had become a self-perpetuating body. In 1966 all the retiring Council members were challenged by a separate slate of candidates who included the Rev. William Loftus. The press reported it as a battle between the 'businessmen on the council and clergy-nominated persons'. Counting the votes took nine hours. The church made the results confidential, imposing 'extraordinary security precautions'. The outcome proved to be that one retiring member was defeated, a clergyman, replaced by another clergyman.[20] Council emerged essentially untouched. It had been made more aware that there were forces opposed to it within the church, but it probably drew no conclusions from this because numerically those forces were only a minority.

As union approached, the Presbyterians debated Scotch's future. The continuing Presbyterians asked for Scotch and PLC. The uniting Presbyterians replied that church property was meant to be divided in proportion to the vote on the union, and that since less than a quarter of Presbyterians opposed union, it followed that the continuing church's schools would be small, and not 'the two best schools'. Instead, the uniting negotiators offered Haileybury and Penleigh. Geelong College was out of consideration because it had become co-educational in 1974. When the continuing church's negotiators rejected Haileybury, the uniting negotiators offered St Leonard's. 'When the Continuing negotiators would not ... accept this offer, the Uniting negotiators made a third offer of two country schools' in Ballarat. When this, too, was rejected the uniting negotiators proposed that no school be allocated. Instead, to meet the conflicting wishes of the continuing church and the schools' councils, both churches should seek to amend the act of parliament to allow both churches representation on all the schools' councils. The continuing church rejected this, preferring control of two schools to a minority influence over nine schools. And so for resolution it went to the Property Commission.[21]

At last Council began to worry. As late as February 1977, no-one challenged Lobban's advice that Council assume Scotch would go to the Uniting Church. Then on 30 March Council held a long discussion and reaffirmed 'in the strongest possible terms' its unanimous wish for Scotch to belong to the Uniting Church.[22] Council and its Chairman made strong submissions to the Property Commission but 'in all cases were not permitted a hearing'.[23]

Since the continuing Presbyterians' claims on Scotch were well-known, Council's complacency led it to misjudge its opponents. Opinions differ on whether the final outcome was good for the school, but for Council it was fatal: in 1980 it ceased to exist as the body it was, and of its eighteen members only five found a place on its successor.

At the same time, too late, Council tried to incorporate the school, but this was immediately overtaken on 3 May by the Property Commission's award of Scotch to the continuing Presbyterian Church. The opportunity for incorporation lay in the past—and in the future.

'Here I stand'

How was Council to respond to the Property Commission's decision? This was not a technical change in ownership that would leave the school to continue running its own affairs. Instead, the school's highest authority received notice of its mortality, for the Property Commission announced that Council could continue in office from 22 June 1977 (the date of union) until 1979. It was doubtful whether the Property Commission had the authority to say any such thing, for its task was to allocate property, not to say how it should be managed. It certainly had no power to bind the Presbyterian Church's control over one of its committees, the Scotch Council, for the next two years.

The Property Commission made another ruling that was equally beyond its powers. It told the Presbyterian Church that its rule that two-thirds of Council be communicant Presbyterians should be amended as soon as possible, because no current member of Council would belong to that church. Why the church would do this was not clear.

These legally dubious rulings of the Property Commission were perhaps an outcome of bargaining among its members, and were presumably intended to soften the blow of its awarding Scotch to the Presbyterian Church. This belated attention to the school's sensibilities clashed with the Commission's insistence that schools were mere property and not human communities entitled to be consulted on their own fate.

The continuing Presbyterian Church's intentions were soon aired. The Moderator, the Right Reverend William Loftus, said Scotch's existing freedoms would not be restricted but then added that 'The only possible changes would be to the "religious and moral tone" of the school'.[24] The next Moderator, the Right Reverend Hector Dunn, said the church would prevent Scotch 'falling into the hands of a pressure group, or of secular humanism'.[25] (Did a rejection of secular humanism imply an end to teaching evolution? This view spread widely at PLC.[26]) Bradshaw spoke of a possible need to eradicate an undesirable element in the school. For the church could do whatever it wanted. Douglas Bain, when Chairman of Council, had assured prospective donors in 1962 that 'while retaining control of the College, the Church has granted it a charter within which the School may function freely'[27] but Bain was wrong. Only convention gave independence to the school, and, eighteen months after Sir John Kerr sacked Whitlam, convention was little protection against the revival of dormant powers.

The Rowing Pool, 1951, among the workmen's wooden sheds that Selby Smith replaced with better accommodation.

Scotch's leaders experienced what had happened as an attack. The minutes of Council and the Foundation used the word 'protect'.[28] One Old Boy supported any step that 'freed' the school from the Continuing Church.[29]

Council's prompt certainty came from earlier encounters with the local Hawthorn parish, which remained Presbyterian and whose leaders, like Bradshaw, were leaders of the continuing church. Council already saw Bradshaw as willing to damage the school by imposing ecclesiastical restrictions. Council believed it had already seen what the continuing church would be like, and wanted none of it.

More personally, many Council members assumed they were the undesirable elements Bradshaw would eradicate. At its most atavistic, therefore, we could see Council's response as that of a group of men (there was one woman) whose power was challenged. To sit on the Council of Scotch College was a mark of distinction in Melbourne society. Many members, moreover, had spent their lives working for Scotch and felt their impending deposition very personally. Many had sat on Council for decades. Council's coherence as a body was fortified by personal connections (Nicholson's son married McCaughey's daughter; John Blanch and Glenn were brothers-in-law). Lithgow and future Council members, Randall, Malcolm Taylor (1943) and John Richards (1950, OSCA President 1979, Chairman of the Victorian gaming and casino authorities 1992–97) lunched regularly. Richards, Lithgow and Randall were successive Presidents of OSCA.

Council was rooted within the Scotch community. Three had been School Captain (Nicholson, Blanch and Philip). One had played in the First XI (Lithgow), and four in the First XVIII (Addison, Blanch, Glenn and Nicholson). In rowing, Nicholson, Blanch and Philip had stroked the First Crew, and Addison, Glenn and Bill Swaney (1937) had rowed in it. As sportsmen, Council inclined less to the finesse of cricket and more to the rough and tumble of football, combined with the intense teamwork and sheer endurance of rowing. Bradshaw had taken on a tough crowd.

One group of Old Boys on Council came there by a ladder requiring years of dedication to Scotch, that of rising up through OSCA. Five had been its President—Addison, Blanch, Nicholson, Philip and Pat Wood (1930, OSCA President 1970)—and Lithgow would become so. This link between Council and OSCA made co-ordination easy.

Opposition to giving Scotch to the continuing Presbyterians was more, however, than a ruling elite's wish to protect its own position. Rather, the award was opposed by almost everyone. Of Scotch's Presbyterians, most joined the Uniting Church and wanted to take their school with them. (Of the 60 000 Presbyterians in Victoria who voted on union, 76 and 80% voted (there were two motions) to join the Uniting Church.) Most Scotch families, moreover, were not Presbyterians. These families preferred the larger group of Presbyterians, as being in what Tony Conabere (1960) called 'the ecumenical main-stream of Protestants'.[30] In a survey in 1965, only 25% of parents put a desire for a church school as their first reason for choosing Scotch.[31] In 1979, OSCA had Irving Saulwick and Associates survey Old Boys and current and future parents on the future control of the school. Opinion across these groups was consistent: 86% favoured incorporation, compared to 9 and 5% for the Continuing and Uniting Churches respectively.[32]

This weight of opinion was irrelevant, because Scotch was merely property; and the response to *that* was a repeated affirmation that Scotch was not chiefly property at all. Indeed it had already changed almost its entire property several times when it relocated, without ceasing to be Scotch. Rather, 'the school is comprised far more of living people than of the real estate'.[33] This view that Scotch is its people now became an accepted way of talking. Thus Bond in 1985 said that what distinguishes Scotch is 'the people who love it'.[34] Donaldson soon paraphrased Bond as saying that 'the difference between this and another school is the people who love it'.[35] The *Collegian* two years later credited Ken Field with this view.[36] Credited to two different sources, it was already an epigram with a life of its own.

Valuable Hawthorn real estate though Scotch was, its wealth was not the issue because none of the parties contemplated selling it. Loftus said 'that ownership means little in material terms. The church has never taken any profit out of the schools but it accepts responsibility for losses.'[37]

This was like a red rag to a bull. That the church accepted responsibility for the school's losses was news to a school that had run deficits as recently as 1956 and 1964. The late 1930s saw deficits of between £800 and £11 000 that doubled the school's debt to £40 000 (1000 times annual fees).[38] That debt, moreover, was to the Presbyterian Church, to which Scotch owed money for much of the century. (In 1902 Scotch owed £12 000, 500 times annual fees). The church charged commercial interest rates. It was a straightforward business arrangement and neither party suggested that the church should support the school or carry its losses. Between 1923 and 1934 Scotch clawed its debt back from £72 000 to £23 000.[39] It did so by paying a steady £3000 per year off the debt, and it raised this money entirely from running at a surplus. That is, the money came from fees. Council's need to earn a surplus put iron into its strict treatment of overdue fees. Many boys helped pay off the debt by leaving Scotch before they wanted to, to make place for someone who could pay, during the 1920s, 1930s and 1940s. In the 1950s the debt rose by £45 000 when the school borrowed to build, and this too was paid off by 1969 out of the annual surplus from fees.

Argument erupted on whether the church had ever actually contributed any money to Scotch. The evidence showed that the school's land in Hawthorn and at its various camps, and all the buildings thereon, were paid for by fees, bequests, appeals and government grants. Since 1954 the church had made no direct grant, and for earlier years the Bursar, Field, 'conducted an exhaustive search of all records pertaining to Scotch held at the Church Office and found no indication of any such grant or gift'.[40] In the 1960s, when the question was not controversial, Healey during fundraising assured an Old Boy that the church provided no resources for the school.[41] Glenn said in 1998 that the church 'never put a penny into the school'.[42] Other than cash, the church had long provided services to the school—secretarial, account-keeping, auditing and insurance costs—but always had the school pay for them, right down to very small sums like postage.

Scotch, by contrast, had long subsidised other parts of the Presbyterian Church. It did so by fee concessions to boys who intended to be Presbyterian ministers, and to the sons of Presbyterian ministers, trainee ministers and medical missionaries. It even gave concessions to ministers' nephews. From 1956 Scotch charged ministers' sons only one-third tuition. In that year ministers' sons received £475 worth of concessions, in 1975 $40 000, and in 1977 $73 000.

Despite this one-way flow of support, the church had somehow acquired a reputation as a benefactor. The Finance Committee recorded in 1939 that 'from the Church, the Old Boys and from parents and friends, the School in the past has received many generous gifts and endowments',[43] and the 1951 *Collegian* proclaimed that 'the Church has always given unstintingly of her support'.[44] Scotch's early borrowing was guaranteed not by the church but by wealthy Presbyterians.

These arguments were anachronistic. Church *members* had certainly been donors. And Scotch had been an integral part of the church, and had relied on its prestige. The fiscal arrangements were a matter of inter-departmental bookkeeping, but now they were recast as arrangements between separate organisations because people were having to choose between church and school and projected that split back onto the past. No-one objected in 1931 when the chaplain, Macneil, thanked God that 'the Church has given to us our school'.[45] It was only when these words were taken literally that the school community felt goaded into pointing out that *it* had given the school to itself.

The same applied to the deeper question of who *owned* the school? Was it not owned by those who had paid for it? Not if they had bought it for someone else. Suddenly, the words the clergy used when new buildings were opened became crucial. When the Longmore Library and Masters' Common Room were opened in 1965, the Moderator accepted the building 'on behalf of the Presbyterian Church'.[46]

Who had paid for the school was a fiery debate but its purpose was to rally support rather than to affect the outcome of the legal proceedings. It became an issue because the Property Commission's ruling dealt with Scotch as property only, and because the case of the Presbyterian Church was that the school was *its* property.

Because from the very start the weight of opinion within the school community was tipped so firmly against Scotch's belonging to the continuing Presbyterian Church, there was no great debate about it, or much attempt by either side to persuade the other. Statements from Glenn, Council and OSCA were intended to keep people informed and, soon, to raise funds for legal expenses. So the arguments above have had to be put together from scraps. Are they sufficient? A thwarted majority and fears of a conservative and interventionist Presbyterian Church—do these explain the fervour with which the school fought the continuing Presbyterian Church?

The struggle over Scotch was so passionate, so bitter, that we may link it also with forces of greater depth. It reflected a struggle between differing views of the world, the one inclusive and the other exclusive. The inclusive view celebrated union with other churches as a reaching out—thus the new church was called not *United*, implying a completed process, but *Uniting*, implying a process that would go on. The exclusive view of the world that insisted on preserving Presbyterianism saw the world in stark terms. In the Last Judgement, Jesus promised to separate people 'as a shepherd separates the sheep from the goats, and he will place the sheep at his right hand, but the goats at the left'. The sheep he will welcome—'Come, O blessed of my Father'—but then he will say to those on the left hand, 'Depart from me, you cursed, into the eternal fire prepared for the devil and his angels' (Matthew xxv.32–41). Such a view requires constant vigilance against groups who risk idolatry (like Freemasons or Catholics; there has been discussion about whether Mozart or the *Ave Maria* can be played at Scotch), and some Presbyterians, although rebuked by the church, in 1998 deplored the didgeridoo as pagan. As Moderator,

> Loftus said there were two different schools of thought in the old Presbyterian church. One school looked at Christianity in the light of today's liberal thought as a social-gospel. They wanted to make a better world this way and opted for the Uniting Church. The other school, to which he belonged, was more evangelical, believing that the world would alter if the people followed the right belief. They opted for the Continuing church.[47]

Perhaps the difference between the uniting and continuing Presbyterians was that the latter embraced the sixteenth-century Reformation but not the eighteenth-century Enlightenment.

The dispute also tapped into a broader liberal/conservative division within Australian society. Loftus described the continuing Presbyterian Church as 'progressive',[48] but it does not now allow women to be clergy or elders. As one Old Boy put it, 'I'm an Anglican, so have no interest to declare here, but … I see the Presbyterian Church is (nowadays) something of an ecclesiastical backwater.'[49]

Although people spoke at the time of the Continuing Presbyterian Church, and it adopted that name itself in the litigation, 'just for the sake of clarity',[50] this was not the official name of those who stood outside the union. They saw themselves as the Presbyterian Church, whereas Presbyterians who joined the union said that at union in 1977 the Presbyterian Church would cease to exist. So there were in the years 1974–77 two bodies of people describing themselves as the Presbyterian Church of Victoria, with rival Moderators. Such schisms are Presbyterian custom. They may well again inconvenience Scotch.

Hard-fought fights
Scotch takes up arms

Council swiftly and firmly met the Property Commission's 'lopsided'[51] award. A two-day Council meeting on 25 May and 8 June 1977 began all the steps that were to dominate its proceedings for the next three years.

First, Council empowered its chairman, Sir Archibald Glenn, to act on its behalf, 'to take all the steps necessary to challenge the legal validity of the Property Commission's decision' and 'to take any other action he considers necessary to protect Scotch College from coming under the jurisdiction of the Continuing Presbyterian Church'.[52] Council took full advantage of Glenn's stature. A knight of the realm, head of ICI, as an Anglican he stood outside the Presbyterian schism. Council's chairman for a decade already, a decisive and energetic leader, he was comfortable in his authority and able to consult and listen, which let Council members enhance his power without feeling that they would be left behind. He had, finally, a fierce love for Scotch. He was a country lad from Sale, and his mother chose Scotch because she liked Littlejohn's Scottish accent, associating it with Scottish commitment to education. He was a prefect in 1929, represented the school in football and rowing, and won a Government Senior Scholarship. At his last Speech Day Sir John Monash presented the prizes, including a mathematics prize for Glenn.

Sir Archibald Glenn (Captain of Boats 1929), Chairman of Council 1963–81. He led the school in the four-year fight with the church from 1977 to 1980 over the ownership of the school.

> When you shake the hand and get the book and you're off, in those couple of seconds Sir John said to me, 'What are you going to do?' I said, 'I haven't made up my mind yet.' He said, 'What are you waiting for, mathematics is the language of the *engineer*.' And those few words made up my mind to study engineering, it changed my whole life, of course. He had those wonderful brown, piercing eyes. He looked at you and said, 'What are you waiting for?' ... That was the only time I ever met him, ... I was only a kid.[53]

Glenn had been looking forward to retiring from Council, but for the next four years he was the school's rock, and stood foursquare whilst the school became a chattel in the courts, while Council's legal authority grew questionable and its continued existence as a body unlikely, and whilst the Principal grew beleaguered and less potent. Glenn grandly dismissed the Property Commission's award of Scotch to the continuing Church as 'purported',[54] and at once took Council's campaign to the OSCA Annual Dinner on 3 June and to the hundreds of parents at the Scotch Association annual general meeting on 6 June. 'On both occasions the applause overwhelmingly indicated an approval of the stand taken by the Council.'[55]

Council crossed its Rubicon at once when it approved expending school funds on legal and other costs, though this might have been illegal.

Scotch now embarked on a succession of legal actions aimed at stopping or invalidating the Property Commission's award. First, Council instructed Blake & Riggall to ask the Commission to explain its decision and to reconsider it. But the Commission unanimously declined to give reasons, or to reopen discussions.

Secondly, Scotch challenged the award's legal validity. The legal aims, outlined by W. R. McKinnon of Blake & Riggall on 8 June 1977, were two-pronged: the Property Commission's decision must either be prevented or reversed.

For prevention there was no time. The transfer of property was to occur almost immediately, on 22 June 1977, the date of church union, and the lawyers could find no grounds to stop the transfer before then.

To reverse the award, over the coming years, the school's legal arguments included assertions:

(1) that the Property Commission did not have the power to make the award;
(2) that even if it had the power, the award was not valid because (among other points) (a) it failed to take into account that the Council was opposed, and 'that the vast majority of boys, teachers, parents and friends of, and donors to, Scotch College were opposed to it being "awarded" to the continuing church'; and (b) that the commission failed to afford Scotch a hearing, and failed to give Scotch opportunity to answer the claims being made about it;[56]
(3) that even if the award was valid it could have no effect because (a) the school was not property within the meaning of the act on church union, and (b) the continuing church could not be the recipient as it was not a legal body.

To challenge the Property Commission's decision, proceedings needed to be brought by a body corporate. Scotch was not incorporated, but OSCA was incorporated in 1934 and at a Special Meeting on 14 June 1977 it unanimously seized the honour of defending the school. It met the costs from its own income and from an appeal, and it was prepared to use its capital, worth $100 000. It was necessary to object to the award before it came into effect, and writs were issued on 21 June.

Although OSCA was officially the plaintiff, the committee organising the legal action was a joint committee of Council and OSCA. It included Glenn, and Council empowered it to make decisions and give instructions. As part of this co-operation, the Council meeting on 29 June 1977 was attended by OSCA's President, 'Ginner' Davidson, its Secretary, Frank

Crawford (1925, OSCA President 1968) and Richards. That Davidson was President at this time was fortuitous in carrying the broad OSCA membership with the steps being undertaken. Vice-Captain in 1927, he was an Old Boy of legend—'the ultimate Old Boy', David Johnston (1968) calls him.[57] His 1927 high jump record stood for 33 years. As a teacher from 1931 to 1973 he had taught Physical Education, so a majority of Old Boys knew him whereas many OSCA presidents are known only to the Association's active members and to Old Boys of their own generation. He had long written the Old Boys' column in the *Collegian*. 'He was', says Sir Laurence Muir (1942), 'always a school boy who treated us as equals ... He was one of the truest and fairest men I have ever met.'[58]

'Ginna' Davidson in 1973. 'He was', says Sir Laurence Muir (Captain 1942), 'always a schoolboy who treated us as equals. He was one of the truest and fairest men I have ever met.'

As well as litigation, a quite different line of attack, discussed at length in Council, was to persuade the Victorian Parliament to amend the existing legislation. It might take less time than litigation, but was less likely to succeed as it had no support from the school's trustees. Even so, 'Council considered that no possibility of having the award reversed should be overlooked' and asked Blake & Riggall to approach the Attorney-General.[59]

A parallel legislative approach involved action by all nine schools that had once belonged to the Presbyterian Church. (These were Scotch, PLC, Haileybury, St Leonard's, Essendon Grammar School, Ballarat & Clarendon College, Hamilton and Alexandra College, Geelong College and Morongo Girls' College.) Council proposed that they jointly seek a uniform independence by act of parliament, linked to both Uniting and Presbyterian Churches. This was an elegant solution to Council's difficulties. Seven of the nine schools were allocated by the Property Commission to the Uniting Church, as they had wished. They might have chosen not to support Scotch or PLC, for fear that if these large schools overturned the settlement then two other schools would be given to the Presbyterian Church. The proposed legislation offered them the prospect of a degree of independence which none could achieve on its own, and so drew them into supporting a new outcome for Scotch and PLC.

Also, the position of all nine schools was still undecided because, in Victoria, the legal status of the continuing church itself was under challenge. This prevented the implementation of all the Property Commission's decisions in Victoria and thus prevented the Uniting Church from taking up its entitlement. (This is why that church was lacklustre in its support for

High jump

The story of high jumping is to leap ever higher while putting the body's centre of gravity ever lower.

Ginner Davidson cleared 6 feet 3½ inches in 1927 with a scissors jump, his body vertical, and a hard landing on the grass athletics track. Next came the Eastern Cut-off which was effectively a type of hurdle. Later, flatter styles of jumping included the Western roll and the Straddle. The break-through came in the 1960s with the Fosbury Flop, where the centre of gravity remained beneath the level of the bar whilst the athlete raised various parts of his body over the bar in sequence. The success-ful competitor is thus much more in command of his body, but the comparison with earlier jumpers is impossible. In 1969 Malcolm Macfarlane set a new Scotch record of 2.058 m (6 feet 10 inches), which remains to this day.

The area they land in has changed from hard ground, to a sandpit, to soft rubber.

In 1927 Ewen Davidson, using the upright scissors style, jumped 6 feet 3½ inches, a record that lasted for decades.

Scotch, as it wanted the whole matter settled quickly.)

Throughout the crisis Scotch acted in concert with PLC. The link with PLC ran deep, because many families with sons at Scotch then had daughters at PLC, and this had bred a habit of co-operation.

Within a month of the Property Commission's award, by the end of June 1977, a three-pronged manoeuvre had been launched. One prong was legal—a writ against the Property Commission through the Attorney-General—and two prongs political—that Parliament should amend the legislation or should incorporate all the former Presbyterian schools. The matter was going to drag on for some time.

At the Scotch College Foundation they faced a different set of problems. As at OSCA, there was a burst of fervour to help Council financially. Foundation members even advocated using Foundation funds to defray Council's legal costs. But the Foundation's particular fears were that donations might dwindle and that the school might lose control of donations received, for they were held by the Presbyterian Trusts Corporation. This was alarming. The Endowment Fund embodied 20 years' work, but the school had no control over it. To keep money raised from now on, Scotch opened a bank account for the Foundation's Building Appeal and the Annual Giving Programme. Scotch also told its solicitor to make sure that Scotch, not the church, received the final settlement of Ross Montgomery's estate bequeathed to the Endowment Fund. Legal action to recover overdue fees was now done in Council's name. In 1979 Struan Robertson (1916) gave the Foundation $600 for an annual award to a piper and a drummer in the Pipe Band. Previously such a donation would have gone to the school and been held by the Trusts Corporation; now donors wished to avoid that.

Foundation Trustees voiced their 'utmost concern of the effect on the future Appeal programme'.[60] Soon, cases arose 'where the Church affiliation has affected Foundation contributions'.[61] Jim Ramsay (1948) made his payments 'conditional upon the Uniting Church having a reasonable voice in the destiny of the School'.[62] Vic Nilsen (1920, OSCA President 1973) warned the Foundation that 'a majority of the contributors to the Foundation, could not support the Foundation knowing the outcome would be to the ultimate benefit of the Continuing Church which is only a minority of the Scotch Family'. Scotch 'should belong to the people who established and maintain it, i.e. Old Boys and Parents, not a minority interest'.[63] To allay such fears, the Foundation toyed with forming a nominee or trustee company (to hold future assets), and with incorporating itself.

Business as usual

Meanwhile within the working life of the school, signs quickly appeared of what would be the two most damaging effects: the paralysis of the building programme and the undermining of the Principal.

The Physical Education centre had just reached the stage where planning was complete and the National Bank had advanced a loan to fund it, subject to approval from the church. The bank understandably now declined to make the loan until ownership was resolved. Scotch deferred the project.

To build without borrowing, in August 1977 Council adopted the architect's suggestion to build the PE Centre in four stages, starting with the east ground floor, including two squash courts. The cost fell within what the Foundation planned to raise, so the school would not need to borrow, but it still needed the approval of the church, as the school's legal owner (albeit under challenge). Any contractor providing services to the school risked not being paid if the church disavowed the contract. The school might have got round this by paying in advance, but that was scarcely prudent. The school duly sought church approval. Two years then elapsed before the Trustees approved. To stall any building, the continuing church did not need to win the litigation, it needed only to raise doubt.

Even had the Presbyterian Trusts Corporation wished to approve, could the Trustees have authorised expenses by a contumacious Council? As it was, refusing permission was a way of putting pressure on the Council to cease its rebellion.

By 1979 other building work was being done. The Music School took over Mackie Hall, which was divided into four rehearsal rooms, whilst upstairs became offices, rehearsal rooms, a workshop and a common room.

Robert Tidd, captain of Soccer in 1992. At Carey his leg was broken by a tackle.

Intense physical coordination: the Scotch 2nd VIII at the Australian Rowing Championships, Penrith, 2000.
Bow: William Hauser, 2. Samuel Troon, 3. Hugh Campbell, 4. Toby Lawrence,
5. Matthew Walpole, 6. Matthew Graham, 7. Robert Westwood; Stroke: Alistair McComus; Cox: George Fordyce.

A boarding house
bedroom, 1998.

Below: Morocco
Olympic Games,
Junior School, 1992.

Simeon Mieszkowski (left) and Andrew Buc at the 1997 Head of the River. The blue jumper is the distinguishing mark of Year 12, and the shorts and red caps are routine summer uniform (a far cry from how boys looked in 1912, see illustration on page 94). The blue motto on Simeon's blazer pocket proclaims him a prefect with half school colours in hockey and athletics.

Rehearsal before the first Tattoo, 1989. As the Unit presents arms, Regimental-Sergeant-Major Ghalib Fareed (left) bellows the order for the Colour Party to march off, led by Cadet-Under-Officer Richard de Visser with sword drawn.

Below: Scotch vs Melbourne Grammar, for the Cordner-Eggleston Cup at the Melbourne Cricket Ground in 1996.

An acoustic consultant said that for the orchestral rehearsal room to have a proper wind response, its volume would need to be increased by 50–60%, which could only be done by raising the ceiling—and the cost. After a second consultant, Council authorised the renovations without increased ceiling heights. By late 1979 Scotch was ready to call for tenders, and sought approval from the Trusts Corporation.

When an organisation suddenly becomes unable to borrow money, effectively losing its credit-worthiness, urgent steps must be taken to forestall any need to borrow. Cash-flow tables had to be scrupulously adhered to, and when Council 'again reiterated' this, the tautology shows their anxiety.[64] Council cut capital expenditure for 1979 (by deleting the planned Prep Year and by staggering work at the Music School over two years), and used the money instead to meet inflation and so hold fees at 1978 levels, no bad thing politically. Outstanding fees drew a newly tough approach, and boys whose fees were a year in arrears were only re-enrolled at the discretion of the Executive and Finance Committee.

A dispute also arose about the length of the Principal's term of appointment. Roff, like his predecessors, was appointed for an initial period of five years, but the church in 1974 decided to stop appointing heads of schools in this way; instead it would stipulate a specific period of notice to terminate, by either party. Scotch believed this applied to current principals,

David Honybun, football, 1979.

but the continuing church said it did not. In June 1977 Council reaffirmed Roff's unlimited tenure, increased his salary and expressed unanimous appreciation for his work. Since at the same time they took the unusual step of praising the principal of another school, Joan Montgomery of PLC, these decisions about Roff seem part of Council's defence of existing Principals against a perceived threat to them from the continuing Presbyterian church.

Next, the position of all staff came under question. In 1979 the Clerk of the Assembly, the Rev. Ted Pearsons, wrote to 'a large majority of the school's academic staff ... concerning the continuity of their appointment'.[65] One of the fears of staff was their security of employment if the church took over (as any employee will fear a change in ownership), and this letter may have exacerbated that.

Council ordered that the school was to go on normally. To a great extent, this policy was successful. Rumours abounded, for instance that 'Roff was going to be replaced by the General Patton of school headmasters ... who would be flying out from Scotland to completely overhaul the running of the school and, like Richard's Crusaders, give us religion whether we liked it or not'.[66] But the schism 'was basically meaningless to us. We were 3rd formers [Year 9s] and becoming interested in girls, so a church wrangle was a bit secondary to the important things in life. ... it did not impinge on our school life at all.'[67] Few boys discussed it.[68]

Incorporation

Council and Roff did well to keep the school's daily work running smoothly, because at the school's upper levels things were awkward. Council's position was irregular, for it had put itself in a limbo in which it answered to neither continuing nor uniting church. Sometimes Council hedged its bets by trying to answer to both, as with seeking approval for building work. Council managed its membership, however, without approval from anyone. The annual nominations from OSCA were for Marshal Addison and Pat Wood, who were duly taken to be reappointed. The annual reappointment of half the Council was ignored, thus effectively extending their terms. When two members died, Council replaced them with Ann Price and John Richards. Price was immediate past President of the Scotch Association, and Richards the next President of OSCA. Their appointment had no legal basis. Council was created and appointed by the General Assembly and it did not have, nor had ever claimed, any power to appoint its own members. This middle-aged or elderly group of respectable people had become revolutionary.

Beside the somewhat dubious position of Council stood OSCA, vigorously expending time and resources on the school's behalf. Its Council acted as co-equal with the school Council. The Chairman of Council and the President of OSCA sent out a joint letter. Key decisions like incorporation were ratified by both Councils, OSCA first. OSCA remained dutifully attentive to Council's wishes, but the son was as tall as the father. OSCA was an independent entity of many decades' organisational continuity, whereas Council ultimately had no organisational existence worth mentioning. If the continuing Presbyterians won they would sack Council and if Council won, Scotch would become incorporated and governed by a council appointed in a quite different way. In court, OSCA was paying, and it was OSCA, not Council, that had to be satisfied with the outcome.

On 5 April 1979, OSCA held a meeting in the Memorial Hall to consider the litigation, drawing 302 Old Boys, parents and friends. For the adherents of the continuing church this was the first time they had encountered in person the overwhelming majority against them, and its anger. It took courage to keep going. One Sunday in the Hawthorn Presbyterian Church Bradshaw and Brian Bayston (1948) 'felt that the Psalm in the service of worship was meant for us, both personally, and as representatives of the Presbyterian Church in the conflict with the rebel Councils of Scotch and PLC':

> Now Israel may say, and that truly,
> If that the Lord had not our cause maintain'd,
> If that the Lord had not our right sustain'd,
> When cruel men against us furiously
> Rose up in wrath, to make of us their prey;
> Then certainly they had devour'd us all.[69]

Meanwhile the lawsuit proceeded 'along its placid way'.[70] Council had no control over this pace but it could speed the proposals of the nine former Presbyterian schools. In May 1978 they agreed that each would seek incorporation under a joint act of parliament. They said:

Hurdlers, 1983.

> The arguments for incorporation are strong. It has been characteristic of the tradition out of which these schools came for the Church to bring into being institutions to meet a need in the community. In their early days such institutions are customarily more closely associated with the Church which founded them. ... But over the years the number of people in the community with experience of the management of educational affairs has grown, and has grown up around particular schools. The processes and techniques of education now require expert knowledge, and ... financial matters and long term planning and policy formulation also require experience and many hours of careful attention on the part of those who accept appointment to the governing bodies of such schools. It is no longer to be expected that either Church bodies such as Synods or Assemblies, or their trustees, could make themselves familiar with the implications of various developments in the schools, except in broad outline. ... We believe that many in the Church would no longer wish to be in a position to interfere in the running of the schools, and will agree that the time has come to give all the schools their appropriate autonomy.[71]

At Scotch, Council would become the body corporate in which the school property was vested. Scotch offered help to the other schools in preparing their constitutions and oversaw drafting the bill, which was submitted for approval to each school council and to the two churches. Each school ascertained the support of its school community in some tangible way, for example by referendums, and then asked the Attorney-General for legislation along the lines of the schools' proposed bill.[72]

Council and OSCA aired incorporation in *Great Scot*, and in a letter to all members of the Scotch Family. Four hundred replies warmly supported incorporation,[73] including one from Healey.[74] 'Fewer than six replies had opposed the move', one berating it as 'autocratic, morally wrong and an insult to the intelligence of us all'.[75]

One reason for the widespread support was that incorporation, although intended as an alternative to control by the Presbyterian Church, did offer that church representation on Council, with an equal number from the Uniting Church. 'A similar arrangement has, with the agreement of both Churches, recently been brought into force at St. Andrew's Hospital, and is working well.'[76] Many people praised this reconciliation as constructive,[77] as common sense—'I cannot think of a more sensible arrangement'[78]— and harmonious. Sir Lenox Hewitt (1933) hailed this 'welcome solution ... glad that Presbyterians, present and past, have come to place their Faith above and beyond their formal division of the Church'.[79]

Others welcomed incorporation for lessening the place of any church. Sir Benjamin Rank (1928) told Glenn that 'For a long time I have thought the Church is over represented on the College council. They provide too little of the wherewithal in underwriting their schools'.[80]

Armed with this strong backing from the great majority of the Scotch Family, Council in late 1979 formally asked the Attorney-General for incorporation. The legislation went before parliament.

The bill's passage was not helped by the Uniting and Presbyterian Churches. Within the Uniting Church were people who would rather not have church schools. Its Moderator took a neutral stance, which weakened the case for the bill and earned him a rebuke from McCaughey. The Presbyterian Church opposed the bill outright. Overriding the views of the Scotch community, in October 1978 the General Assembly unanimously and without debate rejected anything less than Presbyterian ownership of Scotch. The Presbyterians then naturally lobbied Members of Parliament, and in November 1979 succeeded in deferring the bill's passage. Council felt Bradshaw had misrepresented its position to National Party MPs.

The Presbyterian Church was understandably indignant with Council. Council was a church committee and could have no authority of its own. (Letters to this effect were sent to the PLC Council and to its new appointee as Junior School headmistress.) Nor did the church like the school's resources being used against it. The Bursar, Field, was the usual executive officer for most of Council's disobedience and he rallied support among parents. Similarly *Great Scot* was a vehicle for Council's campaign.

Since the entire Council was actively in breach of its duties to the church, the General Assembly in October 1979 sacked them all, and appointed a Commission to run the school. Council in turn repudiated this 'purported termination'.[81] There were thus two bodies each claiming to be the rightful governing body of Scotch College.

The church followed up its decision. Unsuccessful approaches were made to two ministers on Council, Ian Parton (1951) and Donald Macrae, suggesting they resign. Bradshaw and Pearsons (both presumably members of the new Commission) visited Scotch on 5 October. They advised the Principal and the Bursar about the Commission, and the former Council's cessation. 'They indicated that the Principal and the Bursar were to continue the administration of the school.'[82]

Dismissing Council had the reverse effect to that intended by the church, for the Attorney-General, Haddon Storey, QC (1947), decided to regularise the administration of the nine former Presbyterian schools. Pending the outcome of the litigation, he would introduce legislation to appoint interim councils and to indemnify present council members until the coming into operation of this proposed legislation. 'In the meantime Storey advised the Chairmen of the Scotch and P.L.C. Councils to disregard the church's letters of dismissal and continue the administration of the Schools.'[83]

Storey asked the nine schools to make recommendations on the interim councils' composition and powers. The responses were sensible: full administrative powers, except that appointing Principals or making large transactions should be approved beforehand by a commission of three nominated by the Presbyterian Church, the Uniting Church and the

Cricket. 1st XI v Melbourne Grammar School, 1980.

Attorney-General. The councils also suggested that the legislation ratify all their actions since the union.

For the interim council, Council's first advice to the Attorney-General was that he should appoint it, the present Council, as interim council, 'in the interests of continuity'.[84] If not, Council had already, in preparing for incorporation, thought about how to construct a school council. It preferred blocs of members nominated by various constituencies. This managed the competing claims of interest groups. It was reminiscent of what already happened. OSCA had sent representatives for most of the century. Informally, Council gave seats to particular constituencies. There was usually a Reverend Professor from the Theological Hall, a medical man, a parish minister and the minister of Scots Church. In 1959 Council deliberately chose Don Manson (1926) to increase country representation. Another kind of constituency was family-based. Council chose James Aitken in 1940 'in succession to his father', George Aitken.[85] The Marshalls, Addisons and Loves all had a father and son on Council, and Michael Robinson (1955, OSCA President 1989, Foundation President 1993–96), current Chairman, is Sir Arthur Robinson's grandson.

During the 20th century, Council had slowly become less a church committee and more an Old Boy committee. Since 1934 all Chairmen of Council have been Old Boys and usually ex-Presidents of OSCA. The OSCA representatives, though less than one-third of Council, are disproportionately represented among Council's leaders.

Had the schism not occurred in 1977, it is likely that the dominance of OSCA (established in 1913) would have been challenged by the Scotch Association (established in 1972) and the Scotch Foundation (established in 1973), especially because they held the purse strings. Of course, membership of these three organisations overlaps, but they do represent different ways of belonging to the school. As it was, the fight between school and church submerged the differences within the Scotch community and strengthened OSCA's leadership over an alliance of groups that might otherwise have been divergent.

Once the principle of constituencies was adopted, any group could ask that it, too, be a constituency. In 1979 Mappin proposed an elected staff representative on Council, which instead invited staff observers. There were thoughts in the air about the Scotch Association having a representative. If so, it should be a parent who was not an Old Boy.[86] Alexander Millar (1952), a parent and Old Boy, argued for Council members elected by parents—'the "paying customers" on which the School is based'.[87] In 1982 the Foundation closely considered nominating members of Council. A century earlier, great benefactors like Ormond took it for granted that their generosity to the school bought them power in its council. In 1984 the Scotch Association formally discussed nominating members of Council. Council replied 'that while nominations to represent specific areas of the School activities were not desirable, the forwarding to the Chairman of names of suitable people for consideration was to be encouraged'.[88]

In the eventual settlement in 1980, the OSCA representatives are described as representatives of 'the school community'.[89] In fact, parents who are not already Council members and who are neither Old Boys nor Presbyterians are excluded from any choice in the composition of Council, although they clearly have a keen interest in Council's work.

For the *interim* council, Council's advice to the Attorney-General was simpler. It should be the present council or, if not, then it should comprise four representatives from each of the Presbyterian and Uniting Churches, and eight named by the present Council, which was 'already experienced in management of the complicated affairs of a school of this size and history'.[90]

Meanwhile the litigation to upset the Property Commission's award of Scotch to the continuing church was slowly making its way in the Supreme Court as 1979 gave way to 1980. At first Scotch's barristers were Brian Shaw, QC (Dux 1949) and Dr Gavin Griffiths, and later Richard Searby, QC, was brought in to lead them.

SETTLING OUT OF COURT

Litigants settle out of court because either they cannot afford to continue or they fear they might lose. In 1980 the pressure for compromise grew on both sides.

The three-year battle was reported to have cost Scotch and PLC about $700 000. On the Presbyterian side, counsels' fees were well over $100 000. Scotch's Senior Science Laboratories in 1973 cost $728 000, and the Dining Hall in 1970 cost $195 000. Since either side would have appealed if it had lost, the costs threatened to be colossal. Another financial reason Council settled may have been to preserve the school funds held by the church's Trusts Corporation. Glenn feared the church would deny Scotch use of these funds.[91]

The Presbyterians, too, felt a need to settle, for fear that the State Government might yet resolve things by legislation if the case dragged on in the courts.[92] Bradshaw in May 1979, and Pearsons in December, sounded out Lobban and Glenn about joint representation of both churches on Council.[93] The church was hampered, too, by a continuing doubt about the legal existence of the Trusts Corporation. Legislation to resolve this was enacted at the very end of 1979, but the position of the nine former Presbyterian schools was specifically excluded, and the separate bill dealing with the schools, and their interim councils, lapsed.

Neither party welcomed settling. The Presbyterians relished a story that a senior Old Boy dashed his chair to the floor in a rage.

In the second half of 1979 Scotch saw that it might have to settle. Searby gave Council a legal opinion on its status. His view was that the Presbyterian

Church of Victoria joined the Uniting Church. Any remnant was not the Presbyterian Church of Victoria. This reassured Council that it did not derive its authority from the continuing Presbyterian Church, and so was not in rebellion against it. Unfortunately, Council did not derive its authority from anywhere else. When the Presbyterian Church of Victoria ceased to exist, said Searby, so did the authority it delegated to its schools' councils, who therefore had had no authority to manage their schools since 22 June 1977.[94] The legislation granting the councils an interim existence would have rectified this, and its lapse for want of time perhaps meant that the government was hesitating.[95]

With Council's own QC advising it that it had no legal existence, the government of the school ran down. On a day-to-day level, things continued smoothly enough, but at the highest level the school was consumed by the crisis over Scotch's ownership and, as defeat loomed, lost heart in dealing with much else. In the last four months of 1979 the Executive and Finance Committee ceased to meet. This was extraordinary. For half a century it had met every month, apart from January, and become the pivot of the school's government. Now, its minutes, and Council's minutes, reveal an organisation in travail. By 1980 both bodies skipped approving the minutes of their previous meetings, although no single procedure so affirms the continuity of an organisation's existence. When written, the minutes were in disorder and items no longer had a single numerical sequence. Routine business was abandoned, even a Principal's report.

In the negotiations, the key concessions were about incorporation. For the church, to countenance incorporation at all was a big concession. It was made acceptable to them—the key negotiators were Bradshaw, Bayston and Pearsons—by making it 'upon the same trusts as the Trusts Corporation had always held Scotch College, namely for educational purposes in connection with the Presbyterian Church of Victoria. So it was really like exchanging one trustee company for another.'[96]

On the Scotch side, they had to concede to the Presbyterian Church a veto over appointing seven of the 17 Council members. It was 'a concession we had to make'.[97] Glenn hoped that time and the influx of new church people would restore the old understanding that church approval was a formality.

In February 1980 they decided to settle. Searby had already held lengthy discussions with opposing counsel about possible terms. Council thrashed around in its death throes, adopting, rescinding and readopting decisions during one fortnight. In the end, Council abandoned asking for seats for the Uniting Church (which had been little help to Scotch) and dropped its involvement in PLC's settlement. The final shudder came after considering the financial implications of not settling and after input from various lawyers, from OSCA, and from the sub-committee Council had appointed to manage the details of the settlement. It comprised Lithgow, Lobban and Philip. All three were OSCA representatives. As Council's sands ran out, only the OSCA representatives probably had any legitimacy.

On 3 March 1980 Council 'examined in detail' the Articles of Association and Memorandum of Association and 'proposed alterations, deletions and additions'.[98] On 4 March it was done. The Agreement of Settlement, as arranged by lawyers for the Old Scotch Collegians' Association and the Presbyterian Church of Victoria, was ratified.

At the last meeting, with Sir Archibald Glenn in the chair, were Tulloch, Macrae, Parton, Nicholson, Lobban, Lithgow, Wood, Swaney, Philip and Richards. The order in which they are listed (woman, clergy, laymen) echoed Council's formality. McCaughey and Stillwell apologised.

A letter to parents and Old Boys, and a press release, went out over the signatures of the Chairman (Glenn), the President of OSCA (Lithgow) and Roff, this last being a surprise as he had not formally been involved. Apart from voicing optimism for the future, the letter addressed only three points: incorporation, the composition of Council, and the school's religion.

How this settlement worked, we shall trace in the chapters to come.

What made church union such a divisive issue was that it opened up struggles that were otherwise quiescent. All organisations have within them a number of continuing struggles about values and directions, and although at any one time some settlement is reached so that the organisation functions (or is not reached and the organisation tears itself apart), the struggles always continue, or new ones arise, for that is the nature of our talkative and quarrelsome species. In the Presbyterian Church and Scotch, some of the issues were the same. This was encapsulated when Healey took the Presbyterian boarders away from Hawthorn Presbyterian Church and sent them instead to Toorak Presbyterian Church, with the repeated support of all but one of the clergy on Council. Different strands of values could be found within the different parishes of the same church. The effect of church union was to tear two connected strands into separate organisations, so that Scotch was faced with the Hawthorn or Toorak choice on a much larger scale.

To talk of 'Scotch' as a single entity will always be a simplification. Within the school community of the 1970s, different groups with different views about what Scotch was, or could be, or should be, felt enabled or obliged to mobilise to take advantage of the opportunities opened up for them by the structural reorganisation of the school's proprietor. That struggle was always there but was now activated afresh. There always was and will be a variety of views about what is best for Scotch (about what Scotch means) and the holders of those views will always endeavour to see their own views prevail. Usually that is a slow process, occurring over time. Occasionally an event accelerates things. When a new Principal arrives, for example, many old possibilities wilt and new directions are marked out, although after a few years they cease to be new and become the (new) norm. When the church amalgamates (as it did in 1859) or splits (as it did in 1974), then that too generates a period of rapid change, until the many possibilities are reduced to the fewer outcomes that actually emerge. When a large tree is felled there are for a time many saplings competing to establish themselves, until a new stability of slower change is re-established.

18

ROFF'S FALL

S cotch was incorporated under the Companies Act on 30 April 1980, as a company limited by guarantee and not having a capital divided into shares. The name of the company is, simply, Scotch College. This was authorised by the Attorney-General, Haddon Storey (1947). Scotch College *Limited* might have seemed an oxymoron.

THE NEW COUNCIL OF 1980

All members of the Board of Directors, called the Council, were appointed by the General Assembly of the Presbyterian Church of Victoria. Old Boys were variously 'horrified' and 'deeply shocked' at what seemed to be victory in the schism for the Presbyterian Church.[1] Rob Fincher (1959) sent his children to Wesley.[2] But though all members were *appointed* by the church, they were *chosen* in three different ways. Five the church chose itself, five were chosen by OSCA, and the remaining seven, known as Group C, were (in 1980 only) chosen by OSCA from a panel of names put forward by the church. Council was an unknown quantity. Its members had never met before as a body. The balance of forces was not clear, but both the church-chosen and OSCA-chosen groups, energised by their years of dispute, hoped to lead.

'Little pipsqueak'

The first meeting spread over two days 27 May 1980 and 25 June. All 17 members attended.

The sparks began at once when Max Bradshaw objected to Roff's presence. Glenn, in the chair, ruled that Roff remain, as this was normal practice at meetings of the Scotch College Council. Glenn's explanation of his ruling might have been that Roff was present because the Articles of Association said he should be (art. 64), or that he was there as the company's Chief Executive Officer (as the Bursar was present as Company Secretary), but Glenn chose from the start to lead this Council to think and behave not just as the board of a company, but as the board of a school with existing traditions. Bradshaw dissented from this ruling and asked that this be recorded. Glenn was in the position that chairmen dream of: he held the chair by the company's Articles of Association (art. 39). Within reason he could do what he liked, though Council could overturn any particular ruling. This first ruling Bradshaw decided not to challenge.

Glenn then gave the new council a fatherly talk, briefly covering the central issues facing it. He recalled the school's history and achievements: 'we meet as a new Council to carry on this work'. The tribulations of the past few years must be put aside, and he warned against 'point scoring on each other or trying to beat the terms of Settlement by means that in our hearts we know are wrong'. On the school's formal link with the Presbyterian Church, it 'generally has been a very happy one. The Church has historically rarely, if ever, interfered in School affairs because the relationship has been one of trust.'[3]

Having told them their task, he suggested how they might embark upon it. 'We will take a little time to get to know each other as many of us are meeting today for the first time. We also need time to get to know the school ... I say this particularly in the context that decisions taken too early could be unwise and damage the school and those who have made it their

F. Maxwell Bradshaw (1928), Vice-Chairman of Council, 1980–85.

life's work.' The early decisions were thus kept to what was routine or necessary. Council elected a Vice-Chairman, Bradshaw, and chose an Executive and Finance Committee. Council authorised who could sign cheques (Principal, Vice-Principal, Bursar and Accountant). It appointed solicitors and an insurance broker, in each case reappointing those who had exercised these functions under the previous Council because the school was obviously already a 'going concern', as described in the Memorandum of Association, article 3 (1) (d). Council initiated applications for exemptions from various taxes. Roff and Wirth made reports, and Roff explained the Evaluation (see pp. 368–9) in detail, so new Council members would have formed some impression of him.

Then Pearsons and Bradshaw moved to appoint William Morton Mackay, MA, DipEd, of 87 Spotiswoode Street, Edinburgh, as Principal 'from today', to authorise his costs of moving to Australia, to 'Reimburse the Presbyterian Church of Victoria for expenses in securing the services of Mr Mackay as Principal' and, pending Mackay's arrival, to appoint Bond as Acting Principal. There was no talk of dismissing Roff (which required a two-thirds majority at two successive meetings). Rather, Bradshaw held that all positions were vacant. Without conceding that Roff had any claims on the school, Bradshaw and Pearsons also sought a clean break with him by proposing that Scotch pay him $50 000 in return for Roff's accepting that as full settlement for any claims on Scotch he might have.

The Chairman did not accept the motion. Even the official minutes concede that 'a heated discussion ensued in which many members of the Council expressed dismay at the nature of the motion and its lack of notice'. Other evidence tells us that Glenn called one of the church-chosen members 'a little pipsqueak'.[4] The meeting adjourned until 25 June.

Bradshaw's gambit confirmed most people's worst fears about how the Presbyterians would run Scotch. People were appalled at the re-eruption of discord at the very meeting where harmony was to be restored. 'Following the recent litigation I feel it is essential for Scotch to have a period of stable consolidation', wrote a parent, Catharine Pye.[5] Graham Sellars-Jones (1953) told Glenn of his 'utter dismay ... It seems to me to be totally unacceptable, in the light of assurances by all parties that they were pleased with the solution to the problems of the last three years and that the School would now be able to get on with functioning normally, that almost immediately the Head be subject to dismissal.'[6] If 'the new elements in the Council' were successful in replacing Roff, 'then it is my belief that an upheaval of appalling proportions would be the inevitable result'.[7]

As for Scotch's appointing a Principal without advertising, this evoked widespread incredulity. For Scotch, 'Surely nothing less than world wide advertising is good enough'.[8] The Common Room called for 'the normal procedures', that is, 'wide advertisement followed by careful Council consideration'.[9] The Chairman of the Headmasters' Conference of the Independent Schools of Australia warned Glenn that in replacing headmasters

> there are ways of doing so which are proper and some which are not. When done properly the Headmaster, the Common Room, the boys, their parents, the Old Boys and the wider community ... are all able to accept the dismissal and move forward confidently ... otherwise it is very difficult indeed, if not impossible, for a new headmaster, appointed in such circumstances, to be accepted and respected.

Then a threat: in the past the Conference 'has hesitated or refused to invite such a headmaster to join'.[10]

Bradshaw and Pearsons seem to have assumed they would impose Mackay and did not have a plan for selling him. He was formerly headmaster of a boys' school in Peru. Bradshaw had brought him to Melbourne during the schism when the Presbyterian Church expected the Principal's position to fall vacant. Outside Presbyterian circles, his visit was known to the then Council, which refused to meet him, but most people were flabbergasted that he was now produced as a Principal, ready-made. 'That the Presbyterian Church of Victoria has had an alternate principal on its payroll for 2 years seems to indicate a blatant disregard of the principles underpinning the legal settlement earlier this year. ... The deliberations of the Council must be kept ... above factional interests of any group.'[11] Some Council members were 'shocked to learn that Presbyterian officials had been looking for a new principal for two years'.[12]

As well as dismay and disbelief, there was a surge of support for Roff from staff, parents, boys, Old Boys, Foundation and the Scotch Association and its auxiliaries. Letters flooded in to Glenn (who indefatigably found time to reply to them all). The Foundation's Board of Trustees' Executive thundered that it was 'ill conceived, inappropriate and divisive'.[13] The School Captain, Michael Stening, wrote that 'losing Mr Roff would badly blemish this school'.[14] Others said that his 'untimely removal would precipitate the resignation of a significant number of staff (particularly the younger and more innovative ones)',[15] and disrupt the school year.[16] Parents like Gordon and Lesley Spence praised

> the many changes since Mr Roff came to the School. For example, to the House System, so that each junior boy is part of a smaller group of caring masters & boys; a great increase in master-parent contact; introduction of female staff, which, we have found, gives an enriched perspective. ... our sons [at] Scotch ... have found a broad tolerant view of the world and the necessary adaption to change without any sacrifice of basic Christian principles.[17]

Various teachers, including senior staff, like Latham, Director of Music,[18] and Crook, Head of Chemistry,[19] pledged their full support and praised Roff for his humanity, wisdom and administrative ability. Holly, Head of English, found him 'an inspiration'.[20] Phil Anthony, a Group Master, 'found his leadership stimulating and innovative and I have appreciated his willingness to receive suggestions and to discuss his plans. He insists that as professionals we should justify to ourselves and to others not only what we teach but also how we teach it.'[21] Eggleston, the Senior Master, wrote to Glenn 'personally to express my loyalty. ... None of us is perfect, and no doubt there have been mistakes, but I believe that what Philip has done at this school has been with the best interests of Scotch College at heart.'[22] Support from the staff as a whole, however, was not forthcoming. When Herbert moved a motion of support 'the members of the CRA voted that Mr Herbert's motion not be put'.[23] Mappin, Chairman of the Common Room Association, put the best gloss on it by assuring Glenn that the staff had not expressed a lack of confidence.[24] Some staff, also, might have felt reluctant to declare openly against the views of a powerful party on Council who said that none of the staff was any longer employed. If the Principal could be got rid of, then no-one's job was secure. Glenn passed this flood of correspondence on to Council, 'as I think it is important they should understand the warm feelings which have been expressed'.[25]

Council had adjourned on 27 May until 25 June. In between these meetings there was much action off stage. The Presbyterian General Assembly held a special meeting to declare unanimously that Mackay should be Principal. Everyone else, lacking the right to speak in the name of God, rushed to get a legal opinion from a QC.

Roff's QC said that Roff was Principal, appointed for an indefinite period terminable by six months' notice on either side. This opinion was circulated to Council.

Group A, the church-chosen members, acted as a group. They obtained legal advice that Roff was not Principal, and had no authority to act as such, not having been appointed at the sole meeting of Council. To counter the argument that Roff must be Principal because he continued to be Principal, Group A was advised that if Roff's salary was still being paid, it was without the authority or knowledge of Council.

Not to be outdone, Glenn opened the resumed Council meeting on 25 June with two written opinions from S. E. K. Hulme, QC.[26] Hulme (an Old Boy of Wesley College) was advising Glenn personally,

> so that I didn't do anything silly, and he didn't charge a penny for his advice. His reason for that was, during the war Scotch had befriended Wesley, ... and he was so grateful to Scotch that he felt that anything he could do for them was for free. So that was marvellous. So he advised me and he said, 'Well now you are appointed Chairman. They can't sack you, so you can be as firm as you like.' So I was pretty firm.[27]

Hulme's first opinion dismissed the view that Roff was not Principal, his term having expired at the end of Term I, 1980, five years after his appointment. Hulme argued that under the Terms of Settlement the company acquired the school as a going concern. 'That going concern included Mr Roff as Principal.' Indeed, although the company came into existence on 1 May Council did not meet till 27 May because it knew that the Principal and his staff were going about their work. Also, if such staff were not already the company's employees it acted improperly in naming them signatories to its cheques. So to replace Roff required his formal dismissal. Yet, since the company had only operated for a few weeks, Council could not yet have any proper opinion as to Roff's performance. In any case, for a very long time Scotch had obtained its Headmaster as a result of careful enquiry following widespread advertising. Instead, Council was asked to depart from that practice, and 'to appoint a person of whom many of the Council must know absolutely nothing'. Finally, Council was asked 'to give $50 000 of the company's money to someone with whom it is told the company has had no connexion'.

Glenn's second statement from Hulme addressed the behaviour required of directors of public companies. This tackled head-on the implications of Council members belonging to Groups A, B or C. A director cannot justify an action by saying that he is ordered to do it by someone else, even if that other person appointed him and can remove him. While in office, he carries his own responsibility for what he does.

Glenn then summarised Hulme's advice: that Roff was Principal, and could be replaced only after a motion to dismiss him. Glenn therefore refused to accept Bradshaw's and Pearsons's motion. They then withdrew it.

Such was the first meeting of the new Council, angry and divisive. Bradshaw's motion, drafted in advance and sprung upon the Council without notice, was intended to sweep all before it. He would have needed the votes of four of the seven men in Group C, and it was possibly a shock to him to realise that he might not have obtained them. He had not fought the battles of the past years to end up in a minority.

Nor was the matter settled. To fend off the attacks, the Old Boys had encouraged the view that no judgement could be made on Roff until the new Council knew him better, and they said that they would themselves welcome a discussion on Roff in a year's time. The church-chosen members also looked forward to that second bout, and set about trying to win over Council members who had not voted with them.

A divided Council, with an unresolved lack of confidence in its Chief Executive Officer, might well have torn itself apart, and worsened the uncertainty of the past few years. Had it done so, we would have found no shortage of explanations. Instead, this new Council went from strength to strength.

Running the company

The relative strength of each side, and of the chair, being now established, internal politics saw a truce. Once Council had set the shape of the school's government by retaining Roff as Principal, it fell to the new Executive and Finance Committee to make things work under the new arrangement. This Committee was responsible for the 'general management of the College', subject to 'the general control of Council'.[28] It began with eight members, two *ex officio* (the Chairman and Vice-Chairman) and six elected. From a Council of seventeen, it held almost half the Council. It had grown from being a small executive committee in 1934 to being a semi-Council. The mutual distrust among Council's Groups was managed by the six elected members being two from each Group.

The Executive and Finance Committee at once took up its role of a workmanlike management committee. It met before Council and shaped its business. It inspected the school. All the demands of a large organisation rushed in upon it. A 4.2% wage increase added $103 000 to teaching salaries. Rising oil prices suggested converting to gas for $160 000. Long-delayed building gave urgency to the Music School's accommodation needs and to

the proposed Counselling and Careers Centre (the Music School plans were well-advanced, and $80 000 set aside, so it went ahead), pensions, rates, leave … And month by month they watched the deficit blow out to $200 000.

After a year, in 1981, they recommenced building the Physical Education Centre by obtaining a bank overdraft.

They saw to basic sensible things that should have been changed long before. They had the Bursar establish a register of bequests and gifts. They noted that the accounts showed scholarships and concessions as a net loss but gave no indication of the income from scholarship trust funds, and they told the Accountant to rectify this.

Council, too, addressed the pressing task of running the company. Most members of Council probably had to learn a great deal quickly, and discovered that the prestige of sitting on the Scotch College Council exacts a toll of great busyness, a lesson no doubt learnt before and since. Far from excluding Roff, Council now welcomed him, and also the others who attended Council meetings with their knowledge and advice: the Vice-Principal, the Junior School Headmaster, the Bursar and the Accountant.

Everything had to be dealt with for the first time. In effect the new Council conducted a full review of the school. The title to Elliott Lodge needed attending to. The steady increase in staffing abruptly halted when Council asked Roff for a detailed plan and comparisons with other schools. Council took hard decisions, like reducing fee concessions, free from having been party to the previous arrangements. Council questioned priorities and took nothing for granted. Led by its Development Committee, it sorted

Roland Keyboard Laboratory 1986. Electronic music enabled many boys to practise music in the same room.

out what needed to be done and adopted a ten-year plan, endorsing the first two years speedily and allowing 'the balance to be subject to annual review and updating to accord with the needs of the school and its financial resources'.[29]

Council also sought to oversee the syllabus. This was new. A proposal to appoint a teacher in Italian was referred to a Council committee under the Reverend Professor Harman, which asked Roff to outline Scotch's educational policy and priorities in the foreseeable future. This was not an area in which previous Councils had intervened. McCaughey says that 'under Selby Smith we would never have been allowed to discuss the ... syllabus, that would not be a councillor's job',[30] and Healey said that 'Council does not interfere in matters educational, though it likes to be informed'.[31] In rejecting Italian, Council both determined academic priorities and made a ruling on whether or not to teach particular subjects. Roff was unable to resist. But Council stepped back slightly, setting up an Education Advice Committee 'to maintain on behalf of Council a continuing oversight of the School's educational program'.[32]

Besides firmly grasping the reins of government, Council also recognised that it had to win the hearts and minds of the Scotch community. This was a Council imposed on the school against its will, and whilst many welcomed it at least as an end of divisiveness others were hostile, or reserved their judgement. Wirth had to reassure Junior School Mothers about the Council. The Foundation felt unsupported by Council, and the Scotch Association said its communications with Council needed improving. Donaldson, unlike his predecessors, has felt the need repeatedly to say how expert Council is and how hard-working.

This Council had not emerged from within the Scotch community. It was generations since a Council had less than a majority of Old Boys. Since Council lacked the old Council's network of personal links, the solution was deliberately to re-establish them. The Executive and Finance Committee held joint meetings with the Foundation's Board of Trustees. Council dined with the Foundation's Executive and sent Council members to Foundation meetings. (Soon this link was strengthened in the other direction by the appointment to Council of Foundation Board members Peter Buckley (1955, OSCA President 1985) and Brian Randall.) Similarly, Council nominated some of its members to attend Scotch Association meetings. Council selected the church-chosen members for these tasks and also the Rev. Norman Pritchard, both to show these organisations that the Presbyterians were human, as it were, and to show the Presbyterians the hopes and needs of the school's funders and supporters, groups which a hundred years earlier would have overlapped with the church. Council also held a chapel service and buffet dinners for teachers, and the Committees of OSCA.

Within a year, Council had established itself as a hard-working and authoritative body. The tensions of being composed of separately chosen groups were still present. The Executive and Finance Committee continued to be a careful balance of all three groups. Choosing new members of Council proved particularly difficult because that raised the possibility of the working compromise coming unstuck.

OSCA wins Council over

To handle its business, Council set up committees. Much of Council's work happened there. Recommendations reaching Council usually went through on the nod, having already been discussed by half the members. Council's agenda, once shaped by the Principal's report, now came from committee reports. Roff contributed to this, because his reports tended to air issues rather than present matters for resolution, and because he had pushed the old Council into new realms (like long-term planning) that necessitated standing committees. Before 1975, committees other than the Executive and Finance Committee were ephemeral.

Committee work gave members an insight into the workings of the school, and obliged members to work together on non-controversial issues, which presumably helped the new Council develop cohesion.

At first, Council had four committees (Budget, Development, Investment and Superannuation) chaired by three men: Lithgow, Richards and Bill Philip (Captain 1947, who also chaired the Combined Schools Superannuation Fund). All three convenors were OSCA-chosen members, reflecting both their previous experience on Council and their skills and experience outside. Indeed, of the ten men on these committees, four were OSCA-chosen, four were from Group C and only two were church-chosen. In this way the weight of authority on Council slid towards the OSCA group. When in 1981 Randall and Buckley entered Council they at once became committee convenors.

Within a year of the Council's establishment in 1980 the OSCA-chosen men had demonstrated two key things. They showed they had the knowledge, expertise and energy to lead the governance of Scotch, and Council gratefully accepted that the OSCA men shouldered this burden. They showed, also, that they were not as Bradshaw saw them, set upon excluding the church from a role in the school's life. Council decided it could trust the OSCA men without damaging the church.

Bruce Lithgow (1946), Chairman of Council 1981–91. He patiently led a sharply divided Council to find ways of working together.

There were two defining moments in the new Council's early years. The first came at once, when Bradshaw failed to carry his motion to replace Roff. The second was when Glenn retired in 1981 and was succeeded as Chairman not by the Vice-Chairman, Bradshaw, but by Lithgow. Lithgow was the leading OSCA-chosen member, and his accession confirmed that group's leading role. The Group C members, or four of them at least, opted for him. (Bradshaw's supporters would say, by contrast, that he preferred to lead from the side, and that he was wise in 'window-dressing the Council so as to give the appearance of dominance by OSCA'.[33]) Lithgow's rise reaffirmed that the route to the chairmanship lay through OSCA, of which he was President and which he had served man and boy. From 1947, aged 18, he worked for Keith Wilson (1927), Secretary of OSCA, and did much of the routine work and was soon minute Secretary.

Lithgow was affable but tough. As chairman his task was uniting the still-new and somewhat wary Council, and managing the appointment of new Council members of high calibre. In 1981, in the early days of building a working relationship with the church-chosen members of Council, the OSCA-chosen members gave in on one major outstanding bone of contention. They sacrificed Philip Roff.

ROFF'S FALL

Scotch has done well from appointing as principals young men in their twenties (Morrison) or thirties (Selby Smith, Roff, Donaldson), and letting them mature in office.

In the normal course of events, Roff would have followed this path. Taking office in 1975, he would have spent the early years making his mark and by 1981, say, all the major positions in the school would have been held by staff he approved of or could work with. This would have meant new Group Masters and Senior Subject Masters, both from his own actions and from routine retirements. The Vice-Principal, Bond, would have gone around 1978, presumably with special superannuation arrangements, and though his forced departure, if it had come to that, would have been difficult, Council would have backed its new man, as boards of management know they have to do when they bring in new brooms. (In the conditions of appointment, Council said 'It believes it can offer a Headmaster strong support in putting into effect educational activities appropriate to new days'.[34]) In 1981 no boy in the Senior School would remember any principal but Roff, and slowly he would have undergone that transformation into authority which comes to all principals. His personal failings (for all principals have them) would have counted for no more than Healey's temper or the aloofness that came from Gilray's or Donaldson's shyness, and would have been said to be offset by his personal strengths (vigour, purpose). He would have been balanced by the personalities of his new Vice-Principal (Eggleston perhaps? Roff was delighted with him as Acting Vice-Principal in 1978 when Bond was overseas) and his new Senior Master (Tait, perhaps? Holly? Anthony? Mappin?). His idiosyncrasies (all principals have them, too) would have been recounted with affection or irritation but not held up as flaws of character.

None of this was to be. After but two years as principal Roff was ambushed by the Presbyterians' civil war over who owned the school. He lost the momentum crucial to the first years of any Principal's reign. His building programme stalled when the bank would not lend money, and his wish to replace Bond had to be shelved as too controversial at a time when Scotch needed support. These interruptions left Roff like a hiker with one boot off, and he remained so to the end. Also, when Scotch was dragged through the courts and lampooned in the press, the damage to the school's reputation and authority naturally reflected on its most prominent officer, the Principal. Worse, he took sides, openly declaring his opposition to the continuing Presbyterians, whose very first act on the new Council was to seek his disappearance.

The departure of a principal in the prime of his life and professional career, without any official explanation, will always raise questions. As for Lawson, so for Roff.

Unlike the silence about Lawson's departure, in Roff's case explanations abound, but they vary. The historian has dozens of explanations put to him in perfect frankness. It is likely that all these different explanations bear on what happened, and that the departure of a Principal is a many-layered event, on which converge a large number of forces. So there may be no single explanation, but rather a number of factors coinciding or accumulating.

The Principal of Scotch College has to manage six key constituencies: Council, staff, boys, parents, Old Boys, and church. (An outer circle would embrace governments, and other educational organisations like other schools and professional bodies.) Ideally he will keep everyone happy. A Principal who wishes to change things may decide it is worth temporarily offending some of these constituencies, and then the strategy would be to keep at least three or four of the six on side at any one time. The more the Principal loses the support of any key constituency, the more attention he needs to pay to the others, especially Council. The story of Roff's fall is how he lost the support of a majority of his key constituencies. He lost the support of the church, failed to secure the full or formal support of the staff, and eventually was abandoned by the Old Boys and dismissed by Council. Among boys and parents opinion is harder to gauge because the school had no mechanism for ascertaining it.

Roff would concede that he was 'not politically clever enough' in managing the constituencies. Among other Headmasters, Roff knew well Peter Brennan at Xavier and David Prest at Wesley, but felt he could not talk to them too openly, especially at the end, about his lack of support on Council.[35]

The Chairman of Council

Within the school, Roff and Glenn never found a way to work together well. Glenn was only 64, but Roff found 'the generational gap was really quite marked', and looked forward to working with the younger Muir, aged 50, who was Deputy Chairman and due to become Chairman soon. A change in Muir's business arrangements meant that this did not happen, and by then the pattern between Roff and Glenn was set. They met at the Executive and Finance Committee, but had no other regular meeting that might have built up a relationship. Their only long conversation was the two or three hours they spent talking about Bond.[36]

Glenn kept saying 'Now if there's anything that worries you at all … Don't hesitate to come and talk to me about it', but Roff

> rarely ever came to me about anything—or to anyone else for that matter. He was so sure of his own judgement that he didn't need advice. He probably thought I was 100 years out of date in my thinking. But that wasn't my point. I sometimes think if you've got someone you can go and open your heart to, it's half the battle in solving the problem regardless of what advice you get … The relationship between the Chairman of the Council and the Headmaster should be one of great friendship and trust where each one can consult the other about what is happening. You can't always consult a whole Council but you can talk to the Chairman—but it didn't apply. Time and time again I would say to Philip 'My door's open but you never come'. 'I will,' he would say, but he never did.[37]

Instead, Glenn often dropped in on Roff, but to no avail.

Meanwhile, Glenn came to think that Roff lacked the milk of human kindness and had an impatient lack of understanding of the need for a 'Mr Chips' or two, men who may not appear useful but with whom boys bond deeply.[38]

The church

In the case of the church, it was not so much that Roff lost the church as that the church left Roff. Between his arrival and departure the number of Presbyterians shrank, as four-fifths of them joined the Uniting Church. Roff had little in common with those who remained. He was not deeply religious, and was alarmed for his school if it became controlled by conservative anti-ecumenical Presbyterians because he and they saw differently things that he held important, like co-education, liberalism and a reduction in hierarchical power structures.

He particularly damned himself in Presbyterian eyes by seeing religious education as moral rather than evangelical. Religious education, he said, 'does not ensure that children will develop into Christians and we should not necessarily expect this'. Rather, 'children need a proper model during the years when they are working out their own morality. [Scotch] should set forth the Christian morality and an orderly and considerate standard of behaviour. … Without such a model children become confused, self-doubting and unlikely to establish a moral code of their own.'[39] In saying this, Roff reflected what had already happened under Healey's chaplain,

Crow, whose assistant chaplain Melville, believed that religious education had moved away from dogma towards helping boys' personal quest for meaning. Staff aimed to broaden and deepen insight, and to teach religion as a historical, social, and psychological phenomenon with various forms of religious expression. Religious education asked not just '*What* ought the pupils to know?', but also '*How* can they be equipped to deal with religious questions and understand religious phenomena?'[40] Such talk of 'tools to understand phenomena' aligned religious education with the way in which many other subjects described their task.

Barrett Copse's deciduous trees allow a winter view of the Chapel over goalposts in the 1960s.

Roff also broke with the Presbyterians more explicitly. He thought it 'monstrous' for the school to be treated as property, as a chattel, for his idea of a school was that it was a community.[41] As an Anglican he could have stayed outside the dispute over who owned Scotch, and Glenn told him repeatedly not to be involved, but Roff was not a cautious man, nor could he sit quietly while a battle raged for the soul of his school. Speaking out did him no good, but Scotch's own rhetoric urges its boys to stand up for what they think is right, without counting the cost, and its Principal could do no less.

Even had he been circumspect, Roff believes that 'probably whoever was in my position had to go',[42] just as Joan Montgomery at PLC was not kept on (but was replaced by William Mackay). Although Roff survived the Presbyterians' attack in the new Council in 1980, his detractors were not reconciled, and from then on he was weakened as is any chief executive officer when his company's board has directors, including the Vice-Chairman, publicly declared against him. Though he retained Council's support, the very fact of needing to fend off a challenge swept away the mystique of being the heir of Morrison and Littlejohn.

The news of the move against him made him an icon of the school's independence, but that may only have hardened the Presbyterians against him. As McCaughey said, 'it was inordinately bad luck that he ran into church union'.[43]

The staff

Roff's loss of staff support was less complete and more complex.

In his early years Roff is said to have got rid of elderly staff and replaced men in senior positions. Encouraging elderly staff to retire was nothing new, for Selby Smith upon arriving promptly farewelled Bowden, Kirby, Ric Marshall, Orton and 'Nutty' Wilson. What was said to be new was the breadth and speed of Roff's sweep, which thus offended people. Yet it is hard to find evidence for this representation of Roff. In contrast to most incoming Principals, Roff caused little staff turnover. Most who left were retiring (Owen, Lyne, Harold Hill, and Butler). Bower left slightly early, but he was dying and if Roff lessened the school's demands on him, this was out of kindness. The only controversial replacements seem to be those discussed in Chapter 16, Roff's removal of two Group Masters, Scott and Elliott. Elliott's case gave Roff a reputation for callousness. Another Group Master (and Elliot's close colleague), Stan Brown, became openly critical of Roff outside the school.

It is the task of new chief executives to change things, and mostly they choose to do so quickly, both to establish their authority and to get the discomfort over with. Roff was not at loggerheads with all the senior staff, as we have seen. Moreover, to offend senior staff is not necessarily to offend other staff, who might be glad to escape an unwelcome tutelage. Younger staff might have welcomed the arrival to power of the generation that had not fought in World War II. They might have thought it was time to be modern. Senior staff sat at their own table in the common room, and made a point of not talking to new teachers in their first few years. (This senior staff table lasted until the common room moved buildings in 1998.)

What did alienate many in the common room was the matter of Michael Achurch. Achurch, an Englishman, was liked and respected by most boys and staff. He was nicknamed Zulu for his curly black hair, or because he came to Scotch from a school in Africa. He joined the staff in 1964 and was Senior Geography Master from 1975 and influential in Geography teaching circles. He ran Geography excursions to all parts of Australia in the August–

September holidays. (After the 1975 trip five fifth-form (Year 11) boys went back to spend a week living and helping at Ernabella Mission.) He had been Group Scoutmaster and was still a Venturer leader. 'He ran the beginners Rowing and was an invaluable help in Hockey. He was a man of incredible energy and fine organization who gave himself unstintingly in the service of his students and his fellow staff members.'[44] He was House-master of Arthur Robinson House, a boarding house, and lived in the attached flat with his wife and children. (His wife, Helen (staff 1974–81) was Director of the Sub-Primary School from 1978.) His wide and enthusiastic participation in the academic and extra-curricular life of the school was common among staff, but he certainly held his own. Old Boys remember him as 'gifted',[45] 'compassionate & considerate'.[46]

In June 1979 a boarder complained to Roff that Achurch had made sexual advances to him. Roff made a characteristically fast and firm decision and told Achurch that he and his family were to move out of their flat, which they did. A second boy soon came forward. The police were brought in. Some months later, on 9 November 1979, Achurch died when the car he was driving struck a roadside pole.

Scotch plunged into angry debate, fuelled by Achurch's popularity among his fellow staff, by Roff's swift and thorough action, and by Achurch's death. Such an issue raised questions of policy about how the school should deal with complaints of this nature, but what seized people's attention were more immediate questions. Were the boys telling the truth? What, if anything, had Achurch done? Should Roff have responded as he did? Did Achurch commit suicide? If so, did that confirm his innocence or his guilt?

As to whether the boys could be believed, some held that these particular boys were not trustworthy, whilst others felt that they were credible, that their stories gained further credence by corroboration and by the fact that they held to their story. According to Roff the boy said Achurch had come to his bed the night before and handled his genitals.[47] The boy slept in a 15-bed dormitory. Healey, as an informed outsider, and one to whom many seemed to talk, came to the view that a misunderstanding had occurred: that Achurch had been told these two boys were leaving the House at night without leave; that he went to their beds to check if they were there; and that, expecting them to be absent and to have left body-shapes of rolled-up clothes under the blankets, he was not careful, but plunged his hands into the beds. One of the boys was new to boarding, and had perhaps been warned by his father to beware of sexual advances in a Public School boarding house, and so construed Achurch's conduct in that light. Healey's musing is entirely conjecture, of course, even if each step is plausible. Many Scotch boys have certainly had fatherly warnings. 'I remember Dad telling me before I went to my first scout camp—"if someone tries to interfere with you, knee him in the crotch, hard" ' (1948). 'I recall my father taking me for a walk the day before I started as a boarder, and warning me to watch out for older boys who might want to do things to me. I spent the next 6 years watching out, but nothing happened that I noticed' (1977).[48]

Roff now faced one of the most serious matters that can come before a Principal, that of a pupil experiencing an unwelcome sexual advance from a teacher. In a boarding house, the matter is even more serious, since so much opportunity exists for an unscrupulous master.

Such things had happened at Scotch before, of course, inevitably in a large and long-lived school. Of their nature most were dealt with quietly. Selby Smith says he dealt with no such case. Under Gilray, Lyne recalls that a boy made an accusation against one of the masters; 'nothing had happened, but ... Gilray had talked to [the master] and got an assurance that it wouldn't happen again and if it did it was instant dismissal'.[49] Old Boys recall masters who left suddenly under a cloud, shrouded in the circumlocutions of masters and parents.[50]

In 1952 a member of the non-teaching staff was charged with interfering with a boy from another school. He was vouched for in court by Yarnold and by Eric Raven (Mayor of Camberwell, and until 1947 Scotch's foreman carpenter) and received a three-year good behaviour bond. He 'vanished from the place overnight. He was a popular man too and he had nephews at the school which was tough on them. But there were never any details. I remember his name because for quite a while if there was any sort of homosexual indication or banter whoever was involved would be called a "Ewan".'[51]

By contrast one master remained at Scotch for decades despite his proclivities being known to generations of Old Boys.[52] They write of 'the obvious sexual ambivalence shown by his "slicing" of junior boys' (1969), ' "slicing" with a ruler on the buttocks of a boy bent over double had a sense of homosexuality about it' (1968), the 'closest to child molestation I saw at Scotch' (1975). 'These days he would be the subject of much attention!!' (1950). Yet he remained at Scotch for a large part of his professional life, and was well regarded by his colleagues. In any large organisation, things that are known perfectly well at one level can be quite unknown at another. The chorus about this one master both confirms that this happened at Scotch whilst showing that it was limited to one man.

This inconsistent collection of cases gave Roff little precedent within the school as guidance, even had he wished for it. The small number of cases, however, meant that he was not under pressure to deal with a problem already held to be present or on the rise.

Whatever one makes of the charges and of the background, Roff's handling of the matter generated controversy. No doubt this was unavoidable, when accusers and accused rejected each other's statements and no independent evidence existed. It was before the time of sexual harassment protocols which today make us aware of the options open to Roff, and it would be anachronistic to suggest that he could have considered these possibilities.

After the 1934 flood swept the boatshed away, Sir Clive Steele designed a new one with rounded corners to resist floodwaters.

Roff seems to have acted as though his only choice was either to believe the boys or believe Achurch. Even accepting this as the choice, he could have spent more time deciding, putting each party through some sustained questioning, and bringing them together, perhaps with others present such as the Vice-Principal. He could have taken advice about how to proceed, from senior members of Council, (for example, McCaughey was Master of Ormond College at the University of Melbourne), or from a fellow Headmaster. In the meantime, Glenn believes, Roff could have avoided precipitate action by telling Achurch that the boarders' area was off limits.

But to Roff the matter had a more personal urgency. 'The boy was on my doorstep the first thing the following morning.' The central aspect of Roff's action is that 'I believed him and no subsequent conversation either with him or with Michael Achurch changed that'.[53]

Why did Roff believe the boy?

> It's difficult to say. I suppose it was partly age, he wasn't a tiny boy, he was about 15. Partly the fact that, apart from going and getting hold of me from my house, ... there was just no delay, he was there waiting on my doorstep when I got down to school at half past seven the next morning. And just the way he spoke about the thing. ... It's difficult to put into words but sometimes when people talk to you, you get a strong impression that what they're saying is the truth. So then, of course, I spoke to Michael about it. I spoke with each of them separately probably three times that day. And the first impression that the boy had left didn't leave me.[54]

Roff asked Achurch to move out of his flat on the Hill by the end of the following week. Many people have different memories of the deadline. Some are sure it was as short as immediately, or 24 or 48 hours, others believe it was longer.

At once everyone knew, and the Common Room was plunged into several simultaneous debates. 'Could Michael have done something like that?' Some thought perhaps he might have. Some thought he couldn't possibly, and had entrusted their sons to him on camps and excursions. Generally, staff felt bewildered. At the same time, Roff found a resentment that, whether it happened or not, it should have been brought home to roost because of what Achurch had to offer in so many other ways.[55] It was very divisive, recalls Beattie. 'You had to take sides as to … whether you were going to support the headmaster or your colleague. … It became a discussion at dinner parties throughout Melbourne, what was happening at Scotch, like the Azaria Chamberlain case it just grew and grew like topsy.'[56]

Roff's judgement today is that 'the thing that I would have done differently would be to have sought immediate legal advice. That would have raised different possibilities for action and different timing.'[57] It was three weeks after the event when Roff called in the police at the suggestion of Glenn and McCaughey. Achurch's legal advice was 'that prosecution was unlikely but, if initiated, conviction would be difficult to obtain on the available evidence.'[58] 'Police wheels grind exceedingly slow … and it was November before they made a decision … to prosecute Michael and … he died in a car that afternoon.'[59] The story in the telling nowadays usually compresses events so that the death follows Roff's asking Achurch to move out, effectively implying that Roff killed him.

Did Achurch commit suicide? The coroner said it was death by misadventure. Lyne, Achurch's colleague and predecessor as Senior Geography Master, says that suicide 'was just not characteristic of the man'.[60] Others think it possible. Whether Achurch crashed deliberately or out of distraction or anguish was a moot point to his supporters. The very imponderability of the question meant that the debate on Achurch would not go away, but would continue as a permanent wound to Roff's headmastership.

It was soon public knowledge that there were differences between Roff and some staff. Among the staff the discussion was passionate, and at the time of the attempted Presbyterian putsch against Roff in 1980, the Common Room preserved its own cohesion only by neither supporting nor opposing Roff. In doing so, it followed the advice of its chairman, Mappin, that it was best to avoid the open divisiveness of a vote on so controversial a motion.

The Council

In the last months of the old Council, John Blanch launched a stinging attack on Roff in Council, with pages of typed accusations which ranged from grave to trivial. One of these charges was 'the rope incident'. Roff was indignant at a reported theft of two sailing ropes, at a time of widespread theft, and became exasperated in Assembly when he raised this and the school, as Blanch put it, 'responded with its usual derisive tones'. Roff then

> announced that school would not start for the day until the boy or boys concerned came to his office and returned the ropes or told him where they were. ... He then left the Hall, with no further instructions to the Vice-principal or the staff, who remained in the Hall, along with the boys, wondering what the next move was to be. Naturally no boy would admit the theft in front of the whole School under such circumstances, so all sat and waited amid rising temperature and noise levels. Eventually, after 10.00 am the Head returned [and said] that the boys would ... go out in single file. He would stand at the door and expect every boy to look him in the eye as he passed. Nothing came of this, nothing more was heard of the ropes, as far the Staff know, and the boys thought the whole exercise was a great joke—and a good way to miss first period.[61]

A boy of the time liked Roff's asking boys to look him in the eye, as reflecting Roff's 'cooperative' approach. 'Many people highlighted this error in judgement and that wasn't fair. In 1982 "Chesty" Bond demonstrated worse judgement when he suspended [Bond says he merely sent them home] six sixth formers for wearing hats to assembly and that barely raised an eyebrow.'[62]

The rope incident is a story that people still recount as archetypal of Roff, and it is often finished with the flourish of saying that the rope had not been stolen at all, but merely misplaced. Certainly Roff's gambit misfired. Yet had it succeeded, it would have been a legendary *coup de théatre*, worthy of Morrison or Littlejohn. Indeed, in 1927 'School did not stop till four o'clock on account of there being five minutes on to each period until the boys who had a chalk fight in a classroom own up'.[63] But the boys did not own up and Littlejohn had to back down. In that year also Littlejohn several times lectured the boys in Assembly, well into first period.[64] Headmasters of Scotch can fumble things. Roff's misfortune was that there were people eager to carry the news to members of Council, and members of Council who found what he had done to Achurch unforgivable. Council's minutes do not record Blanch's attack. He might have had support from Swaney and Macrae, but the

Soccer, 1976.

majority of Council continued to back the man they had appointed.

The new Council that took office in May 1980 was a different matter. The Presbyterian Church at once proposed to replace Roff, but was defeated. Fifteen months later, on 1 August 1981, Council asked Roff to resign. What had changed in that year? Council itself had taken up the reins of governing the school, and in August 1981 was in the full excitement of exploring new ways of organising its work under the stimulation of a governing bodies seminar run by the National Council of Independent Schools.

In analysing some other issue, like government funding for private schools, Roff knew that 'In order to fight effectively for a belief it is necessary not only to believe in it, but also to have political support for it'.[65] He does not seem to have applied this to his own situation. Perhaps the most striking example of this is that he seems to have felt no need to take the trouble to keep Glenn on side. 'He would not consult', complained Glenn in 1990. 'He had a very strong feeling about his own opinions, that he didn't need to consult. Probably felt that I was old fashioned and wouldn't add anything to his knowledge.' Over Achurch, Roff 'didn't seek help. He just rushed headlong into throwing his weight around. If he had come along and had a chat the whole thing might never have happened. … I went to speak to Mrs Achurch privately to try to console her over the matter and you can imagine what a difficult job that was.'[66]

The August meeting at which Roff's case arose formally was also the meeting at which Council handled its first annual renewal. Perhaps Council wanted first to settle its most intractable problem. Also, Glenn was about to retire from Group C, and the OSCA group wished to avoid any weakening of its position by ensuring Buckley as a like-minded replacement. Concessions by Group B to Group A about Roff might win reciprocal concessions about Council membership.

It is hard to reconcile the different versions of what happened.

Glenn's role was central. 'It went from bad to worse. It got to the stage where I consulted with one or two close friends like Davis McCaughey and Alan Lobban.' In July 1981 Glenn

decided we would call a full council meeting and thrash it out and we did this in confidence. Philip [Roff] did not attend, didn't even know the council meeting was taking place, which sounds rather an underhand way of doing it but it had to be done in the circumstances. Then the whole thing was aired and when we discussed it I went around the individuals at the council meeting and asked each one to honestly express his views on the situation, forgetting whether they represented the Church or anyone else. I said, 'We are discussing the headmastership'. Everyone was there, and it was absolutely unanimous. I was amazed at the strength of the attitude against him. You know, with a big group of people like that you would expect someone to speak up in favour of him, but not one.

The meeting was held at the home of Barrie Orme (1951) and was attended by Council members only. It was not, technically, a meeting of Council at all, merely a meeting of its members, but having had that meeting, Glenn knew 'that action would be taken and there'd be no backlash at a proper Council meeting'.[67]

By summoning such a meeting Glenn signalled that matters had come to a head. He 'sensed that other members of the Council whose opinion I could trust' were shifting stance.[68] It may be that Lithgow had manoeuvred beforehand and that Glenn's ambivalence and exasperation about Roff was mirrored among the OSCA-chosen members. However much they admired Roff (and Lithgow thought he was excellent), they saw that the deep divisions among the staff and among Council would never be resolved so long as Roff remained. Roff says:

> it was apparent to me subsequently that the members of Council who weren't appointed by the Presbyterian Church … realised that they would never get anywhere while I remained as Principal, that there would be no possibility of agreement between the two potentially warring halves of council, and so they agreed that I should go. … I think the Achurch business had a big effect.[69]

Conversations took place at some stage between the OSCA-chosen and church-chosen members. Lithgow's group would abandon Roff if Bradshaw's would abandon Mackay. Lithgow would agree to Roff's departure if Bradshaw agreed to his replacement being filled by the usual world-wide advertising and rigorous selection procedures. Mackay could apply, of course, but he would have to take his chances with the rest. Bradshaw accepted this.

'So it was resolved that Philip should go but in view of his young age we didn't want to ruin his career completely so the idea was that he would be given the opportunity to resign.'[70] Bayston was delighted: 'the resignation came through. I remember telling Ron Bond of what had happened. I rang him at his home and he was very relieved. We had great confidence in Ron and were very happy when he became the Acting Principal.'[71]

Roff learnt the news

> a day or two later. Which was a combination of shock (which it oughtn't have been)—it was a complicated emotion between shock, relief, insult … That was pretty hard for both of us, because there are always some who put some mischievous connotation on it—that I must've done something dreadful [like] absconded with funds, all sorts of bizarre stories of that sort. But then towards the end … there's a process of withdrawal and things become more comfortable. You're looking forward rather than back. … in the end I think Barb and I handled ourselves pretty straightforwardly. …

> Within a couple of months of leaving Scotch a couple of schools and the Association of Independent Schools of Victoria had asked me to do consultancy work, and this was an enjoyable precursor of the future.[72]

He contemplated forcing the school to dismiss him, but decided not to fight.

> In the end I think we probably did the right thing because the less fuss, the easier it is to get on with the next bit of your life. I don't think it does the school any good. I don't think in the long run it would have done us any good, because people don't get re-instated as a result of those things. Just too much bad blood. ... Council weren't ungenerous in terms of a retirement package. I mean it wasn't anything to live on but we were able to survive a year without having to get a job and by that stage we'd set ourselves up [as educational consultants], so ... it wasn't as though we were fighting against something unfair from a financial viewpoint.[73]

He remained as Headmaster for another six months and received a lump-sum retirement gratuity as well as his superannuation entitlement.

Council unanimously agreed to accept Roff's resignation on 6 August 1981, and told the school on 12 August in Roff's presence. Since Glenn was interstate, Bradshaw, as Vice-Chairman, and Richards told the staff before Assembly and told the school at Assembly. This was unfortunate. Bradshaw was so publicly committed to removing Roff that for him to preside over Roff's downfall in front of the school risked seeming triumphal. The boys sat in stunned silence. One of the teachers Roff appointed still weeps in recalling the scene.

AFTERMATH

Council publicly recorded its appreciation that Roff had 'worked tirelessly to implement policies directed to the benefit of the boys of the school'.[74] *Great Scot* carried the resignation on its front page but as the third item, and just seven paragraphs. It was a straightforward report—Roff had resigned to undertake study—with a sketch of his career and a 'wish-him-every-success' conclusion. There was no comment at all.

Outsiders were less credulous. 'I don't think anyone was fooled', Roff recalls. 'I mean, who retires at the age of 43?'[75] Outsiders saw Roff's fall as a continuation of the row under way since the schism began in 1977. They saw it as a revival of the previous attempt to depose him, and predicted, accurately, that Joan Montgomery's days at PLC were numbered. They saw it as proving that the church had taken Scotch over. The *Age* reported 'In the past month the Presbyterian Church has won so much control [of Scotch and PLC] that it can decide the appointment of the school principals and influence the choice of staff and what they teach'.[76]

The Standing Committee of the Headmasters' Conference snubbed Council by declining an invitation to dine with it. Mr Justice Northrop withdrew his son from the school.[77] The Foundation noted privately 'a serious breakdown in confidence of the Scotch College community'.[78] Donors withdrew support, and others threatened to do so, like Colin Keon-Cohen who had promised a large bequest.

The life of the school went on. Few teachers left. Enrolments rose in 1982, fell slightly in 1983 and 1984, and then rose again.

The departures of Healey and Roff seem so different—an old man retiring at a time of his own choice, a man in his prime being cut short by others—that one may overlook the similarities. Between them these two Principals reigned during Scotch's two most turbulent decades, when within the school student challenge to authority was at its height, and when the school itself was physically assaulted by the freeway and through Presbyterian divisions reduced to a mere piece of property to be fought over in the courts. Healey and Roff did not flinch from facing these blows, but tried to lead the school as best they could, through affirming the necessary authority of the principalship, and through challenging the school to consider new directions. Neither failed, for the school continued to fulfil its primary task of education, but neither wholly succeeded either, and each departed conscious of the measure of his defeat, Healey concerned at losing touch with the boys, and Roff isolated and abandoned. That two such different men should both have had difficulty shows us what mighty forces from outside were pressing in on the school at that time.

19

DONALDSON
Early years, from 1983

When Francis Gordon Donaldson took office in 1983 he faced the same task that Sir Zelman Cowen (1935) faced in 1977 when he became Governor-General, Scotch's first Old Boy to reach the highest office in Australia. Donaldson's and Cowen's predecessors, Phillip Roff and Sir John Kerr, were controversial figures who had presided over controversial events. The challenge for the new men was to restore stability. What Scotch needed in 1983 was not a new broom, in the style of Littlejohn or of Roff himself, but reassurance that a tempestuous epoch was over. Donaldson moved cautiously.

The omens were hard to read. When he arrived, the grounds and garden beds were parched. The first day of school, 8 February 1983, was searingly

Gordon Donaldson, eighth Principal, from 1983.

hot, and the late afternoon brought Melbourne an awesome dust storm of biblical proportions. Bond called Donaldson out to watch it, and Joyce Donaldson, waiting alone in the PLC car park to pick up their daughter, was engulfed in darkness. Bushfires burnt so close that Melbourne's outer suburbs were in flames (to the anxiety of relatives in Ulster), and the ash in the sky meant that when rain came, it rained black. Scotch let Nationwide caterers use the boarding school kitchen's equipment and labour to prepare 500 meals a day for distribution by the Salvation Army, along with money and non-perishable food collected by the boys.

On the second day of school, a Year 7 boy killed himself, in school uniform. In the match against Caulfield Grammar, Robert Hodges broke Colin McDonald's post-war record by scoring 204 runs in 190 minutes. As ever, the painful and the vital forces within the school jostled against each other.

Council had advertised worldwide, and agreed in advance to appoint the person best fitted and to do so unanimously. The selection committee comprised Lithgow, Bradshaw, Richards and Harman, two each from OSCA and the church. Lithgow discreetly asked Healey and Selby Smith to rank the applications. William Mackay (Bradshaw's proposed replacement for

Roff back in 1980) applied, but was eclipsed by other applicants. Donaldson looked likely. He was Vice-Principal of Wallace High School in Lisburn, Northern Ireland. His doctorate in electron collision physics, at Queen's University, Belfast, had included two years' research in Canada. Lithgow whilst overseas flew to Ulster to meet him. Impressed, Lithgow then called him to London where they met in a hot Qantas office at Heathrow and videotaped an interview which Lithgow took home to show Council, asking Donaldson the questions Council had agreed to put to candidates. Council then flew him and Joyce to Melbourne to meet them, and after ten days offered him the job. In appointing Donaldson Scotch reached back for comfort to its roots. A young Celt would once again see Scotch through.

The Donaldsons flew from Ulster in January 1983, and the Lithgows met them at the airport. Lithgow introduced him to the school and to parents. Each side no doubt tried to make sense of the other. As the man who replaced Roff, Donaldson was presumed to be a conservative Presbyterian. Was this impression enhanced by his strong Ulster accent, redolent of the Ulster Protestants on television news programmes? More likely, many Australians thought, as they still do, that his accent was Scottish. Other impressions could only be as superficial, but were favourable, for this tall, boyish man was warm and charming, and could talk even to primary school boys, as the Junior School teachers noticed approvingly. His views on Scotch rang familiar. 'The priorities of the school are to educate boys to the highest level they are capable of, to develop spiritual awareness, physical development, and provide a framework of morality within which boys develop. He stressed the need for honesty, flexibility, willingness to learn, confidence and willingness to attack problems.'[1] He proved to be a strong and conservative Christian, with an evangelical leaning. In the countries in which he has lived he has belonged to Presbyterian or Baptist churches, choosing a parish that suited his family.

For his part, Donaldson had to work out the Australians. They had 'a low regard for protocol',[2] but he saw that their direct questions (a boarder meeting him on the path might ask 'Did you have a good weekend, Sir?') were not meant either to be rude or to challenge his authority. The Australians preferred Donaldson to be equally frank with them. In Ulster, to tell parents the school faced some problem implied that it was vast indeed, whereas he found that Australians preferred him to bluntly spell out a problem. Once they knew what was wrong they would tackle it themselves, or would note that he himself was tackling it.

He spent his first year talking and listening. He met everyone, and everyone made it a point to tell him what Scotch had been through; what the real story was; what he now needed to do; whom to trust. Everyone was still engrossed in the schism, and parents were disquieted at what would happen under the rump Presbyterian Church. Donaldson listened without taking sides. Eventually he began to suggest that 'it was time now to put all that behind us. ... What we really need is for everyone to support the school as it sets its directions for the future. And the school community was ready for that.'[3]

Donaldson seems not to have had a Principal's usual initial tussle with Council. The Principal's powers were now clearly laid down in the new company's articles, so he was not cramped like Littlejohn or pestered like Selby Smith. Perhaps Council was still surprised at its own temerity in dismissing Roff, or was aware how impolitic it would be to undermine two Principals in succession. Powerful though he therefore was, Donaldson yet held his hand for several years in most aspects of the school's life. Bond had led the school throughout 1982, and Donaldson left day-to-day matters mainly in his hands (welcomed doing so, for the school looked solid and in no need of urgent readjustment) whilst he embarked on a steep learning curve about Australia, about Scotch, and about being a Principal. The boys nicknamed him 'Dr Who?' and later 'Flash Gordon' (from F. Gordon) or 'Noddy' (for his large head), or simply and more lastingly 'Dr D.'.

He acted only where he saw a need for immediate action. Of course, everything is relative. Donaldson's limited actions in a school of 1800 boys may have taken more time and energy and money than all of Littlejohn's active reforms in a school of 300 boys. And Littlejohn also attended personally to crockery, linen, desks, and lockers—matters that Donaldson could leave to others.

STAFF

One of Donaldson's most immediate problems was the mood of the staff, polarised under Roff, whose supporters now felt vulnerable. No-one felt secure in a school where even the Principal was not safe. The staff lost its recently acquired observers' rights at Council, was still waiting to discover the implications of Roff's dismissal, and was understandably suspicious of Council's appointment of a possibly highly conservative Ulster Presbyterian. Donaldson found that the Common Room 'lacks the measure of confidence in their Council which we would hope to find in a stable and thriving school'.[4] Soon Council and staff were at loggerheads over an industrial matter, while Donaldson urged 'meaningful discussion' and 'improved relationships between them'.[5] Donaldson's dilemma, presumably, was that he needed to deliver to Council a manageable workforce, and needed to deliver to the staff evidence that he could represent their interests effectively at Council.

The disagreement was over an Industrial Relations Commission Wages Board for academic staff of Victorian Independent schools. The staff voted in 1983 to go under its authority, not least as a protection against Scotch's new post-schism, Principal-sacking Council. Council strongly opposed an outside body having jurisdiction over Scotch's staff, and asked the staff to vote again. To encourage them to get it right the second time, Council's Chairman, Lithgow, came in person to outline Council's position to the entire teaching staff, the only time this has happened. Benignly forceful, he made it clear Council would not back down. Donaldson also asked the staff to reconsider their position. Whatever the industrial issues, he reassured staff that he could give them an informed input into the school's affairs. He readily agreed to meet regularly with their executive. He undertook to report to the staff about Council meetings, and to convene and chair meetings between the Common Room Association executive and Council representatives, about issues of mutual concern. The staff also took legal advice, and learnt that it was best not to go under the Wages Board. They could always do so later if they wished, but once under they could not withdraw. They therefore by a large majority rescinded their earlier decision. Scotch remained outside the Board's jurisdiction.

Staff turnover after Donaldson arrived rose slightly, as one would expect. For example, the Rev. Graeme Hildebrand (Assistant Chaplain 1976–83), who taught Religious Instruction, saw that Donaldson wanted a more Bible-focused approach, and he left. (In the Junior School, too, Wirth tacked with the winds of change by encouraging class teachers to have a short Bible reading each day in addition to the cyclical Bible Study period.[6]) In Art, Donaldson asked for the resignation of Rowton, Senior Art Master, who seemed to Donaldson to believe 'that art was there as a means to give boys some relaxation from the academic pressures they were put under', whereas Donaldson wanted boys to be challenged in everything they did.[7] Yet Donaldson reports that he recently met an Old Boy who swore by Rowton.

Several senior staff left. Stan Brown, Group Master of Forms I and II (Years 7 and 8) retired. Donaldson split the position in two, with a Group Master for each form. That allowed more focus on helping boys' transition into Scotch. Brown had begun Year 7 camps in 1972, to accelerate new boys' friendships and to allow scientific observation of nature. Donaldson sympathised with new boys, 'because my first week or two here were very daunting and I was supposed to be the Principal!'[8] So Scotch hurried less to make boys adjust.

> In 1983 a boy would arrive at the flag pole and had to have with him what he needed for that day, plus his sports gear because in the afternoon he would have sports training, and be selected to play for the school on Saturday. Now, we are in not such a rush to get boys playing competitive sport. It takes two or three weeks rather than two or three days, … They are here for six years, … It's alright to take a term or two to get boys eased into the place.[9]

Donaldson's compassion was stirred by one new boy's suicide. Devastating for the family, it also hit the new Principal, who had never been involved in a school suicide before. Donaldson's reign has paralleled the rise of youth suicide in Australia, and Donaldson chose from the start to call suicides by that name rather than by a euphemism, although the *Collegian* preferred to give no cause of death. The handful of subsequent suicides

1983 staff
photograph.

over the next two decades brought the usual sense of bewilderment: the second suicide, at the end of Donaldson's first year, was of a sixth-form boy who seemed busy and competent.

Reshaping the Group Masters of Years 7 and 8 also allowed Donaldson to suggest merging Grade 7 classes in the Junior School with the equivalent classes in the Senior School (Form I). It was anomalous that boys of the same age should be taught in two different ways. In the face of the assumption that the merged classes would all be taught in the Senior School way, the Junior School Headmaster, Wirth, calculated that in their final exams, ex-Junior School boys did better than other Scotch boys.[10] Wirth spelt out the advantages of the Junior School's teaching methods. Grade 7 had a class teacher whereas First Form had subject teachers.[11] The Junior School's class-teacher system allowed teachers to vary the time spent on subjects according to need, unhindered by bells or interruptions. An overall vigilance of each boy's progress overrode subject and timetable constraints. 'It could be described as a "holistic" approach as opposed to one which divides learning into a jig-saw framework in which pupils are taught to see the world as a complex mass of separate entities.'[12] Also, in the 1970s the Junior School's increased numbers had necessitated three 'temporary' classrooms for Grade 6, built on the hill below the hospital. They precipitated 'a good deal of cooperation between the three teachers, and of inter-

Key to 1983 staff photograph.

Back Row: 1. Peter Rickard, 2. Paul Hardy, 3. David Biltoft, 4. Patricia Holdaway, 5. David Hosking (Tenth Vice-Principal 1987–1994), 6. David Baillieu, 7. Ken Clayton, 8. Doug Galbraith, 9. George Tsangaris, 10. Ken James, 11. Peter Hauser, 12. Neil Rumble, 13. Roger Southern, 14. Nick Hale, 15. Jim Scotford, 16. Steve Kong, 17. John Prior, 18. Rob Newton;

Sixth Row: 19. John Francis, 20. Daniel Coase, 21. John Graham, 22. Peter Krumins, 23. Ian Harrison, 24. Edward Hellier, 25. David Perry, 26. Patrick Tobin, 27. Richard Smith, 28. Brian Woolacott, 29. Paul McNamara, 30. Miles Mudie, 31. Geoff Wemyss, 32. Vic Nash, 33. Ernie Hobdell, 34. Euan Walmsley;

Fifth Row: 35. Malcolm Kennedy, 36. Dr Roger Slade, 37. Andrew Tait, 38. Enid Evans, 39. Ben Shearer, 40. Rob Hortin, 41. David Paul, 42. Ken Mappin, 43. John Lewis, 44. Dr Peter Lewis, 45. Wes Thomas;

Fourth Row: 46. Kevin Purcell, 47. Ian Wood, 48. Ron Smyth, 49. Richard Hall, 50. Colin Black, 51. David Blue, 52. Ian Savage, 53. Colin Christie, 54. Robbie Torrick, 55. Tim Hurst, 56. Noel McWhinnie;

Third Row: 57. Dr Michael Elliott, 58. Ken Evans, 59. Geoff Walker, 60. Paul Turner, 61. Warwick Barry, 62. Peter Crook, 63. Graham Hildebrand, 64. Baxter Holly, 65. Carl Statton, 66. Steve Ritchie;

Second Row: 67. Scott Crozier, 68. Geoff Orrin, 69. David Scott, 70. Ivo Beattie, 71. Alan Shugg, 72. Mirko Fluher, 73. David Boykett, 74. Chris Latham, 75. Bob Grant, 76. Neville Taylor, 77. Philip Anthony, 78. Dick Shirrefs;

Front Row: 79. Rex Saunders, 80. David Pryer, 81. Don Macmillan, 82. Leon Bates, 83. Ron Bond, 84. Dr Donaldson, 85. Mick Eggleston, 86. Stan Brown, 87. Archie Crow, 88. Keith Darling.

mingling of the three groups for some activities'.[13] A decade later the Senior School brought in team teaching in Year 7.

The lack of space in the Senior School postponed the merger until 1988, and Donaldson's attention shifted to co-ordinating the curriculums for both groups of boys in Year 7, and to rethinking the curriculum for Years 7 and 8.

As well as Brown, other senior staff also left in 1983–84: Tait (Form VI Group Master), Holly (English), and Harrison (Drama). Holly became a Principal and Tait a Vice-Principal, but Donaldson felt sufficiently sensitive about their exodus to remind Council that it was 'to be expected that … experienced teachers at Scotch will make very strong candidates for senior positions at other schools'.[14] Their replacements dispelled any fear that Roff's

departure meant applicants of lower quality—the new Senior English Master, Watkinson, brought 'scholarship and breadth of academic and technical skills'.[15] Michael Evans (Head of Mathematics 1988–) received an honorary LLD from Monash University in 1999.

The Vice-Principal, Bond, retired at the end of 1985. Before then, Donaldson ended Scotch's custom of having only one Vice-Principal. (He had been one of three Vice-Principals at Wallace High School.) He appointed 'Mick' Eggleston, the Senior Master, as another Vice-Principal from the start of 1985. When Bond left, Colin Black became a Vice-Principal. He was Form VI Group Master, hard-working and good at administrative detail. An effective teacher, in drama he had directed often-inspired productions, for example of *Journey's End* and *My Fair Lady*. Eggleston had charge over timetable, discipline, pastoral care, sport, and other pupil activities, and Black over the curriculum, assessment, reporting, and liaison with Group Masters and Heads of Department. Despite this clear delineation, the school's culture was shaped towards one man having authority, and staff played one Vice-Principal off against the other.

In 1999 Michael Evans (Head of Mathematics from 1988) received the rare honour for a schoolmaster of Doctor of Laws from Monash University.

In 1987 Eggleston retired with a brain tumour, aged only 57, and soon died. The school felt shock and disappointment.[16]

> He was traditional, old-school in his appearance, well educated, he knew the boys, he was tough and you couldn't get much past him. … When he told you to do something, you did it in quick time. At the same time, I remember Mr Eggleston as being very approachable, and one that you could have a quick joke with, although not too many and not for too long! [1990][17]

In executing discipline, he was 'not personal' and was understanding in times of personal crisis (1965).[18]

When Black also left, in 1987, to become a Principal, Donaldson reverted to having only one Vice-Principal, appointing David Hosking, Head of Economics since 1972, Group Master since 1986, and an enthusiastic sportsman. When Hosking left in 1994 to become a Principal, his successor was the Head of Year 11 and former Head of History, Ian Savage.

During the 1980s, Scotch had a new and inexperienced Principal and four Vice-Principals. If this created a power vacuum of any kind, it was probably filled by the new Council (which was more managerial than its predecessor) and by the Bursar (whose authority was already enhanced when the school's incorporation made him Company Secretary). In 1985 Field retired after over 30 years as Bursar, and was replaced by Neil Roberts, Bursar at the Armidale School, NSW. The departure of a senior staff member always creates an opportunity for review, especially if the incumbent has been there so long. In 1984 a committee, chaired by Ralph Morris (Captain 1952, OSCA President 1982, Council 1983–95) and including Field, adopted a consultant's recommendation to improve Scotch's financial reporting systems. When Donaldson arrived, the school was in debt and even had to use an overdraft to pay salaries, because income ran behind expenses. By 2000, the school was in a solid financial situation, operating always in the black and with significant assets. Lithgow and Morris on Council, skilled and hard-headed accountants, were instrumental in achieving this turnaround, as was Roberts, who brought a sharper edge to the school's financial management.

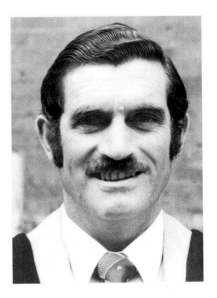

Mick Eggleston (1947), eighth Vice-Principal 1985–87. His sudden death from a brain tumour left a feeling of shock and disappointment.

The Vice-Principal also reached a new level of authority. Since at least the 1940s he had managed the teaching staff. Healey in 1971 felt that in order to attend to his external and fundraising responsibilities he wanted Bond to have 'a firm control of the school and [be] closely associated with me in its running',[19] but this development lapsed under Roff, although Bond still exercised great influence. He 'was the person with whom we all dealt on all matters of a day-to-day nature. He also wrote the school timetable.'[20] Donaldson felt it was unhelpful that everything had to depend on the Principal, and preferred that others take up their authority in their areas of expertise. Donaldson's declaration that he was not the sole educational authority on every topic shocked some teachers, but it merely accelerated what was happening under Roff, as each attribute of a great 19th-century headmaster was divested to a senior staff-member.

Eggleston, Black, Hosking and Savage each brought different personalities and strengths to the task, built his own relationship with the Principal, and saw the role differently. Whilst Hosking adopted a watching brief, Savage actively sought to improve processes and policies. For example, he played a significant part in curriculum reform, in opposing bullying, and in moving Assembly from the start of the day. Savage also introduced continuing, unthreatening staff development through a three-year, three-tiered self-investigation of one's involvement in the school.

PARENTS

Within a month of Donaldson's arrival, the Hawke Labor government took office in Canberra, intending to reduce financial support to independent schools. Susan Ryan, Minister for Education, was a former government-school teacher with little sympathy for private schools. At the state level, the Premier, John Cain (1948), was an egalitarian with a strong commitment to government schools. Scotch mobilised its lobbying resources. Donaldson, like Roff, acted through independent school umbrella organisations, and he also galvanised the members of the Scotch Family.

This had the added advantage of drawing parents and friends back into the life of the school. During the schism they had overwhelmingly opposed Scotch's belonging to the Presbyterian Church. The outcome showed them how little influence they had in the school's affairs, and left them dispirited and suspicious. Now, as Scotch faced a likely 13% cut in Commonwealth and State funding, Scotch was fortunate that the schism was over. Donaldson asked the Scotch Association and OSCA to influence politicians. The Association produced a kit for Scotch parents and held a meeting of 500 parents in the Memorial Hall, addressed by Donaldson and speakers from the Victorian Parents' Council and the Association of Independent Schools of Victoria. The Executive and Finance Committee warmly endorsed the Scotch Association's campaign. By the end of 1984 Canberra agreed to continue funding independent schools, at 1984 levels at least. Funding would be for 1985–88, giving a stability that allowed schools to plan. Also, funding would be on a needs basis not a per capita basis. Scotch replied that the needs in question should be reckoned according to pupils' families' income, not schools' wealth, but the Commonwealth Schools' Commission developed a needs assessment index (Education Resources Index) categorising schools.

As well as revitalising the Scotch Association, Donaldson also had to rein it in, encouraging but channelling its energy. This applied particularly to parents. In 1984, parents' representatives proposed a Parents' Association, to link parents with each other and with the school and to tap their energy. They said 'that parents new to the school often experience loneliness and detachment, even alienation from the school'.[21] The unstated complaint was that the parents provided the bulk of the school's revenue but had no say in how it was spent. The explicit complaint was that the Scotch Association did not represent parents' interests. This was true enough, for the Association was a federation of the auxiliaries, designed to serve the auxiliaries' work. Information went to the small minority of parents engaged in the auxiliaries, and the Association did not inform parents about the general activities of the school. Nor could Donaldson use the Association, as he would have liked, as a vehicle to raise broad issues with the parents as a whole.

The answer seemed to lie in a specifically parental organisation, but Scotch preferred the administratively simpler step of containing matters within the Scotch Association, by expanding its committee to include two parent representatives from each year group in the Senior School. This broadened and strengthened the Association. It also headed off another confrontation: that a Parents' Association would have asked for its own seats on Council. Council had recently firmly rejected the Scotch Association's hopes of making nominations for membership of Council. This was not the time to tinker with Council's structure, so recently and painfully put together. To attempt to change even a small part of it would allow debate on the whole and pick at sores that had not healed. Parents had to 'understand that there are many questions about the school which are not the province of a parents' association'.[22] In the long run that sort of line would be hard to hold, but in the short term a strong Principal at the head of a successful school can do so. A wise chairman, moreover, ensures that Council contains current parents.

When the Foundation, however, wanted to nominate members to Council, it could not be headed off so easily. Donaldson suggested that whoever was its Chairman should be invited to sit on Council, thus linking 'those deciding the future direction of the school and those who will provide much of the funding'.[23] In practice, the Foundation Chairman has often had a seat on Council already.

THE FOUNDATION

Donors were wary in the early 1980s about giving money to a school run by continuing Presbyterians. That was the problem the Foundation faced when the schism ended, and was repeated when Roff fell.

The Foundation responded, under the acting presidency of John

Family Day 1983. Staff from left: Geoff Orrin, Brian Woolacott, Richard Smith, Rob Hortin, Phil Anthony, Don Macmillan, Mick Eggleston, Miles Mudie, Neil Rumble.

McIlwraith (1940), by using its money in several new ways to which no-one could object. It sponsored school drama and the Foundation Day Concert. It underwrote the cost of Drug Identification Cards that police and the Health Commission recommended for distribution. It funded Foundation Fellows, thereby blessing Scotch with a succession of stimulating visitors. The first in 1985 was (quite rightly) a historian, Dr John West. Scotch used these Fellows for an intense look at particular matters, like Mathematics education; communication; computers; computers' use in education, especially in teaching languages; Design and Technology; and boys' education. Thus we glimpse the school's preoccupations over the last fifteen years.

Also, the Foundation formed what became the East Melbourne–Glen Chapter for Old Boys aged over 75. The Foundation's minutes list this initiative under the heading of Wills and Bequests, which would not surprise the members.

The Foundation also took up a visionary goal of giving Scotch financial independence by the year 2000. This was in response to the 1983 government funding cuts. The Foundation set up a corpus, the interest from which could limit fee increases if government grants were withdrawn. Donations to this corpus were not tax-deductible, so most donations went instead to the Building Fund. The amount of money the corpus required was large. In 1985, government grants totalled $1 302 000, being 15% of an expected school revenue of $8.5 million. (By 2000, government grants represented about 10% of the school's revenue and a corpus of $4.5 million had been created.) Donaldson welcomed this bold aim and was happy to fan the fears that underlay it: 'the Labor government intends to seek a degree of regulation and control in return for funding of non-Government schools, and we could well be faced with the need to consider if independence is more important than funding'.[24]

At last the Foundation recovered enough self-confidence to end the interregnum in its leadership, when Sandy Murdoch (1957), already a Life Governor, became Chairman 1984–90. His view, bluntly, was that 'All Old Boys have an obligation to support the School in whatever ways they can to ensure that those who come afterwards have the same opportunity they had'. To spread the load of fundraising, people should have to give only a couple of years of their time.[25]

The Foundation experimented with new kinds of fundraising. Corporate matching gifts allowed companies to match an employee's donation to education. Anomalously, such donations were tax-deductible if made to tertiary institutions but not if made to secondary schools. A Cash Deposit Plan started in 1985, whereby donors allowed the school to have the interest on their deposits. This soon drew questions in the Senate, for the donors would have to pay tax if they had received the interest themselves. Scotch, which had Tax Department approval for the scheme, took its public relations consultant's advice and issued only a brief statement.

Council's Budget and Superannuation Committee urged the school to reduce its overdraft, which had leapt with the resumption of building, and at a 16% rate of interest. One economising response in 1983 was to charge interest on overdue fees, which stood at around $150 000. Scotch hesitated to take this step, but receipts soared when it did so. In 1984 instead of interest, Scotch imposed a levy on unpaid fees. The Principal had discretion not to apply either interest or levy in cases of financial hardship. Reasons for unpaid fees included drought, bushfire, the growing number of divorces and separations, and business failures galore in 1987. In 2000, the dollar amount of unpaid fees is less than it was in 1983. Instead, Scotch provides generous help, and it is rare that a Senior School boy has to leave for financial reasons.

In the 1990s, the Foundation increasingly advocated scholarships for 'deserving and able boys who otherwise would have no opportunity to attend Scotch ... thereby helping to avoid the situation where Scotch becomes a school only for the sons of the wealthy'.[26] The Foundation pointedly compared Scotch's endowments unfavourably with those of American schools. The presence of scholarship boys at Scotch is hidden because they are not usually described as such—although earlier in the century they were clearly identifiable among the entrants in the Removes. Recently Old Boys such as David Copolov (1968) and the family of Will Roddick (entered 1891) have publicly acknowledged their debt to the school as scholarship boys.[27]

COMPUTERS

Donaldson's first action at the Executive and Finance Committee was to give impetus to computerisation, which now suddenly moved forward apace.

Computer Club, 1982. A domestic television set serves as the screen.

The Turtle, an early robot, 1982. Junior School boys could program its movements under the tutelage of Mack Jones.

In retrospect computers seem inevitable, but at the time a Council member dismissed them as a passing gimmick. Donaldson upon arriving was dismayed to find only one computer, a Mathematics Department card-reading machine used only for academic work. Scotch was behind Ulster. Within weeks, Scotch bought a VAX 750, its huge cost of $160 000 being shared with the Foundation. The choice was made by Donaldson, Taylor (from Council), and John Graham (Director of Computing 1983–86 and Chairman of the VISE Computer Subject Committee 1984–86).

Like many new technologies, computers were developed to solve current problems and few foresaw their future uses. At first Scotch contemplated merely a single computer, for administrative tasks. In 1976 OSCA had the mailing list of Old Boys and the Scotch Family stored, for a fee, on the Melbourne Stock Exchange computer, into which the data were typed by employing two members of the school's Computer Club, a body fostered by Ken Evans, Senior Mathematics Master. The new VAX 750 soon held an integrated database of OSCA, Foundation, current parents, finances and, from 1985, academic results, which previously went on White Cards. A terminal for teachers was installed in the Common Room. The old gym became the Keon-Cohen Computer Centre (with access and facilities for disabled people).

For teaching, in 1974 Evans secured a personal grant from the Schools Commission Innovations Program to buy a computer for the new

Mathematics and Science Block, so the school could construct and evaluate a computer course. As early as 1968, John Cromie (1970) recalls that Bob Money (staff 1965–70) 'in addition to the full regular syllabus, taught his entire Fourth Form [Year 10] maths class full Fortran IV programming [which] must have taken quite some effort so early in the computer era'. Programs were transferred laboriously by hand onto 'computer cards which had the little squares (chads) already perforated. They could be poked out with a straightened paper clip.' Programs were run over night at Monash University, the cost met by an anonymous donor. Mistakes could be corrected by pushing the chads back into the holes. 'This worked sometimes.'[28]

In the Junior School, Wirth enthusiastically committed time and resources. In 1981 he bought a 48k Apple II computer with money from the Junior School Mothers' Association. Costa and Mack Jones (staff 1976–87), teachers in Year 6, studied 'Computers in Schools' at Preston Institute of Technology, and Jones set up a lunchtime Computer Club. The first computer had a Turtle, a robotic, plastic dome that boys could make move. But the Turtle developed a bug. Wirth's educational aims for computers were to teach boys to use them, and teach staff to use them in teaching. He had Dr Alan Rogerson (staff 1980–85) develop a computer course from Grades 1 to 7. Wirth could not recall any innovation that had attracted such parental support.[29] Costa and Jones ran Saturday morning computer workshops attended by over 80 families, including brothers and sisters. Wirth called it 'family learning'.[30] Parents learnt something of their sons' new jargon, and learnt that it was better to buy a cheap computer than an expensive video game.

From its initial idea of having just one computer, Scotch spent the 1980s and 1990s repeatedly adjusting its sights. By 1986 the Junior School had an Apple computer in every classroom. The Senior School first taught programming to large numbers of students on one central computer, then had students using micro-computers, which entailed changes in course format and operating procedure. Next, the micro-computers in the upper laboratory were linked to the VAX 750. Later, stand-alones were linked. In 1995 all Year 11 boys had to bring their own portable computer to class, either IBM-PC or Macintosh. (As the VCE made drafting Common Assessment Tasks the norm, so the ability to amend a draft drove the spread of computers.) In 1998, Scotch estimated that well over 90% of parents had computers at home; but that connection to the internet was much less common. Back in 1990, possession of a computer was all, but in 2000 it is merely a starting point.

For staff, in 1983 Donaldson secured two Apple IIE computers. By 1993 all departments were to have a computer and access to the main computer. In 1990 Scotch considered a computer for every staff member, though Greg Baker (Director of Computing 1987–) thought this was excessive.[31] Soon he thought it mundane. Such was the rapid pace of change. The Lithgow Centre's staff section (1998) gave each teacher access to email and desktop publishing facilities through school-supplied laptops, replacing all the old technologies of typewriters and duplicators.

Educationally, at first computers seemed to offer scholars only what they offered administrators: doing the same things, faster. Scott, Senior Physics Master, in 1971 imagined no more than computations, or simulated experiments such as playing with data on salinity.[32] In 1974 Tait, Senior Physics Master, sampled computer-assisted instruction in Los Angeles, and felt 'that he learnt something in spite of himself'.[33]

Computers modified the power relationship in the classroom. Students might know more about information technology than the teacher (as with radio in the 1920s). A good teacher accepted this fact, and changed teaching strategies. Staff became facilitators. The dais was gone but it was the computer that now drew staff out among the boys. 'With computer screens, unless you can see from behind, you can't actually see what's going on.'[34]

Computers were more than a new technology, like the electric calculators that had earlier replaced slide rules. Computers allowed boys to access, handle and evaluate information in an entirely new way. From 1960 to 2000, boys' learning-tools progressed from textbooks to libraries to computers to the internet, that is, from a single authoritative source, to a range of locally held sources, to an unlimited range of sources. Parallel with this, teachers' task changed from reading the textbook aloud or setting pages to be read, to guiding boys on how to locate sources and on how to assess and use sources that differed. Computers let boys work independently and develop judgement in the use of facts. The technology gives access to facts, but teachers' task in an information technology age is, as ever, to teach boys how to assess the facts, and marshal them; to teach boys about appropriate content, proper editing, and rigorous analysis.

Computers changed the way boys worked. Drafting became more common, because it was easier. This increased boys' and teachers' workload. In teaching languages, computers helped boys, at their own pace, to develop listening, speaking and writing skills, and to use them directly with organisations and people in the target country. In Music, boys can create and compose music, experimenting with sounds and structures, without knowing anything about musical notation, and can record a cassette of the result. The school is still developing clear statements of what skills boys should acquire at each level of education, and it is not clear in all subjects how computers are integrated into the curriculum. These problems are the concomitant of a new technology, and their solution may be provisional for some time.

By 2002 Scotch plans to have an intranet accessible from school or home to link all staff and boys to each other and to the internet. The effects of this on learning and on the school community are incalculable.

Before the computer, Scotch spent little on teaching and administrative technology. In 1971 Scotch spent $4079 on boats, oars, a trailer and outboard motors, $2077 on office machines, and $2658 on teaching aids and equipment. Even as late as 1984, Scotch cancelled expenditure on audio-visual equipment and typewriters, in order to buy a new racing eight. This sort of 'huge misallocation of resources away from the curriculum to extra-curricular activities' troubled those who wondered 'Why should the rowers receive the latest in boat technology year in year out when the language laboratory was sorely lacking? Old equipment and even older tapes were used to teach us Russian and German' (1995). Later, the building of a dedicated Language Centre redressed this imbalance. Donaldson finds that parents judge the school by its academic rather than sporting achievements, whilst Old Boys often prefer to hear about premierships.

CHARACTER
Learning through challenge

The school's outdoor programme was, like computers, another matter already under way but to which Donaldson gave impetus.

Extra-curricular activities had grown over the previous century either because the school or individual masters offered activities that they felt boys should want (cadets, scouts, sports, debating, a Science Club) or because boys persuaded the school to let them do their own thing (riding, wireless, Constitutional Club, archery). The system and its contents were always slowly changing. Donaldson admired the range but wanted integration.

There were five extra-curricular domains: sport, music (which was also curricular), clubs, an outdoor programme, and compulsory Thursday afternoon activities. The first three (sport, music and clubs) were straightforward. (In sport and music the pattern was simply an increasing variety of games or instruments played by an increasing number of boys. Clubs rose and fell with boys' enthusiasms.) It was on the fourth and fifth that Donaldson focused—outdoor activities and Thursday activities. He combined several broad changes, already under way, into a co-ordinated programme. In the process, outdoor activities were called outdoor education, and extra-curricular became renamed as co-curricular. Such changes in name formalised the school's more holistic approach to education.

As Donaldson arrived, Eggleston was evaluating the whole Thursday programme, which many staff thought unsatisfactory. Eggleston's report led the Senior School to a co-ordinated six-year programme, including and combining activities previously operating separately under cadets and scouts. Donaldson believed this embraced all that was best of the existing programme while providing a more efficient and attractive programme.[35] The aim was 'to foster self-reliance, initiative, leadership, loyalty, self-discipline, and community awareness, by teaching a variety of skills and providing a range of challenging experiences'. The programme varied according to boys' age.

Forms I and II (Years 7 and 8) did sports practice or scouts. Forms III and IV did outdoor or service activities—scouts, cadets, Venturers, sea scouts, pipe or military band, St John Ambulance or adventure training. (Adventure training in 1987 provided 200 boys with brief exposures to bushwalking, boardsailing, canoeing, canoe maintenance, cooking, cross-country skiing, cycling, first-aid, horse-riding, leatherwork, orienteering, photography, rifle-shooting, rock-climbing, self-defence, skier awareness, and surf survival,[36] and later included sailing, scuba-diving, (sea) kayaking, self-defence (kung-fu), and snorkelling.[37] Richard van Wachem (staff 1986–89) even gave a demonstration dive in a kayak from the high diving board.[38] In 1998, over 240 boys took part in the Adventure Program.[39]) Forms V and VI did Social Service activities or took up leadership roles in the younger boys' activities.[40] In the 1990s the Junior School also began an outdoor programme.

Inevitably accidents happened. In 1986 the road subsided under a bus travelling back from the 24-Hour Hike in Tallarook State Forest. The bus tumbled 60 metres down a steep hillside before trees halted its progress, tossing the passengers about like 'being in a cement mixer'. Miraculously no one was killed. There were bruises and fractures, and several people were knocked unconscious. Staff and boys in a second bus were soon on hand, with the St John Ambulance Brigade assessing injuries and applying first aid and comfort 'in a fashion which later earned enormous praise … There was no panic, rather a scene developed where well-trained staff and students put into practice in exemplary fashion the lessons they had been learning and rehearsing for months and even years.'[41]

By 1982, as the memory of war faded, cadets broadened into outdoor activities.

Donaldson praised the committee that developed the outdoor programme, and soon made its leader, Eggleston, Vice-Principal. Unlike Roff, Donaldson did not extol the concept of staff participation in decision-making but in practice, in the areas he chose, he was able, even determined, to delegate and repeatedly tackled issues by appointing committees which included staff. Similarly, the independent unguided democracy of the General House Committee was not to his taste, and he allowed it to die. He did not always attend. Even when present he told it 'that he would not immediately give information on some motions as there are some which cannot be answered spontaneously',[42] so that it lost one of its great strengths, its chance to hear the Principal think aloud, for Healey, Roff and Bond had usually held forth. Donaldson also reminded the GHC that it was not a decision-making body,[43] reissuing Roff's charter that it existed to allow boys' suggestions and viewpoints to be presented and discussed.[44]

Fifteen years later Donaldson asked Stephen Kong, Dean of Students, to set up a Student Forum 'designed to provide students of Scotch with opportunities to contribute to discussion of aspects of the school and its operation'. Comprising boys from Year 8 and above, it is based on Tutor Groups, each of which is represented at a year level forum. The Forum brings together each year-level. Participation may train students in structured meetings and help develop skills of advocacy and representation.[45]

Whereas Healey began by decreasing the number of exams, Donaldson at once reintroduced them in Forms I–II (Years 7–8): boys needed experience in examinations to become good at them when it mattered. These examinations were no more than the tests the teacher might have done anyhow, but they were made to look serious enough to perhaps induce nervousness and provide the experience of examinations. Some teachers were dismayed, and a motion against the exams was moved at the GHC, but failed. Donaldson also set up slight hurdles so that moving up through Years 10, 11, and 12 was not automatic, to teach boys that 'you just need to get better and better and better, that the challenges get harder and you need to be ready for that'.[46] After 1990, the new Victorian Certificate of Education would lessen examinations' importance, until that, too, seesawed in 2000.

Donaldson disapproved of Junior School sport's stress on participation over achievement. He moved the sportsmaster, Norm Emerson (staff 1963–98), to other duties,[47] overriding Wirth's warning of the 'danger of a school relying solely upon the class-room and the sports-field to develop self-reliance and individual adaptability'.[48]

Booze, smokes, dope and sex

Outside the school, steadily Donaldson won recognition. The number of applications for entrance scholarships held up at over 400, and he joined the Headmasters' Conference, which laid to rest the threats made when

Roff left. (In 1997 Donaldson, like Littlejohn, Gilray, and Healey, became Chairman of the Conference's successor, the Association of Heads of Independent Schools of Australia (AHISA), a body made up of 280 Heads of Australia's leading independent schools. Similarly, in 1992 Graham Nowacki, Donaldson's appointee as Headmaster of the Junior School, became Chairman of the Junior School Heads Association of Australia.)

Other aspects of the school also extended beyond its boundaries, as Scotch reflected changes in Australian society. Donaldson was soon disturbed to find a widespread problem with alcohol among senior boys. Boys drinking spirits had caused substantial damage at school dances. When parents did not mind their sons drinking, or encouraged it, then the school faced an uphill task, but Donaldson intended to supervise the school dance and ensure that no alcohol was available.[49] With other Principals he urged parents always to be present at parties and not to allow alcohol or smoking.[50]

Schools have little chance of preventing drinking among Australian youth. By 1996, boys attending a Scotch 'formal' (Dinner Dance) began, as one enthusiastic participant said, with 'excessive consumption of beer, wine and champagne at private houses—which were endorsed by parents I might add. Then the actual formal which was really a non-event. Then cabs to the secret destination of the after party which was fully pre-arranged.' The

Monash Drive, 1983.

tradition was 'that we had the biggest, most outrageous after parties ... The whole year group would come and everybody would rock on until 4 in the morning then head to champagne breakfasts around Melbourne. Assembly was filled with coughing and cigar breath of half drunk, hungover Yr 12s' (1996).

Donaldson was determined that 'our boys learn the highest standards of behaviour with regard to smoking and drinking'. He knew it was difficult to stop day-boys smoking once they had left the school grounds, but comforted himself that it was 'well within our grasp with the boarders'.[51] This inequality of treatment angered the boarders, who were punished for behaviour at parties that went unpunished for day-boys. Also, a mock diary of a 1985 School House boy had entries like 'Hide durries in pillow during dorm search' and 'Tape cup over fire senser so I can durry without setting off alarm'.[52] Donaldson increased the punishment for smoking, and 'much useful manual work has been done around the grounds on recent Saturday mornings'.[53]

Some boys had always smoked and, during much of the century, so had many staff. Only the boys' age made it a problem, as they tried, too young, to adopt adult behaviour. As a problem it was familiar. The discovery of boys smoking marijuana seemed new, although boys had smoked it at least from 1970 when Healey wanted to develop education against it[54] and when Alan Hartman recalls 'the sweet smell of marijuana at my mate's place in Fordholm Rd. in year 12—I was too scared to smoke it.'[55] In 1985 Donaldson disciplined 15 boys. Nine who had provided the drug left the school. *Truth* published a report, initiating a flood of enquiries from the media, and Donaldson issued a succinct statement giving the bare details. Overall, Donaldson believed the reputation of the school was enhanced rather than damaged by its 'preparedness to tackle a problem which is undoubtedly prevalent in all Victorian secondary schools and beyond'.[56]

Also in 1985, other publicity broke out. In the June edition of *Outrage*, 'Australia's Gay News Magazine', the cover portrayed in colour two male models, one wearing a Scotch blazer.

> Within the magazine two further photographs of the two models, again with the Scotch blazer prominent, accompanied an article entitled "What are they teaching our kids?" The article discussed the lack of any teaching on homosexuality within schools' sex education programmes, without mentioning any specific school. Apart from the photographs, there was no reference to Scotch College.[57]

Whilst Scotch boys who were gay were delighted, they dared not say so, for other boys 'were very angry about the inferred involvement of Scotch students in homosexual practices', and Donaldson was deterred from suing only because his legal advice was to do nothing. 'There is a danger inherent in most proceedings for defamation that the matter complained of will be given much greater publicity than ever attended upon it originally.'[58] When the *Bulletin* in 1979 ran an article on Australia's Public Schools, with a cover picture of an old school tie, Scotch noticed that they had naturally used the Old Scotch tie. When *Outrage*, too, saw Scotch as *the* Australian Public School the compliment was less well received.

In any case, it would have been difficult to assert that no Scotch Collegians were gay. Instead, Scotch was discovering, like the rest of Australia, what was in its own closets. Peter Blazey (1957) had already in 1978 stood for election under the beguiling slogan of 'Put a Poofter into Parliament'.[59] Contested wills, where a widow challenged what her Old Boy husband had bequeathed to Scotch, occurred occasionally, and in 1981 for the first time a contestant, though unsuccessful, said he was the bereaved gay partner of a leading Old Boy.

In managing these matters Donaldson took advice from a public relations consultant. In 1984 Scotch began to use consultants not just for specific tasks, as in the past, but for broad areas like planning and public relations. After years of civil war, Scotch needed to refocus the media on the school's work and achievements, but the precipitating cause was the planned bike path along Scotch's levee bank (Chapter 10). Scotch opposed this, but risked looking mean. In 1985 the MMBW proposed to amend zoning regulations on riverside land, and this, too, Council opposed, and told the Principal to engage a public relations organisation 'to alert the community to this major threat to the School's independence'.[60]

At the end of 1985 Council authorised Donaldson to renegotiate the public relations consultancy to his satisfaction. This voiced Council's trust in his judgement and endorsed his management of the year's drugs and *Outrage* crises, and must mark one of the points that occurs between Councils and Principals, at which Council allows itself the pleasure of feeling that it has chosen the right man. Later Donaldson used various public relations consultants as needed.

Donaldson never came to like Vegemite,[61] but he made the transition to Australia and to Scotch. He became an Australian citizen in 1990. As he and Scotch nudged each other into place, a great tension subsided. After Roff's nervous energy and unpredictability, and the strain of the schism, Scotch entered calmer waters.

Donaldson had asserted the authority of his office against Council, teachers and parents. He had begun to put his stamp on the school through senior appointments and through shaping directions. The watershed that marks the end of these early years was his three months' advanced management course at Harvard in 1987, from which he returned as a new man. From then on, staff felt that his leadership was stronger.

20

THE 1980
SETTLEMENT IN
PRACTICE

Having seen Donaldson successfully ensconced, let us now turn back to 1980 to explore the school's new life as an incorporated company. The 1980 settlement, still in operation today (2000), included a religious settlement (so we must ask what it meant that Scotch was still Presbyterian), a financial settlement (it took Scotch decades to extricate its scholarships and prizes funds from the Presbyterian Trusts Corporation), and a division of the spoils of power on Council (who did control Council and what did this mean?) In short, who owned and ran the school?

COUNCIL'S BALANCE OF POWER, 1980–2000

As we have seen, Council comprises three Groups, imaginatively called A, B and C. All members are *appointed* by the church, but its choice is limited by the members being *nominated* in three different ways: Group A by the church itself, B by OSCA, and C by Council. Groups A and B have five members each and Group C has seven members. The arrangement reflects the struggle that gave it birth, bringing together equal representations of the two litigants who fought for control of the school in 1977–80, and adding another seven. Appointing or removing the Principal requires a two-thirds majority, that is, 12 votes; this means 5 plus 7, so Group C and either Group A or B can suffice.[1]

Group A, the church-chosen group, has been the most fluid in membership. The church has been chiefly concerned, understandably, with appointing men to ensure Scotch's adherence to the church, and less attentive to giving Scotch a stable Council. Its members have changed twice as often as other groups' members. Three sat for just one Council meeting. Several have been deposed and reseated by coups and counter-coups within the church, whereas the other groups' members have held office until they wished to retire.

At least one church-chosen member protested over an issue important to the church but not to the Scotch community at large: Freemasonry. The church deems this incompatible with Christianity, and deplores the existence of the Scotch Collegians' Lodge, independent of the school but associated with OSCA. (It was set up in 1925 by the Rev. Farquhar Chisholm (chaplain 1919–24), and its members have included Bowden, Arthur Waller and Field.)

As early as the second meeting of the new Council, the church replaced G. E. Morgan with Brian Bayston. Although Morgan had attended only a single (two-session) Council meeting, he was honoured with a minute of appreciation longer than that of most previous Council members. That his friends might have written it is understandable; that the rest of Council acquiesced shows how hard they were all trying to find avenues of co-operation. From the Minute, Council learnt that Morgan had taken office 'knowing full well' that the Church intended 'to replace him after the first meeting,'[2] when Bayston returned from overseas. Bayston was then, with Max Bradshaw, an elder of the Hawthorn Presbyterian Church.

Morgan's removal began a pattern of instability among the church-chosen members. Pearsons soon resigned. His Minute of Appreciation, again disproportionately long, said that he had stayed on Council only 'until it was clear that the new structure was serving the interests of the School as a school in connexion with the Church'.[3] In 1985 the church dismissed two of its five men and then, in 'a coup engineered by Norman Pritchard',[4] restored those two and dismissed the other three.[5]

Group B comprises the five OSCA-chosen members. The church cannot reject OSCA's nominations, and even if it does not appoint them they 'shall nevertheless be deemed to have been duly appointed'.[6] In choosing its five members of the new Council, OSCA followed the recommendation of the retiring Council, which balloted five of its members. Of the 17 members of the new Council, only these five had sat on the old Council; they included the only woman, Ann Price.

Group C decides the balance between Groups A and B. Each year the full Council nominates seven people for the seven Group C places. This requires only a simple majority. If four Group C members side with Group A, they could nominate all seven Group C members to be of like mind, thereby creating the two-thirds majority needed to take full control of the school. Once such a majority came into being, it could not be unseated. On the PLC Council, Group C did behave in this way, to the ultimate exclusion of all opposition.

The balance within the first Council was thus crucial, as it promised to be self-perpetuating. The first seven Group C men were therefore chosen jointly by OSCA and the church.[7] (OSCA, however, rejected the church's wish to appoint only Presbyterians.) Much interest focused on this middle group and on how they would behave. The Rev. Norman Pritchard was the Scottish-born minister of Scots' Church, Melbourne, and Werner Brodbeck was an elder there. Dr Bob Gillies was married to Mrs Bradshaw's cousin. John Ball and Professor Brian Spicer were leading Baptists. The sixth member was Professor Peter Gilmour (1961) and the seventh was Sir Archibald Glenn. Initially the church would have thought it could count on all but Glenn.

As we have seen, however, Council at its first meeting did not adopt the Group A motion to replace Roff. Had there been a vote, it seems that Group C members such as Gilmour or Pritchard might have voted against it. 'After the meeting', Pritchard soon recounted, 'I was waited upon by eight colleagues within the church and, to put it mildly, threatened'.[8] They told him that his behaviour was unacceptable. He was a representative of the church and should fall in line with their policy. He replied in very direct terms that he would come to Council with an open mind and that his loyalty to the church required him to vote according to his conscience. They could count on him for his support if they were right in what they were doing but if he felt otherwise he would vote as he wished.[9]

The entire Council is reappointed every year, and in late 1981 faced this hurdle for the first time. Of the Group C members, Glenn and Gilmour were retiring and Council nominated Peter Buckley and Russell Eves to replace them. We may presume that these two preserved the existing balance of power. Buckley was an active Old Boy, whilst Eves had Presbyterian links. For the other five places, Council opted for continuity and lack of complication, by nominating the five sitting Group C members: Ball, Brodbeck, Gillies, Pritchard and Spicer. The motion to do this, carried unanimously, was moved by Pearsons of Group A and seconded by Lithgow of Group B, and may have been worked out beforehand. The church, however, preferred to appoint people more likely to support Group A, and did not approve Pritchard's nomination. The *Age* said that Bradshaw supported this purge.[10]

Group C's membership was in dispute because people disagreed about how to conceptualise it. Pritchard said that there were different interpretations of the 1980 settlement and that the 'basic unresolved question is what came out of it. Was it an interim arrangement to allow the heat to die down, then the church to move in and take over? Or, was it for the middle group on the school councils to be "the leaven in the lump", intelligent amateurs in the middle deciding each issue on its merits.'[11] It is the essence of compromise that each party, whilst conceding something of value, believes it has retained something worth more. We can presume that OSCA and the church, so recently at war, each hoped that they would exercise the leading influence within the new Council. OSCA thus imagined that Group C would be independent members. Bill Tingate (1955, OSCA President 1990), protesting at Pritchard's rejection, told the Moderator that the Group C members were to be an 'independent' group of 'wise heads'. He saw Pritchard's unseating as an attempt 'to manipulate the system to destroy that element of fresh, independent thought on the Council, one can only presume with the intention of gaining some advantage, if not outright control, in complete contempt of the hard won settlement which gave both parties equal representation'.[12] The church, however, 'always intended', said Bayston in 1992, that Council would have a majority of 'people who were committed to the connection with the Presbyterian Church of Victoria'. 'Later on, the argument was advanced very strongly that Group C was meant to be an independent group, … honest brokers between two warring factions. That was never the way the Settlement was structured and it's a misrepresentation of what the Settlement was.'[13]

Pritchard rebuked Pearsons for moving his reappointment at Council and then opposing it within the church.[14] The Foundation warned the church that donors were 'reconsidering their position'.[15] Two months later the church reappointed Pritchard. (He remained on Council until 1996.)

Another crisis came in 1985. Ball of Group C retired, and whilst Council renominated the six retiring Group C members, it was repeatedly unable to choose a replacement for Ball. The vote was tied between Grant Lawry (1937), nominated by OSCA-chosen Richards, and Robert Allen, nominated by church-chosen Bradshaw. Some members warned Council that the issue hinged on the desire by the church representatives to control voting numbers.[16] The six renominated members were reappointed and took their seats. The deadlock on the seventh seat lasted for months and was broken only when the church reshuffled its representatives. (During the process, the church sacked all five church representatives at one stage or another.) Two areas thought to need strengthened representation were parents and the Foundation, so the seat went, unanimously, to the chairman of the Foundation, Murdoch, and (when he declined) to Philippa Barber, President of the Scotch Association. In the church's eyes she and Lawry were linked to OSCA.[17]

Her election confirmed that Council's balance of power leant towards people arising out of the Scotch community (OSCA, the Scotch Association, and the Foundation) rather than towards people whose Council membership derived from the church. That balance of power had already been made clear at the end of 1985 when the incomplete Council unanimously chose Pritchard to replace Bradshaw (who had retired) as Vice-Chairman. This marked a shift in the politics of Council, for although Pritchard was a Presbyterian minister he was not in the church-chosen group. That group's position of leadership on Council was thus diminished.

In 1986 Council chose Lawry, one of the two deadlocked candidates a year before, to replace Eves. Lawry was a former General Manager (Victoria) of the Commonwealth Bank. The OSCA-leaning majority delivered by Pritchard was self-perpetuating and so Group C nominees would continue to combine two attributes: they would be from within the Scotch family, and they would bring to Council the professional expertise the company needed to run the school.

Now that it was clear that the church party on Council did not have the numbers to shape the selection of Group C, the struggle to do so moved from within Council and lay between Council and the church. During the late 1980s and the 1990s, the church insisted that Group C members were not meant to be independents, and it protested at Council's giving 'a high place to business skills and not to Christian commitment'. To remedy this, in 1988 the church announced that Group C members must have 'a vital church connection'. That is, they must regularly attend a Christian church.[18] Lithgow saw this as an abuse of the 1980 settlement. Of course either side would try to generate Group C members favourable to their cause, but neither side had stipulated in advance the kind of person they would or would not countenance. The church denied it had done anything new. Even before incorporation it would always have hoped to appoint active Christians. (What was certainly new about the church position was that it accepted that most of Group C would not be Presbyterians.)

The policy was tested at once, when in 1989 Council nominated Sir James Balderstone (1939) for Group C, intending him to follow Lithgow as chairman. Bayston, no longer on Council but a member of the church commission that vetted nominations, wrote to Sir James that 'our perception of the erosion of the Church's position in the Council, would make it difficult to support your appointment as a member of Group C'.[19] Instead, he could seek nomination in Group B. Given Sir James's eminence as chairman of BHP and AMP, the church was persuaded that to reject him would damage Council's reputation as a serious body. The church compromised by appointing him to Group A, from which it could dismiss him at any time. He became Chairman of Council in 1991.

A succession of similar encounters followed. In 1992 Council nominated for Group C Pam Marshall (President Junior School Mothers' Association 1979, President Scotch Family Association 1990). The church did not consider her a regular churchgoer but it neither appointed nor rejected her. She thus took her seat, for the Articles of Association provide that, when Council nominates someone, the church must respond within thirty days.[20] A person not rejected within thirty days shall be deemed to be appointed.[21] Even so, the church asked that in future Council not nominate non-churchgoers.

In 1996 Council nominated Jill Spargo, and this time the church replied that it did not approve. Oddly, it did not actually say that it *rejected* her, and so once the thirty days had elapsed Council declared her to be a member. The church protested, but the Chairman of Council, Michael Robinson, held firm, bolstered by legal advice from S. E. K. Hulme, QC, he who had advised Glenn back in 1980.

Sir James Balderstone (1939), Chairman of Council 1991–95. He was chairman of BHP and AMP, but the church was reluctant at first to appoint him to Council.

Earlier in the 1990s, however, Council did back off from nominations when the church demured. Even so, whilst Council hoped to find qualified churchgoers, Council's stronger preference was for members with necessary skills and with boys at the school. Council finally asserted this preference in 2000–2001.

The Articles of Association require the church, when it rejects more than two nominations in any year, to state in writing why a person rejected is

'not reasonably suitable'.[22] This has now occurred. To fill a Group C vacancy in 2000, three successive nominations from Council were rejected by the church as lacking a vital church connection. To ask people to allow their names to go forward to a probable public labelling as 'unsuitable' was no easy matter. Robinson turned to OSCA, harking back to the earlier alliance between Council and OSCA against the church.

When the church rejected the third nominee, John Simpson (1975), a parent, as lacking a 'vital church connection', Robinson's legal advice from Neil Young QC was that the church had no authority under the school's constitution to reject a nomination for that reason, and that therefore (the rejection being invalid) Simpson was a member of Council. Council duly passed a resolution to this effect in April 2001. If the church objects, it will have to take legal action.

Michael Robinson (1955), Chairman of Council from 1996. Previously President of both OSCA and the Foundation, and Sir Arthur Robinson's grandson, he personifies the confident control of Council by the Scotch Family at large.

As this book goes to press, the church has not done so. The Group A members of Council opposed all these nominations and decisions strenuously, but were outvoted.

Whether Christians go to church often enough to have 'a vital church connection' is ultimately a dispute within the Christian community. Beyond that, the number of churchgoers in Australian society is declining, and thus so is the pool of Christian expertise available for Council membership. The five OSCA seats are now the only undisputed route by which non-churchgoers can enter Council. This may explain a recent change in Group B members. For a century, the OSCA-nominated members of Council have been leading figures in the Old Boys' organisations. This continued after incorporation: eight of the twelve Group B members have been President of OSCA. But from the mid-1990s OSCA has reached beyond its office-holders and nominated leading educationists, like Professors David Penington (1947) and Stuart Macintyre (1964), and financiers like Ross Bradfield (1952) and Robert Prowse (1962).

The church's doubts about Group C continue. During the 1990s the church has called new nominees to Group C for an interview. It has responded to a Council nomination by suggesting alternatives! Council, in response, has set up a Nominations Committee, comprising the Chairman and one member from each group, and expects the church to consult this committee even before appointing Group A members (who, Balderstone told the church, should have expertise appropriate for company directors).

None of this tussle is necessarily cause for concern. Council itself works well. All organisations are pulled in different directions simultaneously, and need to be if they are to remain healthy. The Articles of Association anticipate and channel these rivalries. Perhaps the tension will become too difficult to contain, as the number of Presbyterians within Victoria dwindles to a few parishes, or as the number of Christians declines. Or perhaps the present settlement will be overturned by a pressure for representation (from parents, perhaps, or from excluded groups like staff, or Muslims, or the boys themselves) or by a pressure from within the community for elections.

The tidiness of three named groups ought not conceal that other groups also exist on Council. Council has always contained struggles among its members between Old Boy and outsider, cleric and lay, reformer and conservative, Chalmers Church and not, Trustee and not. Currently, divided votes in Council are rarely along group lines.

On the Executive and Finance Committee, from 1980 the OSCA-chosen men took the lead. Despite initially balancing the Committee between its three Groups, Council soon turned to its available expertise. In 1983 four of the five OSCA-chosen members of Council were on the Committee and were a majority of its seven members. This leadership has continued.

The achievement of the three Chairmen of Council over the past 20 years (Lithgow 1981–91, Balderstone 1991–95 and Michael Robinson 1996–) is to have shaped Council into a body where in its day-to-day work the groups are not visible. At PLC most votes are polarised by group. At Scotch, group members do not vote as one, nor sit together, and Donaldson feels sure they do not caucus beforehand.[23]

THE FINANCIAL SETTLEMENT

The financial settlement took 20 years. The Presbyterian Trusts Corporation held in trust the money bequeathed to the school for prizes, scholarships, and other benefactions. There were over 100 separate trusts. Their value, in 1989, was $550 000, earning interest of $95 000, of which the church withheld $16 000 as coming from unworkable trusts.[24]

The terms of the settlement required these funds to be handed over to the school. Initially hampered by the school's lack of a common fund, negotiations dragged on, apart from a period after 1986 when they so broke down that Council contemplated legal action.

Only in 1999 was the deed of change of trustee for the Prizes and Scholarship Fund from the Presbyterian Church to Scotch signed.

The religious settlement

Legally, the company that is Scotch College exists 'for educational purposes in connection with the Presbyterian Church of Victoria',[25] and its chaplain must be an ordained minister of that church.[26] Sir Archibald Glenn's view of the 1980 settlement is that the church had 'a right to the Christian side of the school, but not to running the school ... in any other way'.[27] Perhaps this is the key to an unspoken contract reached by the conflicting parties.

Legally, the Memorandum of Association directs the curriculum, in that Scotch exists to teach 'an education of a humane, scientific and general nature' which is limited to what is 'consistent with the teachings of Christianity'.[28] In practice, approaches by individual Christians have not persuaded the staff to deviate from teaching a traditional liberal curriculum. For example, books have remained on the reading list or in the Library despite occasional parental complaints of immorality (one of John Marsden's popular series mentions masturbation). Halloween has been studied in class (as a cultural phenomenon) despite parental protests that it was unChristian and superstitious. Cam Stewart did not prevail in his fulminations against Tolkien's *The Hobbit*.

Tension on curricula seems likely in the future as Scotch grapples with issues such as sexuality and drug-taking, where modern curricula prefer harm minimisation rather than prohibition. At the same time, no comment is made about the staff members whom earlier generations would have described as living in sin: unmarried staff living in relationships.

Side by side with the church's not interfering in the curriculum, the status of religious education was strengthened. For the second time in the school's life (the first was under Healey), Christian religious instruction is obligatory for all boys.[29] The neutrally named Religious Instruction or Religion-In-Life became Christian Education. In practice at present Scotch teaches the boys the basic tenets of Christianity in a way that makes use also of what other religions teach.

The position of Christianity in the school has come full circle. Just as Lawson was advised to think of himself as a missionary and Morrison muttered at how little the boys knew their Bible, so today the chaplains deal with boys who are mostly not Christian and have neither read the Bible nor studied Christian teaching. In 1990 the average attendance at the weekly Christian Fellowship was 15–20 boys, 1% of the school.

Assembly is no longer daily or at the start of the day. It is no longer the consecration of each day's work. Yet it retains its religious purpose and effect. 'In about Year 11, I was sitting in [Assembly] and it seemed like that for the first time I was actually listening (and not just hearing) some of the words Rev. Bradbeer was saying. ... The moment probably marked the beginning of my thoughts regarding religion and hence philosophy towards life' (1996).[30]

The school's official discourse is Christian. When Donaldson told

Senior School as seen from the Chapel steps in 2000.

teachers one of their colleagues had drowned, he told them also that the best thing to do in such circumstances was to turn to the Lord in prayer for comfort. (Miraculously, the teacher, Scott Beynon (staff 1997–98), was soon arrested for robbery in Wollongong, having only faked his death.) The chaplain, Bradbeer, is impressive. Many boys and Old Boys draw upon him in crises, so that he is in a sense chaplain to the Scotch community. There are boys who find through him a Christian calling. His prayers, free of liturgy, engage God directly in conversation.

The discourse among the boys is harder to gauge. It seems not so much anti-religious as, simply, irreligious. 'It's just not a talked about thing any more ... it's just not relevant to how you judge someone else ...nowadays.'[31] A Vice-Captain of the School hears only indirectly about his Captain's denomination. A level of superstition has probably always existed. Boys might have a lucky rabbit's foot (1935),[32] or a 2-cent coin worn around the neck 'whenever I need luck (ie exams)' (1996).[33] Gordon Fisher (Captain 1941) would 'blacken and polish my footy boots and wash the laces on the night before inter-school matches. Failure to do so would mean a poor game!'[34]

Many boys seem unaware of the concept of original sin. Rather, they seem to think that whatever they feel strongly and purposefully is also somehow intrinsically good. Recent School Captains have told their successors: 'the only one who can say if you did a good job, is that face in the mirror'.[35] 'Be yourself. Do things the way you want to do them and set out to achieve goals your way. ... Go with what you believe, don't do something or be hesitant just because of what previous Captains have suggested. Try to trust your instincts, generally they will be right.'[36] This sounds at odds with Christ's teaching that 'If any man would come after me, let him deny himself' (Mark viii.34). As the heirs of Nietzsche, boys are told to have the 'will-to-win' (Peter Thompson, Captain 1978), as though this is in itself a virtue. 'At Scotch I learned that I could focus on a target and plan my way to achieve it. What you wanted could be gained through as much hard work as cunning and sometimes just sheer force of will it seemed.'[37] Drew Ginn (1992) was Scotch's first Olympic gold medallist, winning at Atlanta (where Marty Aitken (1974) coached the Swiss gold-winning rowers). Ginn told Scotch that 'I thought hey, I'm a Scotch Collegian, I can do anything ... because at this school ... we learn to believe in ourselves'.[38]

Being a church school allows Scotch to remind boys of the spiritual side of life, and, as Tapp put it, 'to combat the insistent voice of self-interest and material wealth in the world today'.[39] This has particular relevance at a time when boys' reviving interest in the occult is following a direction unconnected with morality. Beyond formal religious occasions like Assembly or instruction in class, the fact that Scotch has religion and learning under the one roof

> offers the vital opportunity of linking together in the child's mind the ordinary business of living and the service of God—of giving the child the idea that, whether he is doing his homework or playing football, he is doing it as a man walking in the sight of God, and that even these apparently secular activities can be, and should properly be, regarded as done to the greater glory of God.[40]

Like Greenpeace's injunction to 'think globally and act locally', boys are challenged by the idea that everything they do has a value, has a place, and has to be answered for.

The apparent policy of leaving unto education what is due to education and unto God what is due to God may perhaps explain the apotheosis of the Rev. James Forbes. Forbes played a central part when the church founded the school, but he died before the school opened, had no influence on its development, and was never mentioned. For example, only a generation after the school began, at the first annual dinner of the Old Collegians' Society in 1879, Morrison talked of the school's beginning and praised Lawson but made no mention of Forbes.[41] Similarly, the annual smoke concert in 1926 saw the presentation to the school of the portrait of Frank Shew, whose life at Scotch began in 1860 and spanned most of the school's 75 years. It was an occasion full of history-reciting. Littlejohn referred at length to Lawson but not at all to Forbes.[42]

Suddenly, in the few decades at the end of the twentieth century, Forbes has sprung to prominence. Symbolically he now ranks with the Principals. His portrait hangs on the southern side of the Memorial Hall reserved for the Principals, and it appeared with theirs also on the cover of the 1991 *Collegian*. The new drama and music complex is to be named after him, though it is Gilray who is credited with bringing these things fully to life at Scotch, whilst Forbes's extensive writing on education contain no mention of music or theatre. Indeed, as a Presbyterian of his generation he may well have disapproved of both. Forbes has become a focus of the sesquicentenary. A torch will come to the school from Scotland, starting at Forbes's home village rather than Lawson's or Morrison's.

Similarly, the Foundation honours Scotch's most generous benefactors with membership of the Forbes Society rather than a society named after the Foundation's own predecessors, Scotch's earliest lay benefactors, Bonar and Armstrong.

The Old Boys of the nineteenth century saw Morrison as 'virtually the founder of the Scotch College',[43] and only as the last of them died could the title of 'Founder' be transferred to Forbes. So this striking invention of a tradition began in 1967 when the Rev. Gordon Powell (1929) preached a eulogy of Forbes in Assembly, soon published in the *Collegian*. Powell told the boys of Forbes's passionate integrity and he urged the boys to be ready, like Forbes, 'to sacrifice all for conscience sake'.[44] Powell was minister of Forbes's first church, Scots' Church, and preached again about Forbes when Healey briefly took the boarders there on the Sunday nearest to Foundation Day to honour Forbes's memory. In 1985 Donaldson read Powell's sermon 'with interest and delight' and hoped to redress the neglect of Forbes.[45]

It is too soon to say whether this Forbes tradition will take root. Perhaps it will. It is not how nineteenth-century Scotch saw itself, but that is no longer relevant. Traditions live or die in the continuing present, and Forbes offers a founding father more vivid than the shadowy Lawson, more personal than that the founder was the church as an institution.

The Rev. James Forbes, whom the Free Church of Australia Felix authorised in 1850 to write to Scotland to ask for a schoolmaster for Melbourne.

THE FUTURE

The relationship with the church has been tempestuous. Without the church, Scotch would neither have been born nor survived its infancy. But once the school could stand on its own feet it repeatedly wanted its own way. The church, for its part, has probably felt disappointment at how little the school has met the original goal of producing clergymen. Some Old Boys have become Presbyterian clergy—including a Moderator-General, Sir Francis Rolland (1895)—but Scotch has no reputation as a seed-bed for clergy.

The Presbyterian Church of Victoria will continue to change as it has done several times in the last 150 years, though we cannot tell how. In at least three ways its changes may affect the school.

Firstly, Presbyterianism regularly reinvigorates itself through its tradition of splits and unifications. One or other of these will come again to the present Presbyterian Church of Victoria in the fullness of time, and this will have repercussions for Scotch whose Council the church appoints.

Secondly, the church's own internal cycles may bring it to the stage it reached in the 1960s when some Christians were embarrassed by the church's connection with a school that was privileged in a society of social inequality, and with a school that trained boys to be soldiers. In the 1990s, those who attended the Presbyterian Church's services were predominantly white, elderly females,[46] not a group likely to be especially interested in the education of teenage boys.

Thirdly, the church has declined in membership since the schism from 9 500 to 6 500 and looks likely to continue to decline, although it will continue to exist, as does the Free Church that founded Scotch. At some point, the church and OSCA will change places in relative size. OSCA's current membership is 5 000, it regularly seats 800 or 900 at its annual dinners (the largest annual event of their kind in Australia), and 1200 Old Boys contribute to its Annual Fund. That OSCA should grow larger than the church reverses the balance of the school's first 150 years.

If the future brings another struggle about the school's religious affiliation, it is perhaps noteworthy that the religious affiliation of boys and their parents has changed since the school incorporated in 1980. Among entrants, the number of Anglicans has fallen by one-third (from 74 in 1980 to 54 in 2000), and the number of Uniting Church boys has more than halved (79 to 29). The number of Presbyterians has plummeted from 47 to 6. The number of families with no religious affiliation has leapt threefold, from 20 to 72.

If the future brings another struggle about the composition of Council, the school community might protest at the fact that Council is entirely unelected, despite *Great Scot's* recent description of a new Council member as having been 'elected'.[47]

The future's most obvious moment of difficulty in the short term will come when Donaldson retires, by 2009. Then, there would be dissension on Council if the best regular churchgoer seems to many members of Council to be significantly inferior to an applicant who is not a regular churchgoer.

It is also possible that, between Donaldson's departure and his successor's arrival, Council or the staff might play while the cat is away. It was between Littlejohn and Gilray that Council undercut the Principal's administrative independence with a Finance Committee, and it was between Gilray and Selby Smith that the staff set up the Common Room Association.

The future of the 1980 settlement offers more of the past, as the school's various interest groups nudge and nestle.

21

RECENT YEARS

Something held close to the face is hard to see properly. The same is true when we try to look at Scotch's recent years. Half a century from now, people may see that the most significant thing for Scotch in the 1990s was something that we have not much noticed. This chapter nevertheless hopes to trace some of what seem—surely!—to be the important themes of the Donaldson era.

BRICKS AND DOLLARS

Huge physical changes swept the last fifteen years. New and larger buildings arose. In providing educational facilities, the long-term trend has been to do so with dedicated buildings. The Senior School at Hawthorn began with a separate Science Block, and soon a library and a theatre. The Language Centre (1994) continued this pattern, with its three storeys of classrooms and facilities, as do the new library and the Forbes building for music and drama.

The new library (1993) epitomised why so much new building was needed. Not only was the old library, the Longmore, too small, but also the whole educational and technological environment had changed. The Victorian Certificate of Education (VCE) from 1990 emphasised research-based learning, which increased library usage. Moreover, Darling's goal of integrating the Library into the school's curriculum was overtaken during the 1980s by the idea that libraries had something of their own to teach—the rapid manipulation of information, which promised to be a key skill in the next century. In 1990 Donaldson appointed a new librarian, Dr Desmond Gibbs (staff 1990–99). Rather than being in the logistics business of providing access to books or other resources such as the new CD-ROMs which he introduced, Gibbs recast the Library's task philosophically and pedagogically as fostering 'information literacy'. He introduced a computerised catalogue giving boys access over the internet from wherever they might be and he oversaw the design of the new library in the Lithgow Centre.

Bruce Lithgow (1946) and Gordon Donaldson— Chairman and Principal— in 1983. Lithgow plucked Donaldson out of Ulster to settle Scotch down after the schism.

Lithgow (Chairman 1981–91) led Council into funding building in the 1990s without borrowing. Building funds came from the Foundation and the school's investments. The Forbes Academy's $23 million dollars (1900 times annual fees) will be funded without borrowing. Until the early 1990s, Council's policy was to allocate 1% of tuition fees towards building. Balderstone (Chairman 1991–95) discontinued this and today fees do not pay for building. Even so, the cost of depreciating expensive buildings does add to the fees. In setting fees, Council now aims to make only a tiny surplus, and more or less breaks even each year.

A new architectural style appeared from Garry Martin. The Randall and Forbes buildings' revived Edwardianism evokes an earlier age. The message is that Scotch is venerable and traditional. This contrasts with earlier buildings. In the 1930s Council wanted Scotch to look modern. New brick cladding was added, and Glen House soon demolished. Even as late as 1994, Martin's new Language Centre flaunted a modern style suggestive, perhaps, of Scotch's up-to-date multiculturalism. Similarly, his Cardinal Pavilion (1994) had the strong lines of modern materials and design. Only in the Junior School did the extensions in 1990 perpetuate the original architectural style.

In Martin, also, Scotch at last found an architect interested in public spaces. The fountain area inside the Lithgow Centre is a busy and welcoming space, the like of which the school has not seen before. Outside the tuckshop, tables and seating turned a thoroughfare into a social area. Healing the wounded hole where Glen House once stood on the Hill poses a greater challenge.

Scotch's buildings range from old to new. Boys sense this in their daily lives. Daniel Barrie (1995) inhaled 'the wet, mouldy smell of the boarding house showers. The metallic odour of the old heaters in the boarding house (and classrooms). The smell of the classrooms first thing on a Winter's morning. The smell of the new carpet etc. in the new Resource Centre.'[2] Jonathan Hiller (1996) relished what must be among Scotch's oldest smells— the quadrangle lawn being mowed on a winter's morning when the air was still but cool; the smell of hot food in the tuckshop; and in the Junior School Gymnasium, the warm musty smell of wooden floor and rope nettings.[3]

THE SCHOOL-IN-THE-MIND BECOMES FLESH

Many aspects of organisations exist only in the mind. At Scotch the Junior and Senior Schools have a physical existence, but other subdivisions have been less tangible, especially the academic departments, which have gained a physical location only in the last few decades.

Departments

Under Donaldson the academic disciplines have become physical entities. A department now has offices, a small staff room, a small library (ordered and catalogued through the main library) and dedicated teaching space. This was emerging since Selby Smith, but leapt ahead under Donaldson.

In the 1960s there were a few small departmental libraries (no more

'After being told to keep away from the builders and not to annoy them because we didn't want a strike, two Grade 2 boys bought ice-creams and took these down to the builders near the fence. They became friends with the shop steward and we didn't have any delays' — Graham Nowacki.[1]

DAVID BOYKETT

The Cardinal Pavilion doubled the boatshed area and crowned it with the Boykett Room. David Boykett (1952, staff 1963–96), twice an Olympian, epitomised much about Scotch. A thoughtful sportsmaster, he belonged to the Common Room Association's Education Committee in the 1960s. He chaired that Association 1991–93. As a colleague he was considerate and supportive. A big strong man, he had a caring, gentle side,

Building the Heart of Huon *in the 1990s. Davey Boykett shows boys the power of team strength.*

and was perceptive about young people. He believed he understood their difficulties but he felt some frustration at how this might be addressed within the school. Boys targeted him because of his deafness and would try to say things he couldn't hear but he surprised them, being a good lip reader.

He was at Scotch man and boy, a pupil for 13 years and a teacher for 34. As Rowing Master for 15 years (1963–78), he saw Scotch win the Head of the River six times and he coached the victorious 1978 crew. Later, between 1985 and 1993, he introduced beginners to sculling.

His forte was engaging boys in practical, unconventional ways. He was dedicated to the outdoors and to sail training (he was a founding Governor of the Sail Training Ship *Alma Doepel*). His Sea Scouts and scuba camps were legendary. In 1965 he conditioned cadets to march to Puckapunyal. In his last years at Scotch he, shipwright Tom Whitfield, master mariner Bob Lachal and many boys built the 35-foot sailing cutter *Heart of Huon* (oft called, of course, the *Hard of Hearing*). He took over the bank of the Meares Oval to do it, typically recruiting the school into his exploits. A bas-relief of the enterprise graces the Lithgow Centre.

Through his activities, many a difficult student remained connected to the school. He had an ability to inspire spirit and loyalty and to demonstrate to boys the power of combined team strength. By the time he retired, he was a 'living legend ... A unique individual that influenced me greatly. ... an incredible man ... a true gentleman.'[4]

than cupboards in classrooms) and the Junior School Art Subscription Library. Few staff had their own rooms. As late as 1985, the Vice-Principal had only a pokey rectangle, less than 4 by 3 metres, and English's Head and secretary shared an office. Group Masters who had to talk to a boy used an interview room.

Physics and Chemistry always had a separate building at Hawthorn. Under Selby Smith and Healey, other departments acquired at least a 'headquarters' room.[5] Geography's new room above the tuckshop had the latest geography-teaching equipment. Room 39 became the English Room, with a record-player for the likes of Olivier reading Shakespeare. In the 1980s, departments asked for more. English wanted offices, storage space, and a room for staff to meet or work in (previewing material, preparation, and correction). Nearby, five dedicated classrooms should be clustered so they could open up into a large classroom for small lectures, team teaching or group work.[6] In the new Language Centre, English gained the whole top floor, with seven classrooms and a common room for some of its staff. In one generation, it was a giant leap from Room 39. The drawback was that it split the department's staff into two groups, the others moving to the Lithgow Centre (1998) where new staff quarters replaced those designed in 1965 for 60 staff and by 1991 holding 107. The new Centre gave pagers to all staff.

The Middle School

Adding flesh to the concept of the Middle School was less successful. It shimmered into a passing existence in the 1960s–80s. It was to have its own buildings, staff and facilities, its own library, tuckshop and common room. It was floated by Healey, pushed by Roff, and buried by Donaldson, only to be revived, perhaps, in 1999.

The term *Middle School* in the 1960s referred to Forms I to IV (Years 7 to 10). In 1964 this put 658 boys in the Middle School, and 469 above. Boys aged 11 to 16 could be said to have particular needs that were best dealt with separately, and they were less subject to the academic pressures of the final years of secondary schooling.

During the 1970s, *Middle School* came to refer only to Forms I and II (Years 7 and 8), numbering 350 boys in 1981. Their needs were psychological, educational and physical, and focused on the transitions to puberty and to secondary education.[7] A Middle School delayed boys' entry to the Senior School for a year or two, enabling them to take their own measure rather than be on the bottom rung, without authority. For a time Scotch believed these benefits could come only from a Middle School that was physically distinct. In 1975–77 Scotch created it out of the Old Science Block. This building became empty when the new Maths and Science Block was completed. As happens in any organisation when space becomes available, everyone made a play for it, and by early 1976 the plans also included remedial classes, OSCA and the Foundation, a Library and Media Centre, a Group Master's Office, and the Bookroom. The 'Forms I and II Block' came into use in 1977, complete with carpets, an innovation. The trappings of a separate school emerged. It had its own library, squalid, but well-run and popular under John Francis (staff 1962–89, Group Master 1984–89) as part-time Librarian.[8] Further development ceased as funding dried up during the schism, and in 1981 the Middle School staff room was still only under contemplation, though it was needed to relieve congestion in the main staff room. In 1981 Roff persuaded the Development

Committee of the new Council to endorse the idea of a Middle School, housed in a new building on the site of the invincible green grandstand, 'close enough to make use of the specialist facilities of the Senior School such as Art, Music, Physical Education and Science [but] separate enough for those boys to pursue a different programme in a different way'.[9] The building would solve the accommodation problems of both the Junior and Senior Schools which would shed their Grade 7 and Form I and II classes.

Instead, Forms I and II remained in the Old Science Block. In 1986 the Library and special education facilities were upgraded, but the Middle School's prospects withered. On its site the Lithgow Staff Centre arose. By the late 1990s *Middle School* was again only a concept (for example, middle-school curriculum issues), much as one might talk about boys-in-their-teens.

The Middle School died for several reasons. True, a financial chill froze its buds. But it was, also, at odds with another line of reform, which preferred to educate boys in larger age ranges. This gave boys the reassurance of growing up within their peer group and yet at the same time in association with older and younger boys. Young boys had 'the potential force for good of having the example and leadership of older boys', and older boys benefited from the obligation to think for those younger than themselves.[10] For such reasons Selby Smith built the Memorial Hall gallery so as to seat the whole school in Assembly.

Ian Savage, 11th Vice-Principal, 1995– .

The arguments for *not* having a Middle School applied equally to not having an Upper School. In 1985 the Blackburn Report suggested senior secondary colleges for Years 11 and 12. Had they eventuated, Scotch would have faced parental pressure to follow, although 'to locate Years 11 and 12 at Scotch in a separate teaching and living facility would not only be enormously expensive but would also fragment the school, removing the invaluable contact between senior and junior pupils and the attendant opportunities for leadership and influence'.[11] These Upper School possibilities died away, as did the earlier Sixth Form Common Room.

In 1999 Donaldson created two new positions over the Heads of Years, called Heads of the Middle (Years 7–9) and Upper Schools (Years 10–12), to ensure innovation. We may see this as one more attempt to tackle a problem that recurs but is not amenable to easy solutions. It reflects, also, that the final years of schooling are determined by external curricula and assessment, whilst schools have more freedom in managing the earlier years.

TEAM TEACHING YEAR 7

In the meantime, from 1993 Scotch changed the teaching structure of Year 7, containing around 200 boys. Instead of each class having six to eight separate teachers, it had only three or four teachers working as a team (perhaps with a couple of specialists) to teach the entire core curriculum: History, Geography, English, Mathematics, Science, Christian Education, perhaps languages, perhaps Art.

It grew out of discussions between Donaldson, Boydell and Slade about the number of students per day an effective teacher would see. A teacher at Scotch saw about 160. Could one be effective seeing so many different people? Similarly, boys who in Grade 6 had one main teacher would abruptly in Year 7 have many more.

The Year 7 programme succeeded most in the pastoral area, although that was not its primary target. Year 7 was chosen because it was the base of the Senior School structure, and because it was the difficult transition stage for students entering the Senior School, 'who feel disoriented, a bit unloved, small fish/big pond'.[12] The intensive personal contact of the Year 7 team-teachers quickly made this pastoral aspect rewarding and exciting— and it was probably easier than the curricular aspects. Team teaching drew a positive response from boys, parents, and staff. It reduced the number of staff that students dealt with. It reduced the number of students that staff dealt with. It enabled staff (because they saw so much of the students) to detect pastoral and academic difficulties, and (because all a boy's teachers meet regularly) to co-ordinate help.

Team teaching fostered staff development. People from different disciplines had to talk. They met for two periods a cycle to discuss what they did. This generated a grassroots movement for curriculum change, as staff rethought their own discipline or immersed themselves in another. Creativity was encouraged by making the teams responsible for working out how to cover the curriculum. At first, team-members were volunteers and able to be open about their lack of comfort in teaching subjects not their own, but these aspects declined as the programme expanded.

Team teaching cuts across Scotch's usual location of knowledge and teaching within academic departments. Heads of Department had to let their subject be taught by teachers from other departments. Such teachers received special tuition but some Heads felt uncertain about using teachers who lacked a profound understanding of a subject's underlying principles. Would the boys get an adequate preparation for Year 8? Departments instinctively doubt that anyone else can teach what they teach.

Departments thus resisted the pressure to spread team teaching to later years. But half of Year 8 is in 2000 taught by teams. Departments prefer to characterise Year 7 as a foundation year, and to start teaching boys 'properly' in Year 8. Departments who see teaching as cumulative (where each year's work builds on the previous year), like languages or Mathematics, are most desirous to corral team teaching to Year 7. All departments teach particular knowledge and procedures, and all face the fact that they are judged by how well their boys do in Year 12. Departments are already defending their time from the many other claims on a boy's time at Scotch, and this is one more.

TEACHING: SKILLS, KNOWLEDGE, CHARACTER
Skills

This same set of forces applies to another emergent educational approach, that of how to teach skills. At the end of the 20th century Scotch tries to teach social skills and also thinking skills separate from the content of disciplinary curricula, although this means prising time loose from the departments.

Skills themselves go through periods of acceptance or disdain. The very way of talking about them changes. In the early 1990s, educationalists spoke of 'competencies'. In 1992 Donaldson called them 'higher order skills' and in 1999 'generic skills'. The lack of a solid name shows the educational community grappling with a new concept. Scotch defined such skills by asking itself, and outside business leaders, what boys would need in the 21st century. As well as the fundamental knowledge and skills that have long characterised liberal education, Scotch noted the importance of other attributes: independent thinking and learning skills, communications skills, information technology skills, team membership skills, and an understanding of cultural differences. Scotch boys already win very good Tertiary Entrance scores (in 1995–99, 30–40% of Scotch's Year 12 achieved 90 or above ENTER scores) and over 90% of boys go on to tertiary education. There, however, in the first year they can find the transition difficult as it requires some different skills. Similarly, how do they perform in the modern workforce? How do they perform as members of society? What values do they have? How are such things to be taught? These are the perennial questions that Morrison first wrestled with.

Communication skills involve skills in writing or talking, in pitching the message at an appropriate level, and in checking that the intended communication is getting through. The new VCE from 1990 stimulated oral skills as well as written communication. The English Department had begun Speakers' Forum back in 1978, where boys presented talks before their year group, and Holly (Senior English Master) defended inter-house debating at the GHC, as an important part of learning English.[13] In 2000, Year 7 boys making a presentation were assessed for content, clarity, and continuity. Content covered knowledge and accuracy; clarity embraced a boy's speech and body language; continuity required a logical sequence, and a connection to the accompanying visual presentation. A separate Communications Studies Unit in Year 10 taught aspects of public speaking other than the 'word', such as body language and semiotics (in this case visual and graphic material, such as advertisements, where the traditional tools of textual analysis were not adequate). Begun by Boydell as an unattached unit, it now resides in the Department of Drama and

Communications rather than in English. Drama thus became Drama and Communications, probably also to strengthen fundraising for the Forbes Academy. Not all boys are interested in theatre or drama, but communication has suddenly acquired respect.

Group-work skills, co-operation between men, is easiest to find in situations of conflict. Team spirit builds on having a foe to defeat. Co-operation that is built more on our species' enjoyment of shared tasks is less exhilarating but is more akin to boys' professional and family lives after school.

The thinking and learning skills boys needed were: to be able to work independently, to pursue ideas, and to collect data, analyse it, and report. VCAB targeted these skills in its new VCE. The emphasis of education shifted from examinations towards year-round assessment by Common Assessment Tasks (CATs). Boys learnt to be organised. Independent research, analysis and reporting dovetailed with the appearance of computers.

Boys learnt about learning. This has always been a breakthrough. 'Ike Collins in 6th grade junior school taught us it was fun to learn new things and it was good to be inquiring.'[14] Karl Lang (staff 1973–80) taught Bruce Lyman (1979) with tenacity: 'what has intrigued me ever since is the fact that he ... showed me what my mind could do if I applied it. He did not teach me chemistry formulas although there were plenty of them. He taught me how I could learn them. ... The sudden dawning when I received a test back with 100% that this academic adventure could be beat.'[15] Teachers also have learnt more about learning, and now use terms like meta-cognitive that were once unknown. A discipline's skills cannot be taught in isolation from content, and yet 'the important residue' from teachers' work is a boy's skills and understanding of how a discipline works.[16]

> There are really two types of teachers ... those that teach interactively, and those that employ the 'like this, do that' method. ... Those that teach interactively are really the ones that seem to have a passion for their subject ... they know it and they live it. It doesn't matter if it is Chemistry, Maths or History, they are able to teach a subject without relying on writing extensive notes on the board, or reading paragraph by paragraph from the text book. Mr Ian Savage was a teacher in this category ... he was able to teach history just by talking to us. The other kinds of teachers are those that write lines and lines on the board and have you copy them word for word. They might stop now and then to expand on a point, but mainly they rely on imparting the learning by getting you to copy what they write ... which makes it a lot harder. Perhaps it is a matter of experience ... but I don't think so, I think it comes down to a passion for the subject that they teach.[17]

One set of skills was introduced and institutionalised because they were more subject-related. Technological Design and Production (TDP), later Design and Technology, later Technological Design and Development

Officers of Cadets, c. 1985.
Back row (from left): Tony Birch, Shane Mawer
Middle row (from left): Tony Glover, Ross
Campbell, Geoff Wemyss, Richard Smith, Miles
Mudie
Front row (from left): Philip Anthony, Steve Kong,
Neville Taylor, Richard Shirrefs, Rev. Archie Crow,
Ken Baker

(TDD), introduced students to technological processes involving wood, plastics, metal and electronic components, and to basic graphic communication and design principles. It was a far cry from making ashtrays in Sloyd or Craft. Its many names reveal a new area of study trying to define itself. The Junior School introduced a design and technology unit in 1991. Boys designed everything from remote-controlled cars to candle-powered boats, then constructed them and tested the product, then modified or redesigned it. In the Senior School during the 1990s it began in Year 7 (at the same time as each Year 7 boy had to have a computer), became compulsory in Years 7–8 and an elective in Years 9–10, and reached Year 12. In 1996 Sir Ian McLennan endowed within the school a Chair of Design and Technology, Scotch's first such chair.

Schools once taught an academic programme and assumed that skills would be picked up along the way. Thus Healey used to say that every boy must go out the gate with a body of knowledge between his ears.[18] There is now a concern that unless skills are targeted they may not be picked up.

Scotch therefore asks itself how the curriculum develops skills and how they are assessed in each boy. Teaching generic skills raises problems in a school where teaching is based in departments. To create space to teach skills, team teaching might create cross-curricular subjects in which two or more disciplines could be covered at the one time. Such subjects might be developed by staff who were stimulated by teaching in disciplines not their own. But no genuinely cross-curricular programs have emerged (most are still basically taught from one stance with additions). In 1997, in an explicit attempt to create space to teach skills, departments had to reduce the content of their Year 7 course by 10%. Scotch then had to ascertain whether the 10% reduction had happened, and, if so, whether this 10% of time was used to teach skills, and, if they were being taught, how that could be measured. Such preoccupations were characteristic of the 1990s.

Whilst any single discipline is able to experiment and renew itself, overall reform of the curriculum is difficult when its pillars 'are guarded so jealously by the Heads of Department and the structures allow no room at all for any other kind of knowledge to be promoted as part of the classroom agenda'.[19] Scotch continues its quest to develop a way to institutionalise the teaching of skills.

Social education

The emerging commonplace in academic subjects, that to learn skills was as important as learning content, sanctioned the idea of teaching social skills in their own right. Boys had always received a barrage of social injunctions to *stand up straight, don't interrupt, only fishwives fold their arms*, and so on. But now social education became a *timetabled* subject. It tackled areas of behaviour (like drugs or sexuality) and modes of behaviour (like managing conflict).

In a school built round departments, Scotch could best teach Social Education by making it a department. By 2000 it has half taken this step, by appointing someone Head of the area, successively Ron Anderson, a secular humanist; Nick Browne, a high Anglican; and David Paul, a cheerful son of the manse with experience as Head of Department and Head of Year. It is taught in a number of areas and largely on an incidental basis as teachers seize the moment. One of the school's challenges is how to co-ordinate this, to ensure that certain key programmes are covered.

One long-existing area is alcohol. Scotch used to tell boys never to drink. In 1961 'there was one lecture (unbelievable really) in 3rd form in Mackie Hall organised by Miss Tyrell Gill when someone came out of the ark and taught fire and brimstone about the evils of alcohol'.[20] 'Presbyterian influence meant a glass of wine consumed with dinner was treated indistinguishably from a bottle of cheap scotch/vodka swilled at cadet camp or at school parties' (1975).[21] In the 1990s, in contrast, Scotch taught harm minimisation. That is, rather than prohibit, Scotch educated boys about deleterious effects and about reasonable dosages. Such information is now offered to boys from Year 9. Given that boys are likely to drink, the aim is to teach them alcohol's effects and help a boy control his drinking. 'Sexuality (including contraceptives and Sexually Transmitted Diseases) is explored in the Year 10 Christian Education programme in the context of male/female relationships', and further explored in a Human Relations Day held with girls' schools.[22]

Harm minimisation recognises that, whether Scotch likes it or not, many youngsters *are* involved in drinking alcohol and in sexual activity, and some in taking illegal drugs. Scotch knows that a significant number will have tried marijuana, even if few use other illegal drugs like the opiates. The dilemma with drug-taking is that many people see harm minimisation as inappropriate with illegal substances. The school argues that there is no virtue in ignorance and that boys facing a choice about such drugs need to hear a responsible counter-balance against peer-generated risk-taking myths.[23]

Harm minimisation teaches skills rather than morals. Like modern academic subjects, it emphasises approaches as well as content. In other behaviours, too, boys learn that they have a choice of approach. For example, boys are encouraged to be assertive rather than aggressive, and to handle bullying or conflict. Such 'pro-social skills' are taught in a social context.

A 'Skills for Adolescence' course began in 1991 in Year 7, teaching the social skills needed in the classroom and beyond, but fell victim to Year 7 team teaching, and is planned for revival in 2001. This parallels the way in which General Studies fell victim to Australian Studies. Since the introduction of General Studies a generation ago, the subjects that aim to educate boys as men and citizens have contested with each other for a limited amount of space. This paralleled what happened within other disciplinary clusters, for example in languages between Latin, Russian and Chinese. The human-skills subjects, when seen in this light, are undergoing the same healthy winnowing as academic subjects.

The external academic regulatory system

A federal initiative, the National Curriculum Standards Framework (CSF), began in the late 1980s. Its Key Learning Areas (KLAs) were intended to be the same in every Australian State, but Victoria (for one) undermined it, and Scotch's various departments absorbed it selectively.

State requirements, however, had the force of law. The new VCE was phased in over three years, 1990–92. Already, from 1987, it occupied much of the school's attention and energy.

The VCE raised several problems. It required teachers to certify that a boy's work in Common Assessment Tasks (CATs) was his own, which was hard to do for work done outside school. VCE assessed work simply as satisfactory or not satisfactory. Scotch, preferring more incentive for excellence, evaluated quality. This quickly led to boys and teachers spending more time than was productive, because many drafts were allowed, and the school had to develop ways of restraining this. By 2000, CATs had given way to SACs (School Assessed Coursework) produced at school rather than at home.

Also, the VCE had an egalitarian approach that included all subjects in the same certificate. Donaldson characterised the Minister of Education, Joan Kirner, as wanting all subjects to rank equally, dance and physics alike, which he publicly excoriated as 'patently absurd'.[24] Scotch also regretted that the new subject of Australian Studies, being compulsory, obliged boys to drop something else. Modern languages suffered until the universities gave them a 10% bonus.

Schools' responsibility for designing Year 11 was overtaken by imposed regulations. As VCE displaced Scotch's Year 11 General Studies course, so it smothered other initiatives. David Paul

Neil Cracknell in 1997, Head of Year since 1995.

had for many years taken about 10–15 Year 11s who were doing Maths/Sci and a language (and who therefore could not fit in a history subject) for 'extra' History on a Wednesday morning from 8.30 am through Assembly time. This was their only face-to-face tuition, but because they were motivated and very bright, they could cover the entire course in that time. In exams and research activity, they performed at least as well as the general run of boys who had regular classes! Provan ran an extra French class on similar lines.[25]

VCE's bureaucratic insistence on a minimum number of contact hours, however, meant that boys continuing to do these subjects would receive no recognition. Much as the school experienced the VCE as clumsily imposed from outside, however, Scotch had at least seconded three teachers (Boydell, Peter Hauser (staff 1983–96, Head of Commerce 1987, Year 12 Group Master 1987–96) and David Paul) to help VCAB develop the VCE.

A long readjustment had occurred. At the start of the century, the University of Melbourne shaped secondary-school curricula, doing so through various boards to which it admitted school representatives. In the second half of the century, educationalists pushed the universities out and shaped secondary education as something in its own right. Scotch had more influence under the old system. The context in which the school now operates is one determined by others. Nevertheless, powerful Principals like Donaldson and Paul Sheahan of Melbourne Grammar work together to influence events.

Outside academic matters came a more general rise of regulation and litigation. This both curtailed the school's freedom (even in matters as central as, say, staffing), whilst at the same time it increased the administrative burden on the school as it checked to ensure its obedience to the increased number of laws and regulations—like health and safety, or equal opportunity—which make today's environment so different from what once was.

Curriculum

Scotch continued to expand its curriculum. Mandarin began in 1991, as did Technological Design and Production. As well as new subjects, existing subjects spread into later years. As the century ended, Drama reached Year 12 and Psychology Year 11. The extent and the pace of change in the 1990s exceeded what happened in any earlier decade. In 1999, Year 12 students chose from 30 different study areas. Timetabling these was a problem in its own right, managed by the flexible Slade and his computer, whereas Bond's timetable was a large hand-written document. Arrangement of programmes by semester in Years 9 and 10 allowed a greater number of units.

The increased number of subjects helped Scotch meet the wide range of boys' abilities. In his second year Donaldson set up a steering committee to advise on 'how best to handle the problems of both gifted children and those with learning difficulties'.[26] An extension programme was begun in 1986 for Form II (Year 8) boys identified as having 'particularly high ability' and for other boys who expressed interest.[27] Maths Extensions Groups, or special classes in Chemistry and Physics for their Olympics, became routine. Electives also grew, and in years below Year 12, as when a handful of boys did Latin in a class containing boys from Years 9 to 12. Donaldson in 1996 created the position of Director of Educational Research and Development, and appointed Boydell, thereby formalising his role as one who thought creatively about what can be done in a school.

Scotch trumpeted ever-higher percentages of boys performing ever better.

By 1990, Ken Evans worried that middling boys were being neglected.[28] This is the complaint of generations of Old Boys right up to the present: 'If you didn't show an immediate talent for the subject then [they] had no time for you' (1990).[29] Many boys with no academic or sporting ability feel that Scotch ignored them. This was acknowledged most recently in the report of the 1999 Foundation Fellow, Rollo Browne, whose report mentions invisible boys—those who are neither very good at something nor troublemakers.[30] In a large school this is a perennial problem.

For each boy to be good at something: Clubs fade away

Following on the heels of the new tutorial system, in 1990 Donaldson appointed a Senior Master—Students, Kong, with a wide brief covering all Scotch's non-academic aspects. For the first time, Scotch conceptualised and administered its non-academic activities as a single domain, in 1991 coining a new name for it: co-curricular and pastoral.[31]

Success outside the classroom, Donaldson believes, builds confidence and helps a boy win academic success.[32] Old Boys concur: success in sport 'gave me confidence in other spheres' (1963).[33] Scotch hopes that each boy will find something he is good at but it hopes, too, that he will find it among the extensive range of programmes offered. Letting boys choose even more widely is not efficient, as it requires either the provision of facilities or the use of existing facilities in new ways, possibly unwelcome ways. For instance, Ferguson set his face against rock music, and forbade rock-oriented boys to play the drums as loudly as they wanted to, although the Forbes building will contain a specially soundproofed Rock Room.

Scale Plastic Models Club, 1982. 'Please do not handle the models.'
From left: Andrew Mansell, James Barber, Phil Vabre. Since then, clubs have faded.

Meanwhile, clubs, so energetic since the 1920s, largely disappeared. Whilst individual clubs had always come and gone, overall they were numerous and many were long-lasting. New clubs had continued to emerge under Healey (like Coin, Surf and United Nations) and under Roff (like the War Games Club). By the late 1980s, however, only a handful of clubs remained. A mere four lasted more than one year: Christian Fellowship, Astronomy, Scuba and Rifle. Even this slight presence still showed the club system's threefold offering, catering to religion, education and enthusiasm. The Christian Fellowship, like its predecessors, was a quasi-official programme. On the day it met, no other meetings were allowed to compete with it. This has been the rule since Healey at least. Astronomy took boys' enthusiasm and steered it in educative directions. The Junior Computer Club in 1987 did the same. A Theatre Sports Club in 1990 gave small groups of boys a topic and 20 seconds to think of a two-minute sketch. The Scuba and Rifle Clubs, with others such as the Snorkel Club in 1987, were physical activities not undertaken as competitive school sports.

The Scuba Club also reflected the club system's flexibility in catering for new interests. So did the Black Mamba and Sharemarket Clubs in 1987. In 1989 a Games Club, with 15 members, played Warhammer, Dungeon, Russian Front, Imperial Rome, and Futuristic Galactic battles.[34]

Donaldson attributes the demise of clubs to the fact that 'boys don't have hobbies any more. Instead, the computer absorbs a lot of their time,

WIRELESS CLUB

One night in the early 1920s Littlejohn realised that the boarders were suspiciously quiet and not in the prep room. He found them upstairs, where Bruce Mann (1924) had strung a wire across the courtyard and was working the valve wireless receiver he had built. Littlejohn was fascinated. He ran off to fetch Mrs Littlejohn, although she left when the programme changed from classical to dance music at the Palais, St Kilda. Littlejohn asked Mann to set up a Wireless Club, and allowed the gymnasium flagpole to support an antenna. When Kay, the Senior Physics Master, bought a wireless he asked Mann's advice, and to get it working would have Mann round to his house where Mrs Kay served afternoon tea.[35] In 1956, the Common Room's retirement present to Bowden was a wireless, the first he had ever owned.[36]

In 1933 the Radio Club had 60 members, and Rowlands in charge. Perhaps members were encouraged by the example of the Rev. John Barber (1890) who in the 1920s was the practical organiser behind the Flying Doctor Service, or by the example of Sir Hugh Denison (1878), managing director of Amalgamated Wireless (Australia) and chairman of the Macquarie Broadcasting Services. Russell Wright (1939) was soon a prisoner of the Japanese and constructed hidden radio-receivers from scrounged and improvised parts.[37]

In the 1950s the club was the Radio Section of the Applied Sciences Club, and had two groups, one for less experienced students from the crystal-set stage upwards and the other with a reasonable knowledge of electronic theory. Ferres tapped their enthusiasm to encourage them to learn about radio, electronics and physics. 'There were many experiments and lunch time fun in the physics lab.'[38] In 1957 they built a receiver that could pick up Radio Moscow.[39] In 1958 two amateur radio stations operated under Duncan Eales (1958), VK3LQ and Michael Boudry (1958), VK3ZFZ. By 1960 the cadet unit provided most of its own signalling equipment, where enthusiasts relished 'using real equipment to do something genuinely interesting. Learnt a lot';[40] some went on to become electrical engineers. In the 1960s transistors made radios both portable and more reliable. When Bob Cowper scored his triple century boys listened in class to transistor radios with ear plugs, and the masters were just as interested but pretended not to be.

At the end of the century, the pattern of radio's development recurred with computers, when some boys' initial enthusiasm enabled them to lead the masters, and when the school later responded in an organised way to channel and educate the boys.

The Radio Club, 1982. From left: Simon St Hill, Iwan Tumewa VK3XIT, Csaba Veres.

in playing games or doing other interesting things.'[41] Also, David Paul believes that 'Teachers' energies have been redirected into extra demands on their time, particularly curriculum changes and the VCE, extra duties, committees, etc.'.[42] Yet boys can be found engaged in a wide range of pastimes such as breeding rabbits or birds, or fishing, or working on cars and bikes, to judge from the recreational magazines and books used in the library.[43] It may also be that the Adventure Programme's provision of photography, cooking, cycling or whatever, may absorb boys' interest in these and similar activities, although it means that the enthusiast has to share them with boys only doing them because they are compulsory. Clubs' decline, finally, may reflect the fact that fewer Australian adults now join voluntary associations.

It may also be that the attention of the school and its staff was on involving boys ever more closely in organised official activities, manifested by the ever-increasing number of sports and outdoor programmes, so that staff saw no need to encourage or facilitate boys' random enthusiasms, nor had the time to do so. The educational benefits of ensuring that every boy was fully occupied prevailed over the benefits of unleashing boys to do what they could think of themselves.

Clubs' demise has thus paralleled the arrival of a full panoply of compulsory non-academic activities. The classic justification of compulsory activities comes from Kurt Hahn (later Headmaster of Gordonstoun), that although a school has no right to coerce boys into opinion, it has a right and a duty to *impel boys to experience*.[44] Healey often used this phrase,[45] and Donaldson uses it today.[46] To force a boy to develop may seem inherently contradictory, since the boy does not learn how to develop by himself, but boys themselves are inherently contradictory, too. One Old Boy regrets that he 'was never pushed to participate/grow up' whilst admitting 'although at the time I would have hated to be pushed' (1989).

SPORT

The four old sports (athletics, cricket, football, and rowing) still have pride of place. They alone grace the honour boards in the Memorial Hall. In number of participants, hockey, basketball, and soccer each burst into popularity among Australian boys, whilst rugby declined, and Australian Rules football also fell away, perhaps especially in the Junior School where mothers were concerned about injuries. Soccer, having long averaged 12 to 14 teams, has recently vaulted to 17 teams, and the Lower West Oval (formerly for hockey) has become a second soccer pitch. In the winter of 2000, football occupies 430 boys in 19 teams, soccer 280 boys in 17 teams, basketball 220 in 18 teams, hockey 208 in 13 teams, rugby 146 in 6 teams, gymnastics 45 boys, cross-country running 35 boys in five age groups, and winter tennis 17 boys in 2 teams. Seven boys are exempt, and the very precision of this figure reveals how thoroughly required sport now is. (Of

CRICKET, SCOTCH VERSUS CAREY, 1987

We went into this match knowing that to win was to win the A.P.S. premiership. Carey sent us in to bat, and we got off to a great start, with Sinclair and Steele playing solidly and taking us to 1/58. Earle replaced Steele and our score was steadily increased by a fine partnership that added 114 before Sinclair was stumped. Two quick wickets fell before Meggitt took the crease and steadied us, and we finished the day with 4/194.

With every minute counting, we hoped to score runs quickly and declare. After an hour and a quarter, during which Earle completed an outstanding century, we declared. Although Wes Anderson tried to ease James' tension by showing his score as one less than it really was, it just resulted in him hitting a two. We declared at 6/293.

Meggitt got us off to a great start, clean bowling their opener on his sixth ball. Baker took three valuable wickets, but a couple of good middle-order partnerships took them to 181 before Sinclair took the first of three great catches. We had begun to lose our grip on the match when some Scotch boys arrived from the Head of the River, and the sound of the war cry coming from the scoreboard lifted our spirits, and we took three more wickets. But a ninth wicket partnership added 72 runs, during which Carey changed from holding out for a draw to playing for the match. The last couple of hours were the tensest imaginable, and when, with 16 runs remaining, the last batsman struck a perfect lofted drive our spirits sank. But following the path of the ball our eyes suddenly found … David Manderson underneath it, and the match and the premiership were ours!

Many thanks must go to all the people who helped us throughout the year. Enough cannot be said about the superb efforts of Mr Rumble in training and inspiring us. Thanks also to the many parents and friends who were loyal supporters. Best wishes to next year's captain and team!

James Sinclair, Captain of Cricket[47]

course, such figures risk being fantastical and the reality may be that boys have their names on lists but do not play sport in practice.)

As with academic subjects, Scotch has widened its offering, and now has 23 sports. Newcomers in the last 20 years include badminton (catalysed by the rise in Asian students), triathlon, lawn bowls, orienteering and European handball.

Other sports were rejected although greatly popular with teenage boys. The trampoline took up too much space and staff-time supervising. Skateboarding was likely to be dangerous. Cycling and BMX and dragster racing were rejected. Perhaps their time will come. Table tennis, long called ping-pong, was played throughout the century but become a sport only in 1977 (and later an APS premiership sport). Others, like trail riding in 1993, became activities rather than sports.

Facilities were steadily upgraded. Bob Montgomery (1922) donated a new sports field. Built on the site of the old horse-grazing paddock, its synthetic mod-grass surface transformed 'a sub-standard hockey area used three months in the year to a high-class surface useable all year'[48] as a winter hockey pitch and summer tennis courts. The old grass tennis courts immediately east of the Memorial Hall acquired the same surface, virtually maintenance-free compared to the one-third of a groundsman's time the grass courts had required.

Ian Bowman takes a mark at Wesley, 1976.

Sport has become serious. As well as having teachers as coaches, Scotch had long used Old Boys or parents. In 1989 Scotch hired Paul McGann (staff 1989–94) part-time to coach rowing after an eleven-year drought. Since then other sports have also acquired paid professional coaches. At the same time, teachers who coach have received training as coaches, a shift from the previous amateur approach. Intensified coaching has led to intensified sport. Boys train more often and more thoroughly. A boy hoping to get into a First team has to train all year round.

To reward boys' greater involvement in sport, Championship Team awards recognised the best performance in each sport by a team other than the Firsts. This recognised a team's ideals and commitment. A variety of age groups have won it, a counterweight to celebrating only the Firsts. Some sports or coaches dispense a Best and Fairest Player award, rewarding enthusiasm and courtesy.

A LIVING ORGANISM

Hindsight is a great clarifier. It is easy to give Scotch's recent decades a rational pattern. Subjects, sports and activities all increase in number and gain enhanced facilities. Curriculum responds to governments, and circles

HOCKEY

'Hockey is the best sport in the world. Just ask any hockey player.' It is 'a kind of mobile golf',[49] and its penalty for play is that 'when I received a ball it often shot up my hockey stick and struck me in the balls'.[50]

It was played at Scotch occasionally after 1900 and gained a more regular existence from the 1930s. In the 1950s Scotch fielded four teams and repeatedly won the Victo-

rian Under-19 Championship. Its rivals were varied (for hockey was not an APS game), such as YMCA, Old Wesley, Teachers Training College, and RAAF.

In 1959 it became a house and Public School sport. Scotch won the premiership with an unbeaten record. Thereafter the number of boys increased until in 1988 Scotch fielded as many hockey as football teams.

between skills and knowledge. Social trends raise the problems of drugs and sex to new levels of difficulty, pushing the school into new levels of response. Much of this makes sense looking back from today, and might have been predictable looking forward from 1980.

Other outcomes were more unexpected, and remind us that developments in society and in Scotch itself are alive (and dangerous!).

Composition

The composition of the school changed. Groups that once were small increased in size, such as Catholics (reflecting Australia's lessened religious divisions) and Asians (reflecting their increased number within Australia).

Before the discovery of antibiotics, boys commonly had extended absences, even for relatively minor problems like an ear infection. Malcolm McKenzie (1947) 'missed most of Year 5 in Junior school... I always felt that I missed a lot of the bonding during those years.'[51] Although these absences disrupted boys' education, Scotch did not handle very well these boys' return to school. Indeed, they were left to catch up or not, as best they could. Now the challenge is set to revive in a new guise. Improved treatment of cystic fibrosis means more boys with this disability are living longer and so are more likely to be at school. The challenge to the school is how to educate someone who has frequent intervals in hospital. Also, 'many become averse to attending school because they do not have the stamina for strenuous physical activity and may be teased by classmates—consequently problems of social adjustment or isolation may develop'.[52]

The death of young Old Boys is nowadays uncommon. Earlier generations suffered an undertow of deaths from infectious diseases we now regard as vanquished, from illnesses like appendicitis, and from war. That young men die less often perhaps explains modern families' strong response. When Ned Shergold (1987) died the year after he left school, his family paid to change the old Sub-Primary in 1991 into the Shergold building, a specialised Junior School music and drama facility. When Ashley Perelberg (1992) died aged 18, his family endowed a memorial award for exemplifying the 'true Scotch spirit' of personal excellence and service. Its winners include Professors Hugh Taylor (1964) and Rob Moodie (1970). As schoolboys Taylor was caught 'borrowing' a car (see p. 501) whilst Moodie 'got nabbed for smoking at Murph's milk bar on the corner of Glenferrie and Cotham Rd— we ... used to go there after school, and Murph sold single cigarettes. Got a Saturday morning detention for my troubles.'[53] As well as allowing us to draw the moral that today's rule-breaker isn't all bad, we may also speculate that the boy who breaks rules may be more likely to be creative or to achieve discoveries in science by questioning its rules too.

New traditions

The entire pupil population of the Senior School changes every seven years. Few human societies or organisations undergo such a total turnover so frequently. One effect of this is that any custom older than six years is literally beyond the reach of memory. It is a tradition. Take for example, the haka, a Maori wardance performed by Scotch. Jason Andrew (1990), of Samoan descent, recalls the Scotch rugby tour of New Zealand in 1989:

> At an after-match function of our last game on the tour, at a little town about 50 kms South of Christchurch a couple of the local Maoris asked to see our Haka. Our initial response that it didn't exist was not well received and they jokingly threatened to cut our half-back's hair (Luke Daley, '90), which at the time was a bit below the collar. Forced into the corner and keen to preserve Luke's locks I improvised a few moves to a chant that had been bantered around throughout the duration of the tour by Andrew Fortey ('89) and Michael Sutherland ('89)—*Scotch is hot to go, H.O.T.T.O.G.O.* Not very intimidating but certainly a crowd pleaser, and Luke got to keep his hair.
>
> Upon returning to Melbourne and after further editing the Haka made its inaugural appearance at the 1989 APS athletics, performed by members of the rugby team.[54]

The Torch Ceremony is an older tradition of which the beginnings are hard to locate. This ceremony occurs at the end of each year in the Memorial Hall. A flaming torch is passed from hand to hand between the often tearful boys about to leave school. Departing senior staff also pass the torch. The school sings 'Jerusalem'—what Savage calls 'a green and pleasant incongruity. It provides a rousing cacophony.'[55] At the end, the School Captain entrusts the torch to the youngest Form Captain and it is he who rekindles the torch at the next year's ceremony.

It is not easy to say when this ceremony was first held. Boys who were contemporaries have contradictory memories as to whether the ceremony occurred in their time. This illustrates how quickly a human community can create immemorial customs. Scotch finds it tempting to link the ceremony with the relay at the 1951 centenary when a torch was carried on foot and by boat from the school's former sites to Hawthorn. But this event had no immediate successor. The present Torch Ceremony appears to have begun in 1959 and to have been scheduled annually from 1967. The torch itself is almost certainly the one used in the 1951 relay, but people also talk of it as a replica of the one used in the 1956 Melbourne Olympics. (Indeed, the school owns such a replica, acquired through Herb Engel.)

Views on the Torch Ceremony have varied. Its retention was questioned in 1976 because of its stilted nature, and because whilst the torch went round there was much noise and lack of attention. 'Boys chatter and joke while it is on, especially the 4th Formers [Year 10s, in the balcony] who are

MEN OF INFLUENCE, MEN OF WEIGHT

As the 20th century ends, Scotch's Old Boys seem everywhere.

At Princeton, Peter Singer (1963) has become a world figure as a champion of animal rights and human ethical issues. Sir Ninian Stephen (1940), a High Court judge since 1972, was Governor-General of Australia in 1982–89, succeeding Sir Zelman Cowen. In 2001 Peter Hollingworth (1951), Archbishop of Brisbane, and previously an ardent advocate for social justice at the Brotherhood of St Laurence, became Scotch's third Governor-General.

Sir Ninian Stephen (1940), Governor-General of Australia 1982–89.

At the apex of their professions, Alastair Nicholson (1955) is Chief Justice of the Family Court of Australia, Lieutenant-General Peter Gration (1948) was Chief of the Defence Force and his brother Air Marshal Barry Gration (1952) Chief of the Air Staff. Ken Hayne (1962) is a Justice of the High Court of Australia, Ron Taft (1936) is a leading psychology scholar, Creighton Burns (1941) was editor of Melbourne's *Age* newspaper (1981–89). Professor Rod Tucker (1965) won the 1997 Australian Prize. Charles Goode (Dux 1956) is Chairman of ANZ Bank (1995–) and Woodside Petroleum (1999–), two of the top 15 companies in Australia, and John Landels (1947) is Chairman and Chief Executive of Caltex. Evan Thornley (1982) is CEO of LookSmart in Silicon Valley, and John Craven (1969) is CEO of Spike Cyberworks Australia.

Hugh Stretton (1938) is the doyen of Australian social science, one of Australia's most original and creative intellectuals, and author of the enormously influential *Ideas for Australian Cities*.

John Williamson (1963) is a leading Australian singer and song-writer: boarding at Scotch gave him 'a deep knowledge of cricket and church music. [He] took from it all he needed for his career.'[56] Richard Tulloch (1966) has written over 100 episodes of *Bananas in Pyjamas*. Tim Coldwell (1969) was the founding artistic director of Circus Oz.

As well as premiers in Victoria and Tasmania, Andrew Refshauge (1960) is Deputy Premier of NSW, Andrew Peacock (1957) was federal Leader of the Opposition and Michael Wooldridge (1973) Deputy Leader. Jim Kennan (1963) was Leader of the Opposition in Victoria. Tony Staley (1957) was federal president of the Liberal Party.

Old Boys are filmmakers like Chris Warner (1969), architects like Bruce Trethowan (1969), art dealers like Stuart Gerstman (1966) and vintners like the Brown, Campbell, Chambers and Morris families.

Among the youngest prominent Old Boys are Chris Merry (1989), a Vice-President in the Australian Medical Association, and Cameron Milner (1989), Queensland State Secretary of the Australian Labor Party.

The earliest known photograph of the Torch Ceremony, dated 1968.
The staff, from left, are: Leon Bates, Dr Gregor Mendel, Frank Nankervis, Alec Lyne, Frank Paton, Ron Bond, Wilbur Courtis, Stan Brown, Rev. David Webster (obscured), Keith Elliott, Mark Stump, Rev. Archie Crow.

not able to see the torch for several minutes.' But boys in their final year found it 'meaningful'.[57] The youngest Form Captain certainly found it memorable.[58] In 1977 it was cancelled when, as a punishment for several boys' misdemeanours, the entire leaving year was suspended on their final day.[59] Others see it as an emotionally charged but rather empty ritual, even pagan. Nowadays it is much esteemed. Jonathan Hiller (1996) underwent an epiphany, when his 'realisation of the power of harmony, unity, loyalty, confidence, energy and totality culminated at the Torch Ceremony'.[60]

THE PRINCIPAL

Donaldson has proved a boon. At the time of his arrival, the Scotch community was tempestuous, riven and disheartened. The controversy of Roff's fall threatened to taint any successor. Two decades later, the school is united and successful, with sound finances and vigorous building funded without debt. Donaldson is the first to protest that many people helped achieve this outcome, but the Principal's key role made him the focus and fulcrum. Unfairly, the very longevity of Donaldson's administration makes it liable to inertia, which is made even more likely by his increasingly sure touch in creating an enduring team of senior staff. To address this risk he deliberately seeks to stimulate and challenge the school, for instance by using Foundation Fellows, by appointing a Director of Educational Research and Development, and by twice revamping the Head of Year system untouched since Gilray.

In his doctoral research Donaldson studied actual atomic behaviours, as a practical accompaniment to the work of theoreticians. Rhetoric should not run too far ahead of reality. As Principal, Donaldson does not put himself forward as a visionary, but he behaves as though he does have a vision of where he wants the school to be when he retires. Whatever the difficulties (so varied from year to year), there is a sense that the school is purposefully under way and certainly not becalmed.

Donaldson's strategic choices include pushing ahead vigorously with building and with information technology (and the educational changes it entails), keeping the school on one campus, keeping the school a school for boys, introducing team teaching, and encouraging research into the school's functioning. Whilst it is possible to argue against these strategies (that the money spent on building might have been spent in other ways; that his focus is more physical than social; that the school would benefit from a separate country site or from co-education), the school's general mood is firmly to endorse Donaldson's strategic decisions.

Charming, firm, even fierce if crossed, with a whimsical humour, Donaldson radiates a genial authority. Most boys scarcely meet Donaldson and do not know him. Scotch has grown six fold since Morrison's time, utterly altering the relationship between Principal and pupil. Boys who do feel that they have taken Donaldson's measure speak favourably:

> His height and confidence is projected, but not intimidatingly—he is
> approachable. He has the utmost respect for history and tradition, but is at
> the forefront in the quest to expand and revolutionise Scotch's technology,
> equipment, and didactic methods. As a young boy he left an incredible
> impression on me (and no doubt others) as a man you simply know will do
> the right thing; he is a leader to emulate.[61]

Thus a young man idealises male power and influence.

Donaldson has already overtaken Lawson, Selby Smith, Healey and Roff in length of tenure, and in 2002 will surpass Gilray's 19 years. Littlejohn's 30 years lie beyond Donaldson's retiring age of 65 in 2009, 27 years after his appointment. Alexander Morrison, in length of tenure and in so much else of his legacy to the school, remains unassailable.

22

BEING A MAN

A young man is in English called a *youth*. There is no equivalent word for a young woman. Clearly, our society feels the need for a word here to describe a person in a particular state. The youth is neither boy nor man but is in between. One role for a school is to guide that transition.

In the 50 years since Scotch's centenary in 1951, Western society has developed in several ways, not the least of which has been the widespread impact of feminism. This changed women's perceptions of themselves and how they wished to educate themselves. It also led to a change in women's relationships with men and conversely in how men related to women. This in turn has prompted men to re-evaluate both how men see themselves and also how men think boys should be educated. Masculinity, once so self-evident and straightforward, has become a subject to ponder.

Outside the gates, Scotch's teenage boys have had to adjust to the ways of female friends. Inside the school, feminism is mentioned little if at all. It is unmentioned even in discussions of masculinity, and such discussions appear therefore with only a limited or practical focus, lacking any broader intellectual framework. It is as if Scotch cannot see any use for feminism in a boys' school.

Nevertheless all this has impacted greatly on Scotch in four central aspects of life: men's relations with women, and with other men, and men's relations with the gentle and violent aspects of themselves.

We have touched upon some of this already. In Chapters 13 and 21 we saw how one view of girls (as sexual objects to conquer) wars with another view of girls (as people and companions). We saw, too, in Chapters 13 and 19, that Scotch stigmatises some relationships that boys form with each other, refusing to acknowledge the occurrence of homosexuality and considering it a slur on the school.

This chapter looks at the less explicitly sexual ways in which the inhabitants of a boys' school treat each other. Here, too, we find that the choice is between conquering and caring.

MANLINESS

Morrison wanted 'manliness of character' (1869),[1] 'a manly tone of feeling and conduct' (1877).[2] Littlejohn's reference for the future Sir Thomas Ramsay (1924) said that 'He has grown into a fine manly lad'.[3] Manliness appears in the blue cards as late as the 1960s—'A boy with plenty of courage,

486

RAILWAY CLUBS

Railway enthusiasts formed a club in the 1950s, averaging about 50 members a year. Under Dr Mendel, it held weekly meetings, films and excursions. They built a model railway layout in a hut near the rowing pool, and rebuilt it in 1965. In 1966 a boy was caned for damaging it. *Satura* carried advertisements for Hornby model railway items, and for lengths of Marklin track, and a Mashing Board.[4]

The Club also revelled in real trains. In 1955 they hired a train to Maldon, the first train on the line for fifteen years. Everyone turned out to meet them. In 1956 they linked their excursions with study, chartering a train to the Western District along with the senior Geography classes. From 1956 members took part in reopening the Gembrook narrow-gauge railway track for Puffing Billy, toiling on work parties and raising money. In 1978 an attempt failed to re-establish a model-railway club.[5]

common sense and manliness' (1960)—but fell into disuse and was replaced by the idea of masculinity—'Not a bad masculine type of lad. Restless at times' (1963). Ling in 1972 thought the school should teach 'an appropriate masculine social role'.[6] Alec Fraser's prayer for 'the generation now growing to manhood'[7] was reprinted for forty years after 1947, until Bradbeer dispensed with formal liturgies.

What are we to make of the fact that a boys' school no longer uses words like manly, manliness or manhood? Somehow Australian society, though it urges boys to adult behaviour, keeps such language genderless and shrinks from asking boys to become adult *men*. Somehow a phrase like 'be a man' has become comic, or suggestive of violence, or a synonym for having no feelings. None of these meanings is very helpful. The boys themselves were aware of society's doubts about them, and in the 1990s started to call themselves men, albeit in a rhetorical way: 'the men of Morrison [House] have a hard reputation', 'the men from Bond have always prided themselves …'.[8] *The men of* was a popular phrase in speeches, 'but people are certainly never told to "be a man",' writes Lindsay Rattray (1999). Rather, 'being a man was reserved for disciplinary talks to older students, and always prefixed with the adjective "young". Speeches in the vein of "You are about to become young men, so" and "I will not be spoken to like this, young man" were not rare in the school's proceedings'.[9]

Manliness is a social thing. It varies between social classes and between eras. During 150 years its meanings have changed. Scotch has taught boys not just to behave like men but to behave like men of their class and generation. Can we trace Scotch's differing views of manliness? One way to do so is to look for the points of contrast or change.

For instance, acceptable male behaviour slides up and down an age scale. Behaviours that were once the prerogative of male adults have become more openly acknowledged in youths. At adult-like occasions such as the

Sixth-Form (Year 12) Dinner Dance, the 1991 *Collegian* reported that boys stayed out all night—as dawn broke, tuxedo-clad figures offered to help the Hawthorn paper-boy—and came to school 'in various states of disrepair'.[10] The appearance of such a report in the *Collegian* reflects a change in social attitudes.

Acceptable male behaviour also slides back and forward along a manly–effeminate spectrum. Some boys' behaviours can seem to others as effeminate. In 1979, a country lad was amazed to find Scotch boys took dancing lessons, as 'this was not my measure of manliness'.[11] Earrings, once worn only by women, are now commonly sported by young Australian men, but Scotch still forbids them, so boys arriving by public transport remove them on the way. From girls, there is 'greater social pressure for boys to become more "SNAGs" (Sensitive New Age Guys). In this sense, the archaic notion of "manliness" has been lost as this previously implied a

Guy Mason, Junior School Headmaster from 1998, and Matthew Chan (Prep) in 1999.

boy who was chiseled, resolute, and (relatively) insensitive. Today, women still like their men to be "manly" but sensitive as well' (1996).[12]

A parallel scale measures toughness/weakness. An Old Boy of 1948 recalls what manliness required in his day: 'Cold showers in the pavilion. The outdoor and unheated swimming pool. However, when I wonder if today's boys are soft, I marvel at those who hike in the Alps, the 24-hour hikers … those who camp in unlikely places with the Scuba Club, the Sea Scouts and their boat building and so on.' Some modern educators now allow male children to be fragile. Newcomers to the Preparatory School in the 1990s brought a teddy bear, and were eased into school life in a way that acknowledged boys' apprehensions rather than forcing them to be men.

The 1999 Foundation Fellow was an expert in the educational and social needs of boys, Rollo Browne.[13] He advised Scotch to 'emphasise the mature masculine (where power is used for the service of others) in Scotch structures, rituals and practices and move away from heroic images where winning is what matters most (power for its own sake)'.[14] This is today's version, couched in terms of masculinity, of one of the school's oldest internal discussions, the right use of power and authority. Scotch's teachers and older boys have always modelled adult men's behaviour, in all its variety and changes in emphasis. Browne recommended a focused recommitment in this task.

In the past, the widest set of changes in the meaning of masculinity are found, in this largely male environment, in the ways in which males interact with each other.

CONQUER OR CARE: DAY-TO-DAY MASCULINITY
Physical violence

A 1999 brawl involving boys from Scotch and other Public Schools drew considerable public disapproval and no favourable comment at all. A century earlier, the 1905 *Collegian* was openly unapologetic about a 'scrimmage' between Public School boys.

> Delicate issues will always arise which schoolboys will always settle in their own way. And the Australian boy has not lost the fighting propensities of his sires. He is not gentle or mild; he has no desire to be canonised ... The Debating Society took the matter up and almost to a man voted that a boy, if challenged, has no option but to fight. Nor do we ... condemn ... such a wholesome instinct ... It makes for manliness.[15]

Over the century, views have changed about the level of acceptable interpersonal violence. As early as 1917, the APS Headmasters cancelled some inter-school sport because of repeated hostilities at matches.[16]

For most of human history, however, adult men had to know how to fight. Gentlemen once carried swords, and more recently were expected to know how to use their fists. Scotch taught boxing to various boys, though it left them 'bashed and bleeding' (1951). Littlejohn introduced boxing in 1905 at the same time as he revived elocution, 'the one showing you how to spar with the tongue, and the other how to talk with the hands'.[17] Davidson taught boxing in the Junior School as late as the 1960s, when it fell out of fashion. Recently, Physical Education reintroduced it in Year 10, without controversy, in an already varied programme of fencing, squash, badminton, roller-blading, indoor hockey and self-defence.[18]

Until quite recently there was a major fight once a week (1996).[19] There is still a good deal of physical bumping and thumping between boys. 'Fights were fairly common, but as we got older the fights were fewer. ... serious, out-to-hurt fights were very few' (1990).[20] Sustained action by the school means that Savage in 2000 now judges them rare.

Bullying

Many organisational norms flow downwards; the rises and falls of bullying among the boys may reflect its frequency among masters. Masters' violence towards boys is bullying in today's terms, because it involves violence by a larger person against a smaller, and by a person with power against a person with less power. Even so, for most of the school's history, masters' violence against the boys was not seen as bullying.

Masters used to hurt boys, as we saw in Chapters 2 and 3. Throwing chalk and dusters at boys was common into the 1990s.

> I am sure that many boys other than myself witnessed cruelty perpetrated by some teachers on students. ... I witnessed [a] PE teacher hit another student,

and my brother was forced to participate in a PE class, having trodden on a tack during a craft lesson earlier during that day. He had a letter from the Group master excusing him from PE, but this was ignored by the PE teacher [1991].

In trying to understand why some teachers were bullies, Healey perceived in bullying 'the expression of the desire to teach. Its object is usually conformity; it may be manliness, hence initiations; or equality, another form of conformity—and so on'. Teachers might think that a boy 'must learn how to take hard knocks—let's give him a few.'[21] This extends even to non-physical knocks, so that even the behaviour of some of the topmost staff was experienced as bullying (1967).[22]

Bullying also flowed upwards. 'Pretty well the only thing I regret about school was the treatment given to a wonderful young Physics teacher who was full of enthusiasm, but had no control. Boys were pretty relentless with him, and he left after a year.'[23]

Sixty-five years after he left Scotch, Dud Gay (1935) still remembers how another boy

bullied, hounded me and called me names at every conceivable opportunity. I hated him. ... I shake when I think of him and at this moment I'm having trouble writing this. ... I tried to fail everything in the classroom, thinking I may get expelled but it didn't work. So as soon as I turned 15 years of age I left, ... the happiest day of my school life at Scotch. I was almost sick with relief.[24]

Yet in 1868 Morrison had hoped 'to make my boys ... kind to each other'.[25] To be kind to each other is no small aim in a boys' school, where mockery and scuffling abound as boys test their prowess. Morrison urged kindness upon them explicitly, and forbade unkindness in its organised forms of bullying and fagging.[26]

'Though each individual member of a school staff can often be easily recognized as a human being, groups of them together tend to clot into lower organisms—dark, vicious, and sinister,' wrote Arthur Davies (1924).[27] This joke only works because it reverses what adults say about boys. In fact boys and teachers are part of the same system.

Bullying at Scotch has come in waves. In the 1940s it was bad—'a very savage environment compared to state school. One learnt to strike hard without mercy. Glory only to the approved bully' (1946). Perhaps the war unleashed such aggression. Some bullying dealt with boys who stood outside school spirit, 'loners or non-sporting' (1947).[28] Other victims were small. 'The way [——] brutally bockered Graham ... on the outer muscle of his left arm, to leave Graham—a little lad—*almost* in tears was horrifying! I saw this. This was in class—perhaps the master was temporarily absent' (1945).[29] Or perhaps not. 'The first two years in Junior school ... I was shy and timid and subject to considerable bullying. Looking back at it, why could not teachers see what was happening and do something about it? I had a stammer then which could have been a clue' (1949).[30] Glen Boyes (1951), 'Noso' Boyes's son, was thought to receive favourable treatment and was bullied until his father arranged for him to get boxing lessons from Davidson and 'more importantly, suggested I get into rowing!'[31]

To stand up to bullying was difficult. 'Dobbing causes you to be universally despised in school like nothing else does—and how good the reason you have for dobbing, how intense the persecution that prompts it, doesn't even come into it' (1970).[32] Bayston (1948) recalls

an outbreak of bullying. Boys were being "done over". It was sometimes to the chant of "Do him over. Do him over" in imitation of the Hallelujah Chorus. One day, … I said that if it did not stop I would go to Mr Gilray! The matter brewed for several days. Then … My bluff was called! I walked … to Mr Gilray's office. I had made up my mind not to name anybody, but to expose the problem. He was very good: he had the class-rooms locked at recess and lunch-time. Later he came to the class and called me out, and asked how things were. I had been pushed into a few dust-bins and down a few banks, but generally I was all right: it was rather the threats of what was yet to be that had me frightened. I had not intended to go to Cadet Camp, but the threats of what was going to happen to me there made me feel that it would be cowardly not to go. In the result, a group was formed, not by me, and indeed by people I hardly knew, who provided me with protection throughout the Camp. Some Jews at the camp suffered blackening and other forms of bullying, but I escaped. This experience made me very sympathetic with conscientious objectors during the Vietnam conflict, and with oppressed minorities generally.[33]

Scotch takes the mark at a football match in 1982 on the Main Oval with Mackie Hall in the background.

Old Boys since the 1940s make fewer reports of bullying. In the late 1950s one boy 'was bullied a lot by other students because I was overweight. One teacher—"Chook" Fowler—once called me fatso … in front of the class.' The same Old Boy adds: 'Bullying … was not a big deal, school-wide, but there were a few senior boys who picked on some of the younger ones. I don't think bullying was a part of Scotch's culture.' Even so, no other senior boys intervened to help him. The prefects' response to bullying was mild. In 1966 a bully's punishment was only a one-hour detention,[34] whilst smoking and uniform infractions brought the cane. In 1967–68 bullies suffered only severe reprimands, even though one victim 'received a black eye and had to have his head X-rayed'.[35] One boy was so persecuted that he felt like committing suicide, 'but it made me not worry about what people think of me. (bullying and persecution were very common at Scotch) Boys can be very cruel … I was reasonably confident so I coped. I pity boys who were sensitive (I saw it destroy at least 2 boys)' (1967). Another boy in 1967, however, arriving from Scotch College, Adelaide, found the bullying much less and the staff more inclined to step in.[36]

Some bullying occurred in organised settings. At the start of the twentieth century, the *Collegian* openly reported 'initiation' ceremonies like soaping new boys and compelling them to sing—or be wetted and manhandled.[37] In 1919 Littlejohn forbade this, over the strong objections of boarders' leaders who insisted that roughing up, socking and roasting were positively good for people.[38] Around 1940, 'new boys were fair game for a certain amount of harassment' and yet senior boys welcomed new boys and showed them around.[39] Initiations lingered in sub-cultures like the Hill, or scouts (where in 1967 two recruits were 'castrated'[40]), or Scotch-at-Cowes (where initiations drew increasingly heavy official disapproval well into the 1990s).

A 1994 survey of boys in Years 7–9 revealed boys who were very apprehensive about coming to school, or even refusing to do so, because they were being teased or bullied. A quarter of boys reported being bullied. Ken Fisher (staff 1986– , Head of Year 1997–) rejects the notions that *boys will be boys* or *it's part of growing up, they have to learn to cope with it*.[41] Instead, he and Savage developed a written harassment policy. In 2000, Boydell commissioned a survey of 1122 boys of whom 11% reported being bullied weekly and 5% had stayed home at least twice to avoid bullying. By contrast, 61% said they were never bullied.[42] Half the respondents said that bullying occurs in the classroom (not necessarily physical abuse, this could be taking pens and refusing to give them back, for example). The survey shows that the school is trying to manage bullying. That is not a task open to an easy solution, for it is over a century since Morrison urged boys to be kind to each other.

Verbal violence

Short of physical contact, sarcasm is a well-established inter-male means of discourse. Most Old Boys would insist that we hear what follows simply as good humour. The 1910 *Collegian* was not embarrassed to report a master's insults: Shew told one class they were 'only fit to dig potatoes'.[43] Several later masters enjoyed invective. 'Noso' Boyes, Kirby and Bond are famous for sayings like:

Boy, if your brains were ever turned to ink, there wouldn't be enough for a decent sized full-stop.

Boy, if your brains were multiplied by two, you'd be a half-wit.

Boy, if your brains were made of dynamite they wouldn't even blow your cap off!

You ought to get a job in the railways as a sleeper.

Laddy your name might be Baker, but you aren't well bred.

You'd better get your wares on the market now before the rush comes.[44]

'Cakey' Adams mocked Ian Roper (1952) as 'Tawonga born, Tawonga bred, Strong in the arm, but weak in the head'.[45]

Where teachers led, boys followed. McCaughey found 'there is a harshness to his fellow conspicuous in the Australian boy. "Knocking" is as much a part of the Australian character as "mateship". If Scotch could deal with "knocking" it would really have achieved a great thing.'[46] Healey not only discouraged sarcasm but also proposed 'a determined effort to substitute mutual praise for disparagement. ... Can we teach our boys to encourage each other more? Can we use the leaders—the Sixth Form—in Houses to help younger boys not only to take part in sport, but also in their hobbies and in their work?'[47]

How to survive?

Boys respond to violence, bullying and sarcasm in many ways. In the above and in earlier sections on the Hill and on minorities we have seen anger, despair, stoicism and denial that anything was amiss. 'Survival' is the word Scotch's recent outside expert uses[48]—and the very word tells us how much some boys suffer.

More actively and strategically we have seen boys decide to avoid behaviour that invited attention. Another survival strategy is co-operation. Michael Edwards (1970) writes:

As a practical joke, boys took to locking me in steel lockers in the changing rooms. Those lockers were quite tiny: only 36" x 18" x 12", [90 x 45 x 30 cm] but, believe it or not, I could curl up inside one of those lockers quite easily, and the door could be completely closed and locked. It was totally inescapable, and I was completely helpless.

This prank was reasonably good-natured rather than malicious, and I sort of half-went along with it, while putting up a token struggle, and it grew and grew, and I ended up being locked in dozens of times by various boys. The whole thing was known throughout the entire school from about 1968 to 1970, and I became ... one of the best-known boys in the whole senior school ...

I'm not claustrophobic, and being locked in didn't scare me, and no harm came of it. ...

I've never known whether staff at the school were aware that this was going on.[49]

The most common survival strategy is to seek protection in a group. Even here, some thumping and 'knocking' occurs but at a lesser level.

Friends

There are boys who have retained no friendships from their school days,[50] and others who made 'wonderful life long friends'.[51] One set of middle-aged Old Boys lunched so regularly that they became the Climsdow Club, from the first letters of their surnames.

For many boys, what they liked most about Scotch was their friends. Yet Scotch is cautious in talking about such things. Scotch celebrates the bonds made in task-focused teamwork, but no song or speech addresses friendship's other aspects. Old Boys often talk about *camaraderie*[52] (rather than, say, mateship[53]). Their choice of a foreign word (and their many ways of spelling it!) suggest that Scotch itself has not provided a way of talking about this behaviour. John Cumming (1967) says: 'My best achievement was probably helping some of my friends through with work they had difficulty with'.[54] For all the testimony to friends from Old Boys, few say that their *best* achievement was helping their friends. Somehow the commandment to love one another is drowned out by the injunction to love the school or the team.

Friendship 1978.

Friendships gave safety. 'Having lunch and talking to friends. The pressure was momentarily off' (1967).[55] Friendship's aimlessness gave a vantage point from which to ponder life's mysteries. Doug Batten (1946) talked with friends ' "of shoes—of ships—and sealing wax, of cabbages and Kings". I used to look forward greatly to the luncheon recess when this activity mainly took place, but … on rare occasions some of us also skipped a class, for a quiet smoke and a yarn on the banks of Gardiner's Creek'.[56] Ken Foletta (1964) and Peter Waddell (1965) were sitting down on the Yarra at Kew. "God is mother nature," we profoundly and reassuredly decided. That's what was good about Scotch, the kids there could as much be left-wingers, atheists and subverts as they could be perpetuaters of the system. The School set itself up to push bullshit and the kids learned from their secure middle class backgrounds to see right through it.[57]

Friendships fortified rebelliousness: 'such special friendships, but we did tend to lead each other astray, and find ourselves at the ivory end of the cane—once at the hands of Mr Gilray, whose shoulders (on that day) looked about three feet wider than usual' (1944).[58]

As boys grew, friends changed because 'patterns of enjoyment changed over the years but the most continuous was the enjoyment of other people and the diversity of the person contacts both in terms of personalities, activities and interests' (1954).[59]

Abrupt losses were awful. When William Adam died of peritonitis in 1912, aged 17, having delayed an appendectomy so that he could sit his exams, J. D. Burns grieved: 'Why God leaves the weak, and takes the brave / We cannot tell, but know that such must be'.

Early *Collegians* are full of physical affection, but for most of the 20th century men have been uncomfortable about touching each other much. In the last decade, this 80-year chill has ended. The *Collegian* and *Great Scot* have published just a few photographs that show the occasional hand on a shoulder.[60] Such a personal action breaks out of the rigid conformity of the school's visual representations of itself, where each boy matches his neighbour's clothing and body posture, his individuality muted.

Caring

Aggression and affection are both found at Scotch. How is the school to manage this combination?

A drawback of mixing boys of different ages, in Donald Telfer's (1974) experience, was that the greater the age difference, the more likely the bullying, as 'when 12-year-olds are left under the thumbs of 18-year-olds 24 hours a day … with limited staff oversight'.[61] This happened more in scout camps, and less in cadets and sea scouts where the disparity in age (and size) was reduced because students had to be in Form III (Year 9) before they could join. Size gives power. 'One thing I've learnt at Scotch College', reported a Year 7 new boy in 1990, 'is to never expect a bigger boy than you to get out of your way.'[62] To transform this into kindness is to seek to impose civility on nature. Scotch has wrestled with how to regulate the relationships between boys of different ages.

From Healey to Roff to Donaldson, Scotch has seesawed between structuring Houses vertically (with boys of different ages) or horizontally (with boys all the same age). The question is whether boys grow best in groups of their own age or in groups more like families with a spread of ages. Presumably the best system has both aspects, hence the prevarication.

Healey wanted the House system to be pastoral but saw this as done by masters rather than by older boys, and so settled on age-determined horizontal divisions. Roff wanted to generate a family-like structure, and imposed a vertical system of small Houses containing the full range of ages. Donaldson in 1989 reintroduced the horizontal system: each House had a full range of ages, but boys were grouped by age. Each group had a teacher as tutor, and a boy remained in the same Tutor Group, with the same tutor, from Years 8 to 12. This provided a sustained contact with that teacher and a predictable social base among peers, built into daily life by allocating adjacent lockers to each Tutor Group. Boys seem neither to like nor dislike this system. It 'served as a method for the school to carry out administration... distribute news, hand out forms etc. Certainly my tutors never took anything more than a cursory interest in my progress.'[63] So long as a boy got on well enough with the tutor, one could be content.[64] Combined with this change, Roff's 18 Major and Minor Houses were kaleidoscoped into 12 houses of equal rank.

Houses' horizontal structure in Tutor Groups freed the horizontal Head-of-Year system to tilt towards the vertical. Donaldson made the Heads of Years into rotating pairs (Years 7–8, 9–10, and 11–12), so that each Head stayed with the same cohort of boys for two years rather than one. A boy passing through the Senior School thus had only three Heads

Scouts. Venturers, Unit C, 1983. From left: Shane Poulton, Sam Broadhurst, Roger Syn, John Prince.

ZODIAC: THE 12 HOUSES

Half of the new Houses in 1989 kept the names of the six major Houses, except that Lawson–MacFarland became simply Lawson. Five Houses thus commemorated the first five Principals, Lawson, Morrison, Littlejohn, Gilray and Selby Smith. The sixth House was Monash.

The other six Houses were named Bond, Davidson, Eggleston, Field, Fleming and Forbes. Forbes was described as the school's founder,[65] and since this idea was so un-known he was the subject of a superlative-filled hagiography in the *Collegian*.[66] Fleming, Bond and Eggleston were recent Vice-Principals, Davidson a sportsmaster and Ken Field a bursar. Donaldson thus continued Roff's policy of naming Houses after staff rather than Old Boys. Honouring Vice-Principals was uncontroversial, but Field's and Davidson's place of honour here could be challenged by the enthusiastic advocates of many another teacher.

The perennial problem of developing House spirit was addressed by slogans and nicknames, like 'Awesome Lawson'.[67] Selby Smith House's colour was ice blue, and so its boys called themselves the icemen, and warned other Houses that 'The Iceman Cometh'.[68] Houses of older names kept their old colours but seem to have had more fun with them than earlier genera-tions. Yellow Gilray became the Golden Boys, Littlejohn the Boys in Black, and Morrison the Green Machine.[69]

of Year instead of six, with a greater likelihood that boy and Head of Year would know each other better.

With Houses structured horizontally, also, the elder-brother function became separated from Houses and was instituted in its own right in 1996 as the Peer Support Programme. Pairs of approved Year 11 boys trained to have a small group of Year 7 boys under their wing, later expanding to Year 8. The youth was encouraged to become responsible and caring, and the child was invited to feel secure and have someone to look up to. Similarly, in the Junior School by 1998 each Grade 5 boy had a buddy in Prep or Grade 1 and worked with him for one period per cycle.[70]

Are boys intrinsically caring or heartless? Is care to be taught or elicited? The Christian doctrine of original sin defines humans as intrinsically sinful, and a church school must start with this assumption. Yet Scotch in its practice seems to assume that boys just might be basically good. Even so, care is not something left to occur randomly, humanly, but something structured through Peer Support.

In July 1990, four boys on a skiing trip to Mount Buller became lost during a heavy snowfall. Deep snow thwarted them from retracing their steps, and night fell. Overnight conditions were severe and there were concerns for the boys' survival. They were aged from 12 to 14. They made a snow cave in the manner they had seen demonstrated in a snow safety video. The two older boys, Matthew Gray and Charles Millis, took the outside positions to protect the younger ones. When dawn came all were still alive and the two younger boys, feeling the fitter, walked out to find help.[71]

Masters also model care. 'During a cadet bivouac I fell out of a tree skylarking and broke my collar bone. Personally F.A.F. [Fleming] looked after me for the next 2 days when he could easily have delegated the task.'[72] Masters spearheaded new ways of talking. In 1989 an obituary of John Francis, Form I Group Master, spoke of his 'sensitivity',[73] not a word previously applied to Scotch masters.

Teaching as caring

The caring task that is essential in schools is the task of education. This is not how staff usually think about teaching, but Old Boys praise the teachers who cared, and deplore those who did not. Care had many aspects: Frank Paton's 'gentle guiding leadership' (which so impressed Mike Reid (1958) that he aimed to give the same to his own children),[74] 'Wally' Butler's 'high level of personal interest in and commitment to his students' (1967),[75] Neil Cracknell's 'never ending encouragement and support' (1985). Ron Anderson and Mark Dwyer (staff 1991–95) were 'truly committed to getting the best from their students … always ready to give of their time' (1995),[76] and Bruce Brown (1960, staff 1985–, Form III Group Master 1987–) '(affectionately known as Brucie) was … inspirational and much liked by Year 9s and fantastic as Year 12 International Studies teacher … for his endless enthusiasm, hilarious discussions and teaching style' (1996).[77] Dozens more laudatory descriptions clamour to be recorded.

Where there is a gap between teacher and pupil, it can be one of personal chemistry but it can also be an intellectual gap, followed by indifference. Whilst clever boys thrived under eminent masters, other boys complain, for example, that Kay was 'a brilliant man, who could not bring his explanations down to our level of understanding' (1943),[78] and that Alan Ross and Ferres were 'really academic … unable to transfer their vast knowledge to average students' (1952).[79] By contrast, George Mullenger (staff 1935–65) 'was not a true academic, however he was more knowledgeable than his pupils and could transfer his knowledge in a simple and learnable fashion' (1952).[80] The same tensions arose in non-academic areas. A boy in the music school who 'had no idea about any instruments' felt the teachers 'expected us to be geniuses' (1992).[81] To know something is not the same as being able to teach it. Thus Melville, Assistant Chaplain, suggested that the best person to teach Religious Education might not be the chaplain but someone trained in teaching it.[82] This issue lies at the heart of teaching: how to educate boys who fail to share one's enthusiasm. Most disciplines had someone who could teach the boys who were slow at it, although PE often did not and humiliated or neglected the unsporting kids (1980).[83]

a smart-arse Jock who liked the kids that were good at sport and didn't have much time for anyone else. He could be quite rude [1980].[84]

He had no respect for the students and ill treated those without sporting ability. He was officious, arrogant and small-minded and ridiculed the boys who could not achieve the standards he set [1980].[85]

the epitome of everything Scotch could do without [1996].[86]

Yet it was a PE teacher who

took us out onto the main oval one day (the oval was always sacred, I think I went onto it only a handful of times all my years at Scotch) and he sat us all down. It was a beautiful warm, cloudless day. He told us to look around, feel the sun on our skin and said—'isn't it wonderful to be alive!' Thankyou Mr Davenport [staff 1977– , Teacher-in-charge of Athletics 1988–], whenever I am not feeling good, I look up and think about how amazing our world is and how good it is to be alive [1989].

And 'Gym was made enjoyable thru Ginna [Davidson]'s relaxed but firm style. He always encouraged, and made sure the able did not mock the weak' (1959).[87]

EDUCATING BOYS

Around 1980, when co-education was topical, keeping Scotch all-male arose from tradition or a fear of female distractions (or even of female competition). Today, whilst many boys still regret being unable to get to know girls in a casual day-to-day way, a burgeoning literature argues that boys gain from a boy-focused education. For example, a school solely for boys may open up areas that might otherwise be taken by girls. Thus in music 'there is a tendency for girls to play cellos (and violins to some extent) and flutes, and for boys to play heavy brass and wind. This is reduced in an all-boys environment—we have lots of cellos and over 150 violinists, and some flutes etc.'[88]

Concentrating on boys' education alerts one to how boys learn. Unlike girls, boys seem to prefer incidental conversations to a 'sit-down-and-talk-about-it' occasion. Knowing this, a boys' school arranges shared activities over an extended period. The teacher participates in some way in the activity, while mentor-style conversations casually take place.[89]

Concentrating on boys' education alerts one to boys' emotional development. In 1974, the chaplain, Crow, attended a Transactional Analysis course in California and came back telling staff to help boys develop their 'life-scripts'. Boys needed to overcome injunctions like 'Be perfect', 'Hurry up', 'Be strong', 'Try hard' and 'Don't think, don't be yourself, and don't feel'—Crow thought the latter were particularly of school origin.[90] Boys' emotional development was the school's concern, said Donaldson in 1989,[91] the year he introduced the new tutorial system. Attending to emotional development has taken the school into new realms. Upon incorporation in 1980, Scotch committed itself to develop boys' personality, a quite new aim, reflecting how psychology has entered mainstream thinking during the school's 150 years. Before 1980, personality development was not mentioned as a goal for the school. Indeed, it is not clear where this wording came from or what it was thought to mean.[92] Is it merely a modern way of talking about character, a word that now sounds old-fashioned? Littlejohn said Scotch aimed to 'help a boy to develop and express his personality, ... his one and only possession, the great gift he can make to the community when he leaves school'.[93]

'To encourage each student to achieve the highest standard of which he is capable in all his activities and the full development of the personality and sense of responsibility of each student and respect for others and capacity to work with them to promote the development of Christian ideals of citizenship, personal character and a spirit of reverence in the entire life and work of the College'. *Scotch College Memorandum of Association, art. 3 (1) (b).*

However alert the school might be to boys' ways and needs, the boys themselves arrived with their own set of interests and inclinations. One boy, for instance, 'was in love with making machines, and everything else in the universe was an unnecessary mosquito to him. He had all the signs of an Elizabethan lover: wild hair, careless clothes, a fixed eye. It was clear that his soul was for ever turned to his mistress, the machine.'[94] More than at a girls' school, pupils seem inclined to adore machines and tools, and the school is best advised to run alongside. Scotch has had Aeronautical, Radio, Camera, Railway, Rifle and APT Clubs.

Some technologies are particularly associated with the coming of manhood. A boy's first fountain pen, sleekly phallic, was a source of pride and often coincided with puberty. A boy's first watch used to arrive on a birthday in his second decade.[95] Nowadays regular watch-wearing begins earlier, in Year 4, perhaps because watches are no longer so expensive.

Risk-taking

Other devices are more risky, especially weapons and cars. These are the prerogatives of manhood. To combine one of these with that schoolboy hobby, stamp collecting, achieved a double coup, as when the 1954 Stamp Club ran an exhibition called 'Weapons through the ages'.[96]

Cars seem so fast, powerful and invincible—what every boy wants to be—and their link with manhood is emphasised by the age restrictions on licences. Much time was spent on cars. Ken Foletta (1964) thinks his best achievement at Scotch was 'drawing cars during class'.[97]

Masters' cars are of great interest. Pawsey was the first master to own a car.[98] Few owned one until the second half of the century. '45' Clayton walked from Canterbury every day, and sat in Assembly mopping his brow (1951).[99] Reggie Clayton, a boarding house master, undertook weekend preventive maintenance. As he removed each nut he carefully lined them in order, but because he lay under the car it was easy for boarders to rearrange them, and it did take longer for him to reassemble the car (1934).[100] Masters' new cars were noted in *Satura*.[101] Tim Luke (2001) can name every teacher's car.

Nicholson when School Captain in 1936 had his own car.[102] Boys without cars acquired them one way or another. Hugh Taylor, recent Perelberg Prize winner, confesses that in 1963 he and two others at a scout camp 'borrowed (stole?)' the Kombi van of Dugald MacLeish (scout master) to go into Gembrook. 'On the way back [the driver] rolled the Kombi and squashed in the roof and 1 side. Only later he admitted he had never driven before—well we all got into BIG trouble over this unfortunate and silly episode.'[103]

Twenty years earlier, two boys on their way home from dancing class

had to pass a cinema with many cars parked nearby. Ken knew how to get into certain makes of small car and connect up the wiring to start the engine and, I regret to say, we often took a 'joy-ride', but always returned the vehicle unharmed to its parking spot before the movie finished. This pleasant, though illegal, activity we both agreed was much better and more satisfying than messing about with girls! One night, however, when we returned the car we found its owner waiting for us (perhaps he hadn't gone to the movie, but had been visiting friends), so we took off, running as if for our lives through the back lanes of Malvern with the car-owner in hot pursuit. I didn't know I could run so fast—certainly much faster than during the annual Athletics Standards at school—but we avoided capture, and our 'joy-riding' ceased from that time on!

House athletics timekeepers, 1981. Upper (from left): Stephen Kong, Peter Lewis, Andrew Tait, Mick Eggleston. Lower (from left): Miles Mudie, Colin Fox, Syd Boydell.

Nevertheless, it gave this Old Boy in his later years a 'tolerance of the foibles and escapades of youth' (1946).

Old Boys who died accidentally in the 19th century were more likely to do so by drowning, or in the 1930s from flying accidents. The 1950s saw a rising number of deaths from recreational activities such as water-skiing or spear-fishing. But from 1950, deaths in car accidents surpassed all other causes, with the peak in the 1960s. Selby Smith warned final-year boys that 'it was likely one of us would be killed in an accident within 12 months on our past records and on this account he was correct'. Healey told each parting cohort about his own driving accident as a young man when, through no fault of his, he maimed a motorcyclist and killed his side-car passenger.

In 1963 *Satura* rejected the idea of teaching boys to drive, but soon advised boys with licences to 'Watch the car behind the one in front of you'.[104] Scotch ran road-safety programmes for pedestrians and cyclists from the 1950s, and for car drivers from the 1970s. 'The course is not so much aimed at teaching driving skills. Rather the teaching and practice of driving skills is the carrot to encourage in boys a better understanding of what is involved socially, biologically and mechanically in the whole business of driving.'[105]

As with radio, boys' love of cars was harnessed by the cadet unit. Its own signalling equipment and transport played a useful part in the 1960 annual camp. Adrian Jones (1962), a renegade, nevertheless loved cadets and 'was responsible for restoring the 1st school jeep…. Ron Bond gave me a free hand and allowed me to do my own thing—we also pinched petrol

Home time, 1954. Note the Gladstone bag.

from the school tractor and went for evening joy rides' on the levee bank. The Army had put a big 'Never to be re-registered' sticker on it. 'Needless to say, we got it going and had the only left-hand drive Victorian registered vehicle at the time.'[106]

In the 1960s, boys still had to be driven by their parents, but more as chauffeurs than chaperones. David Ashton (1965) 'went out several times with a girl from Greensborough, whom I had met at dancing class—much to my father's inconvenience, because he had to drive me out there to pick her up, and then take her home'.[107] Cars also brought sex to the movies, for instead of cuddling in the back row of a theatre, the new drive-ins 'seemed ideal for such encounters, but always difficult to arrange unless some poor creature could be encouraged to borrow her father's motor car.'[108]

Cars and weapons involve risk-taking. Boys take risks. How much risk to allow is a problem that taxes schools and parents. Once, the school allowed more risk-taking. Bill Callister (1941) camped at Walhalla and rode the 'railway trolley at night-time … down the mountain at the Thompson River—great fun'.[110] Barrie Johns (1955) recalls a scout camp where a handful of Year 11 and 12 boys had charge of two dozen younger scouts. 'No adult! The nearest telephone was probably a couple of kilometres away and we didn't have any bike or electricity. Never was there an anxious parent [with] hand on their solicitor's business card, ready to sue for damages. Times have changed'.[111] Today's outdoor activities are more carefully supervised, not least because of the risk of litigation. And yet as well as outdoor activities that encourage self-reliance and social interaction, Rob McLaren argues that activities must involve challenges and allow boys to be risk-takers.[112] At heart, this is the uncomfortable end of a wider debate, for Donaldson believes that boys' capacity for learning is developed by challenges.[113]

The family was objecting to its son's girlfriend, insisting he ought to be a little more particular about the feminine company he was keeping. 'I'm sorry, Dad', said the boy, 'but that's the best girl I can get with the car we've got.'[109]

FATHERS AND FATHER FIGURES

Relationships between men and boys are shaped by society, so they change over time. The last few decades have seen fathers ever more involved in the school and in their sons' education. From the 1970s fathers took more part in the auxiliaries. The Junior School Mothers' Association changed its name to the Junior School Parents' Association, though it took more than one attempt to do so. From the 1960s, churches and other schools ran father-and-son events as part of sex education programmes. Scotch never did this. Instead, in the late 1970s the Cowes Auxiliary ran 'Father and son working weekends'.[114] Was it very Presbyterian to make the father–son movement into something so practical and money-saving? Bonding no doubt happened, but the stated intention was 'to help the fathers meet *each other*'.[115]

The changed relationship between boys and their fathers affected the relationship between boys and those father-substitutes, the teachers. The rising idea of fathers as friends led to the idea that teachers, too, might be friends. A few teachers were always boys' friends, even as far back as Robert

WEAPONRY

Guns appeal to boys as fine pieces of equipment, as a means of projecting power, as a means of testing and improving one's accuracy and skill, and as a phallic symbol spewing forth power. Shooting requires a good eye, a steady hand and controlled breathing. It comes with a satisfyingly loud noise, the smell of cordite, and a manly thrust of recoil against the shoulder. When Scotch opened, shooting was a common gentlemanly pastime. William Skene (1868) in his holidays shot kangaroos, and boys ever since who were farmers' sons have gone shooting when back home. Marksmanship was a main inter-school sport in the late 19th century, as rifling brought increased accuracy.

During World War I shooting ceased to be a school sport and fell within the cadets. There, it still gave the pleasures of mastering a skill and of companionship—'Me and Mick Eggleston were the only two in our company who got a score of 40-plus at the shooting range.'[116]

Boys also owned air rifles (traded in *Satura*[117]), but they knew that adults used real guns. When Arthur Mitchell left to become Headmaster of Timbertop, former Scotch-at-Cowes boys gave him a double-barrelled shotgun.

Shooting continued as a non-military

Archers, 1982. Despite, or because of, its potential danger, archery had its enthusiasts.

recreation outside the school, as shooting accidents show,[118] and though it did not revive as a sport, in 1958 a Rifle Club began, with 34 members. Like all clubs, it rose and fell. Revived in 1975, membership was limited to boys who owned their own rifles, although the club hoped to buy some. Bob Grant, sportsmaster, ruled that it was not a sport, although Challoner, the Marshal, was willing to act as coach.[119] It revived again around 1990.

Another hunting and killing skill, archery, was championed in 1973 by Andrew Rubins in Year 9 and Andrew Fuller (1974) in Year 11. Bows and arrows would be supplied by the boys themselves, several of whom were experienced archers, and the boarders also had some bows and arrows (and presumably had been using them). Cross-bows were being made in the craft room! For safety, the archers used the rifle range, supervised by Cracknell.[120] Courtis protested that 'these weapons are extremely lethal, possibly more so than a .22 rifle' and preferred that boys join a local club,[121] but Rubins successfully argued the case before the GHC.

Fencing, another ancient military skill, arose briefly in the wake of the Melbourne Olympics. In 1956 an Olympic coach named O'Brien trained a class of seven in the gymnasium and hoped to make it a Public School sport.[122] Instead it became a club in 1957, and again in 1973. Less formally, boys fought with sticks, and in 1928 a boy 'got his nose cut sword-fighting'.[123] Generals Sir Julius Bruche (1890) and Sir James McCay (1880) presented their swords for the cadet guard commander and his second-in-command on ceremonial parades.

Boys' fascination with martial technology is matched by the school's use of war-like phrases. A sportsman's aim is 'not to have triumphed but to have fought well' (1959).[124] 'The swimming sports were once again a closely contested battle' (1996).[125]

Archery and fencing, though once key male activities, are now limited to enthusiasts, and cannot catch boys' interest in the way that guns do. Guns in their turn are not as enticing as cars.

Morrison—'the friend of them all; they were all his friends'[126]—and Frank Shew. But between most boys and most staff there was always a gulf. Around 1900, 'the attitude of the schoolmaster was to drive the boys and punish them if they did wrong' and the boys' attitude to teachers was 'not quite hostility, but sort of obstruction. Certainly not companionship, ... "Sucking up" was a heinous offence and you had to do very little in the way of co-operation to earn the reputation of sucking up to somebody. ... if the staff or *The Boss* wants to do something and asks for the co-operation of the boys, the attitude was: Don't offer.'[127] By the 1920s Littlejohn hoped that in clubs the master would be the boys' friend.[128] In 1934 Ingram said boys used to fear masters but now saw them as elder brothers.[129] Was this a half-way house on the road from father-figure to friend?

The changing relationship between master and boy appears, perhaps, in accounts of staff–student sport. Jokes there always were. In 1909, the masters played the First XI and one teacher promised to excuse his class homework for a week if he scored 50, but unfortunately 'he only made one of the figures (0)'.[130] From the 1960s there seems a new tone of affection. In hockey the masters' team, said *Satura*, knew the rules or could conceal their lack of knowledge from the umpire.[131] In cricket, in 1965, 'Mr Briggs was run out when he forgot that, although the bat might be in the crease, it always helps to have a hand holding it'. There was 'a good diving catch by Mr Darling and a nonchalant boundary catch by Mr Moore'.[132]

Friendship between boys and staff appeared bit by bit over decades. There are Old Boys from as early as the 1940s who already speak of teachers as friends.[133] Yet in the 1960s 'it was not done to be friendly with teachers. Students kept somewhat distant to avoid being accused of being cheeky or too forward'.[134] The 1979 staff–student seminar felt that 'them and us' still prevailed. Until aged about 16, students thought it is not the done thing to be in too close contact with staff.[135] In the 1980s Scott Crozier (staff 1979– 87) 'treated his students as friends'.[136] Old Boys of the 1990s talk about having a teacher as a friend,[137] even as 'someone I invited home to dinner, someone I would spend a lunch time chatting to and someone I would have had no hesitation in telling has a too messy office and a too short hair cut'.[138]

The most striking sign of the new relationship between teachers and boys is that in the last few decades of the twentieth century staff nicknames disappeared almost entirely. Although some teachers were known by variations on their surname, like 'Jamesy' for the affable Ken James (staff 1978– , Head of Geography 1980–),[139] only Norm Bain was known by a nickname so universally that the 1990 *Collegian* confidently labelled a photograph of him merely as 'The Grey Domino'.[140] In itself, nicknames' disappearance seems trivial, but it indicates a profound change. Teachers have become professionals. There are few characters, few idiosyncratic eccentrics. The modern relationship between parent and child means that boys now expect to be engaged rather than talked at, expect activity rather than imprisonment in a desk and expect group work. There is less a gap between teacher and pupil, and perhaps it was this gap that nicknames bridged.

Such changes seem an extension of Hansen's recommendations that teachers come down from their daises and start using forenames. Yet though the daises are gone, Senior School boys still sit at tables lined up facing the front where the teacher sits or stands. In the Junior School, however, by 1992 Nowacki reshaped classrooms. Instead of rows of desks facing the teacher and the blackboard, classrooms had activity centres, reading corners and computers. These enabled small group discussions and helped students learn by working together co-operatively.[141]

As authority leached from teachers, some of it flowed to boys. Ferguson gives boys a say in appointing senior music staff. The musical world regards auditions as routine, and applicants have to audition by running a master-class or conducting a band or a choir which then comments. The Junior

School in the 1990s emphasised developing boys' leadership skills, not previously talked about much for pre-pubescent boys. As part of Personal Development, Cross-Age Tutoring lets older boys work with, and help, younger boys.[142]

Even so, the essential nature of the boy–teacher relationship is still the same: the boys still aim to trick the teachers. Ask an Old Boy about his schooldays and he usually starts talking about the masters, and the tricks he played on them. We may regret this and wish he would talk about his *education*. Or we can accept that this *was* his education. Scotch would hope that what was educative about the teachers was that they provided role models. And of course Old Boys do recall teachers they emulate to this day. But more often Old Boys' tales are about teachers they mocked or teachers whose abiding legacy is not their virtues but their idiosyncrasies. What was educative about the relationship with these teachers? It was not the education of sitting at the feet of Christian models, but something older and more pagan.

One might say that sons have two choices with their fathers—and with father-figures like teachers. Sons can choose either to destroy their fathers, as Chronos did, or to trick them, as Zeus did. The second way is preferable psychologically. Killing your father gains you control but hampers your ability to use it creatively, either through guilt or through fear of your own sons (or younger colleagues or employees) which makes you unable to let them grow. In this context, we could see schoolboy pranks as an important part of boys' development, as a healthy, Zeus-like way of challenging the father-figure without risk of harming him.

Conversely, fathers and father-figures like teachers also have a choice. They can fear boys' challenge and launch a pre-emptive strike by devouring the boys first, or they can allow the sons to test their strength by challenges that are welcomed, or at least tolerated, as appropriate rather than seen as destructive. As Old Boys reflect later about played-upon masters, they often think, now, that the master was much more aware of what was going on— much less a dupe and more a sage.

In Greek mythology, Uranus was castrated by his son Chronos. Chronos was then understandably suspicious of his own children and ate them as they were born. One child, Zeus, eluded this fate when his mother, Rhea, fed Uranus a rock instead. When Zeus grew up he slipped Chronos a potion that made him disgorge all the eaten children who, with Zeus, then deposed him.

GENDER ROLES

Female teachers have appeared in numbers in the last two decades. Many are young, because women with families are deterred from applying by the obligation to engage in co-curricular activity in evenings and weekends. The appearance of women creates new dynamics, and shifts the dynamics between the men and boys. Women precipitate different sexual nuances in the classroom, and introduce mother–son psychological projections. Boys in activities involving both male and female teachers will find themselves caught up in the full range of parental projections. Women also allow new discourses that had not occurred before. A female teacher talking to a group of Year 12s casually told one she liked the coloured tips in his hair. Other

NOOKS AND CRANNIES

Apart from teachers, many men have worked at Scotch in kitchens, sheds or cubby-holes, tucked away in places to do with their work. Huddled in these secret men's places, many boys found the welcome companionship of an adult who had the time and patience to listen and chat. 'After school we boarders loved to lounge around the Pavilion and listen to Bob [Horne]'s reminiscences and his comments on the world at large. A truly remarkable man' (1932).[143] In the rowing shed, 'Ron Roberts used to let us have a swig after school if no-one was around' (1962).[144] John Richards (1950) lived near Scotch and would get up before dawn to help old Wal Fowler (staff 1929–71) light the boiler on the Hill.

Many boys sat at the feet of Jim Baird (staff 1930–79, rising from groundsman to Caretaker), Arthur May, Albert Kitchener 'Jack' Fraser (staff 1947–81), and Bruce Tydeman (staff 1953–96), all rising to Maintenance Officer, and Hugh Aitken and Geoff Prestegar (staff 1977–86), Curators, and their men.

The Mackie Hall caretaker Charles Northcote 'once told me what it meant to him that his only son died in the war, and it stayed with me and has occasionally comforted me. No other adult at Scotch gave me anything like this! Scotch's education of character comes in many guises!' [1964]. In 2000, Norm Bain has a vast storage area below the Lithgow Centre (the building is designed to take in flood water!). Bain's realm has been expanded by student-muscled excavations. Socially this buried world offers a place to boys who might feel they have no place.

Adult female staff have also talked to boys in a dialogue outside the academic curriculum. First, matrons and nursing sisters and then, more recently, librarians, teachers, secretaries, and technicians, have provided a friendly ear, in offices and corridors and in classrooms after class.

Maintenance men in their shed, 1960.

discourses are suppressed. Hosking and Savage expunged girlie posters from boys' lockers, though not from staff areas. A century ago, boys called the school 'she', but today it has long been neuter. The advent of women in significant numbers once again permits a balancing feminine aspect to Scotch.

The school itself encourages boys to move away from gender stereotypes. In the Junior School Grade 6 boys in 1989 learnt knitting,[145] and Nowacki congratulated a Grade 5 boy chosen to dance with the Australian Ballet.[146]

(Long before, the dancing career of David McIlwraith (1940) led him to the Folies Bergères and Walt Disney.[147]) Such steps indicate large social changes. As recently as the 1970s, sexual stereotypes meant that when the Scotch-at-Cowes Parents' Auxiliary was fundraising, the women cooked and the men arranged transport, erected tents and lighting, carved meat and served wine.[148] Work was allocated according to gender preconceptions: 'gloves, buckets, detergents, etc (Ladies) and motor mowers (Fathers)'.[149] 'Washing up—6 daughters needed',[150] although in 1973 'one son also helped',[151] the first swallow of a new summer. As recently as 1981 the organisers divided into a Men's Group and a Ladies Group.[152]

Among Scotch staff, women have spread into most positions. Around 1960, there was only a handful: Woolcock and a few centrally-located support staff (the Principal's secretary, a typist and a book-keeper). Donaldson put them everywhere. Jean Clark (staff 1988–2000) was rowing coach in 1988, Anne Colman was Housemaster in 1989 and Head of Department in 1991, Madeleine Scott née Klug (staff 1990–92) and Libby Mulcahy (staff 1989–97) were cadet officers in 1991, Pauline Westmore (staff 1995–) was football coach in 1995, Fay Leong (staff 1991–2000) was resident boarding-house teacher in 1995, Liz Pratt (staff 1986–99, Director of Studies 1996–98) was Deputy Head of the Junior School in 1998, Michelle Maloney (staff 2000–) was rugby umpire and Keiron Jones (staff 1998–) was Head of Year in 2000.

Until Pratt and Jones, Scotch had lacked a female role model in a position of real power or influence as far as boys or parents could see (Heads of Year

Anne Colman. In 1989 she became the first female Housemaster—she told Donaldson, 'I am nobody's mistress'—and in 1991 the first female Head of Department.

sit in the front row of the staff at Assembly). Colman's leadership was dynamic and intense. In History she emphasised formal academic research. She refused to be called House-Mistress, understandably, and in 1997 Savage renamed all Group-, House- and Senior Masters in gender neutral terminology as Heads or Deans.

Liz Pratt (left), Junior School Deputy Head 1998 and Graeme Nowacki, Junior School Headmaster 1986–98.

Women—young women—in the boarding houses was the most controversial step. When Don Davenport, Senior Boarding House Master, invited Leong, she recalls that 'there was a bit of an uproar about it. McMeckan got used to it pretty quickly but the other houses never really did until they got their own female boarding staff. I gather that somewhere in past history there had been a matron who had enjoyed flirting with the boys and this caused some problems. In the end, the dust settled and it's fairly commonplace.'[153]

Whilst Scotch resolves to remain a school for boys, it has been changing what it means by this. It pays more deliberate attention to how boys learn and it reassesses what boys need. Boys' education still focuses on boys, but the teachers need no longer all be men. This inevitably changes the whole experience.

Being a man involves behaviours ranging from the boisterous to the noble. Take two brief scenes. Suzette Boyd, the new Librarian in 2000, came from a girls' school and soon faced a situation in the Library when the fire alarm went off. At the Methodist Ladies' College the girls would have fallen quiet to receive instructions. At Scotch the boys all spoke at once and there was uproar. Or again, Donaldson in Assembly 'from time to time with remarkable success' asks boys to own up to something. 'I'll say "I've observed the following and I was not able to identify the boys, but please come and see me after assembly." And sure as fate, they turn up.'[154]

Scotch's task is to harness this manly energy and this sense of honour.

CONCLUSION

TO LIVE FOR 150 YEARS

Scotch's survival for 150 years is an uncommon achievement. Scotch is older than the City of Hawthorn, the Commonwealth of Australia, most countries and most companies. Perhaps a few of the school's river red gums have lived so long.[1]

If asked to explain this achievement, Scotch tends to reply out of its own myths, alluding to one or more of: Christian education, character, the staff, school spirit, the Old Boys, or the Principals. Such replies extol the school as much as they explain it. Other factors in its success were more down-to-earth—that from the start Scotch was open to a wider social and religious range of boys than most other private schools, that it offered an education both progressive and conservative, catering for mercantile and scholarly needs, that its academic streaming system kept boys challenged, that Morrison was a businessman of aplomb, and that Littlejohn in the twentieth century made Scotch the first large school in Victoria and deliberately generated attractive myths and symbols.

Along the way, Scotch adopted and discarded things as seemed fit. It thereby acquired its current busy life bit by bit. Organising boys into Houses began in 1917, and into small Houses in 1977. Organising boys under Heads of Year began in 1935. Sport began under Morrison in the 1860s. Extra-curricular activities became widespread under Littlejohn in the 1920s. Music, art and drama grew serious under Gilray in the 1930s. All these are not so much woven together as inserted side by side, like slats in a beehive. The Houses slat has been removed for alteration often. Houses' number and size have changed beyond recognition. Houses' purpose was originally competitive sport, then widened to include music and debating, and was then refocused to support pastoral care.

Scotch has thus achieved and kept its eminence by constantly changing. It emphasises its traditions, but it has repeatedly adapted itself to new circumstances and invented new traditions. Its complexity of disciplines, teaching systems and co-curricular activities means that at any moment in time change was happening at many speeds and in many directions.

HOW TO TALK ABOUT THE PAST?

We might think about these changes musically. For instance, as notes rise higher and higher, so have Scotch's enrolments, staff and income. The number of boys playing sport started growing under Gilray and reached effective full participation under Roff. The number of boys learning an instrument for at least one term began to grow later still.

Other aspects of music offer other models. Like a metronome, some things at Scotch swing back and forth. Caps, for instance, come and go. Government aid was at first indispensable, was then condemned by the church until the 1960s, and then resumed. It is hard to imagine the school ever again declining such support, much less questioning it.

Other things neither rise nor oscillate, but become a sequence of items that are connected but separate, like a symphony's movements. For example, Scotch has had successive perceptions of leadership, starting with no formal leaders at all, to having only a small number of god-like prefects (natural leaders), to having a general leadership spread widely within Year 12 (and trained). In a different, parallel sequence of changes, leadership by example has been a constant but it has moved from being bolstered by the power to punish through to largely relying on persuasion, whilst the power to punish has shrunk as caning ceased.

All the above models postulate movement in straight lines, but we also find ourselves circling ground already familiar as in a minuet or in a song with choruses. For example, the arrival of each new Principal sets off similar disturbances. The school fought the church in the 1870s and in the 1970s. Donaldson is sometimes called 'The Doctor',[2] just as Morrison was a hundred years ago.

Other patterns are more complex, like fugues. The never-ending counterpoint between individuality and conformity is an example. We might think that this would be linear, that is, that boys are less regimented now than they were a hundred years ago. In fact, the reverse is the case. Then, boys wore what they liked and no boy had compulsory sport or co-curricular activities, yet this produced Old Boys loyal enough to build the new school at Hawthorn. Educationally, however, a modern boy is more free than his predecessor and is meant to develop independence of thought. Ultimately, the school dances as best it can between the need to learn things by heart and the need to be creative.

HOW TO TALK ABOUT THE FUTURE?

Will Scotch retain its repeated and skilful adaptiveness? Will it keep up with the pace of technological change and of curriculum and pedagogical reform, which have already brought more change in the 1990s than in any previous decade? Will it meet the dual need to provide an education that both prepares the individual for a productive life and also contributes to the well-being of nations? Will it continue to build and to expand in size, or will it limit its physical development and refocus on the quality of the human experience? Will it become ever more expensive and socially narrower, or will endowments help the sons of families of modest means? Will the dwindling size of the Presbyterian Church raise problems?

If these sound like clichés, that is because they belong to the future we can imagine, whereas the future will of course be one that we cannot imagine. Who in 1950 would have anticipated female senior staff, or the schism, or 20% inflation, or Roff's fall, or personal computers, or the freeway, or the Principal's name burnt with weed-killer in the lawn, or team teaching, or the parish disciplining the Vice-Principal, or a Japanese Regimental-Sergeant-Major of cadets? The list could be doubled and trebled, and our own future will be similarly unexpected.

HOW THEN SHALL WE CONCLUDE?

Shall we end this story by recalling that the school is the culmination of its past? It is a boys' school, from preparatory to Year 12, with an annual enrolment of over 1800 boys, on a single site at Hawthorn, providing boarding facilities, with an emphasis on academic education, and seeking the development of the whole man, especially through Christianity and sport. That sounds straightforward but, as we have seen, each phrase in this description has been thrashed out over the decades. 'The chief focus of the school', says the 1998 *Annual Report*, 'remains as it has been throughout the College's 147-year history—the provision of high quality education'.[3] This is true, of course, but it is also true that this was not one of Lawson's four original goals from Edinburgh. Even in this central focus, Scotch has had to grow and develop.

Shall we note the school's internal rivalries, where the Hill and rowing have been the school's indulged children? Where the departments shape or stifle the emergence of new and inter-departmental disciplines? Where skills and content compete?

Shall we mention what the school would prefer we not mention: bullying and bumping and sarcasm; and the authoritarian behaviours and structures, and the internal systems of privilege, that are so useful in managing 1800 boys?

Shall we remind ourselves of Scotch's status and privilege, about which Scotch feels both proud and yet also awkward?

Shall we try to assess Scotch's contribution to education? It has been a seed-bed for principals, text-books and teachers' associations, and has seconded staff to teacher training and curriculum development. As a successful school it has been a model for others, often innovative and often cautious. The innovations run from Morrison's class-allocation, through Littlejohn's reporting system, Gilray's sports standards and sunburst of cultural activities, Healey's General Studies or introduction of an Asian language, to Donaldson's team teaching in Year 7. Today, senior staff are appointed specifically to think about education. Foundation Fellows keep ideas simmering.

Shall we try to assess Scotch's contribution to the community? Its Old Boys are scattered throughout the world, in roles of power, creativity and service, and also in less laudable roles, even before the courts and in prisons.

Shall we end triumphantly, proclaiming Scotch's confidence in its future. At an OSCA luncheon in 1986 Bond said: 'Let us not be too bashful, but rather let us quietly and confidently give notice to all and sundry that we intend to be in business five hundred years from now, by which time the wood in the Chapel pews will have subtly mellowed, and the carillon bells set high in my clock-tower will resound up the Gardiner valley.'[4]

Or shall we note how Scotch lives in the memories of the Old Boys:

… cet autre monde moyenâgeux … Ici était une mentalité qui datait des siècles, commençant avec la prière, passant par la canne aux autres punitions corporelles. … Cette tradition de scolarité quasi-féodale dans laquelle j'étais incarcérée pendant quatre ans équivaut à quatre ans volés de ma vie. C'est une chose entièrement impardonnable … J'avais une seule envie—de quitter l'école. [Robert Abbey 1959].[5]

[… this other, mediaeval world. Here was a centuries-old state of mind, starting with prayers and then through the cane to other corporal punishments. … This tradition of quasi-feudal education in which I was imprisoned for four years meant four years stolen from my life. It is utterly unforgivable. … I had but one longing—to get out of the school.]

Scotch was more an adventure than a school. From the candid honesty of experiences such as Scotch-at-Cowes and war cries at the Head of the River to the formality and circumstance of cadet parades and chapel services, Scotch provided me with the opportunity to test and establish the foundations of a value system that I carry with me today [Ian Mackenzie 1982].[6]

In 1935 [in] Leighwood House discipline here was enforced by the masters per medium of an extremely cruel horse whip … bruising was seen by the school doctor and the whip barred. What was not known was that two little boys in the middle of the night entered the master's study and hid the whip and so there was some trouble in locating it in order to have it destroyed— perhaps this is a good example of self-reliance. (I know who the other boy was but ain't saying) [Doug Aitchison 1945].[7]

Really, the entire package had a profound influence on me. The values, lifelong habits which were instilled in us such as, in my case, a love of and commitment to health and fitness so much so that I still run 4–5 days a week. Also, of course, that select handful of lifelong friends made during my 4 blissful years at Scotch [Ric Dillon 1965].[8]

He quite unfairly, I still believe, labelled me as a trouble maker … Sensitive to injustice I became frustrated and eventually a real trouble maker—leaving Scotch with scholarships etc. unexpired. … Over this distance of 40 years, he is the only person I've ever hated [Geoff Cadogan-Cowper 1958].[9]

Most of the good things in my life (and there are many) come from my connection with the school [George Anderson 1932].[10]

Just being there and being part of a highly motivated group with a great sense of pride and tradition. Enjoyed the facilities and the variety of extra-curricular activities (Scouts, Rovers, Music etc.). Great spirit of camaraderie. Learning was fun. One of the happiest periods of my life [Alan Hamley 1957].[11]

Stinking hot summers in the classroom, sweating after running around at lunch, listening to the crickets outside, feeling the cool breeze through the open windows and trying to concentrate on the subject [Angus Mackenzie 1983].[12]

A FINAL GLANCE

The illustration below shows a picture of the senior school buildings on a fine spring day. Even a cursory glance shows a school built in stages. The oldest building is immediately discernible from its crenellations and gothic windows. The brick addition on its south (the organ) must logically be later. The style of the other buildings makes them later, too, although their order might not be clear. Different aspects of the buildings suggest continuities and departures. The smooth brick of the Hall was discontinued for later buildings in favour of a textured brick.

As well as what is apparent, one thing is hidden. The brick on the picture's left is mere cladding, covering the original smooth brick. The new brick deliberately conceals the old, and there is no reason to imagine what lies beneath.

The flowering peach tree indicates the opposite kind of hidden feature. The tree was planted in the 1920s, probably by Bob Horne. Perhaps this tree echoes a row of flowering peaches beside the house belonging to the previous owners, and obliterated when the school was built on top of them.

This photograph, like this history, is just a snapshot. Even as it was taken, off camera to the right of the picture the bulldozers were digging the foundations of the new James Forbes Academy. The tennis courts, there from the beginning, are gone and Mackie Hall's days are numbered. Their ground will be taken by the Academy until it too, one day, is demolished ...

To look at Scotch is thus to see patterns overlaying each other. Sometimes they co-exist, and sometimes one replaces or conceals another. Always they blend into the living present. Behind, shimmers the school that still lives in the memories of its staff and boys. Ahead beckons the Scotch College yet to come.

History encapsulated. Some of the school's history is obvious here, and some of it is hidden.

Timeline

Year axis: 1851 · 1876 · 1901 · 1926 · 1951 · 1976 · 2001
(1851 · 1860 · 1870 · 1880 · 1890 · 1900 · 1910 · 1920 · 1930 · 1940 · 1950 · 1960 · 1970 · 1980 · 1990 · 2001)

Chairmen of Council
- Rev. William Miller 1851–56
- Rev. Dr Cairns 1857–65
- Rev. Mackenzie Fraser 1874–79
- John Cumming 1879–83
- Rev. Dr Alexander Marshall 1897–1919
- H. Brenner Lewis 1945–47
- James Aitken 1947–50
- Douglas Bain 1959–63
- Sir Archibald Glenn 1963–81
- Sir James Balderstone 1991–95
- Michael Robinson 1996–

Principals
- Rev. James Nish 1872–74
- Rev. John Mackie 1890–97
- Sir John MacFarland 1919–1934
- Sir Arthur Robinson 1934–45
- Sir Clive Steele 1950–54
- Dr Archibald Anderson 1954–59
- Littlejohn 1904–33
- Gilray 1934–53
- Selby Smith 1953–64
- Healey 1964–75
- Roff 1975–81
- Campbell 1964–67
- Bond 1968–85
- Donaldson 1983–
- Eggleston 1985–87
- Black 1986–87
- Hosking 1987–94
- Savage 1995–

Vice-Principals
- Lawson 1851–56
- Morrison 1857–1903
- Moir 1867–69
- Robert Morrison 1870–1904

Head of Junior School
- Waller 1916–45
- Jamieson 1907–22 (E. Melb. Prep. School)
- Bradshaw 1945–53
- Tapp 1954–77
- Wirth 1977–85
- Nowacki 1986–98
- Mason 98–

Internal
- First Head of Department
- First Dux
- First Head Prefect/Captain
- Old Scotch Collegians' Association
- Old Scotch Collegians' Club
- First House Master
- First Group Master/Head of Year
- First Senior Master/Dean
- Common Room Association
- Junior School Mothers' Association
- General House Committee
- Scotch Association
- Scotch Foundation
- Scotch moves to East Melbourne
- Last class at East Melbourne
- First class at Hawthorn

Sports & Activities
- Collegian
- First Foundation Day Concert
- Satura
- Scotch wins Cricket, Football, Rowing two years running.
- Bowden kicks 21 goals against Xavier.
- Ian Fleming scores 293 runs against Xavier.
- Ginner Davidson sets high jump record.
- Sir Edward Cohen sets oldest surviving record, 100m in 11.64 sec.
- Head of River dead-heat. Scotch wins in row-off.
- John Smith takes five wickets in six balls.
- Scotch's Grand Slam, winning Cricket, Rowing, Football and Athletics.

Scotch's Old Boys
- William Shiels, First Old Boy Premier of Victoria
- Sir George Reid, Prime Minister
- Sir John Monash commands an Army
- Sir John Latham, Chief Justice
- John Cade publishes 'Lithium Salts in the Treatment of Psychotic Excitment'
- Sir Zelman Cowen, Governor-General
- Sir Ninian Stephen, Governor-General

ENDNOTES

NB. Quotations in the text without endnotes are from
questionnaire responses that did not authorise citation by name.

Introduction

1. A. G. Serle (1940) calculated that in the first 14 volumes of the *Australian Dictionary of Biography*, Melbourne University Press, Melbourne, 1969–[2000], (hereafter cited as *ADB*), Scotch's Old Boys have 134 entries compared to 113 for Melbourne Grammar, 66 for Wesley, and 38 for Geelong Grammar. Among Sydney schools Sydney Grammar has 168 entries, Anthea Bundock, emails of 30 Nov and 15 Dec 2000. For *Who's Who* in 1962, 1980 and 1988 see Mark Peel and Janet McCalman, *Who went where in* Who's Who 1988: *The schooling of the Australian elite*, Melbourne University History Research Series No. 1 (1992), p. 28.

2. The eight surviving older schools are said to be: The King's School, Parramatta (1831), St Patrick's College, Campbelltown (1840), Launceston Church Grammar School (1846), Hutchins School, Hobart (1846), Mercedes Catholic Ladies' College, Perth (1846), St Peter's College, Adelaide (1947), Pulteney Grammar School, Adelaide (1847). Two primary schools are also older: St Andrews (Primary) School Walkerville, South Australia (1850) and Essendon Primary School, Victoria (1850?).

3. Peel and McCalman, *Who went where in* Who's Who 1988, p. 12.

4. A. G. Austin, *Australian Education, 1788–1900: Church, state, and public education in colonial Australia*, Sir Isaac Pitman & Sons, Melbourne, 1961. C. E. W. Bean, *Here, my son: An account of the Independent and other corporate schools of Australia*, Angus and Robertson, Sydney, 1950. G. M. Dow, *George Higinbotham: Church and state*, Sir Isaac Pitman & Sons, Melbourne, 1964. I. V. Hansen, *Nor free nor secular: Six Independent Schools in Victoria: A*

first sample, Oxford University Press, Melbourne, 1971. R. J. W. Selleck, 'State education and culture', in S. L. Goldberg and F. B. Smith (eds), *Australian cultural history*, Cambridge University Press, Cambridge, 1988, p. 81. M. R. Theobald, *Knowing women: Origins of women's education in nineteenth-century Australia*, Cambridge University Press, Melbourne, 1996.

5. Minutes of Diamond Jubilee Celebrations, 6 May 1911.

6. R. B. Coutie (1930–32), Q. 'Q' indicates a questionnaire response; the dates indicate the respondent's years at Scotch.

7. D. C. McClean (1943–52), Q.

8. R. K. Mollison (1976–81), Q.

9. J. S. Lawson (1949–52), Q.

10. G. W. Fisher (1948–51), Q.

11. R. L. Davies (1937–41), Q.

12. A. McC. Moorehead (1926), *A late education: Episodes in a life*, Hamish Hamilton, London, 1970, p. 12.

13. L. C. Birch (1925–35), letter to author, 10 Dec 1998.

14. A. R. Edwards (1964–69), Q.

15. J. K. Dempster (1939–50), letter to author, 16 June 1999.

16. A. Morrison, *Annual Report*, 1890.

17. R. Selby Smith, 'A Victorian Independent school: Reflections on the development of Scotch College 1953–1964', in *Melbourne Studies in Education 1965*, ed E. L. French, Melbourne University Press, Melbourne, 1966, pp. 225–250. C. O. Healey, 'Scotch College, Melbourne, 1964–1975', in *Melbourne Studies in Education 1978*, ed Stephen Murray-Smith, Melbourne University Press, Melbourne, 1978, pp. 67–106.

18. D. T. Merrett, 'The school at war: Scotch College and the Great War', in *Melbourne Studies in Education 1982*, ed Stephen Murray-Smith, pp. 209–233.

19. George Wood (ed.), *Scotch College, Melbourne Diamond Jubilee, 1851–1911; Historical sketch with scholastic and sports records, October 6, 1911*, Brown, Prior & Co., Melbourne, [1911]. (For Wood's role, see *Collegian*, 1917, p. 273.) *The Scotch College and its seventieth anniversary*, [Melbourne], 1921. *History of Scotch College Melbourne, 1851–1926*, Scotch College History Committee, Melbourne, 1926. G. Harvey Nicholson (1936) and David H. Alexander (1925) (eds), *The first hundred years: Scotch College, Melbourne, 1851–1951*, Brown, Prior, Anderson, Melbourne, 1952.

1 Lawson, 1851–1856

1. James Fleming (or Flemming), record of Charles Grimes's journey, in James Bonwick, *Port Phillip Settlement*, Sampson Low, Marston, Searle & Rivington, London, 1883, p. 12.

2. James Forbes, *The Port Phillip Christian Herald*, June 1849, p. 44.

3. Synod of the Free Church of Australia Felix, 6 Mar 1850, p. 71.

4. Rev. John Tait, Moderator of the Free Church of Victoria, letter of 16 Aug 1852 to the Colonial Secretary, PROV, VA 856, VPRS 2878/P, Unit 9, A52/2447, listed in Kathryn P. MacKinnon, 'Scotch College … A summary of some of the documents held by the Victorian Public Record Office relating to requests for Land grants and Government financial support'.

5. Colonial Committee of the Free Church of Scotland, 16 July 1850. A Mr Blyth was considered, 17 Dec 1850.

6. Ibid., 17 Dec 1850. To make up to this sum as much as was not brought in by fees.

7. Ibid., 18 Feb 1851.

8. Synod of the Free Presbyterian Church of Victoria, 9 Sept 1851, p. 130.
9. Colonial Committee of the Free Church of Scotland, 15 Apr, 21 May 1851. 'Suggestions for instructions to Mr. Lawson in his conducting the Free Church Academy at Melbourne', National Library of Scotland, Dep. 298; Vol. 262.
10. In the meantime the Synod would take responsibility for a third of Lawson's lease costs, up to £400, Free Presbyterian Church of Victoria, Synod, 5 Aug 1852, p. 155.
11. Ibid., Synod, 9 Nov 1852, p. 155.
12. Austin, *Australian Education*, p. 123.
13. J. L. Row (1868–77), *The Scotch Collegian* (hereafter cited as *Collegian*), Dec 1953, p. 161.
14. A. S. Anderson (1906–9), speaker's notes for OSCA Annual Dinner, 1948 or 1949.
15. Clement Hodgkinson, letter of 13 Dec 1870 about the 'parks and gardens under my control', A. Morrison, *Annual Report*, 1870, p. 8, note.
16. A. Morrison, *Annual Report*, 1868, p. 10.
17. For red see *ADB*, v, 118; for black see J. D. Law (1858) in *The Scotch College and its seventieth anniversary*, p. 24.
18. Wood, *Diamond Jubilee 1851–1911*, p. 14.
19. *Some early history of Mount Blackwood*, p. 267; photocopied excerpt in school's archives.
20. *Collegian*, 1912, p. 48.
21. A. W. Dawes (1917), *Argus*, 28 Sept 1951, p. 2.

2 Morrison, 1857–1903

1. Education Committee, 15 June, 23 Sept, 15, 19 Oct 1857. The dispute with Miller arose when Cairns inspected a parish school said not to be under his jurisdiction.
2. *Argus*, 10 Jan 1857.
3. *Collegian*, Dec 1951, p. 165.
4. Eliza F. Mitchell, Lady Mitchell (née Morrison), *Three-quarters of a century*, Methuen, London, 1949, p. 3.
5. Wood, *Diamond Jubilee, 1851–1911*, p. 19.
6. Mitchell, *Three-quarters*, p. 4.
7. Education Committee, 23 Sept, 15, 19 Oct 1857. Soon after, the

Committee insisted on paying an account out of Morrison's share of the revenue, even in the face of his formal opposition, College Committee, 19 May 1858.
8. Morrison, *Annual Report*, 1868, p. 4.
9. College Committee, 28 Dec 1857.
10. A. Morrison, *Report*, 1860, p. 3.
11. E.g., a promissory note of the Hon Niel Black dated 23 June 1867, due 26 June 1868, promised to pay the London Chartered Bank or order the sum of £75. In 1868 it was down to £65 and in 1869 to £50.
12. Morrison, *Annual Report*, 1890.
13. The Committee, 30 Sept 1861.
14. A. Morrison, *Report*, 1861, p. 28.
15. Ibid., 1864, p. 4.
16. Ibid., 1868, p. 6.
17. Ibid., 1861, p. 8.
18. Ibid., 1866, p. 5.
19. P. A. Gullett (1870), *Collegian*, 1913, p. 64.
20. Morrison, *Report*, 1861, p. 27.
21. T. P. Hill, *The oratorical trainer: A system of vocal culture*, 4th edn, G. Robertson, 1868, Melbourne, Harrild, London, p. iii.
22. Nancy Adams, *Family fresco*, Cheshire, Melbourne, 1966, p. 11.
23. *Young Victoria*, Scotch College, Melbourne, 1877–85, No. 2 (1877), p. 14. Morrison, *Annual Reports*, 1883 and 1897.
24. *Herald*, 6 Sept 1858.
25. *Herald*, 23 Aug 1858.
26. 'Proceedings of the General Assembly … November, 1864', p. 22, in *Proceedings of the Commission of the General Assembly of the Presbyterian Church of Victoria … May, 1864*, Mason and Firth, Melbourne, [1864].
27. *Proceedings of the General Assembly … August, 1861* [sic = 1862], Fergusson and Moore, printers, Melbourne, [1862], p. 13. *Proceedings of the Commission of the General Assembly … May, 1863*, W. H. Williams, [Melbourne, 1863], p. 30.
28. *Proceedings of the General Assembly … November, 1860*, Alex. Anderson, Melbourne, [1860], p. 13.
29. Rev. T. McKenzie Fraser, 'Report of the Special Committee on the educational policy of the Church', in *Proceedings of the General Assembly … November, 1872*, Mason, Firth, and M'Cutcheon, Melbourne, [1872], p. 82
30. *Proceedings of a Pro re nata meeting*

of the General Assembly … July, 1869, [Melbourne, 1869], p. 1. *Proceedings of a pro re nata meeting of the General Assembly … July, 1870*, Egerton and Moore, Melbourne, [1870], p. 5. *Proceedings of the Commission of the General Assembly … November, 1870*, Mason, Firth, and M'Cutcheon, Melbourne, [1870], p. 33.
31. *Proceedings of a Pro re nata meeting of the General Assembly… July, 1870*, p. 5.
32. Education Committee, 24 June 1869, 9 May 1870.
33. For a report summarising this affair see *Business of the General Assembly … November 1871*, Mason, Firth, & M'Cutcheon, Melbourne, 1871, pp. 46 ff.
34. Education Committee, 9 May 1870.
35. Rev. Dr A. Cairns, Moderator, letter of 1 Feb 1854 to the Colonial Secretary, PROV, VA 538VPRS 242, Crown Reserves Correspondence, Unit 23, Letter 54/F1266.
36. *Satura, Newspaper of Scotch College*, Scotch College, Melbourne, 1936— , 3 Mar 1950, p. 1.
37. *Collegian*, June 1952, p. 75.
38. L. C. Birch (1925–35), Q.
39. J. Macdonald (1991–96), Q.
40. R. K. Pickford (1932–36), Q.
41. C. Wallace-Crabbe, 'Losses and Recoveries II', *Selected Poems 1956–94*, Oxford University Press, 1995.
42. *Proceedings of a pro re nata meeting of the General Assembly … July, 1870*, p. 3.
43. A. S. Anderson (1906–9), interview with H. Webster, 19 Apr 1968.
44. J. W. G. Meyer (1944–47), Q.
45. G. S. Blanch (1957–69), Q.
46. L. M. Muir (1937–42), Q.
47. H. R. Taylor (1953–64), email to author, 21 Oct 1999.
48. F. G. Boyes (1941–51), letter to author, 22 July 1999.
49. D. M. Bruce and B. R. Stewardson, 'Regatta patter', *Collegian*, Dec 1954, p. 114. Morrison House wore green.
50. C. W. Johnson (1963–68), Q.
51. A. J. Abell (1988–91), email to author 2 July 1999
52. C. N. McKay and G. M. Dallimore (1919), 'Rowing', *Collegian*, 1919, pp. 155–156.
53. *Satura*, 17 Mar 1965, p.5.
54. D. E. C. R., [D. E. Clunies-Ross (1953)], 'Barwon batteries', *Collegian*, June 1953, p. 31.

55. *Collegian*, May 1951, p. 61.
56. E&F Committee and Council, 28 June 1961.
57. Letter, *Satura*, 17 Mar 1965, p. 5. Reply from J. A. E. Thomson, Captain, *Satura*, 9 Apr 1965, p. 4.
58. D. L. D. Brand, letter to his mother, postmarked 13 Apr 1970.
59. *Collegian*, 1950, p. 16.
60. Irving Hetherington and others, petition to Parliament, quoted in *Business of the General Assembly ... November 1871*, p. 54.
61. Ibid., p. 59.
62. *Proceedings of the Commission of the General Assembly ... November, 1870*, p. 31.
63. Rev. P. Mercer, letter, 20 Sep 1871, in the *Argus*, quoted in *Business of the General Assembly ... November 1871*, p. 52.
64. Education Committee, 13 Nov 1871.
65. Ibid., 23 July, 8 Nov 1872.
66. *Proceedings of the General Assembly ... November, 1872*, p. 36. *Proceedings of the Commission of the General Assembly ... May, 1873*, Mason, Firth, and M'Cutcheon, Melbourne, [1873], pp. 11, 13.
67. Fraser, 'Report of the Special Committee on the educational policy of the Church', p. 79.
68. I. F. Hamilton, *Collegian*, Dec 1953, p. 102.
69. *Proceedings of the General Assembly ... November, 1874*, Walker, May, and Co., Melbourne, [1874], p. 47.
70. Education Committee, 17 Apr 1871.
71. Morrison, *Annual Report*, 1897, p.8.
72. *The Christian Review*, Feb 1875, reprinted in the *Collegian*, Dec 1953, p. 164.
73. Mitchell, *Three-quarters*, pp. 29–31.
74. J. T. Collins, diary, 9 Apr, 24 June, 2 July 1927. By 1911 having to be at school on Saturday was a bitter sorrow, *Collegian*, 1911, p. 20.
75. K. A. Foletta (1961–64), 'Before it all' (unpublished MS).
76. G. R. Baker (1936–38), Q.
77. E. W. W. Peatt (1925–32), Q.
78. A. S. Thomson (1972–77), Q.
79. Council, 25 Mar 1959.
80. Healey, 'Towards a school community' (unpublished MS), pp. 55–6.
81. G. C. McInnes (1930), *The road to*

Gundagai, Hamish Hamilton, London, 1965, p. 92.
82. *Collegian*, 1908, p. 83, 1978, p. 101.
83. *Age,* 20 Mar 1997, p. 3.
84. R. M. Campbell (1958), at OSCA Annual Dinner, *Great Scot*, 64 (1992), p. 18.
85. A. S. Anderson (1909), interview by H. Webster, 1968.
86. Marjory McKay, *Cecil McKay: It wasn't all Sunshine*, Hawthorn Press, Melbourne, 1974, p 46.
87. Mitchell, *Three-quarters*, p. 66.
88. A. Morrison, diary, 9 Feb, 3, 20 Sept, 4 Oct 1884.
89. A. Barnard, 'Elder', *ADB*, iv, 133.
90. A. G. Serle, 'Shiels' *ADB*, xi, 596.
91. J. McI. Young, 'Hood', *ADB*, ix, 359.
92. R. Wright, 'Martin', *ADB*, x, 425.
93. R. Bennett, 'Clendinnen', *ADB*, viii, 28.
94. A. G. Serle, 'Maloney', *ADB*, x, 389.
95. W. J. R. Turner (1901), *Blow for balloons: being the first hemisphere of the history of Henry Airbubble*, Dent, London, 1935, p. 205.
96. Adams, *Fresco*, p. 64.
97. Mitchell, *Three-quarters*, p. 111.
98. MacFarland, Council, 15 June 1903.
99. *Age*, 25 Aug 1934.
100. Morrison, *Annual Report*, 1898.
101. Gilray, *Collegian*, Dec 1950, p. 195.
102. D. O. Shave (1946–52), Q.
103. J. N. Denham (1934–38), Q.
104. G. N. Ingham (1925–32), Q.
105. P. G. Petty (1947–51), Q.
106. D. J. Ashton (1953–65), Q.
107. W. A. Shattock (1974–79), Q.
108. D. G. Barrie (1990–95), Q.
109. *Satura*, 12 Oct 1962, p. 8.
110. Selby Smith, report to Council, 26 June 1963.
111. W. R. Walker (1970–75), email to author, 4 May 1999.
112. *Satura*, 9 May 1958, p. 1.
113. D. J. Ashton (1953–65), Q.
114. H. M. Brown (1955–63), letter to author, 16 June 1999.
115. J. C. H. Spence (1964), email to author, 17 July 2000.
116. F. A. Fleming cited by R. G. Kennedy, 'Cadet Notes', *Collegian*, May 1951, p. 41, repeated by J. P. Sennitt, 'Cadet Corps', *Collegian*, June 1953, p. 25.
117. *Collegian*, June 1952, p. 24.
118. G. P. Cook (1940–46), Q.
119. D. G. Barrie (1990–95), Q.
120. I. C. Teague (1947–52), Q.
121. G. F. Cadogan-Cowper

(1954–58), Q.
122. W. R. Walker (1970–75), email to author, 4 May 1999; J. B. Cumming (1957–67), Q; S. F. Macintyre (1959–64), Q.
123. 'New Principal of Scotch College Mr Gilray arrives', press clipping, 20 July 1934.
124. D. R. Hindle and B. C. M. Knappett, 'Editorial', *Satura*, 9 May 1968, p. 2.
125. Healey, report to Council, 29 Apr 1970.
126. K. R. A. Shirrefs, note to author, Sept 2000.
127. *Scotch College Cadet Unit Handbook*, 1982, p. 2.
128. F. G. Donaldson, *Annual Report*, 1998, *Collegian*, 1998, p. 9.

3 A thorough and liberal education

1. Selleck, 'State education and culture', p. 81.
2. Morrison, *Report,* 1861, p. 28.
3. Morrison, *Report,* 1864, pp. 6–7.
4. 'Mr M. D. Close', *Diploma of survival for fifty years from IIIc Scotch College 1939. 24th February 1989*, [Melbourne, 1989].
5. B. A. Johns (1946–55), Q.
6. J. B. Pettigrew (1932–34), Q.
7. Turner, *Blow for balloons*, p. 207.
8. J. B. Pettigrew (1932–34), letter to author, 17 Sept 1998.
9. R. Stott (1935–40), Q.
10. C. Bridges-Webb (1948–51), Q.
11. A. Edwards (1964–69), Q.
12. M. A. McKenzie (1939–47), Q.
13. G. D. Fisher (1929–41), Q.
14. M. J. Edwards (1967–70), Q.
15. W. K. Fullagar (1936–45), Q.
16. Morrison, *Report*, 1860, p. 4.
17. Ibid., 1861, p. 6.
18. Chris Worth, '"A centre at the edge": Scotland and the early teaching of literature in Australia and New Zealand,' in Robert Crawford (ed.), *The Scottish invention of English literature*, Cambridge University Press, Cambridge, 1998, p. 211. English literature had emerged first among women, for they were not taught the classics, and became academic first in Scotland.
19. E. A. Samson (staff 1866–70), English Department Report, in Morrison, *Report*, 1866, p. 11.
20. B. A. Johns (1946–55), Q.
21. *Young Victoria*, 3 (1877), p. 27.

22. Samson, English Department Report, p. 11.
23. Morrison, *Report*, 1860, p. 11.
24. Ibid., 1865, p. 28.
25. Hill, *Oratorical trainer*, p. iii.
26. Turner, *Blow for balloons*, pp. 206–7.
27. *Scotch College Speech-Day. Christmas, 1862. St, George's Hall. His Excellency Sir Henry Barkly, K.C.B., in the chair*, [Melbourne, 1862].
28. J. A. Lyne, *Collegian*, 1978, p. 166; D. H. Hare (1922–29), Q.
29. P. R. Wilson (1935–47), Q.
30. R. Jackson (1975–78), Q.
31. D. G. Batten (1943–46), Q.
32. P. R. Wilson (1935–47), Q.
33. B. A. Johns (1946–55), Q.
34. A. A. Laing (1933–40), Q.
35. B. W. Bainbridge (1951–53), K. A. Foletta (1961–65), QQ.
36. D. C. M. Ward (1968-79), Q.
37. B. A. Johns (1946–55), Q.
38. A. Morrison, 'Statement made to the Special Committee on Education ... relative to the religious instruction given at that institution', and Fraser, 'Report of the Special Committee on the educational policy of the Church', in *Proceedings of the General Assembly of the Presbyterian Church of Victoria ... November, 1872*, pp. 85, 78.
39. G. J. Carrick (1928–35), Q.
40. McInnes, *Road to Gundagai*, pp. 94–5.
41. J. C. Blaine (1925–32), Q.
42. Morrison, *Report*, 1860, p. 14.
43. D. M. Annand (1930–38), Q.
44. D. O. Shave (1946–52), Q.
45. Turner, *Blow for balloons*, p. 207.
46. Ibid., p. 215.
47. Ibid., p. 223.
48. J. G. Paton (1920), *Collegian*, 1920, p. 106.
49. W. J. Patterson (1908) and A. R. Vines (1910), *Collegian*, July 1908, p. 82
50. *Collegian*, Dec 1953, p. 132.
51. *Collegian*, Dec 1958, p. 166.
52. C. O. Healey, *Annual Report*, 1974, p. 8, Healey, report to Council, 30 Oct 1974.
53. A. P. Williams (1966–71), email to author, 26 July 2000.
54. Morrison, *Report*, 1864, p. 7.
55. Ibid., 1862, p. 7.
56. *Scotch College, Eastern Hill, Melbourne. Prize List, 1857*, Goodhugh & Hough, Melbourne, [1857]. P. A. Mishura, 'Note books

from 1858 found', *Great Scot*, 85 (1997), p. 24.
57. Morrison, *Report*, 1860, p. 15.
58. Ibid., 1861, p. 8.
59. *Young Victoria*, 6 (1878), p. 76.
60. A. G. Serle, *John Monash: A biography*, Melbourne University Press, Melbourne, 1982, pp. 11–12.
61. Turner, *Blow for balloons*, pp. 207–9.
62. Morrison, *Report*, 1864, p. 7.
63. R. M. Carmichael (1956–64), Q.
64. R. Jackson (1975–78), Q.
65. W. N. Hurst (1939–50), Q.
66. M. W. Reid (1953–58), Q.
67. G. E. D. Brooke (1967–73), Q.
68. R. C. Schurmann (1941–45), Q.
69. R. W. McDonald (1943–44), Q.
70. F. G. Boyes (1941–51), Q.
71. Morrison, *Report*, 1860, p. 19.
72. R. K. Mollison (1976–81), Q.
73. Morrison, *Report*, 1861, p. 20.
74. Ibid., 1860, pp. 16–18.
75. Serle, *Monash*, p. 11.
76. Morrison, *Report*, 1861, p. 28.
77. John F. Ewing, *The unsearchable riches of Christ*, Melville, Mullen & Slade, Melbourne, 1890, p. 19.
78. Morrison, *Report*, 1870, p. 5.
79. 50 by 30 by 20 feet, Fraser, 'Report of the Special Committee on the educational policy of the Church', 1872, p. 82.
80. R. Reed (staff 1862–73), Commercial Department Report, in Morrison, *Report*, 1866, p. 12.
81. A. Morrison, *Report*, 1863, p. 8.
82. *Young Victoria*, 3 (1877), p. 29.
83. Sir J. McCulloch, Speech Day 1878, *Young Victoria*, 9, Christmas Supplement (1878), p. 3.
84. *The Christian Review and Messenger of the Presbyterian Church of Victoria*, Dec 1875, p. 9.
85. J. Forbes, *The Port Phillip Christian Herald*, June 1849, p. 44.
86. J. B. Cumming (1957–67), Q.
87. W. R. Gleadell (1959–66), email to author, 19 Nov 1998.
88. R. K. Blair (1954–63), Q.
89. R. Gittins, 'Old soldiers and young men', *EQ Australia*, 2 (1996), p. 8.
90. R. J. McLaren, written 14 Oct 1999.
91. K. C. B. Bethell (1929–37), Q. Similarly, L.K. Shave (1929), Q, letter to author, 20 July 1999.
92. G. J. Carrick (1928–35), Q.
93. W. R. Gleadell (1959–66), email to author, 19 Nov 1998.
94. F. G. Boyes (1941–51); Respondent 79 (1972), QQ.

95. Turner, *Blow for balloons*, p. 213.
96. J. A. Lyne, 'Memories of Scotch College 1924–28', unpublished MS.
97. A. O. Jones (1957–62), letter to author, Aug 1999.
98. J. K. Dempster (1939–50), letter to author, 16 June 1999.
99. H. K. Oxley (1926–33), Q.
100. G. R. Baker (1936–38), letter to author, 21 June 1999.
101. W. R. Skene (1863–68), diary, 13 Jun 1868.
102. *Young Victoria*, 2 (1877), p. 17.
103. J. L. Row (1877), *Collegian*, Dec 1953, p. 161.
104. *Young Victoria*, 2 (1877), p. 17.
105. Roff, 'Address to the Junior School Mothers' Association', 18 Sept 1975.
106. Turner, *Blow for balloons*, pp. 207–12.
107. A. D. Callister (1937–49).
108. Morrison, *Report*, 1864, p. 9.
109. Fraser, 'Report of the Special Committee on the educational policy of the Church', p. 79.
110. Morrison, *Report*, 1868, p. 29, and 1860, p. 4.
111. Ibid., 1869, p. 5.
112. *Young Victoria*, 2 (1877), pp. 18–19.
113. Morrison, *Report*, 1864, p. 9.
114. *Young Victoria*, 4 (1877), p. 40.
115. Morrison, *Report*, 1864, p. 9.
116. Turner, *Blow for balloons*, p. 205.
117. Morrison, *Report*, 1865, p. 4. Three men came from Scotland in 1860, Morrison, *Report*, 1860.
118. Ibid., 1891.
119. Ibid., 1860, pp. 28, 4.
120. ibid., 1861, p. 28.
121. *The Christian Review*, Feb 1875, reprinted in the *Scotch Collegian*, Dec 1953, p. 164.
122. Morrison, *Report*, 1861, p. 29.
123. Ibid., 1861, p. 8.
124. Ibid., 1860, p. 28.
125. Ibid., 1861, p. 29.
126. *The Christian Review*, Feb 1875, reprinted in the *Collegian*, Dec 1953, p. 164.
127. Morrison, *Report*, 1860, p. 28.
128. *Collegian*, 1904, p. 10.
129. Morrison, *Report*, 1860, p. 28. In England boys were put in classes according to the ability in the classics alone, *Report*, 1864, p. 5.
130. Ibid., 1868, p. 4.

4 Educating the whole man

1. Morrison, *Report*, 1864, p. 11.
2. Ibid., 1861, p. 5.

3. Ibid., 1868, p. 8.
4. Morrison, 'Statement made to the Special Committee on Education,' 1872, p. 84.
5. Morrison, *Reports*, 1861, p. 6, and 1862, p. 9. Forbes took the same view, K. Cardell and C. Cumming, 'North Eastern Presbyterians and colonial education: James Forbes and the Port Phillip District' (typescript), p. 13.
6. *The Christian Review*, Feb 1875, reprinted in the *Collegian*, Dec 1953, p. 164.
7. Morrison, *Report*, 1866, p. 8.
8. Ibid., 1861, p. 29, and 1862, p. 9.
9. Ibid., 1861, p. 6.
10. Mitchell, *Three-quarters*, p. 24.
11. Morrison, *Report*, 1868, p. 8.
12. *Collegian*, 1910, p. 127.
13. *Young Victoria*, 12 (Oct 1879), p. 162.
14. A. S. Anderson (1909), interview with H. Webster, 1968.
15. G. M. Shillinglaw and J. G. Wilkin, Editorial, *Collegian*, Dec 1952, p. 86.
16. A. D. Skurrie (1932–33), letter to author, 2 July 1999.
17. D. S. Clues (1930–32), Q.
18. D. J. Ashton (1953–65), Q.
19. J. M. Hickman (1963–66), Q.
20. Healey, *Annual newsletter*, 1966.
21. McInnes, *Road to Gundagai*, p. 104.
22. A view at CRA Education Committee, 29 May 1972.
23. Morrison, *Report*, 1861, pp. 6, 29.
24. J. R. A. Glenn, interview with author, 20 Feb 1998.
25. Littlejohn, *Annual Report*, 1908, p. 9.
26. A. P. Crow, CRA Education Committee, 10 Nov 1969.
27. Morrison, *Annual Report*, 1887.
28. Littlejohn, *Annual Report*, 1908, p. 8.
29. C. M. Gilray, *Annual Report*, 1946, p. 4.
30. Morrison, *Report*, 1869, p. 7.
31. Ibid., 1869, p. 6.
32. Ibid., 1868, p. 8. Italics added.
33. Ibid., 1869, p. 9.
34. Ibid., 1864, p. 9.
35. Littlejohn, *Annual Report*, 1908, p. 8.
36. Littlejohn, 7 Dec 1928, reference for K. W. T. Bridge (1923).
37. Donaldson, 'Annual Report 1989', *Collegian*, 1989, p. 2.
38. F. A. Fleming cited by R. G. Kennedy, 'Cadet Notes', *Collegian*, May 1951, p. 41.

39. Morrison, *Report*, 1869, p. 9.
40. *Young Victoria*, 10 (May 1879), pp. 138, 140.
41. J. W. Olifent (1936–38), R.L. Hyams (1969–80), QQ.
42. *Young Victoria*, 12 (Oct 1879), p. 163.
43. F. Macrae (1956–67), P. M. Ashton (1957–67), QQ.
44. M. L. Jelbart (1963–67), Q.
45. Sir J. McCulloch at 1879 Speech Day, *Young Victoria*, 13, Supplement (Dec 1879), p. 2.
46. *Young Victoria*, 12 (Oct 1879), p. 163. Morrison, *Report*, 1869. p. 9.
47. W. J. Simpson, in D. G. Paul, 'Scotch College—Commonroom Association. Report of Education Committee Conference held on 13.9.71'.
48. *Young Victoria*, 12 (Oct 1879), p. 163.
49. A. S. Anderson (1909), speaker's notes for OSCA Annual Dinner 1948 or 1949.
50. H. R. Taylor (1953–64), Q.
51. D. G. Barrie (1990–95), C.A. Widdis (1983–90), QQ.
52. Correspondent (1955), letter to author, 21 July 1999. Today, all boarders' lockers are padlocked.
53. *Young Victoria*, 14 (June 1880), p. 215.
54. Newspaper cutting in school archives.
55. A. MacV. L. Campbell, diary, 24 Sept 1929.
56. A. J. M. Davies, *The Fiddlers of Drummond*, Consolidated Press, Sydney, 1945, p. 38.
57. D. B. Telfer (1969–74), email to author, 3 July 1999.
58. R. C. Schurmann (1941–45), Q.
59. K. G. McCracken, Arthur Robinson House notes, *Collegian*, Aug 1950, p. 104
60. N. A. Bromberger, 'Stamp Club', ibid., p. 124.
61. *Rules for the guidance of pupils attending the Scotch College*, Fergusson & Moore, Melbourne, [1867?], rule 21. *Young Victoria*, 14 (June 1880), p. 214
62. G. R. Baker (1936–38), Q; italics added.
63. R. H. Clayton, interview by H. Webster, June 1968. W. H. Callister (1936–41), letter to author, 4 Nov 1998.
64. H. S. Millar (1940–48), Q.
65. R. A. W. Wade (1946–49), Q.
66. D. Goodenough at Junior School

Mothers' Association, 6 Aug 1959.
67. H. E. C. Brook, *Collegian*, Dec 1951, p. 165.
68. Tapp, Junior School Mothers' Association, 12 Nov 1964.
69. Morrison, *Young Victoria*, 13 (Dec 1879), p. 190.
70. A. D. Skurrie (1932–33), Q.
71. I. R. Marks (1950–54), Q.
72. Selby Smith, 'A Victorian Independent school', p. 247.
73. Donaldson, Annual Report 1997, *Collegian*, 1997, p. 11.
74. P. W. Howe (1975–80), Q.
75. Morrison, *Young Victoria*, 13 (Dec 1879), pp. 189–190.
76. Sir J. McCulloch at 1879 Speech Day, *Young Victoria*, 13, Supplement (Dec 1879), p. 2.
77. Littlejohn, *Annual Report*, 1927, pp. 1– 2.
78. L. D. Kemp (1922–27), Q.
79. F. Macrae (1956–67), Q.
80. T. R. Winwood (staff 1969–73), 'The purpose of this paper is to suggest ideas for the establishment of an Adventure Training and Field Study Centre', untitled, undated, unsigned, roneoed document marked in MS 'Ed. Cttee (next meeting)', presumably CRA Education Committee, 8 July 1971, p. 3.
81. *Messenger*, 17 May 1928.
82. Scotch College, Memorandum of Association, art. 3 (1) (b).
83. Rev. A. R. Macneil, *Scotch College Melbourne Divine Service in the Memorial Hall … 7th October, 1934 (Old Boys' and Parents' Sunday)*, Brown Prior & Co., Melbourne, [1934], p. 2.
84. G. D. Fisher (1929–41), Q.
85. Healey, 'Towards a school community', p. 36A.
86. Turner, *Blow for balloons*, p. 213.
87. Morrison, *Report*, 1869, p. 7.
88. Ibid., 1860, p. 5.
89. Ibid., 1861, p. 7.
90. 'Prospectus', *Scotch College, Melbourne. Report and honor list, 1863*, p. 26.
91. Morrison, *Report*, 1868, pp. 19, 22. The earliest known Old Boy activity was sport-related, when in 1859 the [Old] Scotch College cricketers club had 49 members, with J. Tait as Secretary, *Sands & Kenny's Cricketers' Guide*, 1859, cited by Douglas W. Rankin (1947), in *Collegian*, Aug 1950, p. 157.

92. J. L. M. Campbell (1907), 'Some unedifying recollections of Eastern Hill', typed MS.
93. Morrison, *Report*, 1881.
94. Morrison, 'Statement made to the Special Committee on Education', p. 85.
95. *Young Victoria*, 14 (June 1880), p. 215.
96. Morrison, *Reports*, 1892 and 1868, p. 9. Morrison, 'Statement made to the Special Committee on Education', p. 85
97. Morrison, *Reports*, 1881 and 1897.
98. Ibid., 1880, in *Young Victoria*, 15 (Dec 1880), p. 234.
99. A. S. Anderson (1909), speaker's notes for OSCA Annual Dinner 1948 or 1949.
100. W. D. Refshauge (1927–31), Q.
101. A. T. Marshall (1971–76), Q.
102. *Collegian*, 1913, pp. 99, 100.
103. Selby Smith, 'A Victorian Independent school'. pp. 245–6.
104. See Martin Crotty, ' "Loyal scions of the British Race": Sport and the construction of the Australian public schoolboy, c. 1870–1920', in Martin Crotty and Doug Scobie (eds.), *Raiding Clio's closet: Postgraduate presentations in History, 1997*, History Department, University of Melbourne, Melbourne, 1997, pp. 45–60.
105. Morrison, *Report*, 1881.
106. Ibid., 1883. 'To learn to accept defeat, to develop better staff-student relationships', P. J. Wade (Captain 1975), in 'Report on staff/senior students' seminar. September 1975'; 'Winning graciously, losing without rancour and respecting one's opponents', Donaldson, *Great Scot*, 63 (1992), p. 2.
107. W. O. Roberts, School House notes, *Collegian*, Dec 1951, p. 180.
108. A. S. Anderson (1909), speaker's notes for OSCA Annual Dinner 1948 or 1949.
109. *Satura*, 9 May 1958, p. 3.
110. H. K. Oxley (1926–33), Q.
111. Healey, 'School Officers', Feb 1965, p. 5; roneoed document.
112. W. I. Picken (1934–37), Q.
113. Selby Smith, report to Council, 30 Oct 1963.
114. *Collegian*, June 1954, p. 78. The school's list of the dates during which staff held office is incomplete in Clayton's and a few other cases.

115. F. I. R. Martin (1939–47), Q.
116. M. Smith (1938–41), Q.
117. *Collegian*, Dec 1952, p. 167.
118. W. G. Pugh (1947–51), letter to author, June 1999.
119. A. S. Anderson (1909), speaker's notes for OSCA Annual Dinner 1948 or 1949.
120. *Collegian*, June 1952, p. 32.
121. *Scotch College Melbourne Foundation Day Concert October 10, 1913*, Brown Prior & Co., Melbourne [1913].
122. J. M. Hickman (1963–66), Q.
123. H. M. Brown (1955–63), Q.
124. Healy, 'Questions for Senior Day-Housemasters and division masters', May 1972, roneoed document.
125. A. S. Anderson (1909), interview with H. Webster, 1968.
126. Roff, 'Address to the Junior School Mothers' Association', 18 Sept 1975.
127. Donaldson, Annual Report, 1998, *Collegian*, 1998, p. 10.
128. Ibid., 1991, p. 6.
129. W. R. Stern, Gardiner House notes, *Collegian*, Aug 1950, p. 107.
130. L. W. Hall (1918–23), Q.
131. F. W. Paton (1958–63), Q.
132. J. D. H. Bruce, Bond House notes, *Collegian*, 1990, p. 83.
133. C. W. Johnson (1963–68), Q.
134. D. J. Drummond, Littlejohn house notes, *Collegian*, May 1951, p. 23.
135. *Collegian*, Dec 1954, p. 111.
136. F. S. Falconer (1950–54), Q.
137. A. T. Hamley (1953–57), Q.
138. W. G. Pugh (1947–51), Q.
139. I. K. Burnett (1970–75), Q.
140. Selby Smith, 'A Victorian Independent school', p. 245.
141. Littlejohn, *Annual Report*, 1924, p. 12.
142. I. D. Phipps (1946–52), Q.
143. Rev. A. R. Macneil, *Scotch College Melbourne Divine Service in the Memorial Hall … 18th October, 1931 (Old Boys' and Parents' Sunday) and to mark the Eightieth Anniversary of the Founding of the College*, Brown, Prior & Co., Melbourne, [1931].
144. *Great Shot: Scotch College Weekly Basketball Review*, ed. R.C. F. Hortin (staff 1981–), Master-in-Charge, Basketball, vol 1, no 5, 3 July 1990., p. 3.
145. W. H. Callister (1936–41), letter to author, 4 Nov 1998.
146. Healey, 'Towards a school community', p. 20.

147. Healey, 'School Officers', Feb 1965, p. 5
148. Littlejohn, 28 Nov 1924, reference for W. A. Dobbie.
149. R. A. W. Wade (1946–49), Q.
150. Selby Smith, 'A Victorian Independent school', p. 245.
151. Morrison, *Annual Report*, 1883.
152. Sir J. McCulloch at 1879 Speech Day, *Young Victoria*, 13, Supplement (Dec 1879), p. 2.
153. A. S. Anderson (1909), speaker's notes for OSCA Annual Dinner 1948 or 1949.
154. *Collegian*, May 1951, p. 56.
155. Junior School Mothers' Association, 1968 Annual report.
156. *Great Shot*, 3 July 1990. p. 3.
157. K. R. McK. Don (1937–44), Q.
158. A. J. Abell (1988–91), email to author, 2 July 1999
159. A. W. L. Mitchell, *Collegian*, May 1951, p. 61.
160. R. N. Swann (1956–60), Q.
161. W. Comerford, letter 11 June 1986.
162. *Satura*, 12 Oct 1962, p. 5.
163. Geelong College, Geelong Grammar School, Melbourne Grammar School, Scotch College, Wesley College and Xavier College were joined by Brighton Grammar School, Caulfield Grammar School, Carey Grammar School, Haileybury College and St Kevin's College.
164. B. W. Anderson, Selby Smith House notes, *Collegian*, 1989, p. 161.
165. *Young Victoria*, 14 (June 1880), p. 215.
166. Healey, report to Council, 28 Oct 1964.
167. *Collegian*, 1907, pp. 68–9, slightly amended.
168. Roff, report to Council, 27 Apr 1977. Similarly, Donaldson, *Collegian*, 1989, p. 7, but subsequent years reduced the figure to 1000.
169. Gilray, *Report*, 1946, p. 7.
170. Serle, *Monash*, p. 21.
171. Ibid., *Monash*, p. 19.
172. S. D. Kunstler (1970–75), Q.
173. D. G. Paul, 'Report on staff/student 5th Form Seminar: "Choice & Compulsion in the school environment" ', 10 Sept 1979.
174. M. D. Purvis (1969–75), Q.
175. G. A. Bremner, '1929 A very good year: Reminiscences 1929–32', typed.
176. R. A. Stott (1935–37), Q.

177. A. S. Anderson (1909), 'Appeal Dinner 1962',
178. GHC, 30 Sept 1976.
179. W. Norris (1942–45), 1943 diary, comments written in 1992.
180. W. Norris, diary, 19 Nov 1944.
181. P. Tainsh (1980–85), letter of 14 Ocotber 1998.
182. D. G Paul, 'The Fifth and Sixth as Years of Transition', 1971—typed speaker's notes.

5 The Boss, 1904–1933

1. *Collegian*, 1904, p. 6.
2. 'His unfailing courtesy, ready sympathy and genial presence', H. Stewart, Principal of Wesley, *Herald*, 7 Oct 1933. 'He had a warm and genial personality combined with a natural dignity which easily assured respect for authority', *Herald*, 7 Oct 1933.
3. A "Littlejohn" Old Boy, 'Our Principals—No. 2 "The Boss" A man of immense dignity', *News from Scotch*, [No. 2. headline: 'Start on first of the new buildings'], [1962], p. 4.
4. *Age*, 9 Oct 1933.
5. G. G. Powell (1926–29), Q.
6. Bremner, '1929 A very good year'.
7. A. S. Anderson (1909), interview with H. Webster, 1968
8. Ibid.
9. G. H. Reid, *Collegian*, 1904, p. 95.
10. *The Australian Encyclopaedia*, 10 vols, Grollier Society, Sydney, ca. 1956, vii, 402.
11. *Great Scot*, May 1981, p. 1.
12. Council, 24 Sep 1903.
13. Roff, report to Council, 28 Apr 1976.
14. Council, 24 July, 25 March, 7 Dec 1906, 19 June 1908.
15. Council, 22 Apr, 4 Aug 1904.
16. Council, 29 June 1904.
17. Littlejohn, *Report*, 1908, p. 10.
18. McInnes, *Road to Gundagai*, p. 103.
19. Ingram, Speech night, 1933, newspaper clipping.
20. Thus Ron Testro, 'Empire's Biggest Public School', *The Australasian Post*, 1 Mar 1951, p. 9. *Collegian*, Aug 1951, p. 132
21. A. G. Mackay (1965–70), Q.
22. A. C. Watson, (1942–47), letter to author 15 Sept 98.
23. *Scotch College, Melbourne. Examination Results*, Ford & Son, Printers, Carlton [1897?], pre-printed with the names of the subjects and with notes on the back about 'Written examinations' and 'attendance'; with an attached *Subject Report* slip for J. McA. Howden (1898).
24. Bremner, '1929 A very good year'.
25. *Scotch College Melbourne Preparatory School, Report on* A. A. Buchanan, term III, 1913.
26. *Middle, Lower and Preparatory Schools. Scotch College, Melbourne Report* for 1919 on A. A. Buchanan.
27. Littlejohn, 'General remarks', *Scotch College Melbourne Preparatory School, Report on* A. A. Buchanan, term II, 1913.
28. *Forms IV., V., VI., and Remove. Scotch College, Hawthorn and East Melbourne Report on* A. B. Cameron in Remove B in 1926.
29. E. H. Thorpe (1925), unpublished memoirs.
30. Jas. Jamieson, Headmaster of Preparatory School, Report, 13 Dec 1918.
31. Jas. Jamieson, 'General remarks', *Scotch College Melbourne Preparatory School, Report on* A. A. Buchanan of the Senior Preparatory Form, term III, 1915.
32. Jas. Jamieson, *Scotch College Melbourne. Preparatory School. Report* on L. W. Galvin, of the Senior Preparatory Form, term III, 1914.
33. Ingram, Speech night, 1933, newspaper clipping.
34. E.g., 1927 School Diary. Similarly, Bond, 'Prefects and School Officers', Feb 1982, 'Staff Manual', Section B. 12.
35. Littlejohn, testimonial for J. R. A. Glenn, 17 Dec 1929.
36. *Satura*, 18 Feb 1957, p. 3.
37. A. S. Anderson (1909), speaker's notes to Junior School Mothers' Association, 5 Oct 1950.
38. A. S. Anderson (1909), 'Appeal Dinner 1962',.
39. R. A. W. Wade (1946–49), Q.
40. T. C. C. Downing (1991–99), interview with author, 4 May 1999.
41. D. L. D. Brand (1969–72), conversation with author, 24 June 1999.
42. Bremner, '1929 A very good year'.
43. J. A. Lyne (1924–28), Q.
44. C. J. Adam (1975–81), Q.
45. W. R. Fleming (1969–76), Q.
46. R. A. W. Wade (1946–49), Q. Similarly, M. A. McKenzie (1939–47), Q.
47. B. Andrews (1941–45), Q.
48. K. R. McK. Don (1937–44), Q.
49. P. H. R. Sargeant, "Prologue for Summer. To C.F.M. [C. F. Munro, his co-editor], *Collegian*, Dec 1950, p. 206
50. G. K. Bolger (1946–49), Q.
51. Bremner, '1929 A very good year'.
52. R. M. Campbell, *An urge to laugh*, Wildcat Press, Sydney, 1981.
53. Littlejohn, *Annual Report*, 1908, p. 8.
54. W. F. Ingram, 'Public schools in a changing age', *Herald*, Week-End Magazine, 8 Dec 1934, p. 33.
55. A. F. Reid, 'Science Club', *Collegian*, 1950, pp. 126, 193.
56. M. J. Spargo, School Captain's Speech, Speech Night 1998.
57. A. S. Anderson (1909), speaker's notes to Junior School Mothers' Association, 5 Oct 1950.
58. J. B. Pettigrew (1932–34), Q.
59. Healey, 'The House System', Sept 1965; roneoed.
60. Healey, 'The Day-Boy Houses. 1971'; roneoed.
61. *Collegian*, 1998, p. 43.
62. B. R. Stewardson, *Collegian*, June 1954, p. 10.
63. Littlejohn, *Annual Report*s, 1924, p. 14; 1925, p. 14.
64. D. Goodenough at Junior School Mothers' Association, 6 Aug 1959.
65. *Satura*, 16 July 1956, p. 8.
66. P. M. Ashton (1957–67), Q.
67. R. C. Schurmann (1941–45), Q.
68. B. Andrews (1941–45), Q.
69. R. M. Carmichael (1956–64), Q.
70. *Old Scotch Collegians' Association … Annual re-union November 29, 1929*, Brown, Prior & Co, Melbourne, [1929].
71. Foundation Day Concert 1913.
72. 'When the days are growing short, / And we strip for Winter sport, / Then we look for exercise and honour too; / When we get into our stride, / Then the School can feel some pride / In the team that wears the cardinal, gold and blue', *Scotch College School songs*, Ford and Son, [Melbourne, 1911–13?].
73. Ibid. The third version was 'BUCK IN SCOTCH the boys are calling. / How the game delights their souls! / When the Scotch boys take the field, / Then the foe will have to yield, / For they revel in the task of kicking goals'.

74. *Scotch College Melbourne Foundation Day Concert October 9, 1914,* Brown, Prior & Co, Melbourne.

75. McInnes, *Road to Gundagai,* p. 109.

76. Details of programme, *Collegian,* Dec, 1914, p. 144; for authorship, *Collegian,* 1915, p. 5.

77. *Public Schools Boat Race 7th and 8th May, 1926. Dinner to the Crew of the Scotch College Saturday, 8th May. Menzies Hotel.* Hosted by Sir Arthur Robinson. Similarly at *Old Scotch Collegians' Association Dinner … October 10, 1930. At The Wattle,* Brown, Prior, Anderson, [Melbourne, 1930].

78. R. A. Reyment (1942–44), email to author, 22 July 1998.

79. R. D. Fincher (1956–59), email to author, 28 Apr 1999.

80. R. A. Reyment (1942–44), email to author, 22 July 1998.

81. *Herald,* 23 Apr 1924.

82. *Old Scotch Collegians Association Scotch College, Melbourne. Eleventh Annual Report* [Melbourne, 1924].

83. R. A. Reyment (1942–44), email to author, 22 July 1998.

84. Littlejohn, *Annual Report,* 1908, p. 8.

85. *Collegian,* 1904, p. 4.

86. Ibid., 1913, pp 133, 192.

87. Ibid., 1914, pp. 62, 117.

88. D. J. Ashton (1953–65), Q.

89. F. C. Findlay (1924–27), Q.

90. B. W. Bainbridge (1951–53), email to author, 13 Nov 1999.

91. C. R. Parsons (1984–86), Q.

92. A. S. Anderson (1909), interview with H. Webster, 1968.

93. Council, 27 Apr 1906.

94. Minutes of Diamond Jubilee Celebrations, 29 Apr 1911.

95. *Collegian,* 1917, p. 274.

96. Ibid., 1913, pp. 129, 188–91.

97. Ibid., 1919, p. 116. Littlejohn, *Annual Report,* 1919, p. 9.

98. M. W. Reid (1953–58), email to author, 12 Oct 1999.

99. Nicholson, *First hundred years,* p. 90.

100. Bremner, '1929 A very good year'.

101. *Collegian,* 1918, p. 3.

102. Littlejohn, *Annual Report,* 1918, p. 8.

103. R. Taft (1929–36), email to author, 13 Sept 1998.

104. Campbell, *Urge to laugh,* p. 30.

105. A. S. Anderson (1909), interview with H. Webster, 1968.

106. Donaldson, report to Council, 24 July 1986.

107. J. G. Paton (1914) cited in *Great Scot,* 26 (1981), p. 9.

108. P. R. Wilson (1935–47), Q.

109. Littlejohn, *Annual Report,* 1926, p. 17.

110. Ibid.

111. Ibid., 1916, p. 9.

112. *Collegian,* 1916, p. 34.

113. Ingram, 'Public schools in a changing age', p. 33.

114. Healey, 'Report on the Seminar of masters and Sixth Form boys held on Monday 11th September [1972] to discuss the care of boys exercised at Scotch College'.

115. J. D. McCaughey, 'Final summing up', 'Report on the Seminar of masters and Sixth Form boys [on] the care of boys exercised at Scotch College', 1972, p. 8.

116. Blue card of a boy in Form III in 1976.

117. J. R. A. Glenn, interview with author, 20 Feb 1998.

118. D. G. Penington (1940–47), email to D. E. McC. Hunter, 28 Sept 2000.

119. Macneil, *Old Boys' and parents' Sunday,* 1931.

120. Ibid., 1934, p. 2.

121. *Collegian,* Dec 1955, p. 207.

122. D. M. Hart (1936–41), Q.

123. A. C. Watson (1942–47), letter to author 15 Sept 1998.

124. R. K. Blair (1963), letter to author, 15 Apr 1999.

125. M. J. Edwards (1967–70), Q.

126. *Scout Scoops. The official organ of the 1st Hawthorn Scout Group.* Anniversary Issue, vol. 3, No. 1, July 1939, p. 6.

127. R. J. Moran (1949–54), letter to author 22 Oct 1998.

128. A. D. Callister (1937–49).

129. *Satura,* 18 Feb 1957, p. 6.

130. *Satura,* 17 Mar 1965, p. 12.

131. Roff, report to Council, 27 Apr 1977.

132. C. H. Campbell, Acting Principal's report to Council, 29 July 1964; Roff, report to Council, 25 Mar 1981.

133. Littlejohn, *Annual Report,* 1924, p. 12.;

134. 'Report on the Seminar of masters and Sixth Form boys [on] the care of boys exercised at Scotch College', 1972, Form V Group, p. 5.

135. Ibid., Form I and II Group, p. 7.

136. G. D. Fisher (1929–41), letter to author, 5 Jan 2000.

137. G. J. Carrick (1928–35), Q, and also R. K. Pickford (1932–36), J. C. Blaine (1925–32), QQ.

138. A. D. Skurrie (1932–33), Q.

139. G. D. Logan (1932–33), Q.

140. D. S. Thomson (1941), Q.

141. P. S. Colclough (1929–36), Q.

142. B. L. Adams (1939–43), Q.

143. G. N. Ingham (1925–32), Q.

144. G. J. Carrick (1928–35), Q.

145. P. S. Colclough (1929–36), letter to author, 30 Oct 1999.

146. R. A. Stott (1935–37), Q.

147. L. W. Hall (1918–23), Q.

148. W. G. Pugh (1947–51), Q and letter to author, June 1999.

149. D. O. Shave (1946–52), Q.

150. R. A. W. Wade (1946–49), Q.

151. D. L. G. Zwar (1949), *The soul of a school,* Macmillan, South Melbourne, 1982, pp. 16, 96–9. See Michael Cathcart, *Defending the National Tuckshop: Australia's secret army intrigue of 1931,* McPhee-Gribble, Melbourne, 1988, p. 89.

152. The computerisation of the school's enrolment records will allow a thorough examination of fathers' occupations over time. What is clear already is that the range spreads well down any scale of income or social standing. Thus a glance at nineteenth-century boys' fathers' occupations reveals occupations suggestive of wealth and social standing, headed by 'squatter', 'gentleman' and the leading professions. Other fathers, however, were salary- or wage-earners: clergyman, journalist, pier master, railway station master, police sergeant, and teacher. Others' income would depend on the size of their establishments: blacksmith, butcher, clothier, draper, ironmonger and saddler. Others' income sounds small: actor, book-keeper, carpenter, comedian, commercial traveller, despatch clerk, government clerk, master mariner, post office clerk, railway employee, sailor, tinsmith, warehouseman and writing clerk.

153. W. G. Pugh (1947–51), Q.

154. Moorehead (1926), *A late education* p. 13.

155. J. C. Kelso (1947), letter to author, 30 July 1999.

156. R. W. McDonald (1943–44), Q.

157. B. W. Bainbridge (1951–53), email to author, 13 Nov 1999.

158. G. R. Baker (1936–38), Q.

159. R. C. Schurmann (1941–45), Q.

160. I. D. Phipps (1946–52), Q.

161. I. C. Teague (1947–52), Q.

162. *Collegian*, Dec 1957, p. 163.

163. E. M. Davidson referring to Graham Seccombe (1936), *Collegian*, Dec 1956, p. 116.

164. *Collegian*, June 1954, p. 62.

165. L. C. Birch (1925–35), letter to author, 10 Dec 1998.

166. S. F. Macintyre (1959–64), note to author, May 2000.

167. Draft VII Form Arithmetic, term III, 1952.

168. C. B. Mackey (1970–75), Q.

169. Hansen, *Nor free nor secular*.

170. A. S. Anderson (1909), speaker's notes to Junior School Mothers' Association, 5 Oct 1950.

171. David Dunstan, 'Morell', *ADB*, x, 584.

172. B. R. Speed (1954–62), email to author, 19 July 1999.

173. Healey, report to Council, 30 Oct 1974.

174. *Old Scotch Collegians Association Scotch College, Melbourne. Twentieth Annual Report* [Melbourne, 1933].

175. McInnes, *Road to Gundagai*, p. 102.

6 To Hawthorn

1. Ronald East (1917), 'Cattanach', *ADB*, vii, 591.

2. *Age*, 5 Nov 1926.

3. *Collegian*, Dec 1950, p. 170.

4. *An Appeal to the Old Boys and Friends of the School. From the Principal*, [Melbourne, 1914], p. 5

5. McInnes, *Road to Gundagai*, p. 90

6. Littlejohn, *Annual Report*, 1926, p. 13.

7. *Collegian*, May 1950, p. 15.

8. Gilray, *Annual Report, 1949*, p. 5.

9. A. S. Malcolm (1938–42), Q.

10. *Collegian*, Aug 1951, p. 88.

11. *Old Scotch Collegians' Association Year Book 1937*, Brown, Prior, Anderson, Melbourne, 1937, p. 13.

12. *Collegian*, Dec 1952, p 124.

13. G. D. Fisher (1941), letter to author, 5 Jan 2000.

14. *Collegian*, 1953, pp. 23. 101; 1954, p. 21. My thanks to Leonie Robbins for comments on this list.

15. *Year Book of the Old Scotch Collegians' Association 1942*, Brown, Prior, Anderson, Melbourne, 1942, p. 5.

16. Finance Committee, 24 Apr 1945.

17. J. G. Hiller (1985–96), email to author, 20 Apr 2000.

18. Healey, *Annual Report*, 1973.

19. D. S. W. Reid (1962–67), Q.

20. Council, 29 Aug 1919.

21. *Great Scot*, 55 (Apr 1990 [mistakenly dated 1989]), p. 31.

22. I. D. Phipps (1946–52), conversation with author, 19 Apr 1999.

23. *Collegian*, 1915, p. 25.

24. *Satura*, 9 May 1958, p. 9.

25. A. S. Anderson (1909), speaker's notes to Junior School Mothers' Association, 5 Oct 1950.

26. H. K. Oxley (1926–33), Q.

27. *Satura*, 9 May 1958, p. 9.

28. E. W. W. Peatt (1925–32), Q.

29. Bremner, '1929 A very good year'.

30. R. D. Fincher (1956–59), Q.

31. R. C. Gabriel (1932), conversation with author, Nov 1998.

32. J. N. Ferguson (Director of Music 1991–   ), interview with author, 23 Feb 1998.

33. *Old Scotch Collegians' Association Year Book 1932*, Brown, Prior & Co., Melbourne ,1932, p. 10, and for years thereafter.

34. A. J. Abell (1988–91), email to author, 2 July 1999.

35. Healey, report to Council, 28 Oct 1964.

36. W. R. Gleadell (1959–66), email to author, 19 Nov 1998.

37. I. C. Teague (1947–52), H. Hall (1932–34), W. R. Gleadell (1959–66), QQ.

38. J. T. Collins, diary, 26 Apr 1926.

39. A. W. H. Chandler (1918–22), email to author, 24 Feb 1998.

40. A. P. McCaughey, 'Images from a train', *Collegian*, June 1958, p. 41.

41. A. P. McCaughey, 'The seat', ibid.

42. *Year Book of the Old Scotch Collegians' Association 1941*, Brown, Prior, Anderson, Melbourne, 1941, p. 18.

43. E&F Committee, 2 Feb 1955.

44. I. D. Phipps (1946–52), Q.

45. J. B. Cumming (1957–67), Q.

46. J. T. Collins, diary, 24 Mar 1925, 25 Mar 1926.

47. B. R Speed (1954–62), email to author, 21 July 1999.

48. W. B. Harvey (1944–50), letter to author, 17 May 1999.

49. D. R. Head (1963–68), letter to author, 7 July 1999.

50. W. Norris, diary, 26 Dec 1943.

51. W. Norris, aged 14, ibid., 2 Dec.

52. D. M. Taylor (1945–49), Q. Similarly, I. D. Phipps (1946–52), Q, and D. B. Telfer (1969–74), email to author, 30 June 2000.

53. G. J. Carrick (1928–35), Q.

54. *Satura*, 12 July 1963, p. 5.

55. OSCA, *Year Book*, 1941, pp. 5–6.

56. *Collegian*, Dec 1952, p. 89.

57. B. R. Stewardson, 'Upon Gardiner's Creek Bridge', *Collegian*, Dec 1952, p. 136.

58. Roff, report to Council, 30 July 1975.

59. Ibid., 28 Apr 1976.

60. J. A. Goldsmith (1949–51), Q.

61. See also P. B. Blazey (1957), *Screw loose: Uncalled-for memoirs*, Picador, Sydney, 1997, p. 37.

62. *Satura*, 30 June 1961, p. 2.

7 In search of a new identity, 1920–1950

1. 'Prelector', 'The schools', [an obituary], newspaper clipping [1934].

2. For evidence that he did so, see Serle, *Monash*, pp. 20–1.

3. F. H. U. Baker (1907–17), interview with John Bannister, 7 Dec 1998.

4. National Fund Raising Counsel of Australia Pty Ltd, 'Scotch College Building Appeal Appraisal and Plan 30th October, 1963', Council, 30 Oct 1963, attachment.

5. A. C. Moyle (1921), *Collegian*, 1922, p. 69.

6. J. C. M. [J. D. C. Moyle (1950)], 'The mill', *Collegian*, Dec 1951, p. 213.

7. *Collegian*, 1922, p. 124.

8. Moorehead, *A late education*, p. 13.

9. Littlejohn, *Annual Report*, 1924, p. 9.

10. *Scotch College, Melbourne Divine Service in the Memorial Hall at the Unveiling of the Roll of Honour of the Masters and Old Boys of the School who fell in the Great War. Anzac Eve, 1936*.

11. W. Norris, diary, 1943, comment written in 1992.

12. *Old Scotch Collegians' Association Year Book 1935*, Brown, Prior & Co., Melbourne, 1935, p. 7.

13. OSCA, *Year Book,* 1941, p. 18.

14. Donaldson, Welcome at 50th anniversary of chapel, 19 Oct 1986. Donaldson to Sir Ninian Stephen's Deputy Official Secretary, 18 July 1986.

15. *Satura*, 22 Oct 1936, p. 1.

16. *Scotch College Melbourne Dedication of the Littlejohn Memorial Chapel Sunday, 18th October 1936*, Brown, Prior, Anderson, Melbourne, [1936]. OSCA *Year Book*, 1941, p. 18.

17. Rev. A. P. Crow, *Collegian*, 1975, p. 8.

18. J. Kirk Robertson, of Scarborough, Robertson, and Love, typed document, signed.

19. C. W. Hill, *Edwardian Scotland*, Rowman and Littlefield, Totowa, NJ, 1976, p. 5.

20. R. W. McDonald (1943–44), Q.

21. Finance Committee, 23 Mar, 21 Sept 1937.

22. Quoted in *News from Scotch*, [No. 3. headline: 'Scotch plans big day'], [1962], p. 4.

23. E&F Committee, 2 June 1965.

24. Ibid., 25 Nov 1970.

25. Newspaper clipping in school archives.

26. A. S. Anderson (1909), speaker's notes for OSCA Annual Dinner, 1948 or 1949.

27. Mary Lord, *Hal Porter: Man of many parts*, Random House, Sydney, 1993, pp. 29–30.

28. H. Porter, *The Paper Chase*, Angus and Robertson, Melbourne, 1966, p. 175.

29. McInnes, *Humping My Bluey*, Hamish Hamilton, London, 1966; *Goodbye Melbourne Town*, London, Hamish Hamilton, 1968.

30. D. R. McNicoll, *Luck's a fortune*, Sydney, Wildcat Press, 1979.

31. Blazey, *Screw loose*, see p. 29.

32. Gordon Matthews, *An Australian son*, William Heinemann, Port Melbourne, 1996; J. R. A. Glenn, *Things to be remembered*, Diana Gribble, Melbourne, 1991. See also W. S. Robinson, *If I remember rightly*, ed. G. N. Blainey, F. W. Cheshire, Melbourne, 1967.

33. E. M. Pike, *New every morning*, Essien, Melbourne, 1996.

34. A. E. Pratt, *Dr W. S. Littlejohn: The story of a great Headmaster*, Lothian Publishing Company, Melbourne, 1934.

35. A. G. Serle, *Colin Gilray*, History Department, University of Melbourne, 1999.

36. R. Coleman, *Above renown*, Macmillan, Melbourne, 1988.

37. R. Matthews, *David Bennett: A memoir*, Australian Fabian Society Pamphlets No. 44, Melbourne, 1985.

38. P. S. Cook, *Red barrister: A biography of Ted Laurie QC*, LaTrobe University Press, Melbourne, 1994.

39. J. S. McCalman, *Journeyings: The biography of a middle-class generation. 1920–90*, Melbourne University Press, Melbourne, 1993.

40. Comment in a Year 7 diary, 1990.

41. Year 7 comment 1991, recorded by D. G. Paul.

42. Littlejohn, *Annual Report*, 1924, p. 9.

43. McCalman, *Journeyings*, p. 70.

44. Council, 17 Aug 1994.

45. McInnes, *Road to Gundagai*, p. 89.

46. T. F. Healey, J. G. Bryce (Gilray's grandson), and E. W. R. Littlejohn.

47. *Collegian*, Dec 1955, p. 208.

48. G. R. Baker (1936–38), letter to author, 21 June 1999.

49. *Satura*, 17 Aug 1965, p. 12

50. *Collegian*, Aug 1950, p. 156; similarly, 1919, p. 187.

51. W. K. Fullagar (1936–45), Q.

52. I. R. Roper (1950–52), Q.

53. R. A. Reyment (1942–44), Q.

54. L. D. Kemp (1922–27), Q.

55. N. McH. Ramsey (1934–41), Q.

56. R. L. Hyams (1969–80), letter to author, 2 Feb 1999.

57. Littlejohn, *Annual Report*, 1912, p. 13.

58. Ingram, 'Public schools in a changing age', p. 33.

59. W. T. McKendrick (1925, Bursar 1934–47), letter to Tom ——, 6 Mar 1946.

60. D. C. McClean (1943–52), Q.

8 The Blue, 1934–1953

1. Davies, *Fiddlers of Drummond*, p. 22.

2. D. L. Scott (1940–44), note to author, 4 Sept 2000.

3. R. Stott (1935–40), Q.

4. W. N. Hurst (1939–50), email to author, 10 Feb 1998.

5. P. A. Walker (1936–43), Q.

6. W. H. Callister (1936–41), letter to author, 4 Nov 1998.

7. D. G. Jewkes (1940–44), Q.

8. J. M. Ross (1941–44), Q.

9. G. D. Fisher (1929–41), Q.

10. K. W. Fraser (1930–41), Q.

11. W. H. Callister (1936–41), letter to author, 4 Nov 1998.

12. Bremner, '1929 A very good year'.

13. R. A. Reyment (1942–44), email to author, 11 Jan 1998.

14. G. D. Fisher (1929–41), Q.

15. M. A. Griffith (1939–41), Q.

16. J. S. Green (1936–47), Q.

17. B. A. Johns (1946–55), Q.

18. W. G. Pugh (1947–51), letter to author, June 1999.

19. P. R. Wilson (1935–47), Q.

20. B. D. Bayston (1936–48), letter to author, 22 Mar 1999.

21. J. G. Hiller (1985–96), email to author, 20 Apr 2000.

22. J. N. Ferguson, interview with author, 23 Feb 1998.

23. J. N. Ferguson, email to author, 17 Nov 2000.

24. G. de Korte (1989–94), J. Duband (1977–80), QQ.

25. J. G. Hiller (1985–96), email to author, 6 May 2000.

26. J. N. Ferguson, interview with author, 23 Feb 1998.

27. F. C. Findlay (1924–27), Q.

28. M. W. Reid (1953–58), letter to author, 19 Apr 1999.

29. J. B. Pettigrew (1932–34), letter to author, 5 Oct 1998.

30. M. W. Reid (1953–58), letter to author, 19 Apr 1999.

31. R. A. Reyment (1942–44), email to author, 7 June 1998.

32. S. F. Macintyre (1959–64), Q.

33. A. Edwards (1964–69), Q.

34. J. D. Hawes, 'Art Club', *Collegian*, Dec 1953, p. 99.

35. D. L. D. Brand (1969–72), letter to his mother, 8 Oct 1972.

36. A. Hartman (1965–70), email to author, 4 May 1999.

37. Healey, report to Council, 4 Aug 1970.

38. *Satura*, 9 Nov 1956, p. 7.

39. D. G. Paul, note to author, 15 June 2000.

40. I. T. Harrison, 'Report of Drama-in-Education Study Tour September '73 — January '74', p. 15.

41. G. D. Fisher (1929–41), Q.

42. Donaldson, Annual Report 1989, *Collegian*, 1989, p. 2.

43. G. D. Fisher (1929–41), letter to author, 5 Jan 2000.

44. Morrison, *Annual Report*, 1897.

45. A. H. Tucker (1987–92), Q.

46. W. C. Ch'ng (1973–85), Q.

47. J. M. Watson (1950), 'Library', *Collegian*, Dec 1950, p. 186.

48. A. G. Serle, 'The Russel Ward Lecture', University of New England, 18 Sept 1990, *Australian Historical Association Bulletin*, nos 64–65, Oct–Dec 1990, p. 17, cited in Ian Britain, 'In pursuit of Englishness: Public School stories and Australian

Culture', *The University of Melbourne Library Journal*, 1 (1994–95), pp. 11–17.

49. *Collegian*, Dec 1951, p. 207.

50. Ibid., Dec 1957, p. 163.

51. Ibid., Dec 1952, pp. 139–40.

52. R. E. Marks (1952–64), email to author, 6 Apr 1998.

53. I. C. Teague (1947–52), Q.

54. *Satura*, 24 Oct 1956, p. 11.

55. S. F. Macintyre (1960–64) note to author, May 2000.

56. D. Sawer, *Satura*, 29 Apr 1957, p. 7.

57. *Rules for the guidance of pupils attending the Scotch College*, [1867?], rule 25.

58. I. A. Dudgeon and A. S. Kemp, Editorial, *Satura*, 11 Nov 1960, p. 2.

59. B. R. Stewardson, *Collegian*, June 1954, p. 10.

60. GHC, 8 May 1975.

61. A. S. Kemp, 'Thoughts on a year's Satura editing', *Satura*, 11 Nov 1960, p. 6.

62. W. J. Simpson (1966–71), Q.

63. A. S. Thomson (1972–77), Q.

64. C. W. Johnson (1963–68), Q.

65. D. E. McC. Hunter, 'Editorial', *Satura*, 17 Apr 1989, p. 9.

66. G. D. Fisher (1929–41), letter to author, 5 Jan 2000.

67. C. W. Johnson (1963–68), email to author, 9 Oct 2000; C. A. Widdis (1983–90), email to author, 23 Aug 2000.

68. M. J. Edwards (1967–70), email to author, 24 Nov 1999.

69. G. D. Fisher (1929–41), letter to author, 5 Jan 2000.

70. Ibid.

71. N. Leybourne-Ward (1941–42), Q.

72. J. M. Ross (1941–44), Q.

73. G. D. Fisher (1929–41), Q.

74. Bayston, note to author, June 1999.

75. Ibid.

76. A. G. MacQuarrie (1936–40), Q.

77. J. M. Ross (1941–44), Q.

78. G. D. Fisher (1929–41), letter to author, 5 Jan 2000.

79. L. M. Muir (1937–42), letter to author, July 1999.

80. K. Cole, 'Lamble', *ADB*, ix, 653.

81. A. R. Watkinson, *Scotch College Rugby Club*, Edition 2, 1998, p. 1.

82. K. W. Fraser (1930–41), letter to author, 6 July 1999.

83. Ibid.

84. D. S. Thomson (1941), email to author, 30 May 1999.

85. K. W. Fraser (1930–41), letter to author, 6 July 1999.

86. Roff, report to Council, 30 July 1975.

87. Ibid., 24 Sept 1980; W. C. Ch'ng (1973–85), Q.

88. A. R. Watkinson, *Scotch College Rugby Club*, p. 3.

89. Ibid., p. 1.

90. J. A. Lyne, 'Scotch College 1942–74'.

91. W. H. Callister (1936–41), letter to author, 4 Nov 1998.

92. G. J. Carrick (1928–35), letter to author, 18 Feb 1999.

93. W. G. Pugh (1947–51), Q.

94. G. de Korte (1989–94), Q.

95. *Satura*, 5 Aug 1960, p. 2.

96. GHC Sports committee, 13 June 1978.

97. Correspondent, note to author, Mar 2000.

98. *Satura*, 25 Oct 1963, p. 3.

99. *Satura*, 12 July 1963, p. 3.

100. GHC, 5 Mar 1981.

101. GHC, 14 Oct 1981.

102. GHC, 4 June 1981.

103. M. J. Waldron and M. R. Bell, *Satura*, 15 June 1989, p. 14.

104. A. S. Anderson (1909), speaker's notes to Junior School Mothers' Assocation, 5 Oct 1950.

105. 'Scotch College. 80th anniversary celebrated', newspaper clipping, [1931].

106. J. W. G. Meyer (1944–47), Q.

107. Finance Committee, 23 Mar 1937.

108. Scotch College Financial position as at 31 Dec 1939, Finance Committee, 27 Feb 1940, attachment.

109. W. R. Baxter (1961–64), email to author, 10 Feb 1999.

110. B. A. Johns (1946–55), Q.

111. *Scout Scoops. Jamboree Issue* [1938? 1939?], p. 5. The stamp was the Dantzig current (1924) arms type.

112. David Bradshaw, Campbell, Close, F. L. 'Flea' Edmunds (staff 1937–45), Engel, Fleming, George Gellie (Dux 1935, staff 1941–42), N. E. Lee (staff 1938–42), Ken Luke (staff 1941–65), McKendrick, Mullenger, Scholes, and Henry Tasker (1920, staff 1936–40)

113. R. L. Hughes (1963–69), Q.

114. W. Norris (1942–45), 1943 diary, additional comment written in 1992.

115. M. A. McKenzie (1939–47), Q.

116. D. G. Jewkes (1940–44), letter to author, 5 June 1999.

117. B. L. Adams (1939–43), Q.

118. P. A. Marseille (1942–47), Q.

119. L. M. Muir (1937–42), letter to author, July 1999.

120. G. D. Fisher (1929–41), letter to author, 5 Jan 2000

121. Ibid.

122. L. M. Muir (1937–42), Q.

123. G. D. Fisher (1929–41), Q.

124. L. M. Muir (1937–42), letter to author, July 1999.

125. J. R. Philip (1939–42), Q.

126. *Old Scotch Collegians' Association Year Book 1943*, Brown, Prior, Anderson, Melbourne, 1943, p. 5.

127. A. M. Hilliard (1939–41), Q.

128. J. P. Jones (1939–49), Q.

129. *Collegian*, May 1950, p. 85, citing *Fact*.

130. G. P. Walsh, 'Pennefather', ADB, xv, 588.

131. L. M. Muir (1937–42), letter to author, July 1999, and similarly, G. D. Fisher (1929–41), Q and letter to author, 5 Jan 2000.

132. G. D. Fisher (1929–41), letter to author, 5 Jan 2000.

133. W. B. Harvey (1944–50), letter to author, 17 May 1999.

9 Selby Smith, 1953–1964

1. I. R. Marks (1950–54), letter to author, 26 Feb 1999.

2. Rev. A. C. Watson at installation of Selby Smith, *Collegian*, June 1953 p. 7.

3. *Collegian*, Dec 1953, p. 152.

4. I. R. Marks (1950–54), letter to author, 26 Feb 1999.

5. J. D. McCaughey, interview with author, 21 Oct 1998.

6. Selby Smith, report to Council, 27 June 1956.

7. R. D. Fincher (1956–59), email to author, 28 Apr 1999.

8. J. Duband (1977–80), Q.

9. *Collegian*, 1999, p. 106.

10. J. A. Lyne, 'Scotch College 1942–74', unpublished MS.

11. Ibid.

12. Ibid.

13. D. B. Telfer (1969–74), email to author, 9 July 1999.

14. C. H. Campbell, Acting Principal's report to Council, 29 July 1964.

15. D. B. Telfer (1969–74), email to author, 9 July 1999.

16. Ibid.

17. Development Committee report, Council, 10 Mar 1981, attachment.

18. Selby Smith, 'Memorandum on future development', 29 June 1960. Ibid., 24 June 1959.

19. Selby Smith, 'Notes on the need for an improved Tuckshop in the Senior School', Council, 26 Oct 1955, attachment.
20. Davies, *Fiddlers of Drummond*, pp. 50–1.
21. D. A. Vines, 'Tuckshop techniques', *Satura*, 24 Oct 1967, p. 7.
22. Council, 30 Oct 1963.
23. *Satura*, 2 Aug 1962, p. 4.
24. Lyne, 'Scotch College, 1942–74'.
25. Healey, 'Introductory talk at the Seminar of Masters and Senior Boys at Scotch College September 9th, 1974'.
26. I. D. Phipps (1946–52), Q.
27. A. J. Radford, K. C. Watson, 'Waratah Club', *Collegian*, Dec 1954, p. 129.
28. Lyne, 'Scotch College, 1942–74'.
29. Council, 29 Feb 1956.
30. Healey, 'Draft of speech to be delivered on 22nd July, 1967'.
31. Selby Smith, 'A Victorian Independent school', p. 231.
32. Ibid., p. 232.
33. Ibid., p. 228.
34. Gilray, *Annual Report*, 1949, p. 3. Davies, *Fiddlers of Drummond*, p. 29.
35. Lyne, 'Scotch College, 1942–74'.
36. Lyne, interview with author, 30 Apr 1998.
37. Davies, *Fiddlers of Drummond*, p. 128.
38. Ibid., p. 197.
39. F. S. Falconer (1950–54), Q.
40. *Collegian*, Dec 1956, p. 150.
41. Lyne, 'Scotch College, 1942–74'.
42. Selby Smith, 'A Victorian Independent school', p. 228.
43. D. J. Ashton (1953–65), Q.
44. G. I. Anderson (1928–32), Q.
45. Selby Smith, interview with G. S. Tolson (1939, OSCA President 1983, school archivist 1983–92), 26 Oct 1989.
46. G. D. Fisher (1929–41), Q.
47. Ewing, *Unsearchable riches of Christ*, p. 7.
48. G. D. Fisher (1929–41), Q.
49. J. C. Kelso (1946), letter to Healey, 3 Nov 1965.
50. A. D. Grounds (1946), memoirs.
51. D. M. Taylor (1945–49), Q.
52. J. C. Kelso, letter to Healey, 3 Nov 1965.
53. J. C. Kelso, letter to author, 30 July 1999.
54. A. Hartman (1965–70), email to author, 4 May 1999.

55. I. D. Phipps (1946–52), Q.
56. W. B. Harvey (1944–50), letter to author, 17 May 1999.
57. A. F. McKinnon (1968), *Great Scot*, 67 (1993), p. 39.
58. M. W. Reid (1953–58), email to author, 12 Oct 1999.
59. A. Hartman (1965–70), email to author, 4 May 1999.
60. S. D. Kunstler (1970–75), Q.
61. A. Hartman (1965–70), email to author, 15 July 1999.
62. S. D. Kunstler (1970–75), Q.
63. GHC, 8 July 1971.
64. C. O. Healey, *A Guide to Scotch College*, [1972], p. 6.
65. W. McKay (entered 1880), *Collegian*, 1935, p. 292.
66. 'Jottings from Sydney', *Collegian*, Dec 1951, p. 236. Dr Julian (1919–27), A. V. (1916–24), E. (1918–20) and H. A. Kaw (1918–25).
67. J. S. Green (1936–47), email to author, 8 Jan 1998.
68. W. C. Ch'ng (1973–85), email to author, 1 June 1999.
69. A. S. Anderson (1909), speaker's notes for OSCA Annual Dinner, 1948 or 1949. Also, I. R. Roper (1950–52), Q.
70. D. C. M. Ward (1968–79).
71. A. R. Frater and B. R. Stewardson, Editorial, *Collegian*, Dec 1955, p. 108.
72. A. S. Anderson (1909), speaker's notes for OSCA Annual Dinner, 1948 or 1949.
73. *Satura*, 17 Mar 1965, p. 16.
74. A. Edwards (1964–69), Q.
75. A. S. Thomson (1972–77), note to author Aug 1999.
76. W. A. Shattock (1974–79), Q.
77. W. C. Ch'ng (1973–85), Q.
78. D. L. D. Brand (1969–72), letter to his mother, 6 Mar 1972.
79. Ibid., 17 June 1972.
80. R. K. Mollison (1976–81), Q.
81. D. G. Paul, *Great Scot*, 58 (1991), p. 16.
82. Roff, report to Council, 27 Oct 1976
83. Ibid., 28 Apr 1976.
84. M. W. Reid (1953–58), email to author, 11 June 1999.
85. Selby Smith, report to Council, 30 Oct 1963
86. Selby Smith, 'A Victorian Independent school', pp. 245–6.
87. D. L. D. Brand, letter to his mother, postmarked 22 June 1970.
88. Ibid., [1970].

89. I. C. Mackenzie (1972–82), email to author, 16 Aug 1999.
90. A. J. Radford, K. C. Watson, 'Waratah Club', *Collegian*, Dec 1954, p. 129.
91. K. F. Field, Minute Book Scotch at Cowes Parents' Auxiliary, 1972.
92. I. C. Mackenzie (1972–82), email to author, 16 Aug 1999.
93. 'Circular. Bookings for 1978 camps. July 1977'.
94. *Collegian*, 1936, p. 247.
95. D. L. Bardas, 'Ski Club', *Collegian*, June 1954, p. 24.
96. D. H. Hare (1922–29), letter to author, 24 Feb 1999.
97. R. K. Pickford (1932–36), Q.
98. W. G. Pugh (1947–51), Q.
99. R. B. Jane (1984–90), Q.
100. Healey, *Annual Report*, 1973.
101. D. C. McClean (1943–52), Q.
102. G. A. Rush (1937–45), letter to author, 1 July 1999.
103. *Satura*, 9 May 1968, p. 2.

10 Hawthorn as a place for a school, 1950–2000

1. R. D. Cowley, 'Traffic lights', *Collegian*, Dec 1952, p. 145.
2. F. S. Falconer (1950–54), Q.
3. W. H. Melville, quoted in *The Littlejohn Memorial Chapel, Scotch College, Melbourne*, Old Scotch Collegians' Association, Brown, Prior, Anderson, Melbourne, [1938?], p. 11.
4. *Old Scotch Collegians' Association Year Book 1934*, Brown, Prior & Co., Melbourne, 1934, p. 11. *Old Scotch Collegians' Association Year Book 1935*, p. 10.
5. *Year Book 1939. Old Scotch Collegians' Association*, Brown, Prior, Anderson, Melbourne, [1939], p. 10.
6. A. C. Watson (1942–43), Q.
7. Council, 25 June 1958, 24 Apr 1974, 31 July 1974.
8. Scotch College, Memorandum of Association, art. 6 (2).
9. *Collegian*, Dec 1954, p. 200.
10. E&F Committee, 22 Aug 1961.
11. B. D. Bayston, interview with G. S. Tolson, 17 Aug 1992.
12. E&F Committee, 29 Mar 1961. Council, 29 Mar 1961.
13. Council, 28 June 1961. For a copy of the form, see *Collegian*, Dec 1961, p. 210.
14. E&F Committee, 22 Aug 1961. *Collegian*, Dec 1961, pp. 209–10.

15. B. S. Symon, interview with author, 2 July 1997.
16. Maxwell S. Paton (1926), letter to G. S. Tolson, 1991.
17. F. M. Bradshaw, Session clerk, Hawthorn Presbyterian Church, to Fleming, 26 June 1961.
18. F. A. Fleming, Acting Principal, submission to Presbytery, 11 Aug 1961, p. 2.
19. Ibid.
20. Presbyterian Church, Hawthorn, Session, 29 Aug 1961, extract, p. 5.
21. Fleming, submission, 11 Aug 1961, pp. 3–4.
22. Ibid., p. 1.
23. Presbyterian Church, Hawthorn, Session, 29 Aug 1961, extract, p. 4.
24. Healey to Selby Smith, 24 Feb 1964. Campbell, Acting-Principal, letter to Healey, 19 June 1964.
25. Presbyterian Church, Hawthorn, Session, 29 Aug 1961, extract, p. 4.
26. Bremner, '1929 A very good year'.
27. B. D. Bayston, 'Frederick Maxwell Bradshaw: a Memoir', unpublished MS, pp. 7–8.
28. Roff, report to Council, 29 Oct 1975.
29. M. L. Jelbart (1963–67), Q. Respondent 243 (1954), Q, found him 'a most dreary man'.
30. A. G. MacQuarrie (1936–40), Q.
31. P. A. Pullar (1951–57), Q.
32. Bayston, interview with Tolson, 17 Aug 1992.
33. W. L. Sides (1960–64), Q.
34. Council, 28 July 1965.
35. Ibid.
36. Ibid., 27 Apr 1966.
37. D. L. D. Brand, letter to his mother, [1970].
38. Healey, letter to Clerk of Presbytery of Melbourne North, in Healey, report to Council, 4 Aug 1970.
39. D. L. D. Brand, letter to his mother, postmarked 3 Aug 1970.
40. Bond, Acting-Principal's report to Council, 28 Apr 1982.
41. Healey, report to Council, 31 Oct 1973.
42. P. G. Mason, Littlejohn House Captain's report, 1968.
43. D. O. Shave (1946–52), letter to author, 19 Sept 1998.
44. Bremner, '1929 A very good year.
45. Bond, Acting-Principal's report to Council, 28 Apr 1982.
46. E&F Committee, 1 May 1957.

47. Selby Smith, 'Memorandum The proposed Oakleigh Freeway', 4 July 1960.
48. Ibid.
49. Ibid.
50. 'Scotch College Council report to Assembly—1965'.
51. R. N. Swann (1956–60), A. O. Jones (1957–62), W. G. Pugh (1947–51), QQ.
52. Satura, 9 Apr 1965, p. 3.
53. D. L. D. Brand, letter to his mother, postmarked 22 Mar 1970.
54. Healey, report to Council, 4 Aug 1970.
55. E&F Committee, 27 Mar 1968.
56. Ibid., 24 June 1970. Council, 29 Apr, 4 Aug 1970.
57. Healey, 'Scotch College The following are the uses to which Scotch College buildings, grounds …', [1973?].
58. Special Council meeting, 9 Dec 1960.
59. E&F Committee, 26 Oct 1966.
60. Ibid., 31 Oct 1962.
61. Council, 29 Mar 1967.
62. E. D. Lloyd (1945), 'Re: Mrs. Dorum. Advice', 13 Dec 1966, E&F Committee, 25 Jan 1967, attachment.
63. E&F Committee, 31 Oct 1962.
64. Ibid., 25 Jan 1967.
65. Lloyd, 'Advice'.
66. Ibid.
67. E&F Committee, 27 Feb 1973.
68. 'Municipal Rating. Notes of a talk by Mr K. H. Gifford, Q. C. to members of the Headmasters' Conference of the Independent Schools of Australia, Victorian Branch … 19th October, 1966', Council, 26 Oct 1966, attachment.
69. Ibid.
70. E&F Committee, 29 Jan 1969.
71. Council, 25 July 1984.
72. Ibid., 29 May 1985.
73. Donaldson, 'Annual Report, 1998', Collegian, 1998, p. 11–12.

11 Scotch reinvents itself, 1950–1975

1. Turner, Blow for balloons, p. 208.
2. Bremner, '1929 A very good year'.
3. McInnes, Road to Gundagai, p. 102.
4. Littlejohn, letter of 8 Oct 1916, to father of P. C. Young (entered 1909), killed in action in 1916.
5. One of the 'Notes written by fellow boarders during Prep, after tea, in school House, & passed to each other, collected by Bill Norris'.
6. H. S. Dupin (1927), Great Scot, 59 (1991), p. 15.
7. H. V. R. 'Goop' McKay (1946), letter to W. Norris, 26 Sept 1944.
8. 'Scotch College Annual Golf Championship Monday May 30th 1966 At Ivanhoe Public Links', roneoed.
9. R. N. Swann (1956–60), Q.
10. D. York Syme at Annual Smoke Concert, Age, 5 Nov 1926.
11. P. D. Craw and J. C. Moyle, Editorial, Collegian, May 1951, p. 7.
12. 'We thank Thee for the great pioneers of our race, the founders of this our School', Rev. R. C. Foyster (1899), in Scotch College Melbourne Divine Service in the Memorial Hall … 8th May, 1927 (Old Boys' and Parents' Sunday), [Melbourne, 1927].
13. Newspaper clippings.
14. Hugh Trevor-Roper, 'The invention of tradition: the Highland tradition of Scotland', in Eric Hobsbawm and Terence Ranger (eds), The invention of tradition, Cambridge University Press, Cambridge, 1983, pp. 15–41.
15. See above, p. 122, Collegian, Aug 1951, p. 88.
16. Ibid., p. 89.
17. H. M. Knight (1933–35), Q.
18. Satura, 3 Mar 1950, p. 3.
19. Littlejohn, letter to A. B. C. Laing (1906, Hon Sec of OSCA 1929–36, Bursar 1948–53), 27 Feb 1933.
20. Pipe Bands Victoria, vol. 19, no. 5, June 1989.
21. Collegian, June 1954, p. 69.
22. Satura, 12 July 1963, p. 3.
23. Letter, Satura, no 2, 1999.
24. Nicholson, First Hundred Years, p. 45. Great Scot, 85 (1997), p. 34.
25. OSCA, 'Fifty-ninth Annual Report', Old Scotch Collegians' Association … 38th Annual Meeting … 1972', Melbourne, 1972.
26. OSCA Council, 6 Dec 1971, 14 Feb 1972.
27. Scotch College, Melbourne. Break-up Concert and Speech Night, Melbourne Town Hall, December 14th, 1917, Brown, Prior, Melbourne, [1917] p.5.
28. Satura, 17 Apr 1958, p. 3.
29. A verse in the College Song, Foundation Day Concert October 10, 1913, Brown Prior & Co.
30. M. J. Spargo, Head of the River speech to Assembly, 1998.

31. Cf. the *Conditions of Appointment* for the Principal as advertised in 1963 with those advertised in 1952, such documents being the school at its most formal.
32. Donaldson, 'Triple Scotch farewell, Scotch Family farewell dinner for Ron Bond, Ken Field & Archie Crow. Camberwell Civic Centre', 15 Nov 1985, p. 4.
33. *Satura*, 17 Feb 1960, p. 2.
34. A. S. Anderson, 'Memo to Members of Council' [date-stamped 1 Aug 1956].
35. Ibid.
36. *Scotch College, Melbourne. Examination Results*, Ford & Son, Printers, Carlton [1897?].
37. Bremner, '1929 A very good year'.
38. Healey, 'All masters in the Senior School. On Friday 17th June 1966 there will be a meeting for parents …', May, 1966; circular.
39. Healey, report to Council, 4 Aug 1970.
40. Lyne, 'Scotch College, 1942–74'.
41. Junior School Mothers' Association, 1 Apr 1969.
42. [Yellow sheet], Jan 1977, p.1.
43. Scotch at Cowes Parents' Auxiliary, 'Scotch at Cowes minute book' [1959–68], 1964.
44. 'Scotch at Cowes Reference Book 1967– '.
45. Healey, report to Council, 31 Mar 1965.
46. Ibid., 29 Oct 1969.
47. Ibid., 28 Apr 1971.
48. Donaldson, 'Triple Scotch farewell', p. 2.
49. OSCA, 'Annual Report', 1972.
50. Healey, report to Council, 8 Oct 1970.
51. Ibid., report to Council, 26 Apr 1972.
52. E&F Committee, 28 Sept 1971.
53. A. G. Tapp, "The Tapps Abroad 24/5/70 – 5/9/70", Council, 28 Oct 1970, attachment.
54. In 1978, 'Scotch at Cowes Reference Book'.
55. Scotch at Cowes Parents' Auxiliary, Minute Book, 1977.
56. Ibid., 1981.
57. Healey, 'Introductory talk at the Seminar of Masters and Senior Boys at Scotch College September 9th, 1974'.
58. A. S. Murdoch (1957), *Great Scot*, 1989, p. 21.

59. Foundation, Annual General Meeting, 7 Mar 1979.

12 The Hill

1. A. S. Anderson (1909), interview with H. Webster, 1968.
2. Bremner, '1929 A very good year'.
3. J. C. H. Spence (1954–64), email to author, 17 July 2000.
4. D. L. D. Brand, letter to his mother, postmarked 9 Feb 1971.
5. Ibid., postmarked 21 Oct 1970.
6. Ibid., postmarked 29 July 1970.
7. Ibid., postmarked 2 July 1970.
8. W. L. Sides (1960–64), Q.
9. G. W. Fisher (1948–51), Q.
10. A. MacV. L. Campbell, diary, 14 and 11 Apr 1928.
11. D. M. Taylor (1945–49), Q.
12. G. K. Bolger (1946–49), letter to author, 19 June 1999.
13. R. McK. Campbell (1923–28), "On the margin", *Bulletin*, 16 Mar 1968, p. 14.
14. *Collegian*, Dec 1952, p. 133.
15. W. L. Sides (1960–64), Q.
16. J. S. Lawson (1949–52), letter to author, 29 Dec 1997.
17. W. L. Sides (1960–64), Q.
18. H. S. Dupin (1927), *Great Scot*, 59 (1991), p. 15.
19. J. C. Brown (1929–33), Q.
20. T. W. Steer (1953–55), Q.
21. W. H. McDonald (1935–44), letter to author, 3 Sept 1999.
22. D. W. J. Aitchison (1932–45), letter to author, Feb 1999.
23. J. S. Lawson (1949–52), letter to author, 29 Dec 1997.
24. See T. W. Steer (1953–55), Q.
25. W. L. Sides (1960–64), Q.
26. D. L. D. Brand (1969–72), conversation with author, 24 June 1999.
27. A. S. Thomson (1972–77), Q.
28. W. R. Baxter (1961–64), Q.
29. A. S. Thomson (1972–77), Q.
30. D. R. Galbraith, Dean of Boarding, letter to B. R. Stewardson, 9 Nov 2000.
31. Bremner, '1929 A very good year'.
32. W. Norris (1942–45) to G. S Tolson, 3 Oct 1992, p. 12. W. Norris, diary, 1943, additional comment written in 1992.
33. D. O. Shave (1946–52), letter to author, 19 Sept 1998.
34. J. S. Lawson (1949–52), letter to author, 29 Dec 1997.
35. Ibid.

36. D. O. Shave (1946–52), letter to author, 19 Sept 1998.
37. D. M. Taylor (1945–49), Q.
38. D. O. Shave (1946–52), letter to author, 19 Sept 1998.
39. D. O. Shave (1946–52), Q.
40. J. C. H. Spence, email to author, 17 July 2000.
41. T. J. Johnston, Littlejohn House 1985, Captain's report.
42. M. S. Paton (1920–26), Q.
43. T. J. Johnston, Littlejohn House 1985, Captain's report.
44. G. H. Owen, letter to Ian ——, 26 Nov 1965.
45. Roff, report to Council, 27 July 1977
46. A. S. Thomson (1972–77), note to author, 1999.
47. Draft letter from Moderator to Prices Commissioner, Canberra, 19 Nov 1946.
48. E&F Committee, 29 Nov 1961.
49. Council, 25 Oct 1967.
50. Finance Committee, 26 Nov 1947, Council, 22 July 1953.
51. Finance Committee, 26 Nov 1947.
52. Selby Smith, letter to Glenn, 28 July 1960.
53. Finance Committee, 26 Nov 1947.
54. A. S. Anderson (1909), 'Appeal Dinner 1962'.
55. T. J. Johnston, Littlejohn House 1985, Captain's report.
56. E&F Committee, 26 Mar 1969. Council, 31 July 1968.
57. E&F Committee, 28 Sept 1971.
58. Healey, report to Council, 29 Mar 1967, Apr 1968.
59. P. C. Greening, Captain of the Hill, *Collegian*, 1998, p. 69.
60. D. R. Galbraith, Dean of Boarding, letter to B. R. Stewardson, 9 Nov 2000.

13 Growing up: Sex and conversation

1. McNicoll, *Luck's a fortune*, p. 13.
2. L. K. Shave (1929), R. A. Reyment (1942–44), QQ.
3. H. R. Taylor (1953–64), Q.
4. M. W. Reid (1953–58), email to author, 12 Oct 1999.
5. D. J. Symington (1963–68), Q.
6. R. K. Pickford (1932–36), Q.
7. M. W. Reid (1953–58), letter to author, 19 Apr 1999.
8. M. S. Paton (1920–26), Q.
9. B. W. Bainbridge (1951–53), Q.
10. B. D. Bayston (1936–48), Q.
11. R. A. W. Wade (1946–49), Q.

12. G. J. Carrick (1928–35), Q.
13. D. H. Hare (1922–29), Q.
14. D. McK. Sharpe (1942–49), Q.
15. W. N. Hurst (1939–50), letter to author, 10 Feb 1998.
16. J. Ross (1941–44), J. A. McMeekin (1940–43), W. R. Gleadell (1959–66), QQ.
17. *Satura*, 24 Apr 1956, p. 2.
18. W. C. Ch'ng (1973–85), Q and email to author, 1 Jun 1999.
19. P. M. Ashton (1957–67), Q.
20. J. W. G. Meyer (1944–47), Q.
21. M. W. Reid (1953–58), letter to author, 19 Apr 1999.
22. B. A. Johns (1946–55), Q.
23. Ibid.
24. C. R. Parsons (1984–86), Q.
25. A. C. Bales (1985–88), Q.
26. A. G. Mackay (1965–70), Q.
27. Campbell, *Urge to laugh*, p. 29.
28. G. M. Mayor, school diary, 24 Sept 1948.
29. B. A. Johns (1946–55), Q.
30. M. W. Reid (1953–58), email to author, 12 Oct 1999.
31. Campbell, *Urge to laugh*, p. 29.
32. D. O. Shave (1946–52), letter to author, 19 Sept 1998.
33. J. W. G. Meyer (1944–47), Q.
34. M. A. Crow (1935–45), Q.
35. J. A. Goldsmith (1949–51), Q.
36. R. J. Moran (1949–54), letter to author, 22 Oct 1998.
37. P. M. Ashton (1957–67), Q.
38. A. T. Marshall (1971–76), S. F. Macintyre (1959–64), A. Edwards (1964–69), A. S. Thomson (1972–77), QQ.
39. R. J. Moran (1949–54), letter to author, 22 Oct 1998.
40. P. M. Ashton (1957–67), Q.
41. B. A. Johns (1946–55), Q.
42. Ibid.
43. B. R. Stewardson, 'Collegian Diary', *Collegian*, Dec 1954, p. 113.
44. B. A. Johns (1946–55), Q.
45. G. I. Hynam (1928–36), Q.
46. P. A. Walker (1936–43), Q.
47. D. W. Aitchison (1932–45), letter to author, Feb 1999.
48. Bond, Triple Farewell speech 15 Nov 1985, *Scotch Association News. An information bulletin for parents*. Feb 1986, p. 3.
49. D. O. Shave (1946–52), letter to author, 19 Sept 1998.
50. K. R. Thom (1945–51), Q.
51. A. J. Abell (1988–91), email to author, 12 Mar 1999.

52. P. G. Mason, Littlejohn House Captain's report, 1968.
53. Campbell, *Urge to laugh*, p. 30.
54. I. R. Marks (1950–54), Q.
55. R. F. Dillon (1962–65), Q.
56. R. K. Blair (1954–63), Q.
57. G. S. Blanch (1957–69), Q.
58. A. S. Thomson (1972–77), Q.
59. Campbell, *Urge to laugh*, pp. 24–5.
60. McNicoll, *Luck's a fortune*, p. 13.
61. K. W. Fraser (1930–41), Q.
62. G. D. Fisher (1929–41), Q.
63. J. A. Goldsmith (1949–51), Q.
64. R. W. McDonald (1943–44), letter to author, 27 May 1999.
65. J. M. Ross (1941–44), Q.
66. B. Andrews (1941–44), Q.
67. J. A. McMeekin (1940–43), Q.
68. M. W. Reid (1953–58), letter to author, 19 Apr 1999.
69. Turner, *Blow for balloons*, pp. 277–9.
70. B. Andrews (1941–44), Q.
71. G. G. Powell (1926–29), Q.
72. D. J. Ashton (1953–65), Q.
73. W. F. R. Wood (1941–46), C. R. Parsons (1984–86), QQ.
74. H. K. Oxley (1926–33), Q.
75. D. McK. Sharpe (1942–49), Q.
76. H. M. Brown (1955–63), Q.
77. W. Norris (1942–45), 1943 diary, additional comment written in 1992.
78. Campbell, *Urge to laugh*, pp. 24–5.
79. J. M. Ross (1941–44), Q.
80. D. R. Head (1963–68), letter to author, 7 July 1999.
81. D. C. M. Ward (1968–79), Q.
82. I. D. Phipps (1946–52), Q.
83. M. A. Crow (1935–45), Q.
84. J. M. Ross (1941–44), Q.
85. B. Andrews (1941–44), Q.
86. J. W. G. Meyer (1944–47), Q.
87. M. A. McKenzie (1939–47), Q.
88. C. Bridges-Webb (1948–51), Q.
89. B. D. Bayston (1936–48), Q.
90. A. G. MacQuarrie (1936–40), Q.
91. C. Bridges-Webb (1948–51), Q.
92. *Song of Solomon*, vii.1–8.
93. *Young Victoria*, 9 (1878), p. 118.
94. A. O. Rentoul, 'Too many cooks spoil the broth', *Collegian*, 1905, p. 15.
95. *Collegian*, 1909, p. 14.
96. *Satura*, 21 Jun 1963, p. 2.
97. K. A. Foletta (1961–64), Q.
98. Campbell, *Urge to laugh*, pp. 20, 23.
99. P. S. Colclough (1929–36), Q.
100. H. S. Millar (1940–48), Q.
101. K. R. McK. Don (1937–44), Q.
102. G. K. Bolger (1946–49), Q.
103. H. Hall (1932–34), Q.
104. D. H. Hare (1922–29), Q.

105. Rev. K. Prentice, *Collegian*, Dec 1953, p. 97.
106. Macneil, *Divine Service in the Memorial Hall … 1934 (Old Boys' and Parents' Sunday)*, p. 2.
107. *A Guide to Scotch College*, [1972], p. 6.
108. K. C. B. Bethell (1929–37), Q.
109. G. G. Powell (1926–29), Q.
110. D. S. Clues (1930–32), Q.
111. L. C. Birch (1925–35), Q.
112. J. T. Chenhalls (1933–36), Q.
113. A. A. McDonald (1929), Q.
114. L. B. Brand (1930–34), letter to author 1 Aug 1999.
115. M. A. McKenzie (1939–47), Q.
116. M. E. Scott (1944–54), Q.
117. K. R. Thom (1945–51), Q.
118. I. D. Phipps (1946–52), Q.
119. A. MacV. L. Campbell, diary, 8 Oct 1929.
120. Tapp, Junior School Mothers' Association, 12 Nov 1964.
121. J. B. Cumming (1957–67), Q.
122. D. S. W. Reid (1962–67), Q.
123. Campbell, *Urge to laugh*, p. 20.
124. W. B. Harvey (1944–50), letter to author, 17 May 1999.
125. M. W. Reid (1953–58), email to author, 12 Oct 1999.
126. R. R. Briggs (1958), conversation with author.
127. I. D. Phipps (1946–52), Q.
128. G. Cadogan-Cowper (1954–58), Q.
129. J. M. Ross (1941–44), Q. Similarly, W. G. Pugh (1947–51), Q.
130. D. C. McClean (1943–52), Q.
131. A. G. MacQuarrie (1936–40), Q.
132. J. Martin (1947–50), Q.
133. D. H. Dyson (1952–61), email to D. E. McC. Hunter, 17 Oct 2000.
134. I. D. Phipps (1946–52), Q.
135. Campbell, *Urge to laugh*, p. 13.
136. M. S. Paton (1920–26), G. N. Ingham (1925–32), L. C. Birch (1925–35), D. M. Annand (1930–38), Respondent 101 (1939), A. A. Laing (1933–40), Respondent 140 (1945), Respondent 17 (1947), Respondent 106 (1949), Respondent 34 (1950), J. Martin (1947–50), K. R. Thom (1945–51), J. H. C. Nairn (1943–55), I. R. Robinson (1952–57), F. W. Paton (1958–63), R. F. Dillon (1962–65), P. M. Ashton (1957–67), P. G. L. Harkness (1954–67), QQ.
137. W. N. Hurst (1939–50), N. McH. Ramsey (1934–41), A. Edwards (1964–69), D. J. Symington (1963–68), Respondent 55 (1967), QQ.

138. D. E. Johnston (1960–68), Q.
139. W. I. Picken (1934–37), Q.
140. Respondent 77 (1948), N. McH. Ramsey (1934–41), R. C. Schurmann (1941–45), QQ
141. D. McK. Sharpe (1942–49), Q.
142. H. S. Millar (1940–48), Q.
143. R. K. Blair (1954–63), Q.
144. I. D. Phipps (1946–52), Q.
145. A. O. Jones (1957–62), Q.
146. H. M. Brown (1955–63), Q.
147. I. K. Burnett (1970–75), Q.
148. K. A. Foletta (1961–65), Q.
149. See also *Collegian*, Dec 1954, p. 193
150. M. W. Reid (1953–58), email to author, 11 Jun 1999.
151. W. Norris, diary, 4 Dec 1943.
152. I. C. Mackenzie (1972–82), Q.
153. Lyne, 'Scotch College, 1942–74'.
154. *Satura*, 30 Jun 1961, p. 2.
155. K. F. Field, 'Bursar's Leave of Absence — June–November, 1970', roneoed report.
156. R. M. Tasker in D. G. Paul, 'Annual Staff-Student Sixth Form Seminar … The expectations of Sixth Formers at Scotch; and the Extent to which they are unsatisfied', 29 May 1978.
157. Prefects Meeting, 19 Mar 1964.
158. J. H. C. Nairn (1943–55), Q and email to author, 8 Nov 2000.
159. *Satura*, 24 Oct 1956, p. 4.
160. Healey, report to Council, 30 Oct 1974.
161. C. J. Stewardson, 'Hot rock', *Collegian*, Jun 1958, p. 42.
162. D. E. Johnston (1960–68), Q.
163. I. R. Cameron, *Collegian*, 1978, p. 46.
164. D. E. Johnston (1960–68), email to author, 27 Oct 2000.
165. *Satura*, 9 Mar 1956, pp. 5, 8.
166. Campbell, *Urge to laugh*, p. 32.
167. Anonymous letter to G. D. Fisher (Captain 1941).
168. *Satura*, 17 Aug 1965, p. 9.
169. A. Hartman (1965–70), email to author, 4 May 1999.
170. S. D. Kunstler (1970–75), Q.
171. W. R. Walker (1970–75), Q.
172. A. S. Thomson (1972–77), Q.
173. J. E. H. Harkness (1990–96), Q.
174. K. D. Oliver, Littlejohn House Captain's report, 1974.
175. S. J. Bubb, ibid., 1976.
176. A. H. McDonald, ibid., 1984.
177. J. W. G. Meyer (1944–47), Q.
178. R. K. Jackson (1975–78), Q.
179. K. A. Foletta (1961–64), Q.

180. C. B. Mackey (1970–75), Q.
181. D. G. Barrie (1990–95), Q.
182. S. F. Macintyre (1959–64), Q.
183. H. M. Brown (1955–63), Q.
184. R. K. Blair (1954–63), Q.
185. R. K. Jackson (1975–78), Q.
186. I. R. Roper (1950–52), D. A. McQueen (1986–91), J. Macdonald (1991–96), QQ.
187. D. L. D. Brand (1969–72), letter to his mother, 18 Oct 1971.
188. Ibid., aged 16, letter to his mother, 18 Jun 1971.
189. P. D. Ritchie (1965–76), Q.
190. Ibid., email to author, 11 Mar 1999.
191. W. R. Walker (1970–75), letter to author, 4 May 1999.
192. GHC, 16 Oct 1975.
193. G. E. D. Brooke (1967–73), letter to author, 13 Oct 1998.
194. R. L. Hyams (1969–80), letter to author, 29 Oct 1998.
195. R. S. Wootton (1965–71), Q.
196. I. C. Mackenzie (1972–82), Q.
197. *A Guide to Scotch College*, [1972], p. 25.
198. D. C. Ekberg, *Collegian*, 1975, p. 77.
199. D. G. Barrie (1990–95), Q.
200. Ibid., email to author, 7 Apr 2000.
201. D. A. McQueen (1986–91), Q.
202. R. D. Ewing (1995–2000), conversation with author, 7 Nov 2000.
203. D. Tacey, *Remaking men: The revolution in masculinity*, Viking, Penguin, Ringwood, 1997, p. 128, citing, Andrew Fuller, 'Risk-taking as a healing process', in I. Gawler (ed.), *The mind body connection*, Melbourne, Gawler Foundation, 1996, p. 45–54.
204. G. D. Logan (1932–33), Q.
205. H. R. Taylor (1953–64), Q.
206. P. G. Mason, Littlejohn House Captain's Report, 1968.
207. G. K. Oliver, ibid., 1972.
208. I. D. Shimmin, ibid., 1977.
209. G. C. Hearn, ibid., 1980.
210. S. E. McInnes, ibid., 1986.
211. B. G. Whittaker, 'Annual staff-student seminar', 6 Sept 1976.
212. R. L. Hyams (1969–80), letter to author, 29 Oct 1998.
213. Junior School Mothers' Association, 8 Feb 1979.
214. Ibid., 4 July 1983.
215. Junior School Parents' Association, 16 Apr 1984.

216. Ibid., 19 Mar 1984.
217. Donaldson, *Annual Report 1998*, Collegian, 1988, p. 7.
218. T. J. Cade (1994–2000), interview with author, 1 Jun 1999.
219. Wirth, report to Council, Apr 1983.
220. A. H. Tucker (1987–92), Q.
221. M. J. Spargo (Captain 1998), Speech to Assembly on the day of the Corner-Eggleston Cup, and Head of the River speech in Assembly, 1998.
222. J. E. H. Harkness (1990–96), Q.
223. L. G. Rattray (1994–99), email to author, 27 Aug 2000.
224. D. G. Barrie (1990–95), email to author, 7 Sept 2000.

14 *Healey, 1964–1975*

1. Healey, 'Towards a school community', p. 4.
2. P. L. Crook, D. G. Paul and N. J. Cracknell, emails to author of 3, 8 and 10 Nov 2000.
3. D. I. Cliff (1967–72), Q, email to author, 13 June 1999.
4. D. L. D. Brand, emails to author of 23 Oct and 14 Nov 2000.
5. Healey, *Memoirs*, chapter XXXVII 'To Sydney Grammar School', p. 19. Unpublished MS.
6. D. B. Telfer (1969–74), emails to author, 9 July 1999, 1 Oct 2000.
7. D. L. D. Brand (1969–72), letter to his mother, 8 Nov 1971.
8. Rev A. P. Crow, conversation with author, 20 Nov 2000.
9. W. B. Holly, conversation with author, 19 Dec 2000.
10. J. W. Hogg, *Our proper concerns : a history of the Headmasters' Conference of the Independent Schools of Australia*, Stanmore, NSW, c1986, pp. 165–6.
11. Healey, 'Towards a school community', p. 4,
12. A. O. Jones (1957–62), Q.
13. D. J. Symington (1963–68), letter to author, 25 Jan 2000.
14. Healey, report to Council, 28 July 1965.
15. Selby Smith to Healey, 24 Mar 1964.
16. Ibid.
17. M. J. Favaloro (1944–52), Q.
18. Cameron, letter to author, 13 Feb 1999.
19. Healey, report to Council, 31 Mar 1965.

20. J. D. McCaughey, interview with author, 21 Oct 1998.
21. Healey, report to Council, 27 Oct 1965.
22. D. F. Ladbury (staff 1968–2000), 'Maths 6B', MS comments next to boys' names on loose sheet, 1972?
23. [unknown], 'Grade 6B', MS comments next to boys' names on loose sheet 1972?; only some names have comments
24. Donaldson, 'Blue Cards', Feb 1983, 'Staff Manual', Section B. 11.
25. Healey, 'On writing reports', undated, roneoed.
26. Lyne, 'Scotch College 1942–74'.
27. *Great Scot*, 67 (1993), p. 31.
28. Healey, report to Council, 28 July 1965.
29. Healey, report to Council, 4 Aug 1970.
30. Tapp, 'The Tapps Abroad', 1970.
31. A. N. Shugg, 'Education Cttee. Notes of an informal meeting between HM, the Chairman (Ken Mappin) & Secretary (Alan Shugg) on 30/3/71'. Handwritten.
32. Healey, 'Proposals for improving the House system', Jan 1965, roneoed.
33. Ibid.
34. G. B. Wemyss, 'Comments on a document headed "Houses and Day-boy house prefects" (Feb 1971)'
35. Healey, 'The Day-Boy Houses. 1971'.
36. J. G. Miles, CRA Education Committee, 17 July 1972.
37. P. J Wade (1969–75), in 'Report on staff/senior students' seminar. September 1975'.
38. E&F Committee, 30 May 1972.
39. J. D. McCaughey, 'Final summing up by Dr McCaughey', 'Seminar [on] the care of boys', 1972, p. 8.
40. G. B. Lyman (1977–79), Q.
41. K. L. Elliott, Form III report in 'Report on the Seminar of masters and Sixth Form boys [on] the care of boys exercised at Scotch College', 1972, p. 6.
42. Wirth, report to Council, 20 Oct 1977.
43. G. B. Mason (staff 1991–94 and 1998– , Junior School Deputy Headmaster 1992–94 and Headmaster 1998–), email to author, 19 June 2000.
44. GHC, 16 Mar 1972.
45. Roff, 'The General House

Committee Purpose, Structure and method of operation', Dec 1979. Donaldson, 'The General House Committee Purpose, Structure and method of operation', 1 Mar 1983.
46. GHC, 8 May 1975.
47. GHC, 29 Mar 1979.
48. *Satura*, 8 Oct 1956, p. 2. *Collegian*, Dec 1956, p. 116.
49. Healey, memoires, chapter XLIII, p. 37.
50. R. H. Clayton, interview with H. Webster, 1968.
51. Evans, *Collegian*, 1978, p. 37.
52. Heads of Department (HOD), 22 and 29 May 1990.
53. Biology and Geology were poor relations, and were not included in the New Maths and Science Block.
54. Healey, report to Council, 29 Oct 1969.
55. *Satura*, 13 Apr 1961, p. 6.
56. Roff, report to Council, 26 July 1978.
57. Roff, report to Council, 19 Apr 1978.
58. Healey, 'School Officers', Feb 1965, p. 4.
59. W. Norris, diary, 19 June 1944.
60. Boarding House, 'Corporal punishment Book Commenced December. 1966' [to Nov 1973]; below the last entry is written 'End S. F. B. 7/12/73' [=S. F. Brown; he told new boys that his initials stood for what he would not allow: Spitting, Foul language and Bullying.]
61. *Satura*, 29 Mar 1963, p. 2.
62. C. A. Widdis (1983–90), email to author 23 Aug 2000.
63. CRA Education Committee, 2 Aug 1971.
64. Ibid., 28 Sept 1971.
65. Healey, letter to Mr Ling, (Secretary, CRA Education Subcommittee), 1 July 1974.
66. Healey to Mappin, chairman, CRA Education Committee, 31 May 1973.
67. 'Seminars—Term 3, 1974', signed and dated I. M. Ling, 13 August 1974.
68. D. L. Scott, 'To the Principal and Council of Scotch College. Report from D.L. Scott on new physics buildings and facilities seen in the United States and the United Kingdom. Period of leave: May 8 to September 6, 1971', p. 4.
69. R. N. Jefferies (1970–73), in D. G.

Paul, Annual Seminar, 10 Sept 1973.
70. R N. Jefferies, in D. G. Paul, Notes of Master Sixth Form Seminar, 10 Sept 1973.
71. J. P. Simpson (1970–75), in 'Report on staff/senior students' seminar. September 1975'.
72. Healey, report to Council, 29 Apr 1970.
73. CRA Education Committee, 8 July 1971.
74. *Collegian*, 1970, p 156.
75. Selby Smith, 'A Victorian Independent school', p. 249.
76. W. J. Simpson (1966–71), Q.
77. J. D. McCaughey, 'Final summing up by Dr McCaughey', 'Seminar [on] the care of boys', 1972, p. 8.
78. Healey, report to Council, 27 Oct 1965.
79. Healey, 'Towards a school community', p. 31.
80. Healey, report to Council, 27 Oct 1965.
81. L. M. Muir (1937–42), 'Transcript of the tape re-opening of Scotch Building Appeal', 14 Sept 1965, p. 10.
82. Council, 13 Apr 1973.
83. D. B. Telfer (1969–74), Q.
84. Malcolm Fraser, ministerial statement, 13 Aug 1969. Senator J.L. Carrick, Federal Minister of Education, 'Why private schools need Canberra's help', *Age*, 7 July 1977, p. 8.
85. P. M. Ashton (1957–67), Q.
86. *Collegian*, Aug 1951, p. 89.
87. Respondent 141 (1943), Q.
88. M. D. Purvis (1969–75), Q.
89. P. M. Ashton (1957–67), Q.
90. H. S. Dupin (1927), *Great Scot* 59 (1991), p. 15.

15 The times they are a'changin'

1. GHC, 16 Mar, 16 Oct, 4 Nov 1975.
2. GHC Sports Committee, 6 June 1979.
3. Ibid., 22 Mar 1979.
4. G. O. Griffiths (1972), *Collegian*, Dec 1969, p. 152
5. Healey, report to Council, 26 Apr 1972.
6. G. S. S. Yule (1929–35), Q.
7. M. E. Scott, Junior School Mothers' Association, 14 Apr 1955, 27 July 1961.
8. D. A. Evans, Junior School Mothers' Association, 27 Feb 1964.
9. Tapp, Junior School Mothers' Association, 24 June 1954.

10. W. J. W. McAuley (1965–69), phone conversation with author, 28 Feb 1999.

11. M. W. Reid (1953–58), Q.

12. D. L. D. Brand (1969–72), letter to his mother, 29 Mar 1971.

13. Healey, 'To English Masters English Expression', Mar 1971.

14. Ibid.

15. Gilray, *Annual Report,* 1946, p. 4.

16. R. C. Schurmann (1941–45), Q.

17. C. B. Mackey (1970–75), Q.

18. ACNielsen Research Pty Ltd, 'Outcomes of Schooling Report (draft)', Feb 1999, pp. 23–34.

19. R. H. Clayton, interview with H. Webster, June 1968.

20. P. A. Walker (1936–43), Q.

21. Clayton, interview, June 1968.

22. K. R. Clayton (1954, staff 1973–94, Registrar 1989–94), note to author, 24 Aug 2000.

23. R. D. Fincher (1956–59), email to author, 28 Apr 1999.

24. J. S. Green (1936–47), Q.

25. K. R. Thom (1945–51), Q.

26. R. D. Fincher (1956–59), email to author, 28 Apr 1999.

27. B. A. Johns (1946–55), Q.

28. R. A. Reyment (1942–44), email to author, 1 May 1998.

29. M. A. Griffith (1939–41), Q.

30. W. B. Harvey (1944–50), letter to author, 17 May 1999.

31. R. D. Fincher (1956–59), email to author, 28 Apr 1999.

32. J. Martin (1947–50), Q.

33. H. R. Taylor (1953–64), email to author, 21 Oct 1999.

34. Tapp, Junior School Mothers' Association, 24 June 1954.

35. J. A. Goldsmith (1949–51), Q.

36. G. B. Lyman (1977–79), email to author, 2 Mar 1999.

37. D. E. Johnston (1960–68), Q.

38. *Collegian*, 1978, p. 137.

39. Wirth, report to Council, 28 Oct 1981.

40. K. McR. Evans, *Collegian*, 1975, p. 19.

41. 'Some notes for parents on Mathematics: How you can help the school', signed by Healey but written by Evans.

42. S. G Boydell, interview with author, 3 Mar 1999.

43. A. Tait, *Collegian*, 1978, p. 34.

44. Ibid., p. 35.

45. 'The order of celebration of the birthday and 40th year at Scotch of Mr W.R. Jamieson … T.O.R.T. 10th August 1948', roneoed document. The organisers included K. McR. Evans.

46. R. M. Braddy, email to author, 14 July 2000.

47. Ibid., 12 May 2000.

48. D. G. Paul, emails to author, 10, 24 July 2000.

49. I. M. Ling, 'Education Subcommittee Suggestions for 1975 Program', 30 Oct 1974.

50. Healey to I. Ling, 10 Dec 1974.

51. Healey, 'Questions for our consideration', Aug 1968.

52. 'Education Committee Submission on evaluation', CRA Education Committee, 13 Oct 1971, attachment.

53. CRA Education Sub-Committee, 29 Apr 1975.

54. Shugg. Notes of an informal meeting … on 30/3/71'.

55. CRA Education Committee, 21 Apr 1969.

56. 'Cognitive Domain taxonomy headings, listing also Affective and Psycho-Motor domain headings', a purple gestetnered foolscap sheet, presumably attachment to CRA Education Committee of 1 Apr 1970.

57. 'Rating scale for Affective Objectives in Mathematics', roneoed foolscap sheet.

58. D. L. Scott, CRA Education Committee, 1 Apr 1970.

59. K. S. Darling, CRA Education Committee, 5 Apr 1972.

60. K. McR. Evans and I. T. Harrison, 'Mr K. Mappin', *Collegian*, 1987, p. 32.

61. K. S. Darling, interview with author, 10 Aug 2000.

62. K. S. Darling, note to author, 10 Aug 2000.

63. K. S. Darling, in typed summary of various speakers at CRA Education Subcommittee Seminar, 9 Sept 1974, 'Learning at Scotch College—Past, present, and future'.

64. Roff, report to Council, 26 Oct 1977.

65. CRA Education Committee, 25 Mar 1969.

66. Ibid., 2 June 1969.

67. J. W. De Ravin (1974), in D. G. Paul, Annual Seminar 10 Sept 1973.

68. D. G. Paul, 'Concerning proposals to introduce General Studies into the curriculum at Scotch College—with special emphasis on the contribution of and effect on the teaching of history', MS [1972?].

69. Eggleston, 'Report [to the Senior Masters' Committee] of 5th Form General Studies Sub-committee' [Nov 1972].

70. D. G. Paul, 'Concerning proposals to introduce General Studies'.

71. J. A. Lyne, 'General Studies at Form V'.

72. D. L. Scott, 'To the Principal from D. L. Scott, re General Studies at Form V level', 10 July 1972.

73. Healey, letter of 29 Apr 1971 to the CRA, entitled 'General Studies and non-examinable activities'.

74. Healey, Senior Masters Committee, 5 Aug 1971.

75. Interpolated comment in Healey, 'Comments on Scotch College by Mr Wayne Frederick [exchange teacher] of Phillips Academy, Andover, Mass., U.S.A., May 1971'.

76. Eggleston, 'Report of 5th Form General Studies Sub-committee'.

77. Roff, report to Council, 19 Apr 1978.

78. Eggleston, *Collegian*, 1978, p. 36–7, D. G. Paul, email to author, 28 Apr 2000.

79. I. J. Savage, email to author, 10 Apr 2000.

80. D. G. Paul, email to author, 24 Apr 2000.

81. Tapp, 'The Tapps Abroad', 1970.

82. L. D. Kemp (1922–27), P. S. Colclough (1929–36), QQ.

83. J. G. Hiller (1985–96), A. J. Abell (1988–91), Respondent 45 (1949), QQ.

84. F. P. Brown (1905), *Collegian*, 1904, p. 24.

85. R. A. Reid (1960–72), Q.

86. D. W. W. Earle (1960–72), Q.

87. I. K. Burnett (1970–75), Q.

88. W. J. Simpson, 'Scotch College—Commonroom Association. Report of Education Committee Conference held on 13.9.71', D. G. Paul's notes.

89. M.A. Dreyfus (1973), in D. G. Paul, Annual Seminar ,10 Sept 1973.

90. N. Ruskin (1976), in D. G. Paul, 'Annual staff-student seminar', 6 Sept 1976. I. R. Cameron wanted less competitiveness, in D G. Paul, 'Report on staff-student Seminar 5th September 1977'.

91. J. S. Neyland, in D. G. Paul, 'Report on staff-student Seminar', 5th September 1977'.

92. D. C. Coote (1978) in D. G. Paul, 'Annual Staff-Student Sixth Form Seminar ... The expectations of Sixth Formers at Scotch; and the Extent to which they are unsatisfied', 29 May 1978.

93. J. S. Neyland, Annual Staff-Student Sixth Form Seminar, 29 May 1978.

94. F. R. Samuel (1980–85), Q.

95. P. Howe (1975–80), Q.

96. Form IV Group, 'Report on the Seminar of masters and Sixth Form boys held on Monday 11th September [1972] to discuss the care of boys exercised at Scotch College', p. 5.

97. D. G. Paul, 'Annual staff-student seminar', 6 Sept 1976.

98. Council, 8 Aug 1973.

99. T. Swain (1978), in D. G. Paul, MS notes of Annual Staff-Student Sixth Form Seminar 29 May 1978.

100. F. Macrae (1956–67), Q.

101. 'Scheme for a continuing year-long test for Fourth Form History'.

102. Healey, 'Towards a school community', p. 40, citing Donald Barr, Who pushed Humpty Dumpty?, Atheneum, New York, 1972.

103. Healey, CRA Education Committee, 2 July 1970.

104. Healey, Annual newsletter, 1972.

105. Healey, 'Questions for our consideration', Aug 1968.

106. D. W. K. Webster, 'Eleven propositions on examinations', dated 24 Apr 1967, CRA Education Committee, 21 Apr 1970, attachment.

107. CRA Education Committee, 28 Sept 1971.

108. 'David Hosking: Eco', in MS notes of meeting of 28 Sept 1971.

109. R. G. Caro (1973), Annual Seminar 10 Sept 1973.

110. D. F. Schloeffel (1977) in D. G. Paul, 'Report on staff-student Seminar', 5 Sept 1977'.

111. J. B. Pettigrew (1932–34), letter to author, 17 Sept 98.

112. H. M. Knight (1933–35), Q.

113. I. C. Teague (1947–52), Q.

114. Webster, 'Eleven propositions'.

115. Senior Masters' Committee, 16 Nov 1972.

116. Healey, report to Council, 27 Oct 1971.

117. K. McR. Evans, 'Report on Examinations and Testing from the Mathematics Department', [1971].

118. Evans, CRA Education Committee, 2 July 1970.

119. Evans, CRA Education Committee, 28 Sept 1971. Senior Masters' Committee, 16 Nov 1972.

120. A. S. Anderson (1909), speaker's notes for OSCA Annual Dinner, 1948 or 1949.

121. Butler, CRA Education Committee, 28 Sept 1971.

122. Mappin, CRA Education Committee, 28 Sept 1971.

123. Senior Masters' Committee, 16 Nov 1972.

124. B. A. Johns (1946–55), Q.

125. Selby Smith, 'A Victorian Independent school', p. 239.

126. Respondent 243 (1954), Q.

127. A. G. Mackay (1965–70), Q.

128. E. H. Thorpe, Memoirs, chapter 5.

129. G. D. Fisher (1929–41), Q.

130. Healey, 'Introductory talk at the Seminar of Masters and Senior Boys at Scotch College September 9th, 1974', p. 4.

131. Littlejohn, Annual Report, 1927, p. 2.

132. P. D. Craw (1951), Collegian, Aug 1951, p. 85.

133. Selby Smith, 'A Victorian Independent school', pp. 245–6.

134. Collegian, June 1953, p. 12. K. R. Clayton, note to author, 24 Aug 2000.

135. R. S. Groom and J. Marcard, Editorial, Satura, 1 Apr 1957, p. 1.

136. Healey, 'Towards a school community', p. 14.

137. R. Stott (1935–40), Q.

138. A. O. Jones (1957–62), Q.

139. R. B. Coutie (1930–32), Q.

140. G. B. Lyman (1977–79), Q.

141. J. Macdonald (1991–96), Q.

142. D. McK. Sharpe (1942–49), Q.

143. Donaldson, Great Scot, 77 (1995), p. 3.

144. Annual newsletter, 1968.

145. GHC, 1 July 1982.

146. A. O. Dixon (1959) and N. J. Radford (1959), 'New Boy—Stop! Read this!', Satura, 17 Feb 1960, p. 2.

147. Associated Public Schools of Victoria, Head Prefects Meeting, 11 Mar 1960.

148. Prefects' Meeting, 21 July 1961.

149. Ibid., 8 Apr, 12 June and 8 Nov 1963.

150. Satura, 12 Aug 1963, p. 4.

151. Prefects' Meeting, 10 June 1964.

152. D. J. Mason, 'To the School Captain, 1967'.

153. F. Macrae (1956–67), letter to author, 21 Apr 1999.

154. A. G. Mackay (1965–70), letter to author, 19 Mar 1999.

155. P. G. Hammond (Captain 1973), Prefects Minute Book, 1973.

156. Prefects' Meeting, 18 Sept 1975.

157. D. J. Mason, 'To the School Captain, 1967'.

158. Prefects' Meeting, 5 July 1967.

159. Ibid., 3 Oct 1961.

160. E. McG. Fry and J. M. Macneil, Editors, Satura, 3 Mar 1950, p. 2.

161. Healey, 'The Day-Boy Houses. 1971'.

162. Ferguson, interview with author, 23 Feb 1998.

163. Morrison, Report, 1862, p. 30.

164. Field, 'Leave of Absence'.

165. Healey, Guide to Scotch College, [1972], p. 22.

166. GHC, 8 July 1971.

167. Healey, Guide to Scotch College, p. 22.

168. D. L. D. Brand (1972), letter to his mother, 7 June 1971

169. Ibid., 16 Sept 1971.

170. Ibid., 10 Nov 1972.

171. Satura, 9 Apr 1965, p. 12.

172. W. H. Henderson (1972), conversation with author.

173. Healey, 'Proposals for improving the House system', Jan 1965, roneoed.

174. Healey, 'Questions for Senior Day-Housemasters and division masters', May, 1972.

175. Healey's note on his blue card.

176. Matthews, Australian son, p. 63.

177. Annual newsletter, 1970.

178. Healey, Guide to Scotch College, p. 21.

179. D. S. W. Reid (1962–67), Q.

180. Satura, 12 July 1963, p. 2.

181. F. S. Falconer (1950–54), Q.

182. Healey, Guide to Scotch College, p. 22.

183. Satura, 16 Mar 1962, p. 3.

184. Healey, 'School Officers', Feb 1965, roneoed.

185. Prefects' Meeting, 31 May 1966.

186. Ibid., 11 Oct.

187. Annual newsletters, 1968, 1970.

188. T. J. Cade (1992–2000), interview with author, 1 June 1999.

189. Annual newsletter, 1968,

190. Ibid., 1970.

191. Healey, interview with G.S. Tolson, 20 Oct 1989.
192. Healey, *Guide to Scotch College*, p. 22.
193. *Satura*, 29 Mar 1963, p. 3.
194. Annual newsletter, 1968.
195. Council, 30 July 1969.
196. Healey, *Guide to Scotch College*, p. 21.
197. D. R. Head (1963–68), letter to author, 7 July 1999.
198. GHC, 1 July 1982, 24 July, 1 Aug 1979.
199. Healey, *Guide to Scotch College*, p. 26.
200. G. R. D. Keep in D. G. Paul, 'Summary of Staff-Student Fifth Form Seminar … 'Control and Freedom at Scotch College'', 11 September 1978.
201. GHC, 30 June 1983.
202. GHC, 29 Mar 1979.
203. *Satura*, 12 July 1963, p. 3.
204. D. R. Head (1963–68), letter to author, 7 July 1999.
205. W. R. Walker (1970–75), email to author, 22 May 1999.
206. J. K. Dempster (1939–50), letter to author, 16 June 1999.
207. GHC, 29 Mar 1973.
208. Miss Goodenough at Junior School Mothers' Association, 6 Aug 1959.
209. Minute Book Scotch-at-Cowes Parents' Auxiliary, 1969.
210. OSCA Council, 8 Dec 1969.
211. Healey, 'Questions for our consideration', Aug 1968.
212. W. G. Pugh (1947–51), letter to author, 17 Mar 1999. K. R. Clayton, note to author, 24 Aug 2000.
213. D. R. Head (1963–68), letter to author, 7 July 1999.
214. R. A. W. Wade (1946–49), email to author, 18 Aug 1999.
215. S. G Boydell, interview with author, 3 Mar 99.
216. G. B. Lyman (1977–79), email to author, 2 Mar 1999.
217. A. P. Crow, CRA Education Committee, 10 Nov 1969.
218. D. S. Clues (1930–32), Q.
219. L. C. Birch (1925–35), Q.
220. R. Stott (1935–40), Q.
221. Healey, 'Towards a school community', pp. 38–9.
222. GHC, 19 Apr 1979.
223. Rev. K. Melville, CRA Education Committee, 10 Nov 1969.
224. Rev. A. Crow, CRA Education Committee, 10 Nov 1969.

225. Healey, 'Conscription and Vietnam', Apr, 1966
226. Healey, report to Council, 29 Apr 1970.
227. D. S. W. Reid (1962–67), Q.
228. J. Rickard, *ADB*, xv, 156.
229. Healey, report to Council, 28 July 1971.
230. D. L. Scott, email to author, 18 Sept 2000
231. A. Hartman (1965–70), emails to author, 4 May, 15 July 1999.
232. Ibid.
233. Ian Birch, *Age, Good weekend*, 11 Dec 1999, p. 44.
234. McCaughey, 'Dr McCaughey's Address (a summary)', 'Report on the Seminar [1972] to discuss the care of boys', p. 1.
235. Healey, report to Council, 26 Apr 1972.
236. A Hansen recommendation, mentioned in Healey, 'Report on the Seminar of masters and Sixth Form boys [on] the care of boys exercised at Scotch College', 1972.
237. Morrison to Monash, 5 Jan 1881, Serle, *Monash*, p. 22.
238. R. L. Hyams (1969–80), letter to author, 29 Oct 1998.
239. M. L. Santini (1979) in D. G. Paul, 'Summary of Staff-Student Fifth Form Seminar … "Control and Freedom at Scotch College" ', 11 Sept 1978. W. R. McDonald (1978) in D. G. Paul, 'Annual Staff-Student Sixth Form Seminar … The expectations of Sixth Formers at Scotch; and the Extent to which they are unsatisfied', 29 May 1978.
240. Davies, *Fiddlers of Drummond*, p. 42.
241. A. MacV. L. Campbell, diary, 29 Oct 1929.
242. D. R. Head (1963–68), letter to author, 7 July 1999. Also, D. S. W. Reid (1962–67), email to author, 17 July 1999.
243. E&F Committee, 29 June 1971. The Principal 'detailed at some length some of the problems that he was experiencing'.
244. Healey, report to Council, 28 July 1971.
245. E&F Committee, 30 May 1972.
246. Council, 25 July 1972.
247. Roff, interview with author, 8 Dec 1998.
248. E&F Committee, 30 Jan 1973.
249. Healey, report to Council, 2 May 1973.

250. Council, 26 June 1973, attachment. The actual date of his departure was 1 February 1975.
251. Healey, report to Council, 30 Oct 1974.
252. Ibid., 25 July 1971, 25 July 1972.
253. M. J. Edwards (1967–70), Q.
254. D. J. Mason, 'To the School Captain, 1967'.
255. 'Mon' [J. A. E. Thomson], '[to] The School Captain 1966'.

16 *Roff, 1975–1981*

1. Muir, on behalf of the selection committee, Council, 31 July 1974.
2. Moderator of Presbyterian Church, press release, 14 Aug 1974.
3. Roff, report to Council, 30 July 1975.
4. Clayton, interview with H. Webster, June 1968.
5. Roff, in Paul, MS notes of CRA Education Sub-Committee, 15 July 1975.
6. K. McR. Evans, in ibid.
7. Roff, 'Address to the Junior School Mothers' Association', 18 Sept 1975.
8. Ibid.
9. Development Committee report, Council, 10 Mar 1981, attachment.
10. Submission to the church's Board of Investment and Finance and the Educational Policy and Consultative Committee.
11. Roff, report to Council, 19 Apr 1978.
12. A. G. Mackay (1965–70), Q.
13. Council, 30 Mar 1977.
14. P. B. Thompson, *Collegian*, 1978, p. 84.
15. Development Committee report, Council 10 Mar 1981, attachment.
16. Roff, report to Council, 27 May 1980.
17. E&F Committee, 12 Apr 1976.
18. Council, 28 Apr 1976.
19. Roff, report to Council, 30 July 1975.
20. Bond, Acting Principal's report to Council, 28 July 1982.
21. Roff, report to Council, 26 July 1978.
22. Roff at 'Annual staff-student seminar', 6 Sept 1976.
23. GHC, 10 Oct 1974.
24. D. C. M. Ward (1968–79), Q.
25. Roff, report to Council, 27 Oct 1976
26. Donaldson, report to Council, 31 Oct 1984.
27. Roff, 'Council Briefing on Co-Education', 19 July 1978, p. 1,

Council, 26 July 1978, attachment.

28. Roff at 'Annual staff-student seminar', 6 Sept 1976.

29. Roff, 'Council Briefing on Co-Education', 19 July 1978, Council, 26 July 1978, attachment.

30. J. Martin (1947–50), R. K. Blair (1954–63), D. S. W. Reid (1962–67), P. D. Ritchie (1965–76), W. A. Shattock (1974–79), J. Macdonald (1991–96), QQ.

31. C. B. Mackey (1970–75), Q.

32. G. E. D. Brooke (1967–73), Q.

33. D. E. Johnston (1960–68), letter to author in Nov 1998.

34. David Murray Robinson (1963–66), Q.

35. J. G. Hiller (1985–96), email to author, 20 Apr 2000.

36. Satura, 9 May 1968, p. 2.

37. B. Andrews (1941–45), Q.

38. Donaldson, 'No co-ed. at Scotch', Great Scot, 62 (1992), p. 2.

39. Roff, report to Council, 25 Mar 1981.

40. A Hansen recommendation, Healey, 'Report on the Seminar of masters and Sixth Form boys held on Monday 11th September [1972] to discuss the care of boys exercised at Scotch College'.

41. M. E. Scott (1944–54), Q.

42. I. C. Teague 1947–52, Q.

43. R. Jackson (1975–78), Q.

44. Wirth, report to Council, July 1983.

45. Roff, report to Council, 26 July 1978.

46. Ibid.

47. Council, 24 June, 28 Oct, 23 Nov 1981, 24 Feb, 28 Apr 1982. It was Mappin and D. L. Scott, 1 Aug 1981, and Costa and Beattie on 30 June 1982.

48. B. W. Lithgow, Chairman's report, Scotch College AGM, 8 June 1982.

49. Roff, report to Council, 30 July 1975.

50. Roff, in Paul, MS notes of CRA Education Sub-Committee, 15 July 1975.

51. Walmsley, in ibid.

52. D. G. Paul, email to author, 21 June 2000.

53. GHC, 4 Mar 1982.

54. Roff, 'Address to the Junior School Mothers' Association', 18 Sept 1975.

55. A. S. Thomson (1972–77), note to author, 1999.

56. J. P. Herbert, letter to Glenn of 11 June 1980.

57. P. A. Holdaway, 'Outcome of Staff/5th Form Seminar. Deliberation of Student Sub-Committee steered by Holdaway/Galbraith', Apr 1979.

58. Roff, interview with author, 8 Dec 1998.

59. Roff, 'Outdoor activities—Safety Committee', 29 June 1981, in 'Staff Manual', Section B.18.

60. Roff, report to Council, 24 Sept 1980.

61. S. G Boydell, interview with author, 3 Mar 99.

62. G. B. Lyman (1977–79), Q.

63. GHC, 24 July and 1 Aug 1979.

64. R. L. Hyams (1969–80), letter to author, 2 Feb 1999.

65. Roff, Annual Report, 1979.

66. J. R. Cormack (1978), Collegian, 1978, p. 146.

67. Roff, 'Note to Monash House masters and House tutors', 6 Nov 1978.

68. Roff, report to Council, 19 Apr 1978.

69. Roff, Annual Report, 1979.

70. R. L. Hyams (1969–80), letter to author, 29 Oct 1998.

71. Roff, Annual Report, 1979.

72. Roff, interview with author, 8 Dec 1998.

73. C. Taylor, 'McLaren', ADB, x, 324.

74. Ivan Southall, Softly tread the brave, Angus and Robertson, Melbourne, 1960.

75. R. L. Hyams (1969–80), letter to author, 2 Feb 1999.

76. GHC, 2, 23 July 1981.

77. Collegian, 1998, p. 57.

78. Wirth, reports to Council, 23 Mar 1981, 25 July 1984.

79. I. C. Mackenzie (1972–82), email to author, 21 July 1999.

80. 'Questions submitted by Lawson–MacFarland House for consideration', March 16, 1976.

81. GHC, 16 Mar 1976.

82. GHC, 7 June 1979.

83. G. B. Lyman (1977–79), Q.

84. Roff, report to Council, 19 Apr 1978.

85. S. G Boydell, interview with author, 3 Mar 1999.

86. Council, 25 July 1979.

87. I. M. Ling, 'Education Subcommittee Suggestions for 1975 Program', 30 Oct 1974.

88. Roff, report to Council, 28 Apr 1976.

89. Ibid., 29 Oct 1975.

90. Long Range Development Subcommittee, 15 Oct 1976. Council, 27 Oct 1976.

91. G. G. Powell (1926–29), letter to author, 15 Feb 1999.

92. A. S. Anderson, interview with H. Webster.

93. B. D. Bayston, interview with G. S. Tolson, 17 Aug 1992.

94. Scotch Association News. An information bulletin for parents. Feb 1986, pp. 2–3.

95. Roff, interview with author, 8 Dec 1998.

96. P. A. Holdaway, 'Outcome of Staff/5th Form Seminar. Deliberation of Student Sub-Committee steered by Holdaway/Galbraith', Apr 1979.

97. D. G. Paul, 'Staff / Student Sixth Form Seminar. Report on the "Recommendations" Session held after lunch, Monday 28th May 1979'.

98. N. C. Pavlovski (1986–91), Q.

99. David Meredith Robinson (1963–68), Q.

100. GHC, 1 Aug 1973, Appendix.

101. GHC, 10 Oct 1974.

102. D. G. Paul, 'Staff / Student Sixth Form Seminar. Report on the "Recommendations" Session held after lunch, Monday 28th May 1979'.

103. GHC, 1 Aug 1973, Appendix.

104. Tapp, report to Council, 18 Oct 1972.

105. Wallace Ironside, 'Cade', ADB, xiii, 330–1.

106. A. D. Grounds (1946) was contacted by the then Prime Minister's office, letter to author, 16 Nov 1999.

107. Bond, Acting Principal's report to Council, 28 Apr 1982

108. Roff, 'Address to the Junior School Mothers' Association' 18 Sept 1975.

109. Ibid.

110. Roff, report to Council, 30 July 1975.

111. Ibid.

112. A. D. Rubins (1972–76), in D. G. Paul, 'Annual staff-student seminar', 6 Sept 1976.

113. Davies, Fiddlers of Drummond, p. 83.

114. W. C. Ch'ng (1973–85), Q.

115. R. K. Mollison (1976–81), Q.

116. J. G. Hiller (1985–96), email to author, 20 Apr 2000.

117. A. J. Abell (1988–91), email to author 12 Mar 1999.

118. I. C. Mackenzie (1972–82), Q.

119. Roff, report to Council, 30 July 1975.
120. Wirth, report to Council 24 Sept 1980.
121. Ibid.
122. Council, 28 Oct 1981.

17 Schism, 1977–1980

1. Hill, *Edwardian Scotland*, pp. 5–6.
2. J. D. McCaughey, interview with author, 21 Oct 1998.
3. D. R. McNicoll (1932), 'Religious split degenerates into real estate row', *Bulletin*, 3 Apr 1979, p. 52.
4. Glenn, interview with author, 20 Feb 1998.
5. Mark Baker, 'Church union leads to a $500 mil. split', *Age*, 17 June 1977, p. 8. The continuing Church was the Presbyterian Church which was to continue to function after 22 June 1977.
6. B. D. Bayston, interview with G.S. Tolson, 17 Aug 1992.
7. W. G. Philip at OSCA Council meeting, 14 June 1977.
8. R. M. Northrop, interview with author, 16 Nov 1999.
9. McNicoll, 'Religious split', p. 53.
10. F. M. Bradshaw, letter 1 May 1953 to Presbytery of Melbourne North.
11. F. M. Bradshaw, *Scottish seceders in Victoria*, Robertson & Mullens, Melbourne, 1947, pp. 84–6, 97–8.
12. Healey, 'Scotch College, Melbourne, 1964–75', p. 70.
13. Bayston, interview with Tolson, 17 Aug 1992.
14. Healey to Bethell, 16 Sept 1978.
15. E&F Committee, 15 July 1974.
16. J. A. Lyne, letter to Glenn, 27 Sept 1978.
17. W. G. Philip at OSCA Council meeting, 14 June 1977.
18. J. D. McCaughey, letter to Healey, 26 June 1974.
19. J. D. McCaughey, interview with author, 21 Oct 1998.
20. *Age*, 14 Oct 1966, pp. 1, 3; 15 Oct, p. 3; 18 Oct p. 3.
21. 'Submission from the Uniting negotiators for Victoria to the Property commission regarding a school for girls and boys', typed, undated [1977?], pp. 2–3. 'Victorian Negotiators for Continuing Presbyterian Church Submission Regarding a School for Boys', typed, undated [1977?].
22. Council, 30 Mar 1977.

23. W. G. Philip at OSCA Council meeting, 14 June 1977.
24. Mark Baker, *Age*, 8 June 1977, p. 5.
25. Letter to the *Age*, 13 Aug 1979.
26. Bayston, note to author, June 1999. R.M. Northrop, interview with author, 18 Nov 1999.
27. D. G. Bain, 'School Council backs appeal', *News from Scotch*, [No. 2. headline: 'Start on first of the new buildings'], [1962], p. 1.
28. Council, 25 May 1977, 21 Oct 1979. Foundation, Exec of Board of Trustees, 3 June 1977.
29. P. S. Lawson (1958), letter to Glenn, 6 Oct 1978.
30. A. B. Conabere (1960), letter to Bethell, 19 Sept 1978.
31. Healey, 'Towards a school community', p. 36.
32. Council, 12 Sept 1979.
33. W. G. Philip at OSCA Council meeting, 14 June 1977.
34. Bond, quoted in Peter Ellingsen, 'Profile of a Private School', *Age*, 5 Oct 1985, 'Saturday Extra', p. 1.
35. Donaldson, in 'Triple Scotch farewell, Scotch Family farewell dinner for Ron Bond Ken Field & Archie Crow. Camberwell Civic Centre, 15 Nov 1985', p. 6.
36. R. J. Hume, *Collegian*, 1987, p. 40: 'Scotch is to be distinguished by the number of people who love it'.
37. David Elias, *Australian*, 12 June 1977, p. 5.
38. Finance Committee, 23 Feb 1937, 24 Feb 1938, 7 Mar 1939.
39. Ibid., 7 Mar 1935.
40. K. A. Ditterich (Accountant 1969–90), letter to Mallesons, 27 Sept 1977. Mallesons had become the school's solicitors in this matter because Blake & Riggall experienced a conflict of interest, being also solicitors to the church.
41. Healey to J. C. Kelso (1947), 8 Nov 1965.
42. Glenn, interview with author, 20 Feb 1998.
43. 'Scotch College Endowment Fund Appeal by Council and Old Boys', *Collegian*, Dec 1954, p. 182.
44. P. D. Craw and J. C. Moyle, *Collegian*, May 1951. p. 7a.
45. Rev. A. R. Macneil, *Scotch College Melbourne Divine Service in the Memorial Hall ... 18th October, 1931*.
46. 'Scotch College Council report to Assembly—1965'.

47. Elias, *Australian*, 12 June 1977, p. 5.
48. Baker, *Age*, 8 June 1977, p. 5.
49. D. S. W. Reid (1962–67), Q.
50. Bayston, interview with Tolson, 17 Aug 1992.
51. Council, 27 July 1977, and Glenn and Bethell, 'Dear Member of the Scotch Family', 13 Sept 1978.
52. Council, 25 May 1977.
53. Glenn, interview with author, 20 Feb 1998.
54. Glenn, letter to parents, 12 July 1977. Glenn and Bethell, 'Dear Member of the Scotch Family', 13 Sept 1978.
55. Council, 8 June 1977.
56. B. J. Shaw and R. A. Sundberg, 'In the supreme court 1977 no 3271', Scotch's case.
57. D. E. Johnston (1960–68), Q.
58. L. M. Muir (1937–42), letter to author, July 1999.
59. Council, 8 June 1977.
60. Foundation, Board of Trustees, 1 July 1977
61. Foundation, Exec. of Board of Trustees, 16 Dec 1977.
62. J. H. Ramsay, letter to the Trustees, 18 June 1977.
63. O. V. A. Nilsen, letter to B. S. Stillwell, 31 May 1977.
64. Council, 19 Apr 1978.
65. E&F Committee, 12 Feb 1979.
66. I. C. Mackenzie (1972–82), email to author, 21 July 1999.
67. R. L. Hyams (1969–80), letter to author, 2 Feb 1999.
68. R. L. Price (1974–79), letter to author, 6 May 1999.
69. B. D. Bayston, 'Memorandum ... submitted to the Commission of Assembly of the Presbyterian Church of Victoria, meeting in September 1992', quoting from Psalm 124.
70. A. R. Lobban, 'Incorporation of Schools', Council, 25 Oct 1978, attachment.
71. 'The incorporation of former Presbyterian schools' an agreed statement by the nine former Presbyterian schools.
72. Lobban, 'Incorporation of Schools'.
73. E&F Committee, 9 Oct 1978.
74. Healey to Bethell, 18 Sept 1978.
75. E&F Committee, 9 Oct 1978. Council, 25 Oct 1978. Old Boy (1938), letter to Bursar, 18 Sept 1978.
76. Glenn and Bethell, 'Dear Member of the Scotch Family', 13 Sept 1978.

77. E. R. Love (1929), letter to Glenn, 18 Sept 1978.
78. D. U. Macintosh (1922), letter to Glenn, 19 Sept 1978.
79. C. L. S. Hewitt, letter to Glenn, 10 Oct 1978.
80. B. K. Rank, letter to Glenn, 18 Sept 1978.
81. Council, 21 Oct 1979.
82. Ibid.
83. Ibid.
84. Ibid.
85. Council, 27 July 1950.
86. R. B. Negri, letter to Glenn, 8 Oct 1978.
87. A. C. Millar, letter to Glenn, 23 June 1980.
88. Council, 30 May 1984.
89. Glenn, Lithgow and Roff, letter to parents and Old Boys, 24 Mar 1980.
90. Untitled document beginning 'The nine former Presbyterian Schools welcome the suggestion that… ', Council, 28 Oct 1979, attachment.
91. Glenn, interview with author, 20 Feb 1998.
92. Bayston, interview with Tolson, 17 Aug 1992.
93. E&F Committee, 14 May 1979. E. R. Pearsons, letter to Glenn, 19 Dec 1979.
94. Mallesons, 12 Sept 1979, 'Summary of [Searby's] opinion', point B.2.
95. Bayston, interview with Tolson, 17 Aug 1992.
96. Ibid.
97. Glenn, interview with author, 20 Feb 1998.
98. Council, 3 Mar 1980.

18 Roff's fall

1. G. D Fisher (1929–41), letter to author, 5 Jan 2000; L. C. Birch (1925–35), note to author, June 1999.
2. R. D. Fincher (1956–59), email to author, 16 June 1999.
3. Glenn, Council, 27 May 1980.
4. Bayston, interview with Tolson, 17 Aug 1992. Glenn, interview with Tolson, 5 May 1990.
5. Mrs Catharine Pye, 23 June 1980.
6. G. R. Sellars-Jones, letter to Glenn, 20 June 1980
7. Ibid., 5 June 1980.
8. G. J. Howe, Chairman of Scotch Association, letter to Council, 23 June 1980.
9. Mappin, letter to Glenn, 28 June 1980.
10. Chairman of the Conference, letter to Glenn, 20 June 1980.
11. Howe, letter to Glenn, 23 June 1980.
12. Sue Green, 'Principal quits stormy Scotch', Age, 13 Aug 1981, p. 1.
13. J. T. McIlwraith, letter to Glenn, 10 June 1980.
14. M. R. G. Stening (1980), letter to Glenn, 25 June 1980.
15. Sellars-Jones, letter to Glenn, 5 June 1980.
16. P. J. E. Long (1980), letter to Glenn, 24 June 1980.
17. G. H. Spence, L. Spence, letter to The Secretary, Scotch College, 24 June 1980.
18. C. P. Latham, letter to Glenn, 30 May 1980.
19. P. L. Crook, letter to Glenn, 6 June 2000.
20. W. B. Holly, letter to Glenn, 30 May 1980.
21. P. J. Anthony, letter to Glenn, 24 June 1980.
22. A. J. M. Eggleston, letter to Glenn, 24 June 1980.
23. Ibid.
24. Mappin, letter to Glenn, 28 June 1980.
25. Glenn, letter to Crozier, 20 June 1980.
26. S. E. K. Hulme, 'Employment of Headmaster', 23 June 1980, and 'Scotch College Employment of Headmaster', 23 June 1980, Council, 25 June 1980, attachments.
27. Glenn, interview with author, 20 Feb 1998.
28. Scotch College, Articles of Association, art. 55.
29. Development Committee report, Council, 10 Mar 1981, attachment.
30. J. D. McCaughey, interview with author, 21 Oct 1998.
31. C. O. Healey, letter to I. Ling, 10 Dec 1974.
32. Council, 30 June 1982.
33. Bayston, note to author, June 1999. Similarly, S. Green, 'Church tightens grip on schools', Age, 16 Sept 1981, p. 26.
34. The Headmastership of Scotch College Melbourne, Australia. Conditions of Appointment [Melbourne, 1974], p. 2.
35. Roff, interview with author, 8 Dec 1998.
36. Ibid.
37. Glenn, interview with Tolson, 5 May 1990.
38. Glenn, note to author, 26 July 1999.
39. Roff, 'Address to the Junior School Mothers' Association', 18 Sept 1975.
40. Rev. P. K. Melville, 'Visit to U.K. 1972–3', Study Leave Report.
41. Roff, interview with author, 8 Dec 1998.
42. Ibid.
43. J. D. McCaughey, interview with author, 21 Oct 1998.
44. Roff, Annual Report, 1979.
45. R. L. Price (1974–79), Q.
46. K. Thomas (1962–67), Q.
47. Roff, interview with author, 8 Dec 1998
48. A. S. Thomson (1972–77), Q.
49. J. A. Lyne, interview with author, 30 Apr 1998.
50. Respondent 77 (1948), Q, letter to author, 7 Oct 1998. McInnes, Road to Gundagai, p. 97. Respondent 245 (1963), Q
51. I. R. Marks (1950–54), letter to author, 26 Feb 1999.
52. W. N. Hurst (1939–50), 10 Feb 1998. Respondent 22 (1950), Respondent 278 (1968), Respondent 156 (1969), Respondent 79 (1972), Respondent 160 (1975), C. B. Mackey (1970–75), QQ.
53. Roff, interview with author, 8 Dec 1998.
54. Ibid.
55. Ibid.
56. I. H. Beattie, interview with author, 7 Apr 1998.
57. Roff, note to author, 12 Sept 1999.
58. G. P. Mackenzie (1949), Achurch's solicitor, email to author, 13 Nov 2000.
59. Roff, interview with author, 8 Dec 1998.
60. Lyne, interview with author, 30 Apr 1998.
61. J. A. Blanch, 'Information for Council members concerning current school difficulties', typed, [1979?], Addendum.
62. I. C. Mackenzie (1972–82), email to author, 21 July 1999.
63. J. T. Collins, diary, 28 Mar 1927.
64. Ibid., 1927, passim.
65. Roff, report to Council, 27 Oct 1976
66. Glenn, interview with Tolson, 8 May 1990.
67. Glenn, interview with author, 20 Feb 1998.
68. Ibid.
69. Roff, interview with author, 8 Dec 1998.

70. Glenn, interview with Tolson, 8 May 1990.
71. Bayston, interview with Tolson, 17 Aug 1992.
72. Roff, interviews with author, 8 Dec 1998, 7 Dec 1999.
73. Roff, interview with author, 8 Dec 1998.
74. Council, 23 Nov 1981.
75. Roff, interview with author, 8 Dec 1998.
76. Green, 'Church tightens grip', p. 26.
77. R. M. Northrop, letter to the Bursar, 2 Sept 1981.
78. Foundation, Exec. of Board of Trustees, 1 Oct 1981.

19 Donaldson

1. Addressing the Junior School Mothers' Association, 3 May 1983.
2. Donaldson, *Satura*, no. 3, 1998, p. 11.
3. Donaldson, interview with author, 31 Mar 1998.
4. Donaldson, report to Council, 27 Apr 1983.
5. Ibid.
6. Wirth, report to Council, 12 Oct 1983.
7. Donaldson, interview with author, 31 Mar 1998. Donaldson, report to Council, 31 Oct 1984.
8. Donaldson, interview with author, 31 Mar 1998.
9. Ibid.
10. Wirth, report to Council, Apr 1983.
11. Ibid., 31 Oct 1984.
12. Ibid., July 1983.
13. Tapp, report to Council, 22 July 1973. Wirth, report to Council, 20 Oct 1977.
14. Donaldson, report to Council, 31 Oct 1984.
15. Ibid.
16. Donaldson, *Collegian*, 1987, p. 24.
17. C. A. Widdis (1983–90), email to author, 23 Aug 2000.
18. K. A. Foletta (1961–65), Q.
19. Healey, report to Council, 28 Apr 1971.
20. S. A. Ritchie, email to author, 20 June 2000.
21. 'Report of meeting held on 7th November, 1984, between members of the School Council and members of the Committee set up by the Scotch Association to examine the idea of establishing a Scotch College Parents' Association.'
22. Donaldson, report to Council, 25 July 1984.

23. Ibid., 5 Dec 1984.
24. Ibid., 5 Dec, 31 Oct 1984.
25. *Great Scot*, 51 (1989), p. 21.
26. Donaldson, Annual Report 1991, *Collegian*, 1991, p. 16.
27. *Great Scot*, 66 (1993), p. 21, and 67 (1993), p. 33.
28. J. G. Cromie (1959–70), email to author, 29 Mar 1999.
29. Wirth, report to Council, 10 Nov 1982.
30. Ibid., Apr 1983.
31. Baker, HOD, 22 May 1990.
32. D. L. Scott, 'Report … on new physics buildings and facilities seen in the United States and the United Kingdom. Period of leave: May 8 to September 6, 1971', p. 9.
33. CRA Education Subcommittee, 25 Feb 1974.
34. A. R. Watkinson, interview with author, 24 Mar 1998.
35. Donaldson, report to Council, 25 July 1984.
36. *Collegian*, 1987, p. 141.
37. Ibid., 1998, p. 72.
38. G. M. Bradbeer, ibid., 1989, p. 23.
39. *Collegian*, 1998, p. 72.
40. 'Guide to Scotch College— Supplement', photocopied page in Staff Manual, [1984].
41. Donaldson, report to Council, 24 July 1986.
42. GHC, 27 Oct 1983.
43. Ibid.
44. Donaldson, 'The General House Committee Purpose, Structure and Method of Operation', 1 Mar 1983.
45. Donaldson, Annual Report 1998, *Collegian*, 1998, p. 8.
46. Donaldson, interview with author, 31 Mar 1998. Donaldson, report to Council, 27 Apr 1983.
47. Maclennan, Acting Junior School Headmaster's report to Council, 30 July 1986.
48. Wirth, report to Council, Apr 1983.
49. Donaldson, report to Council, 25 July 1984.
50. Donaldson, 'School Circular No. 2. Dances and Parties', Mar 1984.
51. Donaldson, report to Council, 25 July 1984.
52. 'The life of Noel', in '1985 The year and the men who made it', [School House] pink, laser-printed, stapled.
53. Donaldson, report to Council, 25 July 1984.
54. Healey, report to Council, 29 Apr 1970, 28 July 1971.

55. A. Hartman (1965–70), email to author, 4 May 1999.
56. Donaldson, report to Council, 31 July 1985.
57. Ibid.
58. Ibid.
59. Blazey, *Screw loose*, p. 233.
60. Council, 29 May 1985.
61. Donaldson, *Satura*, no. 3, 1998, p. 11.

20 The 1980 Settlement in practice

1. Scotch College, Articles of Association, art. 60.
2. Council, 23 July 1980.
3. Ibid., 28 Apr 1982.
4. B. D. Bayston, interview with G. S. Tolson, 17 Aug 1992.
5. E&F Committee, 16 Sept 1985.
6. Scotch College, Articles of Association, art. 32.
7. OSCA let Council make the choice, Council, 7 Mar 1980.
8. Quoted in Sue Green, 'Church veto on Scotch College appointment', *Age*, 15 Sept 1981, p. 3. See also S. Green, 'Church tightens grip on schools', *Age*, 16 Sept 1981, p. 26.
9. Pritchard, emails to author, 12, 18 Oct 2000.
10. Green, 'Church tightens grip on schools'.
11. Ibid. Councils (plural) refers to those of Scotch and PLC.
12. W. S. Tingate (1955), letter to the Moderator, Rev. C. A. Harrison (1940), 7 Oct 1981.
13. Bayston, interview with Tolson, 17 Aug 1992.
14. Rev. N. M. Pritchard, letter to Rev. E. R. Pearsons, 25 Aug 1981.
15. Sir Thomas Ramsay (1924), Vice–Chairman of Foundation, letter to Moderator designate, 30 Sept 1981.
16. Council, Special Meeting, 16 Sept 1985.
17. B. D. Bayston, 'Memorandum … submitted to the Commission of Assembly of the Presbyterian Church of Victoria, meeting in September 1992'.
18. Council, 21 Oct 1992.
19. B. D. Bayston, letter to Sir James Balderstone, 1 Mar 1989.
20. Scotch College, Articles of Association, art. 33 (3).
21. Ibid., art. 33 (5).
22. Ibid., art. 33 (6).
23. Donaldson, interview with author, 30 May 2000.

24. E&F Committee, 11 Nov 1991.
25. Scotch College, Memorandum of Association, art. 2.
26. Scotch College, Articles of Association, art. 71.
27. Glenn, interview with author, 20 Feb 1998.
28. Scotch College, Memorandum of Association, art. 3 (1) (a).
29. Ibid.
30. J. G. Hiller (1985–96), email to author, 20 Apr 2000.
31. T. J. Cade (2000), interview with author, 1 June 1999.
32. G. J. Carrick (1929–35), letter to author, 9 Nov 1999. G. D Fisher (1929–41), letter to author, 5 Jan 2000.
33. J. G. Hiller (1985–96), email to author, 6 Sept 2000.
34. G. D. Fisher (1929–41), letter to author, 5 Jan 2000.
35. A. G Walkom (Captain 1995), advice to A. T. Simm (Captain 1996).
36. T. C. C. Downing (Captain 1999), 'Notes for 2000 School Captain—Tom Cade'.
37. G. B. Lyman, email to author, 2 March 1999.
38. D. C. Ginn (1992), Great Scot, 83 (1997), p. 5.
39. Tapp, Junior School Mothers' Association, 12 Nov 1964.
40. Quoting from an unnamed school chaplain, The Independent Schools of Australia (Current Affairs Bulletin, vol. 21, no. 3, Dec 1957), p. 39.
41. Young Victoria, 13 (1879), p. 189.
42. Age, 5 Nov 1926.
43. S. A. [S. Atchison (1888)], Collegian, 1905, p. 59.
44. G. G. Powell (1929), 'The Courage of James Forbes', Collegian, Dec 1967, pp. 126–8.
45. Donaldson, letter to H. Ingram, 3 June 1985.
46. J. R. Buchanan (Chaplain 1992–), 'Victorian by name, Victorian by nature. A preliminary investigation into the decline of the Presbyterian Church of Victoria with suggestions on how this decline may be arrested', M.Ed thesis 1999, University of Melbourne, p. 49.
47. Great Scot, 83 (1997), p. 2.

21 Recent years

1. G. T. Nowacki, letter to author, 4 Sept 2000.
2. D. Barrie (1990–95), emails to author, 10 Apr, 11 Aug 2000.
3. J. G. Hiller (1985–96), email to author, 20 Apr 2000.
4. J. Macdonald (1991–96), Q.
5. Healey, 'Introductory talk at the Seminar of Masters and Senior Boys at Scotch College September 9th, 1974', p. 4.
6. A. R. Watkinson, departmental report sheet, 3 May 1988.
7. Roff, report to Council, 27 May 1980; 'a Middle (or Transition) School'.
8. Roff, report to Council, 27 Oct 1976. D. R. Gibbs, note to author, Aug 2000.
9. Roff, report to Council, 30 July 1975.
10. E&F Committee, 30 May 1972.
11. Donaldson, comment on Blackburn Report, report to Council, 29 May 1985. The E&F Committee, 30 May 1972, wondered if there should be a separate sixth-form establishment.
12. A. R. Watkinson, interview with author, 24 Mar 1998.
13. GHC, 27 Mar 1980.
14. H. R. Taylor (1953–64), Q.
15. G. B. Lyman (1977–79), email to author, 2 Mar 1999.
16. M. A. Macmillan (staff 1995–2000), written in 1999.
17. C. A. Widdis (1983–90), email to author, 23 Aug 2000.
18. K. R. Clayton, note to author, 24 Aug 2000.
19. S. G Boydell, interview with author, 3 Mar 1999.
20. H. R. Taylor (1953–64), Q.
21. S. D. Kunstler (1970–75), Q.
22. D. G. Paul, note to author, 3 Oct 2000.
23. D. G. Paul, conversation with author, 3 Oct 2000.
24. Donaldson, Annual Report 1989, Collegian, 1989, p. 8. Great Scot, 56 (1990), p. 2
25. D. G. Paul and B. R. Stewardson, emails to author, 24 Apr, 18 Nov 2000.
26. Donaldson, report to Council, 25 July 1984.
27. Ibid., 5 Dec 1984, attachment.
28. HOD, 30 Oct 1990.
29. C. A. Widdis (1983–90), Q.
30. R. Browne, 'Scotch College. Report. December 1999', p. 8.
31. Donaldson, Annual Report 1991, Collegian, 1991, p. 8.
32. Ibid., p. 5.
33. F. W. Paton (1958–63), Q.
34. C. A. Blair, Collegian, 1989, p. 157.
35. B. R. Mann, 'My lifetime hobby', OTN, The Journal of the radio Amateur Old Timers' club of Australia, no 13, Sept 1994, pp. 14–15.
36. Lyne, 'Scotch College, 1942–74'.
37. J. K. Fullagar, 'Fifty years on—1939 Ninth Form Re-union Dinner', 1989.
38. R. D. Fincher (1956–59), Q.
39. Collegian, Dec 1957, p. 112.
40. J. Cromie (1959–70), Q.
41. Donaldson, interview with author, 16 May 2000.
42. D. G. Paul, email to author, 24 July 2000.
43. D. R. Gibbs, email to author, 13 Nov 2000.
44. Roff, 'Address to the Junior School Mothers' Association', 18 Sept 1975.
45. D. G. Paul, note to author, 15 Mar 2000.
46. Donaldson, Great Scot, 82 (1999), p. 3.
47. J. A. Sinclair, Collegian, 1987, pp. 103–4.
48. Budget and Superannuation Committee, 15 Nov 1984.
49. Satura, 28 Mar 1956, p. 5.
50. R. N. Swann (1956–60), Q.
51. M. A. McKenzie (1939–47), Q.
52. Blue card.
53. A. R. Moodie, email to author, 5 Sept 2000.
54. J. P. Andrew (1990), email to D. E. McC. Hunter, 26 Oct 2000.
55. I. J. Savage, email to author, 21 Aug 2000.
56. J. C. H. Spence (1964), email to author, 17 July 2000.
57. GHC, 4 Apr 1976.
58. W. Walker (1970–75), Q.
59. N. A. S. Brand (1977), letter to Donaldson, 20 Jan 1997.
60. J. G. Hiller (1985–96), email to author, 20 Apr 2000.
61. Ibid.

22 Being a man

1. Morrison, Annual Report, 1869, p. 9.
2. Young Victoria, 2 (Sept 1877), p. 13.
3. Littlejohn, Testimonial for T. M. Ramsay, 8 Mar 1926.
4. Satura, 17 Apr 1958, p. 10.
5. Collegian, 1978, p. 52.
6. Ling, CRA Education Committee, 29 May 1972.
7. W. A. Fraser, Divine Service in the Memorial Hall … 19th October, 1947.
8. R. I. Scambler (1991), Morrison House notes, Collegian, 1991, p. 91.

L. B. Sher (1998), ibid., 1998, p. 108.

K. A. Bhardwaj (1998), ibid., p. 105.

9. L. G. Rattray, email to author, 24 Aug 2000.

10. A. E. Buck and A. N. Jamieson, Editors, 'The Class of 1991', *Collegian*, 1991, p. 46.

11. G. B. Lyman (1977–79), Q.

12. J. G. Hiller (1985–96), email to author, 6 Sept 2000.

13. Donaldson, Annual Report 1999, *Collegian*, 1999, p. 8.

14. R. Browne, 'Scotch College. Report. December 1999', p. 34, Suggested Action N° (x).

15. A. O. Rentoul, 'Editorial', *Collegian*, 1905, p. 69.

16. *Collegian*, 1917, p. 205.

17. B. C. Fuller, *Collegian*, 1905, p. 42.

18. C. J. Hayes (staff 1979–   ), email to author, 14 June 2000.

19. J. G. Hiller (1996), email to author, 6 Sept 2000.

20. C. A. Widdis (1983–90), email to author, 23 Aug 2000

21. Healey, 'Towards a school community', pp. 8–9.

22. J. B. Cumming (1957–67), email to author, 8 Dec 2000.

23. W. J. Simpson, email to author, 1 June 1999.

24. D. J. Gay (1934–35), Q.

25. Morrison, *Annual Report, 1868*, p. 8.

26. *Rules for the guidance of pupils attending the Scotch College*, [1867?], rule 24.

27. Davies, *Fiddlers of Drummond*, pp. 37–8.

28. F. I. R. Martin (1939–47), Q.

29. W. Norris (1942–45), letter to G. S. Tolson, 3 Oct 1992, p. 5.

30. D. McK. Sharpe (1942–49), Q.

31. F. G. Boyes (1941–51), Q.

32. M. J. Edwards (1967–70), Q.

33. B. D. Bayston (1936–48), Q.

34. Prefects' Meeting, 7 July 1966.

35. Ibid., 10 Aug 1967, 21 June 1968.

36. M. J. Edwards (1967–70), Q.

37. *Collegian*, 1909, pp. 15–16; 1910, p. 118; 1911, pp. 4, 15, 17; 1912, pp. 13, 15

38. *Collegian*, 1919, p. 28; 1920, pp. 33, 139.

39. G. D. Fisher (1929–41), letter to author, 5 Jan 2000.

40. Healey, unsigned pencilled note on the blue card of the Patrol Leader whom he censured for not interfering.

41. K. W. Fisher, interview with author, 23 May 2000.

42. Hexadec, 'Peer relations assessment', November 2000.

43. *Collegian*, 1910, p. 115.

44. N. Leybourne-Ward (1941–42), Q. Lyne, 'Scotch College, 1942–74'. W. H. Callister (1936–41), letter to author, 4 Nov 1998. W. G. Pugh (1947–51), letter to author, June 1999. S. F. Macintyre (1959–64), comment to History Committee, 31 Aug 2000.

45. I. R. Roper (1950–52), Q.

46. J. D. McCaughey, 'Final summing up', 'Report on the Seminar of masters and Sixth Form boys held on Monday 11th September [1972] to discuss the care of boys exercised at Scotch College', p. 8.

47. Healey, 'Report on the Seminar of masters and Sixth Form boys held on Monday 11th September [1972] to discuss the care of boys exercised at Scotch College'.

48. Browne, 'Scotch College. Report. December 1999', section 3.3.1(ii)

49. M. J. Edwards (1967–70), email to author, 24 Nov 1999.

50. D. S. W. Reid (1962–67), Q.

51. N. McH. Ramsey (1934–41), Q.

52. Respondent 38 (1929), G. I. Hynam (1928–36), D. C. McClean (1943–52), I. C. Teague (1947–52), A. T. Hamley (1953–57), F. Macrae (1956–67), R. A. Jacobson (1966–70), W. R. Fleming (1969–76), R. L. Hyams (1969–80), J. Macdonald (1991–96), QQ. J. H. C. Nairn (1943–55), email to author, 16 Apr 1999. M. W. Reid (1953–58), letter to author, 19 Apr 1999.

53. J. A. Goldsmith (1949–51), Q.

54. J. B. Cumming (1957–67), Q.

55. Ibid.

56. D. G. Batten (1943–46), Q.

57. K. A. Foletta (1961–64), Q.

58. R. W. McDonald (1943–44), Q.

59. M. E. Scott (1944–54), Q.

60. *Great Scot*, 66 (1993), p. 11.

61. D. B. Telfer (1969–74), email to author, 3 July 1999.

62. Year 7 comment 1990, recorded by D. G. Paul.

63. C. A. Widdis (1983–90), email to author, 23 Aug 2000.

64. D. Barrie (1990–95), email to author, 7 Sept 2000.

65. Donaldson, Annual Report 1989, *Collegian*, 1989, p. 10, and see p. 15.

66. M. R. Bell, ibid., pp. 75–8.

67. A. C. Green, Lawson House notes, *Collegian*, 1991, p. 88.

68. B. W. Anderson, Selby Smith House notes, *Collegian*, 1989, p. 161.

69. D. McWilliams, Gilray House notes, C. W. Johnston, Littlejohn House notes, J. C. Perelberg, Morrison House notes, *Collegian*, 1990, pp. 89, 91, 93.

70. *Collegian*, 1998, p. 51.

71. See Donaldson, Annual Report 1990, p. 9.

72. A. O. Jones (1957–62), Q.

73. C. M. A. Power (staff 1975–90), *Collegian*, 1989, p. 25.

74. M. W. Reid (1953–58), letter to author, 11 March 1999.

75. D. S. W. Reid (1962–67), Q.

76. D. Barrie (1990–95), Q.

77. W. R. Winspear (1985–96), Q.

78. B. L. Adams (1939–43), Q.

79. D. O. Shave (1946–52), Q.

80. Ibid.

81. A. H. Tucker (1987–92), Q.

82. Melville, Study leave report, 1974.

83. P. Howe (1975–80), Q.

84. J. Duband (1977–80), Q.

85. R. L. Hyams (1969–80), Q.

86. J. E. H. Harkness (1990–96), Q.

87. R. D. Fincher (1956–59), email to author, 28 Apr 1999.

88. Ferguson, email to author, 11 April 2000.

89. M. A. Macmillan, written in 1999.

90. Education Subcommittee, 4 June 1974.

91. Donaldson, Annual Report 1989, *Collegian*, 1989, p. 3.

92. McCaughey, phone call to author, 16 June 2000, Bayston, letter to author, 13 June 2000.

93. Littlejohn, *Annual Report*, 1927, p. 2.

94. Davies, *Fiddlers of Drummond*, p. 75.

95. Bremner, '1929 A very good year', on his 15th birthday.

96. *Collegian*, June 1954, p. 21.

97. K. A. Foletta (1961–65), Q.

98. Lyne, 'Scotch College, 1942–74'.

99. W. G. Pugh (1947–51), letter to author, 17 March 1999.

100. J. B. Pettigrew (1932–34), letter to author, 17 Sept 1998.

101. *Satura*, 29 March 1963, p. 2.

102. Prefects Book, 6 Apr 1936.

103. H. R. Taylor (1953–64), Q.

104. *Satura*, 12 Aug, Oct 1963, p. 2.

105. Roff, report to Council, 26 July 1978.

106. A. O. Jones (1957–62), Q and letter

to author, August 1999.

107. D. J. Ashton (1953–65), Q.

108. W. J. W. McAuley (1965–69), Q.

109. *Satura*, 17 March 1965, p. 4.

110. W. H. Callister (1936–41), Q.

111. B. A. Johns (1946–55), Q.

112. R. J. McLaren, written 14 Oct 1999.

113. Donaldson, Annual Report 1998, *Collegian*, 1998, p. 6.

114. Scotch-at-Cowes Parents' Auxiliary, General Meeting, 10 Oct 1979.

115. Scotch-at-Cowes Parents' Auxiliary, Minute Book, 1975. My italics.

116. K. A. Foletta (1961–65), Q.

117. *Satura*, 28 March 1956, p. 7.

118. *Young Victoria*, 5 (1878), p. 59. Selby Smith, report to Council, 26 June 1963.

119. GHC, 26 March, 4 June 1981. R. J. Grant, 'General House Committee Rifle Shooting as a Sport,' [1981].

120. GHC, 8 May 1973, attachment.

121. Ibid.

122. *Satura*, 24 October 1956, p. 4.

123. A. McV. L. Campbell, diary, 10 May 1928.

124. A. O. Dixon and N. J. Radford, Editorial, *Collegian*, June 1959, p. 4.

125. R. Stummer (staff 1992–99), Campbell House notes, *Collegian*, 1996, p. 54.

126. Littlejohn, *Annual Report*, 1908, p. 10.

127. A. S. Anderson (1909), interview with H. Webster, 1968.

128. Littlejohn, *Annual Report*, 1924, p. 12.

129. Ingram, 'Public schools in a changing age'.

130. *Collegian*, 1909, p. 18.

131. *Satura*, 12 July 1963, p. 9.

132. *Satura*, 17 March 1965, p. 17.

133. D. J. G. Cameron (1944–45), R. A. W. Wade (1946–49), QQ. J. K. Dempster (1939–50), letter to author, 16 June 1999.

134. W. L. Sides (1960–64), Q.

135. 'Report of working-group on staff/student relationships' [1979].

136. R. Mollison (1981), Q.

137. J. E. H. Harkness (1990–96), S. O'Byrne (1985–92), QQ.

138. J. G. Hiller (1996), email to author, 30 April 2000.

139. *Great Scot*, 67 (1993), p. 8.

140. *Collegian*, 1990, p. 80.

141. *Great Scot*, 63 (1992), p. 4.

142. Ibid.

143. Bremner, '1929 A very good year'.

144. A. O. Jones (1957–62), letter to author, Aug 1999.

145. *Collegian*, 1989, p. 39, photograph.

146. *Great Scot*, 63 (1992), p. 3.

147. Ibid., 54 (1990), p. 15.

148. 1971 and 1972 in 'Scotch-at-Cowes Reference Book 1967– '.

149. Scotch-at-Cowes Parents' Auxiliary, General Meeting, 10 Oct 1979.

150. 1974 in 'Scotch-at-Cowes Reference Book 1967– '.

151. 1973, ibid.

152. Minute Book Scotch-at-Cowes Parents' Auxiliary, 1981.

153. Fay Leong, email to author, 22 May 2000.

154. Donaldson, interview with author, 25 May 1999.

Conclusion

1. See G. J. Prestegar, curator from 1985, *Great Scot*, 62 (1992), p. 24.

2. T. J. Cade (1994-2000), interview with author, 1 June 1999.

3. Annual Report 1998, *Collegian*, 1998, p. 6.

4. R. S. Bond, *Great Scot*, 41 (1986), p. 4.

5. R. G. Abbey (1956–59), Q.

6. I. C. Mackenzie (1972–82), Q.

7. D. W. J. Aitchison (1932–45), letter to author, Feb 1999.

8. R. F. Dillon (1962–65), Q.

9. G. F. Cadogan-Cowper (1954–58), Q

10. G. I. Anderson (1928–32), Q.

11. A. T. Hamley (1953–57), Q.

12. A. Mackenzie (1971–83), Q.

BRIEF BIBLIOGRAPHY

For reasons of space this bibliography omits most sources that are from within the school and cited in full in the endnotes, such as interviews, letters, testimonials, personal reports, items in the school's publications, and the minutes and papers of the school's committees and associate organisations. It omits, similarly, the school's publications: *Annual Reports, Great Scot, Great Shot: Scotch College Weekly Basketball Review, Scotch Collegian, Satura, Scotch Broth, Scotch College Rugby Club, Scout Scoops,* the official organ of the *1st Hawthorn Scout Group,* the *Yellow Sheet* later the *Scotch Association News. An information bulletin for parents,* and *Young Victoria.*

Rather, for unpublished material it lists, chiefly, items cited more than once.

UNPUBLISHED MATERIAL

ACNielsen Research Pty Ltd, 'Outcomes of Schooling Report (draft)', February 1999.

Anderson, A. S., 'Appeal Dinner, 1962'.

——, speaker's notes for OSCA Annual Dinner, 1948 or 1949.

——, speaker's notes to Junior School Mothers' Association, 5 October 1950.

Bremner, G. A., '1929 A very good year: Reminiscences 1929–1932', typed.

Browne, Rollo, 'Scotch College. Report. December 1999'.

Buchanan, J. R., 'Victorian by name, Victorian by nature. A preliminary investigation into the decline of the Presbyterian Church of Victoria with suggestions on how this decline may be arrested', M.Ed, thesis, 1999, University of Melbourne.

Campbell, A. MacV. L., diaries, 1927–29.

Campbell, J. L. M., 'Some unedifying recollections of Eastern Hill', typed.

Cardell, K. and C. Cumming, 'North Eastern Presbyterians and colonial education: James Forbes and the Port Phillip District' (typescript).

Collins, J. T., diaries, 1925–27.

Donaldson, F. G., 'The General House Committee Purpose, Structure and method of operation', 1 March 1983.

——, 'School Circular No. 2. Dances and Parties', March 1984.

Eggleston, A. J. M., 'Report [to the Senior Masters' Committee] of 5th Form General Studies Sub-committee' [November 1972].

Field, K. F., 'Bursar's Leave of Absence—June–November, 1970', roneoed report.

Foletta, K.A., 'Before it all', unpublished MS.

Free Church of Australia Felix, synod, minutes, 1847–50.

Free Church of Scotland, Colonial Committee, minutes, 1850–51.

Free Presbyterian Church of Victoria, synod, minutes, 1850–67; presbytery, minutes 1854–59.

Fullagar, J. K., 'Fifty years on—1939 Ninth Form Re-union Dinner', 1989.

Healey, C. O., 'All masters in the Senior School. On Friday 17th June 1966 there will be a meeting for parents ...', May, 1966; circular.

——, Annual Newsletter.

——, 'Comments on Scotch College by Mr. Wayne Frederick [exchange teacher] of Phillips Academy, Andover, Mass., U.S.A., May 1971'.

——, 'Conscription and Vietnam', April 1966.

——, 'Draft of speech to be delivered on 22nd July, 1967'.

——, *A Guide to Scotch College,* [1972].

——, 'Introductory talk at the Seminar of Masters and Senior Boys at Scotch College September 9th, 1974'.

——, Memoirs, unpublished MS.

——, 'On writing reports', undated, roneoed.

——, 'Proposals for improving the House system', January 1965, roneoed.

——, 'Questions for our consideration', August 1968, roneoed.

——, 'Questions for Senior Day-Housemasters and division masters', May 1972, roneoed.

——, 'Report on the Seminar of masters and Sixth Form boys held on Monday 11th September [1972] to discuss the care of boys exercised at Scotch College'.

——, 'School Officers', February 1965; roneoed.

——, 'Scotch College. The following are the uses to which Scotch College buildings, grounds …', [1973?].

——, 'The Day-Boy Houses. 1971', roneoed.

——, 'The House System', Sept 1965, roneoed.

——, 'To English Masters English Expression', March 1971, roneoed.

——, 'Towards a school community', unpublished MS.

Hexadec, 'Peer relations assessment', November 2000.

Lyne, J. A., 'Memories of Scotch College 1924–28', unpublished MS.

——, 'Scotch College 1942–1974', unpublished MS.

MacKinnon, K. P., 'Scotch College … A summary of some of the documents held by the Victorian Public Record Office relating to requests for Land grants and Government financial support'.

Norris, W., diaries, 1942–44.

Paul, D.G., Annual Seminar, 10 September 1973.

——, 'Annual staff-student seminar', 6 September 1976

——, 'Annual Staff-Student Sixth Form Seminar … The expectations of Sixth Formers at Scotch; and the Extent to which they are unsatisfied', 29 May 1978

——, 'Concerning proposals to introduce General Studies into the curriculum at Scotch College—with special emphasis on the contribution of and effect on the teaching of history', MS [1972?].

——, MS notes of Annual Staff-Student Sixth Form Seminar 29 May 1978.

——, Notes of Master Sixth Form Seminar, 10 September 1973.

——, 'Report on staff/senior students' seminar. September 1975'.

——, 'Report on staff-student Seminar 5th September 1977'.

——, 'Report on staff/student 5th Form Seminar: "Choice & Compulsion in the school environment"', 10 September 1979.

——, 'Scotch College—Commonroom Association. Report of Education Committee Conference held on 13.9.71'.

——, 'Summary of Staff-Student Fifth Form Seminar … "Control and Freedom at Scotch College"', 11 September 1978.

——, 'The Fifth and Sixth as Years of Transition', typed speaker's notes, 1971.

Presbyterian Church, Minutes 1857–64, 1872–83, of what is called variously the Education Committee, the College Committee, the Committee of the Scotch College, and the Scotch College Committee 1872–83, and some meetings of its sub-committees.

'Report on the Seminar of masters and Sixth Form boys held on Monday 11th September [1972] to discuss the care of boys exercised at Scotch College'.

Roff, P. A. V., 'The General House Committee Purpose, Structure and method of operation', December 1979.

——, 'Note to Monash House masters and House tutors', 6 November 1978.

——, 'Outdoor activities—Safety Committee', 29 June 1981, in 'Staff Manual', Section B. 18.

Scotch College, Staff Manual (comprising numbered roneoed circulars in the 1980s).

——, Cadet Unit Handbook, 1982.

Scott, D. L., 'To the Principal and Council of Scotch College. Report from D.L. Scott on new physics buildings and facilities seen in the United States and the United Kingdom. Period of leave: May 8 to September 6, 1971'.

Selby Smith, R., 'Memorandum on Future Development', 24 June 1959.

——, 'Memorandum on future development', 29 June 1960.

——, 'Memorandum: The proposed Oakleigh Freeway', 4 July 1960.

——, 'Notes on the need for an improved Tuckshop in the Senior School', Council, 26 October 1955, attachment.

Shugg, A. N., 'Education Cttee. Notes of an informal meeting between HM, the Chairman (Ken Mappin) & Secretary (Alan Shugg) on 30/3/71'. Handwritten.

Skene, W., diary, 1868.

Thorpe, E. H., unpublished memoirs.

'Triple Scotch farewell, Scotch Family farewell dinner for Ron Bond, Ken Field & Archie Crow. Camberwell Civic Centre', 15 November 1985.

PUBLISHED MATERIAL

A 'Littlejohn' Old Boy, 'Our Principals—No. 2 "The Boss", A man of immense dignity', News from Scotch, [No. 2], 1962.

Adams, Nancy, *Family fresco*, Cheshire, Melbourne, 1966.

Austin, A. G., *Australian Education, 1788–1900: Church, state, and public education in colonial Australia*, Sir Isaac Pitman & Sons, Melbourne, 1961.

Australian Dictionary of Biography, Melbourne University Press, Melbourne, 1969–[2000].

The Australian Encyclopaedia, 10 vols., Grollier Society, Sydney, ca 1960.

Bain, D. G., 'School Council backs appeal', *News from Scotch*, [No. 2], 1962.

Baker, Mark, 'Church union leads to a $500 mil. split', *Age*, 17 June 1977, p. 8.

Bean, C. E. W., *Here, my son: An account of the Independent and other corporate schools of Australia*, Angus and Robertson, Sydney, 1950.

Birch, Ian, *Good weekend*, 11 December 1999.

Blazey, P., *Screw loose: Uncalled-for memoirs*, Picador, Sydney, 1997.

Bond, R. S. 'Triple Farewell speech 15 November 1985', *Scotch Association News: An information bulletin for parents*, February 1986, p. 3.

Bonwick, James, *Port Phillip Settlement*, Sampson Low, Marston, Searle & Rivington, London, 1883.

Bradshaw, F. M., *Scottish seceders in Victoria*, Robertson & Mullens, Melbourne, 1947.

Campbell, R. McK., *An urge to laugh*, Sydney, Wildcat Press, 1981.

——, 'On the margin', *Bulletin*, 16 March 1968, p. 14.

Carrick, J. L., 'Why private schools need Canberra's help', *Age*, 7 July 1977, p. 8.

Cathcart, Michael, *Defending the National Tuckshop: Australia's secret army intrigue of 1931*, McPhee–Gribble, Melbourne 1988.

Coleman, Robert, *Above renown*, Macmillan, Melbourne, 1988.

Cook, P. S., *Red barrister: A biography of Ted Laurie, QC*, La Trobe University Press, Melbourne, 1994.

Crotty, Martin, ' "Loyal scions of the British Race": Sport and the construction of the Australian public schoolboy, c. 1870–1920', in Martin Crotty and Doug Scobie (eds), *Raiding Clio's closet: Postgraduate presentations in History 1997*, History Department, University of Melbourne, Melbourne, 1997.

Davies, A. J. M., *The Fiddlers of Drummond*, Consolidated Press, Sydney, 1945.

Dawes, A. W., *Argus*, 28 Sept 1951, p. 2.

Dow, G. M., *George Higinbotham: Church and state*, Sir Isaac Pitman & Sons, Melbourne, 1964.

Elias, D., *Australian*, 12 June 1977, p. 5.

Ellingsen, P., 'Profile of a Private School', *Age*, 5 Oct 1985, 'Saturday Extra', p. 1.

Ewing, J. F., *The unsearchable riches of Christ*, Melville, Mullen & Slade, Melbourne, 1890.

Forbes, James, *The Port Phillip Christian Herald*, 1849.

Foyster, Rev. R. C., *Scotch College, Melbourne. Divine Service in the Memorial Hall … 8th May, 1927 (Old Boys' and Parents' Sunday)*, [Melbourne, 1927].

Fraser, Rev. T. McK., 'Report of the Special Committee on the educational policy of the Church', in *Proceedings of the General Assembly of the Presbyterian Church of Victoria … November, 1872*.

Fraser, Rev. W. Alec, prayer, in *Scotch College, Melbourne. Divine Service in the Memorial Hall … 19th October, 1947, (Old Boys' and Parents' Sunday) to pay a tribute to Old Scotch Collegians who have fallen in the war and to mark the ninety-sixth anniversary of the founding of the college*, Brown Prior Anderson, Melbourne [1947].

Fuller, A., 'Risk-taking, as a healing process', in I. Gawler (ed.), *The mind body connection*, Melbourne, Gawler Foundation, 1996, pp. 45–54, cited in David Tacey, *Remaking men: The revolution in masculinity*, Viking, Penguin, Ringwood, 1997.

Gittins, R., 'Old soldiers and young men', *EQ Australia*, 2 (1996), p. 8.

Glenn, J. R. A., *Things to be remembered*, Diana Gribble, Melbourne, 1991.

Green, Sue, 'Church tightens grip on schools', *Age*, 16 September 1981, p. 26.

——, 'Church veto on Scotch College appointment', *Age*, 15 September 1981, p. 3.

——, 'Principal quits stormy Scotch', *Age*, 13 August 1981, p. 1.

Hansen, I. V., *Nor free nor secular: Six Independent Schools in Victoria: A first sample*, OUP, Melbourne, 1971.

The Headmastership of Scotch College Melbourne, Australia. Conditions of Appointment [Melbourne, 1974].

Healey, C. O., 'Scotch College, Melbourne, 1964–1975', in Stephen Murray-Smith (ed.), *Melbourne Studies in Education 1978*, Melbourne University Press, Melbourne, 1978, pp. 67–106.

Hill, C. W., *Edwardian Scotland*, Rowman and Littlefield, Totowa, N J, 1976.

Hill, T. P., *The oratorical trainer: A system of vocal culture*, 4th edn., G. Robertson, 1868, Melbourne, Harrild, London.

History of Scotch College, Melbourne 1851–1926, Scotch College History Committee, Melbourne, 1926.

The Independent Schools of Australia (*Current Affairs Bulletin*, vol. 21, no. 3, December 1957).

Ingram, W. F., 'Public schools in a changing age', *Herald*, Week-End Magazine, 8 December 1934, p. 33.

Hogg, J. W., *Our proper concerns: A history of the Headmasters' Conference of the Independent Schools of Australia*, Stanmore, NSW, ca 1986.

The Littlejohn Memorial Chapel, Scotch College, Melbourne, Old Scotch Collegians' Association, Brown, Prior, Anderson, Melbourne, [1938?].

Littlejohn, W. S., *An Appeal to the Old Boys and Friends of the School. From the Principal*, [Melbourne, 1914].

Lord, Mary, *Hal Porter: Man of many parts*, Random House, Sydney, 1993.

Macneil, Rev. A. R., *Scotch College, Melbourne. Divine Service in the Memorial Hall … 18th October, 1931 (Old Boys' and Parents' Sunday) and to mark the Eightieth Anniversary of the Founding of the College*, Brown, Prior & Co., Melbourne, [1931].

——, *Scotch College, Melbourne. Divine Service in the Memorial Hall … 7th October, 1934 (Old Boys' and Parents' Sunday)*, Brown Prior & Co., Melbourne, [1934].

Mann, B. R., 'My lifetime hobby', *OTN, The Journal of the radio Amateur Old Timers' club of Australia*, no 13, September 1994, pp. 14–15.

Matthews, G. B., *An Australian son*, William Heinemann, Port Melbourne, 1996.

Matthews, R., *David Bennett: A memoir*, Australian Fabian Society Pamphlets No. 44, Melbourne, 1985.

McCalman, J. S, *Journeyings: The biography of a middle-class generation, 1920–1990*, Melbourne University Press, Melbourne, 1993.

McCulloch, J., Speech Day speech, 1878, *Young Victoria*, 9, Christmas Supplement (1878).

——, Speech Day 1879, *Young Victoria*, 13, Supplement (December 1879).

McInnes, G.C., *Goodbye Melbourne Town*, Hamish Hamilton, London, 1968.

——, *Humping my bluey*, Hamish Hamilton, London, 1966.

——, *The road to Gundagai*, Hamish Hamilton, London, 1965.

McKay, Marjory, *Cecil McKay: It wasn't all Sunshine*, Hawthorn Press, Melbourne, 1974.

McNicoll, D. R., *Luck's a fortune*, Wildcat Press, Sydney, 1979.

——, 'Religious split degenerates into real estate row', *Bulletin*, 3 April 1979, p. 52.

Merrett, D. T., 'The school at war: Scotch College and the Great War', in Stephen Murray-Smith (ed.), *Melbourne Studies in Education 1978*, Melbourne University Press, Melbourne, 1978, pp. 209–33.

Mishura, P. A., 'Note books from 1858 found', *Great Scot*, 85 (1997), p. 24.

Mitchell, E. F., *Three-quarters of a century*, Methuen, London, 1949.

Moorehead, A. McC., *A late education: Episodes in a life*, Hamish Hamilton, London, 1970.

Morrison, A., 'Statement made to the Special Committee on Education … relative to the religious instruction given at that institution', in *Proceedings of the General Assembly of the Presbyterian Church of Victoria … November, 1872*.

News from Scotch, [No. 2. headline: 'Start on first of the new buildings'], 1962.

News from Scotch, [No. 3. headline: 'Scotch plans big day'], 1962.

Nicholson, G. H., and D. H. Alexander (eds), *The first hundred years Scotch College Melbourne, 1851–1951*, Brown, Prior, Anderson, Melbourne, 1952.

Peel, Mark, and Janet McCalman, *Who went where in Who's Who 1988: The schooling of the Australian elite*, Melbourne University History Research Series No. 1 (1992).

Pike, E. M., *New every morning*, Essien, Melbourne, 1996.

Porter, H., *The Paper Chase*, Angus and Robertson, Melbourne, 1966.

Pratt, A. E., *Dr W. S. Littlejohn: The story of a great Headmaster*, Lothian Publishing Company, Melbourne, 1934.

Presbyterian Church of Victoria, *Proceedings of the General Assembly of the Presbyterian Church of Victoria … November, 1860*, Alex. Anderson, Melbourne, [1860].

——, *Proceedings of the General Assembly … August, 1861* [sic = 1862], Fergusson and Moore, printers, Melbourne, [1862].

——, *Proceedings of the Commission of the General Assembly … May, 1863*, W. H. Williams, [Melbourne, 1863].

——, 'Proceedings of the General Assembly …

November, 1864', in *Proceedings of the Commission of the General Assembly of the Presbyterian Church of Victoria ... May, 1864*, Mason and Firth, Melbourne, [1864].

——, *Proceedings of a Pro re nata meeting of the General Assembly ... July, 1869*, [Melbourne, 1869].

——, *Proceedings of a pro re nata meeting of the General Assembly ... July, 1870*, Egerton and Moore, Melbourne, [1870].

——, *Proceedings of the Commission of the General Assembly ... November, 1870*, Mason, Firth, and M'Cutcheon, Melbourne, [1870].

——, *Business of the General Assembly ... November 1871*, Mason, Firth, & M'Cutcheon, Melbourne, 1871,

——, *Proceedings of the General Assembly ... November, 1872*, Mason, Firth, and M'Cutcheon, Melbourne, [1872]

——, *Proceedings of the Commission of the General Assembly ... May, 1873*, Mason, Firth, and M'Cutcheon, Melbourne, [1873].

——, *Proceedings of the General Assembly ... November, 1874*, Walker, May, and Co., Melbourne, [1874].

Rules for the guidance of pupils attending the Scotch College, Fergusson & Moore, Melbourne, [1867?].

Scotch College, Eastern Hill, Melbourne. Prize List, 1857, Goodhugh & Hough, Melbourne, [1857].

Scotch College, Melbourne. Break-up Concert and Speech Night, Melbourne Town Hall, December 14th, 1917, Brown, Prior, Melbourne, [1917].

——, *Dedication of the Littlejohn Memorial Chapel Sunday, 18th October 1936*, Brown, Prior, Anderson, Melbourne, [1936].

——, *Divine Service in the Memorial Hall ... 8th May, 1927 (Old Boys' and Parents' Sunday)*, ([Melbourne, 1927]).

——, *Divine Service in the Memorial Hall at the Unveiling of the Roll of Honour of the Masters and Old Boys of the School who fell in the Great War. Anzac Eve, 1936*.

——, *Examination Results*, Ford & Son, Printers, Carlton [1897?].

——, *Foundation Day Concert October 10, 1913*, Brown Prior & Co., Melbourne [1913].

——, *Foundation Day Concert October 9, 1914*, Brown, Prior & Co., Melbourne. 1914.

The Scotch College and its seventieth anniversary, [Melbourne], 1921.

Scotch College School songs, Ford and Son, [Melbourne, 1911–13?].

Scotch College Speech-Day. Christmas, 1862. St, George's Hall. His Excellency Sir Henry Barkly, K.C.B., in the chair, [Melbourne, 1862].

Selby Smith, R., 'A Victorian Independent school: Reflections on the development of Scotch College, 1953–1964', in E. L. French (ed.), *Melbourne Studies in Education 1965*, Melbourne University Press, Melbourne, 1966, pp. 225–50.

Selleck, R. J. W., 'State education and culture', in S. L. Goldberg and F. B. Smith (eds), *Australian cultural history*, Cambridge University Press, Cambridge, 1988.

Serle, A. G., *Colin Gilray*, History Department, University of Melbourne, 1999

——, *John Monash: A biography*, Melbourne University Press, Melbourne, 1982.

——, 'The Russel Ward Lecture', University of New England, 18 September 1990, *Australian Historical Association Bulletin*, nos 64–65, October–December 1990, p. 17, cited in Ian Britain, 'In pursuit of Englishness: Public School stories and Australian Culture', *The University of Melbourne Library Journal*, 1 (1994–95), pp. 11–17.

Southall, I., *Softly tread the brave*, Angus and Robertson, Melbourne, 1960.

Testro, Ron, 'Empire's Biggest Public School', *Australasian Post*, 1 March 1951.

Theobald, M. R., *Knowing women: Origins of women's education in nineteenth-century Australia*, Cambridge University Press, Melbourne, 1996.

Trevor-Roper, H. 'The invention of tradition: the Highland tradition of Scotland', in Eric Hobsbawm and Trevor Ranger (eds), *The invention of tradition*, Cambridge University Press, Cambridge, 1983.

Turner, W. J. R., *Blow for balloons: Being the first hemisphere of the history of Henry Airbubble*, Dent, London, 1935.

Wallace-Crabbe, C., *Selected Poems, 1956–1994*, Oxford University Press, 1995.

Wood, G. (ed.), *Scotch College, Melbourne. Diamond Jubilee, 1851–1911, Historical sketch with scholastic and sports records, October 6, 1911*, Brown, Prior & Co., Melbourne, [1911].

Worth, C., '"A centre at the edge". Scotland and the early teaching of literature in Australia and New Zealand', in R. Crawford (ed.), *The Scottish invention of English literature*, Cambridge University Press, Cambridge, 1998.

Zwar, D. L. G., *The soul of a school*, Macmillan, South Melbourne, 1982.

INDEX

Many people are mentioned only in the acknowledgements and not included in this index.

Bold page numbers indicate illustrations